Canvas Detroit

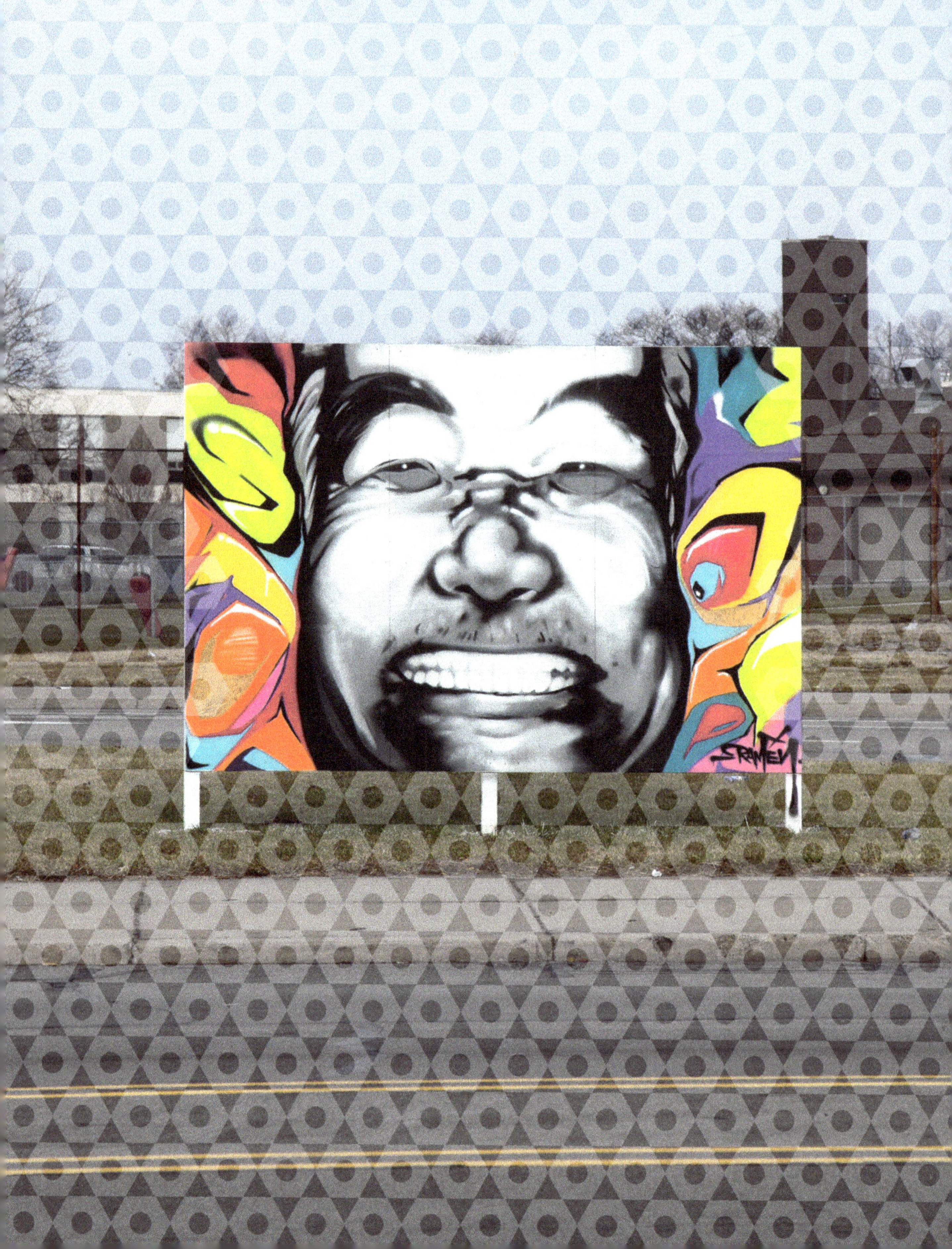

CANVAS DETROIT

JULIE PINCUS | NICHOLE CHRISTIAN

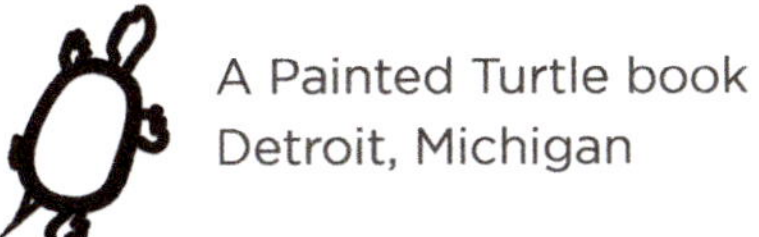

A Painted Turtle book
Detroit, Michigan

ISBN 978-0-8143-4462-0 (paperback)
ISBN 978-0-8143-4023-3 (jacketed cloth)
ISBN 978-0-8143-3880-3 (e-book)
Library of Congress Control Number: 2013950445

Grateful acknowledgment is made to the following for their generous financial support of this volume:
The Leonard and Harriette Simons
Endowed Family Fund
Lois and Avern Cohn
Mandell & Madeleine Berman Foundation
Walter Ohlmann
Broder & Sachse Real Estate Services, Inc.
Mary Lou Zieve
Ellen Kahn
Nancy and Bud Liebler
Ruth Rattner

Designed and typeset by Julie Pincus

Photographs not attributed to individual artists or photographers are by Julie Pincus.

Composed in Gotham, Trade Gothic Bold Condensed No. 20 and Veneer Two and Three.

Frontispiece: An artwork painted in late 2012 by Raman, a Grand River Creative Corridor artist.

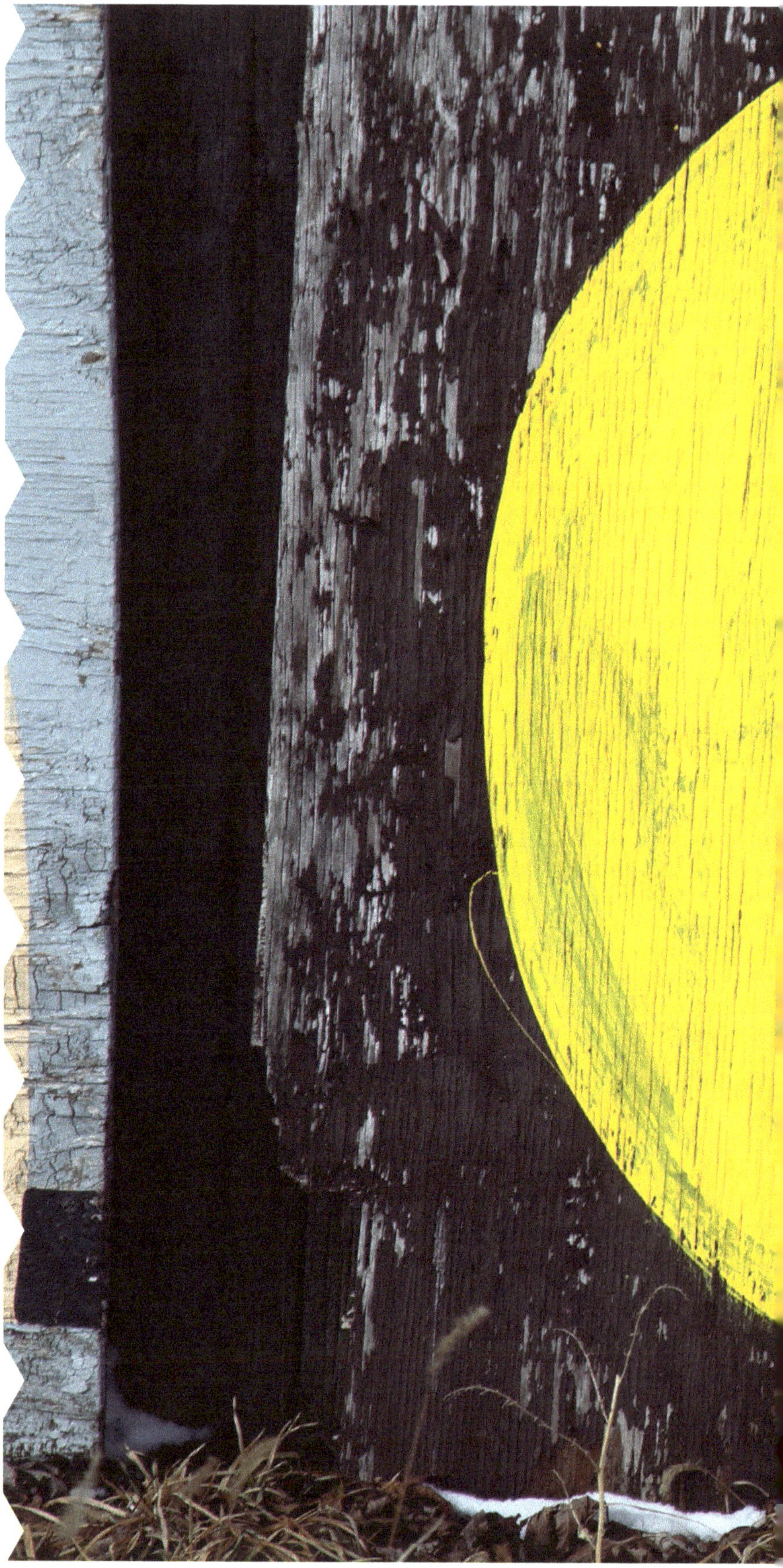

RIGHT: Artwork by Tyree Guyton at the Heidelberg Project, Detroit. Circles are a recurring theme for Guyton and grace the house he grew up in on Heidelberg Street as well as abandoned buildings throughout the city.

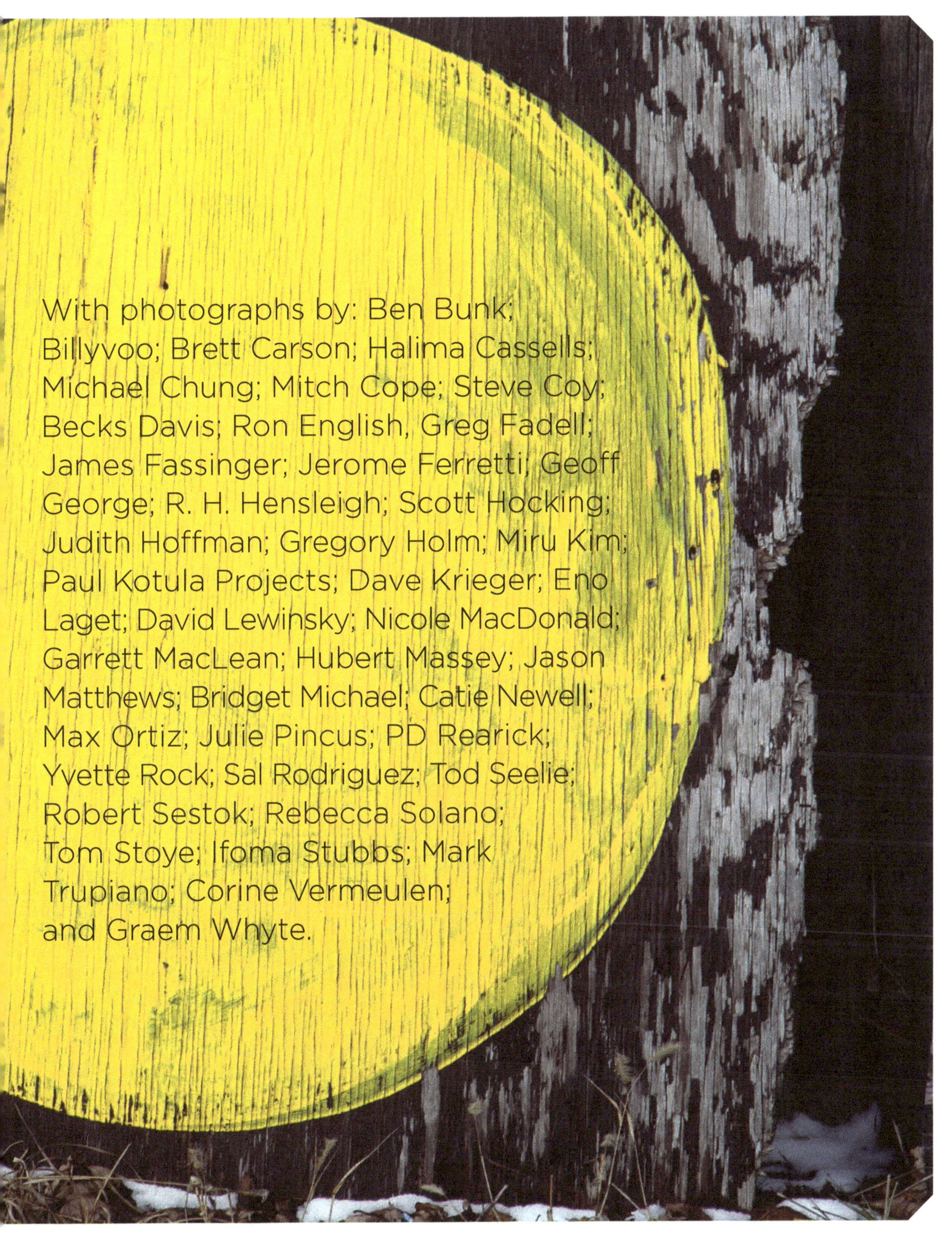

With photographs by: Ben Bunk;
Billyvoo; Brett Carson; Halima Cassells;
Michael Chung; Mitch Cope; Steve Coy;
Becks Davis; Ron English, Greg Fadell;
James Fassinger; Jerome Ferretti; Geoff
George; R. H. Hensleigh; Scott Hocking;
Judith Hoffman; Gregory Holm; Miru Kim;
Paul Kotula Projects; Dave Krieger; Eno
Laget; David Lewinsky; Nicole MacDonald;
Garrett MacLean; Hubert Massey; Jason
Matthews; Bridget Michael; Catie Newell;
Max Ortiz; Julie Pincus; PD Rearick;
Yvette Rock; Sal Rodriguez; Tod Seelie;
Robert Sestok; Rebecca Solano;
Tom Stoye; Ifoma Stubbs; Mark
Trupiano; Corine Vermeulen;
and Graem Whyte.

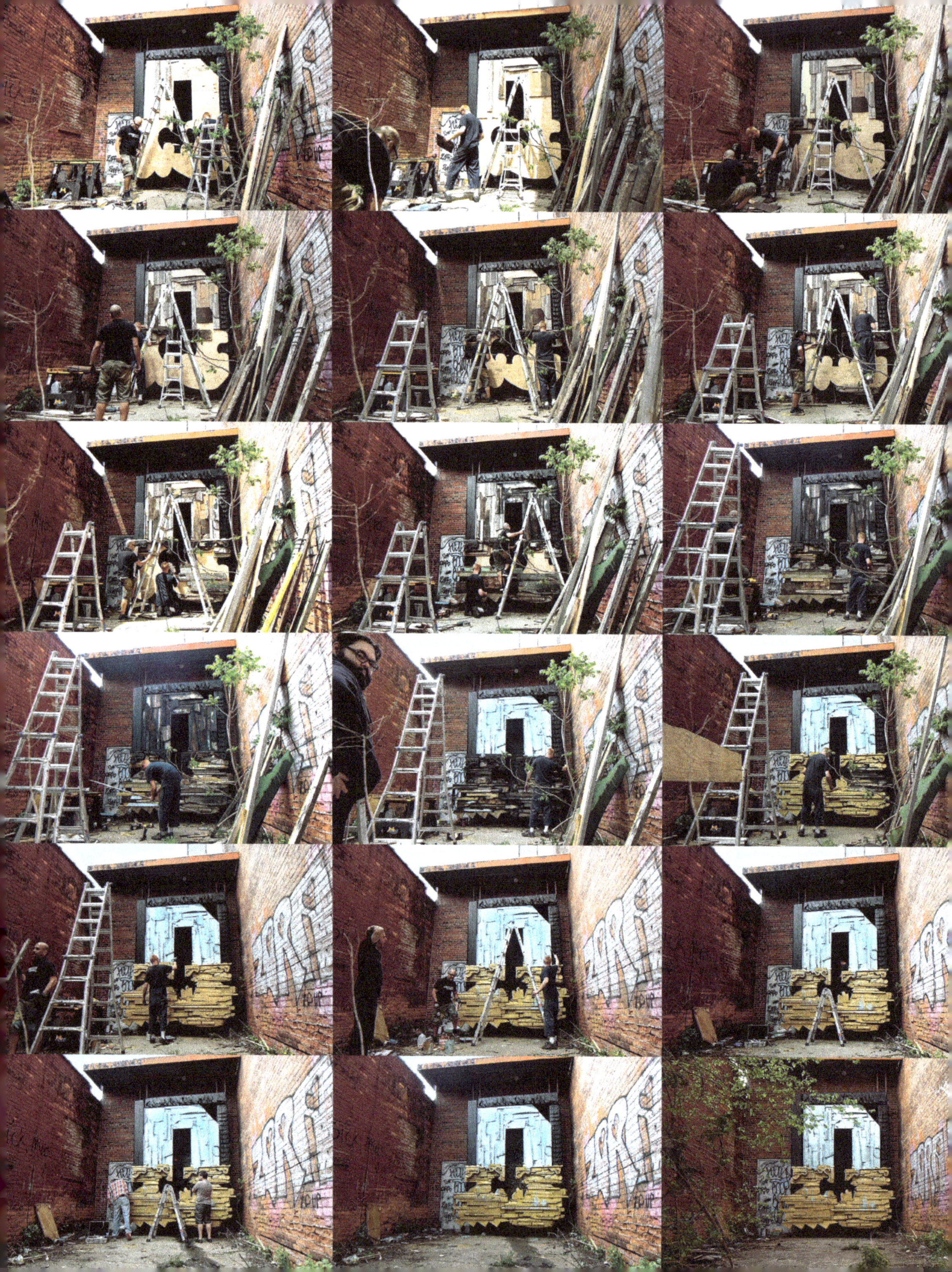

Contents

LEFT: A time-lapse photo sequence of BASK creating an assemblage depicting the letter "D" for Detroit in an empty shipping bay in Eastern Market. (Photos: Sal Rodriguez)

Preface

Julie Pincus: As an art student at the University of Michigan, I was fascinated by Detroit and began trolling its streets for photographs. This was in the eighties, and even then the city was in distress, but I still enjoyed poking around places like Brush Park with its stately mansions, many of which were already in disrepair. Even in the midst of this decline, I remember seeing signs of hope in the poverty and wondering how people managed to keep their spirits up when there was so much working to undermine them.

In the years that followed, many of my generation fled metropolitan Detroit since it held little promise of work. It was not until 2007 when I was working on a monograph about Marcus Belgrave for the Kresge Foundation that I was drawn to photograph Detroit again, this time in search of icons like the Spirit of Detroit, Motown, and the Noguchi fountain. The city was in even worse shape and the mayor promised to raze the abandoned houses mushrooming across its landscape in an attempt to erase evidence of blight. It was in this unlikely climate I became obsessed with Detroit, and soon a theme to my photographs emerged. I was chronicling folk art graphics, beautiful old signage, and funky icons, like an enormous cow on top of a defunct ice cream shop. I even came across antique advertising for cigars, which remained untouched due to its remote location.

I thought I had the makings of a book, but soon learned that books about the despair of this once-great city had already been done. What intrigued the publisher, however, was something altogether different, and a theme I had failed to discern and now embrace. Where buildings were boarded up, weathered surfaces here and there started sporting artwork of striking originality. I would turn a corner, only to spy a bright painting in crimson stenciled with golden pigeons, or walruses frolicking in a blue-green sea. The art was transformative: a fortress became a graphic beauty; an abandoned apartment building, an aquarium.

I was onto something! But what it was wouldn't be revealed until a year or two later, when a critical mass of interventions had been achieved. Soon more artworks were springing up all over the city. Articles about buildings completely festooned with mirrors, or guerrilla branding experiments cropping up on the walls of old hotels or office buildings appeared in national publications. Many artists who had come from afar or who were here all along were using Detroit as their canvas, and their work was astonishing.

The attraction to Detroit was simple. It was vast, affordable, and there was virtually nobody to stop artists from creating moments of sheer brilliance out of the distress. Grant money began flowing into the artists' hands, and they responded in the best way they knew how—they transformed it into beauty. Far-flung pockets of Detroit were coming to life, thanks to the artists, who were behaving like pioneers, and doing the heavy lifting that the broken city couldn't. While downtown was being gentrified by billionaires, the artists were tackling portions of the city that many saw as dismal.

I was hooked, and it became an obsession to locate as much artwork as I could; to track down one elusive artist after another. I was sometimes rebuffed, but more often welcomed with open arms. On the following pages are the fruits of these artist's considerable labors. Detroit is once again the land of opportunity and It is my hope that this book will convey the rich art movement that is rapidly transforming the city from beleaguered to triumphant. Nobody knows where this will lead, but one thing is certain: in

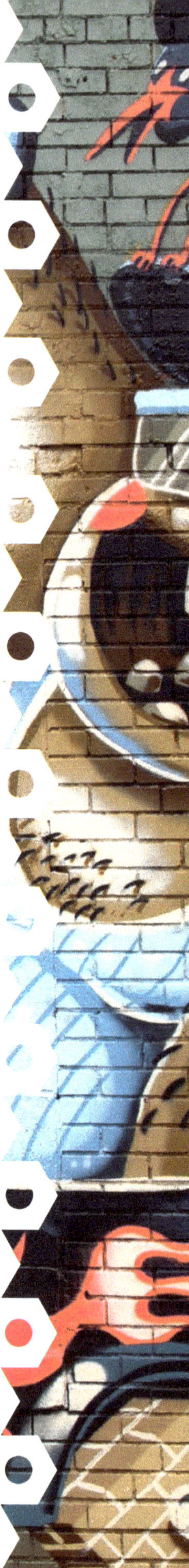

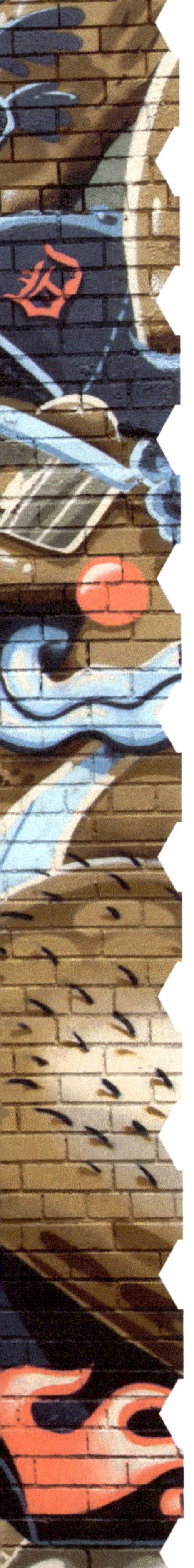

the birthplace of the motor vehicle, it will be a glorious and captivating ride.

Being a graphic designer, I desperately needed a writer, and it was difficult to find the right person with the necessary "chops." While Detroit is a friendly town, it is also becoming increasingly media savvy, camera shy, and self-protective. Detroiters are tired of their city being depicted as a ruin. They are wary of interlopers, and for that reason I realized the writer needed serious street cred. I found that in Nichole Christian, a Detroit native and a veteran national and local journalist. Nichole interviewed almost every artist, and she wrote all but one of the profiles. Like me, she had to be relentless in her pursuit of them and their stories. It was a feat akin to herding cats, but between the two of us we were able to get most artists on our list to meet with Nichole, whose intelligent and quiet demeanor helped win them over.

In addition, we asked several contributors to write essays that will provide context to how the city arrived where it is, and how the arts have and will continue to affect its future. We are gratified to have Marion (Mame) Jackson, Professor Emerita of Art History at Wayne State University, include her insightful introduction. Michael H. Hodges, fine arts columnist for the *Detroit News,* writes from a popular-culture frame-of-reference, John Gallagher, *Detroit Free Press* writer who specializes in writing about urban redevelopment, discusses the notion of place-making, and Linda Yablonsky, a writer about the arts for the *New York Times* and other national publications tells of her impressions about the Detroit art scene from an outsider's point-of-view.

This brings me to the fact that the artists included in this book are by no means everyone I met throughout the last five years, nor are they the only ones who merited inclusion in the book. There were many others whose work I followed and we simply couldn't fit into the book—a frustrating reality.

We set out to include as many art disciplines as we could, including painting, sculpture, community-based projects, architecture, conceptual and figurative work. Since street artists are notoriously publicity shy, I quickly learned that famous artists like Revok wouldn't be accessible. That was the case with Banksy, who remains anonymous. Matthew Barney agreed to participate through the curator Rebecca R. Hart at the Detroit Institute of Arts, and sadly, while we were working on the book, Mike Kelley died. Some artists, like the peripatetic Miru Kim, couldn't be pinned down long enough to interview, and for that reason we have extensive captions describing some of their pieces. During the making of this book, babies were born, countless artists came and went, and I fretted about the "cut-off" date or how I could include the newest cool piece I discovered.

Beyond the artists' contributions of their valuable time, I want to acknowledge the generosity of all the other contributors to this book. First, a huge thank you goes to my husband, **Hugh Broder**, for giving me the time and freedom to be away from home for months on end. I couldn't have done this without your unfailing love and support. A heartfelt thank you goes to **Lois** and **Avern Cohn** for all of their guidance, love, and lodging during the years this project took. Please don't send me a bill! Thank you to my sister, **Lisa Pincus**, for her writing guidance. Since I live in New York, I often relied on photographer **Dave Krieger** to catch the action. Thank you for all of your time and talent. To all the other photographers who donated the spectacular photos seen on these pages, this book is a direct result of your talent and passion for documenting the world: **Ben Bunk**; **Billyvoo**; **Brett Carson**; **Halima Cassells**; **Michael Chung**; **Mitch Cope**; **Steve Coy**; **Becks Davis**; **Ron English**; **Greg Fadell**; **James Fassinger**; **Jerome Ferretti**; **Geoff**

George; **R. H. Hensleigh**; **Scott Hocking**; **Judith Hoffman**; **Gregory Holm**; **Paul Katula Projects**; **Eno Laget**; **David Lewinsky**; **Nicole MacDonald**; **Garrett MacLean**; **Hubert Massey**; **Jason Matthews**; **Bridget Michael**; **Catie Newell**; **Max Ortiz**; **PD Rearick**; **Yvette Rock**; **Sal Rodriguez**; **Tod Seelie**; **Robert Sestok**; **Rebecca Solano**; **Tom Stoye**; **Ifoma Stubbs**; **Mark Trupiano**; **Corine Vermeulen**; and **Graem Whyte**. **Michael Poris** started this project by giving me an extensive tour of Detroit. Michael, this is all your fault! I am most grateful to **Nichole Christian**, **John Gallagher**, **Becky Hart**, **Michael Hodges**, **Mame Jackson, and Linda Yablonsky** for their masterful writing. **Nichole**, you gave this book a dimension I never could. Thank you a million times. Thank you **Zak Rosen** for leading me to Nichole. A special thanks to **Mike Kelley Foundation for the Arts** for their inclusion of *Mobile Homestead* in the book. Thanks to **Marsha Miro**, **Rebecca Mazzei**, and **Mary Clare Stevens** for making that happen. Thank you **Matthew Barney**, **Becky Hart**, and **the Gladstone Gallery** for your valuable contribution. Also, a big thank you to: **Susanne Hilberry**, **Hazel Blake**, **Nancy Barr**, **Nick Tobier**, **Marc Schwartz**, **Ryan Schirmang**, **Matthew Naimi**, **Michael Carabetta**, and **Mary Bisbee-Beek** for your help and guidance. **Matthew Eaton**, thanks for all your help. The Detroit art scene literally revolves around you. Thank you to **Mandell Berman** and **Anne Berman**, **Walter Ohlmann**, **Ellen Kahn**, **Bud Liebler**, and **Ruth Rattner** for your invaluable support. Thanks goes to **Larry August**, **Mikel Bresee**, **Katie Craig**, **Dorota and Steve Coy**, and **John Dunivant** for helping with our video. A very special thank you goes to **Kathy Wildfong**, who must be the calmest person I've *ever* met. I appreciate your sure guidance and unwavering belief in this project. And lastly, thank you **Mary Lou Zieve**. I couldn't have done this without all of your support and enthusiasm. You are the Energizer Bunny. How do you do it?

–Julie Pincus
April 2013

Nichole Christian: On the surface, *Canvas Detroit* is exactly what it appears to be: a book about art.

The images are vivid and lush. They engage. They intrigue and to some small degree maybe they expand, or even assault, our idea of the indescribable thing we call art.

Perhaps the images could stand alone. However, I believe an added value exists in pairing them with a mosaic of voices just as rich and textured. After all, a canvas can only tell a portion of the story. The artist holds the truth of their intention, deciding whether it should be silenced or shared. It is a strength of this book that so many extraordinarily driven and busy people paused to give *Canvas Detroit* life.

See their stories for what they are: mini snapshots of a small group of men and women who, at a specific moment in time, are making new marks in a city with a history of making major marks on the world. I'm grateful for the opportunity to help introduce and reintroduce a few of Detroit's many artists.

I'm also grateful to the artists and architects, for as much as this book is about their work, it's also a personal reminder of the importance of confronting assumptions. This project challenged me to face more than a few, some I didn't even know I still carried. A couple assumptions almost convinced me to say no to the book altogether.

I'm a Detroiter, native born, a child of the nitty-gritty North End.

For much of my adult life, I believed only natives could see the beauty of a city long broken but never buried. I'd watched too many outsiders parachute into town without the slightest bit of interest or the patience to let Detroit speak through its greatest asset: its people. Time and time again, the stories starred pathologies, decades old, yet

For much of my adult life, I believed only natives could see the beauty of

easily reheated and served as the truth of Detroit. If these words read like an admission of chip on shoulder, I'm guilty. Or at least I was.

I was so guilty that when the invitation of this project arrived, I listened mostly out of respect for the friend who'd suggested me. The list of artists, filled with some natives, lots of newcomers, and a few high-profile visitors, was nearly complete. Several of the names had already made headlines in stories hailing the resurrection of a creative Detroit and declaring hip new settlers as its saviors.

I was certain I had nothing to add to or learn from such a well-worn narrative.

But a crazy thing happened on the way to nearly saying no. I looked over my list of reasons and winced at what the list said about me. Here I was about to practice the same brand of easy disregard so often inflicted on Detroit. I'd heard a little hype and I was willing to let it keep me from discovering and experiencing the people behind the stories for myself.

I knew better. I had made a career of doing better, listening carefully, and letting the story lead me. I decided this time should be no different. I set a few ground rules. I vowed to see each person on the list as an individual, not a representative of Detroit's so-called emerging creative class. I was also determined to let them speak without applying my natural super-sensitive Detroit filter to their stories.

The conversations that came about as a result schooled me, challenged me, and in so many ways they left me inspired. Again and again, I heard echoes and metaphors of the Detroit I love.

Like the city, these artists do not live perfect lives. Still they endure. They feed their dreams with sweat and small, steady steps. They greet failure and the promise of a hard day's work equally, welcoming both but fearing neither.

And despite the messiness that is life, these artists do what Detroit has always done: they keep going, sometimes humming, sometimes sputtering, yet always pressing forward.

No writer writes alone.

I owe immense gratitude to an amazing cast of supporters starting with Zak Rosen and Julie Pincus. Julie, thank you for reminding me what fortitude looks like. *Canvas Detroit* lives because of your dogged determination and your willingness to share your dream project with just the right partner. Zak, my friend and fellow journalist, thank you for acting on whatever led you, across thousands of miles, to champion me as "the" person. You are a wonder. Perhaps my greatest fortune was having a chance to work with Kathy Wildfong, who guided a daunting concept into a beautiful creation with the seemingly effortless touch of an Aikido master. Deep bow to her leadership.

I also wish to thank Wayne State University's Journalism Institute for Media Diversity, whose invisible, yet indelible, mark is stamped on every story I write. Finally, a gigantic heartfelt thanks to my husband, Wayne Criner, and my daughter, Asha Criner. Their steady supply of caffeine, creative freedom, and love made all the difference.

-Nichole Christian
April 2013

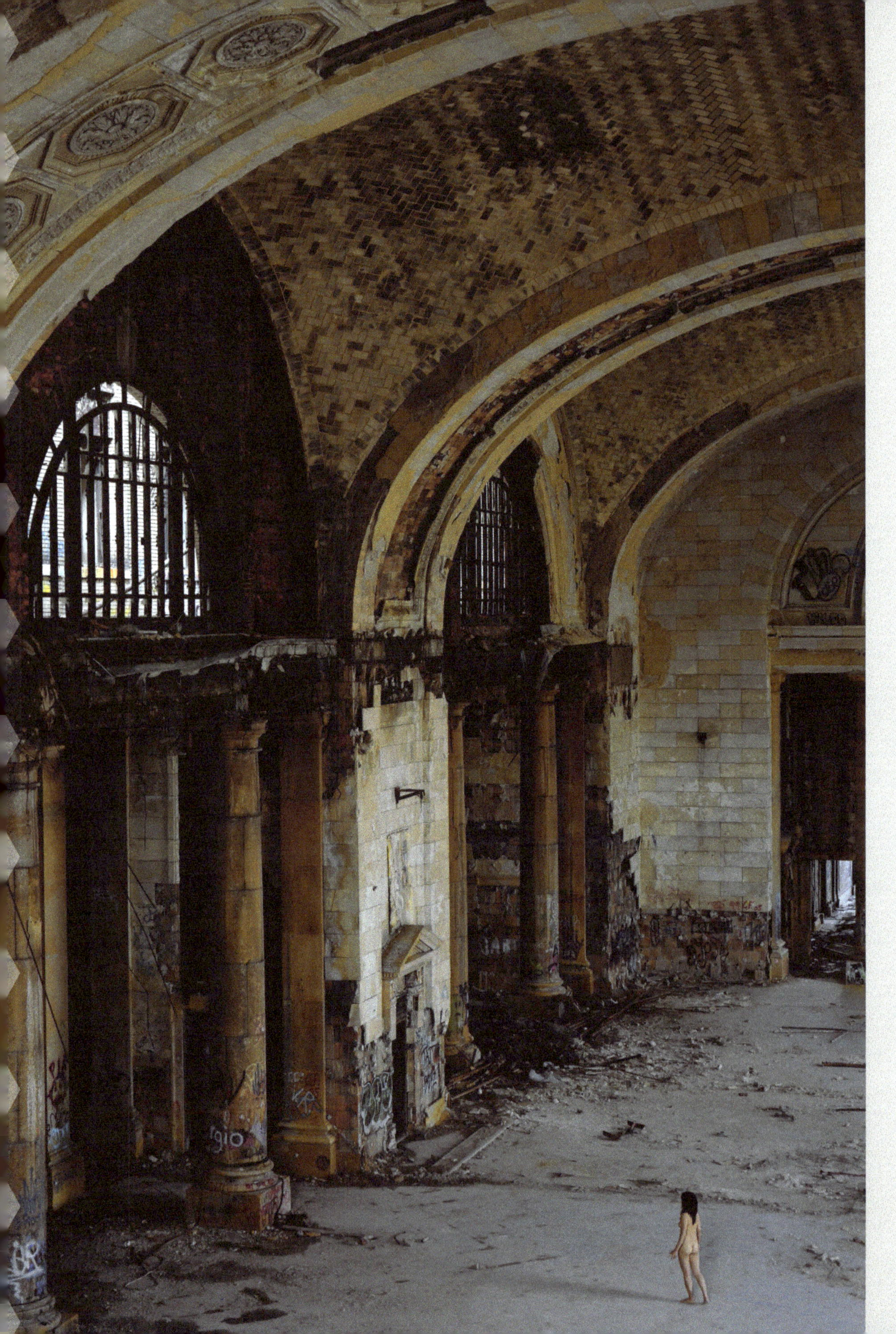

Introduction

BY Marion Jackson

The opportunity to introduce Detroit to friends and visitors—and, especially, the opportunity to introduce Detroit's vibrant arts community—is a pleasure.

And the privilege of introducing such a visually engaging book as *Canvas Detroit* that explores the extraordinarily creative arts of Detroit's streets is a privilege I truly welcome. The book's co-author and principal photographer, professional graphic designer Julie Pincus, responds personally and as an artist to the vibrant, offbeat, ever-changing art that she has encountered in the streets of Detroit and that, for the past several years, has captured her attention and, one imagines, her heart as well. Having grown up in metropolitan Detroit and left the area for "greener pastures," as did many other young professionals in the late 1980s and early 1990s, Pincus revisited Detroit in 2007 to discover a city much changed from the declining, unpromising city she had left more than a decade earlier. Colorful murals, pop-up galleries, impromptu performance art, distinctive neighborhood arts environments, painted windows in abandoned buildings, and enigmatic images in unexpected locations had begun to redefine Detroit's urban landscape. Pincus began documenting this creative and exciting transformation; this book is a record of her discoveries.

LEFT: A piece by internationally recognized artist Miru Kim from her 2009 *Naked City Spleen* series was taken in the Michigan Central Station which has become a symbol of Detroit's fall from its past grandeur. (Photo: Miru Kim)

Though a distinctively edgy urban energy seems to characterize much of the work in this book, the artists whose work is included represent a wide diversity of styles and approaches and identify with differing world views regarding the role of art and the artist in modern life. Not surprisingly, the artists also differ widely in terms of demographics and personal biography. Through interviews with most of the artists, co-author Nichole Christian gained insights into the life experiences and thinking of many of the artists and has contributed biographical sketches that give access to the individuals behind the artworks. Some of the artists are academically trained as artists, designers, or architects, while others have little or no formal training in the arts but are driven by the urgency of their own creativity and vision. Some are mature artists, such as Robert Sestok and Jerome Ferretti, whose seasoned work evidences the thoughtfulness and depth earned through long years of dedication and experience as artists and as human beings. Others are young, filled with youthful energy and imagination, feeling their way through an endlessly-fascinating city that enables them to flex their creative muscles and search for their own authentic artistic voices.

Among the works included in *Canvas Detroit,* many are large in scale, located in highly visible public spaces, and will be easily recognized by all who have followed Detroit's exploding art scene in recent years. Kobie Solomon's unforgettable 8,750-square-foot spray-painted *Chimera* on the side of the Russell Industrial Center facing the Chrysler Freeway not far from Midtown Detroit is seen by thousands driving by each day. Likewise, the proliferation of lively murals in Eastern Market instigated by the Detroit Beautification Project are seen by hundreds of market visitors every week, positively affecting their experience of the city. Other less obvious but equally engaging artworks are purposely placed off the beaten path to surprise and delight unsuspecting viewers. John Sauvé's 40-inch-tall *Man in the City* steel statues painted burnt orange and placed strategically on rooftops around the city delight and surprise us when we encounter them, as do the Hygenic Dress League's seemingly serious images of pigeons, the artists themselves wearing gas masks, and faux advertisements for nonexistant products stenciled by street artists Steve and Dorota Coy in random locations on abandoned buildings.

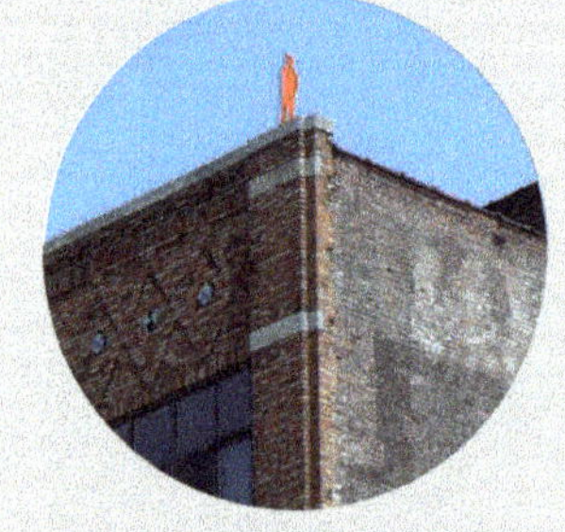

While *Canvas Detroit* presents a number of monumental works of art made to last—such as Hubert Massey's etched granite reliefs in Harmony Park recalling Detroit's jazz era in Paradise Valley and his colorful *Spiral of Life* mosaic celebrating Detroit's Latino culture on the pedestrian walkway near the Ambassador Bridge—many others are intentionally ephemeral. One such work is New York artist Judith Hoffman's *In Hoping We Find.* This work was actually a hand-sewn "slipcover" of bright blue paper covering and mimicking the architecture of a former used-car sales shed on Woodward Avenue and intended to deteriorate naturally through exposure to the elements; the lasting record is a series of time-lapse photographs recording the deterioration. A similarly transitory work was *Ice House*, a frozen sculpture created in winter 2010 by two other New Yorkers, architect Matthew Radune and photographer Greg Holm, who sprayed tons of water on a dilapidated house in an east-side neighborhood. The result was a hauntingly ephemeral ice castle that called attention to economic and social issues of foreclosure. Temporary as well were the sixteen abandoned houses painted between 2006 and 2010 in bright Tiggerific orange by a group of anonymous young Detroit artists known only by their code name, Object Orange. Protective of their anonymity, the young artists adopted guerrilla tactics to paint these highly visible houses by night in order to attract attention to and call for the demolition of such dangerous structures. The strategy was effective; the houses were demolished shortly after they were painted orange. Artist Eno Laget also accepts impermanence in his art; Laget considers the disappearance or defacement of the stenciled images and newsprint posters he applies to Detroit's deserted structures as evidence that his art is provoking dialogue and actively engaging the community.

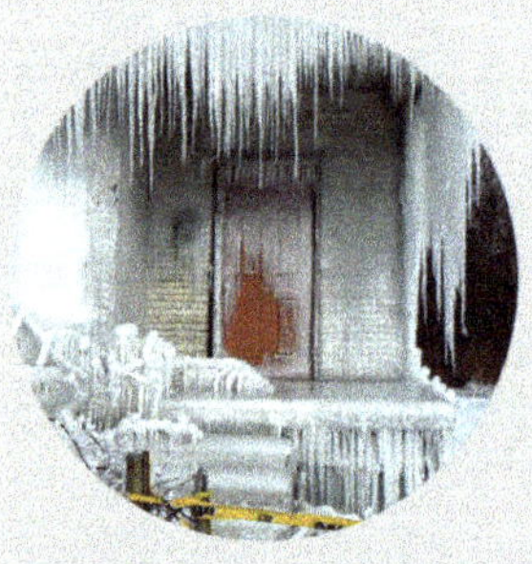

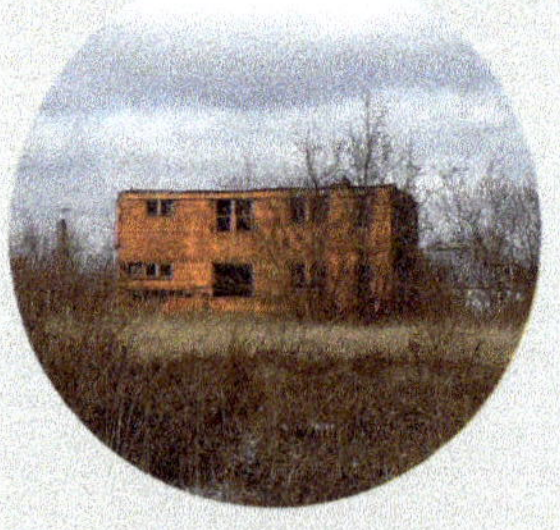

In general, artists who choose to create imagery inside or on the surfaces of deserted buildings are forced to think of their work as ephemeral. At present count, Detroit has an estimated 80,000 abandoned buildings, many slated for demolition to accommodate urban redevelopment. For this reason, a number of ambitious art works in this book, particularly large-scale works in abandoned downtown structures, are known now only through photographs. Kevin Joy's joyous depiction of sunrise on the windows of the once-deserted and now-demolished Lafayette Building in downtown Detroit is one such work; another is the colorful accumulation of Mayan-style hieroglyphics that Joy and friends spent three years painting on the windows of the 18-story United Artists Building near Grand Circus Park, only to have all the paintings washed from the windows in preparation for Detroit hosting the Super Bowl in 2006. The same is true of Scott Hocking's compellingly beautiful, large scale, archetypal sculptures painstakingly constructed of architectural debris on the floors of abandoned factories; these too are preserved only in photographs.

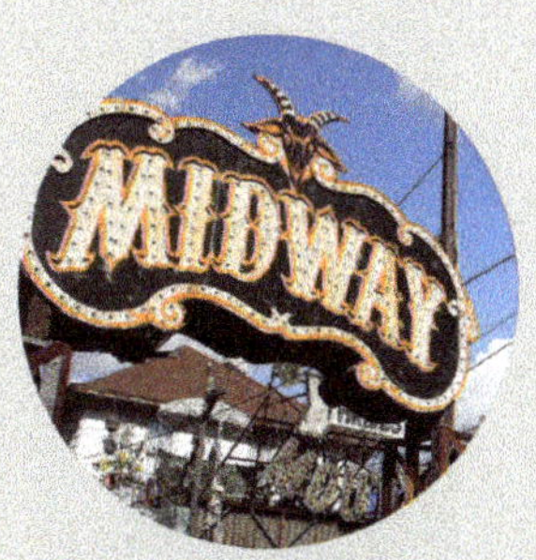

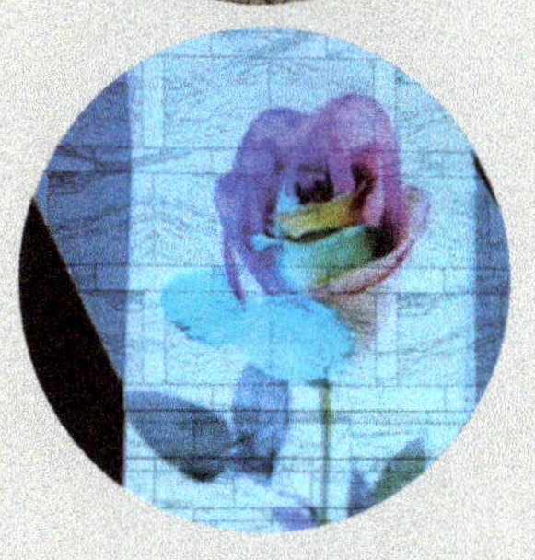

Among the ephemeral works presented in this book—but, like the foregoing, etched into the collective memory of the community—are incredible participatory performance events such as John Dunivant's Halloween night extravaganza, *Theatre Bizarre*, which attracts thousands of paying guests to a night of underground entertainment and reveling but leaves little trace by morning. Likewise, Detroit's newest Midtown festival, DLECTRICITY, conceived and first organized in 2012 by master impresario Marc Schwartz, electrifies Midtown Detroit for a weekend in the fall. Fantastic displays of light and technology energize thousands of spectators with multimedia performances and light projections by dozens of local, national, and international artists.

Some of the artists whose work is featured here consider art to be a strategy for revitalizing the city and its residents, and they actively engage themselves in their communities. Other artists find energy and inspiration in their experience of Detroit but consider their artistic practice to be largely a matter of solitary, individual expression. Artists in the first group, particularly those who are long-time Detroit residents, often integrate a social dimension into their work—tending toward collaboration, teaching, and mentoring—and often engage youth in collective initiatives through which they develop skills, confidence, a DIY approach to life, and an appetite for creative expression. A prominent Detroit artist with an international reputation for the social dimension of art is Tyree Guyton. Guyton's Heidelberg Project is an ever-changing art environment of sculptures and houses covered with polka dots, which has brought life and energy to a deteriorated east-side neighborhood and has served as an inspiration and model for artists and others for nearly thirty years. Olyami Dabls, likewise, focuses on community; his extravagantly colorful African Bead Museum and adjoining sculpture park celebrate Detroit's African heritage and provide educational opportunities for learning about this cultural legacy. Younger artists whose interactive work also engages community participation include photographer Erik Howard, who initiated The Alley Project (TAP) in 2010 to encourage and celebrate the creation of murals and artful graffiti on garages along a previously overgrown alleyway in southwest Detroit and to teach spray painting techniques to youth; painter Katie Craig, whose eye-catching 125-foot-high dripped paint mural in a business district on East Grand Boulevard was created in collaboration with a group of neighborhood teens; and muralist Halima Cassells, who established Detroit Mural Factory to beautify neglected neighborhoods and mentor young artists and now works with ArtsCorpsDetroit to facilitate volunteer participation in neighborhood arts projects across the city. Detroit benefits as well from other community-focused artists whose work is not included in *Canvas Detroit*, such as Chazz Miller, who implements collaborative

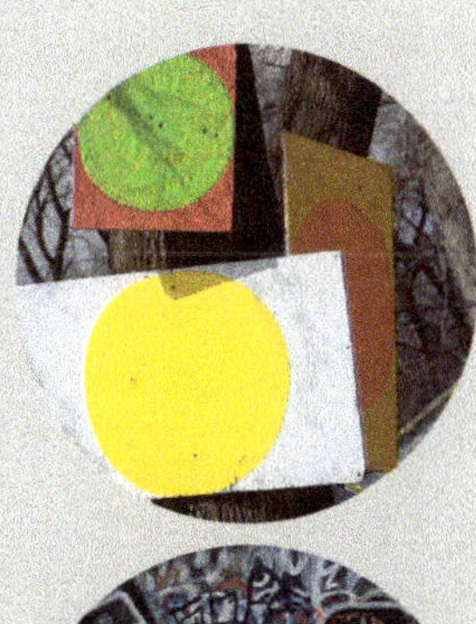

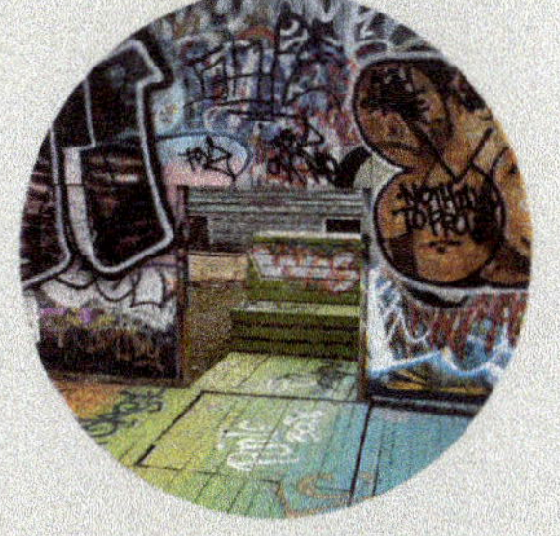

neighborhood mural projects, gardens, and youth art classes dramatically revitalizing the blighted Brightmoor neighborhood in Detroit's northwest section, and artist/teacher Vito Valdez, whose lively murals in southwest Detroit are a source of community pride and cultural identity and whose mentoring and encouragement has launched many young artists. For the artists named here and others like them, the visual rehabilitation of distressed neighborhoods and the empowerment of residents are fundamental objectives. For them, art is a *process*—a process that is itself at least as important as the art objects created.

RIGHT, *top: Mobile Homestead* in front of the abandoned Detroit Central Train Station, 2010. (Photo: Corine Vermeulen. Courtesy of Mike Kelley Foundation for the Arts. All Kelley Works © Estate of Mike Kelley. All rights reserved.)

In contrast, other artists choose to work more independently, often pursuing their actual work in isolation and interacting more deeply with their experience of the urban environment than with the people who inhabit it. Such artists often focus on aesthetic issues and/or the authenticity of self-expression, and include Czech-born Florida artist Ales Hostomsky (aka BASK), who finds that his visits to Detroit and his encounters with the street art here have freed him from the conventions of traditional painting and opened him to experimenting with unconventional surfaces and supports. Others who work in this vein are photographer Greg Fadell, who found inspiration for his series of large paintings -titled *Nothingness* in the aesthetic beauty of light shining through "whitewashed" windows of a deserted building; and architecture professor Catie Newell, who was inspired by charred wood remaining after a house fire in Corktown's Imagination Station to rebuild a portion of the burned building from its charred remnants, creating an aesthetically stimulating micro-environment.

Increasingly, Detroit is a destination for young artists, architects, and designers seeking to experience the city and absorb its celebrated creative energy. Established artists have long been hosted as visiting artists in Detroit through departments of fine arts and design at local institutions such as Wayne State University, the College for Creative Studies, and Cranbrook Academy. Increasingly, however, residency opportunities are emerging through artist-run organizations such as the nonprofit 555 Gallery in southwest Detroit that hosted artists Jane Orr (aka Cupcake Girls) and Ben Bunk. In 2009, a group of students and faculty known as the Five Fellows received a collective grant from the University of Michigan Taubman College of Architecture and Urban Design to purchase a deteriorated house in Hamtramck (a small municipality located totally within and surrounded by the City of Detroit) to serve as a site to pursue experimental design projects. In 2011 and in the same Hamtramck neighborhood, Detroit artists Gina Reichert and Mitch Cope (aka Design 99) received a $150,000 grant from *Juxtapoz* magazine for Power House Productions to invite six artists for two-month residencies to artistically transform abandoned homes in the neighborhood. *Canvas Detroit* covers Cope's and Reichart's collaborative, neighborhood-based art projects and includes, as well, the artistic contributions of these six visiting artists.

RIGHT, *bottom:* The "mobile" section of Mike Kelley's public project, *Mobile Homestead*, 2005–2013, on site at MOCAD in 2010. (Photo: PD Rearick. Courtesy of Mike Kelley Foundation for the Arts. All Kelley Works © Estate of Mike Kelley. All rights reserved.)

While increasing numbers of young artists are drawn to Detroit by its edgy, urban energy and its famously low-cost real estate, Detroit is also a magnet for established artists of international stature. There is circumstantial evidence, for example, that elusive British street artist Banksy made an unannounced pass through Detroit not so long ago; and Rebecca Hart's essay describes the intense interaction that New York sculptor/filmmaker Matthew Barney had with the city in developing aspects of his epic *River of Fundament.* Though not among the artist profiles in this book, New York artist Miru Kim has been drawn to Detroit by the haunting scale and grandeur of the city's "magnificent ruins." Kim has included images of the once-grand Michigan Theatre (now a parking garage) and the deserted lobby of the iconic Michigan Central Train Station in her international series of photographs, *Naked*

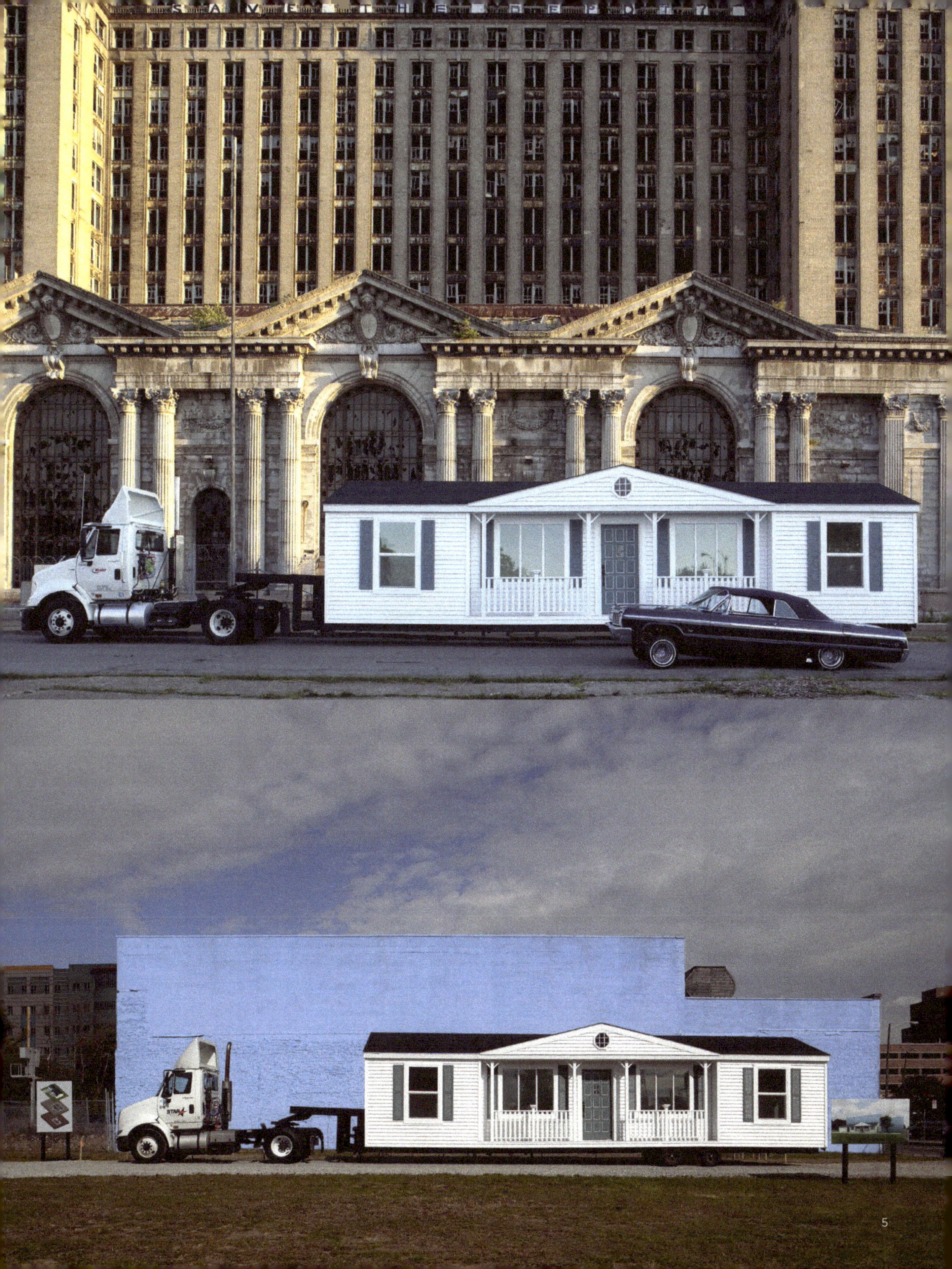
SAVE THE DEPOT

City Spleen, in which she positions herself naked in abandoned urban structures of enormous scale worldwide. Also important in the history of Detroit's contemporary art scene but not included because of his untimely death is Mike Kelley, highly regarded musician/artist who grew up in suburban Westland and whose last major work, *Mobile Homestead,* is now installed at MOCAD, Detroit's Museum of Contemporary Art. A replica of Kelley's childhood home, *Mobile Homestead* will be used to encourage and showcase creative community arts endeavors on its public first floor and to accommodate creative exploration by visiting artists and others in its more secretive, less accessible basement level.

Detroit News writer Michael H. Hodges applauds the exploding energy of Detroit's art scene in his *Canvas Detroit* essay, "How Detroit Got Its Groove Back." Hodges describes the dramatic "uptick" he has observed in the ambient energy and appeal Detroit has for visitors during the past five or six years. Hodges attributes these positive changes to the influx of artists and creative young people seeking the excitement and freedom of a city that is turning a corner on half a century of economic decline, population loss, and social malaise. He relates the effervescence of street art in Detroit to similar turnarounds in cities such as New York, Boston, and Chicago where young artists flocked to shabby, downtrodden neighborhoods, infusing vitality and reversing economic and social decline, making these cities once again interesting destinations for newcomers and visitors.

In his essay, "Art and Public Places," *Detroit Free Press* urban affairs columnist John Gallagher considers the value of arts as a strategy for "place making." In his overview of public art, Gallagher includes Detroit's prominent, officially commissioned public artworks—Marshall Frederick's iconic *Spirit of Detroit* in front of City Hall, David Barr and Sergio DiGiusti's *Labor Legacy Monument* at Hart Plaza, and early civic monuments going back to the nineteenth century—along with "unofficial" art that includes the profusion of stylized graffiti throughout the city and the ever-changing neighborhood art installations of Tyree Guyton and Chazz Miller. Recognizing the role that all art plays in enlivening and humanizing the urban environment and creating an identifiable and engaging sense of "place," Gallagher optimistically posits that the present proliferation of art in Detroit gives witness to the resilience and returning health of the city. Gallagher's optimism is echoed by freelance arts writer Linda Yablonsky in her essay, "Detroit: City of Loss and Wonder." Yablonsky notes the irrepressible energy she observed in the artists she encountered in Detroit, artists she sees as undaunted in the face of formidable odds—evidence to Yablonsky of the tenacious determination of these artists not to abandon their hope for the city nor the city itself—and, through their unquenchable creativity, to "make a difference" in Detroit and in the world.

A good number of artists included in *Canvas Detroit* are native Detroiters or long-term Detroit residents. Others are newcomers or temporary visitors, drawn to the city by its aura of urban collapse and its famous "ruins." While inevitable differences of perspective separate these two groups, a point of commonality shared by all these artists is the centrality of Detroit both as a personal experience and as an inspiration for the making of art. For lifelong Detroiters, this experience is integral to their very being; for others whose familiarity with Detroit is shorter in duration, the experience may be more transitory and less central to their artistic core. But for all of the artists in this book, Detroit is clearly an influence and powerful shaping force in their artistic practice.

Newcomers might see opportunity in apparent emptiness; for them, Detroit's abandoned buildings and deserted streets are an "empty canvas" awaiting and

Canvas Detroit presents neither an empty canvas nor a finished canvas,

inviting their artistic intervention. In contrast, longtime Detroiters might see in the same situation a "crowded canvas" full of life and energy and the traces of a vibrant past. They sense instead the traces of Black Bottom, Paradise Valley, thriving factories, elegant neighborhoods, the artistic spirit of the Cass Corridor, and the music of Motown. For them, the city is not an empty canvas but a rich heritage, which they and their forebearers have worked hard to develop, in which they take ownership, and from which they continue to draw inspiration.

The truth is that both longtime Detroiters and newcomers are *correct* in their perceptions of the city and its possibilities, and both groups—if they hold tightly to their preconceptions—are also *incorrect.* Detroit is *not* an "empty canvas." Generations of artists have been here before and have left their strong marks upon the city. Nor, in truth, is Detroit a "finished canvas" without space for additions from those who bring a new energy and perspective to the city. Among artists in Detroit today, newcomers miss an important aspect of Detroit's vitality if they see the city simply as an empty canvas and overlook its history—and likewise, longtime Detroiters miss an important opportunity if they view Detroit as a finished canvas, a history complete unto itself with nothing to gain from a dialogue with newcomers. Detroit, in the end, is a cosmopolitan city—a city with a rich and varied history and an ability to integrate new ideas and welcome change. *Canvas Detroit* presents neither an empty canvas nor a finished canvas, but a *living canvas* on which many creative individuals are making their marks and from which a fresh new vision of Detroit is being formed. The canvas of Detroit is—as is the city itself—a glorious, complicated, ever-hopeful work in progress.

Marion (Mame) Jackson is Professor Emerita of Art History, Wayne State University, and co-director of Con/Vida y—Popular Arts of the Americas. She is also founding director of ArtsCorpsDetroit, a nonprofit organization established to facilitate volunteer involvement in community-based arts initiatives throughout Detroit.

but a living canvas...

Detroit is suddenly sexy, How'd that happen?

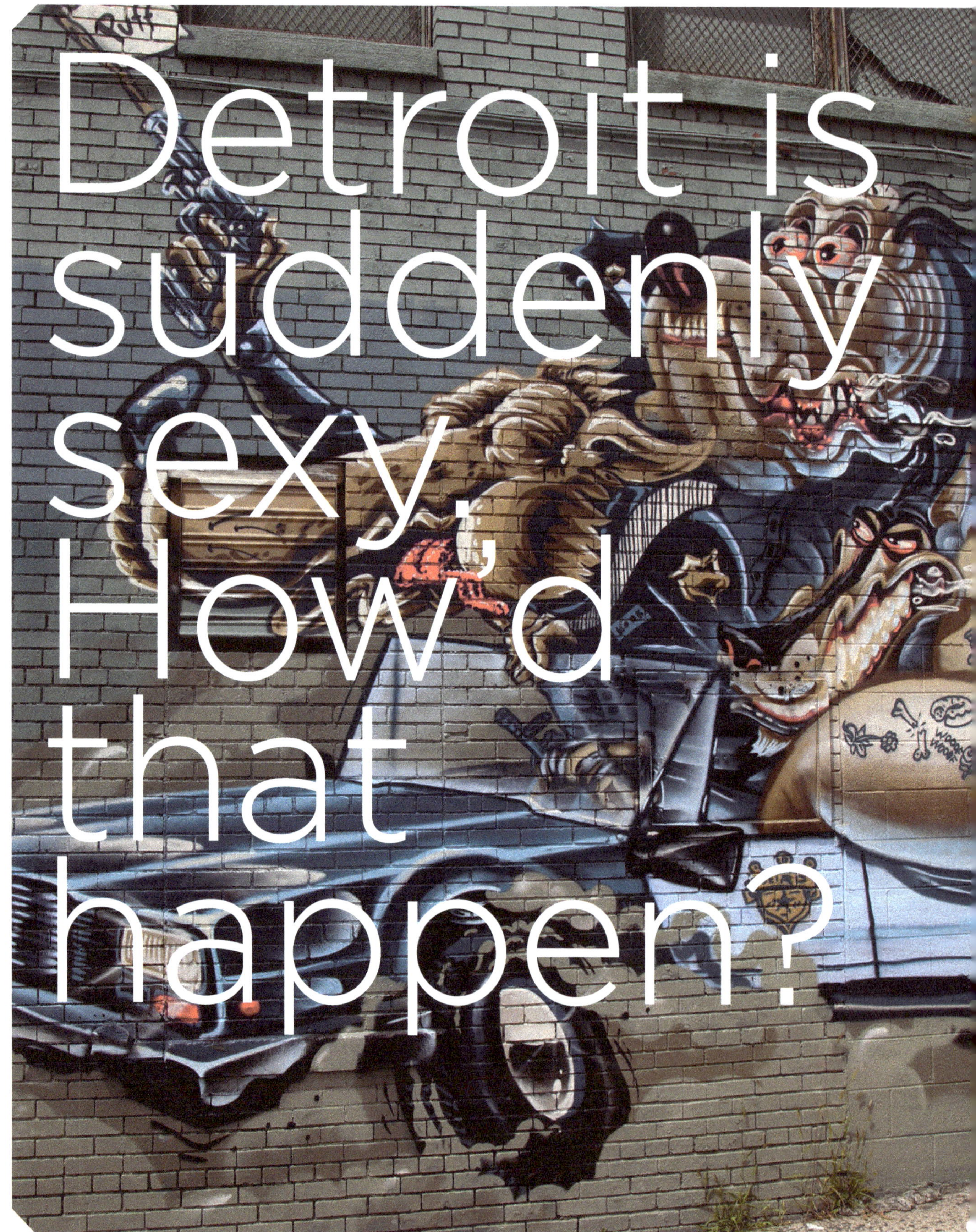

BY Michael H. Hodges

How Detroit Got Its Groove Back

The bikes were the first tip-off. The *Detroit News*, where I work, sits in an urban desert on the far west edge of Detroit's shrunken downtown. For years, the only activity out front on Lafayette Boulevard was the rush of cars, scuttling for the nearest on-ramp to the suburbs.

In my memory, the bikes materialized around 2007—just here and there, but startling for having once been so rare. Even more remarkable were the people pumping the pedals—hip-looking twenty- and thirtysomethings, the privileged, middle-class sorts that in this state have traditionally shunned Detroit for the fashionable suburbs.

These are the neo-yuppie, aspirational kids just starting life who in years past, if they wanted a big city, would decamp for Chicago or New York without a thought. *Detroit? You gotta be kidding me.* Now a significant part of that urban-loving demographic is breaking for the Motor City. How big a percent is hard to say. But downtown's population is visibly younger than twenty years ago and, well, you see bikers everywhere. From their clothes to the groceries in their wire baskets, it's clear these riders didn't commute in from north of Eight Mile Road, the legendary city-suburb divide. They live downtown, probably west of the newspaper in Corktown, suddenly a much-desired neighborhood among the new arrivals.

It's not just the bikes. Go to events like the colorfully raucous Nain Rouge parade, an old tradition revived by young newcomers, or to their haunts like Café D'Mongo's Speakeasy, and there's a palpable fizziness in the air that just wasn't there fifteen years ago. Everyone seems enthusiastic about Detroit and, more to the point, delighted to be here. It isn't that people didn't adore the city in the eighties or nineties, of course, but the affection has recently gone viral. It's suddenly cool in many different circles to be excited about Detroit. And that's new. *Real* new.

Detroit is suddenly sexy. How'd that happen?

Artists, of course, figure large in this budding renaissance. Creative sorts in droves have been drawn to Detroit's raw beauty. And why not? The real estate is famously cheap, and with its stately, abandoned architecture, the city echoes with mystery, romance, and drama. Even cooler for artists, there are no adults in the room. City hall is ineffective at best and overwhelmed at worst, with the result that Detroit is perhaps

LEFT: While in Detroit for a solo show at Inner State Gallery in Eastern Market, Nychos took the time to paint several walls in Eastern Market.

the least-governed city in the western industrial world. You can get away with almost anything—an exhilarating jolt of freedom hard to find in adequately supervised towns like New York. In this respect, Detroit has become a guerrilla artist's dream. A few years back, some puckish soul—an artist I'm convinced—mounted a beat-up bicycle delicately atop a twenty-foot pole in a field not far from downtown. As compositions go, it was at once elegant, forlorn, and funny, and loomed over the surrounding sumac and abandoned tires for months. Just try that in Brooklyn. See how many hours pass before someone complains and the cops show up.

Cause and effect are hard to prove, but just behind these artistic pioneers comes a far more populous wave, mostly washing in from the surrounding suburbs. In my twenty years back in Michigan, I've never seen anything like it. The optimist in me wonders whether we're witnessing proof positive of Richard Florida's thesis in *The Rise of the Creative Class*—that cities friendly to artists and gay people will, in turn, attract young professionals longing to soak up the bohemian atmosphere.

This is how American cities get rebuilt. New York, Boston, and Chicago, to cite three, all benefited from youngsters, white and black alike, sweeping in and taking over entire neighborhoods that had fallen into shabby disuse. Indeed, I'd add sick-of-the-suburbs kids to Florida's list of vital urban catalysts. New York's East Village, once a byword for crime and desolation, was repopulated in the eighties and nineties by this energetic cohort, all desperate for a little romance and urban grit. Which, it's worth pointing out, Detroit has in abundance.

The truth is, Detroit has been the beneficiary of one of the most remarkable rebrandings in recent history—a 180-degree turn that ought to be a case study in all business schools. Ever since the American car industry began to stumble in the 1970s, the rest of the country has regarded this one-time world leader with condescension or contempt. *Look how they fucked up their industry. Look how they fucked up their town.* Americans despise losers, and the fear spread that Detroit might just be a leading indicator for the nation as a whole. Small wonder we got the cold shoulder.

If Detroit's regeneration continues—no sure thing, alas—scholars will argue for years over the proximate causes. But a few things stand out. The big game-changer seems to have been the 2008 financial collapse, when much of the rest of the country suddenly caught up with us in the loser department. On account of the auto bailout, the media—in particular, foreign outlets—anointed Detroit one of the two epicenters of the crisis, along with Wall Street, once so high and mighty. For much of 2009 and 2010, reporters from around the world swarmed the city. It got hard to make your way down Lafayette Boulevard without bumping into a German TV anchor doing a stand-up. Also in 2009, *Time* magazine embedded a team of staffers in Detroit for a year-long intensive on the city. Much maligned at the time, the effort, along with the other media attention, helped generate a more intelligent national discussion of Detroit and its issues than the city had enjoyed for years.

Events of global consequence weren't the only factors. It's hard not to credit the four op-ed pieces that Toby Barlow, creative director at the Dearborn ad agency that handles Ford, wrote over the space of a year for the Sunday *New York Times*. Funny and insightful, Barlow's essays painted a picture of downtown life that was both hip and unexpectedly sophisticated. The pieces introduced an alien concept to Michiganders and the world, to wit: *Detroit can be fun. Who knew?* Barlow also broke what became a humongous media pile-on—the news that artists were buying houses in the city for as little as a hundred dollars, a man-bites-dog story that

The truth is, Detroit has been the beneficiary of one of the most remarkable rebrandings in recent history — a 180-degree turn that ought to be a case study in all business schools.

generated a flood of inquiries to Detroit real-estate agents. (For the record, that one-hundred-dollar house comes with fire damage and a huge hole in the roof.)

Then there's Slows Bar BQ, an immense success that set up shop on one of the bleakest blocks on a dismal stretch of Michigan Avenue, right in front of Detroit's famously abandoned train station. Slows has been cited so often in news accounts as evidence of Detroit's regeneration that it's become fashionable of late to pooh-pooh its impact, as if the Near West Side were always going to start sprouting cool businesses in front of the city's most famous ruin. By locating where it did, with windows gazing right at the Michigan Central Depot, Slows reframed the entire narrative about Detroit's fabulous ruins, converting what had been a humiliating symbol of collapse into a commercial asset. Particularly for those under forty, many of the city's empty landmarks suddenly look sexy, valuable elements in Detroit's haunting, one-of-a-kind cityscape.

Further sealing the deal was the 2011 Super Bowl spot that's come to be known as the "Chrysler/Eminem ad," with its gritty, gorgeous aesthetic and its "fuck you" attitude toward the rest of the country.

Word of Detroit's new coolness has spread far beyond Michigan. Indeed, the city increasingly finds itself on the tourist map, drawing city-loving young people from around the world. One recent visitor, Allison Reedy from Chattanooga, Tennessee, drove up with a group of fellow idealists to collaborate with locals to revive Roosevelt Park, the large, mostly overlooked green space in front of the depot.

I interviewed Allison and wrote an article for the paper about her excitement at being in Detroit, and her conviction that the city is pregnant with opportunity. She returned home before the piece appeared, so I sent it to her and got a nice email back thanking me. But it's the way she signed the note that made me catch my breath: *Jealous you get to live in Detroit.*

Ladies and gentlemen, the earth has shifted beneath our feet. Nobody's said that about Detroit for seventy-five years.

Michael H. Hodges covers the fine arts for the *Detroit News*. His book of architectural photography, *Michigan's Historic Railroad Stations* (Wayne State University Press, 2012), was named a 2013 Michigan Notable Book by the Library of Michigan.

THE ALLEY PROJECT

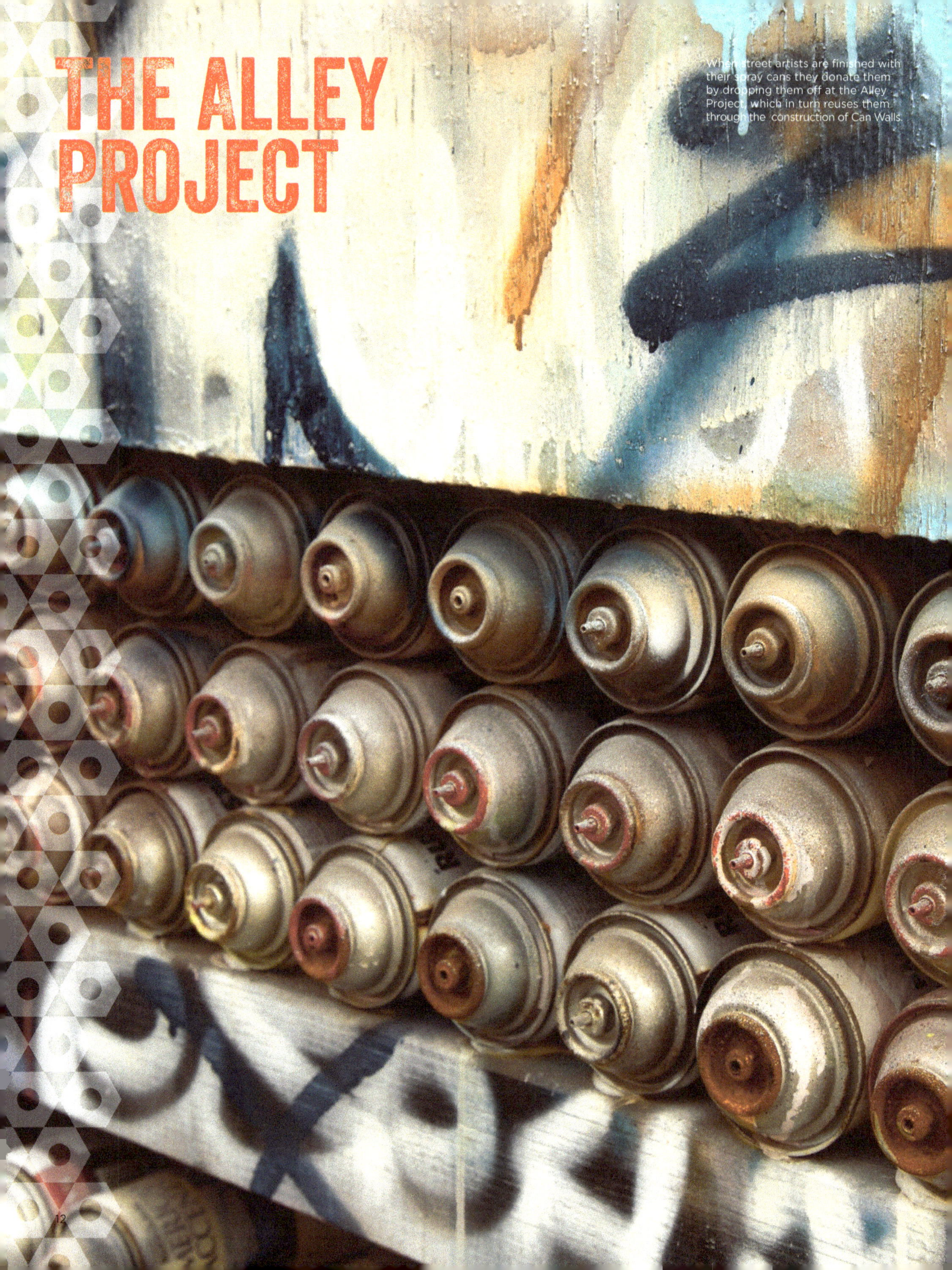

When street artists are finished with their spray cans they donate them by dropping them off at the Alley Project, which in turn reuses them through the construction of Can Walls.

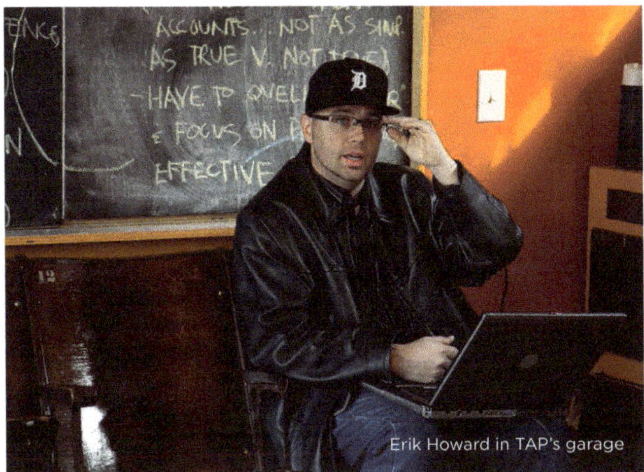

Erik Howard in TAP's garage

In the art world, the alley is the last place one expects to find art. But in Southwest Detroit, creativity has always lurked there.

For years, photographer Erik Howard dreamed of opening the world's eyes to what he witnessed daily in his neighborhood. In 2010, Howard found a way to lift the curtain with the launch of TAP (The Alley Project), an outdoor gallery showcase of street art's possibilities.

Now, people not only know about the alley, they gladly show up to see it just as Howard always imagined. "We get the world," he says.

TAP, located in the Southwest Detroit's Springwells neighborhood, between Avis, Falcon, Elsemere, and Woodmere Streets, includes a garage that functions as studio and gallery space for youth and neighborhood residents. Visitors also have access to two lots that were once abandoned but have since become a common art space for neighbors and other artists who gather and create at TAP.

Yet what's most distinct about TAP are the fifteen to twenty-five garages that have become canvases for young community artists. The garages form a strolling gallery unlike any other space in Detroit. The same young minds behind the art on display, ten- to twenty-five-year-olds, also had a hand in planning and curating the overall use of the space.

As a concept, TAP is counterintuitive in every way. The space is, after all, still an alley. But traffic hasn't slowed nor has support for the vivid way that some say TAP transforms what creative community redevelopment can look like.

"TAP is a prescriptive response based on a community's unique needs and assets," says Howard, thirty-four. "People can walk up and down the alley, meet the neighbors; they can create and see pieces of street art in a way that is legal, safe, and supports learning and relationships."

What was once an area subject to random graffiti, even vandalism, has become a go-to source of community pride. "We have people from all over who come through just to see. We've had people from China, Japan, Canada, Italy, Brazil; you name it," he says. Even urban planners and design experts look to the alley as a blueprint for creative engagement and land use.

"When you come to TAP you're experiencing art in someone's backyard. You're actually in the backyards of six people who happen to see the potential of promoting relationships through creativity," Howard says. "Because we have permission, everyone has a stake— neighbors, youth, organizers. It's clear where you can paint and where you can't. TAP is about an intentional culture-change."

The participatory nature of the project helped grow its fan base far beyond Southwest Detroit. TAP received a thirty-eight-thousand-dollar grant in 2010 through Community + Public Art Detroit (CPAD), an ambitious partnership between the Skillman Foundation, the J. P. Morgan Chase Foundation, and Detroit's College for Creative Studies. Of course, the funding helped to spread the creativity by facilitating the purchase of the lots, which now function as TAP's common space. Bike racks made by local metal artists along with mobile canvases have been added, as have community mural workshops.

TAP's success can't be measured in traditional terms, Howard says. "We measure our success by the frequency and the depth of unlikely relationships that are created because of our process of bringing assets together," he says.

For now, revenue is irrelevant, and so is formal training. The art that's created is sometimes destroyed by the very elements that make the space unique. There are no walls, providing no defense against Mother Nature.

"This is a living, breathing art environment," he says. "We're open and everyone who comes is opened up in a new way to the community and to the idea that learning and transformation can happen through art, through sharing, all in an alley. You can't get any more creative."

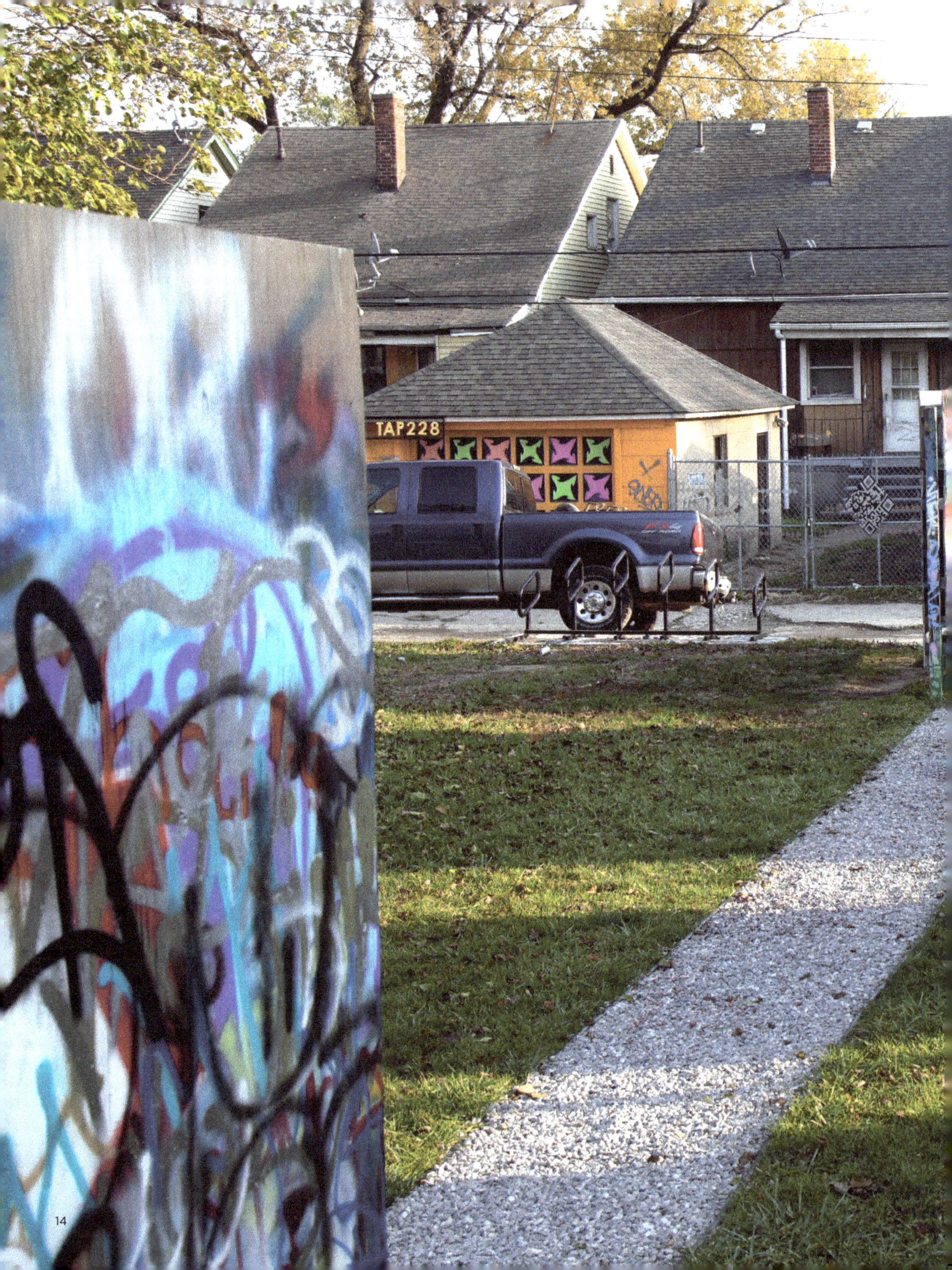
TAP228

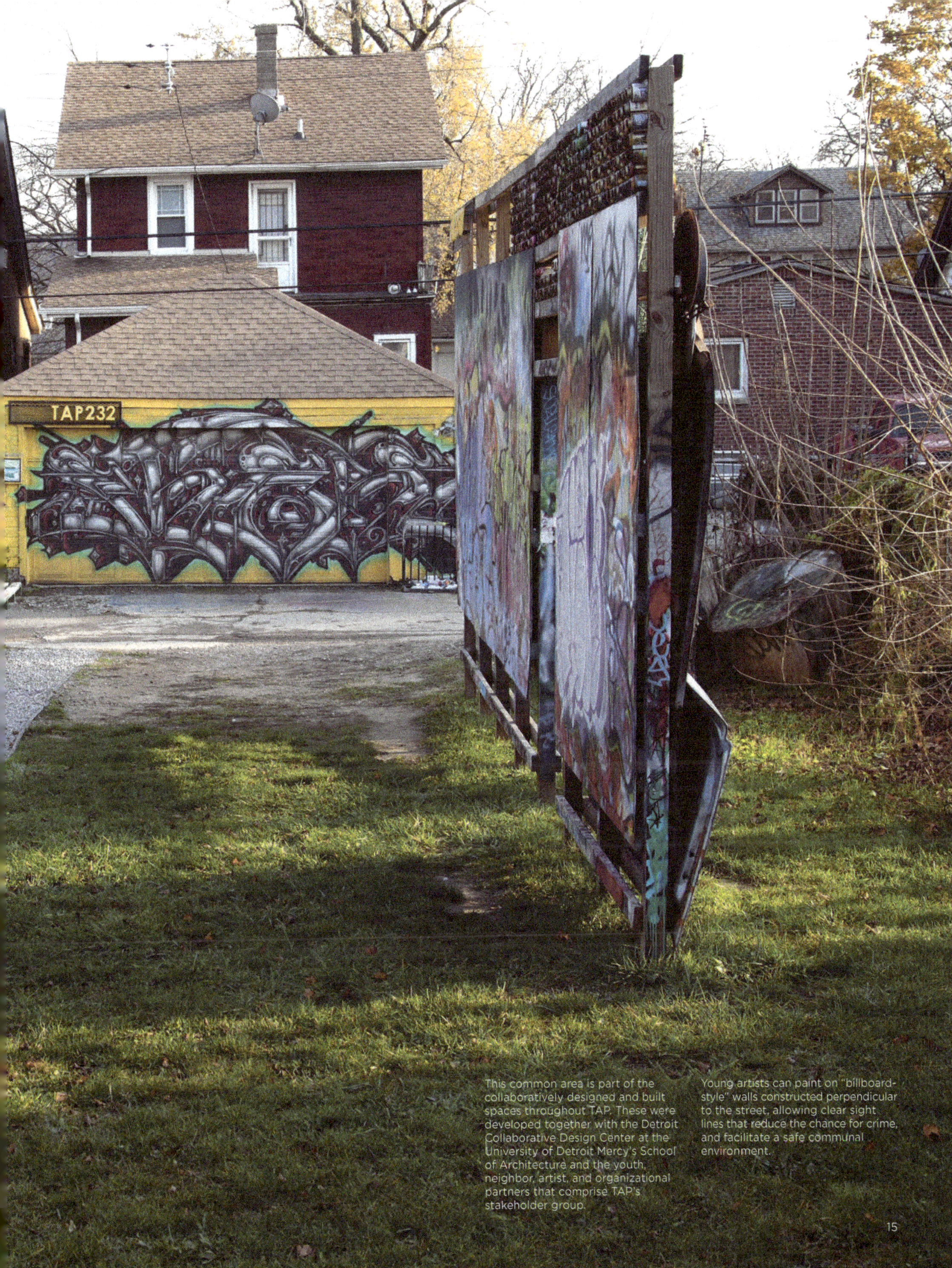

This common area is part of the collaboratively designed and built spaces throughout TAP. These were developed together with the Detroit Collaborative Design Center at the University of Detroit Mercy's School of Architecture and the youth, neighbor, artist, and organizational partners that comprise TAP's stakeholder group.

Young artists can paint on "billboard-style" walls constructed perpendicular to the street, allowing clear sight lines that reduce the chance for crime, and facilitate a safe communal environment.

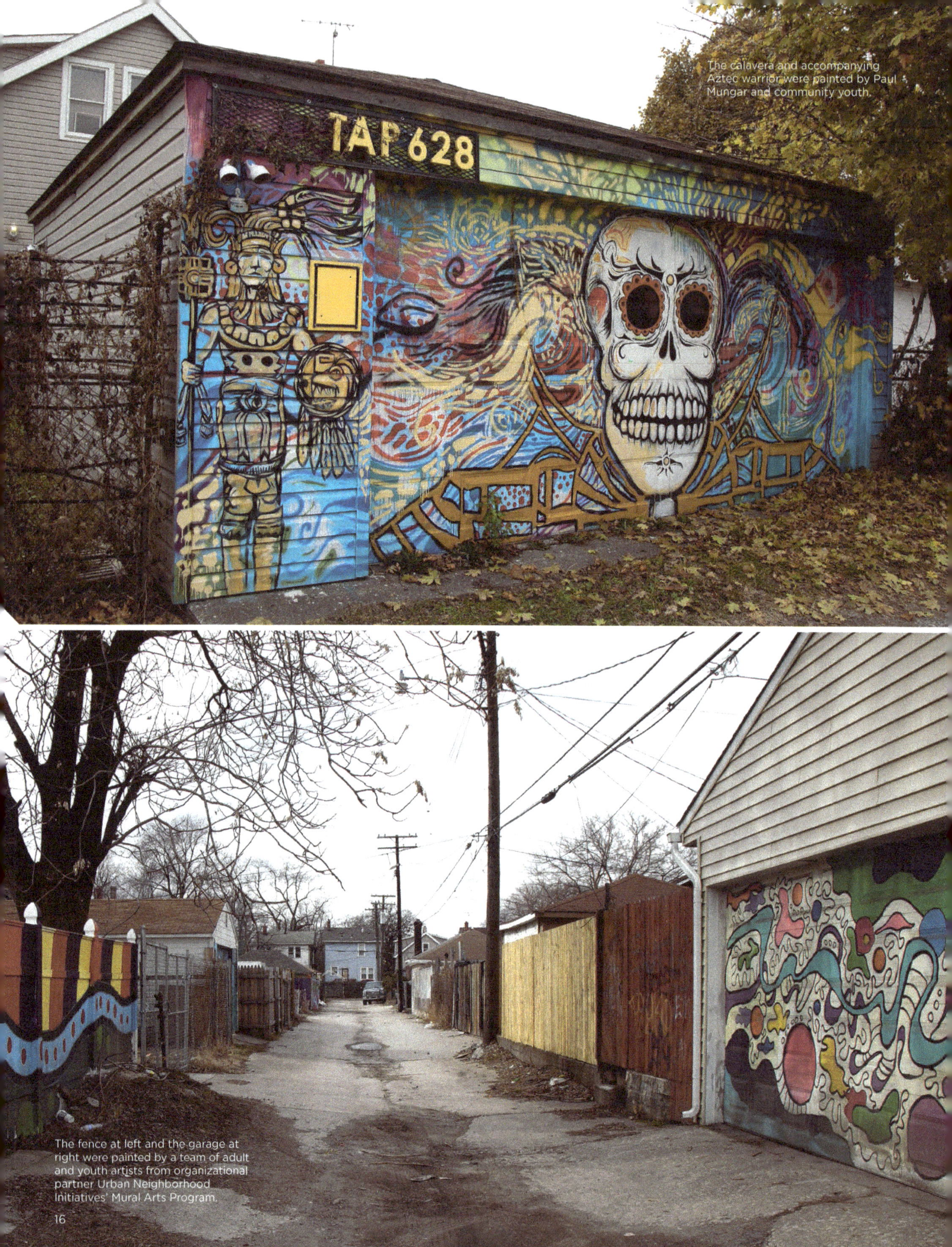

The calavera and accompanying Aztec warrior were painted by Paul Mungar and community youth.

The fence at left and the garage at right were painted by a team of adult and youth artists from organizational partner Urban Neighborhood Initiatives' Mural Arts Program.

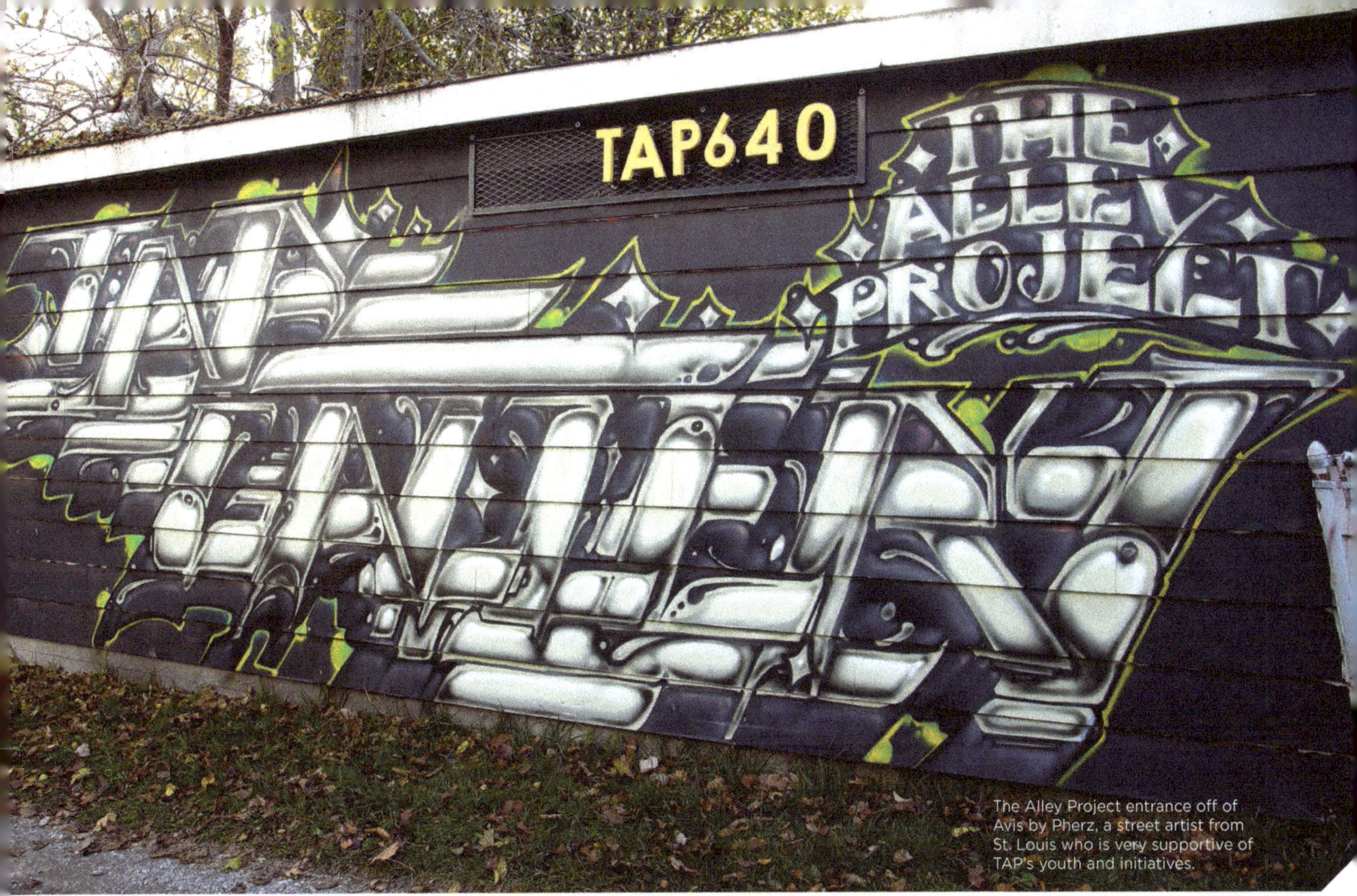

The Alley Project entrance off of Avis by Pherz, a street artist from St. Louis who is very supportive of TAP's youth and initiatives.

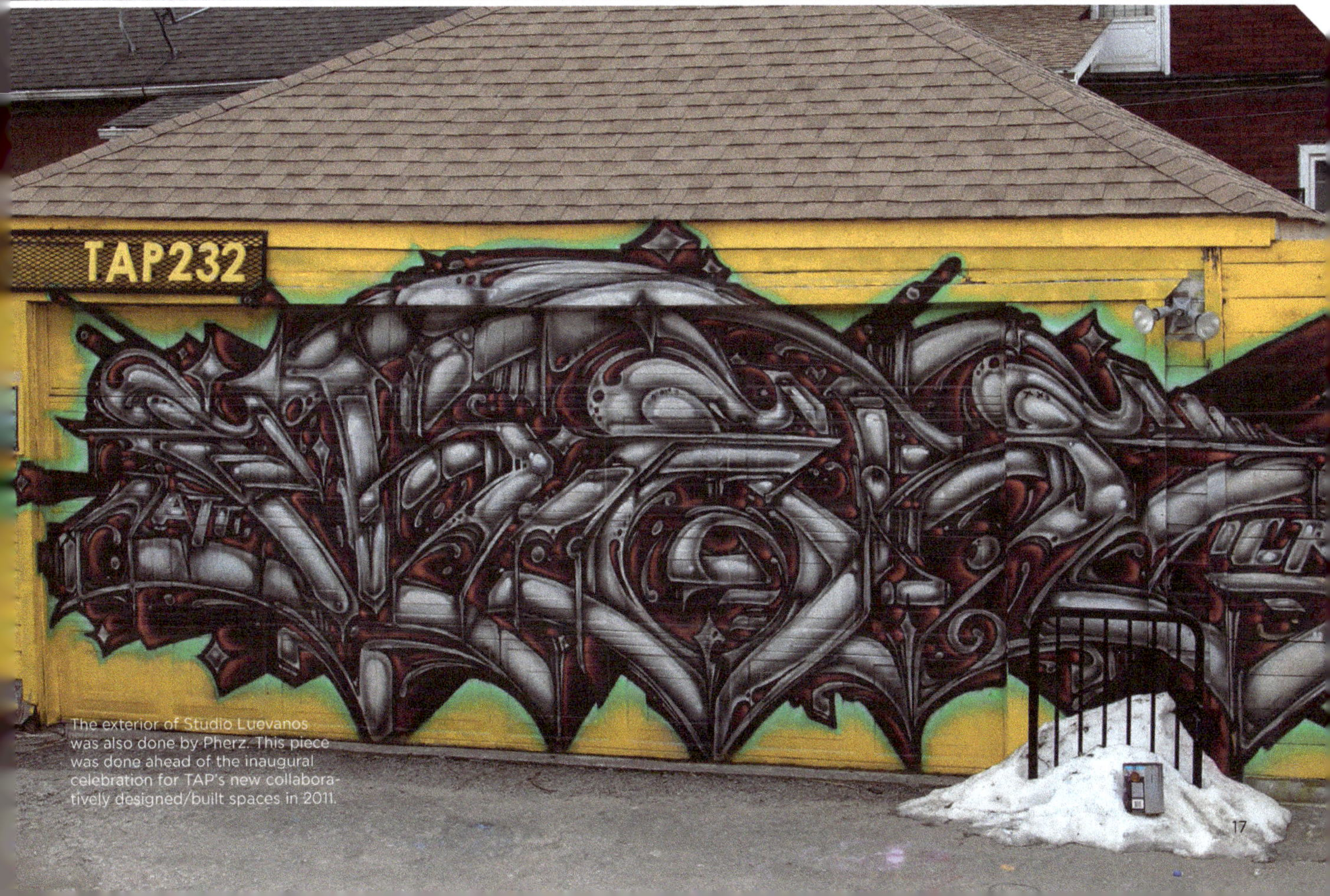

The exterior of Studio Luevanos was also done by Pherz. This piece was done ahead of the inaugural celebration for TAP's new collaboratively designed/built spaces in 2011.

BANKSY

The Banksy is now on public display at 555 Nonprofit Gallery in their new quarters in a repurposed police station in Mexicantown.

A Banksy lives in Detroit

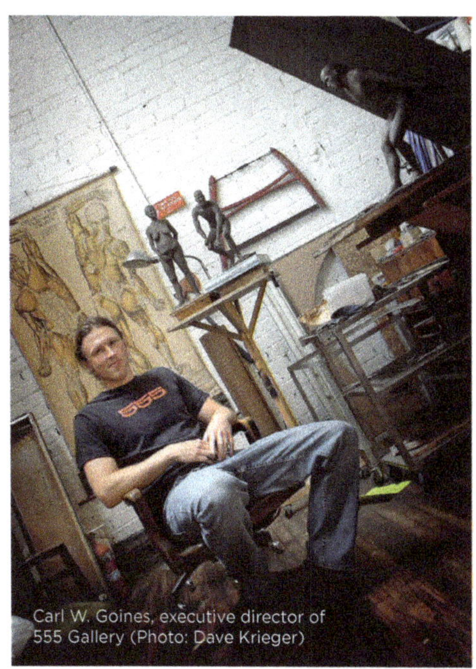
Carl W. Goines, executive director of 555 Gallery (Photo: Dave Krieger)

Legend has it that the famously reclusive British street artist made a pilgrimage to Detroit sometime in 2010 to add his mark to the city's most visited industrial ruin, the crumbling old Packard car plant. Banksy's mark in Motown features a seven-foot-by-seven-foot stenciled mural of a boy artist toting a can of red paint. Next to him are the words "I remember when all this was trees."

The painting was instantly hailed as an original and one more reason for public art and graffiti purists to descend on Detroit.

Only those who moved quickly got a chance to view the mural, as Banksy must have intended, on a wall inside the remains of the hollowed-out Packard plant. Over the years, other images found around Detroit have been linked to the artist, but all were destroyed before they could be traced back to the graffiti giant.

Today, the slab of concrete that Banksy tagged amid the remains of the Packard plant exists in, of all places, a gallery. Artists from Detroit's 555 Nonprofit Gallery and Studios swooped in to rescue the image from destruction. They took the entire fifteen-hundred-pound wall with the help of an oxyacetylene torch, a mini-tractor, and a gas-powered masonry saw. The gallery also took a ton of criticism for boldly disrespecting the location Banksy chose.

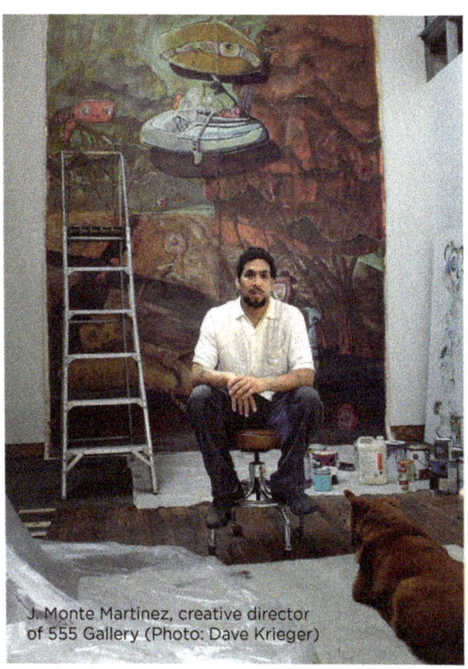
J. Monte Martinez, creative director of 555 Gallery (Photo: Dave Krieger)

The artists have insisted that they were acting in the name of artistic preservation. "We're watching this beautiful city crumble around us and we can't do anything to stop it," Carl W. Goines, executive director and co-founder of the 555 Gallery, told the Detroit Free Press. "So with this fine-art piece—and it's not just everyday graffiti that you might whiz by—here was our opportunity to do something. It would have been destroyed if we didn't make the effort."

Reportedly, gallery supporters helped raise $250,000 to settle a lawsuit brought on behalf of the Packard plant's owner.

Images of Banksy's Packard mural have shown up on the official Banksy website, www.banksy.co.uk. They continue to make the rounds in street-art circles and on the Internet.

Still, the world is left to wonder whether Banksy would approve of the fate that has befallen his only known work in Detroit.

Perhaps he'll make his way back to make another mark on Detroit.

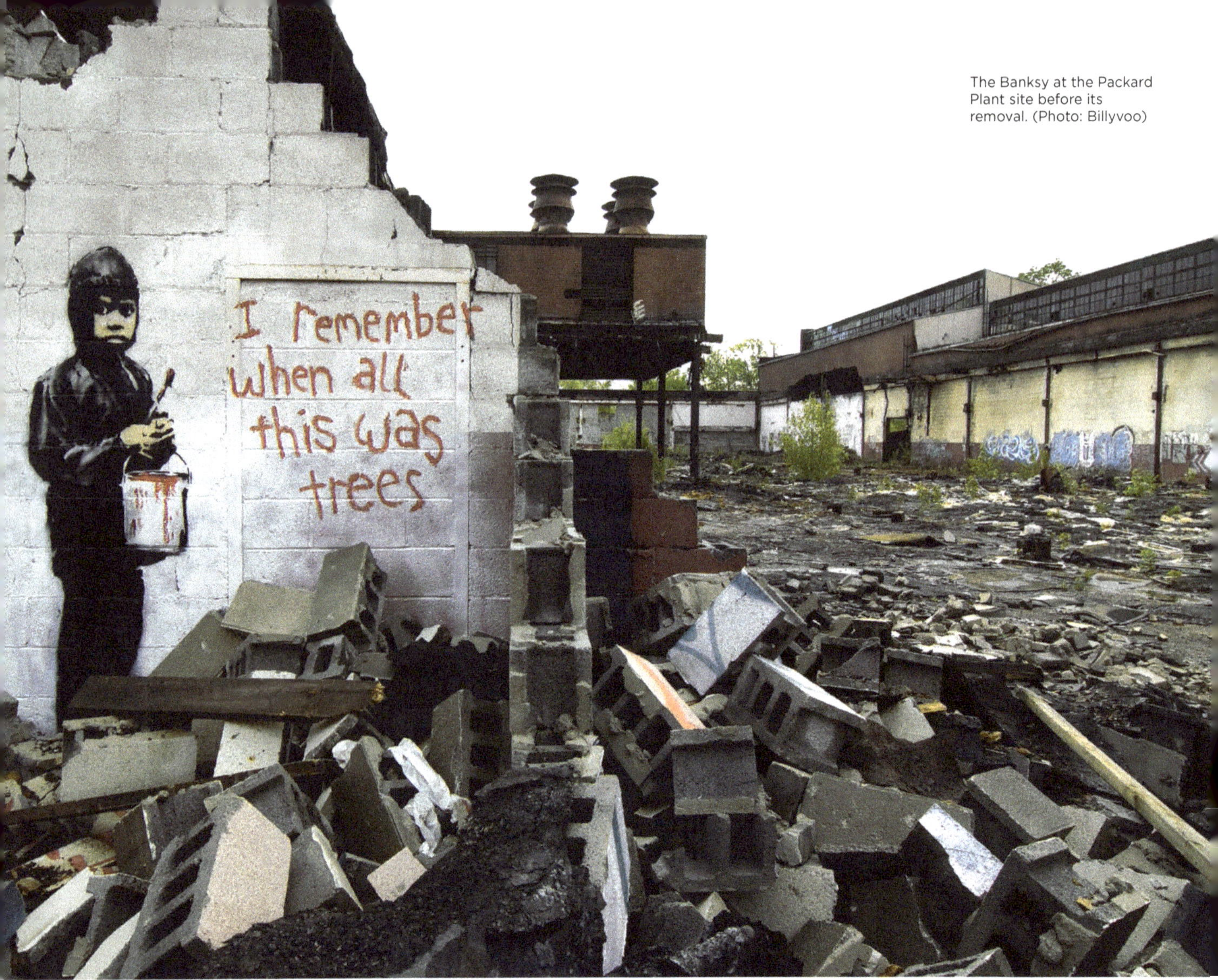

The Banksy at the Packard Plant site before its removal. (Photo: Billyvoo)

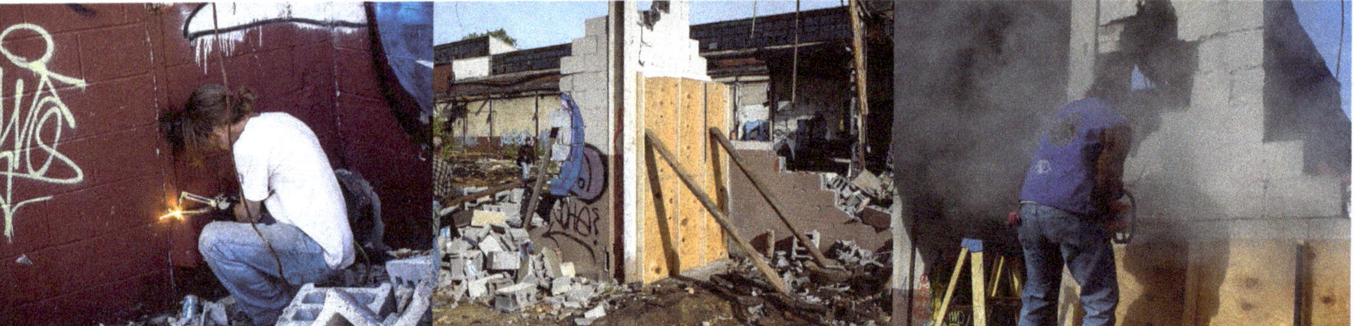

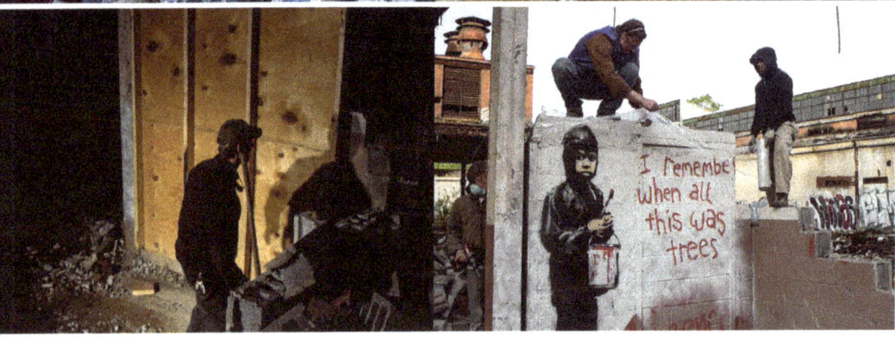

PHOTO PROGRESSION: The removal of the artwork was a difficult undertaking considering its location and immense weight. (Photos: Jason Matthews)

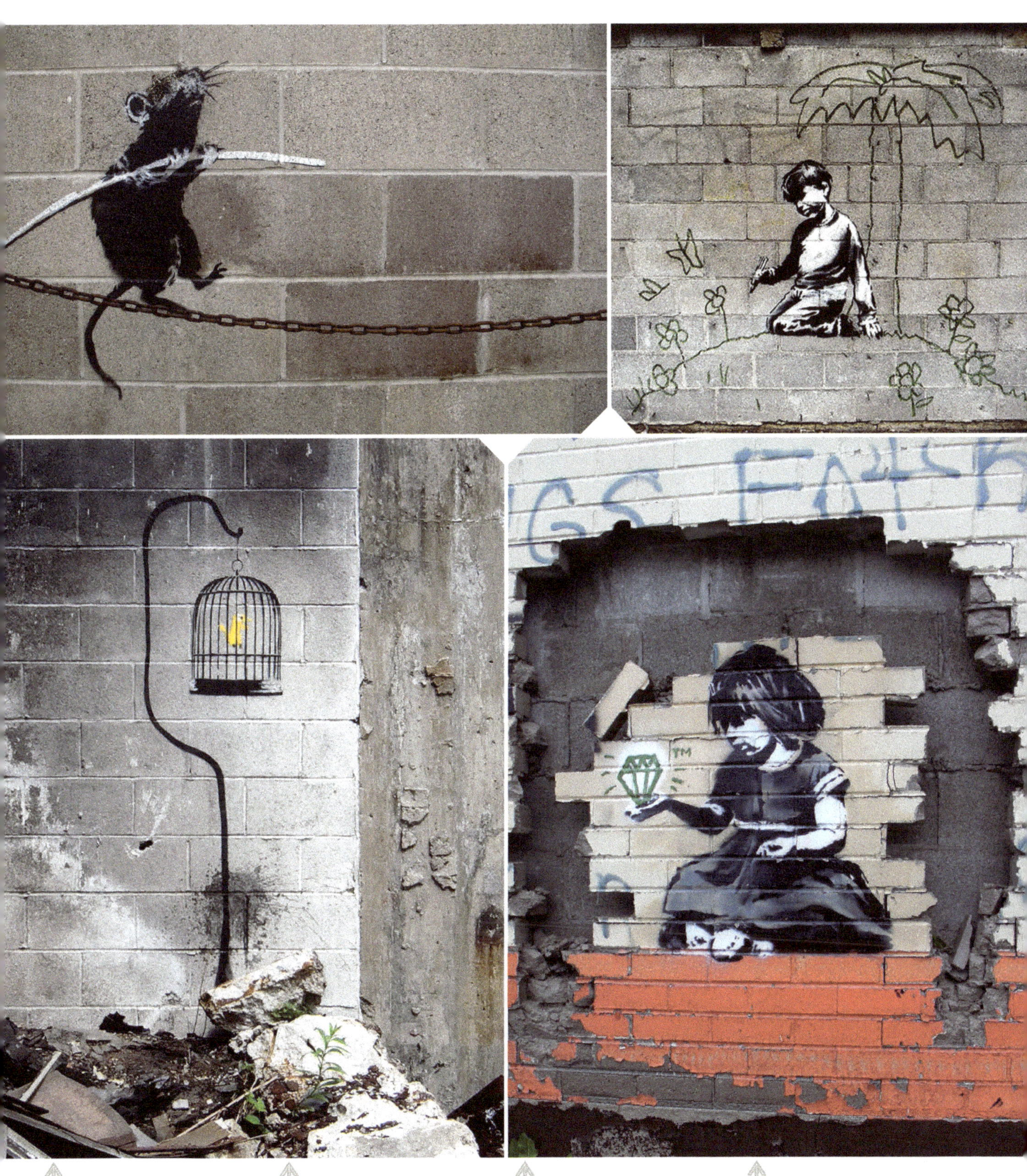

TOP LEFT: The tightrope-walking rat was painted on an occupied industrial building, but was quickly painted over. (Photo: Billyvoo)

TOP RIGHT: This painting was in the Cass Corridor and lasted only a short while before being power washed off the building. (Photo: Rebecca Solano)

BOTTOM LEFT: The canary was painted in the Packard Plant. (Photo: Billyvoo)

BOTTOM RIGHT: The girl with a diamond was on a drycleaner's wall and didn't last long before somebody removed her brick by brick. (Photo: Becks Davis)

MATTHEW BARNEY

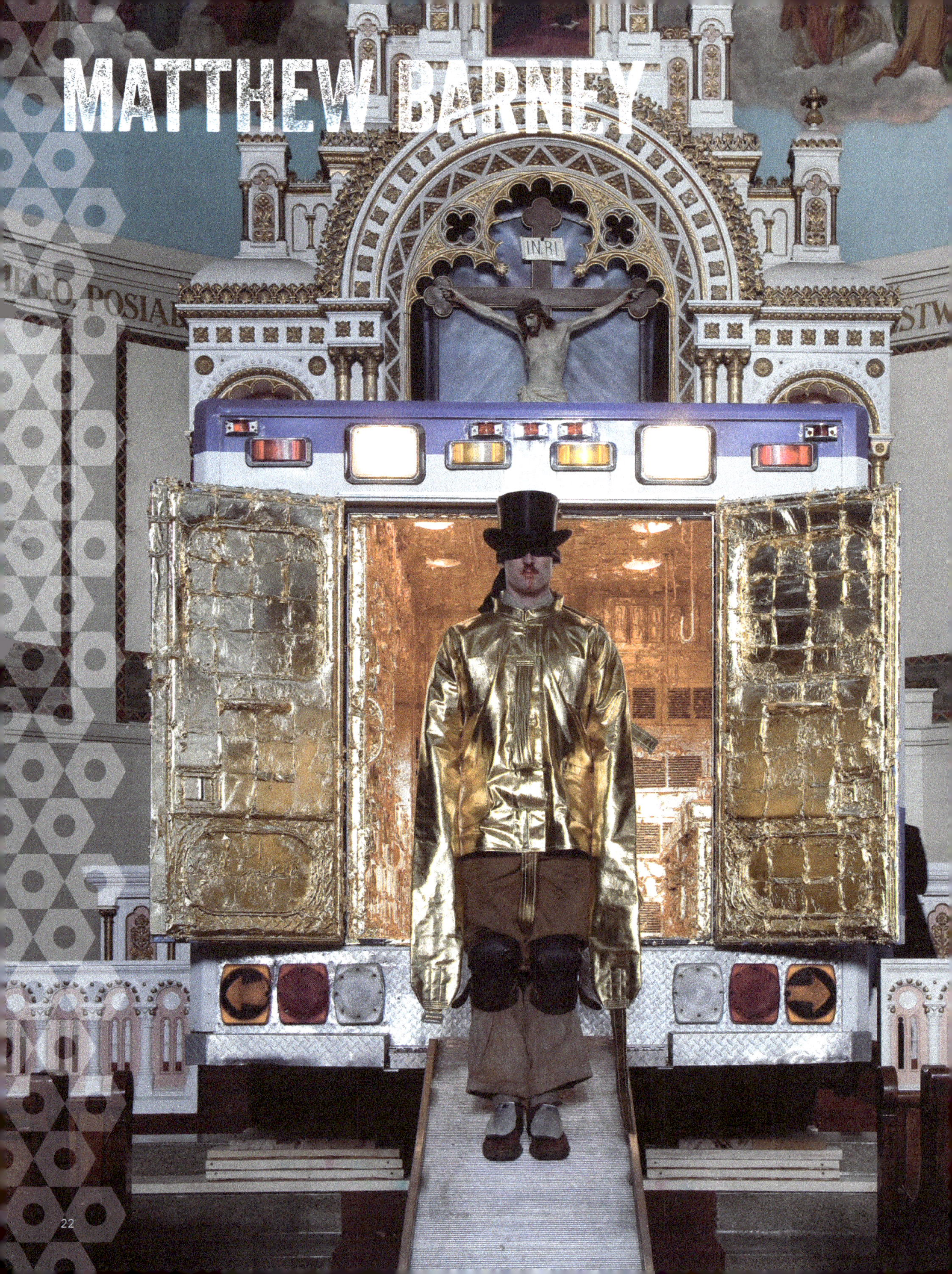

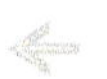

LEFT: Matthew Barney at St. John Cantius Catholic Church during performance of *SEKHEM.*

CREDITS:
Matthew Barney and Jonathan Bepler
SEKHEM, 2010
Production Still
Photo: David Regen
Copyright 2010 Matthew Barney
Courtesy Gladstone Gallery, New York and Brussels

BY Rebecca R. Hart

Matthew Barney, Alchemist

New York-based sculptor and filmmaker Matthew Barney chose Detroit as a location to develop the prologue and second act of his epic opera, *River of Fundament*. The opera considers the afterlife and casts the American automobile, a surrogate for the male ego, as a principle character. Passages from Norman Mailer's novel *Ancient Evenings* based on the Egyptian myth of Osiris inspired the libretto. Barney activated the narrative within the American industrial landscape by staging performances in and near Detroit's Rouge River. Between 2008 and 2010, he researched, wrote, and filmed *SEKHEM* (a prologue, 2009) and the public performance *KHU* (2010) using an international team anchored by a large contingent of local artists. Berlin-based composer Jonathan Bepler was his collaborator throughout the project.

By transposing Mailer's account of Egyptian beliefs about the soul's chthonic journey and rendering it within the geography and lore of Detroit, Barney complicated the narrative of *River of Fundament*: "As I understand the novel *Ancient Evenings*, it takes the Egyptian mythology as a source and it uses the body as a site to abstract that mythology, much in the same way that I am trying to do in some of my projects. In that case, the body is simultaneously the landscape and the literal body."[1]

Detroit was chosen as the location for the performances because of synergies between Barney's practice and the region's geology as well as its manufacturing heritage and social history. Often the artist uses salt as a medium for his sculpture; thus the presence of a deep vein of salt beneath the Detroit River attracted him to the area. This mineral deposit drew him here, yet it was the Motown culture that he experienced while here that seduced him into developing the opera in unexpected ways.[2] Detroit's manufacturing history and status as the world's automotive capital developed from its past reputation as home to a maker-culture during the nineteenth and early twentieth centuries. During the course of *KHU* an automobile is unearthed, cut apart, and then its molten remains are formed into a new regal symbol, a djed. Filmed during the restructuring of the auto industry, the second act of *River of Fundament* had particular resonance with Barney's consideration of death and rebirth.

For the narrative platform of the prologue, Barney turned to the legacy of Detroit-born artist James Lee Byars (1932-97). In December 2009 at Saint John Cantius Church, Barney performed as the protagonist in a sequence that faithfully recalled Byars's work *The Death of James Lee Byars*. The Roman Catholic Church, once in the heart of a southwest Detroit neighborhood, now is surrounded by the municipal sewage treatment plant, a location that echoes Mailer's description of the Nile as the river of feces. For his performance, Barney substituted a gold-leaf-covered interior of an ambulance for Byars's similarly prepared stage and proscenium. The addition of several actors who played detectives shifted the novel's narrative from ancient times into the vernacular of a made-for-TV crime scene investigation. As a performer, Barney emerges from the ambulance as Byars, wearing a goldlamé jacket with long sleeves buckled tight to his body (the figure straitjacketed) and is put into a 1979 Pontiac Firebird Trans Am—a Barneyesque riff. The car is sealed (it is a crime scene) and then races through the city streets before careening off the Belle Isle Bridge into the Detroit River with Barney, still restrained inside. Barney reenacts Byars's performance while echoing details of Harry Houdini's bridge jump here, when he miraculously escaped after being handcuffed, enclosed in a packing box, and hurled from the Belle Isle Bridge in 1906.

On a cold and wet day in October 2010, *KHU* was performed and filmed as an eight-hour event. The performance began at the Detroit Institute of Arts, where guests gathered for lunch and a viewing of the prologue, a special edit of the footage filmed during the previous December. Then guests boarded buses bound for the Rouge River, which deposited the audience in front of an abandoned glue factory. There machinists assembled steel violins. One by one the musicians plucked the instruments off the assembly-line, tuned them, and serenaded guests with a haunting aria that featured passages from the *Book of the Dead*. Next, the chamber orchestra and guests boarded a long barge and set out into the Rouge River. Near Zug Island, the barge stopped to observe an unfolding crime scene. In the performance, a lead investigator, played by Aimee Mullins, supervises as the remains of a 1967 Chrysler Crown Imperial New Yorker are hoisted onto the barge and examined. As if recalling an ancient memory, Mullins's character, "Agent Isis," shifts her personae: she immerses herself in mythological imagination as she conflates the auto remains with memories of the body of her deceased husband, the Egyptian god and king Osiris. Caught within the ancient story, Isis mourns Osiris's death before she is inseminated astride the engine block, a reference to the myth.

The barge then traveled downriver to the dock at McLouth Steel Mill where the plant was converted into a mammoth ironworks to stage the climax of *KHU*. On the bank, Agent Isis offloads the evidence (the recovered auto carcass), as a dispute ensues with a demolition foreman at the steel mill, a character who is based on the personality of Osiris's brother, Set. During the conflict, the Crown Imperial is cut apart further, an allusion to a version of the Osiris story that describes his dismemberment. Agent Isis emerges from the argument still maintaining possession of the vehicle. Its battered parts are transported uphill to a series of huge furnaces. Five iron cupolas are alight as massive amounts of scrap metals are loaded into the smelters. The remains of 1967 Chrysler are added to the molten metal. Just as the iron was ready to run from the cupolas into a mold below, the planned culmination of Barney and Bepler's operatic finale, the weather became extreme, forcing the audience to leave the site.

During the following year, Matthew Barney refined the iron form that was cast on that October evening into the sculpture *DJED*, the symbol of Osiris and Egyptian majesty. Throughout the project, he relied on the support and goodwill of the Detroit artist community, who provided advice and offered material support to facilitate the production of *River of Fundament* in Detroit. The completed project is scheduled to debut in Munich, Germany, during 2014. Those artists who worked directly with Barney experienced firsthand his Promethean vision and work ethic. The Detroiters who joined guests from around the world to experience the live performance of *KHU* had the privilege of witnessing the alchemy of great art, as our native landscape was reinscripted by transformative myths old and new.

Rebecca R. Hart is associate curator in the James Pearson Duffy Department of Contemporary Art at the Detroit Institute of Arts

NOTES

1. Matthew Barney as quoted in Isabelle Dervaux "From Residual Marks to Drawing as Mediation: An Interview with Matthew Barney," *Subliming Vessel: the Drawings of Matthew Barney* (New York: The Morgan Library et al., 2013), 57.

2. Site research included a trip underground to consider the practicality of making a portion of the film in the salt mines. Extensive knowledge was gained through conversations and tours with Severstal NA, the Russian owned plant that was formerly Rouge Steel, and Edward C. Levy Company, which manages slag waste removal at the Rouge.

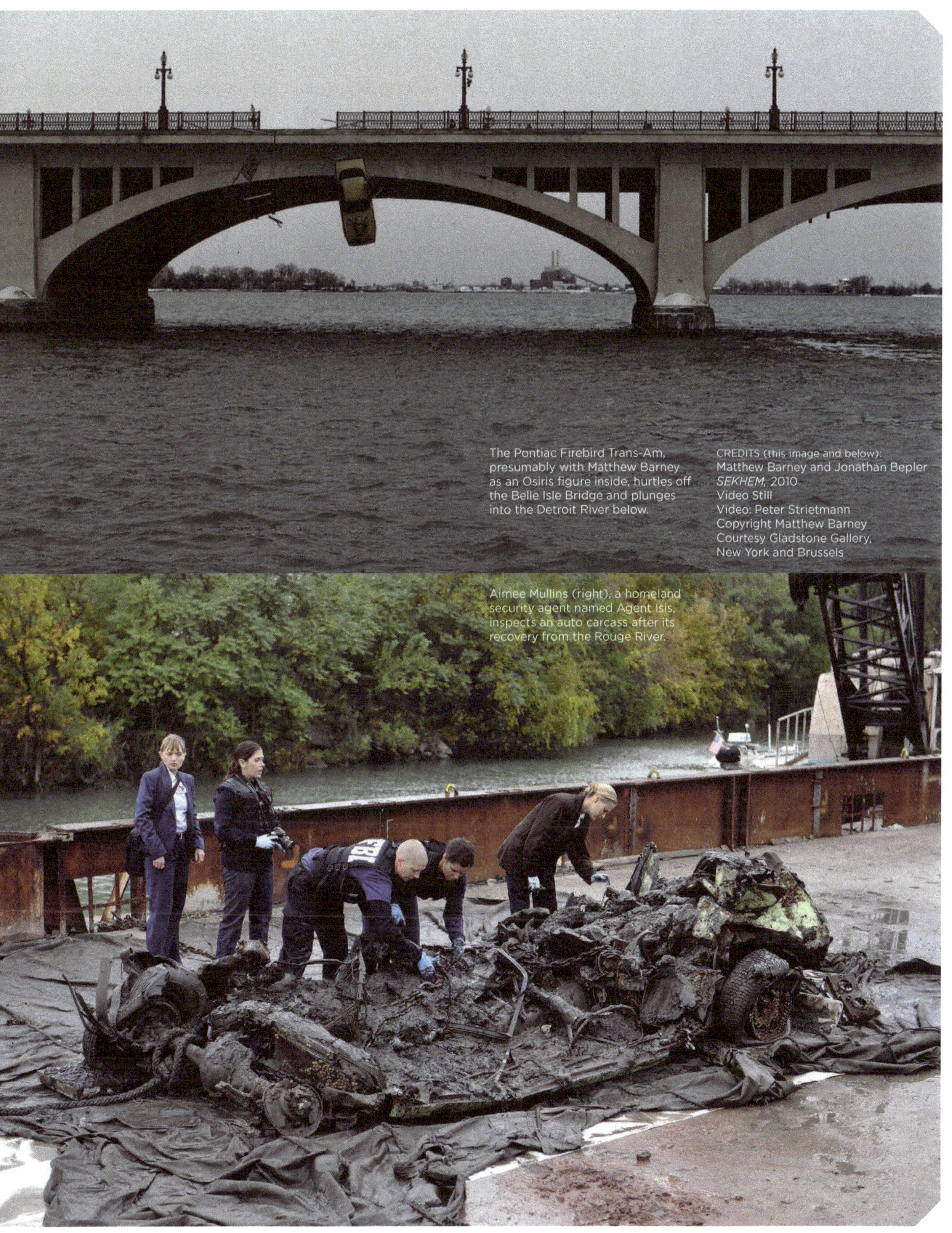

The Pontiac Firebird Trans-Am, presumably with Matthew Barney as an Osiris figure inside, hurtles off the Belle Isle Bridge and plunges into the Detroit River below.

CREDITS (this image and below):
Matthew Barney and Jonathan Bepler
SEKHEM, 2010
Video Still
Video: Peter Strietmann
Copyright Matthew Barney
Courtesy Gladstone Gallery, New York and Brussels

Aimee Mullins (right), a homeland security agent named Agent Isis, inspects an auto carcass after its recovery from the Rouge River.

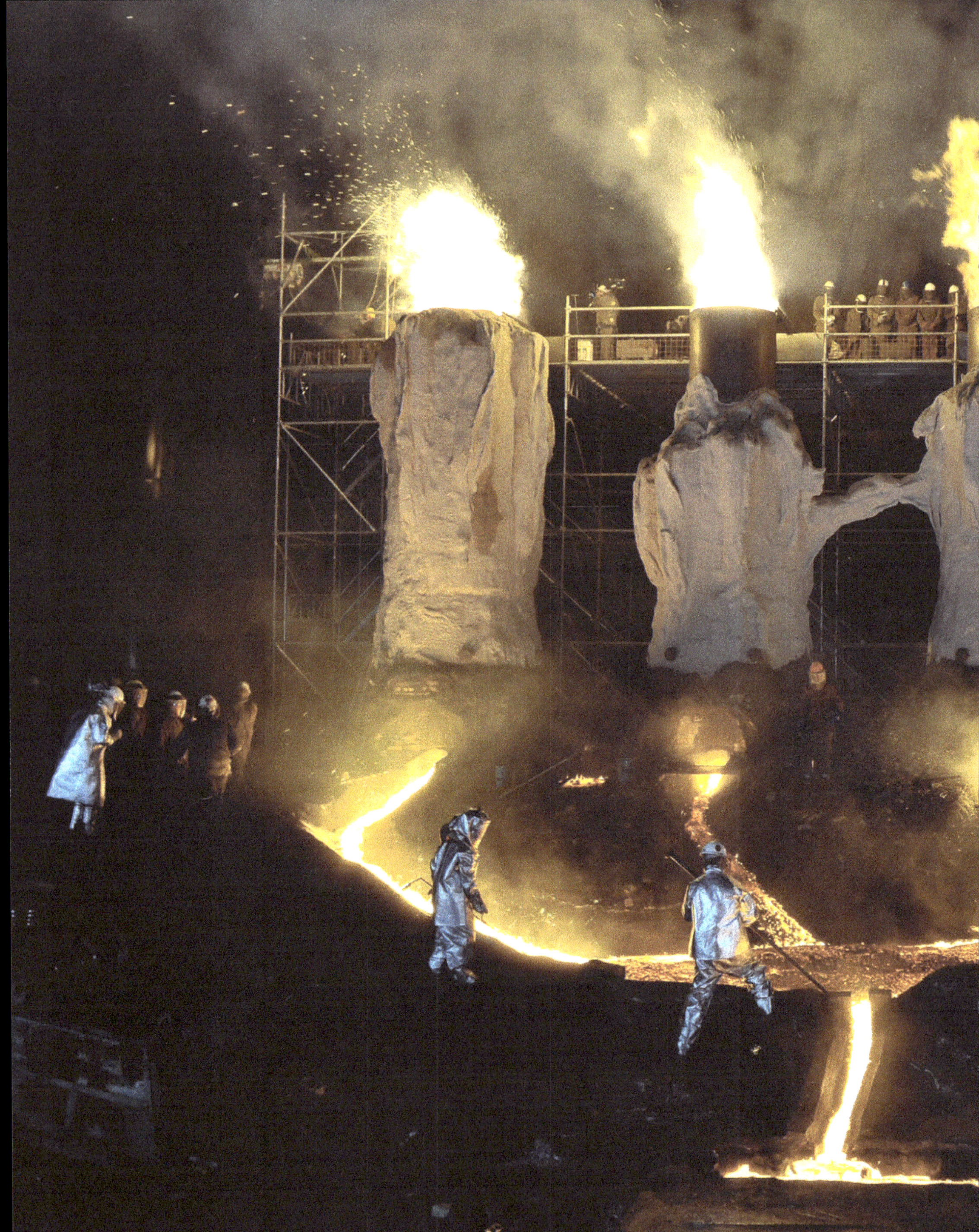

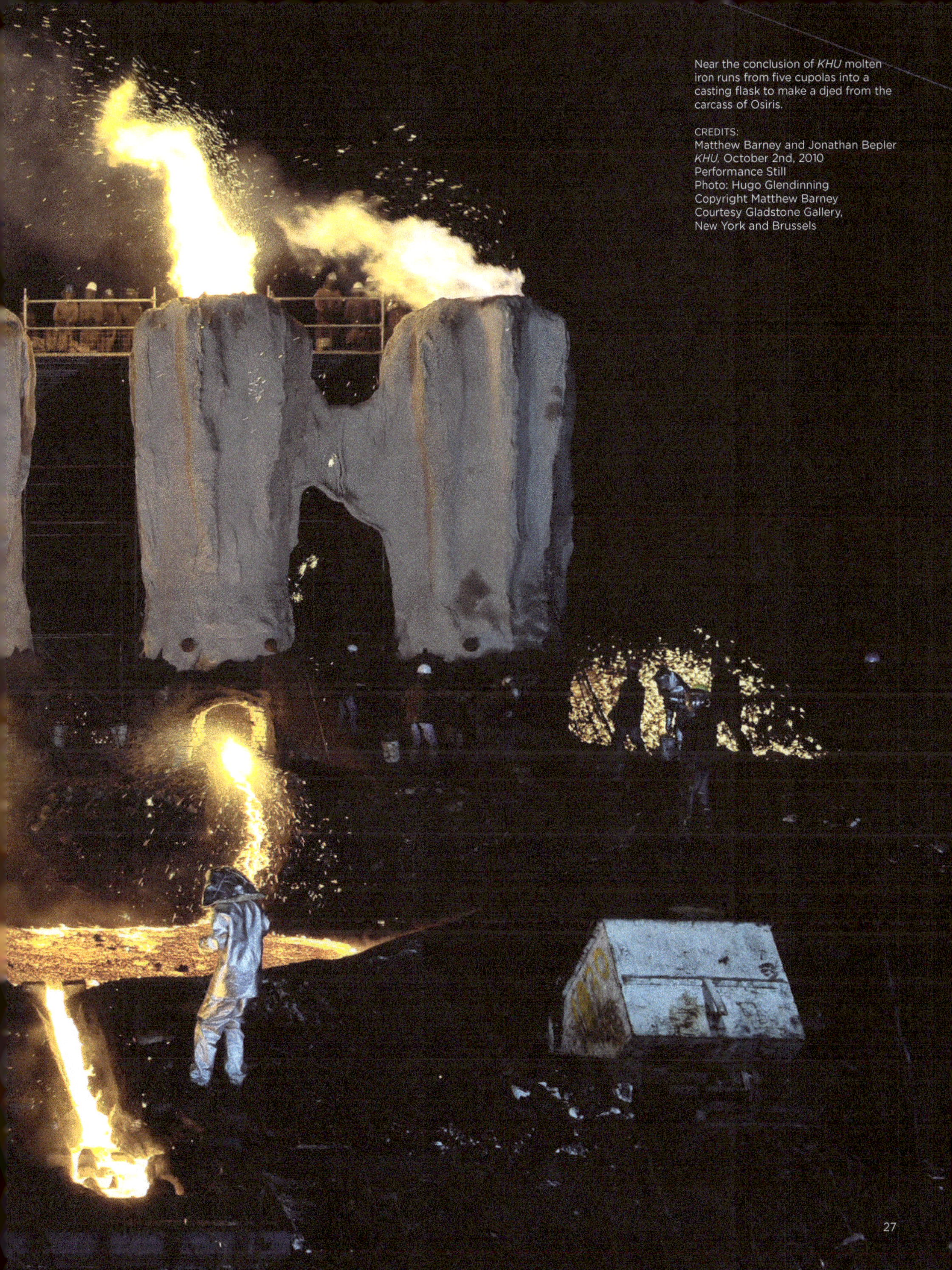

Near the conclusion of *KHU* molten iron runs from five cupolas into a casting flask to make a djed from the carcass of Osiris.

CREDITS:
Matthew Barney and Jonathan Bepler
KHU, October 2nd, 2010
Performance Still
Photo: Hugo Glendinning
Copyright Matthew Barney
Courtesy Gladstone Gallery,
New York and Brussels

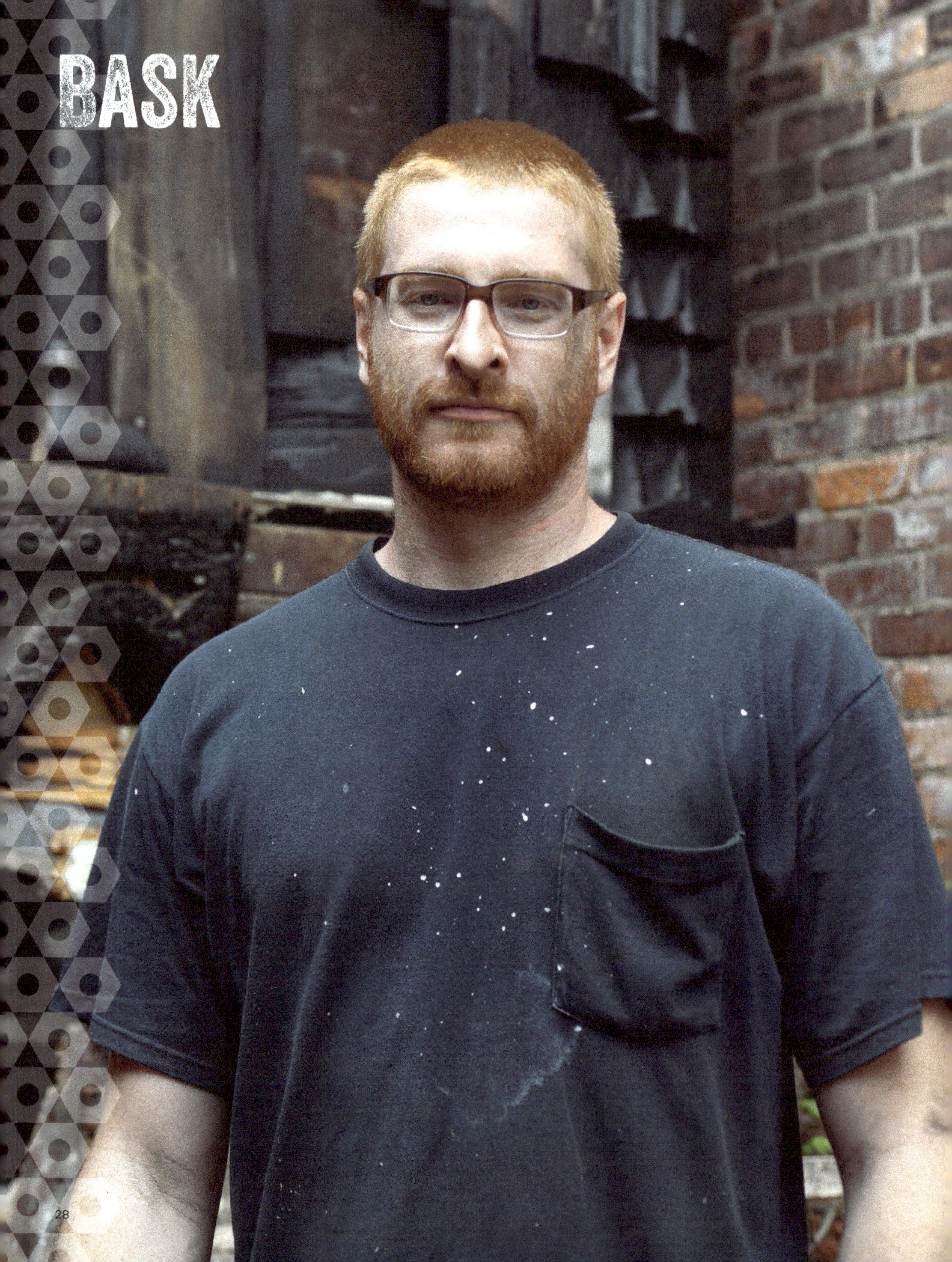

BASK

This may be hard to believe, but Czech-born artist Ales Hostomsky swears it's true.

If not for the lessons he learned in Detroit, a world away from the sun and sand of his St. Petersburg, Florida, home, there might be no BASK, the alias that has made him a self-taught talent known around the world.

Careful eyes might even notice his raw, edgy imagery in the film *Iron Man 3*. BASK was commissioned to do a total of fourteen paintings for the film, including a re-creation of a 2004 piece entitled *When It Rains, It Pours*. The painting features a massive bomb crashing into the Morton Salt Girl.

Wherever he goes and whenever he's asked, BASK traces his creative roots and his subsequent rise to four pivotal years spent living in Detroit. In 2000, a fellow artist who happened to be from Detroit encouraged him to come for a visit. BASK tossed a painting in the back of his friend's car and hit the highway. It was, he says, one of the smartest moves he ever made. "Creatively," says BASK, who dropped out of high school, "Detroit was a total coming-of-age story for me."

His launch started practically the moment he arrived. He sold the only painting he had with him, and he was signed, almost immediately, as a represented artist by Detroit's now-closed C-PoP Gallery.

"It gave me the confidence to put myself out there in a big way. Some of the relationships and contacts I made up there are why I'm able to make my complete living today as an artist. Detroit just opened everything up for me, a huge building block for my art."

While BASK returns to Detroit at least once a year for gallery shows of his work, he's left behind only two major pieces. The most recent is a giant monochromatic "D" covering an old shipping bay in Eastern Market and formed out of found objects. BASK's most notable work in Detroit is an untitled mural just outside the city that looks, at first glance, to be an homage to scrubbing bubbles.

"It can take on different interpretations depending on who's looking at it and based on the fact that my name is up there and it's a verb," he says. "But it's really very symbolic of what the city is in a constant struggle to do, to clean up the city, to put in the work to preserve things."

The streets taught him how to see everything as a potential canvas. "I don't remember the last time I painted on traditional canvas. It's too pretty. I draw zero inspiration from it. Whatever the street discards and finds no longer useful, that's where I start."

BASK has found and lost himself painting on just about every kind of surface, from windows, parts of rooftops, wooden and metal fencing, tarps, and entire sides of buildings. BASK prefers found things.

"I didn't grow up on the streets of Detroit," he says. "But my soul is definitely of the place. When I look at Detroit, all I see is potential. The city's not hiding from anyone. It's been through hell and back, but it's still got this willingness to keep on struggling and surviving no matter what. I travel to a lot of cities that I love to visit, but I've never seen another city that comes close to capturing that raw inspiration."

For BASK, there is one other reason to love Detroit. Even to his surprise, his work always sells.

"The city is broke economically and downtrodden, but I do a show up there and people come out and they support you. You have to see it to really understand it. In Florida I do a show and it's a great party for the hip crowd. But in Detroit, the struggle to be creative means something different. It's like art makes a difference to the city and they want you to know it."

(Photos: Sal Rodreguiz)

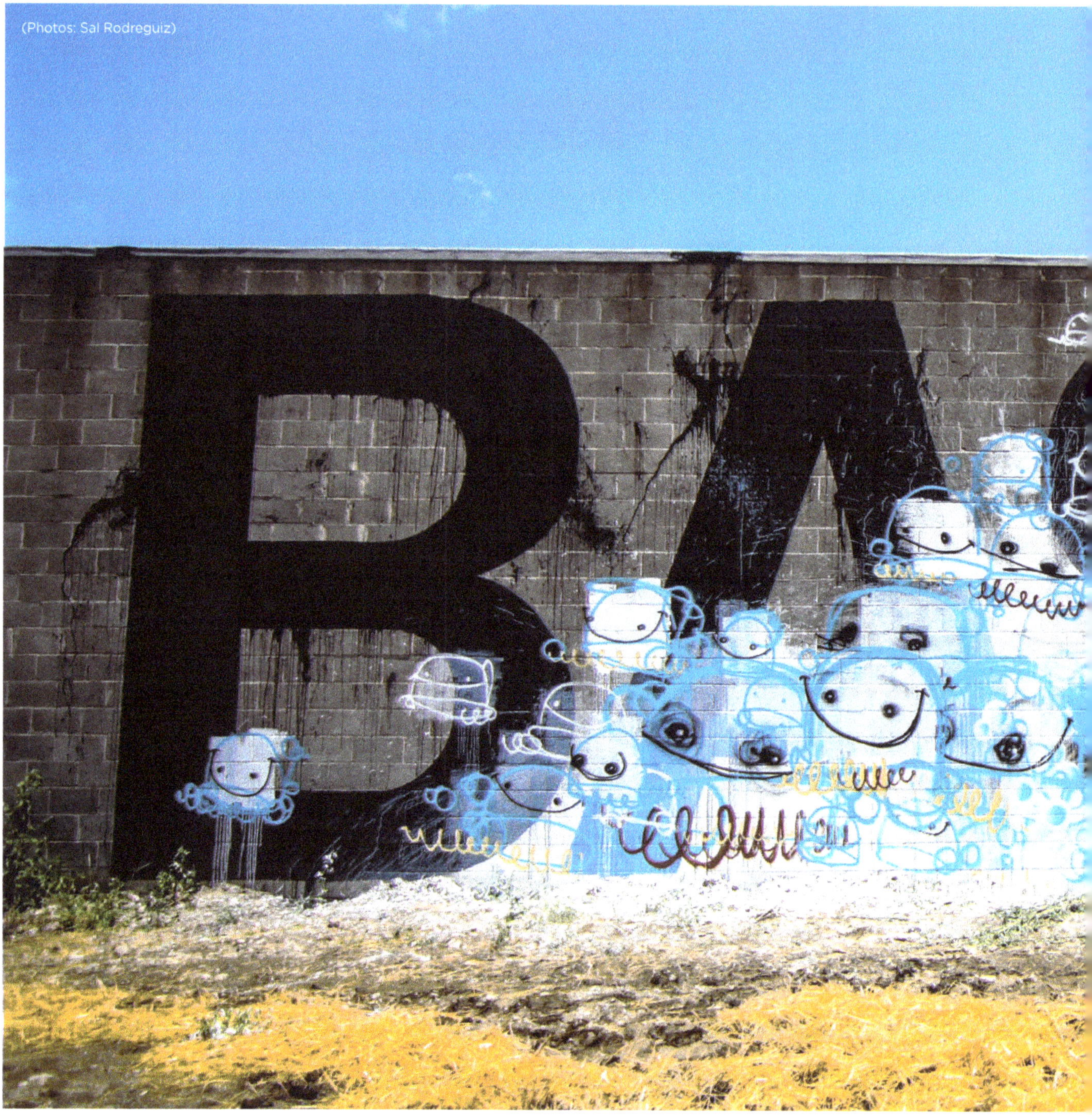

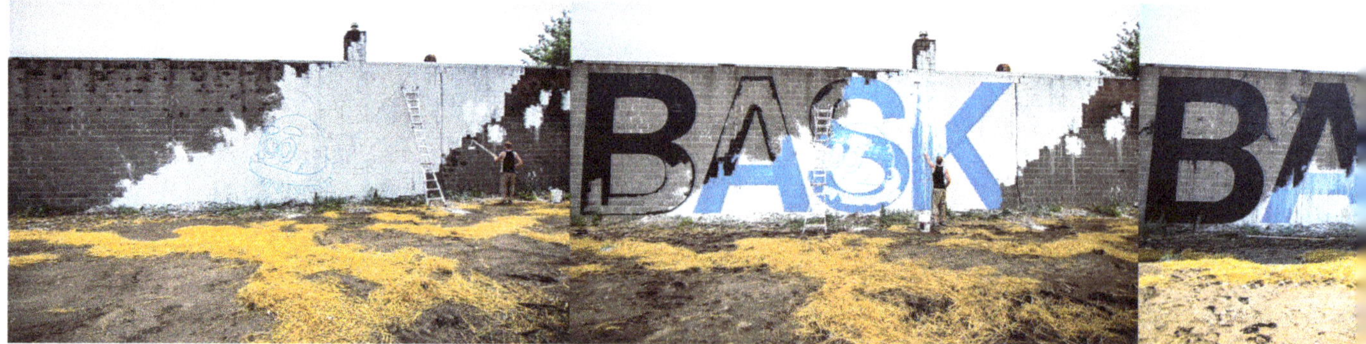

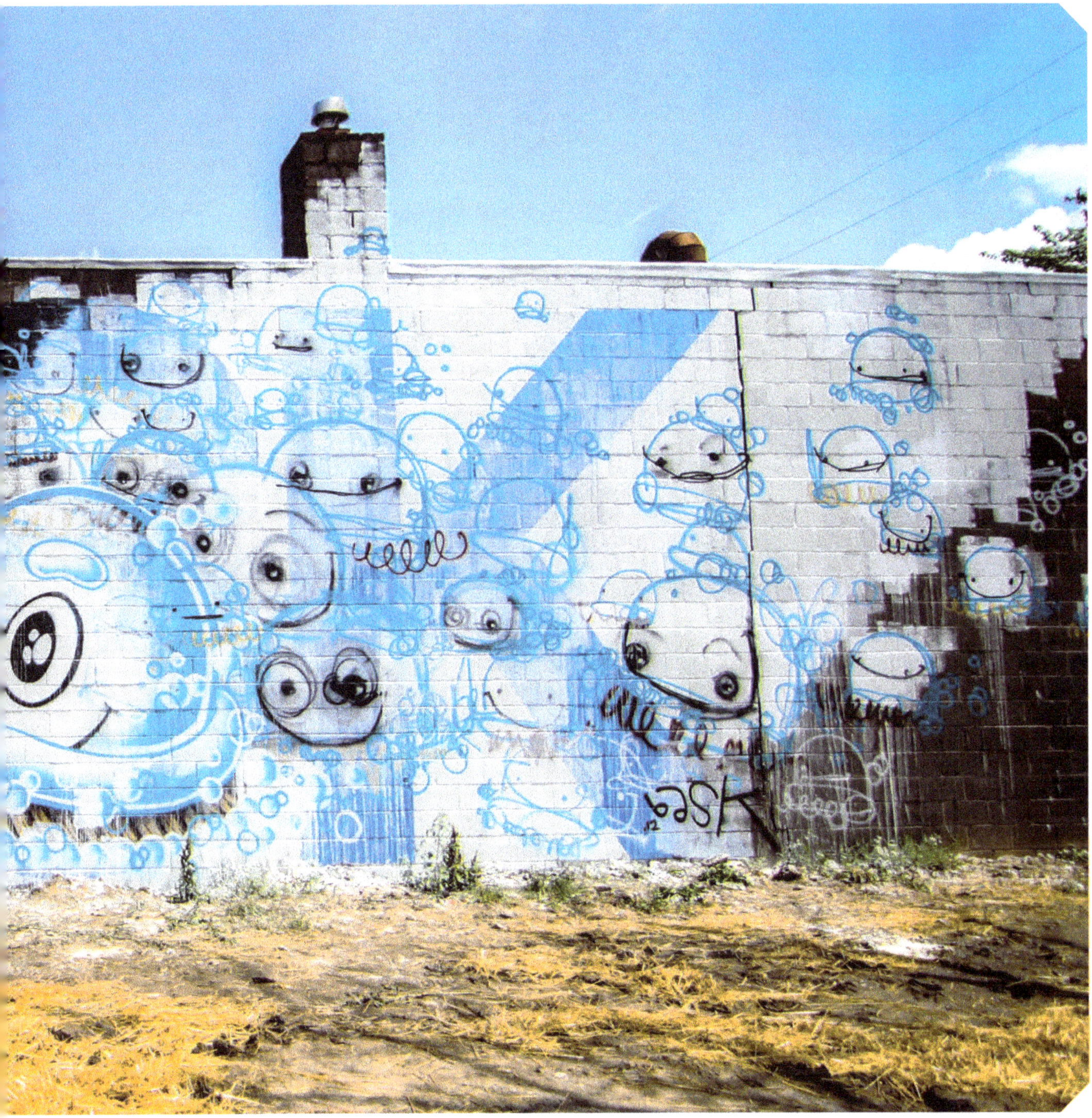

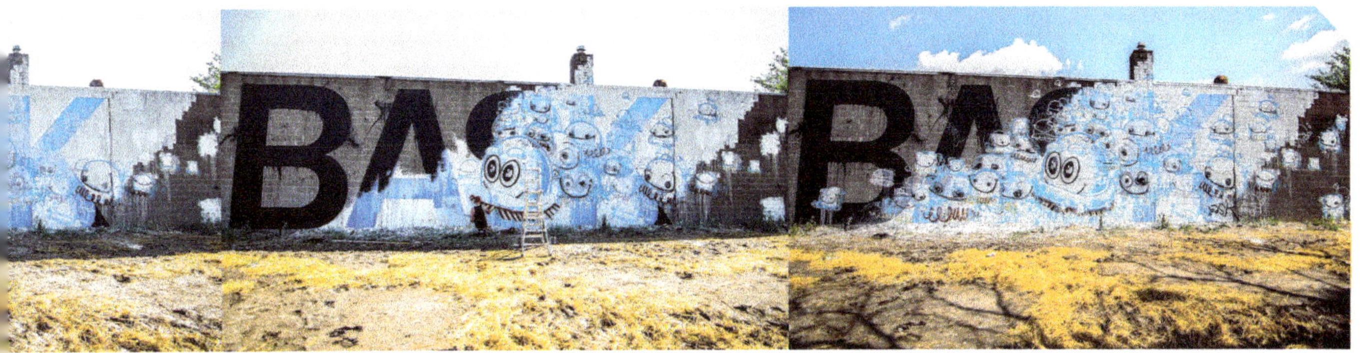

BEN BUNK

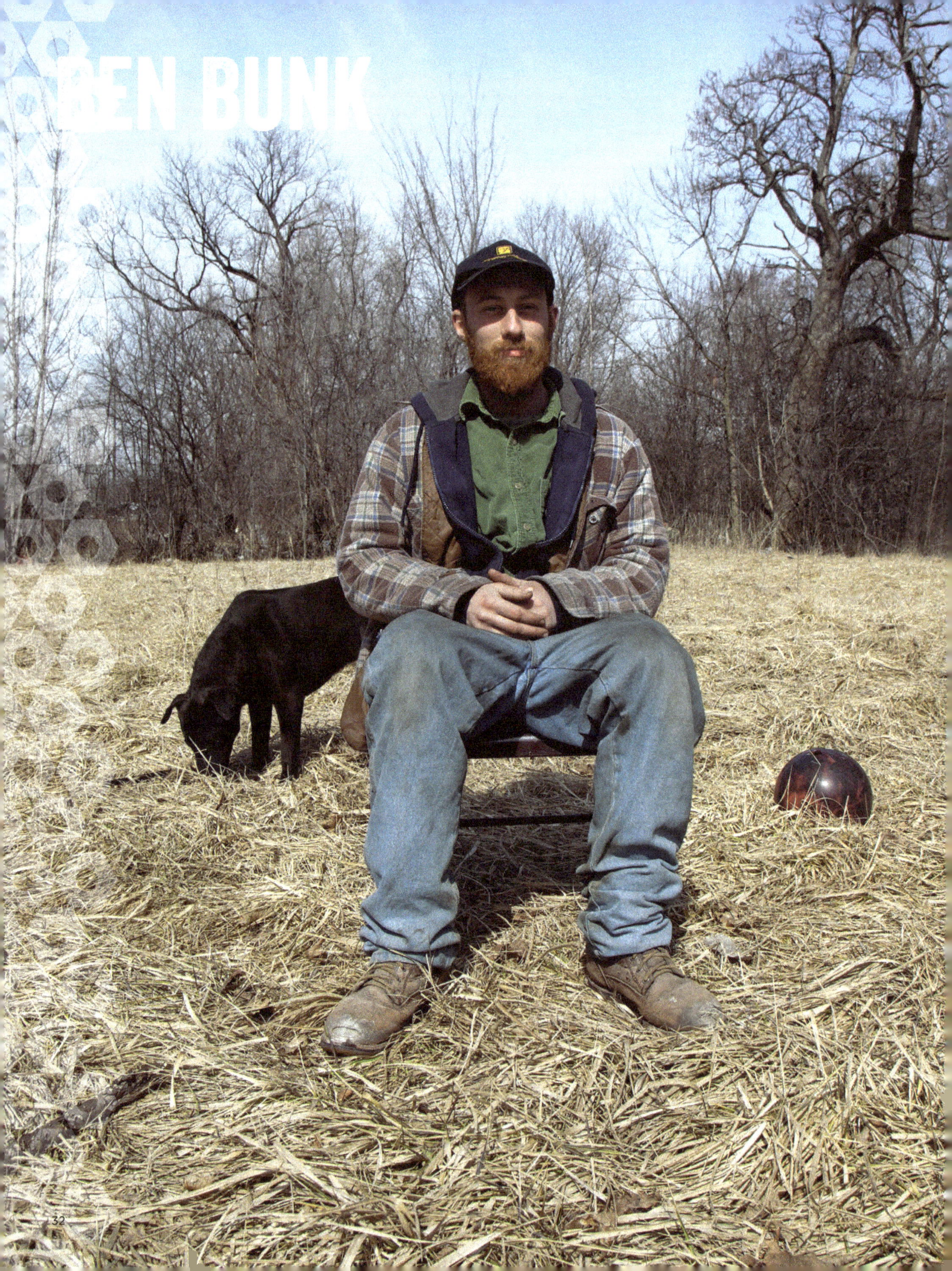

A girl, and a hunger to make things, lured Ben Bunk to Motown.

But once the twenty-eight-year-old native New Yorker arrived, he found something more, something raw. With a bike as his only means of transportation, Bunk traveled the streets, watching the city unfold like a slow-moving animation, linked together by bewildering images of beauty and blight.

The barren blocks and majestic buildings Bunk passed each day lodged themselves in his mind. A daily seven-mile commute to an artist residency at the 555 Gallery in Southwest Detroit made it impossible to turn away. The more Bunk looked, the more he saw.

The route he took soon became his road to an unlikely creative expression. "I was blown away," Bunk says. "Some people talk things out; I figure things out when I draw."

Bunk wasted no time putting his pencils to paper. "I was so confused by the paradox I saw on my bike," Bunk says, recalling how he'd snake his way from Detroit's Eastern Market/Poletown area, through downtown Detroit and into Mexicantown. "I kept thinking, how does this happen to a city? How could we, as a country, turn our back on a place once so rich in culture? We'd never do that to New York. I really wanted a way of understanding what I was seeing."

Images of Detroit, neighborhood houses, buildings, entire blocks spilled out of Bunk, a graduate of the Minneapolis College of Art and Design. First came random doodles and then detailed yet spare black and white drawings.

While the drawings failed to answer Bunk's big questions about the dichotomy in Detroit, the flood of images gave him enough inspiration to fill a ninety-foot scroll of butcher paper. "I didn't come with a concept or a plan to necessarily draw Detroit. I was riding my bike because I had to. The drawings just kind of started happening. In my free time, I'd find myself just drawing the city. It gave me a way to process and to see the hidden beauty that's here."

Each time Bunk unveiled his Detroit, the drawings garnered more fans, native and new Detroiters alike enamored with his simple yet elegant depictions of arguably America's most maligned city. "I went to Portland thinking it would be a great place, but I didn't really like even leaving the house. It was kind of boring being in a city where everyone looked like everyone else; all talking about doing creative things. I wanted to be someplace where I could use my hands and my mind. I thought it might be New Orleans, but I came here and I've never left."

The creative spark Bunk found in Detroit became a solution to a number of problems. "You learn to do and to make things in Detroit because you have to." The scroll helped him fulfill the main requirement of his residency. "I needed something to show. I never thought the thing I'd create would be a scroll of drawings about Detroit."

And the drawings themselves became a source of basic survival as Bunk decided to self-publish a forty-page postcard-sized coloring book featuring thirty of his drawings. "There's opportunity here, but you have to work to make life sustainable." As Bunk poured himself into re-creating his images, again he found unexpected support in Detroit. He won a mini-grant from SOUP, a nationally celebrated community-based micro-lending project. SOUP has raised more than thirty thousand dollars through a model that invites locals to a simple dinner of soup while asking that they vote on funding pitches for various small community projects. The evening's proceeds are awarded to the diners' favorite project.

"When you take a photo of Detroit," he says, "it's almost hard to see what's really here. Somehow, in drawings you see more of the innocence and the possibilities. I wanted to invite people to interact with Detroit, to color the city in whatever way they see it." Bunk's SOUP grant paved the way for the first run of "Drawing Detroit," one hundred hand-bound copies of the book that he marketed and distributed by bike. "I always wanted to make a book," Bunk says. "Detroit gave me the opportunity."

In return, Bunk rewarded Detroit by becoming a home-owner, buying a fixer-upper on an otherwise desolate block. The house is also home to his studio business, Bunkhead Productions. (The girl who first lured him to Detroit? She decided to stay, too.) Bunk's choice to live and create in Detroit, he says, continues to be something of a roller coaster ride: "I go visit friends who live in more established cities, New York and other places, and when I'm there, I just get reminded of how much more Detroit has to offer. It's not easy but it's complex. You can't live here and not be creative. More than any other city, Detroit's alive."

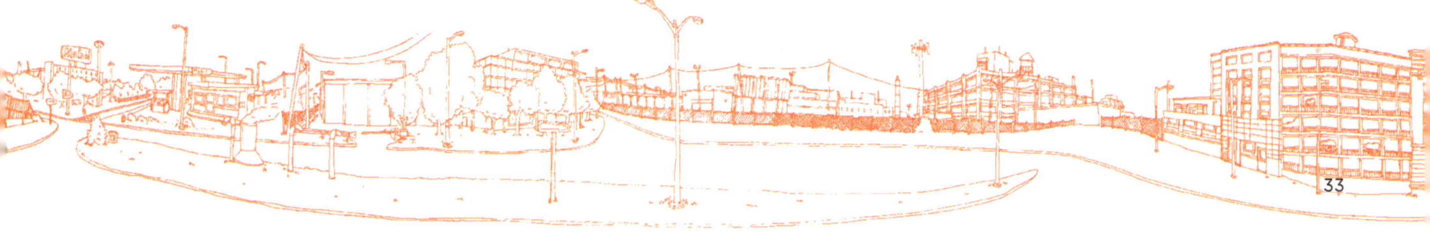

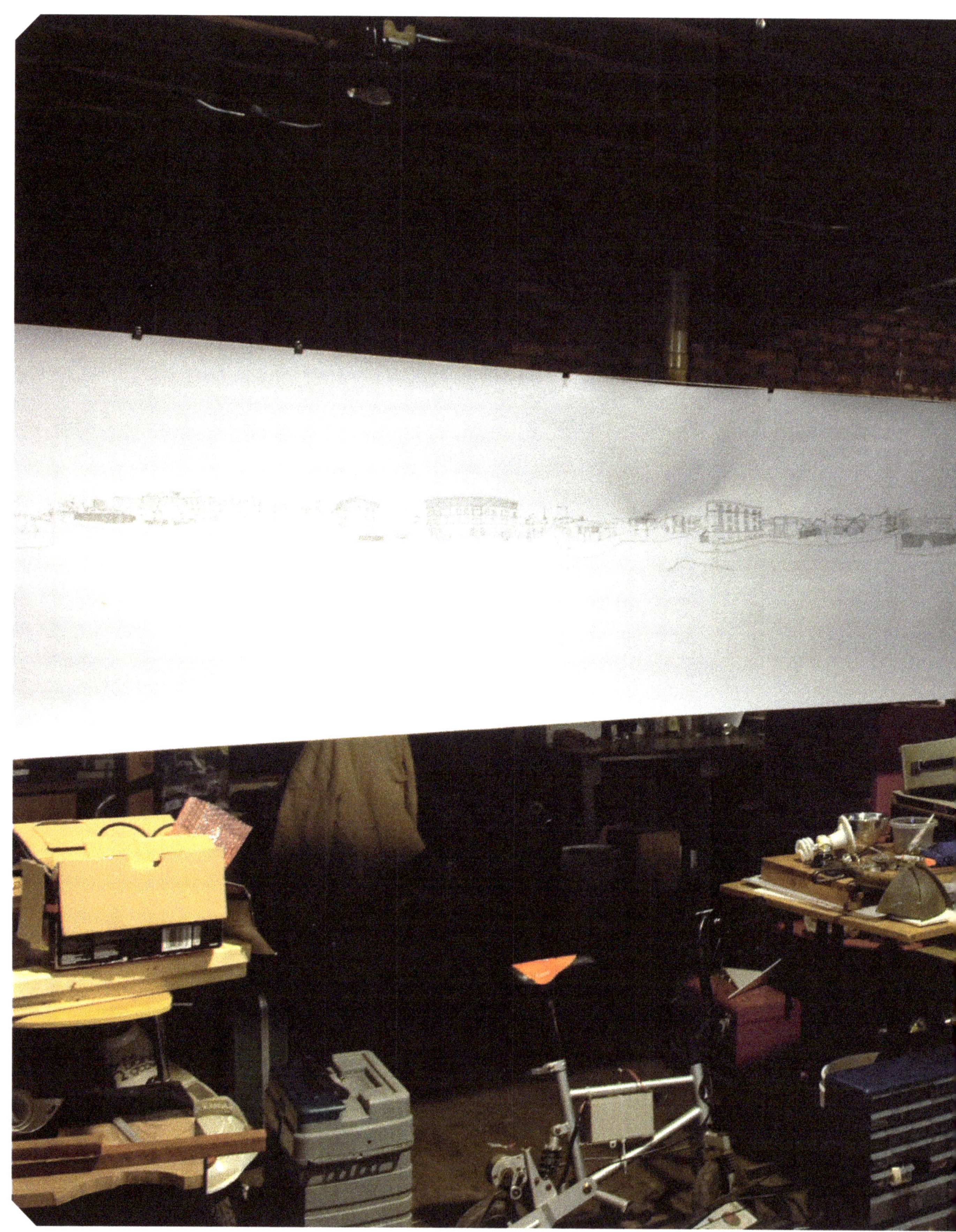

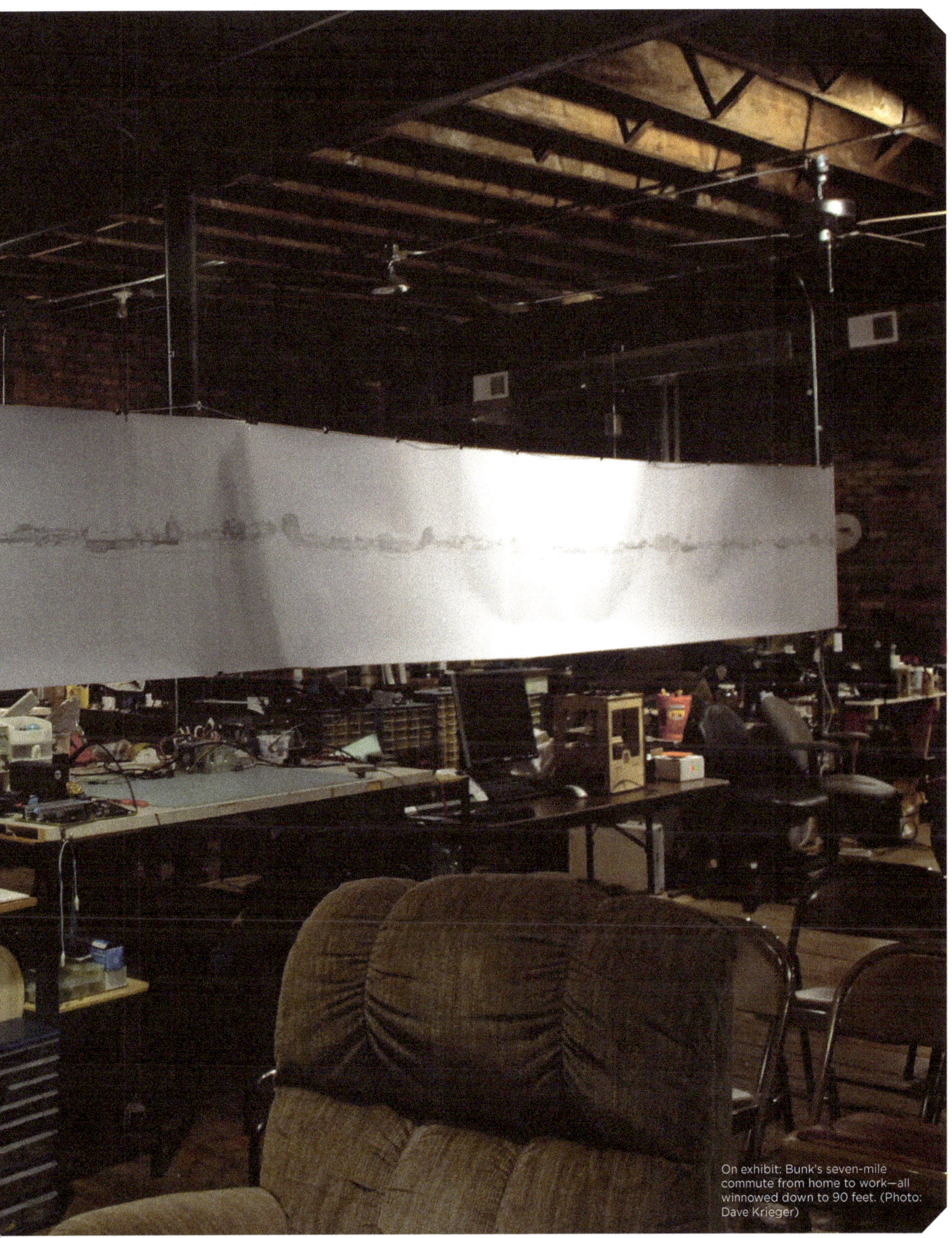
On exhibit: Bunk's seven-mile commute from home to work—all winnowed down to 90 feet. (Photo: Dave Krieger)

HALIMA CASSELLS

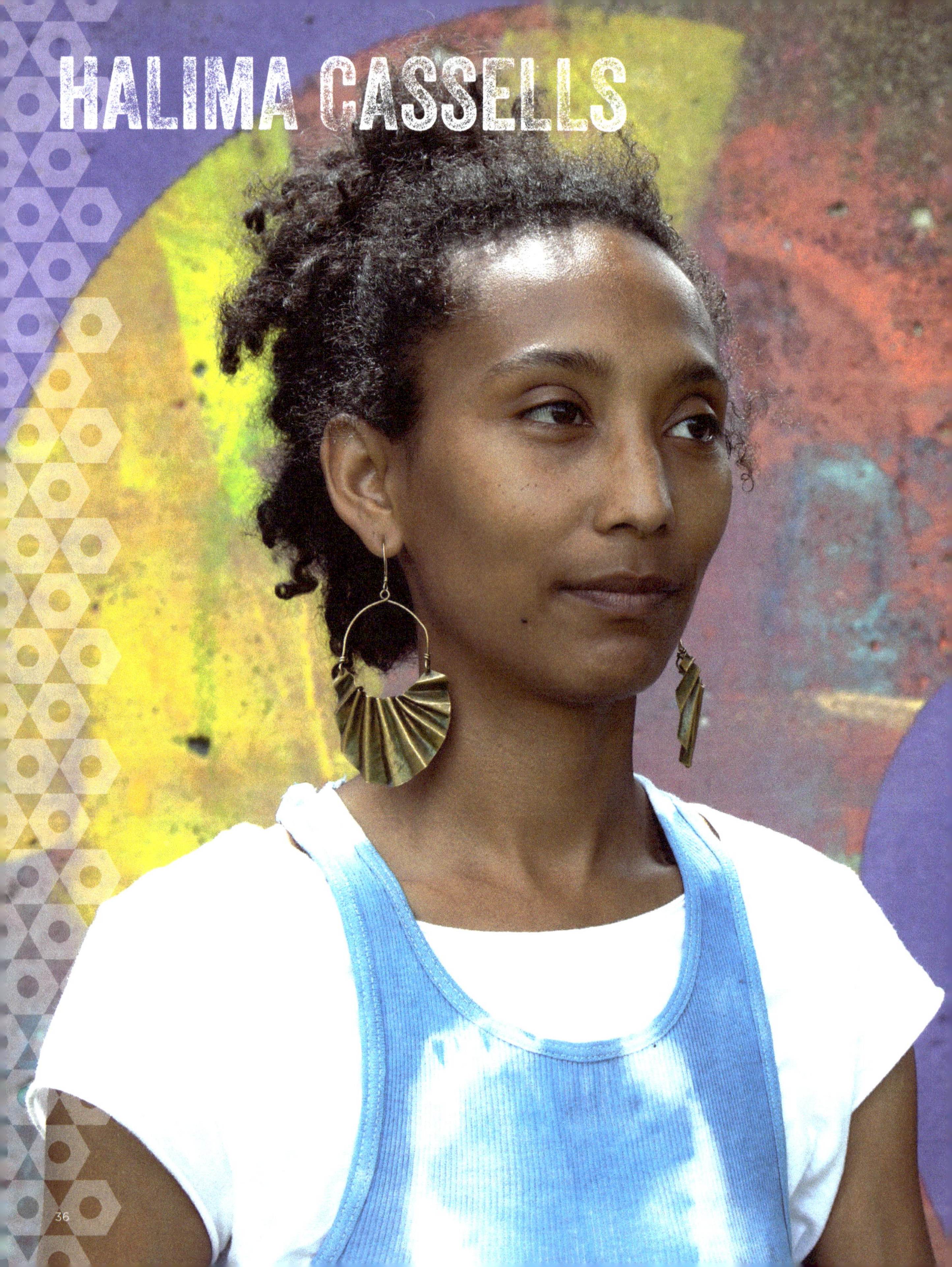

By training, Halima Cassells seemed destined to become a classroom teacher like her mother and grandmother before her.

But the classroom could not compete with the allure of paint and art. They'd always whispered to her. Inevitably they won. "After teaching for six months," says Cassells, who studied secondary education at Howard University, "I knew. I just decided that it was not going to work out for me."

Without a second thought, Cassells immersed herself in art: "I started painting and it just took over." The choice, she says, came as naturally as breathing. "All of my life I'd been really encouraged and nurtured creatively; I grew up completely around art, knowing artists, visiting artists' studios. It's something that had always been with me. I guess it just had to evolve."

Like any evolution, Cassells's happened slowly.

First she found work lending her skills to neighborhood after-school programs in Brooklyn. Teaching painting to young children became a perfect way to marry her classroom training to her newfound passion. Soon, Cassells, thirty-two, found herself on another adventure, painting neighborhood murals and suddenly itching to live as a fulltime artist back home in Detroit. "Growing up I was always inspired by the Heidelberg Project," she says. "I just really started thinking about what it would be like to experience Detroit and its creativity as an adult and as an artist myself."

In 2008, Cassells returned with her imagination fired up and focused on a dream project she called the Detroit Mural Factory. For four years, Cassells recruited other Detroit artists to join her in teaching youth painting through live community mural projects. Students and artists worked side-by-side designing and completing outdoor and indoor works, including some block-long muralscapes. "The experiences I've had and the diverse turns in my career couldn't have happened anywhere else."' In total, the DMF painted fifteen murals and taught painting to more than six hundred young people, she says.

In 2009, Cassells and the DMF won a commission to create *American Beauty*, a project that wrapped the once-iconic American Beauty Irons Building in a visual history of Detroit's industrial past and its effort to grow a more green economy. Cassells worked with thirty-one schoolchildren to complete the six-week project. Though the building was torn down in 2013, the mural, painted on wooden panels, was saved and relocated. One portion of the mural was donated to Americorps' Urban Safety Project for reuse in boarding up other buildings around the city.

While Cassells says she doesn't plan to resurrect the DMF, she remains active in public art projects, including as a community volunteer coordinator with ArtCorps Detroit, a Wayne State University program that offers service-learning opportunities to students and citizens interested in using art as a community revitalization tool.

"I'm super glad that I returned when I did," she says, "and I'm super appreciative to be here now as an artist and a creative when so many people are starting to see and to experience the true Detroit."

BELOW: Co-created by over 300 students, the mural at Loving Elementary School in Detroit stretches across a playground wall with a dual message.

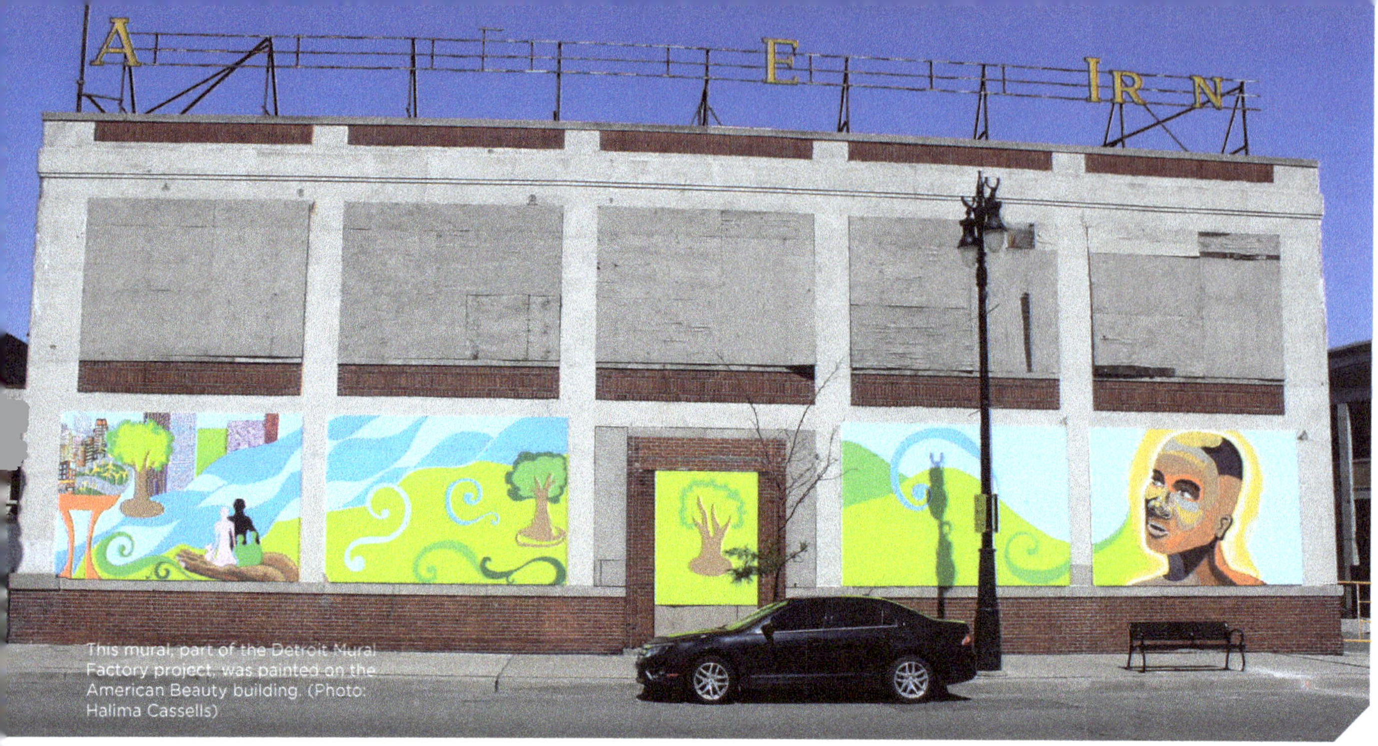

This mural, part of the Detroit Mural Factory project, was painted on the American Beauty building. (Photo: Halima Cassells)

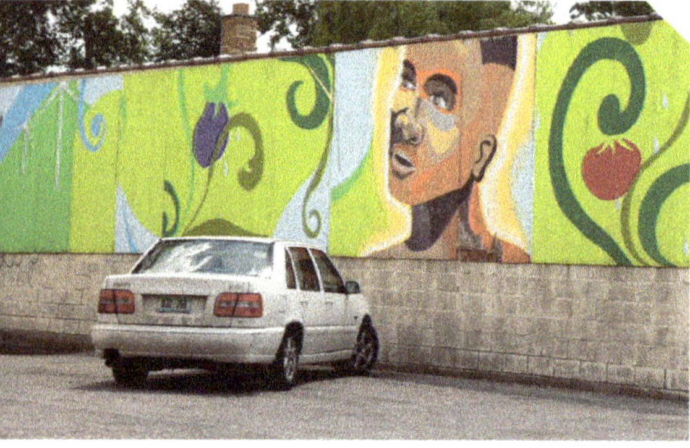

ABOVE: The mural was eventually moved to a new location along Woodward Avenue.

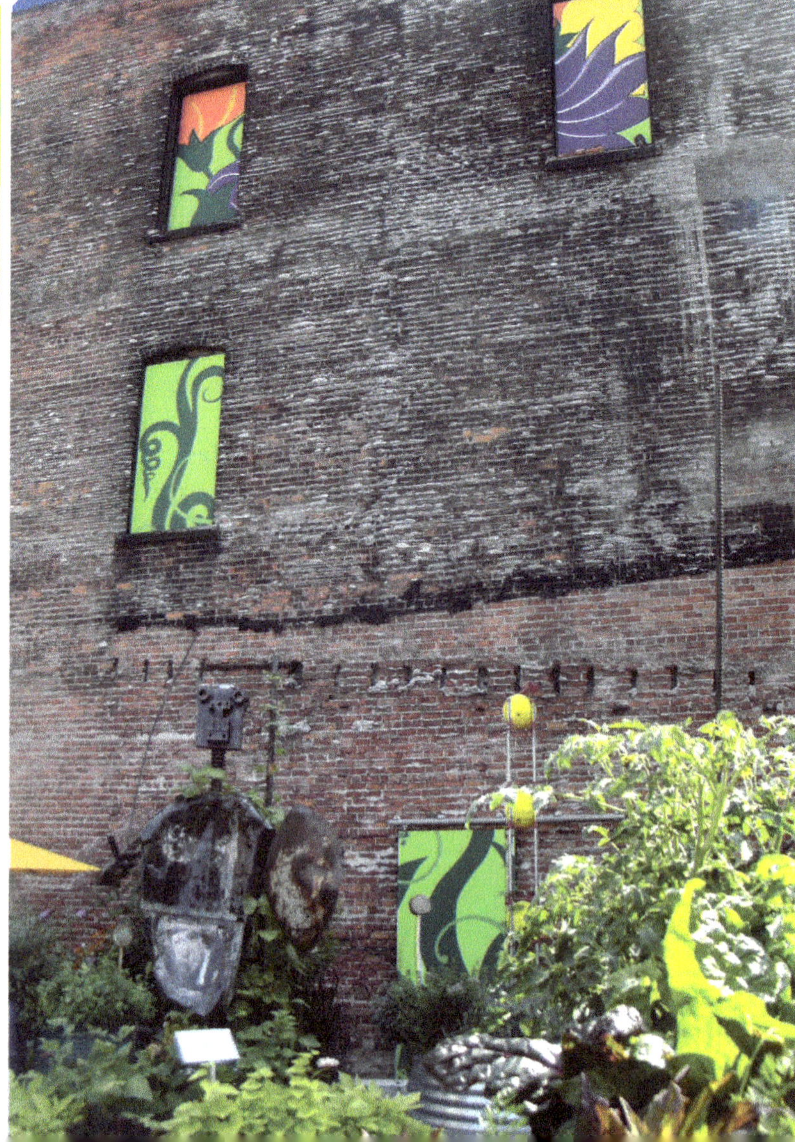

RIGHT: Titled *Climbing Flower*, this modular mural acts as a backdrop for Lafayette Greens garden in downtown Detroit. (Photo: Halima Cassells)

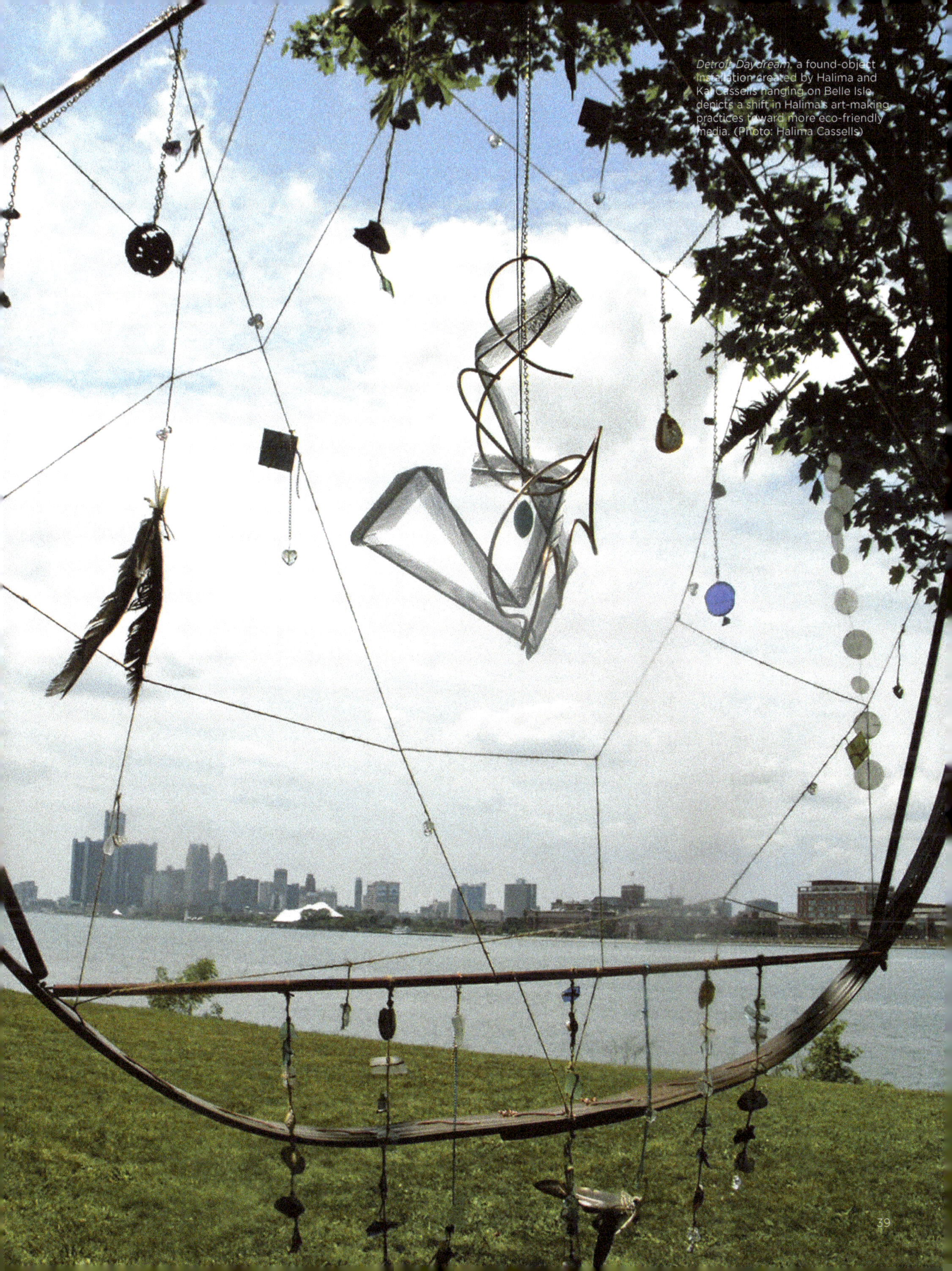

Detroit Daydream, a found-object installation created by Halima and Kai Cassells hanging on Belle Isle, depicts a shift in Halima's art-making practices toward more eco-friendly media. (Photo: Halima Cassells)

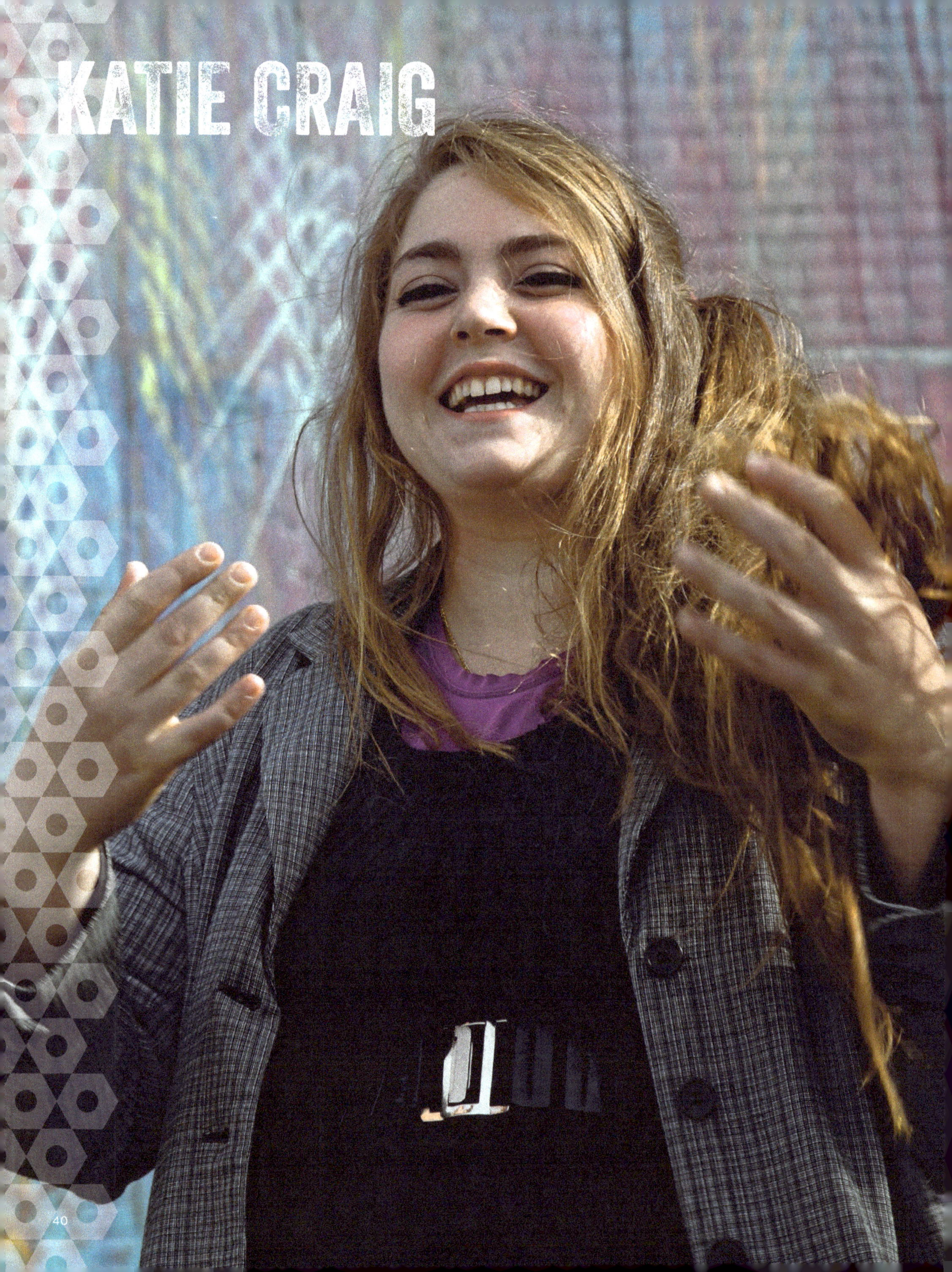
KATIE CRAIG

Katie Craig's most recognized work as an artist is exactly where it belongs: on Grand Boulevard.

Craig's *Illuminated Mural* is giant, nearly as grand as the history of this storied street with its enduring emblems of American ingenuity and creativity. Grand Boulevard, which once spanned twelve uninterrupted miles, is where Berry Gordy transformed his two-family flat into Hitsville, USA, and Motown Records' legendary Studio A.

Decades before Gordy made his house of music, architect Albert Kahn was dazzling the world from the boulevard. Both the Kahn-designed Fisher Building, an ornate precursor to the modern skyscraper, and the former world headquarters of General Motors Company, at one time the largest office building in the world, still stand. Kahn's gems and Gordy's gutsy music studio are each registered as National Historic Landmarks.

It's doubtful that Craig's mural will ever make that leap. But it does tower over the boulevard's less glamorous eastern half, an unofficial yet alluring landmark for a new Detroit: art rising where industrial might once ruled. Anyone who has glimpsed her first major work can understand how Craig comes to be mentioned beside Grand Boulevard's creative titans. It's all about scale. The mural, 100 feet by 125 feet, is beacon-like, daring passersby not to be lured by its vibrant explosion of splattered colors. The eye starts skyward then follows a cascading rainbow of colors as they appear to race, in drips, down one side of a former industrial storage facility.

"At first, it really looks simplistic," she says of the mural. "You don't really see that it happened at a scale so huge that we were able to let the laws of physics and nature help us paint just by pouring paint into one area and letting it drip and fade together."

Those who gawk, Craig included, cannot help themselves. She stares with incredulous eyes, almost wanting to pinch herself into believing that an idea once alive only in her imagination now lives as a testament to public art. "I drive up the boulevard and I'm like 'wow' every time," Craig says. "Detroit gave me an opportunity to amaze people, to amaze myself. That's why a lot of new artists and even established artists are coming, because the city has places and opportunities that make you think about trying new things, impossible things."

From start to finish, Craig's mural challenged the limits of experimental and traditional approaches to street art. The mural called for more than one hundred gallons of paint. Instead of spray cans, fire extinguishers were fashioned into giant splatter hoses to help spread the paint, while Craig spent hours at a time hoisted in the air, painting from a lift. "Even with all the research, learning which equipment was needed, coming up with the different painting techniques; I still didn't know if it could be done. I was so used to working small. But here it is, saying to the world, 'Look what's possible in Detroit.'"

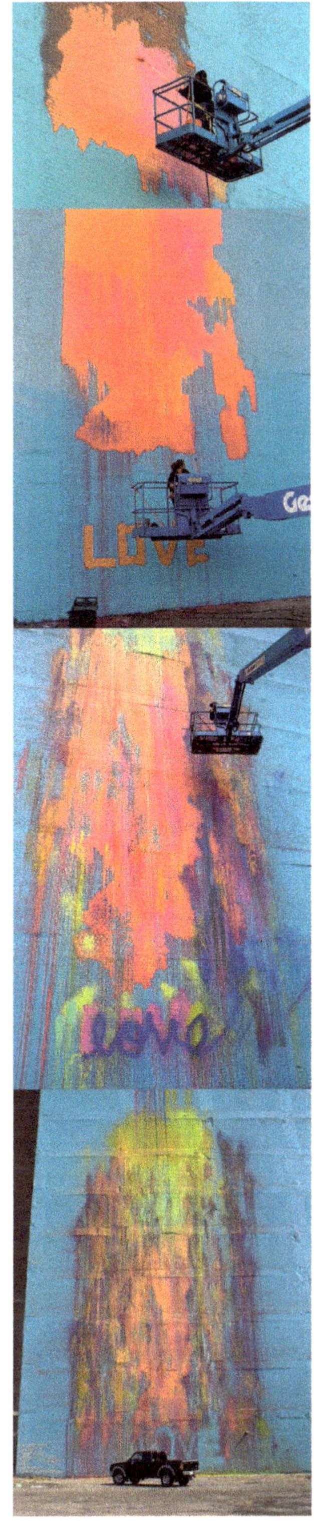

ABOVE: The making of a mural. After the wall was painted blue, layers of bright pink underpaint were applied by Craig with rollers, spray cans and fire extinguishers from a lift. It was physically demanding work that caused her to drop many pounds in the process. (Photos: Ifoma Stubbs)

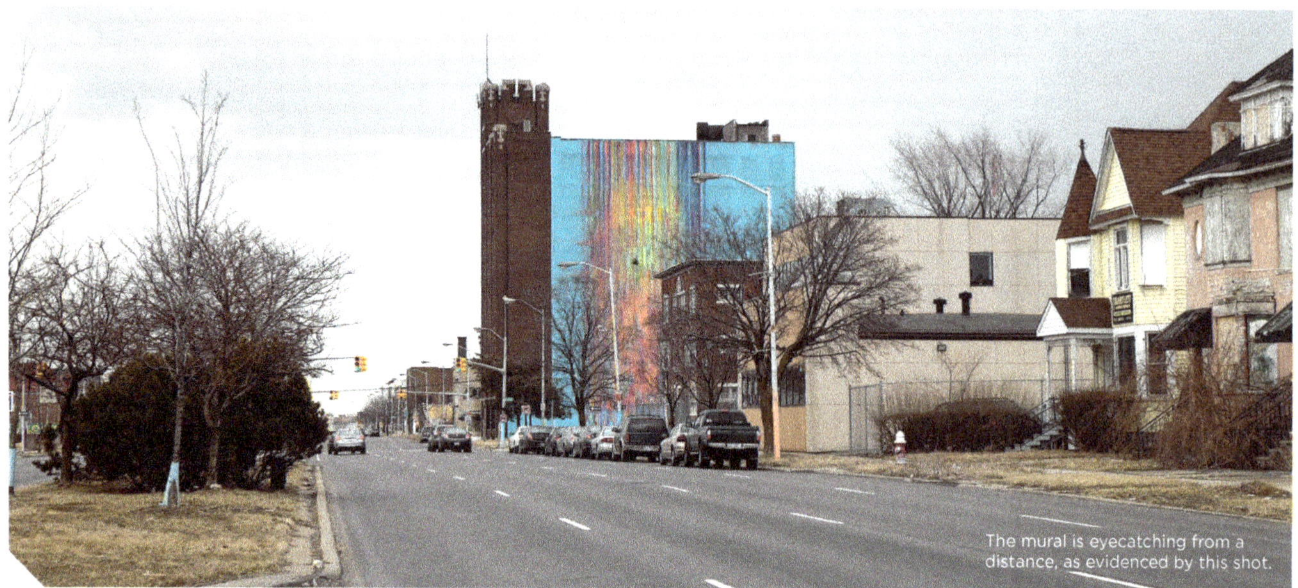

The mural is eyecatching from a distance, as evidenced by this shot.

At twenty-eight, Craig is almost too young to remember Grand Boulevard's more brilliant days or the nights when GM's famed rooftop sign lit up the sky. "There's a lot of memories there for people. I had tons of people telling me their stories about the buildings they remembered and what they meant. It's beautiful to see the way art can help people embrace a space or even their own history."

That the mural even found a home on Grand Boulevard was more a stroke of good fortune than clever design. In 2009, when residents of Detroit's North End approved her proposal to lead a neighborhood public art project, Craig knew only that she wanted to involve area youth as aides in the making of a mural "like no other," a lasting gift to a neighborhood scarred by industrial and residential abandonment.

Beyond the big vision, Craig's mural had one other asset working in its favor: She won a highly competitive Community + Public Arts (CPAD) grant, which included thirty-five-thousand dollars through a collaboration between the College for Creative Studies, the Skillman Foundation, the J. P. Morgan Chase Foundation, and the Kresge Foundation. For Craig, the award unleashed a flood of ideas about experimental painting techniques.

She found eager young partners immediately. The location took more work. "I looked at the whole neighborhood, almost every street, trying to find a location that would really let the community work together in a big, meaningful way."

Craig narrowed her list to six possible sites. But the owners of the East Grand Boulevard site made the choice an easy one with enthusiastic support of the idea and an unexpected pledge to allow the building's first floor to become a studio and staging base. "It took a lot work from a lot of people, and things that they don't teach you in college, to get the project going and to get it finished.

Now, nearly four years after the mural's completion, Craig still enjoys watching drivers pull up for a closer look. Sometimes, she gives a behind-the-scenes tour of the process and what she calls "the hidden jewel." "It looks like this mural just happened; one day someone took the wall," she says. "But the only reason we were able to do this and make it lasting is because we engaged the community. They had a say and they got to put their hearts in, too."

Ultimately, thirty-five neighborhood teens joined Craig at almost every step of the project, from clearing weeds and trees and prepping paint cans, to throwing colors along the bottom of the mural and, for a lucky few, even dripping various hues of paint from the roof to create the illusion of colors raining down from the sky. Craig is especially proud that nearly half of the teens walked away with invaluable creative exposure and a little compensation, grants of a thousand dollars each provided by a federally subsidized youth entrepreneurial program.

"I see a lot of the kids around still," she says. "The pride is still on their faces. It's a huge memory for them and it's the power of the piece. Art gave them a way to see their community in a different light, to add something instead of focusing on all the things that have been taken away."

Nonetheless, Craig is quick to caution against seeing her mural or any work of art as a civic problem-solver: "I'm not one of those people who believes art can put a city up on its shoulders and bring it back to life. There's a lot of real systematic things that need to change. What art can do is to give a voice to people, and spaces and ideas. I think that's big enough."

In Detroit, it's at least a grand place to begin.

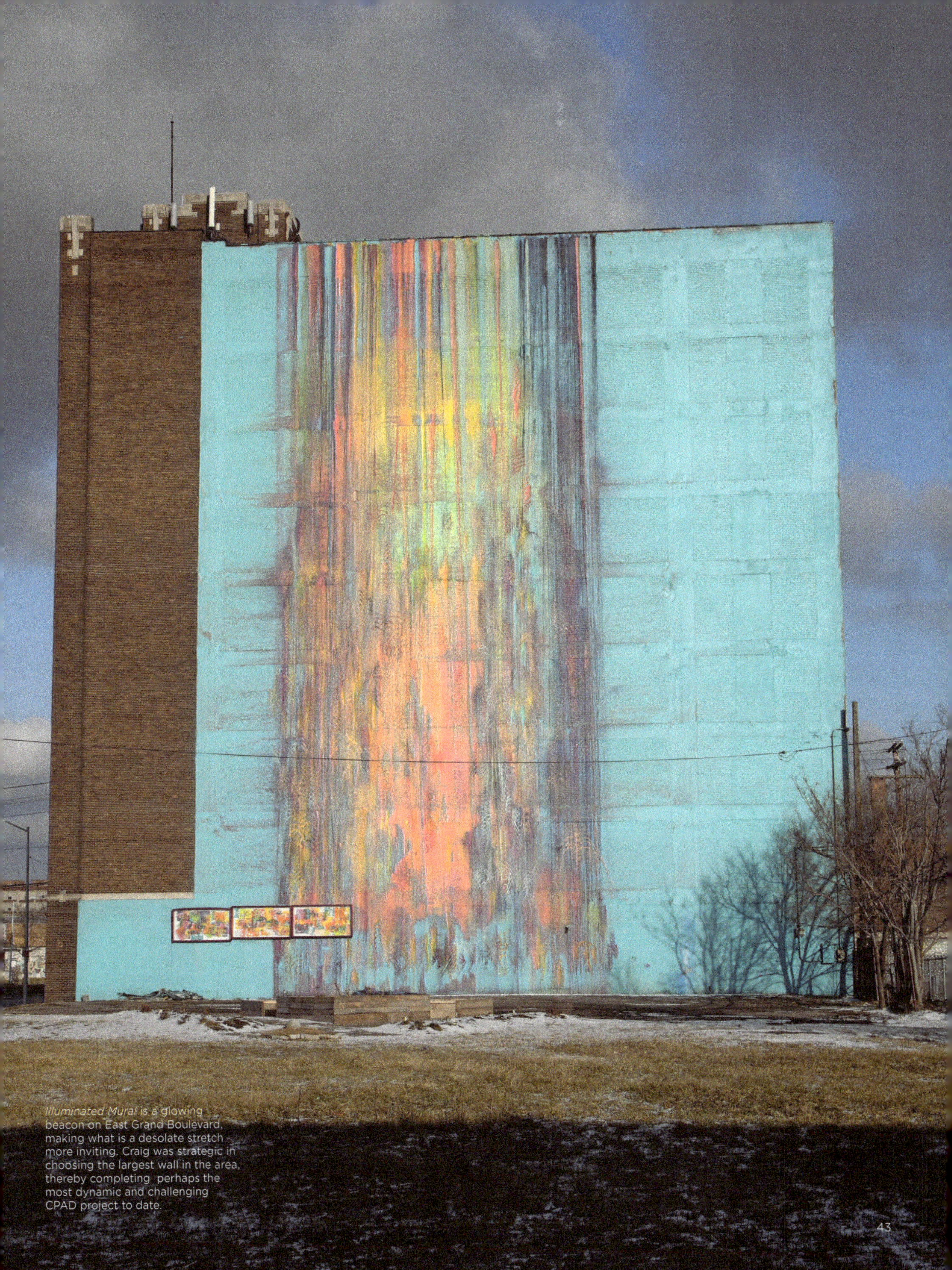

Illuminated Mural is a glowing beacon on East Grand Boulevard, making what is a desolate stretch more inviting. Craig was strategic in choosing the largest wall in the area, thereby completing perhaps the most dynamic and challenging CPAD project to date.

CUPCAKE GIRLS

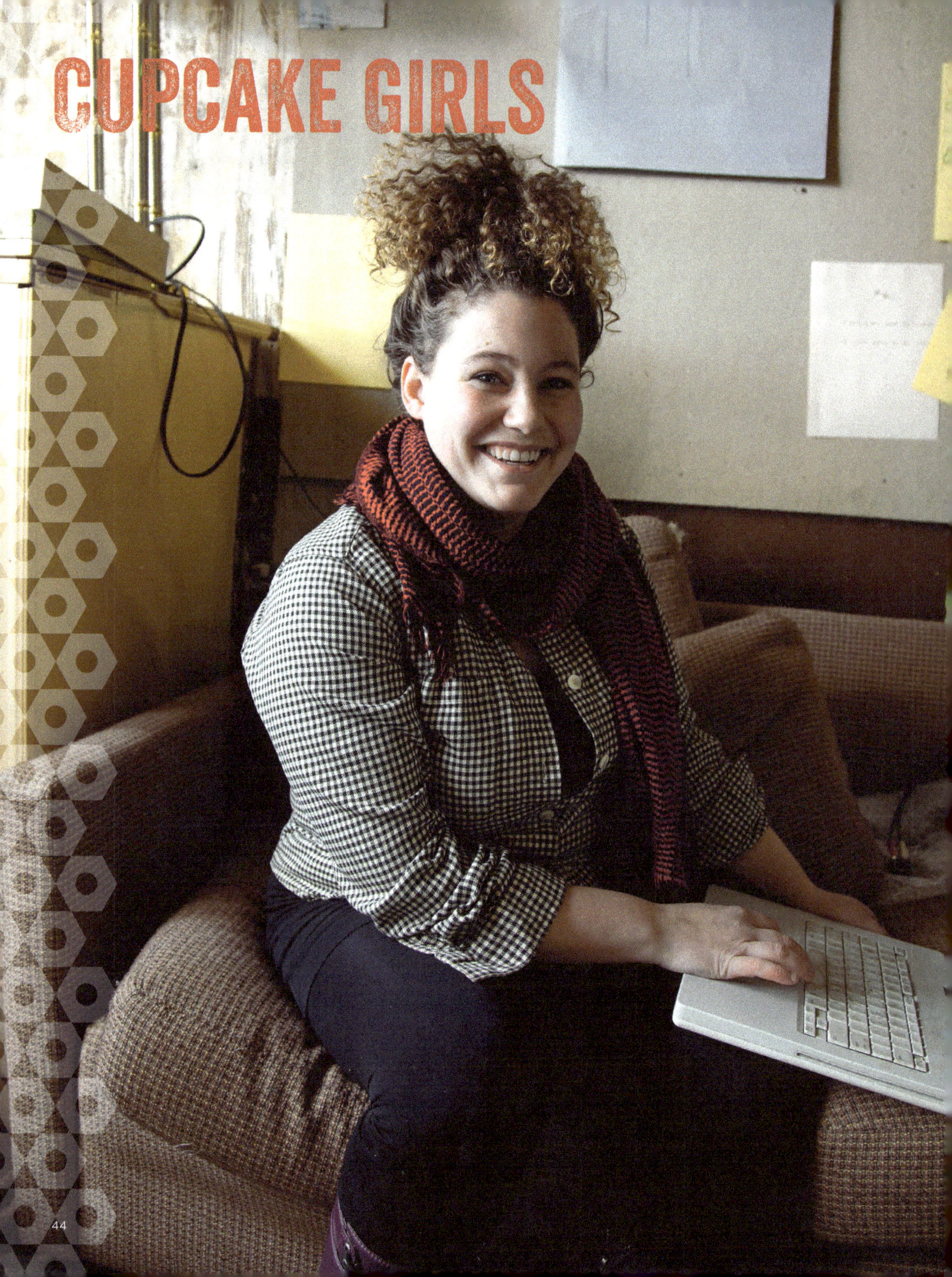

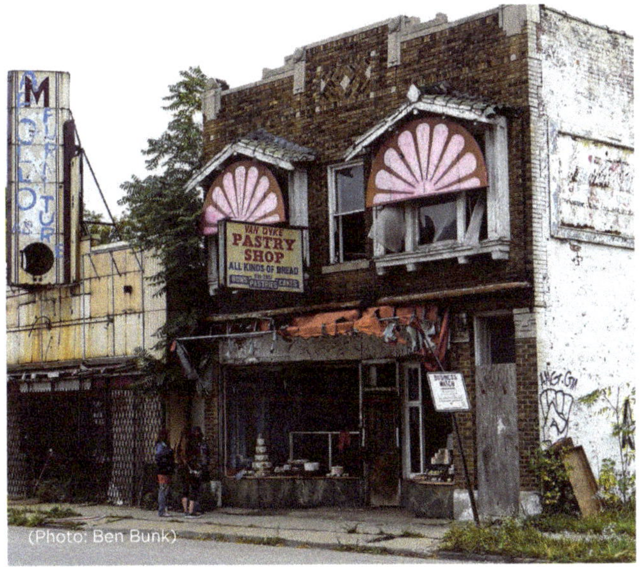

(Photo: Ben Bunk)

Good intentions drove ceramic artist Jane Orr to Detroit.

"I wanted the confidence to know if I could make it on my own as an artist," she says.

In Maine, she'd heard talk that Detroit was the best place to test drive her dream. Friends and fellow grads of the fine arts program at Alfred University in upstate New York were already on their way to the Motor City. "I was working three jobs and surviving," she said. "But I was really thinking about what it means to have a life with art-making at the center."

An offer of an arts residency at the emerging 555 Gallery made the move and Orr's question all the more urgent. So did the swirl of global headlines proclaiming Detroit as a rising arts mecca. Orr arrived in 2008, with a modest shared living space, a bike for transportation, and a mission to hit the ground creating.

"When you first move here, you're hypnotized by the opportunity and what people call an open canvas." With fellow classmate Krysta Kearney, who'd also moved to town, Orr focused her attention on the city's east side and an installation project she envisioned would engage Detroit. The project: building ten-inch realistic cement cakes as window treatments for a stretch of abandoned and burned-out storefronts.

The concept seemed innocent enough. Set a sweet, universally accepted symbol like cakes and cupcakes inside stark and empty storefronts, and just maybe people would begin to take a second look at the possibilities. At least Orr hoped. But instead, the Cupcake Girls got a cruel introduction to the costs of cultural naiveté.

"At the time, I think we thought we'd been sensitive," she said. "But we didn't fully understand the neighborhood we were in. When you come from a place that's completely different, you don't really think to stop and look into the past. So it's easy to see what looks like an open canvas. But it's not blank. There's history and there's tensions. You have to try to understand."

The night after the first display was installed, it was destroyed. "Every other day it seemed like we were refilling the windows, stacking them back up because of the destruction. I don't know how many cakes we ended up making," she recalls.

Though the destruction slowed, the vandals were not done. Two days before the show's opening, they torched the storefront that was to be a main showcase for the project. Fortunately, Orr's creations had been taken back to the gallery to be presented as the culmination project of her residency.

After the fire, Orr made two tough but pivotal decisions. She returned the cakes to the burned-out window, and she also decided to become a student of Detroit. She still smiles recalling how a guy named Juice came out with hammers, nails, and lots of free advice. Several of the firefighters who'd worked to save the building also became protectors of the cakes. "Some of the most beautiful interactions came out of that moment, with the firefighters and with people who were there helping us restack."

While the fire shook her spirit, the lessons Orr learned in the process buoyed her belief in Detroit as the ultimate place to live the artist's life. "Humanity has influenced me here," says Orr, who's since formed a studio collective and declared Detroit home. "The ability to take time and reflect back on things and to be conscientious in my work at all levels is a huge gift," she says.

Whether she'll always call Detroit her creative home, Orr can't say. But the visions of opportunity that first lured her still appeal. "I've found amazing ways to make work here and there's still a lot of work to be done as an artist."

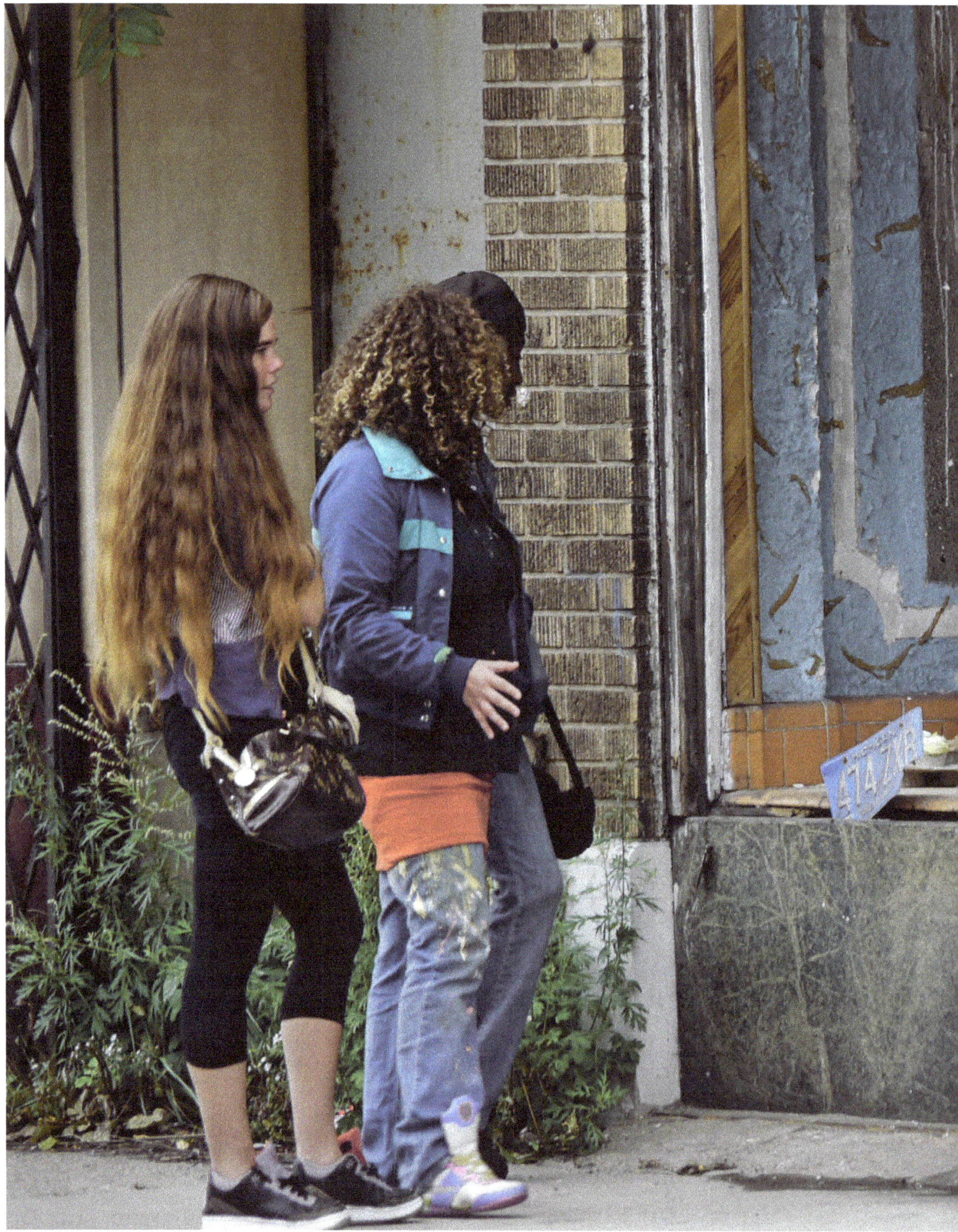

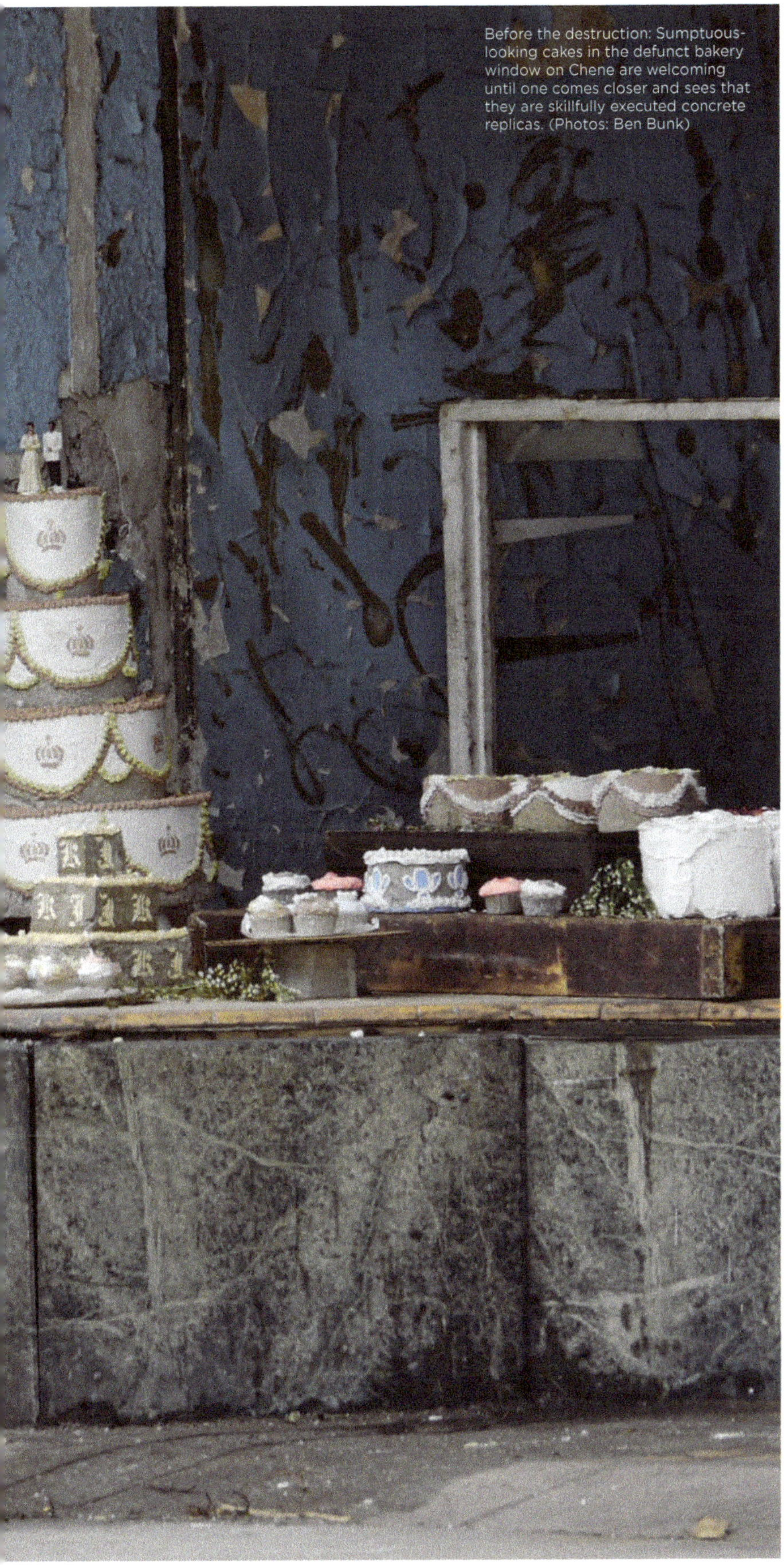

Before the destruction: Sumptuous-looking cakes in the defunct bakery window on Chene are welcoming until one comes closer and sees that they are skillfully executed concrete replicas. (Photos: Ben Bunk)

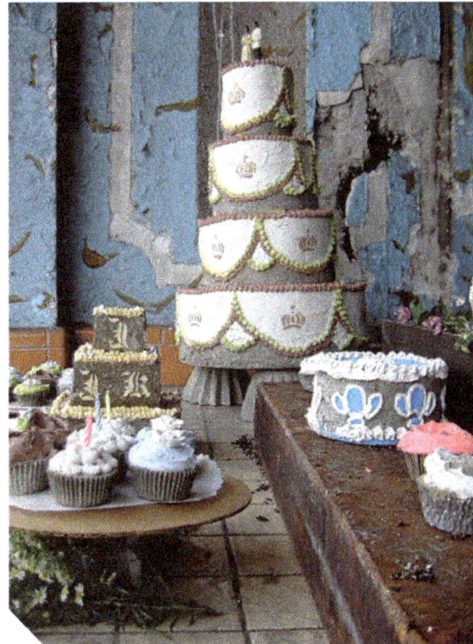

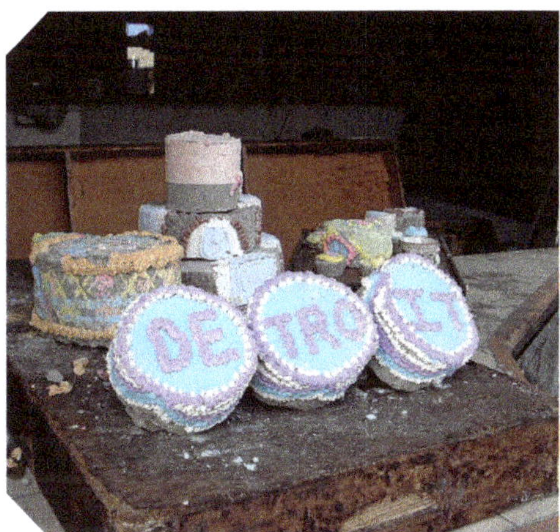

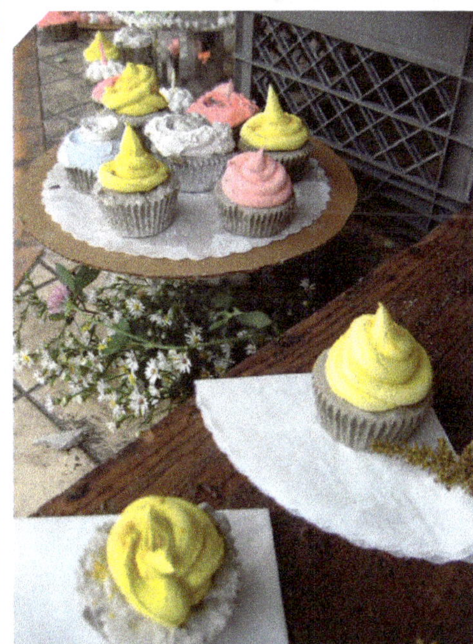

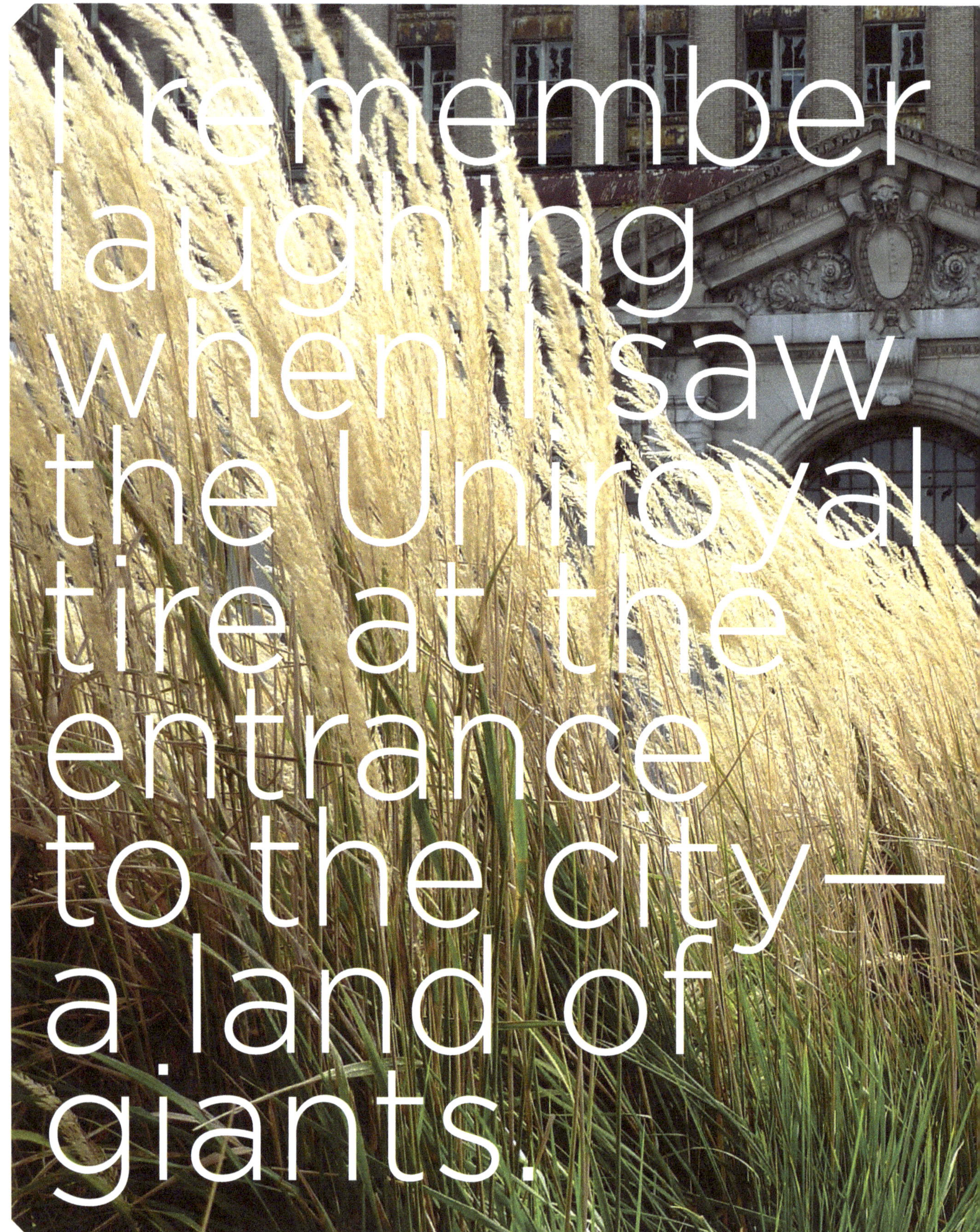
I remember laughing when I saw the Uniroyal tire at the entrance to the city—a land of giants.

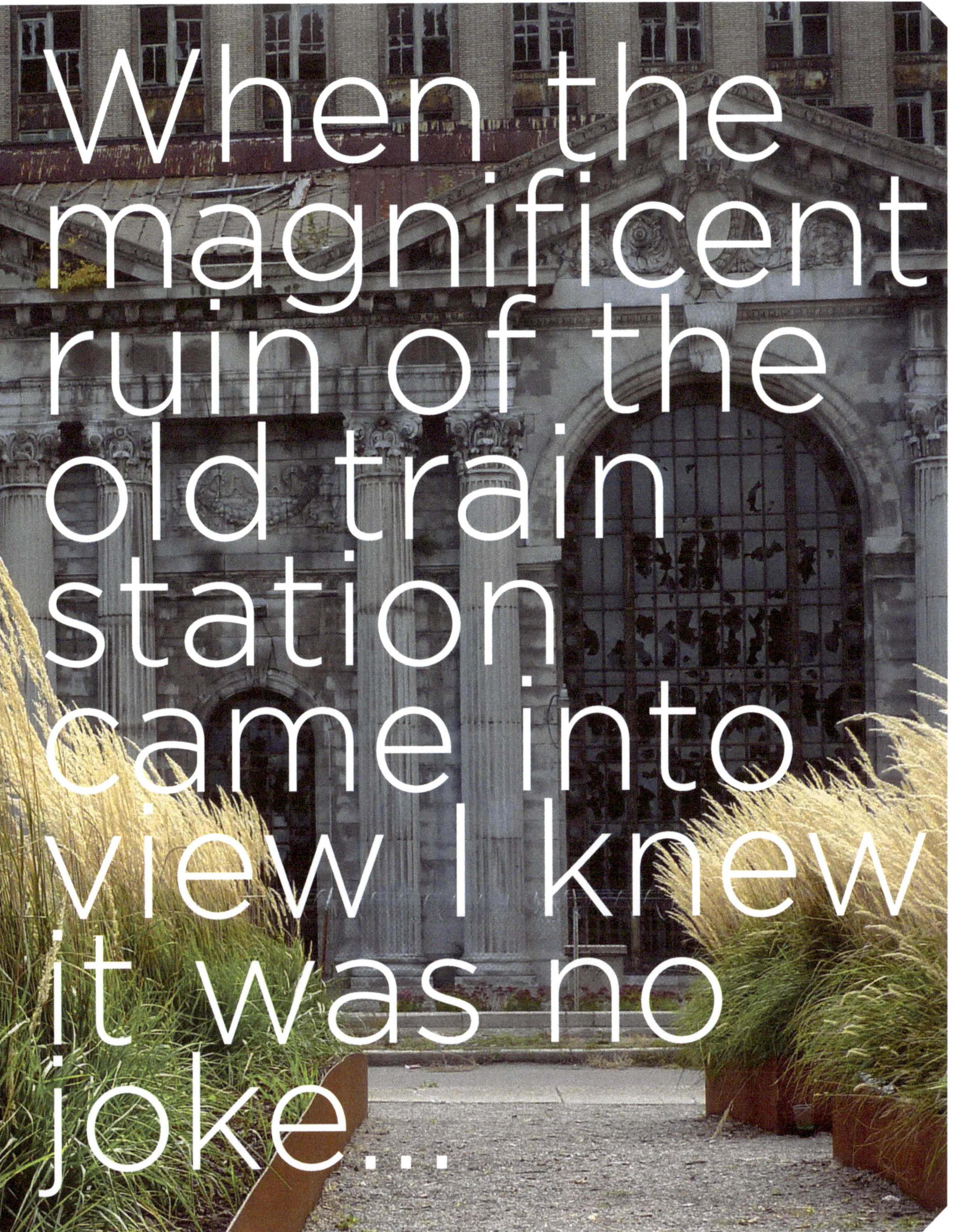
When the magnificent ruin of the old train station came into view I knew it was no joke...

BY Linda Yablonsky

Detroit: City of Loss and Wonder

The first time I saw Detroit there was a bit of snow on the ground but somehow it wasn't that cold. This was early in January of 2005, and the sky was silver-gray and streaked with white. All I knew about Detroit then was what everyone knew: the music (of Motown, Eminem, and Detroit house), the racial tensions, the car companies, the murder rate, and Elmore Leonard. None of it gave me any reason to go there. You could buy records, cars, and books anywhere, and I'd seen enough mean streets in New York. But when three friends told me they were making an overnight to see the new Museum of Contemporary Art Detroit and the city, I tagged along, curious despite myself.

I remember laughing when I saw the Uniroyal tire at the entrance to the city—a land of giants. When the magnificent ruin of the old train station came into view I knew it was no joke. Silhouetted against the steely sky and surrounded by empty space, it appeared to be floating on the air. Like the rest of the city, it conveyed a sense of wonderment in its decreptitude, an indomitable structure that no one knew what to do about. Except stare.

That trip was my rabbit hole into a land as fascinating as it was troubling. What I saw haunted me for years—four years to be exact, when I went back to research a magazine story on the Detroit art scene. I was pretty sure it had one but I didn't actually know. I just wanted another look. In the following three years, I found reasons to go back five or six times. One of them was for an eight-hour performance staged by Matthew Barney for a film. It began on a chilly, rain-soaked October Saturday with a procession of buses from the Detroit Institute of Arts that went through the empty streets at a funereal pace, then moved on to a glue factory and then a barge that drifted down the Rouge River to an old steel mill that he'd turned into a fiery sculpture. I'll never forget that day, and not just because of the pace or the long hours in the rain, but because it gave us an intimacy with Detroit, city of power, city of loss, city of wonder.

The sheer size, the breadth of this place. That was the thing. Detroit had the problems of every post-industrial city but here they were amplified to an incomprehensible degree. The cascading histories, shining at one moment, crumbling the next. The vast prairie lands within the metropolis. The freeways that divided neighborhoods where people lived and also no longer did. And the Fist of Joe Louis—enormous! All of it an incitement to make art.

I was disturbed by the segregation, by the stark contrast between the wealthy suburbs outside and the poverty within, and most of all by the emptiness, whole avenues of boarded-up buildings. Yet people were moving in, and a lot of them were artists and designers who graduated from Cranbrook or Wayne State or CCS and didn't want to leave because they believed they could make a difference. They all said the same thing: "We can make an impact." It wasn't about establishing a career. It was about making art as life support. And no matter who they were or what they did or where in the city they lived, or even if they were there for a single project, they all had the same subject: Detroit.

It consumed them—making art out of Detroit, saving Detroit from itself, largely by repurposing existing structures and materials to serve a larger social purpose. I didn't know if the houses they were fixing up and tricking out as nonprofit residencies or eco-conscious laboratories, if the sculptures they were making with ice, and gas, and pipe metal, and glass added up to art or whether or not they were working in a radical new form, but they went about it as artists and it couldn't have been anything else.

I saw a car in a tree. I saw boats in the road. I saw the alphabet of a nearly extinct language painted on a barn. I saw art made out of rusting paint cans and broken chairs. I saw the polka-dotted blocks of the Heidelberg Project, and my jaw dropped. I climbed through the infinite ruins of the Packard Plant and when I got to the top I cried. I saw clothing made out of vacuum cleaner hoses. I saw an index of medicinal plants growing through cracked sidewalks. I saw galleries in old banks and schools and the shows at the museums. People talk about the landmark Diego Rivera "Industry" murals at the DIA, about the nineteenth- and early-twentieth-century paintings. But the works in the modern and contemporary collections were chosen by someone with a prescient eye for value beyond market share.

So I forgot Motown and murder rates. I saw Mitch Cope and Gina Reichert, and the enduring Dabls. I talked to Tyree Guyton and Jenenne Whitfield, to Phil Cooley and Sabrina Nelson, to Chido Johnson and Monica Bowman, to Scott Hocking and Levon Milross, to Leon Johnson and Megan O'Connoll, to Graem Whyte and Faina Lerman, to Oren Goldenberg and Sterling Toles, to Luis Croquer and Susanne Hilberry and to Hazel Blake, to Julie Taubman and Marc Schwartz and Michele Perron and Michele Andonian, to Becky Hart and Nancy Barr, to Adam Miller and Nicola Kuperus and Hernan Bas, to Lynn Crawford and Steve Hughes and Tate Osten and more—the artists, writers, curators, collectors, and gallerists who excited me with their excitement and belief not just in themselves but in a place. It was the same with security guards, shopkeepers, and educators, all married to the city and working against time to see if they could make a difference.

They did to me. And yet I found myself wondering if Detroit was going to make it—or if it was all going to crash. Yet these people hang on and more are coming, even as Detroit goes through bankruptcy, its material assets threatened by numbers crunchers who have yet to be touched by the soul of this city. Which is real. And wounded. And very, very large. ○

It wasn't about establishing a career. It was about making art as life support.

Linda Yablonsky is a freelance journalist covering the international art world for such print and online publications as Artforum.com, *T: The New York Times Style Magazine*, *W*, *Elle*, and *The Art Newspaper*. She is also the author of *The Story of Junk: A Novel*.

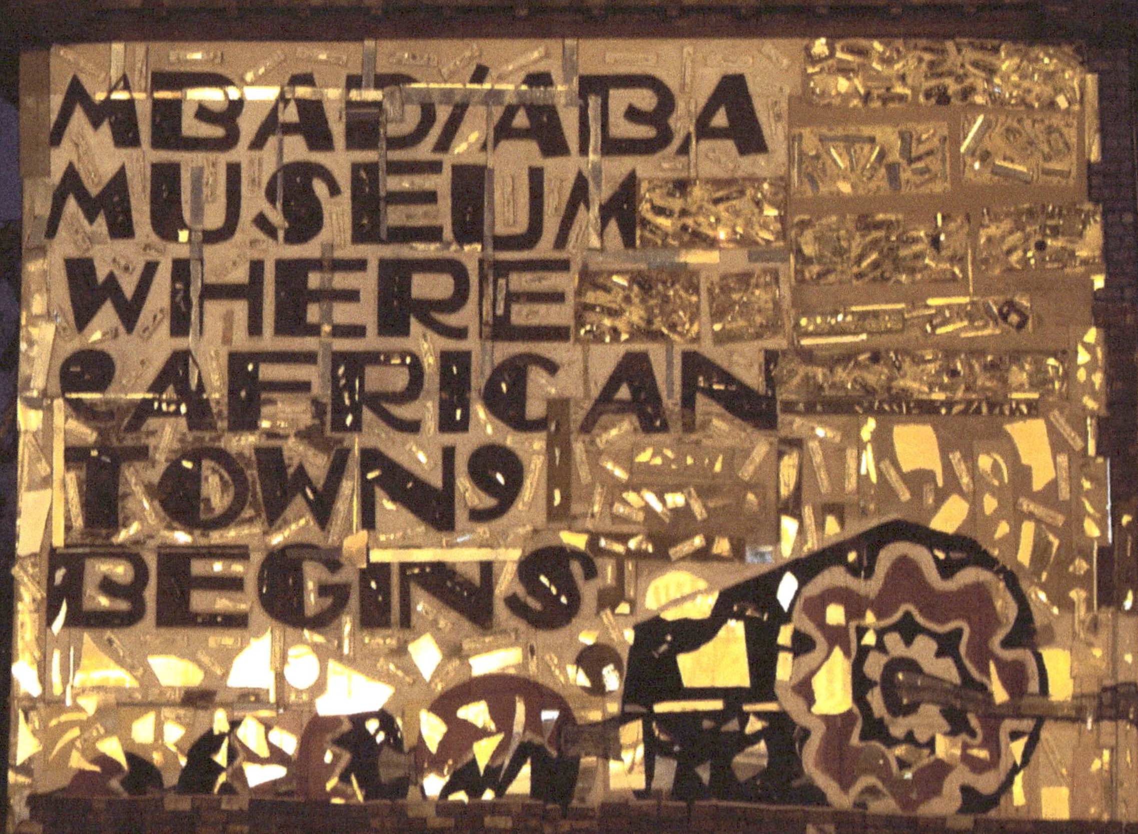

On a cold winter night one building on Dabls African Bead Museum's compound glitters, reflecting car headlights with unexpected energy.

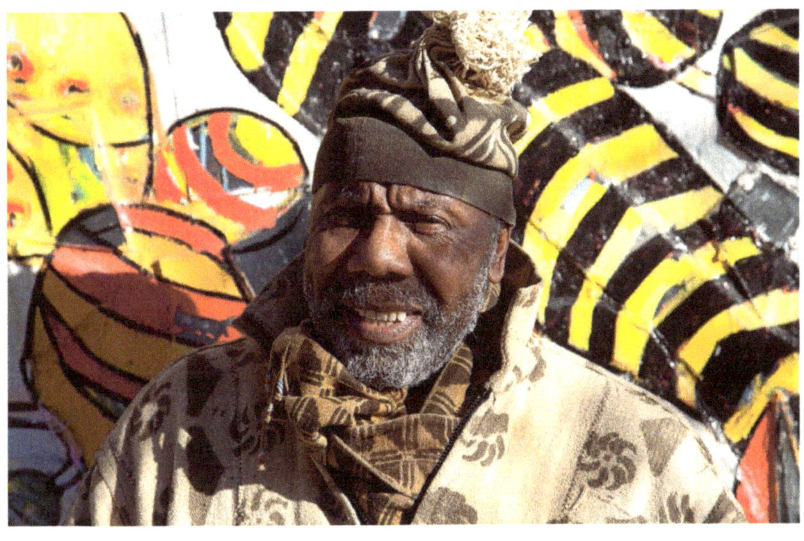

On an otherwise forgettable block in Detroit, the Dabls African Bead Museum doesn't just stand out. It screams, "Come close, see me."

The building is covered in beads, metals, iron sculptures, jagged-cut mirrors: a vibrant slice of creativity pitched in the middle of nowhere.

Most people circle the building at least once before ever going in, transfixed by the odd assortment of objects on display. The man who sits high behind the counter inside the main gallery and gift shop has placed each piece with purpose.

He knows every object's story. He shares the tales freely with visitors from "all parts of the planet." The man, Olayami Dabls, makes only one cautionary request: Do not call him an artist.

"I consider myself a storyteller," says sixty-three-year-old Dabls, who is also the museum's founder, curator, and main creator of its installations. "I may use tools that cross all the various mediums, but I do not see myself as an artist, a painter, or sculptor. I approach my talent the way Africans had the responsibility of doing."

Every inch of the building and the grounds echo Dabls's declaration. "Before we opened," he says, "there was nothing really that you could point to in the city as being reflective of art in a true African experience. In the west, art is supposed to be without purpose and meaning. You like it or you don't. In African systems, art is used for very specific reasons. Artists have great responsibility to educate, to tell the story."

By birth, Dabls is African American, born in Canton, Mississippi. By choice, he makes the preservation of African creative and cultural traditions the heart of his work. "The beads on this building, they have specific meaning to cultures who used them in the past. They could come here today and it would act as a trigger."

The museum, which is really a small campus of outdoor installations and a separate beaded house, is best known for an outdoor work called "Iron Teaching Rock How to Rust." At first glance, it's merely a collection of school chairs facing a rock with rusty pipe in its center.

"Iron is a metaphor for Europeans. Rocks are a metaphor for Africans. It's a political social commentary that deals with cultural indoctrination. The rocks, the people, tell stories."

Perhaps the museum's most engrossing story is the tale of how it came to be.

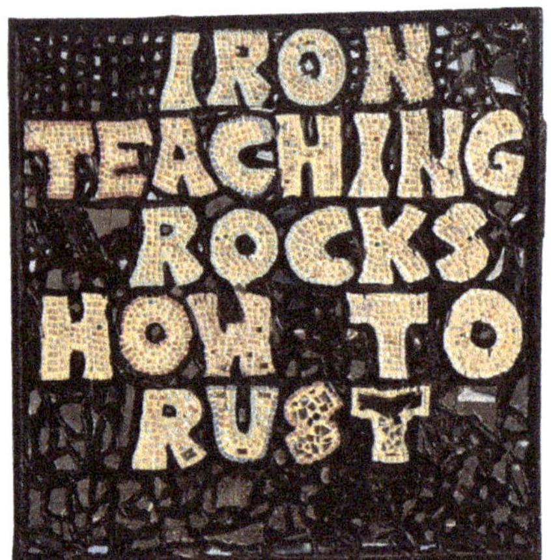

"I could lie and say that what's happened here was my master plan," says Dabls. But the truth starts in downtown Detroit, where he'd operated a bead store. His tastes turned out to be too African for the building's owner. Dabls was eventually evicted, he says, because of a wide-ranging dispute that started with his decision to feature African imagery on a store awning and evolved into issues over the rent. "All my stuff was on the street."

Suddenly in need of storage space, he decided to take advantage of a longstanding offer. "These buildings had been donated to me but they were just sitting here," he says. "I hadn't done one thing with them until I was forced to move."

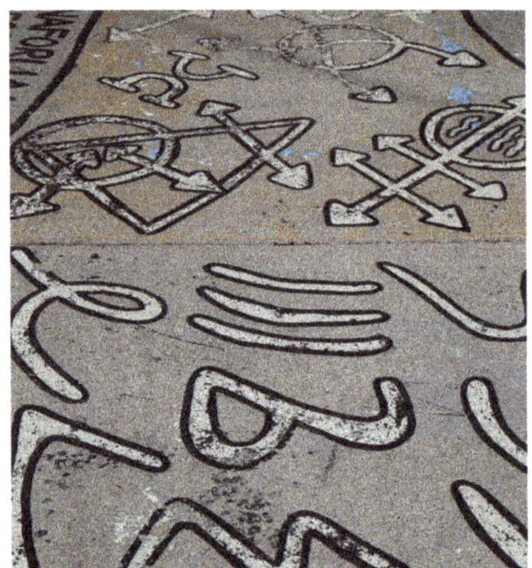

A decade later Dabls's choice to move appears to have been a wise one. "We get people here all times of the day and night, moving around like they're in a safe zone. You can't convince people not to be afraid. But things we call art can make people feel comfortable."

Dabls says the museum's "energy" and great word of mouth partly explain how an Italian billionaire by the name of Luciano Benetton happened to saunter into the gallery in 2012. Dabls's skill as a painter may explain the other half of the unlikely story. The globe-trotting billionaire founder of the fashion company Benetton Group purchased ten of his original figurative watercolors.

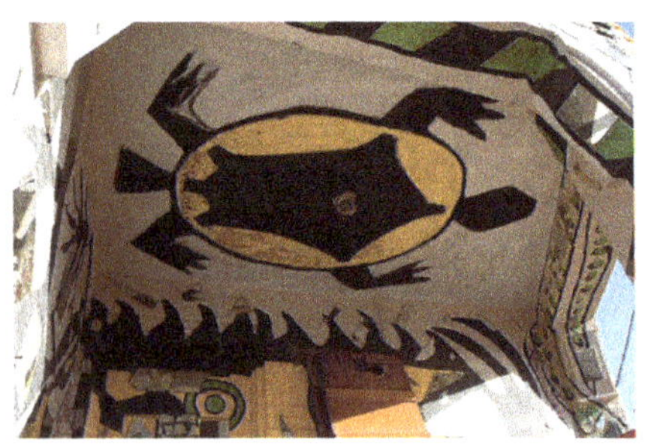

"I always wanted to do something big, but the truth is, we ran out of money and just decided to beautify the place and see what happens," he says. "I never thought it would be global. I didn't even know who he was until he left and I looked him up."

But visits like Benetton's and a steady stream of requests from documentary filmmakers have given Dabls a greater story to tell about his little museum's role in Detroit.

"What we're doing is not just for a particular segment of the community. Europeans, Chinese, Africans, Arabs, they all come here," he says. "And if I didn't tell them about what some of the installations were all about, people could come close to what I did not say just because of the ambience of it. Good energy is universal."

ABOVE: The artwork of Dabls is everywhere on his property, on the sidewalk, the walls, and even on the ceiling of an entrance.

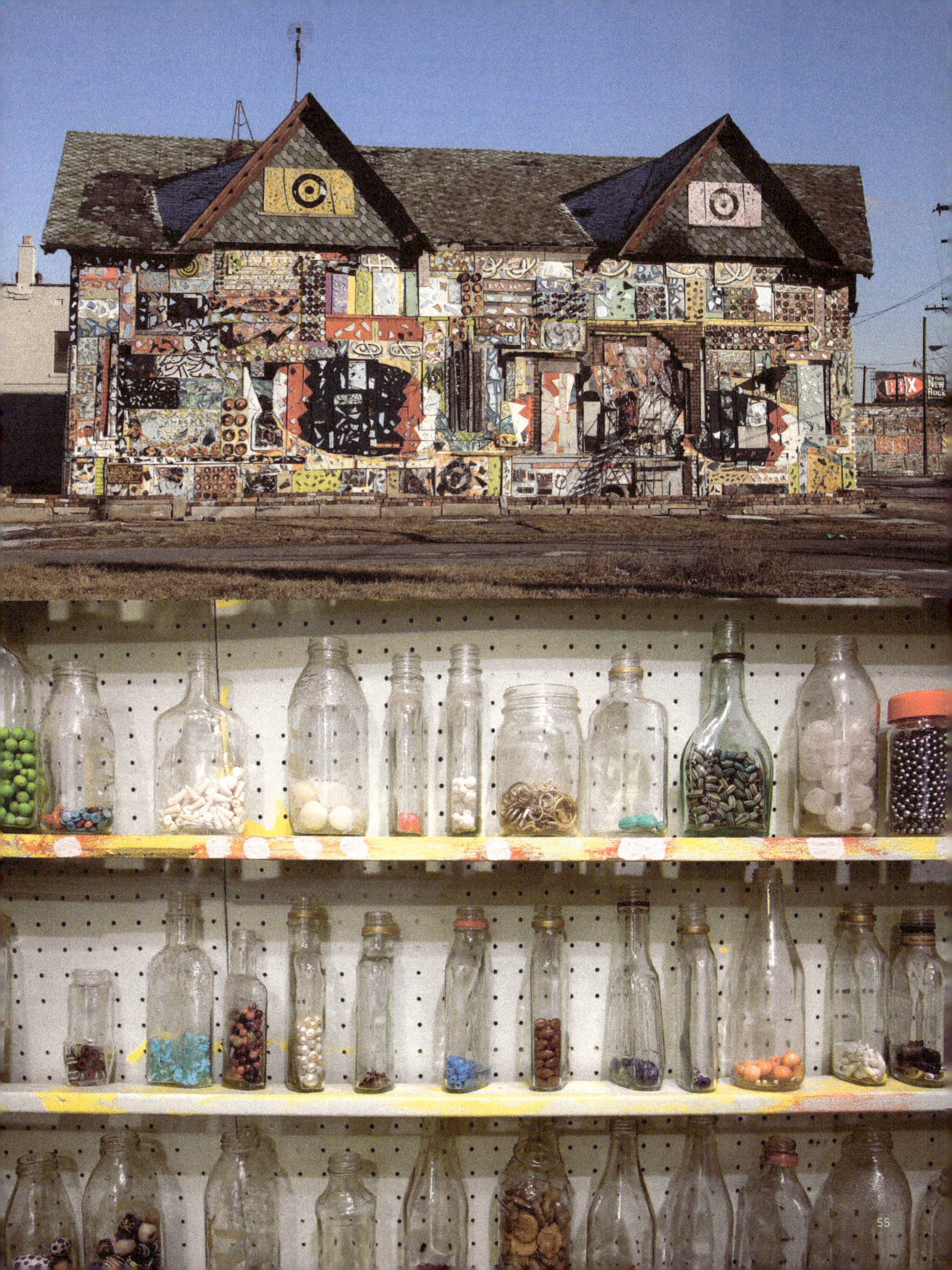
New
Rock

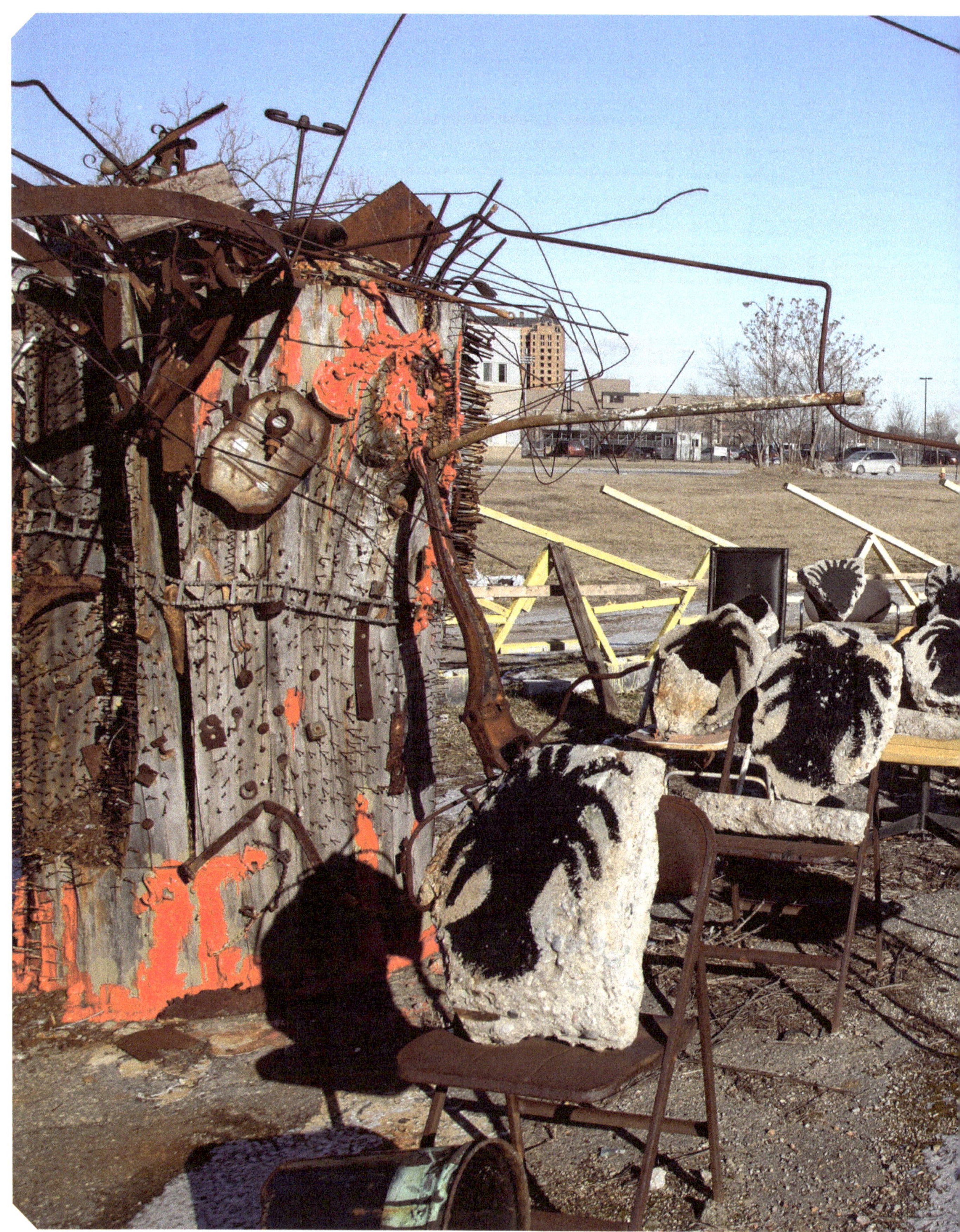

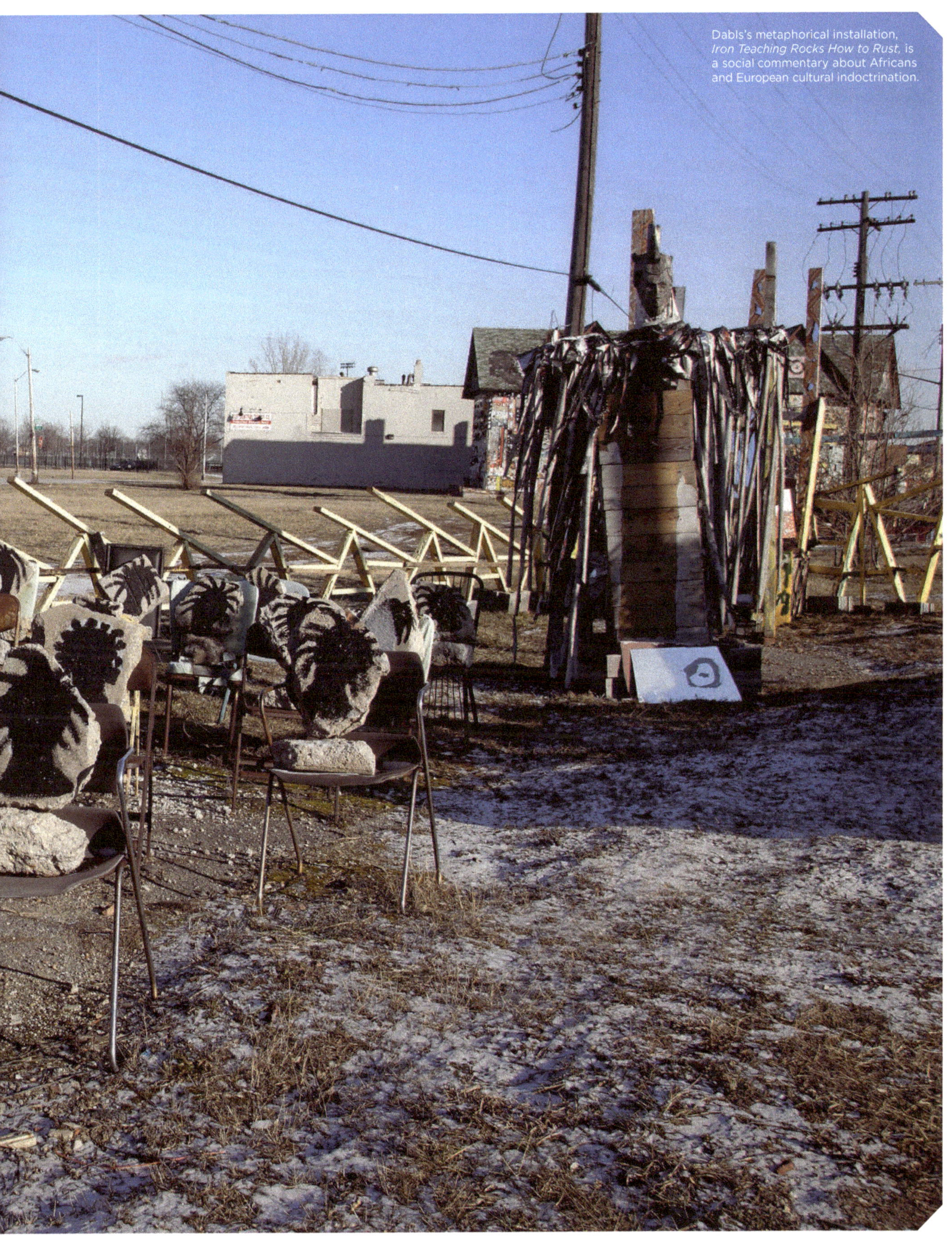

Dabls's metaphorical installation, *Iron Teaching Rocks How to Rust*, is a social commentary about Africans and European cultural indoctrination.

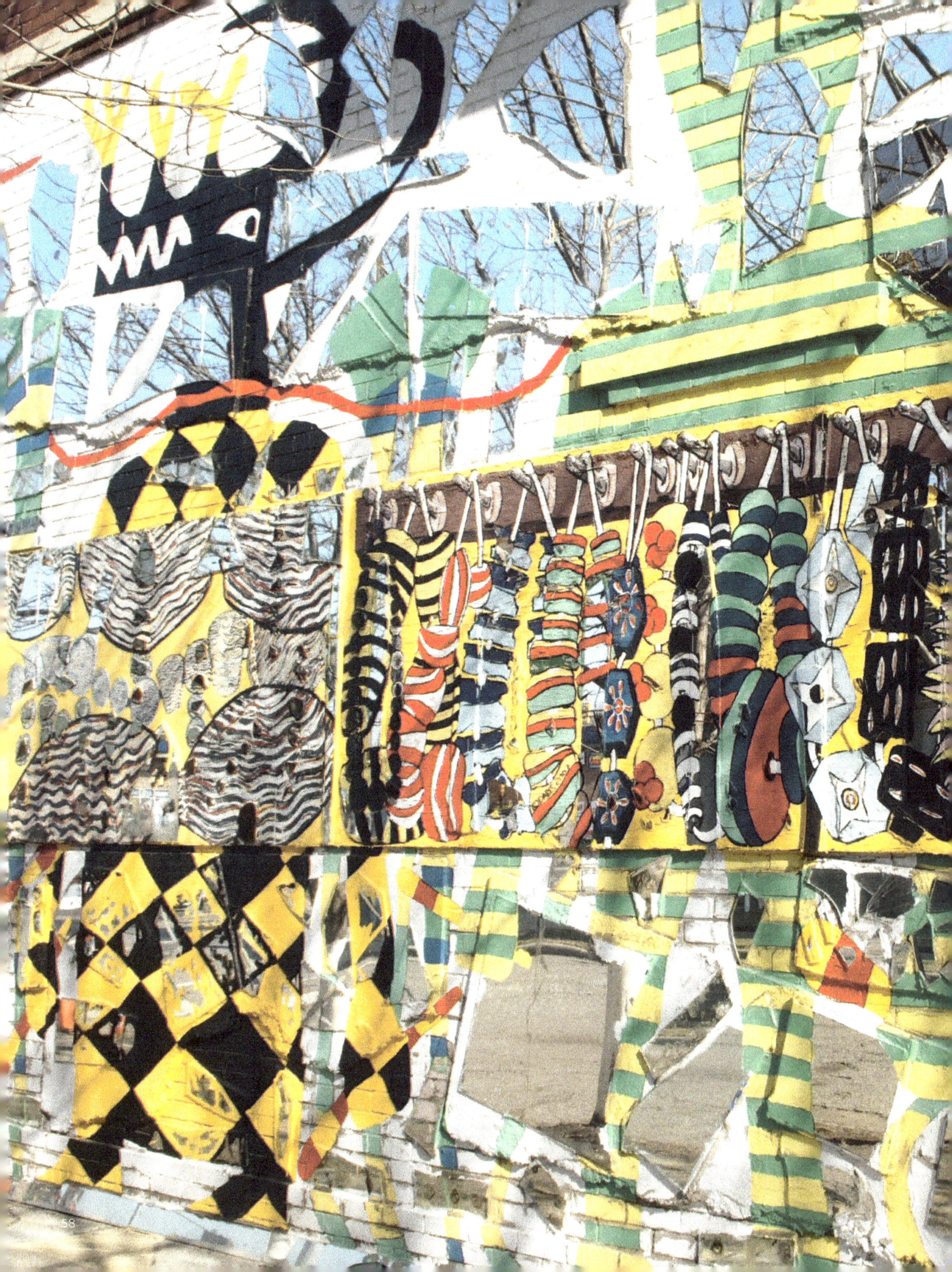

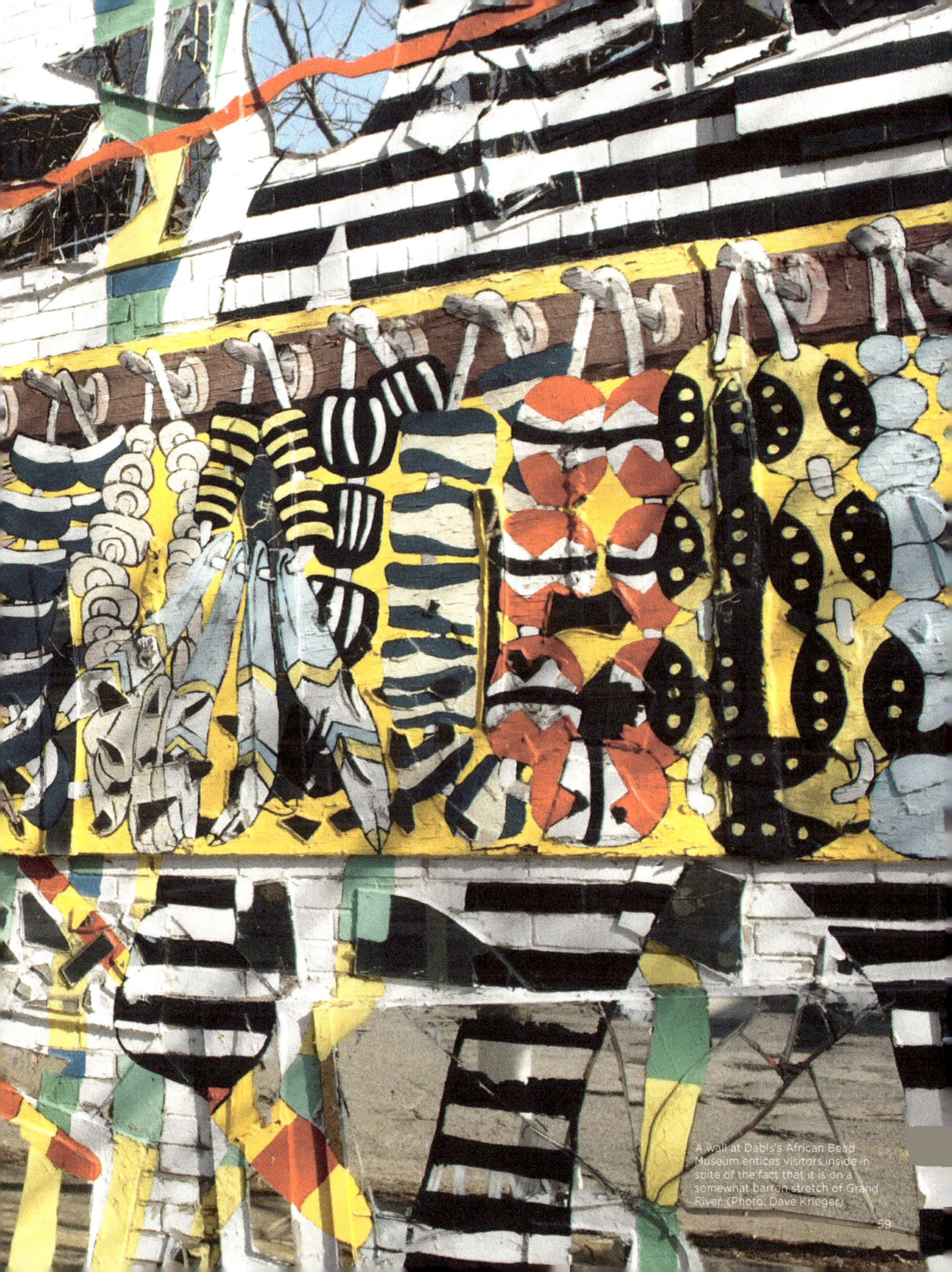

A wall at Dabls's African Bead Museum entices visitors inside in spite of the fact that it is on a somewhat barren stretch of Grand River. (Photo: Dave Krieger)

DESIGN 99 AND POWER HOUSE PRODUCTIONS: MITCH COPE AND GINA REICHERT

In any other city, Gina Reichert and her partner, Mitch Cope, might be branded simply an architect and a painter.

Yet in Detroit creative pioneers are what many people call the duo. The tag seems apt given the ambitious way that they've gone about using art to resuscitate a deteriorating block of abandoned homes and encouraging other artists to join their quest.

Reichert, a graduate of the Cranbrook Academy of Art, and Cope, a College for Creative Studies grad, are co-founders of Design 99, an experimental community-based architecture and contemporary art studio.

They treat the experimental part of their work as serious fun. They've been known to offer ninety-nine-dollar house calls and to offer consultations for ninety-nine cents a minute to encourage more people to consider adding art to their neighborhood. "We don't have a typical art practice," explains Reichert.

While Design 99 generally pays the couple's bills, much of their accolades have come via another endeavor called Power House Productions, a nonprofit they formed to transform abandoned homes into art performance, installation, and residency spaces.

Their work also includes the Power House, a home that's solar powered and completely off the grid, along with the redesign of four vacant lots into the Ride It Sculpture Park. The park's colorful concrete landscapes and sculpture features appeal as much to skateboard and BMX bike enthusiasts as they do to average neighborhood residents.

"A lot of our work is about consumption and worth and creating a comfort level around art so that people who don't normally talk to artists or architects might consider it as an accessible option," says Reichert. "I'm much more interested in talking to my neighbors about art than going to an opening and courting a patron."

Reichert's preference hasn't stopped the wider art world from calling. Buzz about the couple exploded in 2010 when *Juxtapoz* magazine tapped Power House Productions as the beneficiary of a $150,000 grant generated from the proceeds of an international auction celebrating the magazine's fifteenth anniversary.

The sudden windfall kicked their dream of art-in-action into overdrive. The block became a must-see, and Reichert and Cope had enough money to purchase the first wave of houses at auction, many for no more than five hundred dollars.

"It really allowed us to get the ball rolling with some momentum, being able to buy some houses and to set up budgets to do projects in one area. It just legitimized what were just ideas and questions." The grant also helped cover one-month residencies for six visiting artists, each tasked with embellishing the neighborhood with their own artistic style.

The roster included artists Monica Canilao, Swoon, Retna, Richard Colman, Saelee Oh, and Ben Wolf. With their arrival came headlines and the start of nationally held misconceptions about being creative in Detroit.

"A lot of people wanna just parachute in. Yes, you can make work just for the sake of making work. But there's sacrifice and hard work," she says. "It's not just cheap real estate and the thing that doesn't get represented about a $500 house [a running joke among artists in response to news reports about Detroit's cheap real estate], it needs a lot of work. There's a lot of responsibility."

Reichert knows. She and Cope own four houses. Through the nonprofit, they own and manage six additional properties.

As local and international interest continue to grow around their projects, Reichert says she and Cope have become intensely selective about the artists they bring to Detroit.

"When you first come here, it's easy to get caught up in seeing a photogenic quality to the decay," she says. "The whole reason we started with the guesthouses was to help artists get past the surface level. If you're here three months or at least coming back repeatedly, then you start to develop a healthy dialogue about what's really possible in Detroit."

The possibilities as Reichert sees them don't add up to traditional wealth or creative notoriety.

"A number of the projects we take on don't pay for themselves," she says. "But they mean enough to us that we're still willing to take them, hoping that the next grant or next commission will catch us up. The reason we're both happy living in Detroit is because you can take the risk and not go totally broke."

The willingness to risk, says Reichert, is the only reason to be in Detroit. It's how she explains her decision years ago to walk away from a safe corporate job. Right after grad school, she earned a coveted seat in the world of designers and architects, a spot at Gensler's Michigan office.

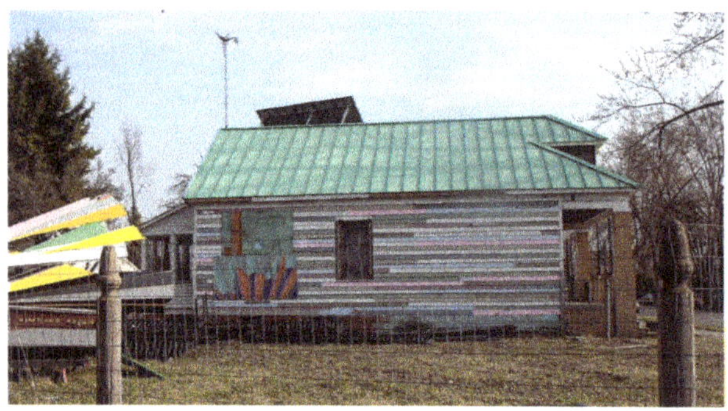

But Reichert felt more restrained than rewarded.

"A typical corporate job just made less sense to me here. I thought, if I'm going to stay, I'm going to find a different way of making a living. Otherwise I could just go back to New York."

She insists she's never looked back: "In a lot of ways there are more choices here. There's definitely been times when I'm at a loss for work. But I have brain space and we're not just scrambling to be artists in a studio. We're living."

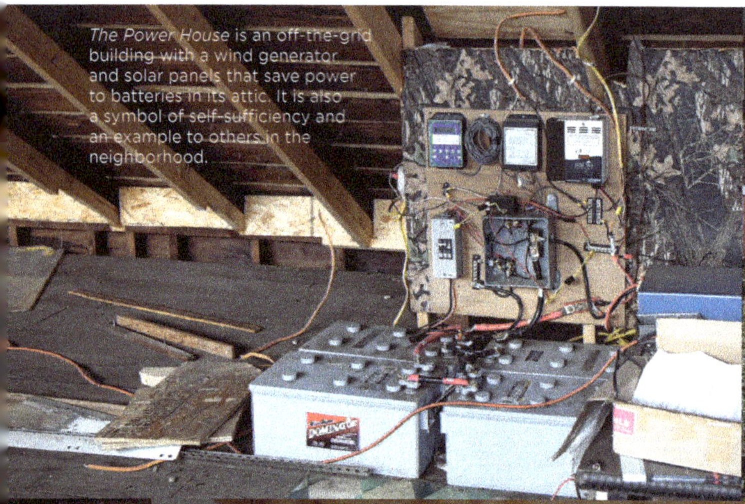

The Power House is an off-the-grid building with a wind generator and solar panels that save power to batteries in its attic. It is also a symbol of self-sufficiency and an example to others in the neighborhood.

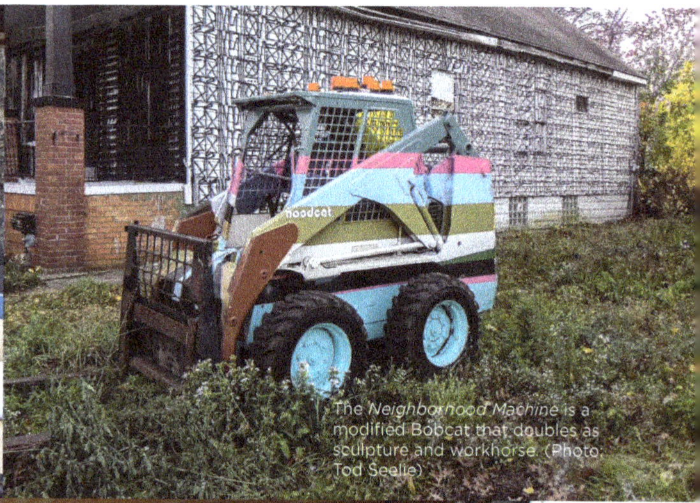

The *Neighborhood Machine* is a modified Bobcat that doubles as sculpture and workhorse. (Photo: Tod Seelie)

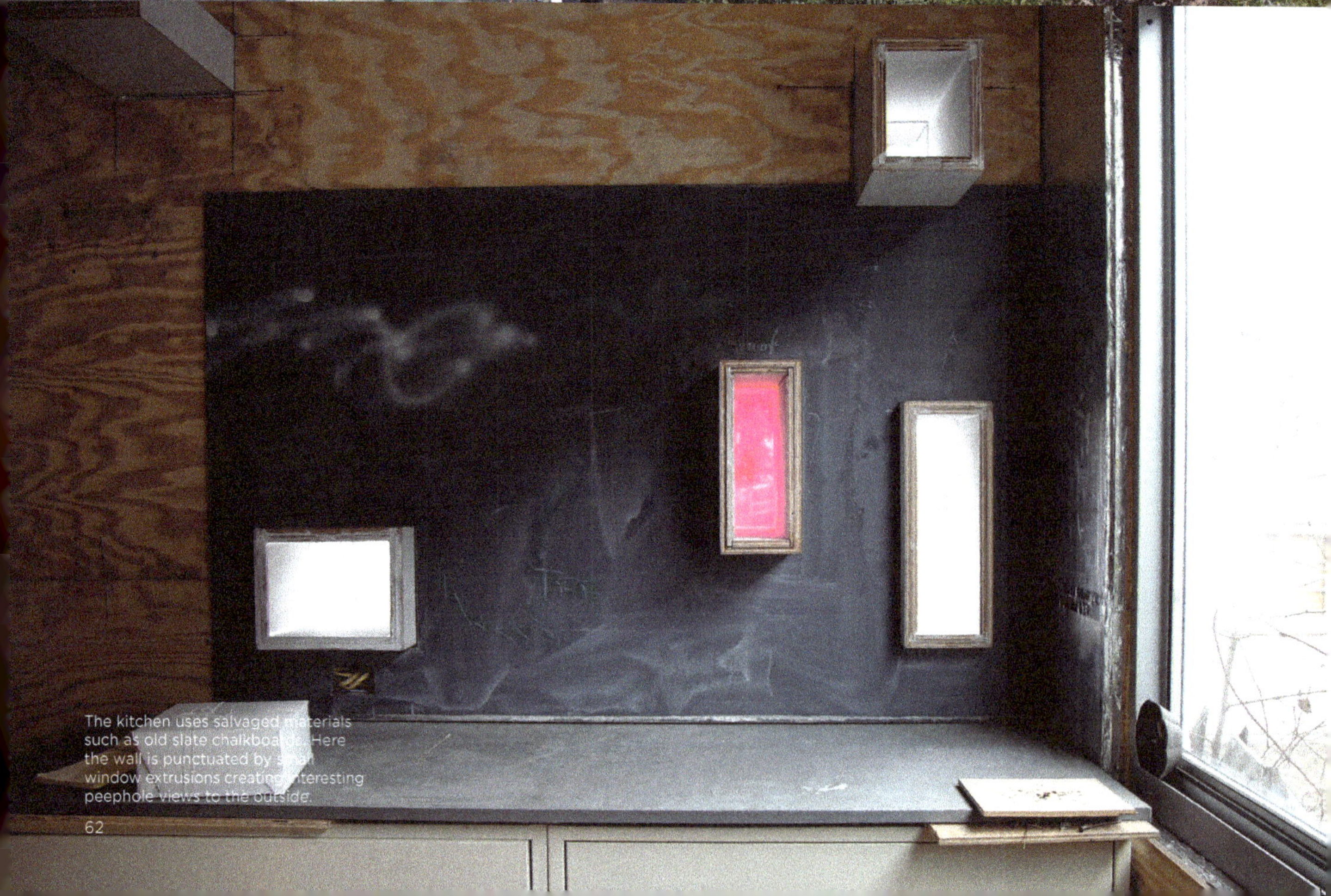

The kitchen uses salvaged materials such as old slate chalkboards. Here the wall is punctuated by small window extrusions creating interesting peephole views to the outside.

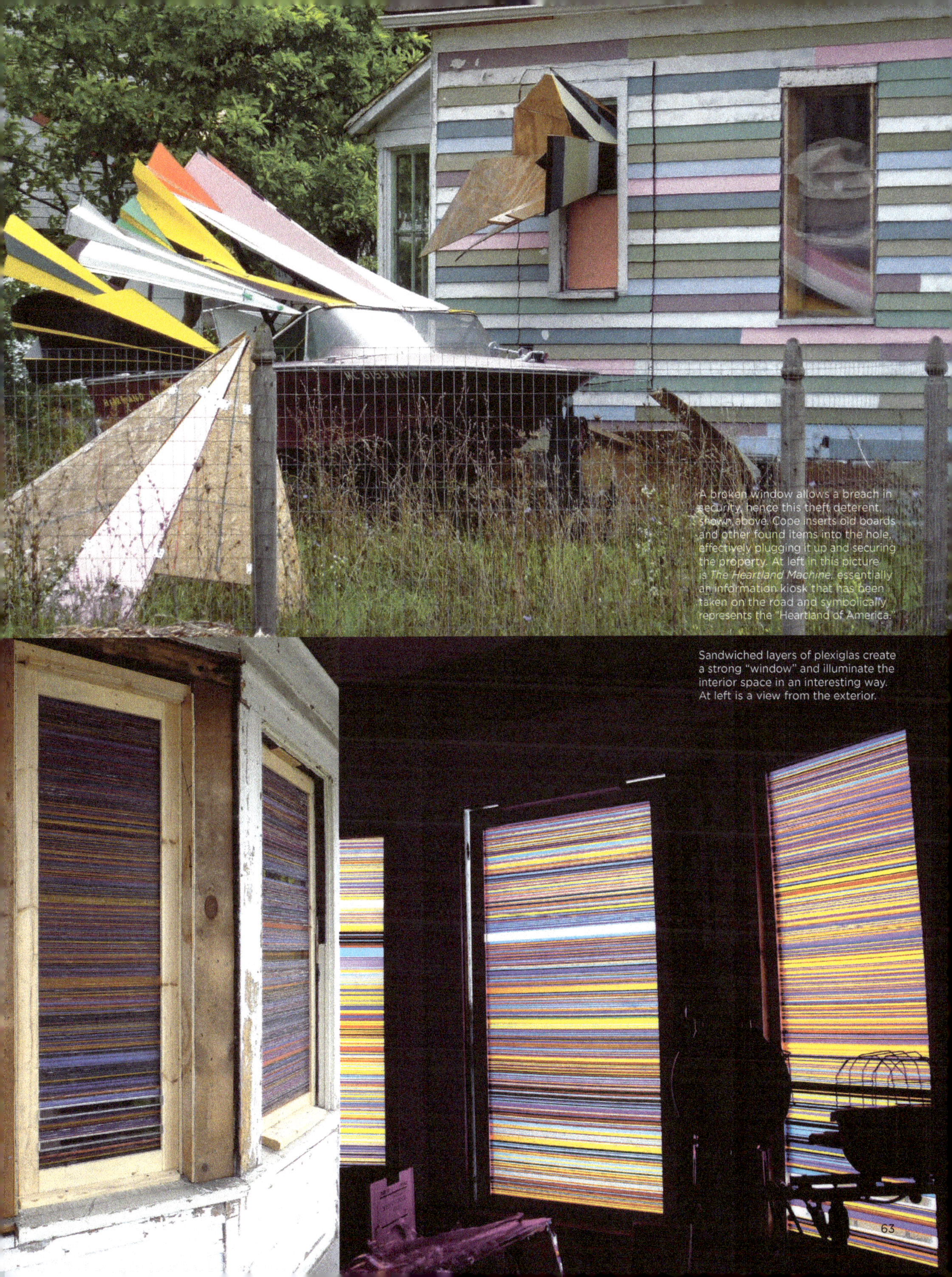

A broken window allows a breach in security, hence this theft deterent, shown above. Cope inserts old boards and other found items into the hole, effectively plugging it up and securing the property. At left in this picture is *The Heartland Machine*, essentially an information kiosk that has been taken on the road and symbolically represents the "Heartland of America."

Sandwiched layers of plexiglas create a strong "window" and illuminate the interior space in an interesting way. At left is a view from the exterior.

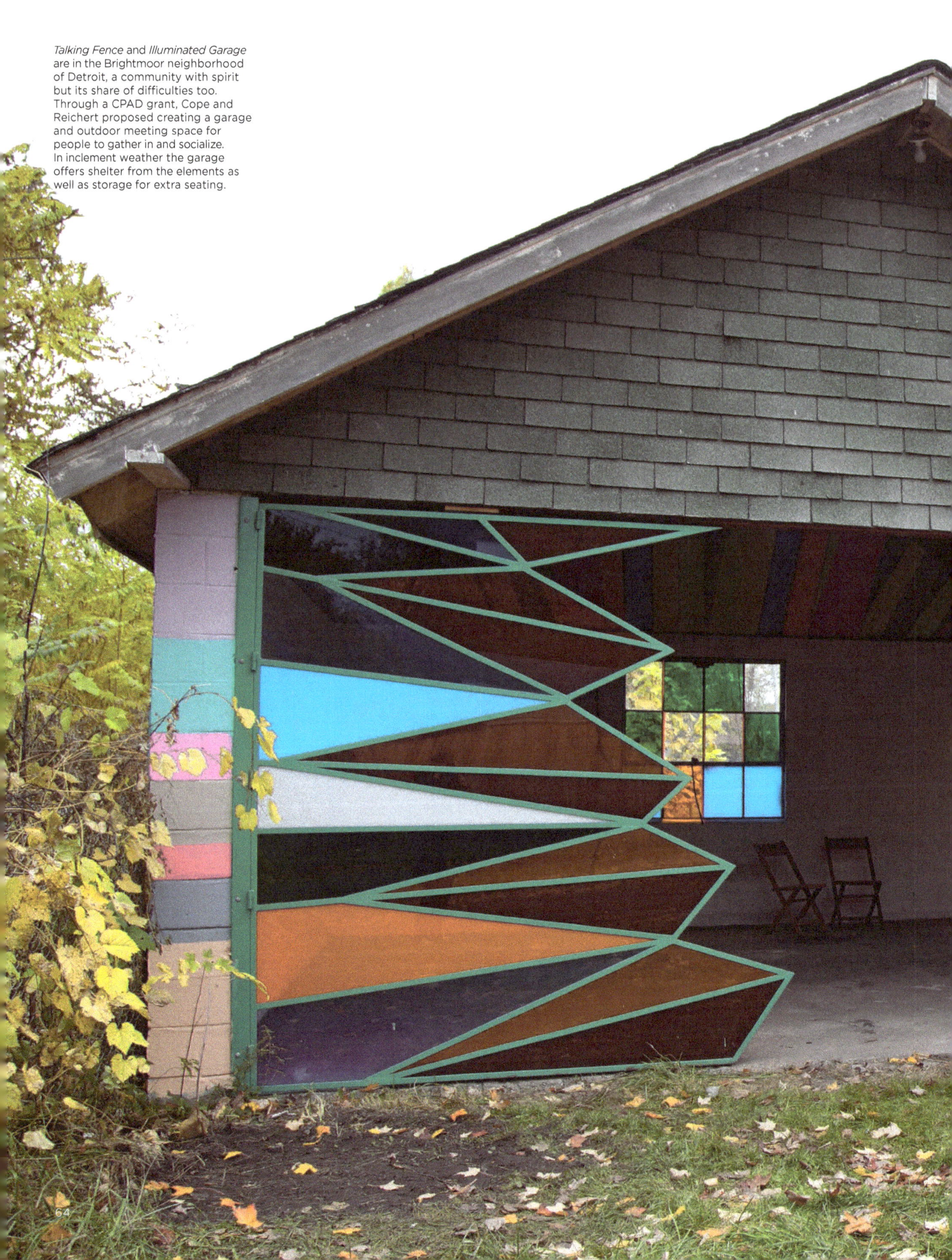

Talking Fence and *Illuminated Garage* are in the Brightmoor neighborhood of Detroit, a community with spirit but its share of difficulties too. Through a CPAD grant, Cope and Reichert proposed creating a garage and outdoor meeting space for people to gather in and socialize. In inclement weather the garage offers shelter from the elements as well as storage for extra seating.

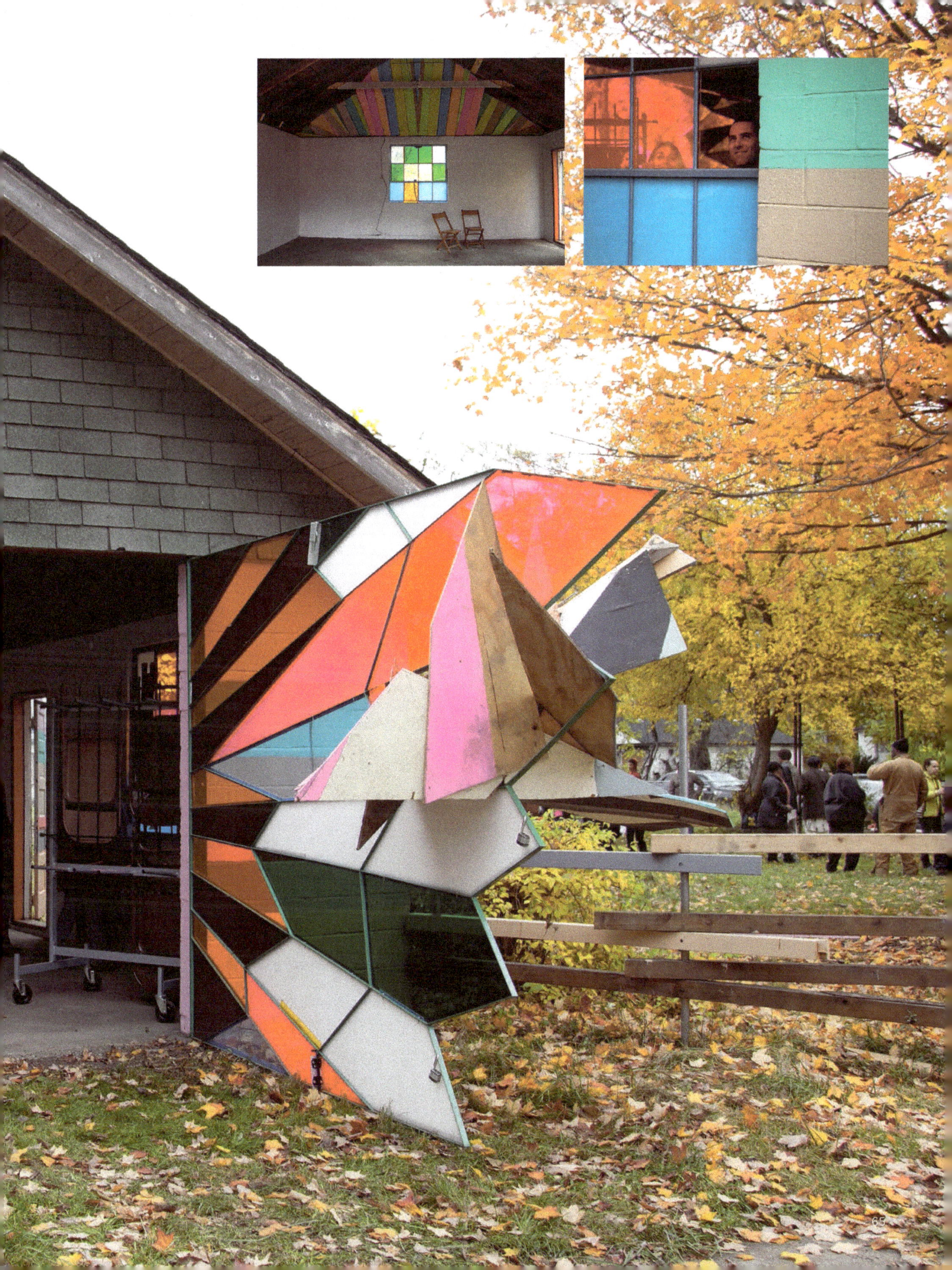

DESIGN 99 AND POWER HOUSE PRODUCTIONS: RIDE IT SCULPTURE PARK

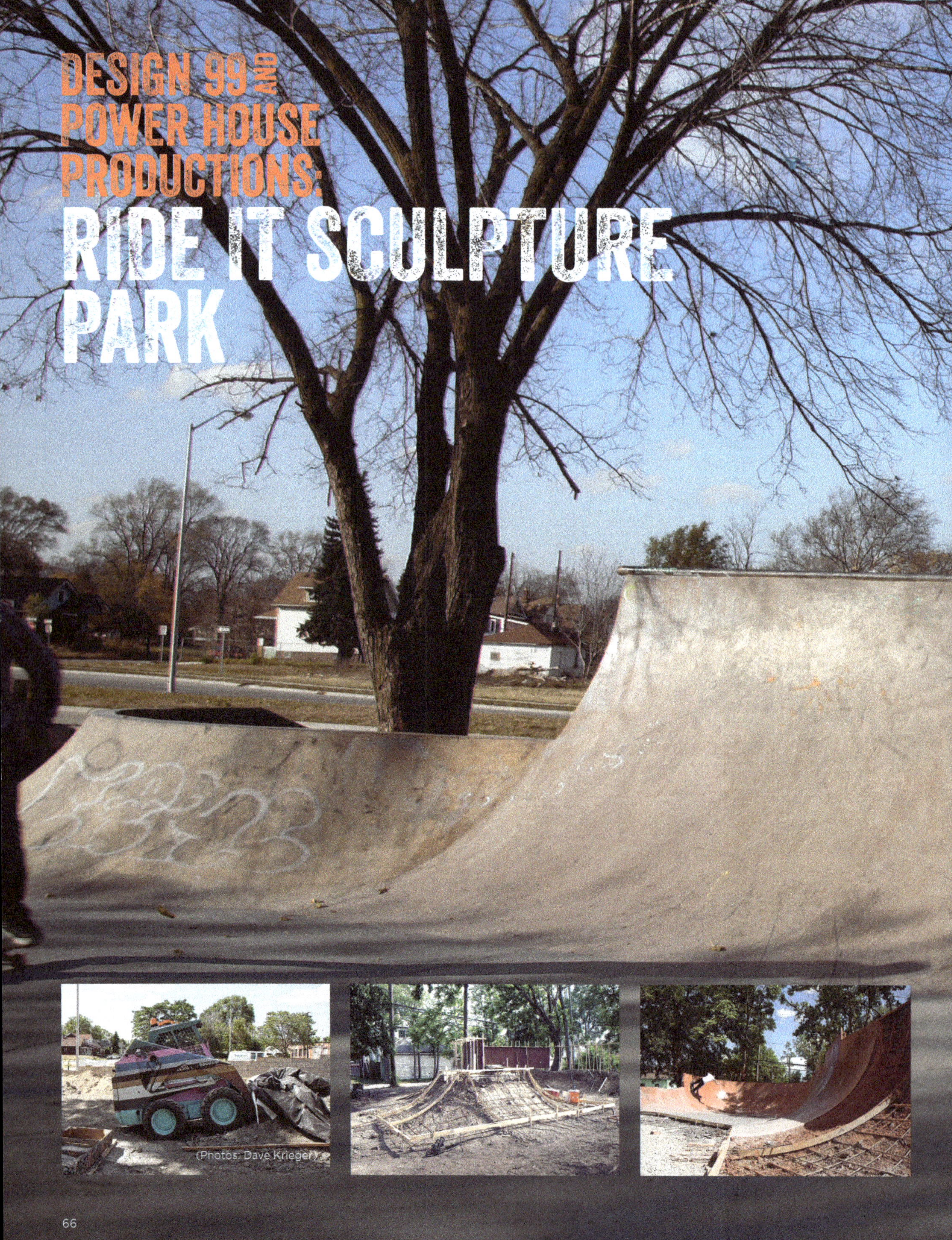

(Photos: Dave Krieger)

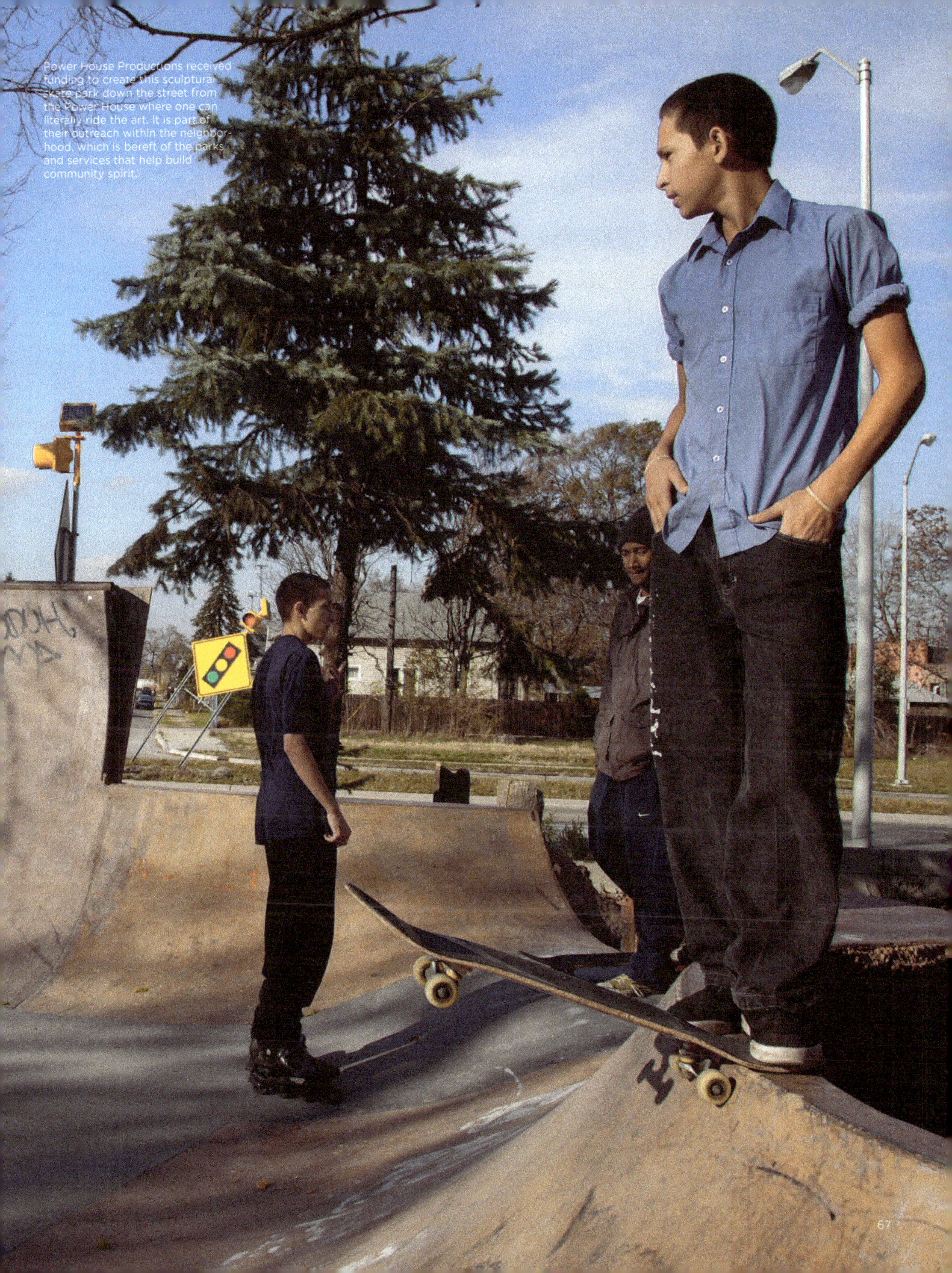

Power House Productions received funding to create this sculptural skate park down the street from the Power House where one can literally ride the art. It is part of their outreach within the neighborhood, which is bereft of the parks and services that help build community spirit.

DESIGN 99 AND POWER HOUSE PRODUCTIONS WITH GRAEM WHYTE: SQUASH HOUSE

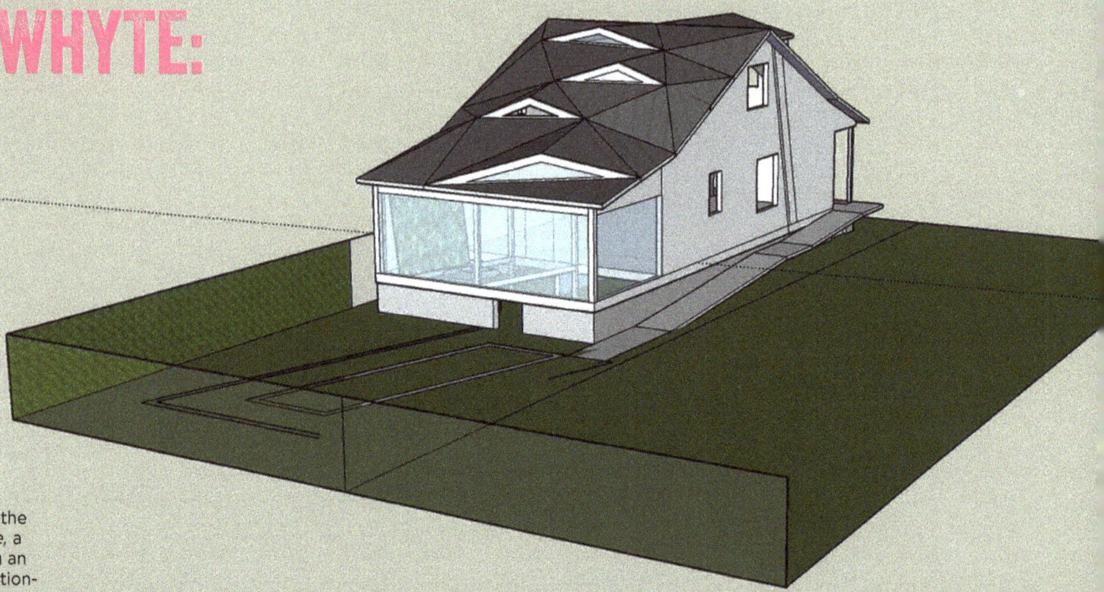

Lead artist Graem Whyte tests the limits of space in *Squash House*, a project with the goal of turning an abandoned house into a regulation-size squash court. (Art: Graem Whyte)

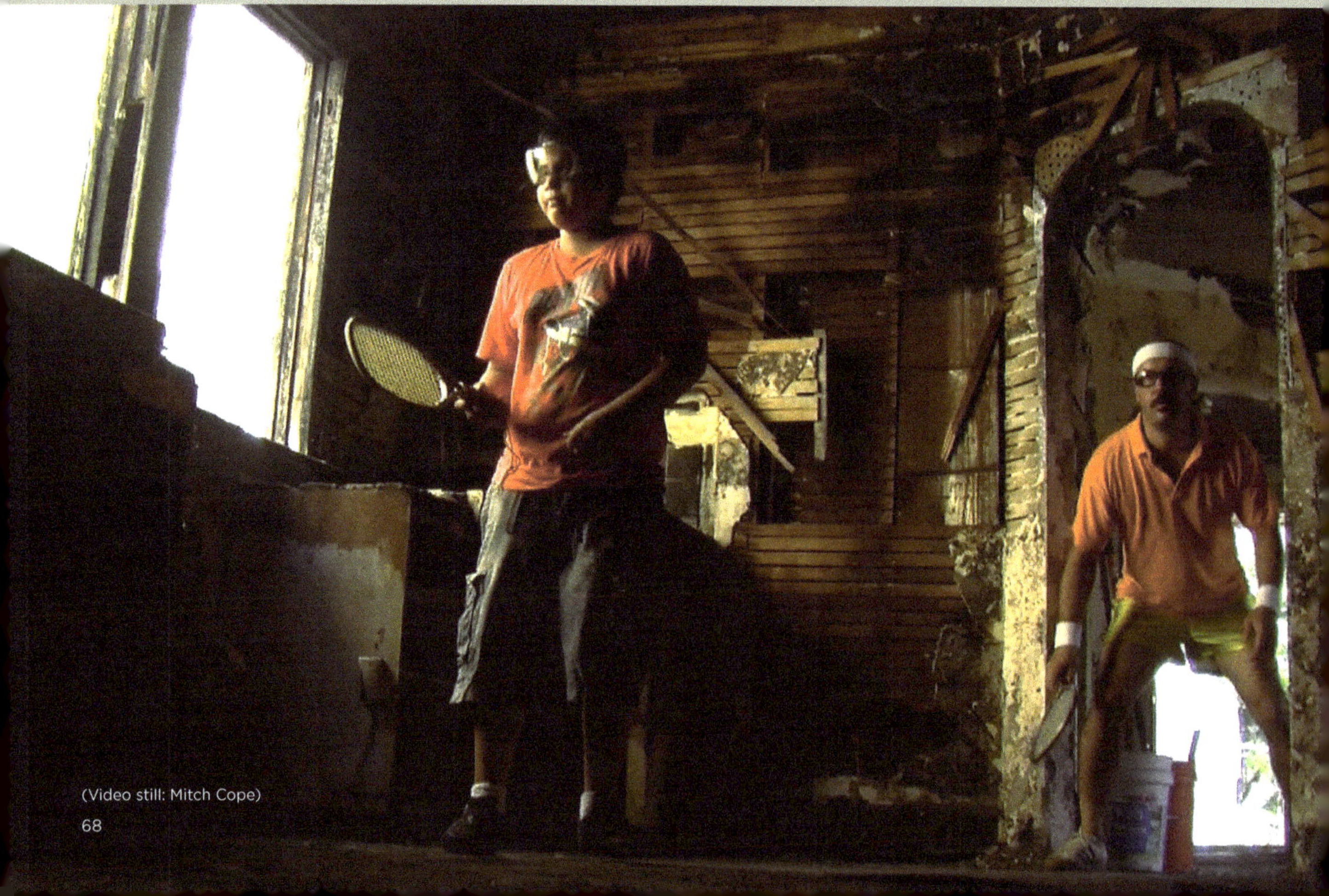

(Video still: Mitch Cope)

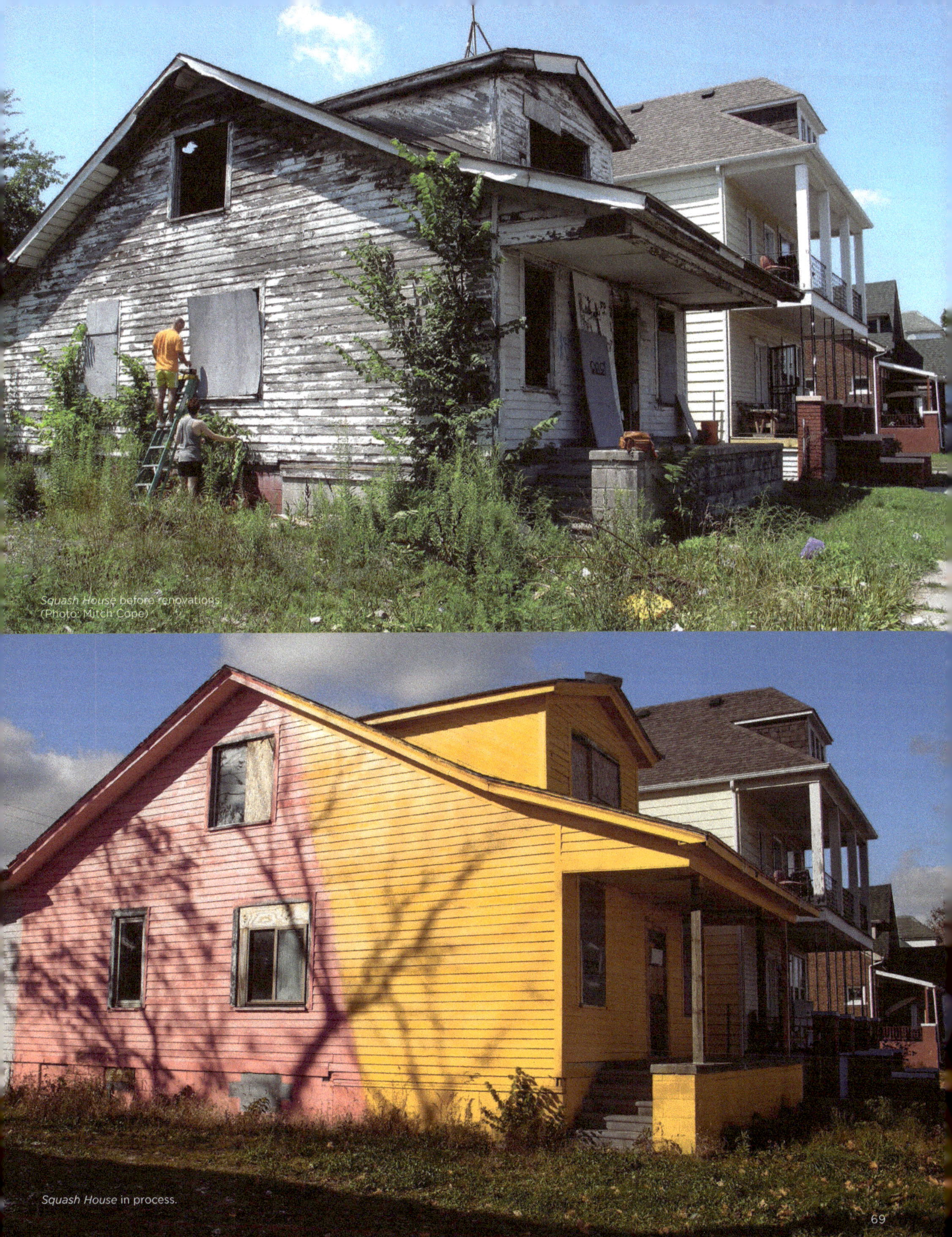

Squash House before renovations. (Photo: Mitch Cope)

Squash House in process.

DESIGN 99: THE *JUXTAPOZ* & POWER HOUSE PRODUCTIONS RESIDENCIES

MONICA CANILAO

With proceeds from the *Juxtapoz* fifteenth anniversary benefit and auction, Power House Productions received funds to purchase several homes on Moran Street, which were turned over to Monica Canilao, Richard Colman, Saelee Oh, Retna, Swoon, and Ben Wolf to use as their canvases. On the followng pages are the fruits of their labor.

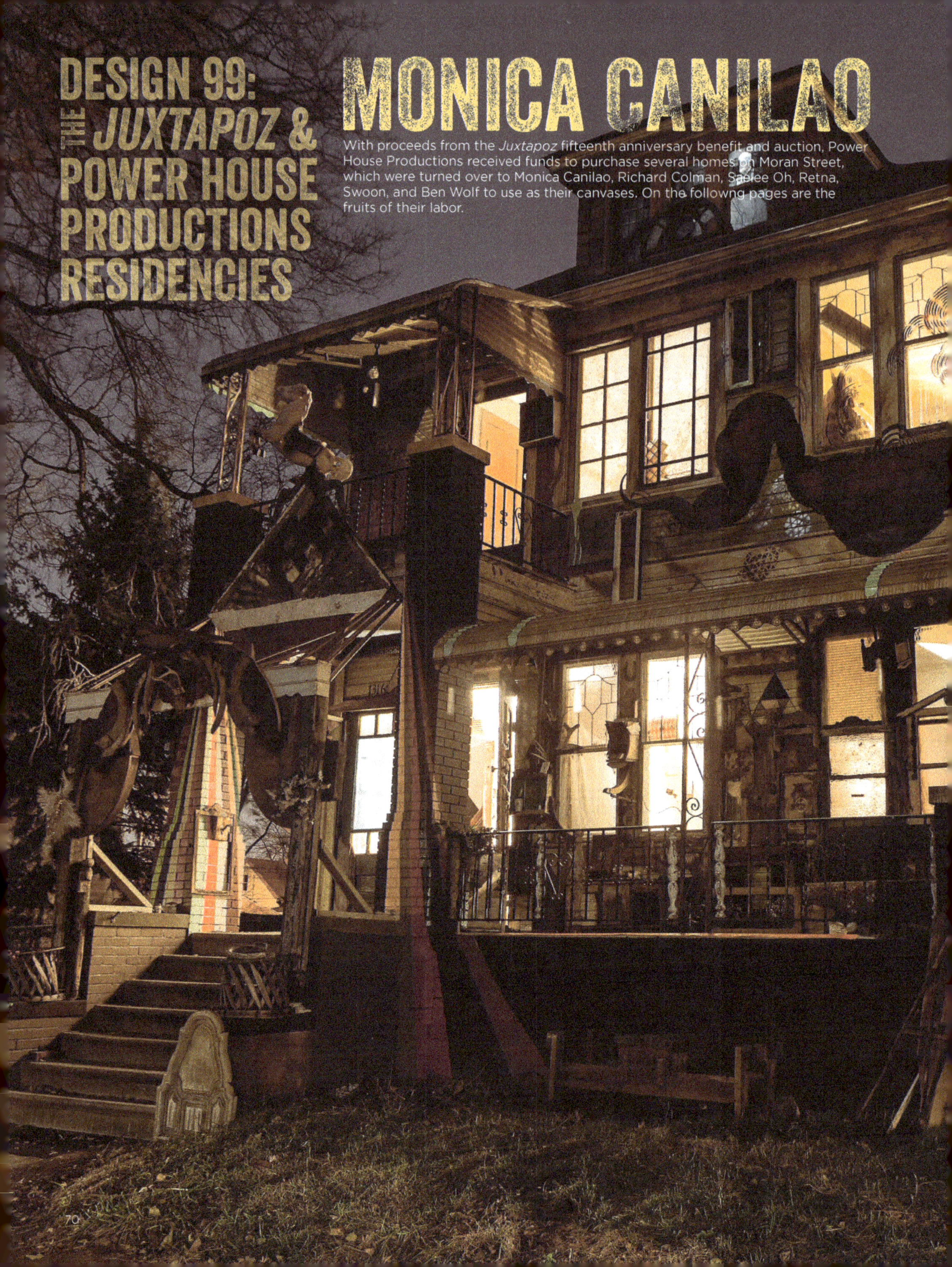

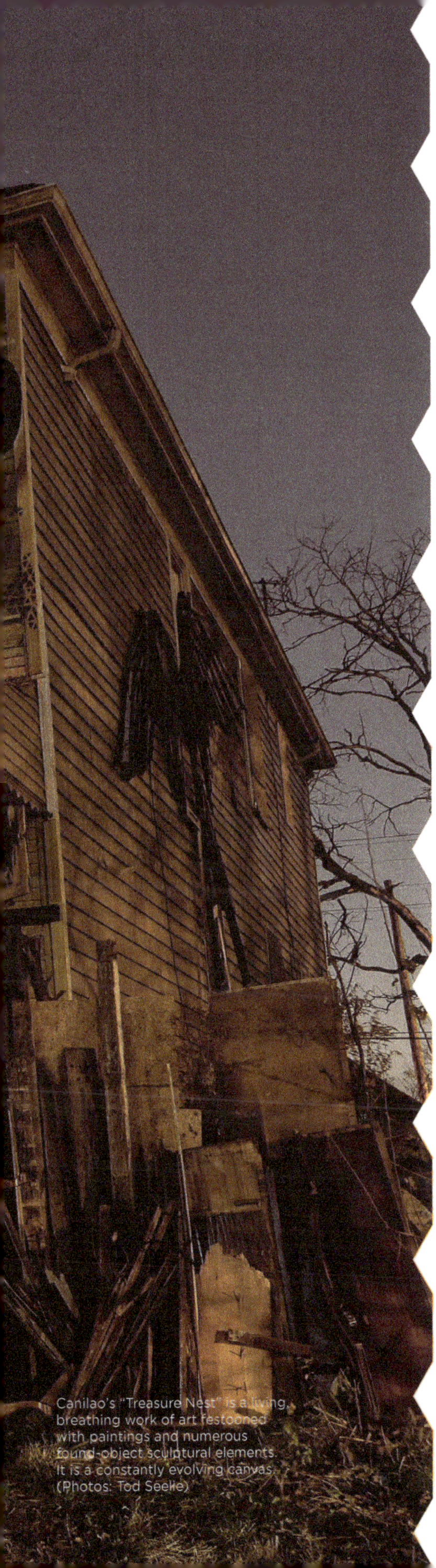

Canilao's "Treasure Nest" is a living, breathing work of art festooned with paintings and numerous found-object sculptural elements. It is a constantly evolving canvas. (Photos: Tod Seelie)

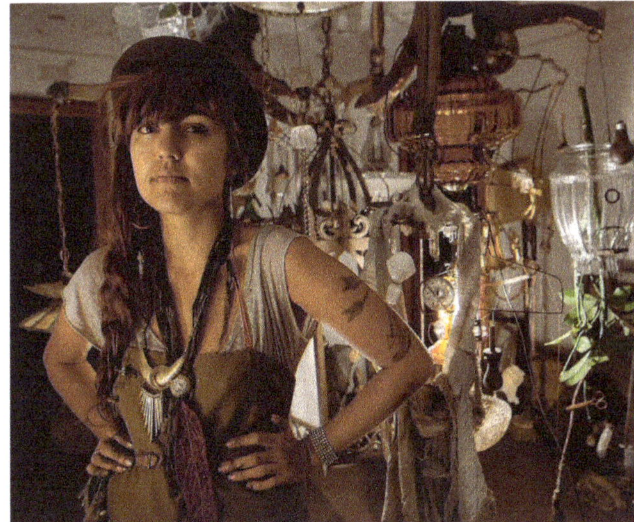

Artist Monica Canilao bought a house in Detroit.

Canilao wants the story told to be that she is one who stayed. "It ended up becoming a part of my life. I just fell in love with the spirit of the city."

A hip two-month arts residency project designed to commemorate *Juxtapoz* magazine's fifteenth anniversary coaxed the California native to Motown in 2011. But the treasures she found on the ground convinced Canilao to make Detroit her home, at least one of them.

"I spend a lot of months out of every year here," says Canilao, twenty-nine. "All of my art relies on using abandoned things. This is just a mecca for neglected things and a really magical city. You're always finding all this crazy stuff and wanting to make things here."

In Detroit, Canilao's attention remains fixed on the "Treasure Nest." That's the name she gave to the house that lured her and later became her own, for only two thousand dollars. Canilao was one of six artists invited to Detroit to participate in the Power House X *Juxtapoz* project, an effort to rehabilitate a neighborhood block overrun with abandoned homes into active art installations and performance spaces.

Even Canilao struggles to fully describe the art that she's made in, of, and around the house. Mostly it is a gallery of found materials, transformed by the eye of a California College of the Arts graduate whose work includes painting, sculpture, drawing, printmaking, illustrations, costume-making, even tattoo design.

"I like that you don't have to spend money to make things. There's so much old lumber and other great artifacts just lying around Detroit. You just have to want to put in the work to salvage," she says.

Often the searching bears surreal fruit. For instance, Canilao created a giant fourteen-panel paper quilt commissioned by the Oakland Museum and made entirely of paper and photographs that she found while salvaging around abandoned schools, churches, bars, and funeral homes. Among the papers, she also found a check for two hundred dollars, made out in 1965, signed by Rosa Parks.

"That was like a magical piece of history that was found, and it was just there disintegrating more and more. It's kind of a really special thing to get to find these artifacts and treasures and do something with them when they're just getting destroyed by time and water and snow and more burning down of buildings."

Canilao knows there are critics who say Detroit is being exploited by creatives who lack concern for the city's past or its future. The charge does not land easily in her ears.

"I don't feel like I'm sucking the soul out of the city, and I don't think most artists who are coming here are coming to exploit the city's resources. There aren't very many resources. I'm completely interested in making art that's alive with history."

Artists who see Detroit as easy pickings have a special kind of welcome awaiting them, Canilao says. "People that come with that in mind find out pretty quickly that's not how it is," she says. "You can't just come and loot a bunch of shit. You have to work and have a reason for being here."

Since choosing to stay, Canilao's reasons for calling Detroit home have multiplied. Even when she's off in Oakland, where she maintains a studio, or back in New Orleans, where she shares space in a 1905 steamboat house built on the levee, Motown remains top of mind.

"I feel really lucky to have gotten to come to the city and just kind of fall in love with it. I have a lot of plans."

There's the residency program she's building. In some ways, mimicking the very process that brought her to Detroit, Canilao envisions using an art auction to fund the arrival of other artists who will help transform a former school, purchased by a friend, into a showcase of installations.

Of course, the house that she continues to adorn will play a role in the residency program. After all, the house is at the heart of why Detroit is home.

"I've been a maker of things my whole life, and I always wanted a house to make a project," she says. "Never thought I'd find it in Detroit."

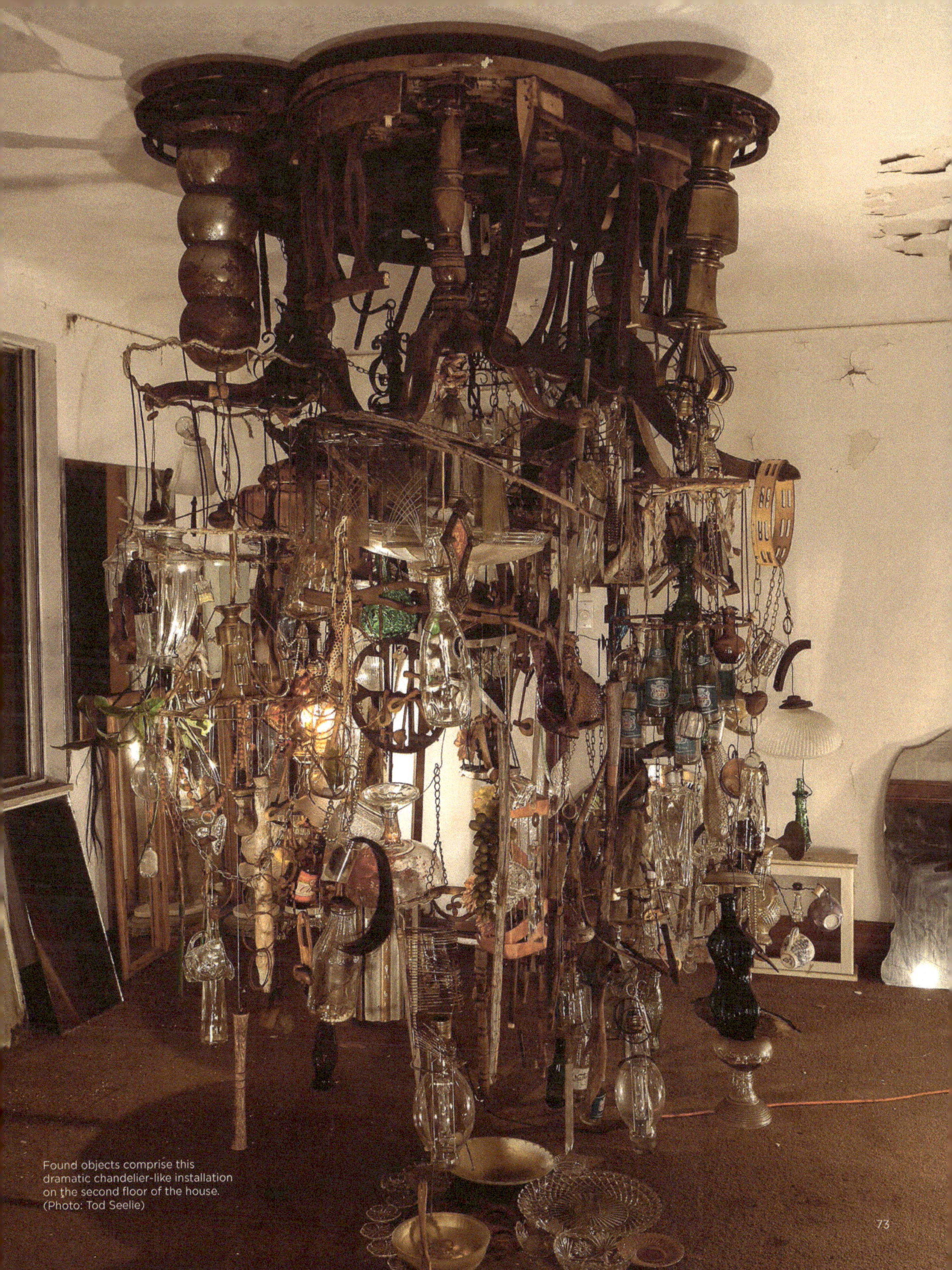

Found objects comprise this dramatic chandelier-like installation on the second floor of the house. (Photo: Tod Seelie)

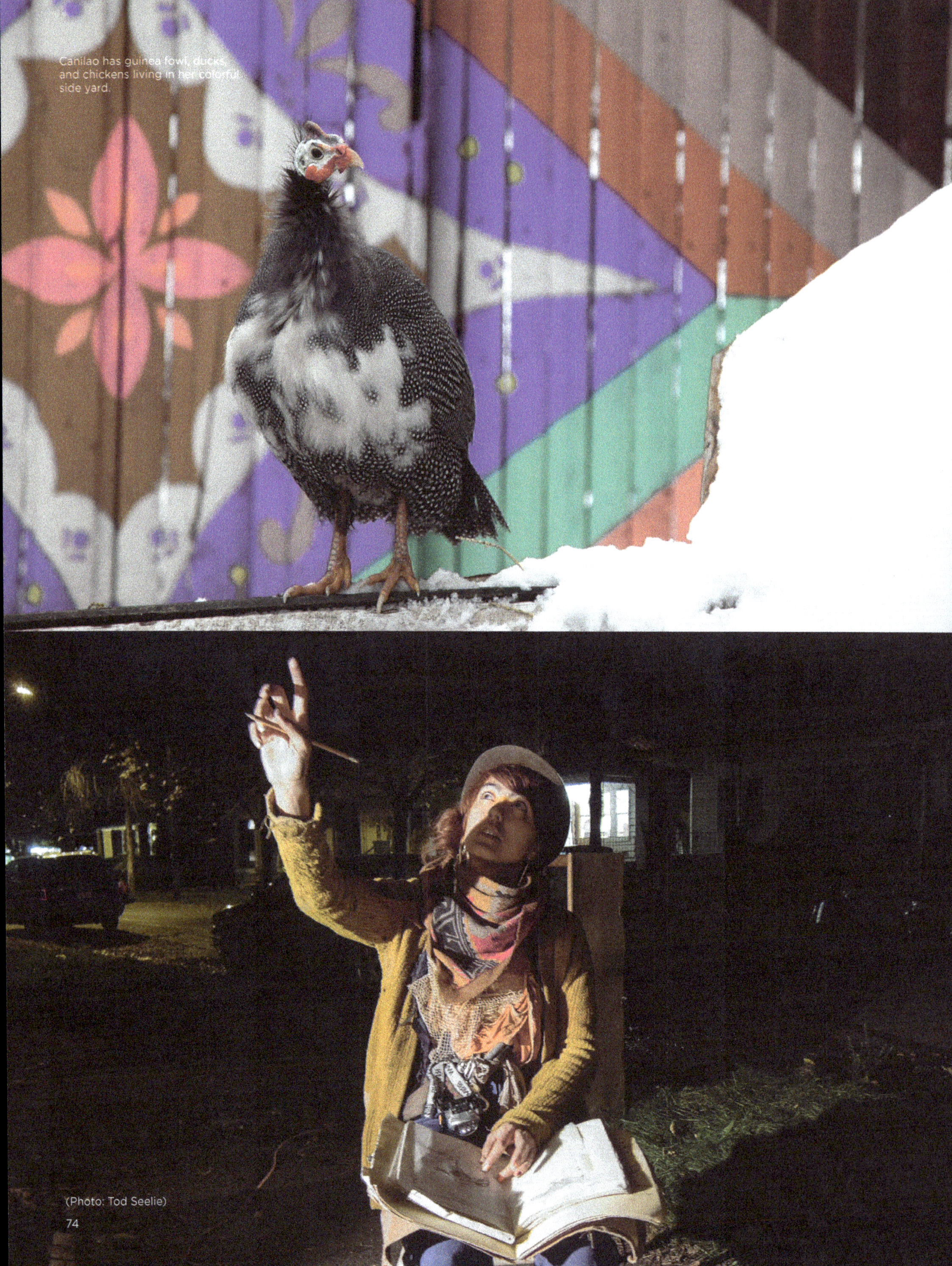

Canilao has guinea fowl, ducks, and chickens living in her colorful side yard.

(Photo: Tod Seelie)

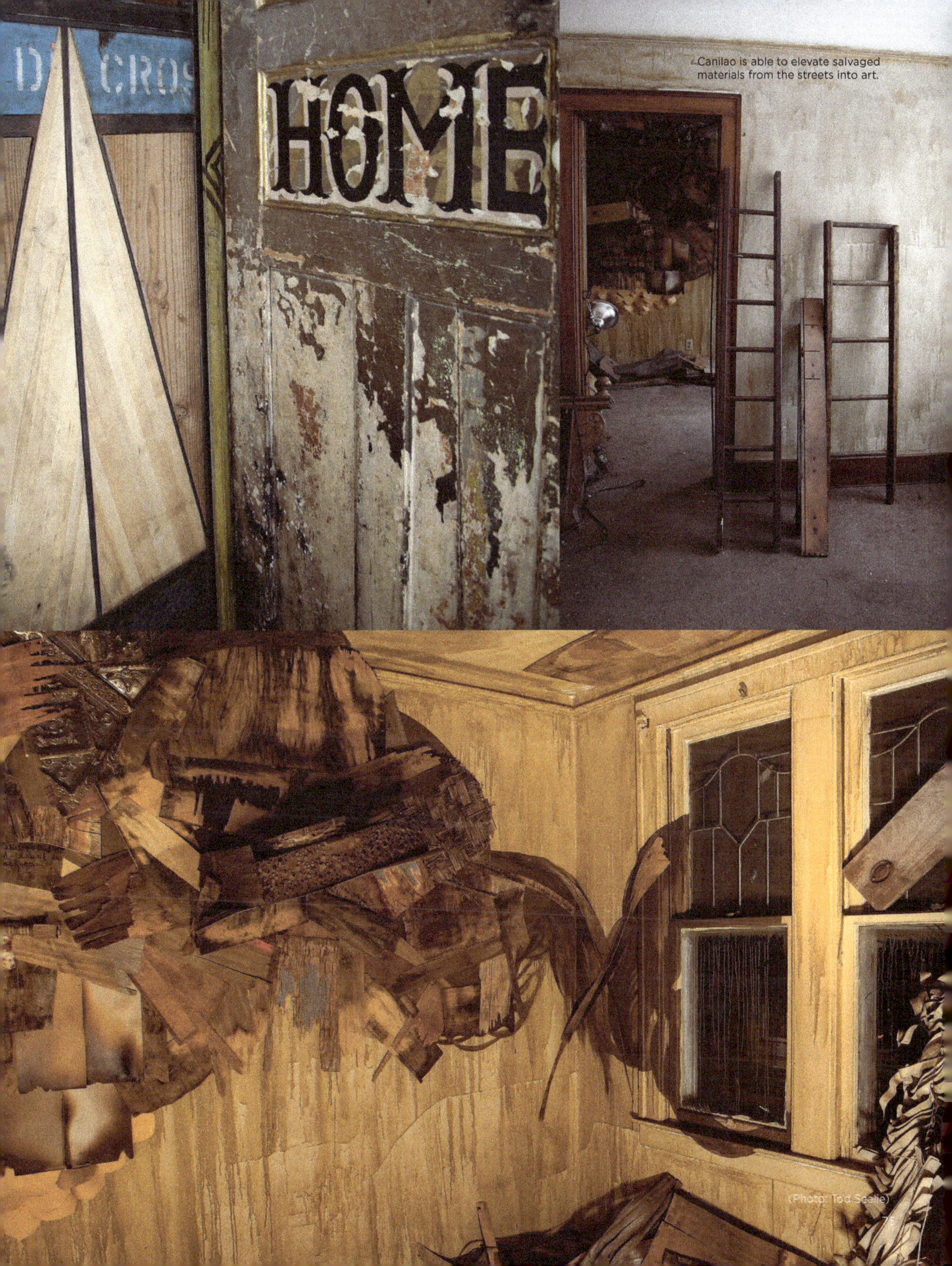

Canilao is able to elevate salvaged materials from the streets into art.

(Photo: Tod Seelie)

DESIGN 99: THE *JUXTAPOZ* & POWER HOUSE PRODUCTIONS RESIDENCIES

RICHARD COLMAN AND RETNA

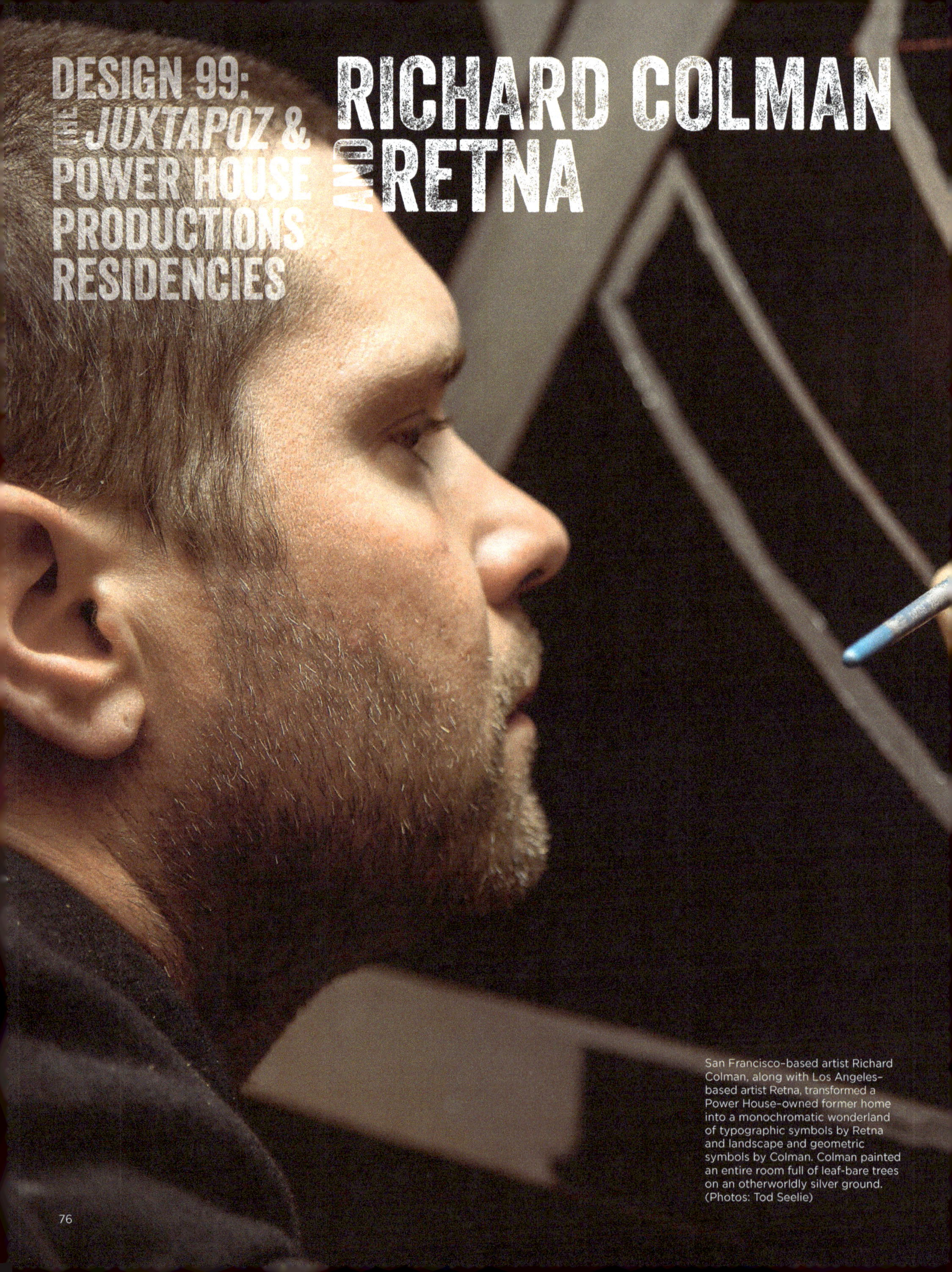

San Francisco-based artist Richard Colman, along with Los Angeles-based artist Retna, transformed a Power House-owned former home into a monochromatic wonderland of typographic symbols by Retna and landscape and geometric symbols by Colman. Colman painted an entire room full of leaf-bare trees on an otherworldly silver ground. (Photos: Tod Seelie)

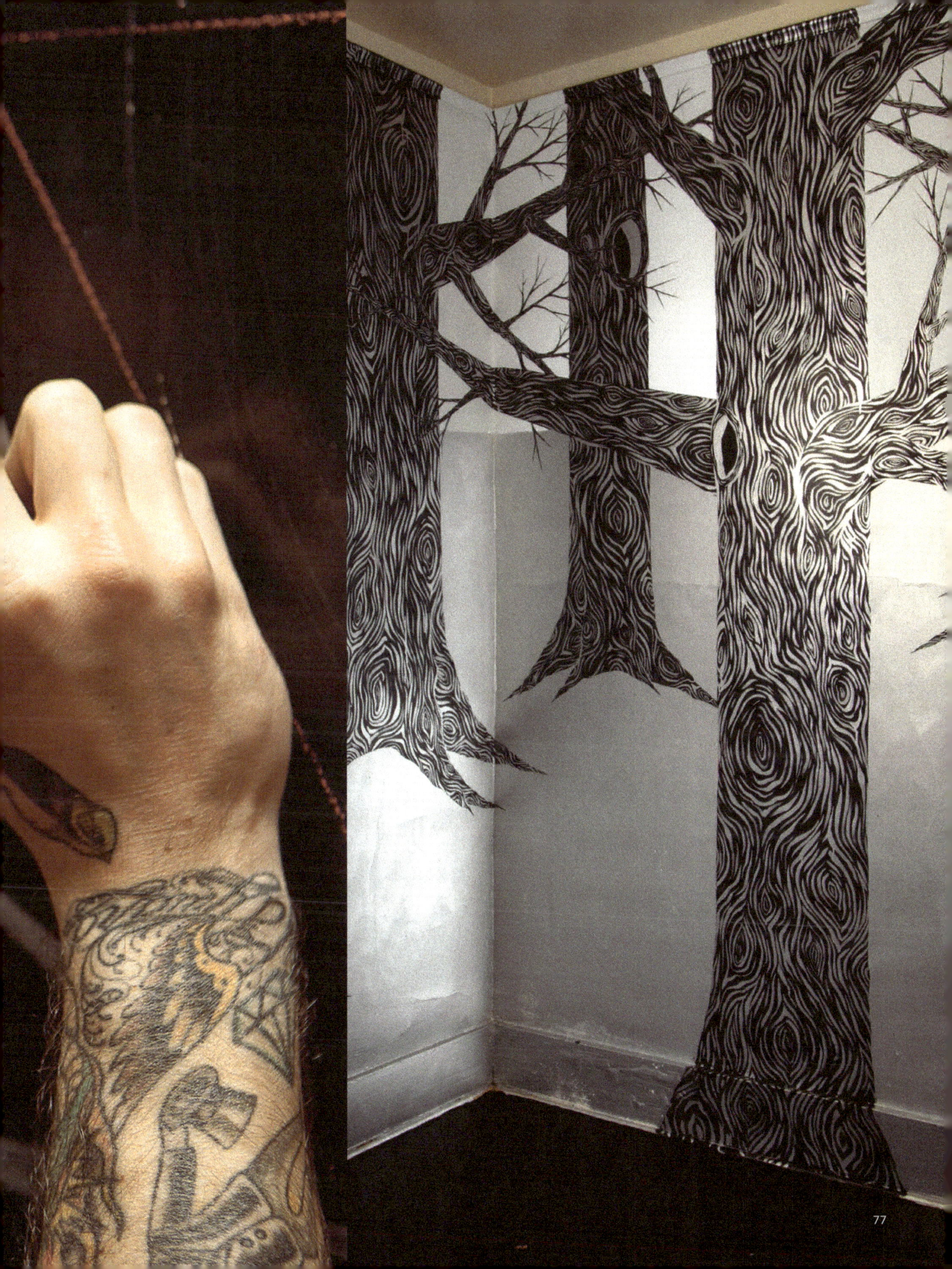

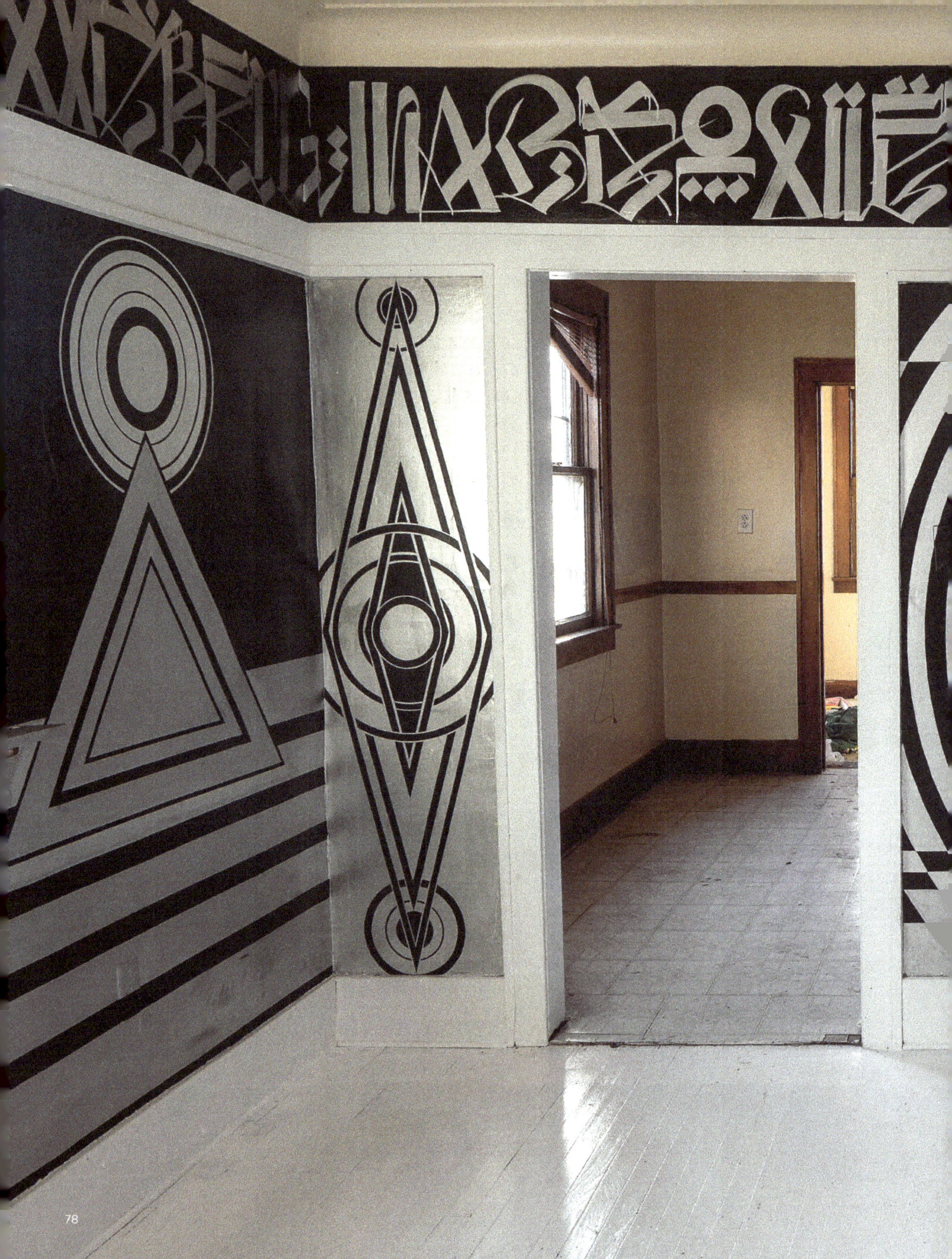

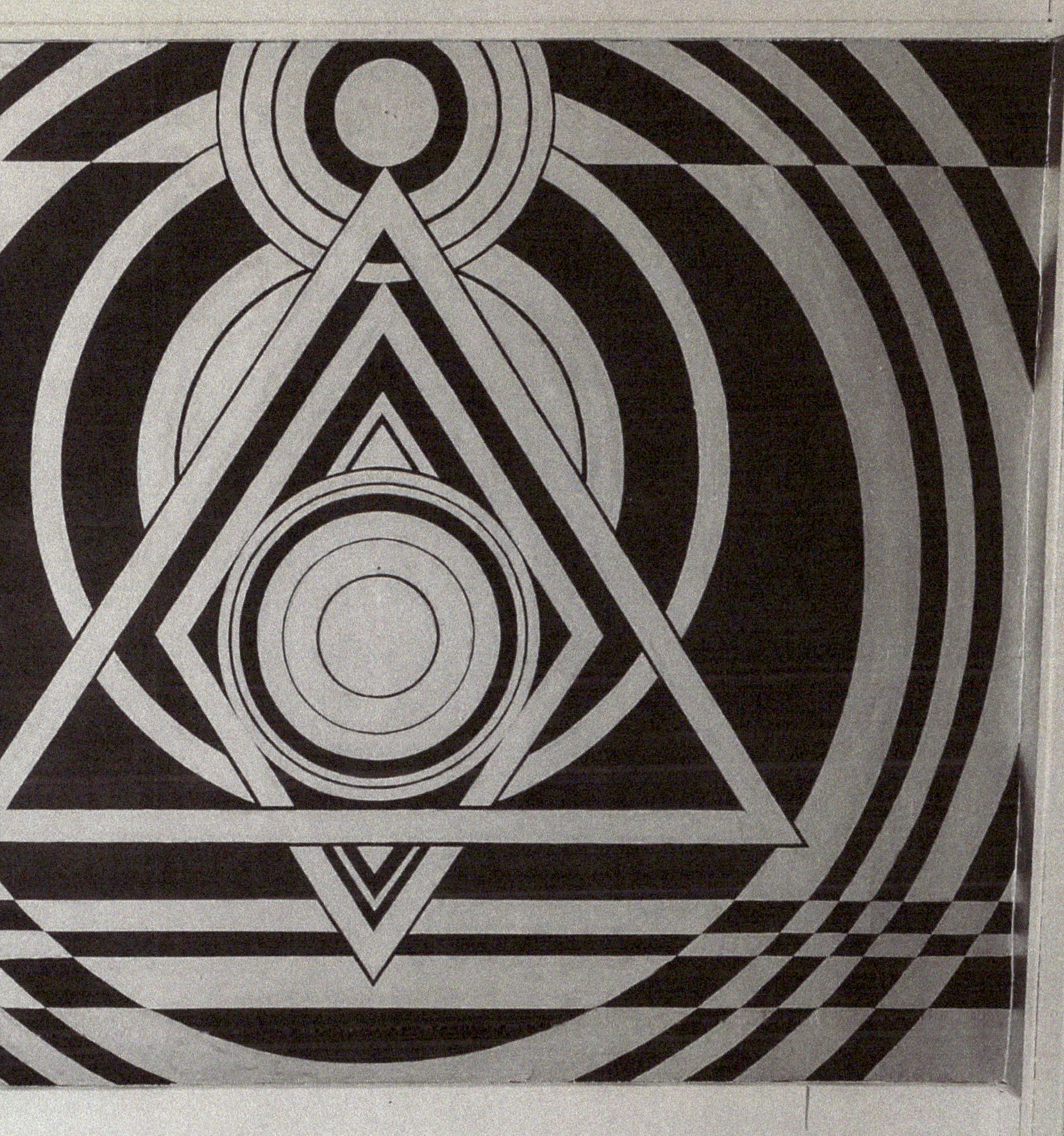

Complicated geometric symbols by Colman adorn the walls throughout the house. (Photo: Tod Seelie)

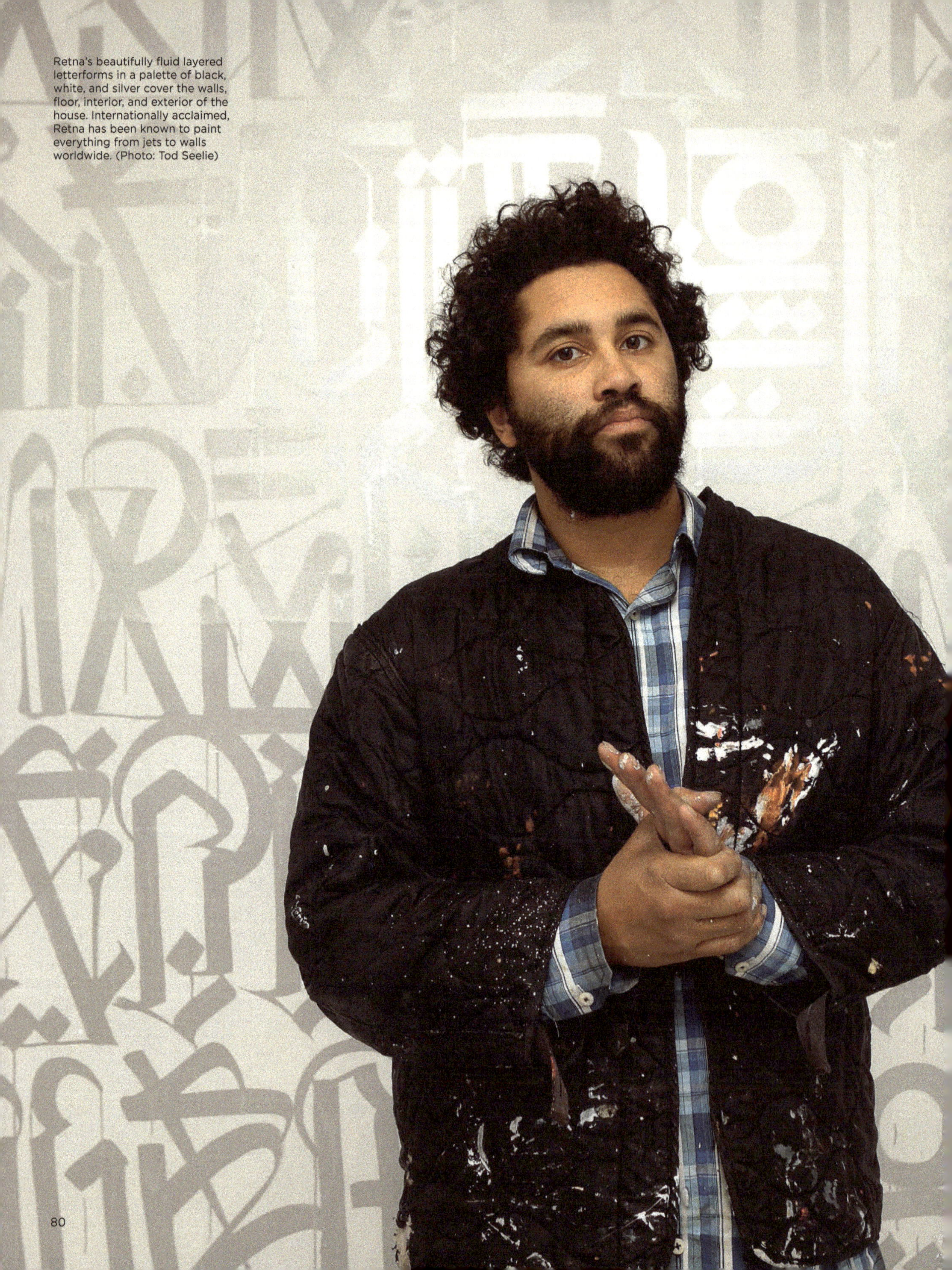

Retna's beautifully fluid layered letterforms in a palette of black, white, and silver cover the walls, floor, interior, and exterior of the house. Internationally acclaimed, Retna has been known to paint everything from jets to walls worldwide. (Photo: Tod Seelie)

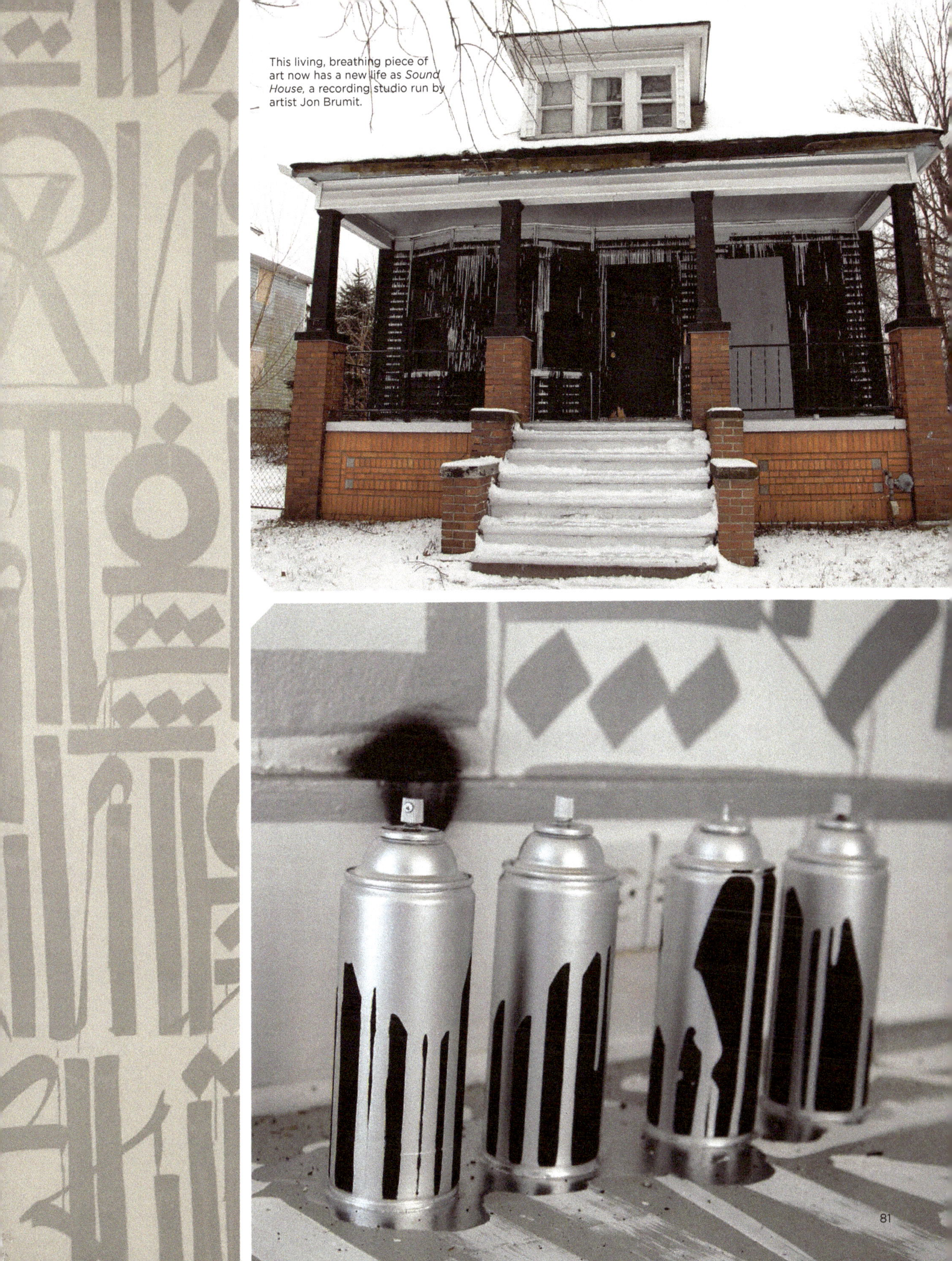

This living, breathing piece of art now has a new life as *Sound House*, a recording studio run by artist Jon Brumit.

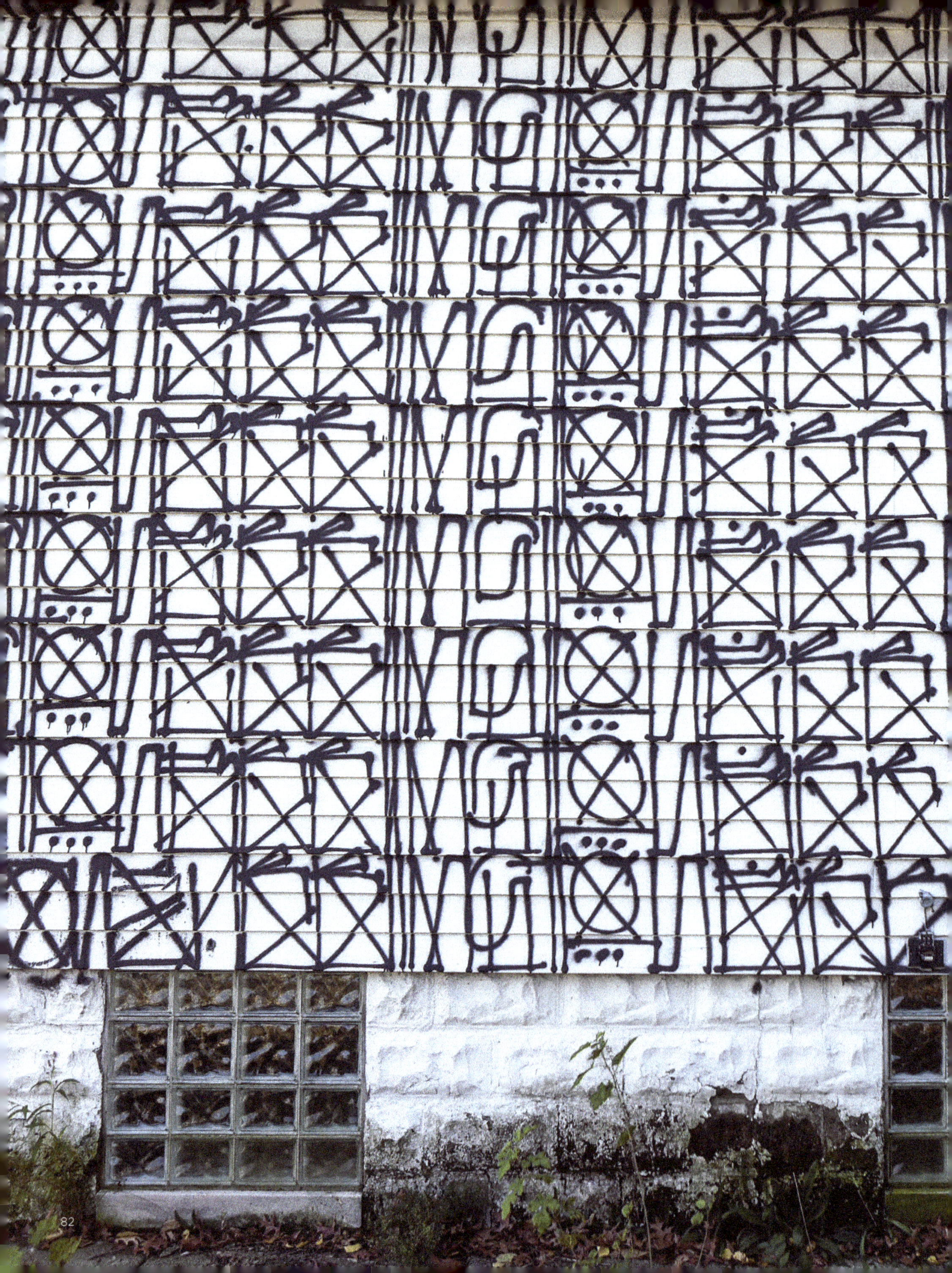

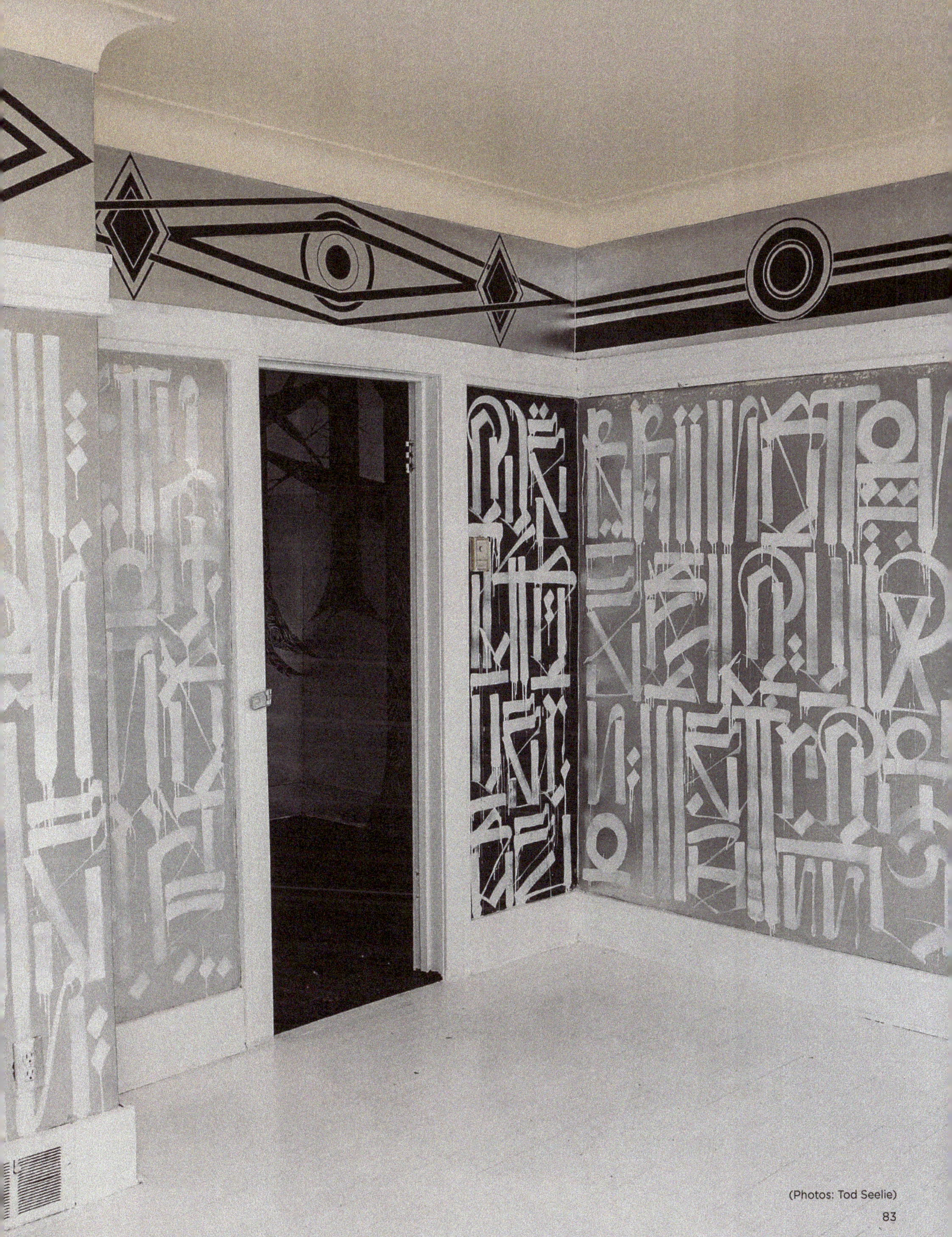

(Photos: Tod Seelie)

DESIGN 99: THE *JUXTAPOZ* & POWER HOUSE PRODUCTIONS RESIDENCIES

SAELEE OH

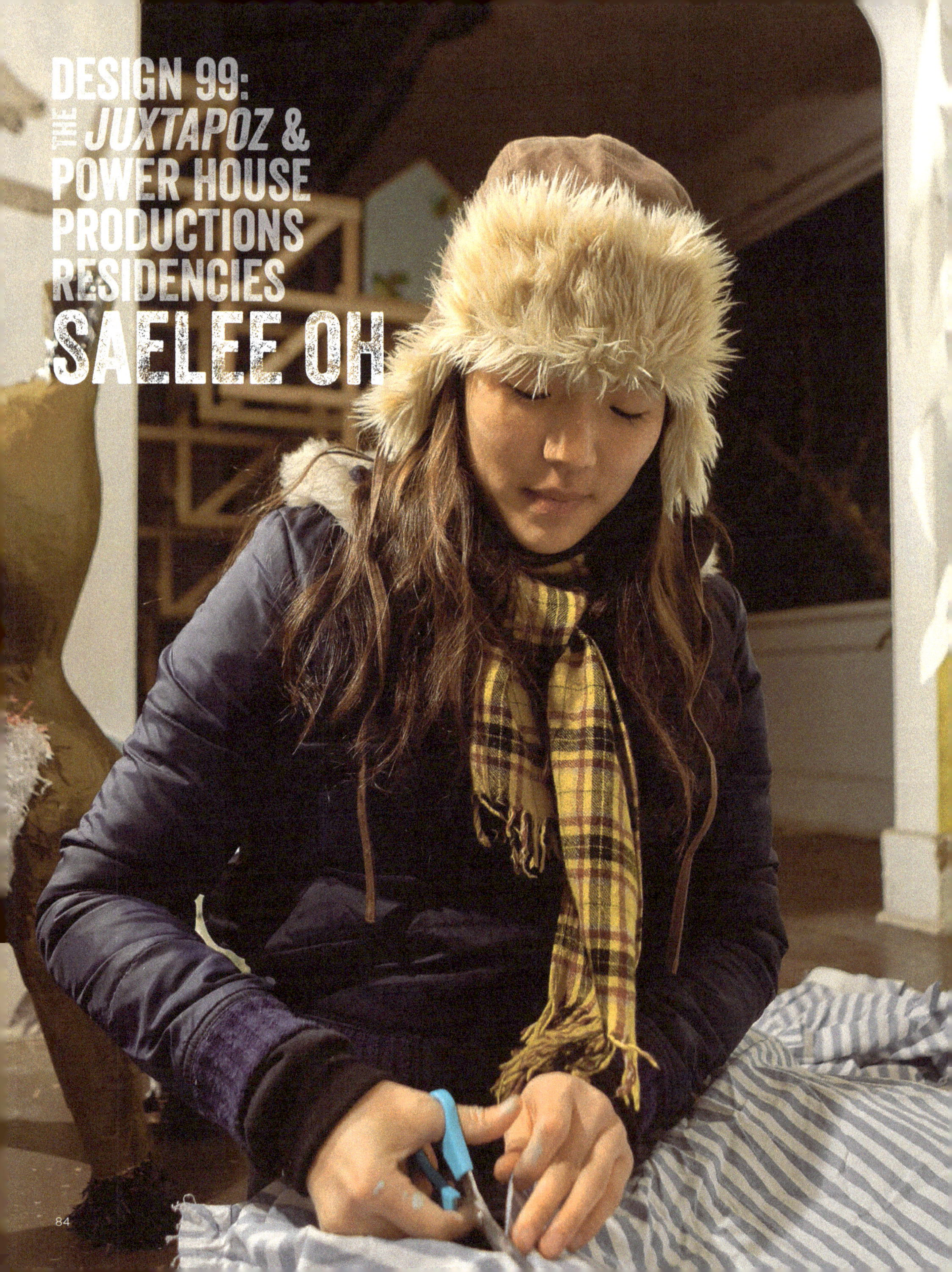

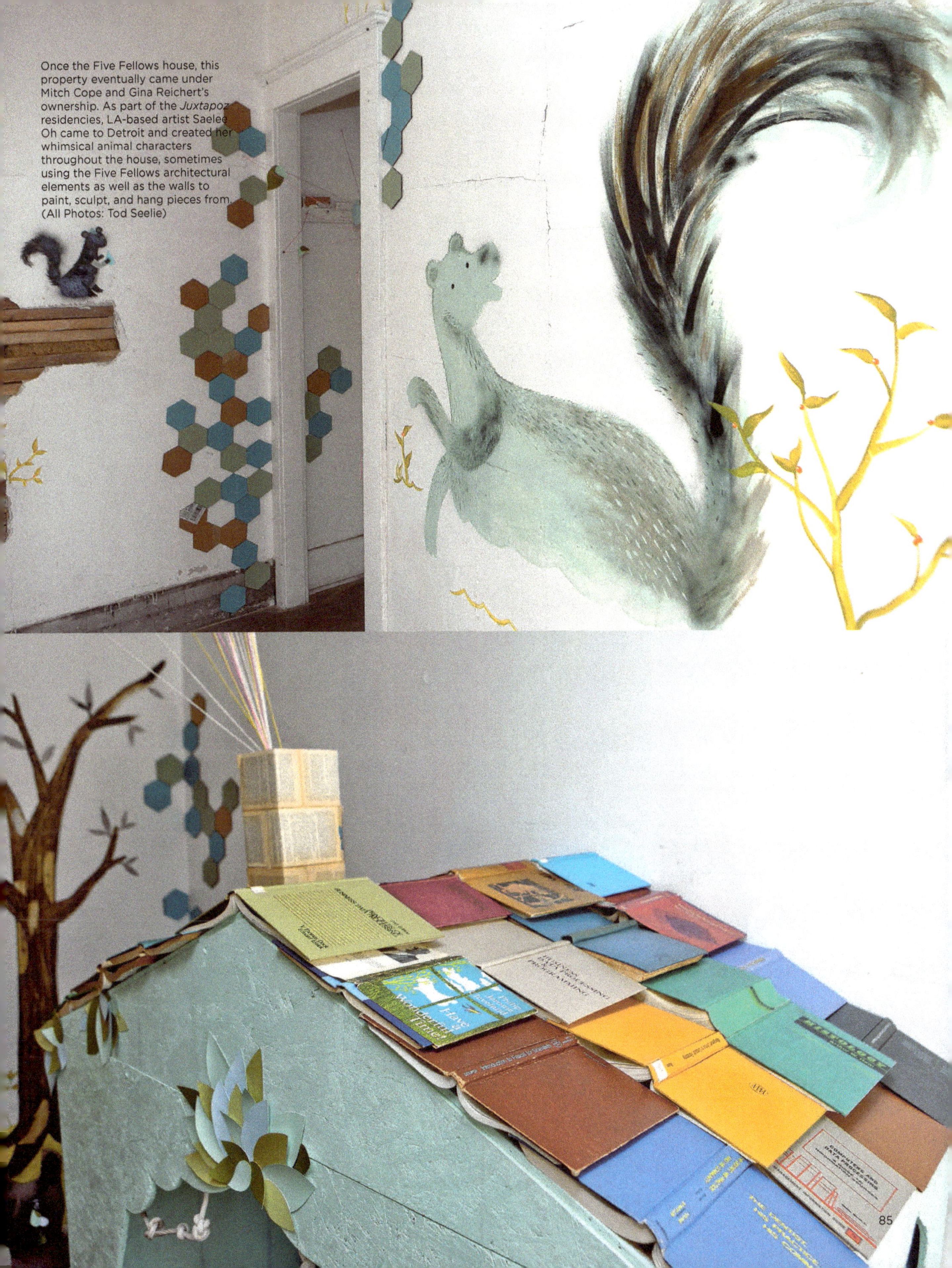

Once the Five Fellows house, this property eventually came under Mitch Cope and Gina Reichert's ownership. As part of the *Juxtapoz* residencies, LA-based artist Saelee Oh came to Detroit and created her whimsical animal characters throughout the house, sometimes using the Five Fellows architectural elements as well as the walls to paint, sculpt, and hang pieces from. (All Photos: Tod Seelie)

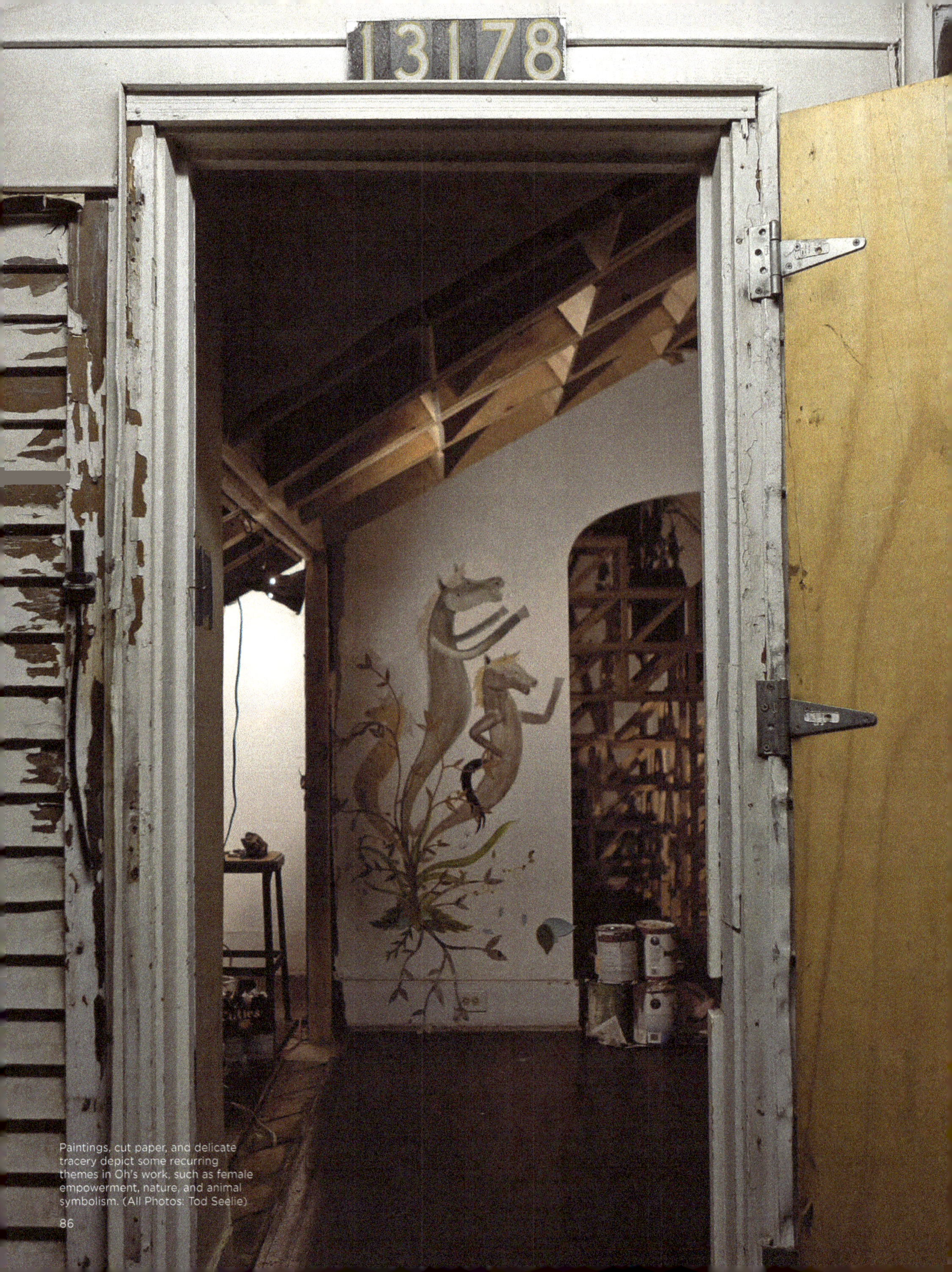

Paintings, cut paper, and delicate tracery depict some recurring themes in Oh's work, such as female empowerment, nature, and animal symbolism. (All Photos: Tod Seelie)

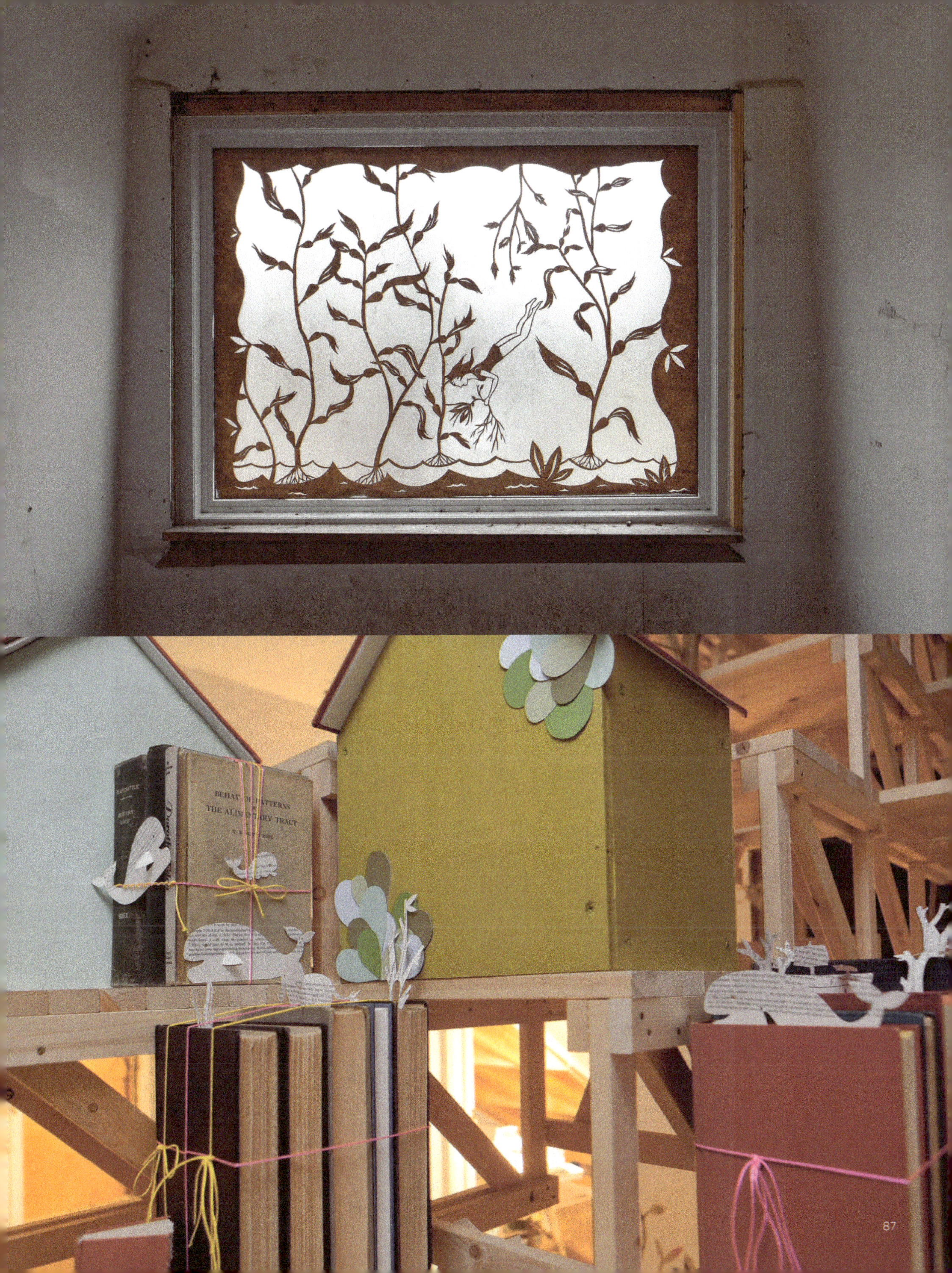

DESIGN 99: THE *JUXTAPOZ* & POWER HOUSE PRODUCTIONS RESIDENCIES
SWOON

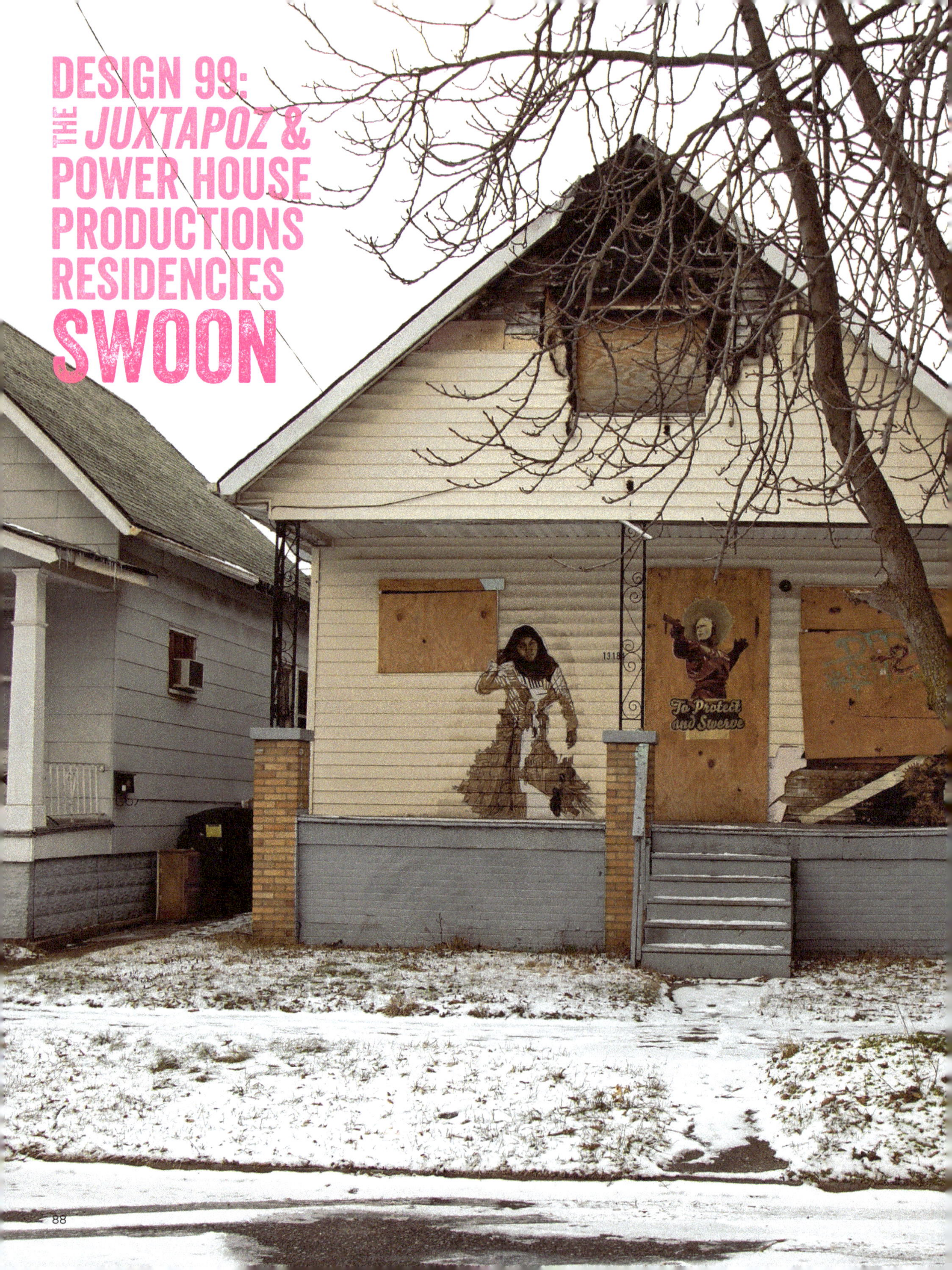

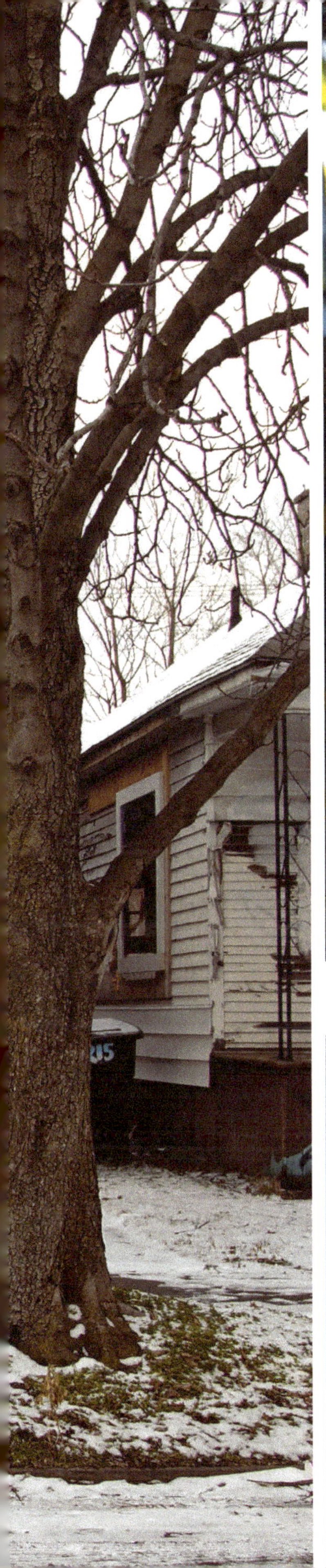

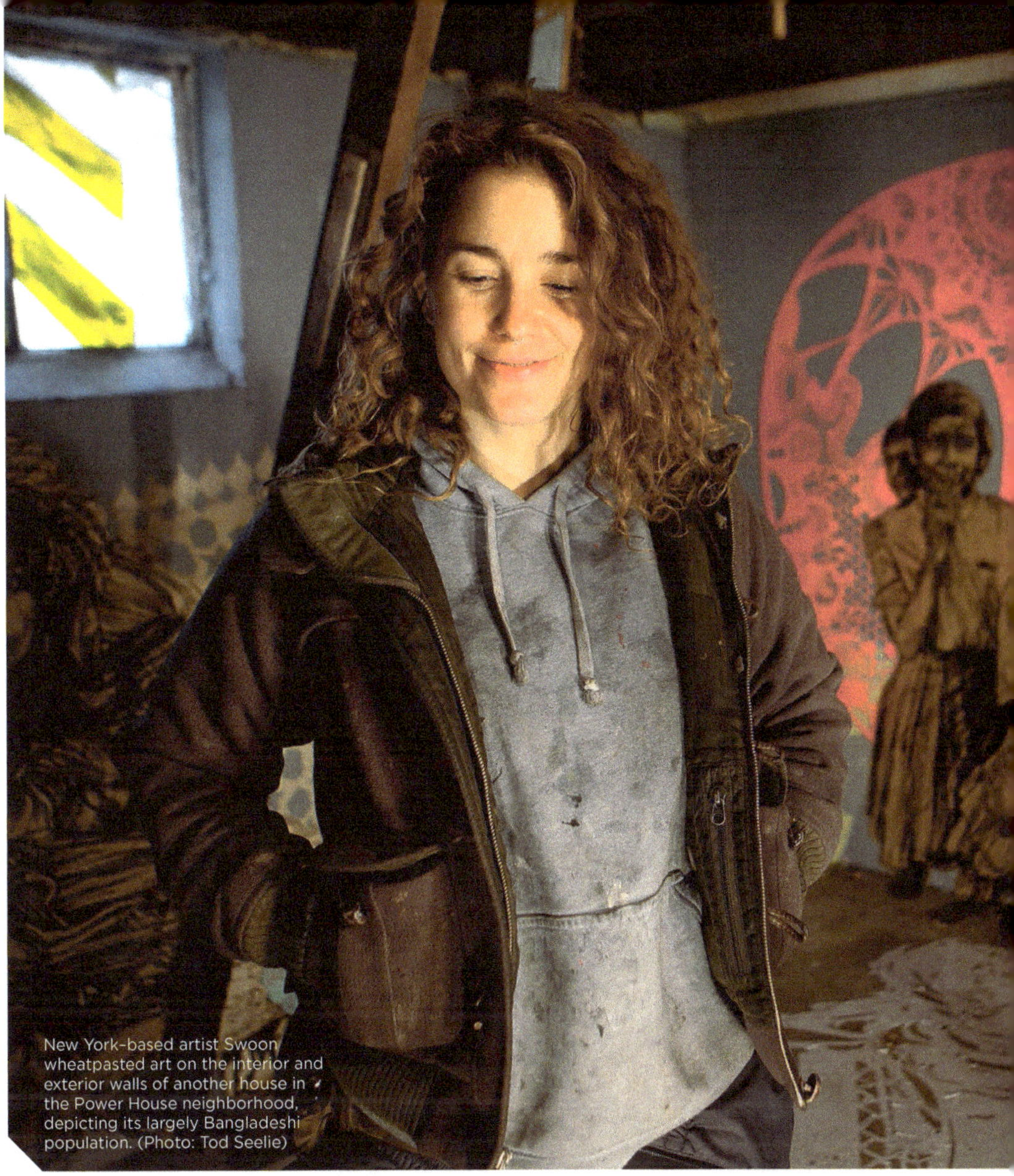

New York-based artist Swoon wheatpasted art on the interior and exterior walls of another house in the Power House neighborhood, depicting its largely Bangladeshi population. (Photo: Tod Seelie)

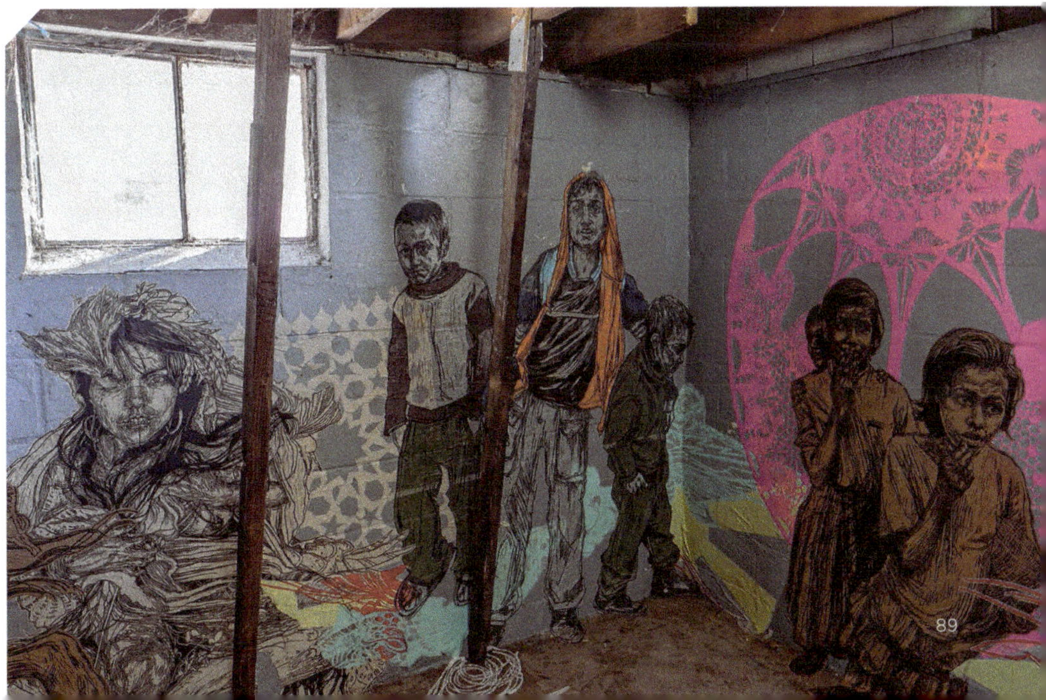

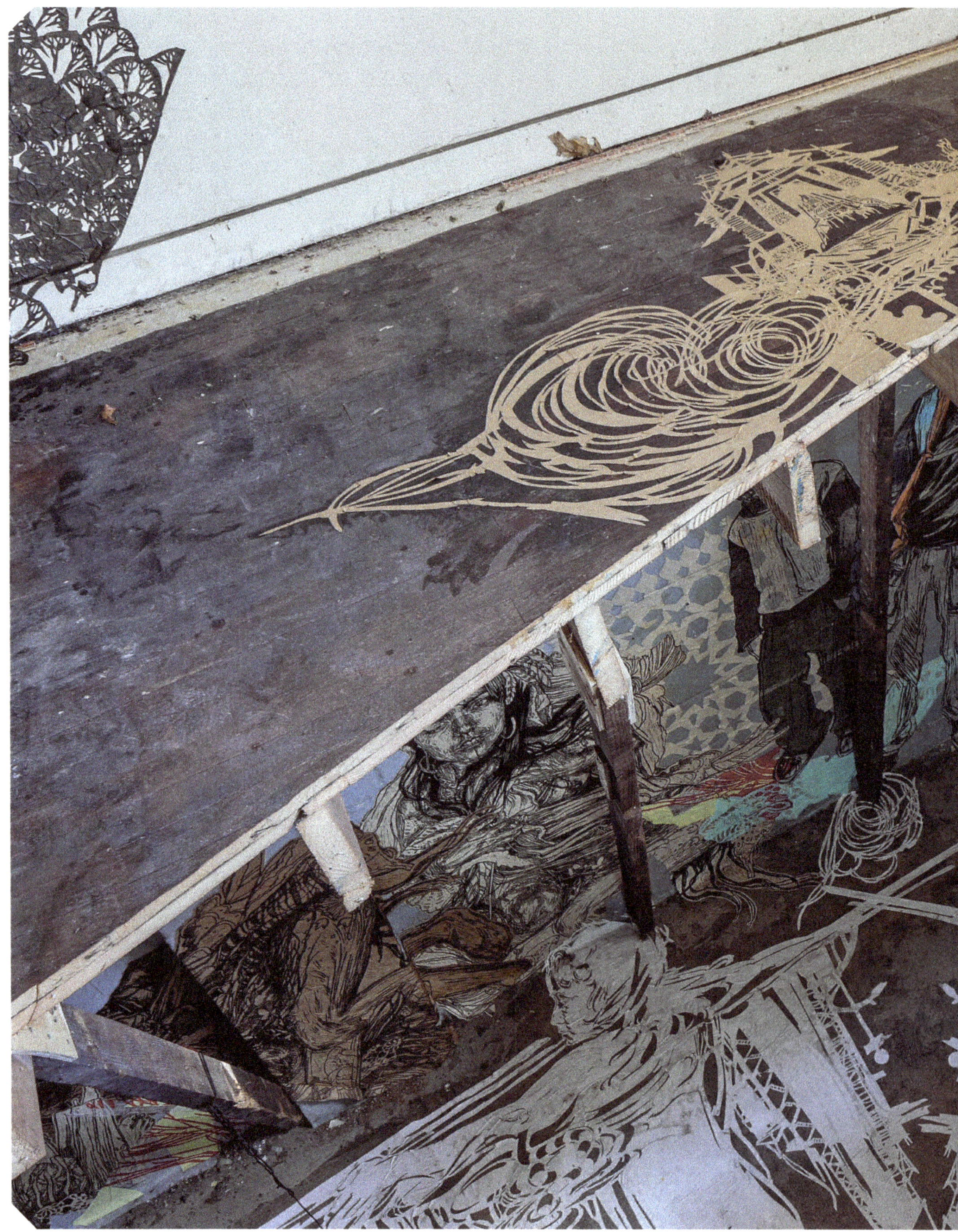

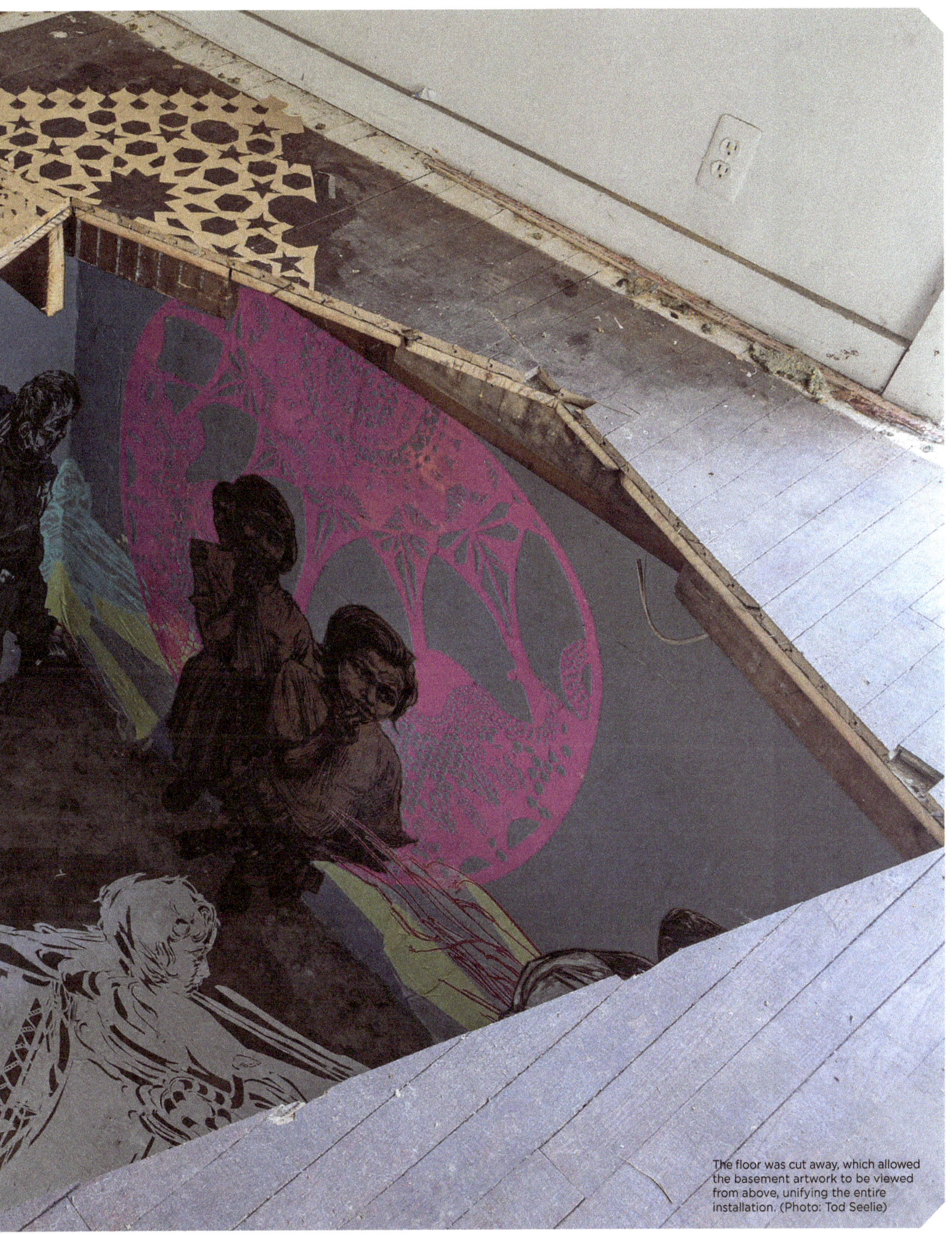

The floor was cut away, which allowed the basement artwork to be viewed from above, unifying the entire installation. (Photo: Tod Seelie)

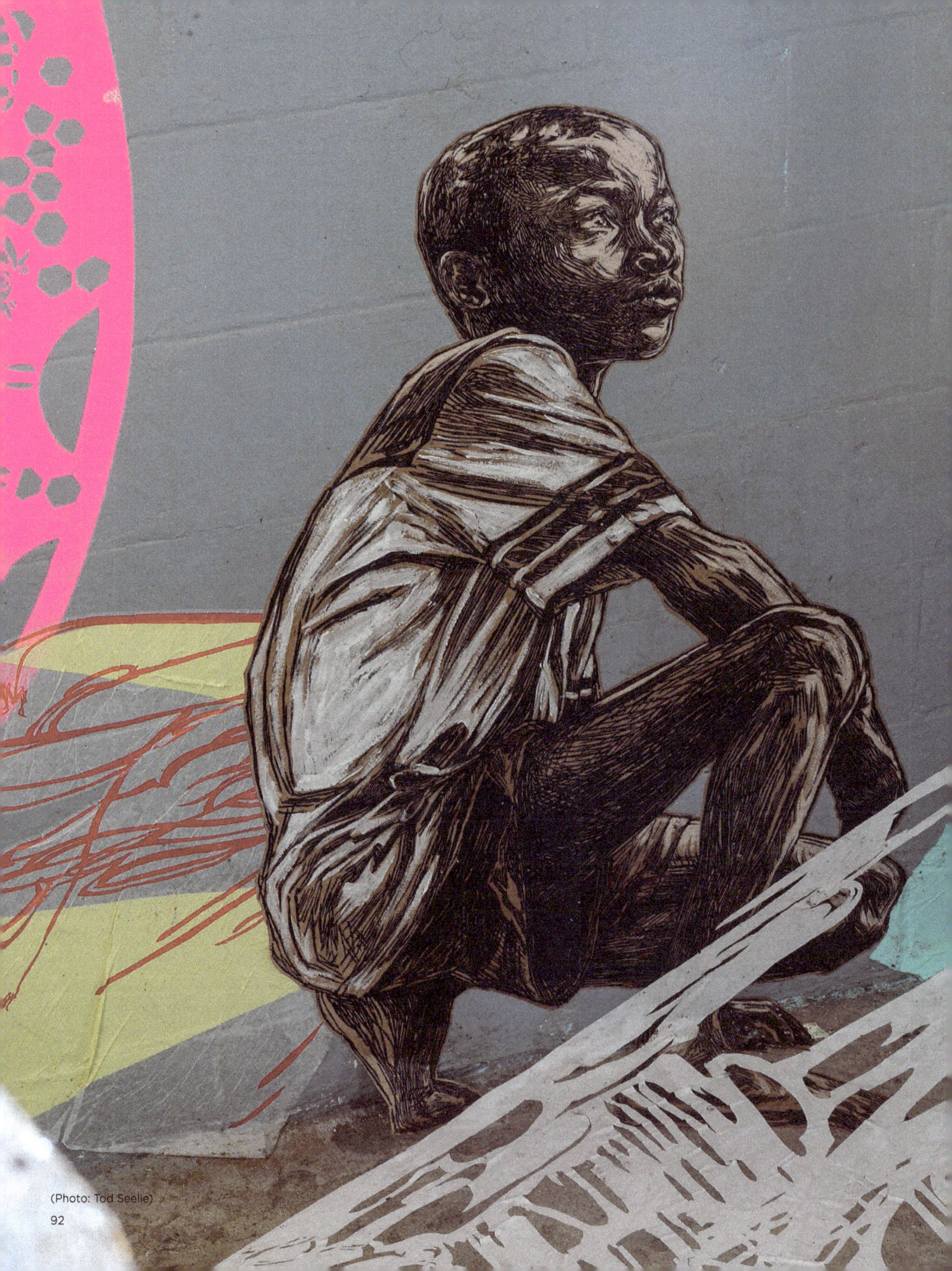

(Photo: Tod Seelie)

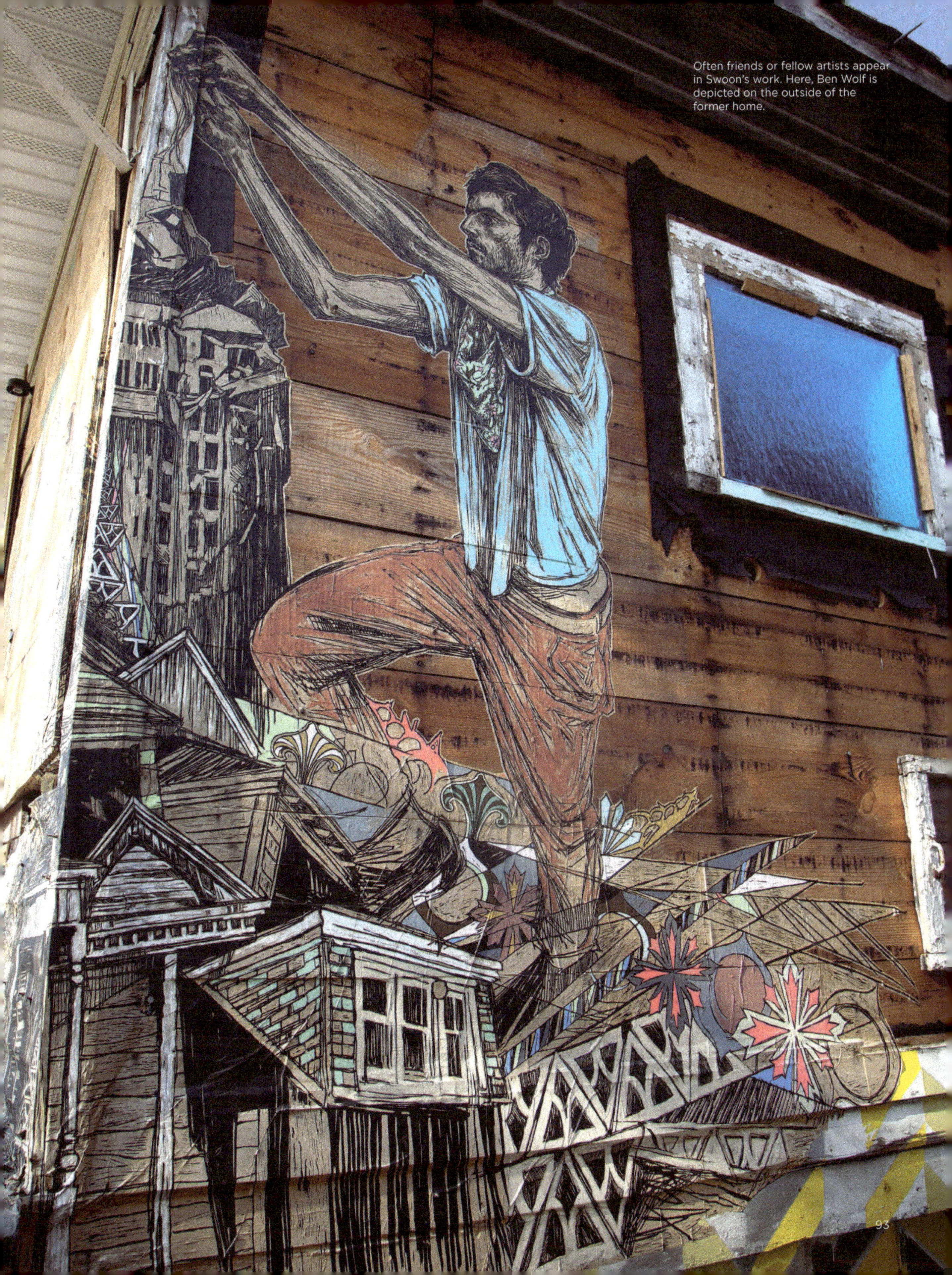

Often friends or fellow artists appear in Swoon's work. Here, Ben Wolf is depicted on the outside of the former home.

DESIGN 99: THE *JUXTAPOZ* & POWER HOUSE PRODUCTIONS RESIDENCIES

BEN WOLF

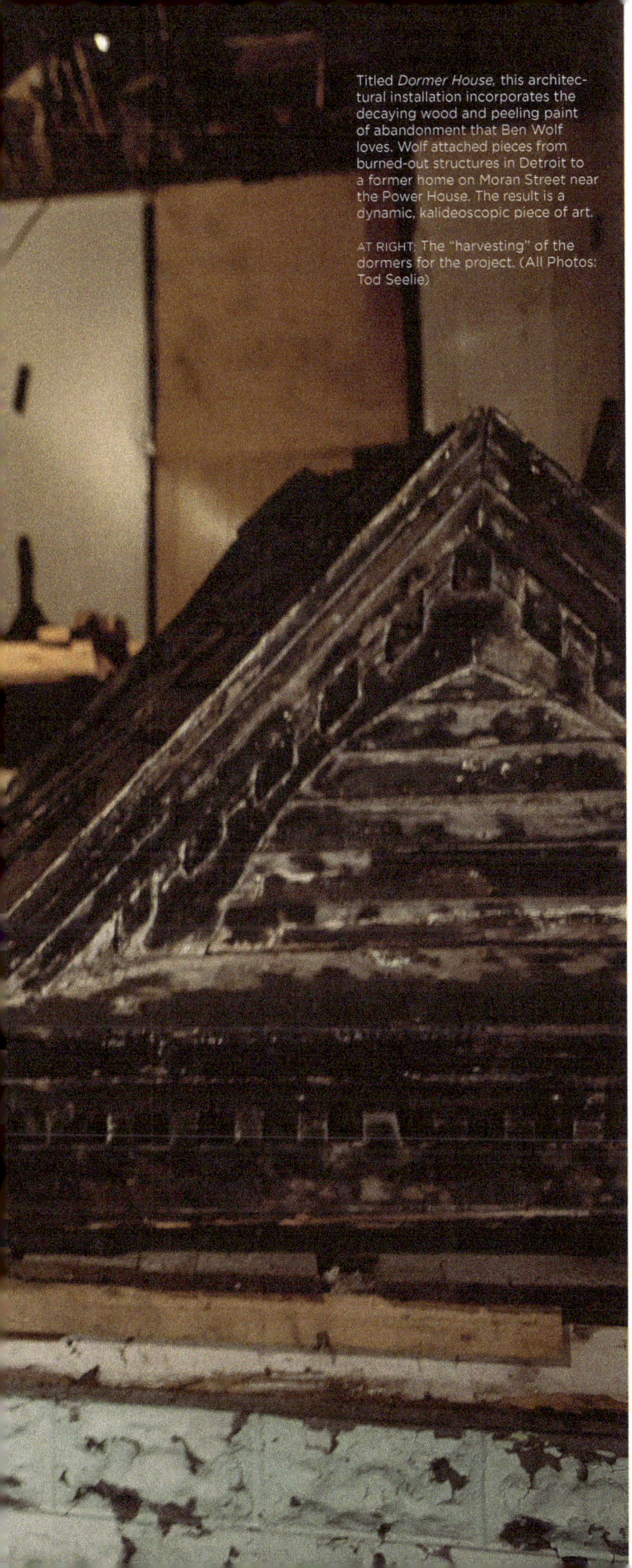

Titled *Dormer House*, this architectural installation incorporates the decaying wood and peeling paint of abandonment that Ben Wolf loves. Wolf attached pieces from burned-out structures in Detroit to a former home on Moran Street near the Power House. The result is a dynamic, kalideoscopic piece of art.

AT RIGHT: The "harvesting" of the dormers for the project. (All Photos: Tod Seelie)

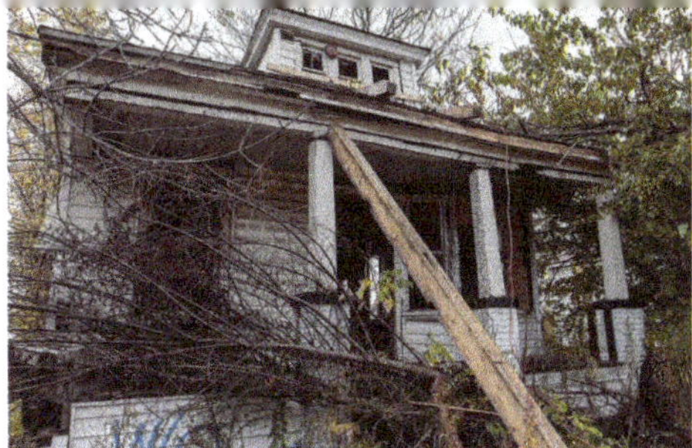

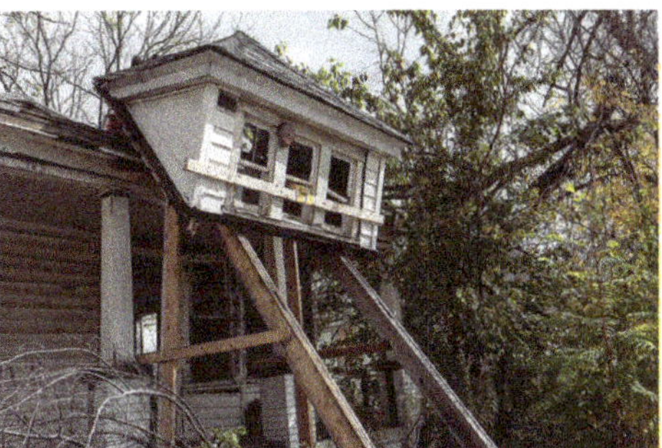

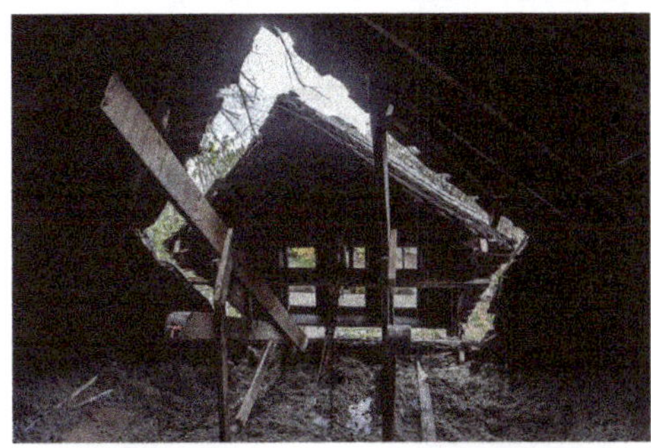

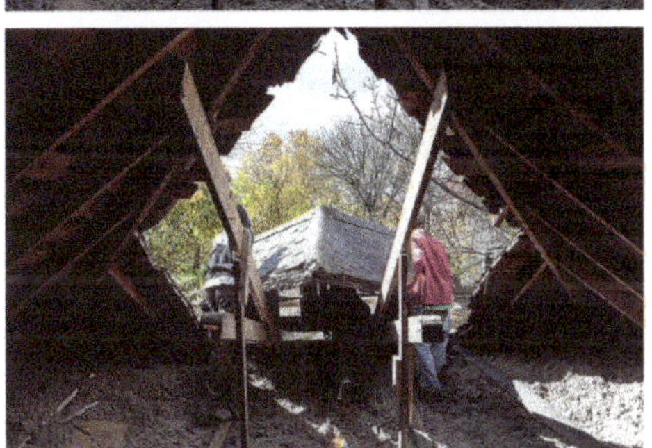

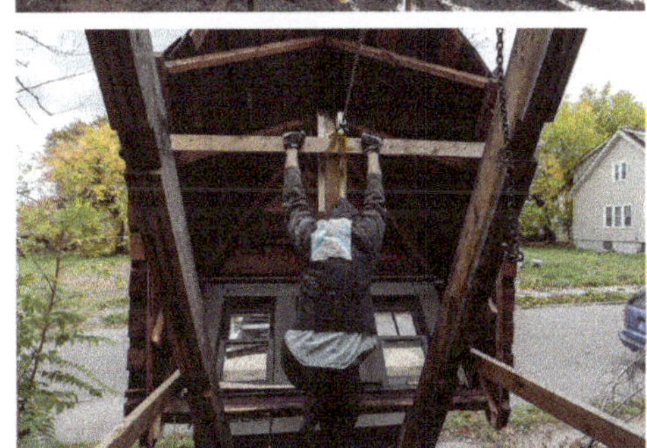

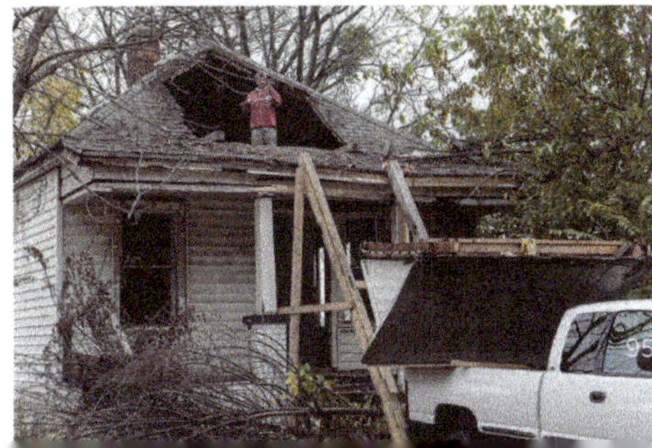

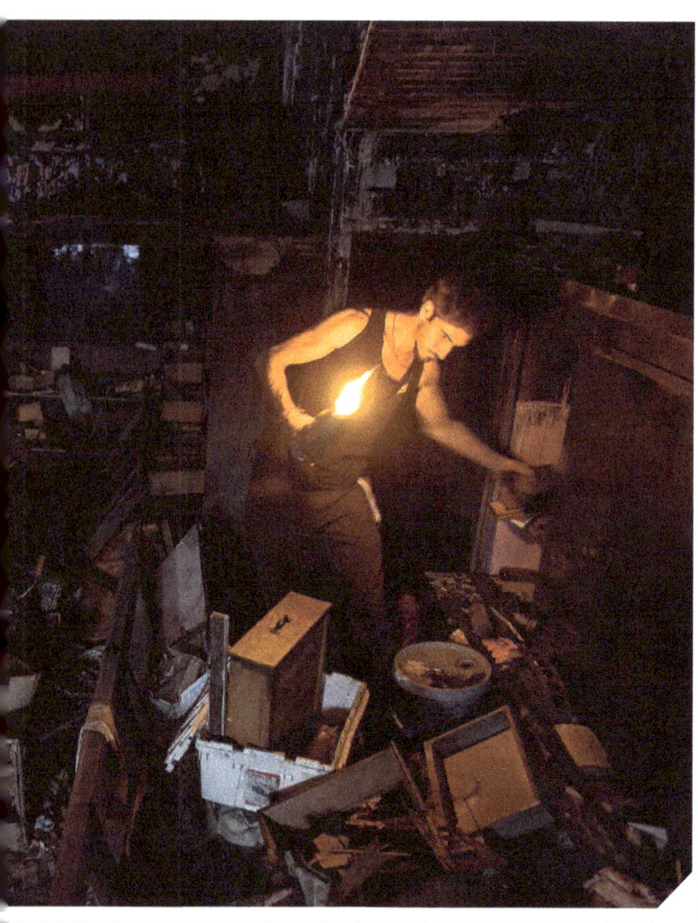

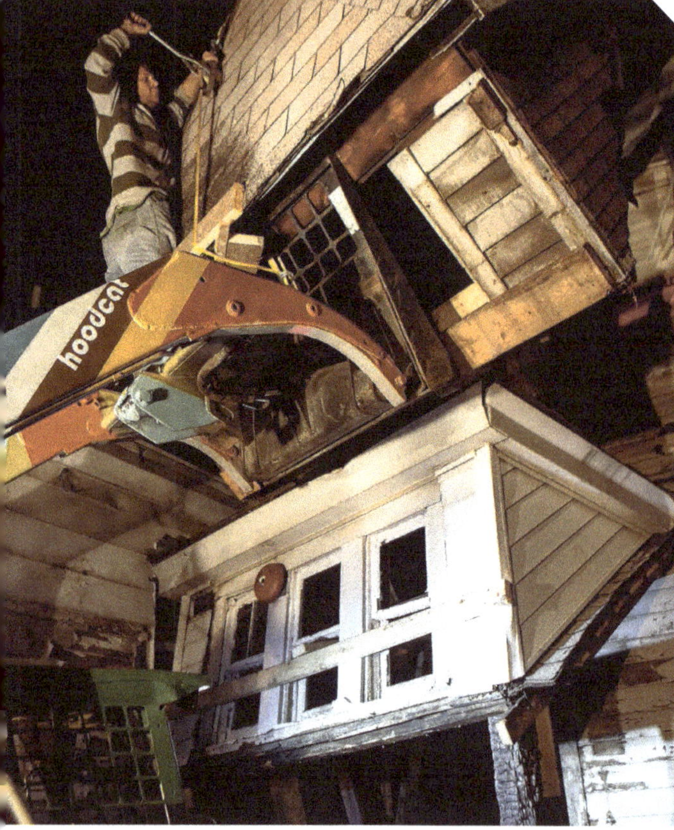
hoodcat

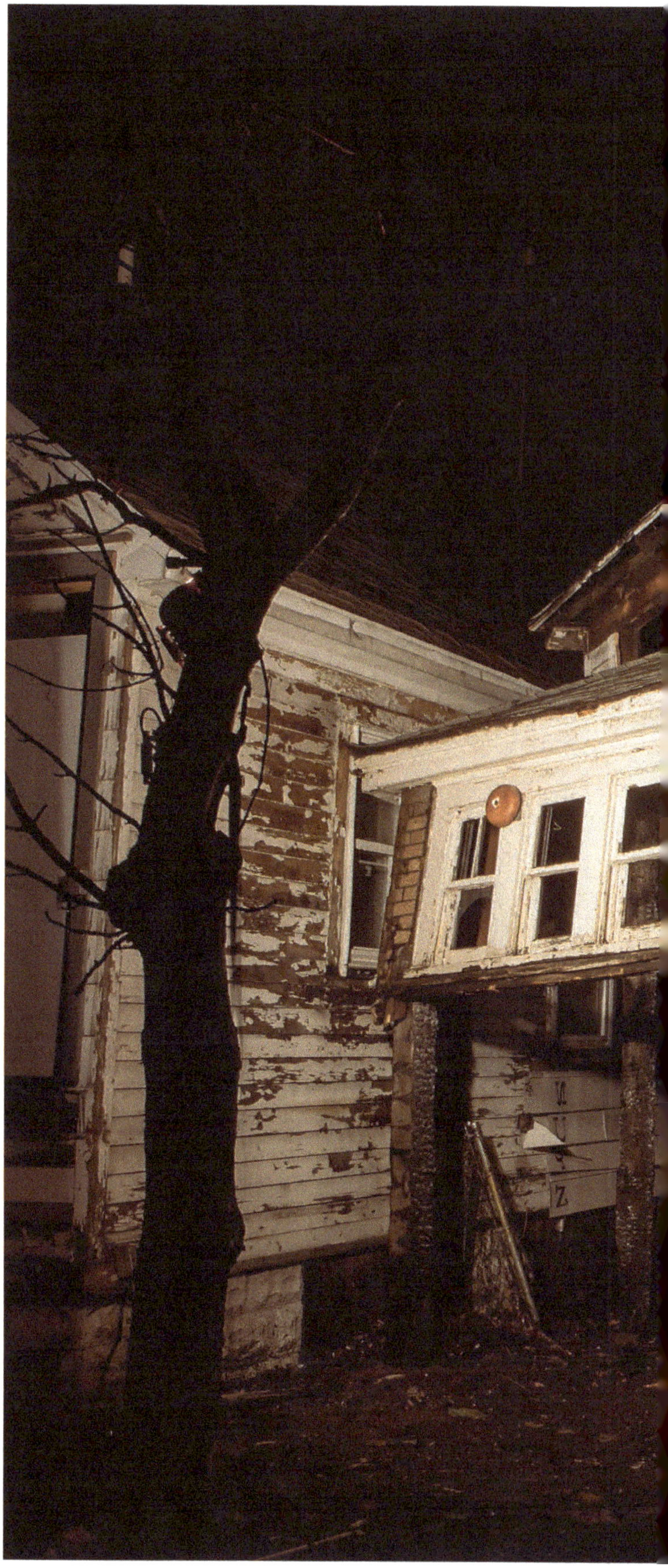

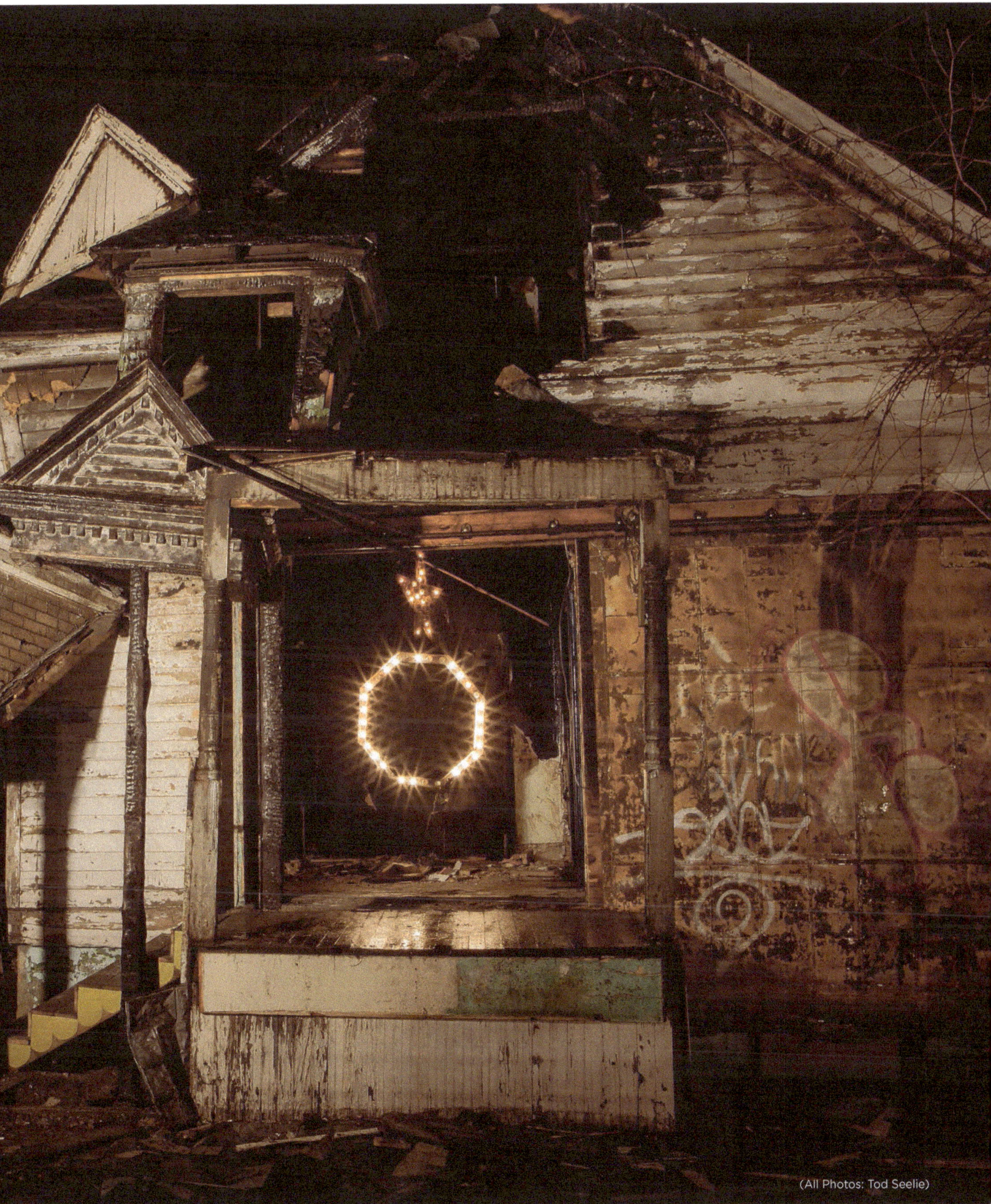

(All Photos: Tod Seelie)

DETROIT BEAUTIFICATION PROJECT

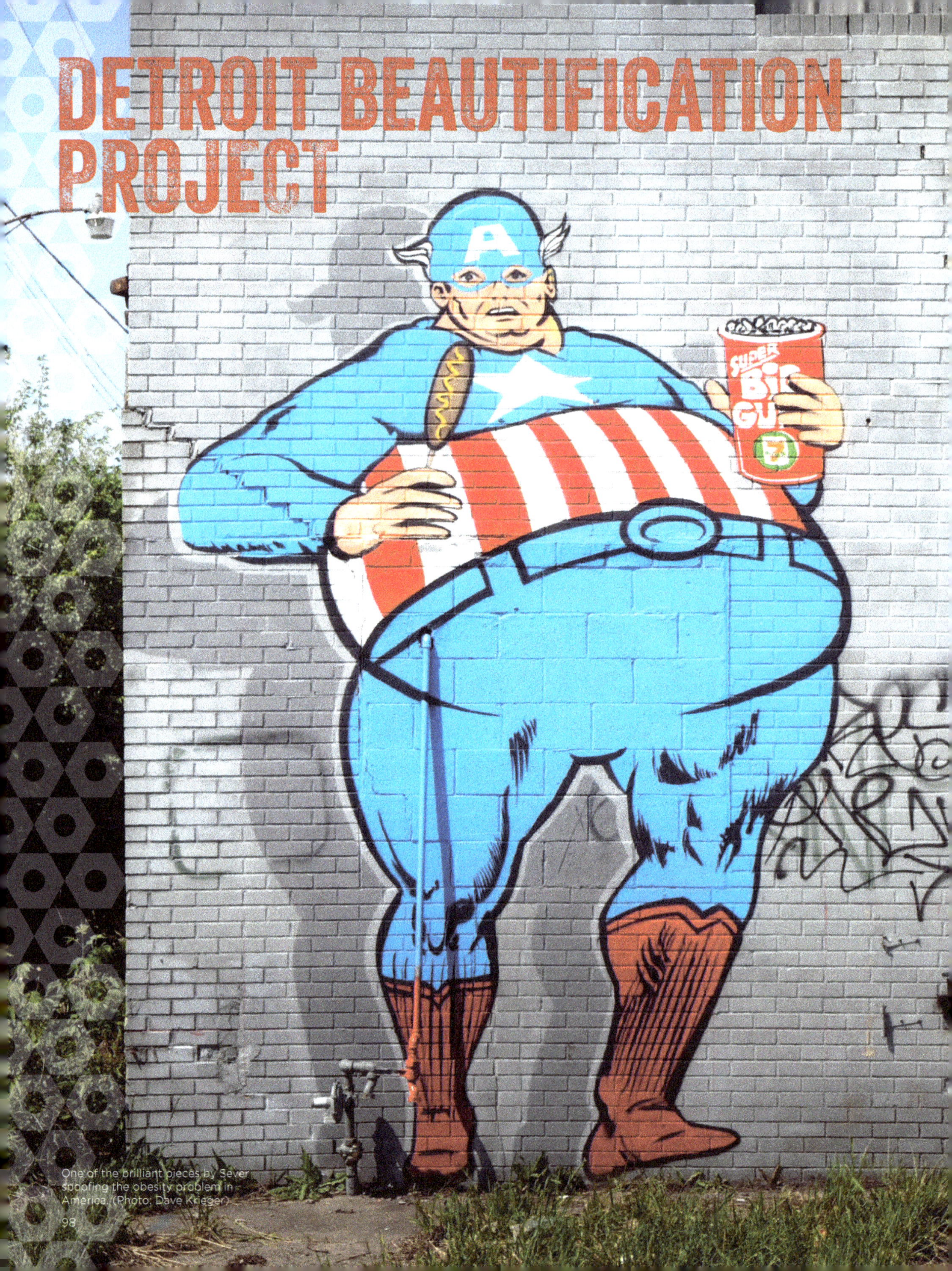

One of the brilliant pieces by Sever spoofing the obesity problem in America. (Photo: Dave Krieger)

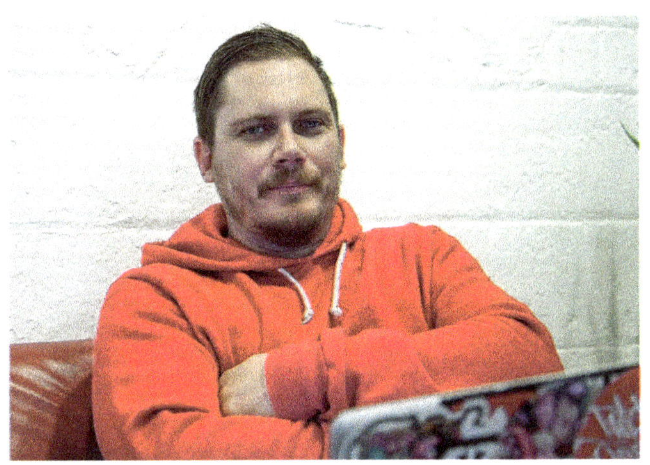

Matthew Eaton was only supposed to be passing through, in town to help his mother sell her house.

"As it turned out," says Eaton, "the market was horrible. The process ended up taking a year and half. I had to find some way to keep myself busy and productive."

Eaton's idea of productive: he co-founded the Detroit Beautification Project, an underground arts collective that invites artists from around the globe to transform the walls of Detroit. The artists have come from as far away as New Zealand.

Since 2012, some of graffiti's biggest names have ventured to the D, spreading seventy-eight colorful and sometimes playful murals around the city as proof of their presence. Eaton, thirty-nine, insists that the DBP is grassroots but has enough sparkle to catch the eyes of high-profile sponsors, including an initial investment of fifteen thousand dollars from Montana Cans, one of the world's largest spray paint manufacturers.

"We don't have a bottomless pot, but for people who want to be here, we work really hard to make it a good experience," he says.

In most cases, artists cover the bulk of travel costs, while project organizers secure prominent sites to paint and a stipend, usually about a thousand dollars.

Of course, Eaton didn't plan on the global interest in DBP any more than he planned to stay in Detroit. "It wasn't even supposed to have a name," explains Eaton, who grew up in Los Angeles but had called New York home for twelve years prior to his accidental move to Detroit in 2010. Eaton's father and grandfather were born and raised in Detroit.

"The idea was more about taking some initiative, getting a bunch of really talented artists to bring a little color to a few neighborhoods and maybe elevate the awareness of Detroit in general," he says.

As a painter himself, Eaton is especially interested in trumpeting artists and guiding art lovers to Detroit: "Detroit is one of those weird places on the map, where it's in a state that you have to want to go to. So, the artists who create are sort of in a bubble and they kind of stall out or become stagnant. The isolation is not a bad thing necessarily. It's just that Detroit could be so much more. "

Enter the Red Bull House of Art and Library Street Collective, the other components of Eaton's passion for art in Detroit. Red Bull is an incubator and gallery space, in the historic Eastern Market section of Detroit, for up-and-coming local artists. Eaton is co-owner of the Library Street Collective, a gallery focused on bringing international artists and collectors to Detroit.

"My intention was always to come here for a little while and then go back. But I'm here, and as frustrating as it is sometimes, my intention is to stay and be involved in the possibilities. There are so many people doing creative things that have no voice and get no attention," says Eaton. "If I was in control, the arts would be in the forefront of everything after the necessities."

Depending on how you ask, Eaton argues that for Detroit, art—of every kind—is a necessity.

"Detroit owes the arts," he says. "It's nothing without the creative genius that started here and went out into the world. That's why we have a city."

Yet for all of his passion about the role of art in Detroit, Eaton says what the city most needs is to appoint a public champion to help show civic leaders just how much art can help enliven streets, even resurrect empty spaces.

"This is a turning point. Artists see it but the people in power, they just don't get it," he says. "We're not Motown anymore. We're not Rock City. We're not even the Motor City anymore, and we're never going to be any of those things again. But we do have this opportunity to define a new Detroit. Why not art? It's the only thing that's still moving the city forward."

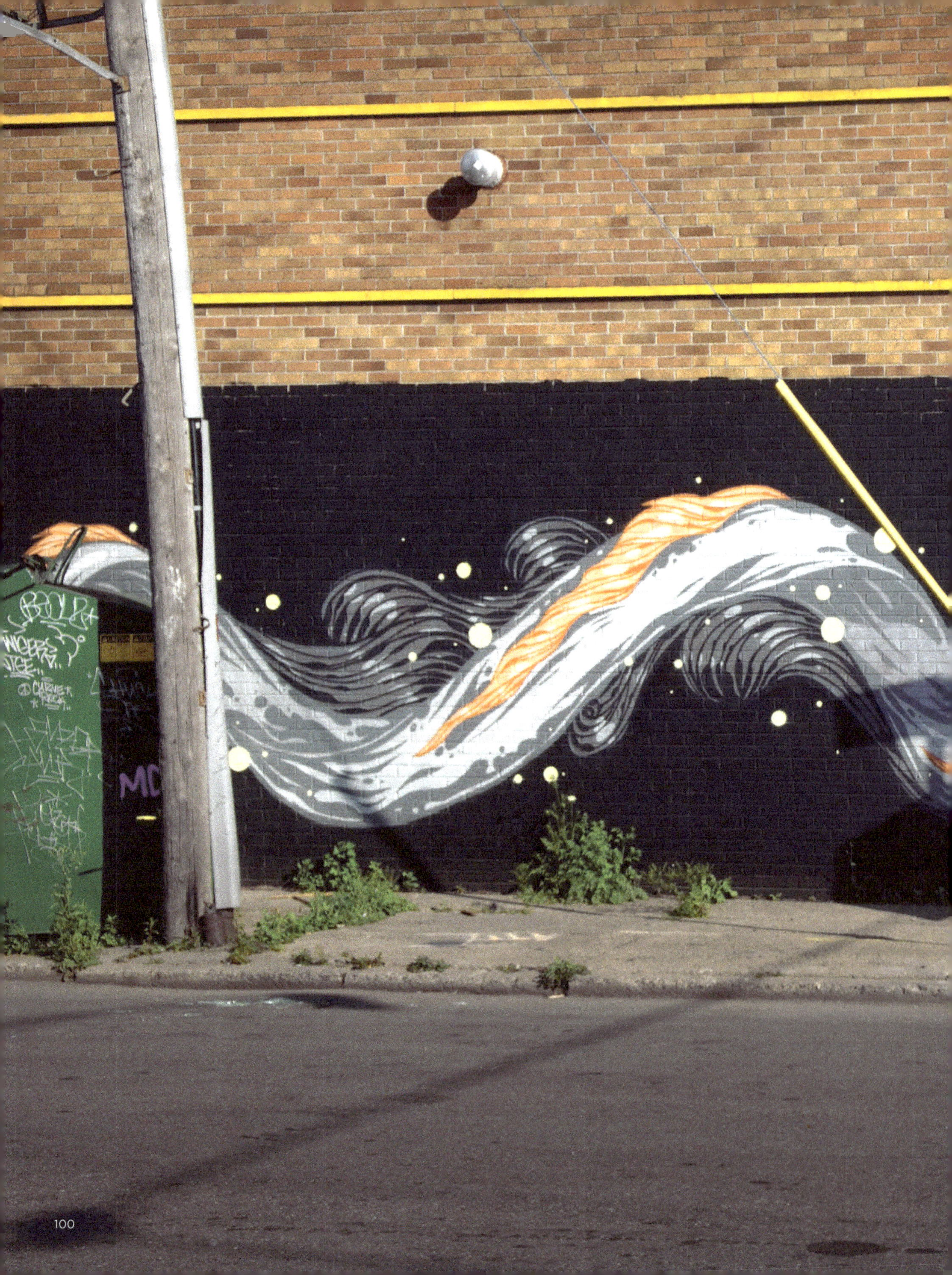

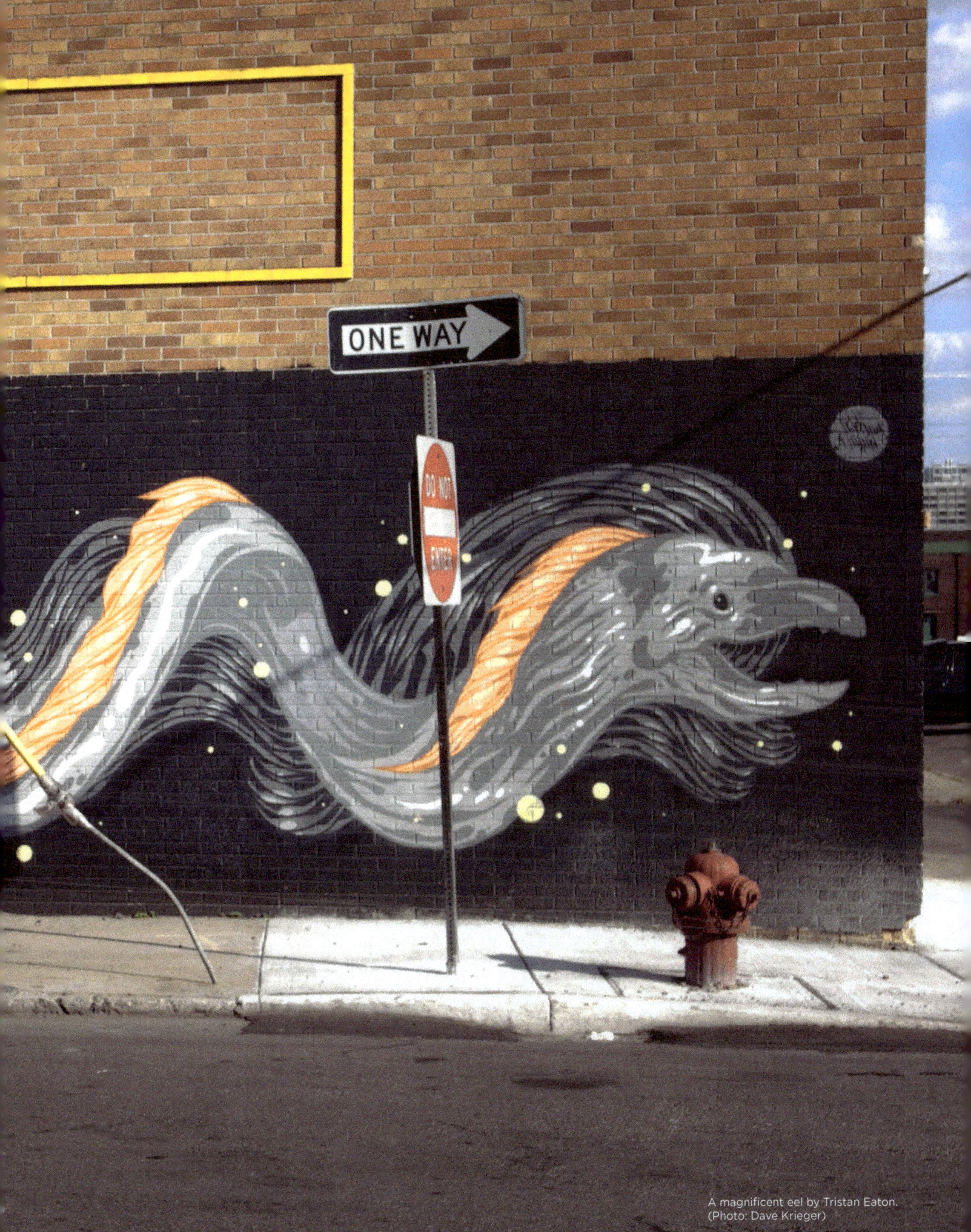

A magnificent eel by Tristan Eaton. (Photo: Dave Krieger)

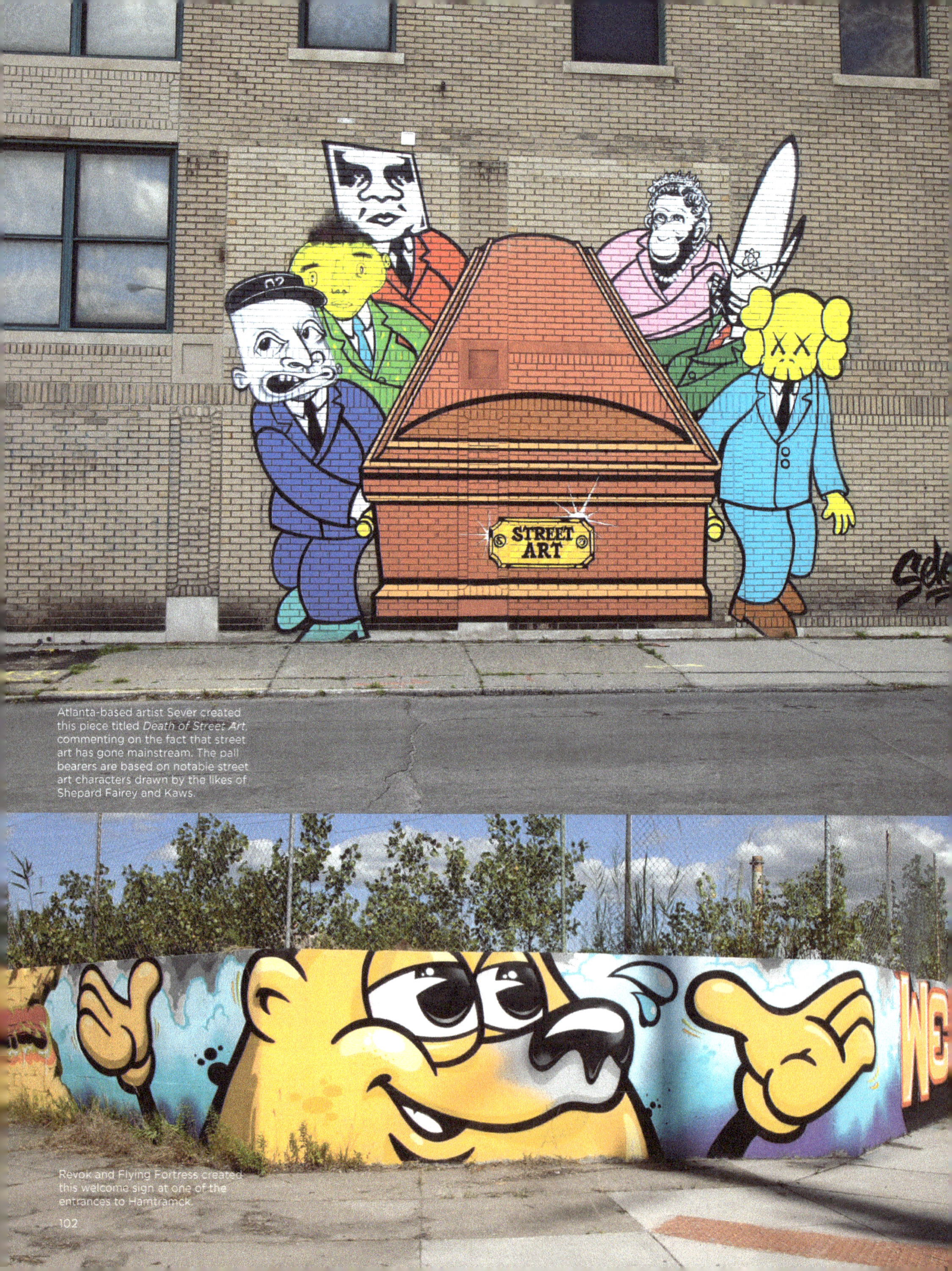

Atlanta-based artist Sever created this piece titled *Death of Street Art*, commenting on the fact that street art has gone mainstream. The pall bearers are based on notable street art characters drawn by the likes of Shepard Fairey and Kaws.

Revok and Flying Fortress created this welcome sign at one of the entrances to Hamtramck.

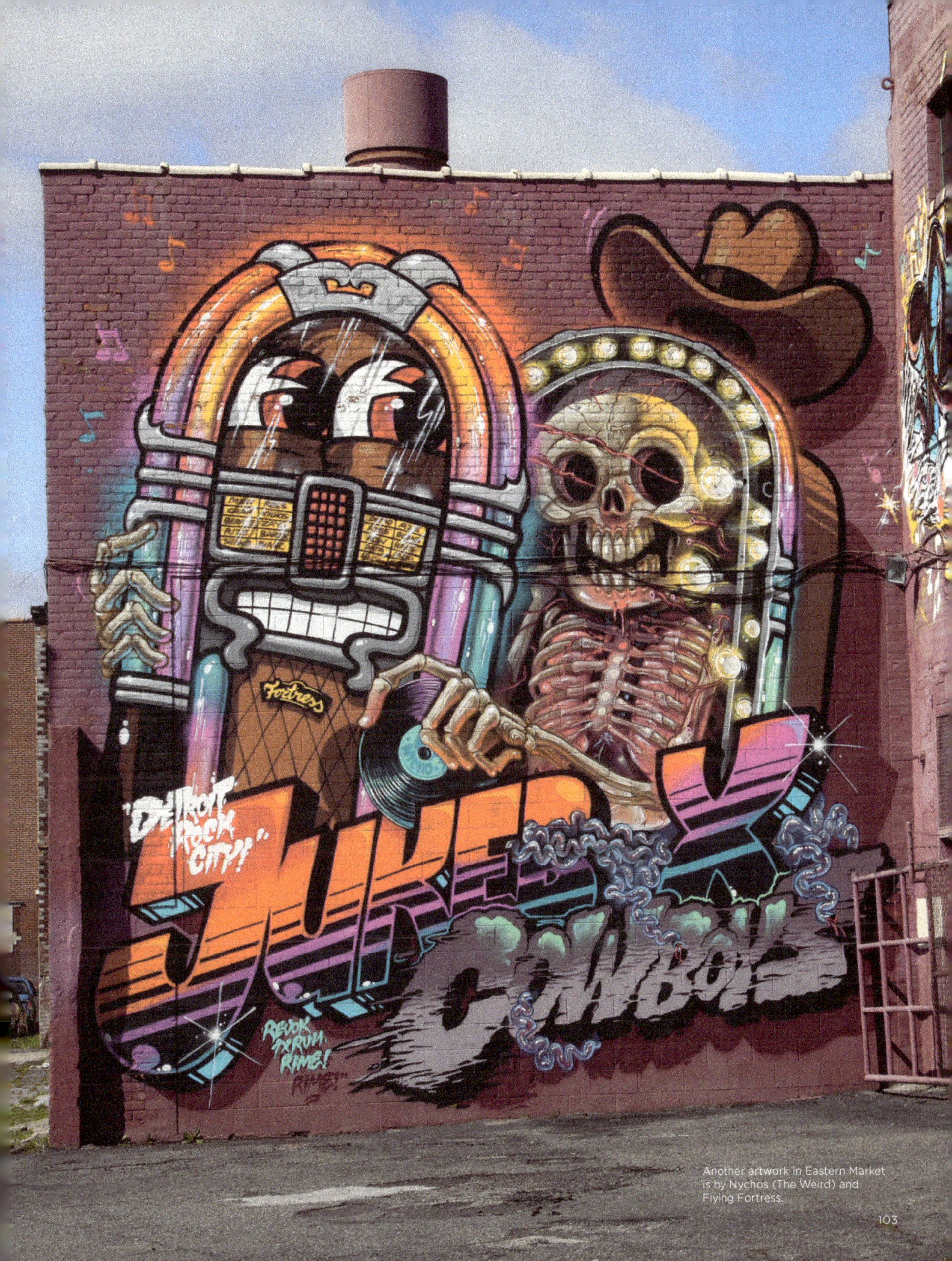

Another artwork in Eastern Market is by Nychos (The Weird) and Flying Fortress.

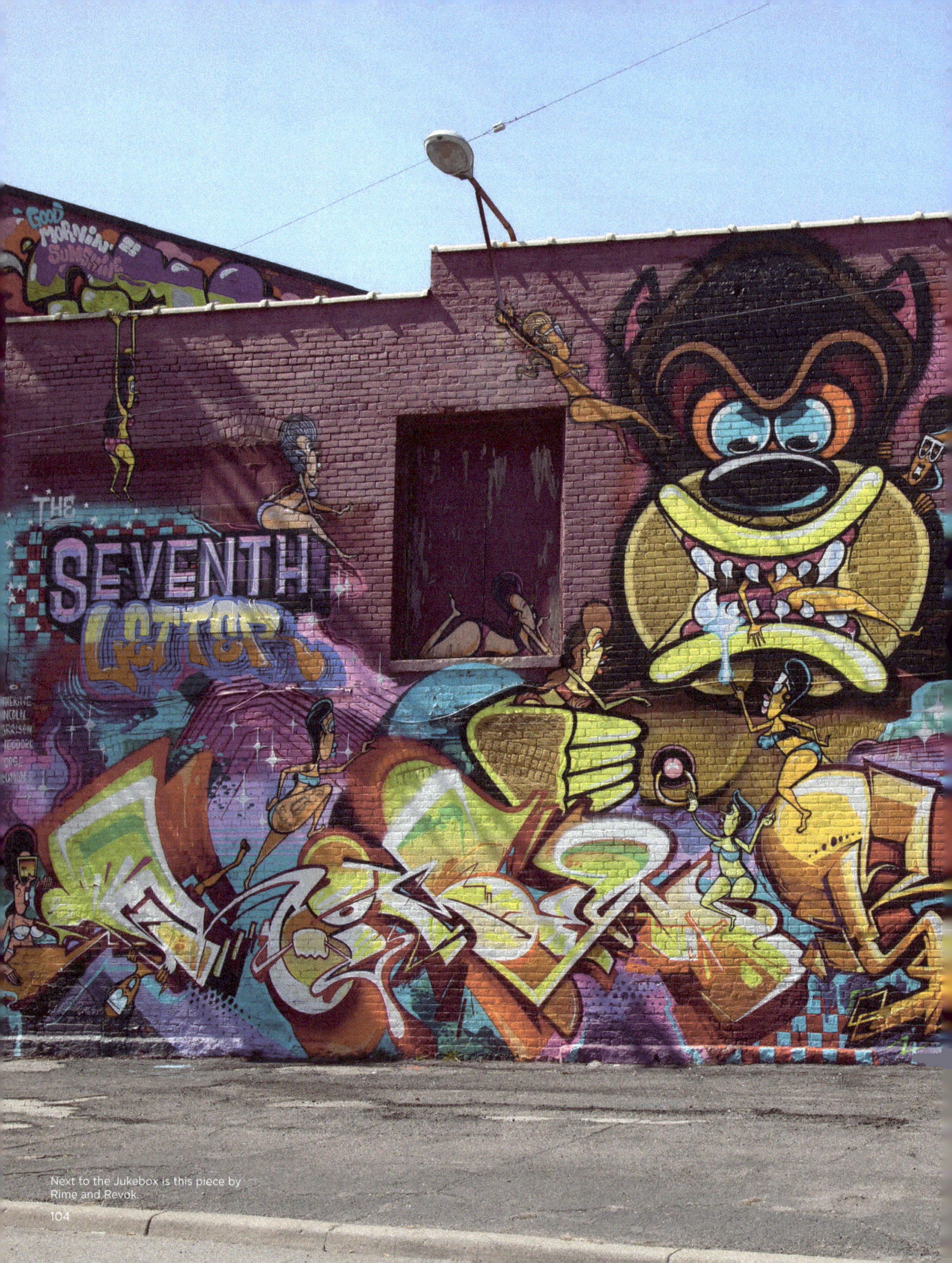

Next to the Jukebox is this piece by Rime and Revok.

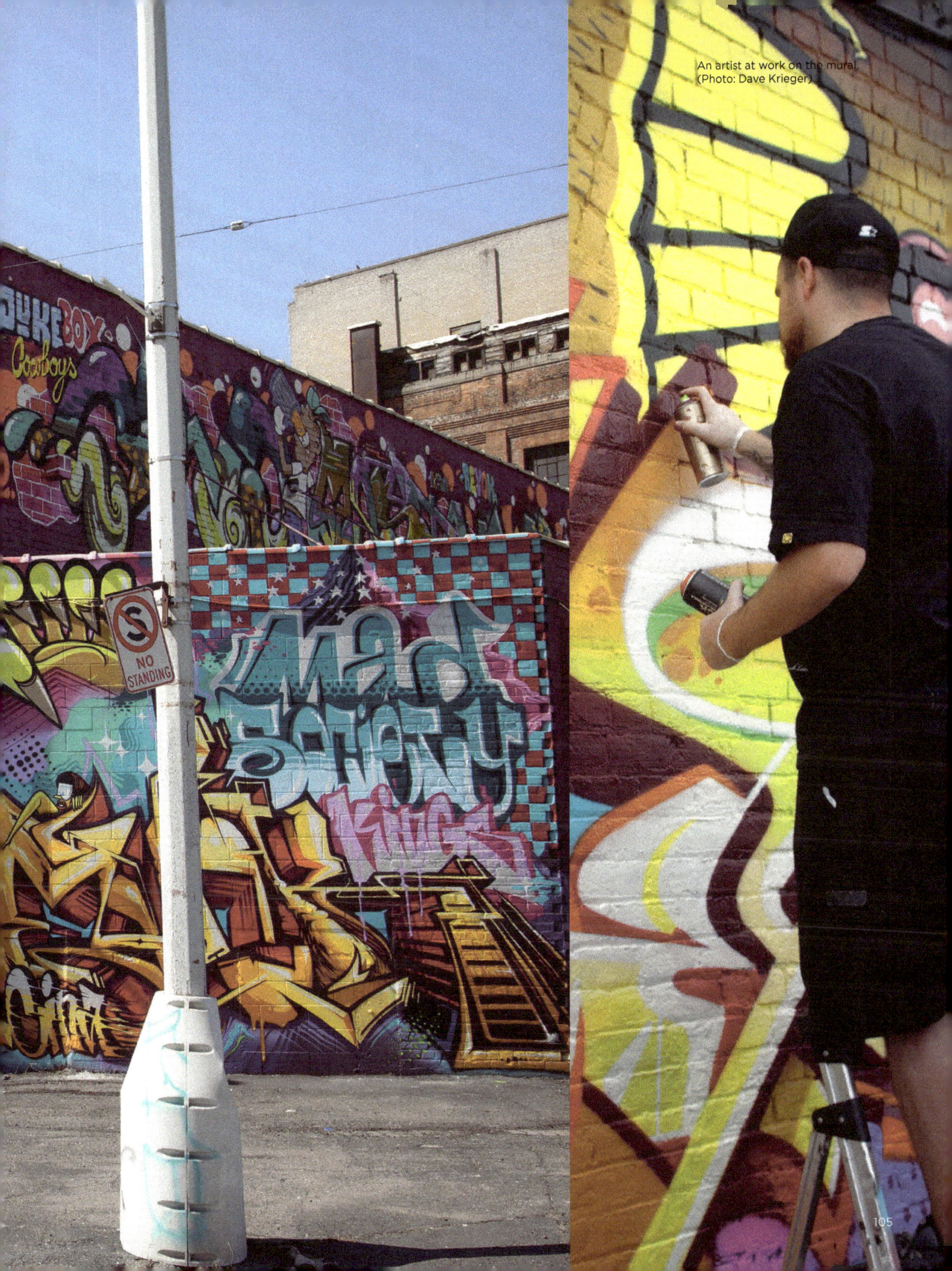

An artist at work on the mural.
(Photo: Dave Krieger)

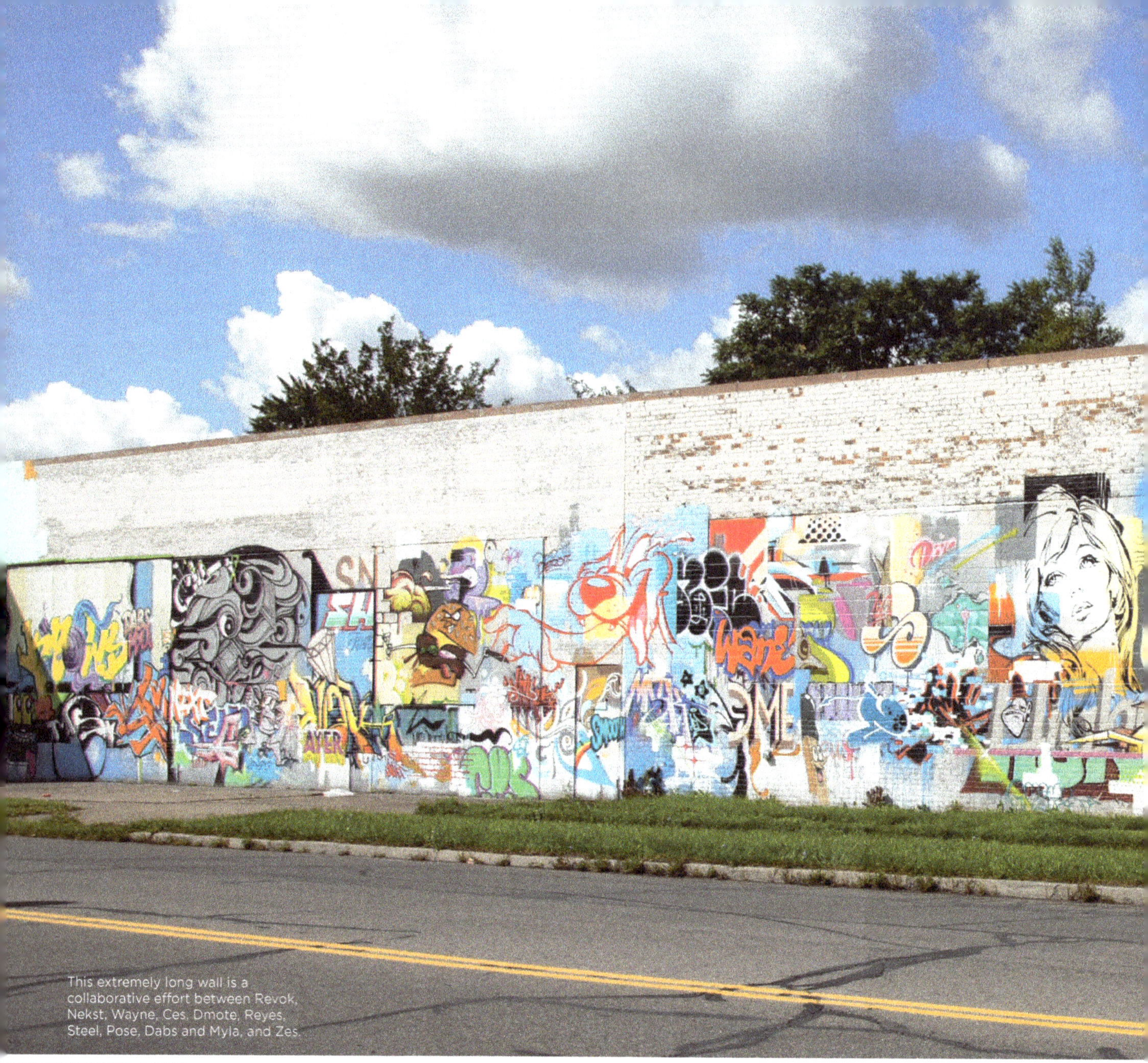

This extremely long wall is a collaborative effort between Revok, Nekst, Wayne, Ces, Dmote, Reyes, Steel, Pose, Dabs and Myla, and Zes.

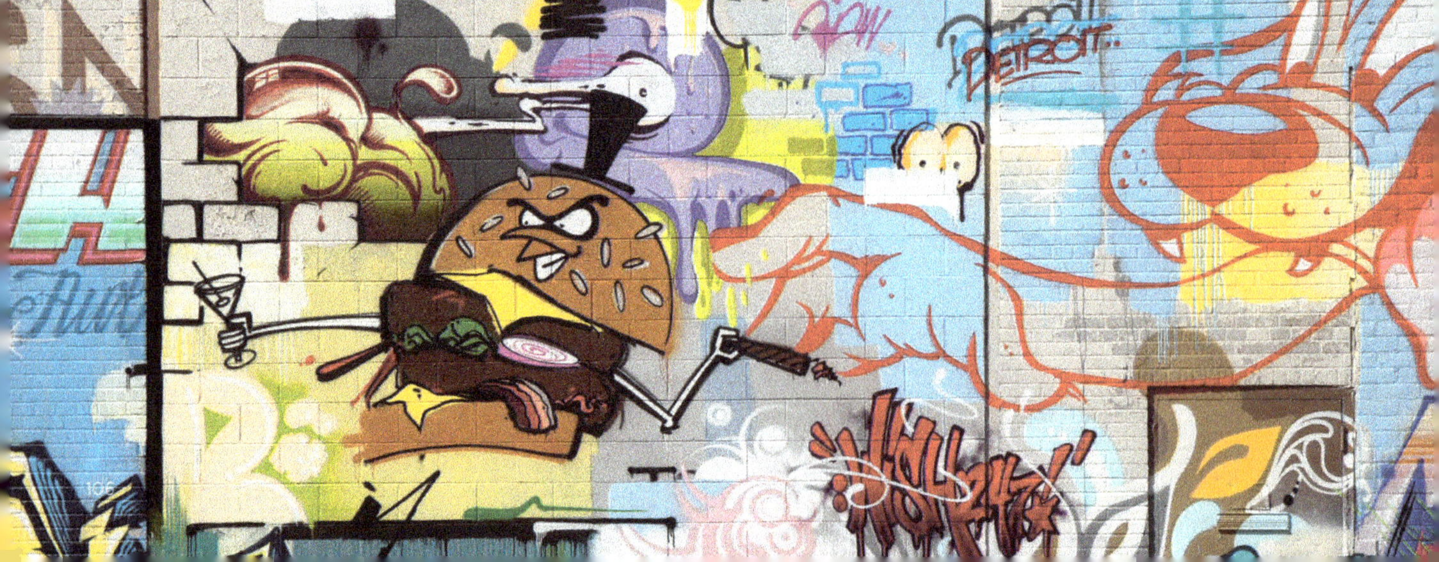

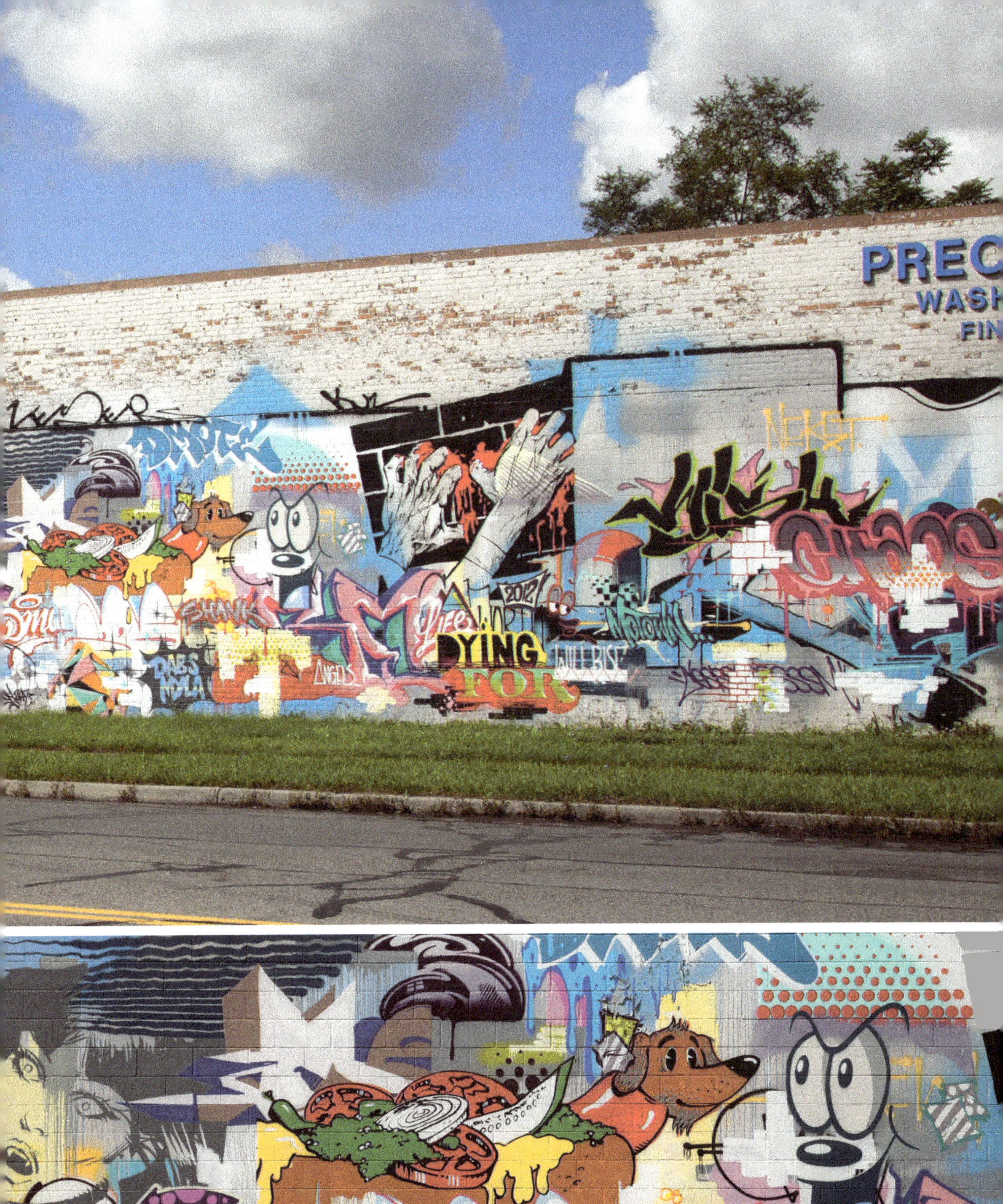
2012
DYING
FOR
SHANK

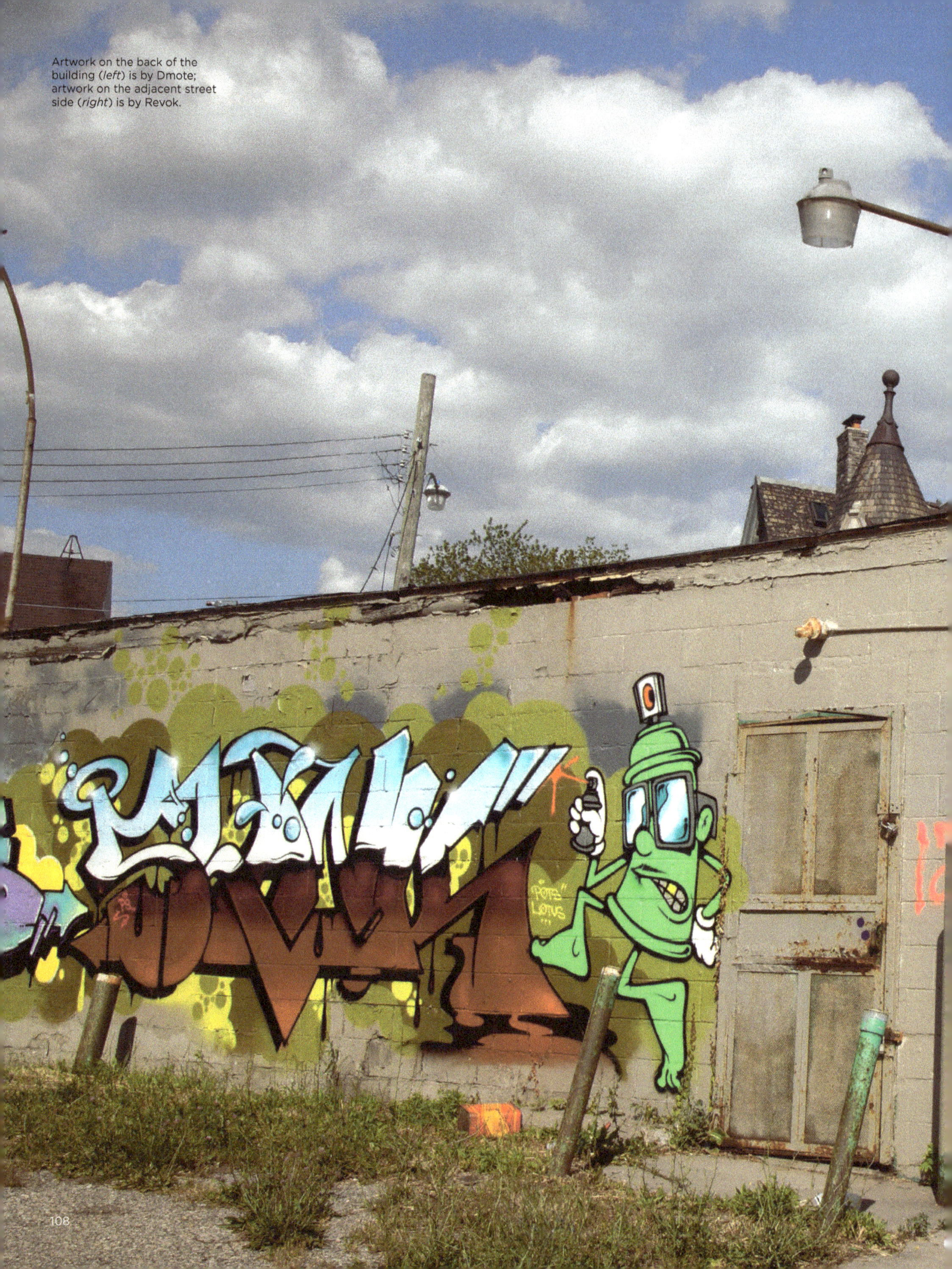

Artwork on the back of the building (*left*) is by Dmote; artwork on the adjacent street side (*right*) is by Revok.

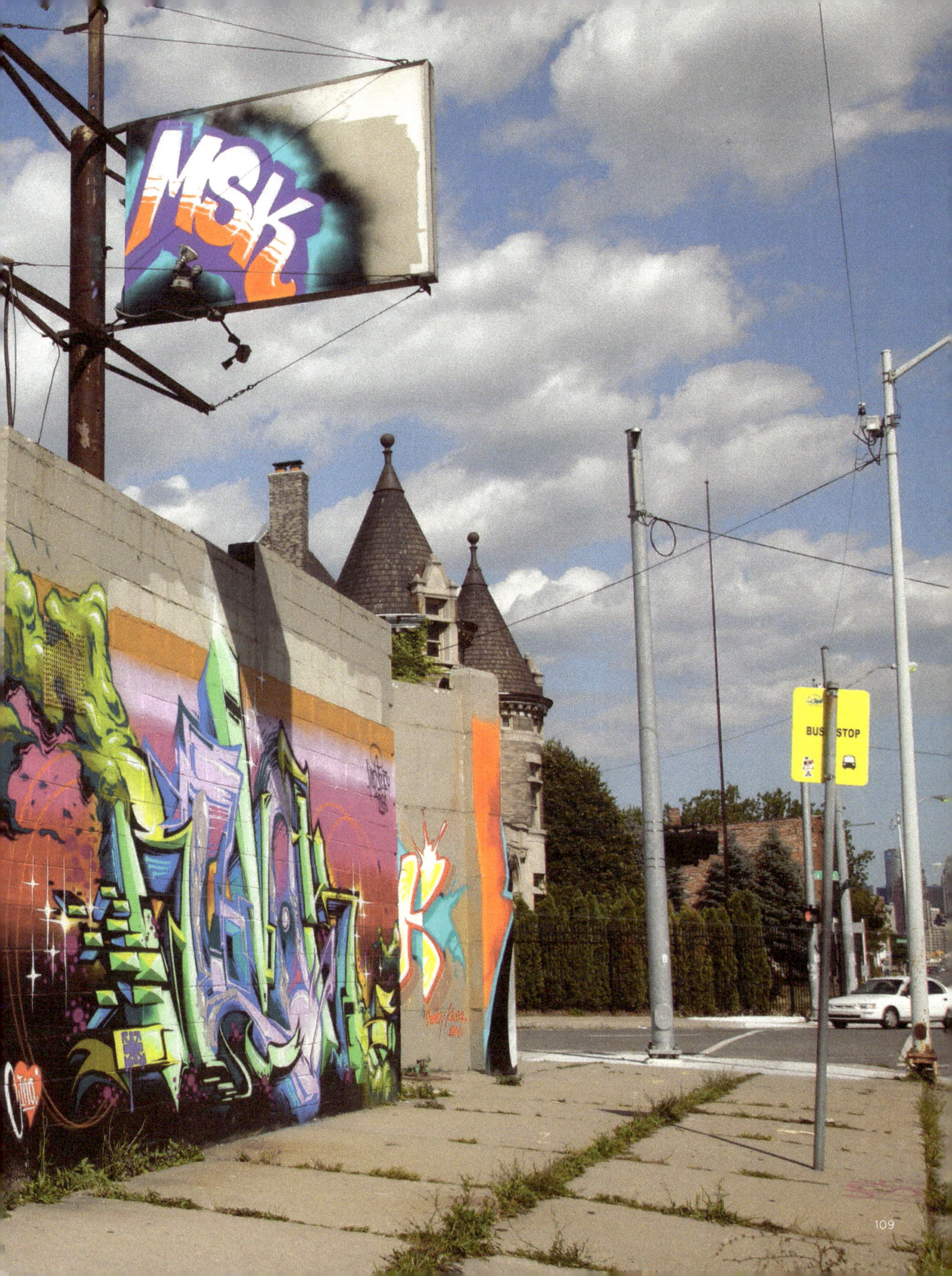
MSK
BUS STOP

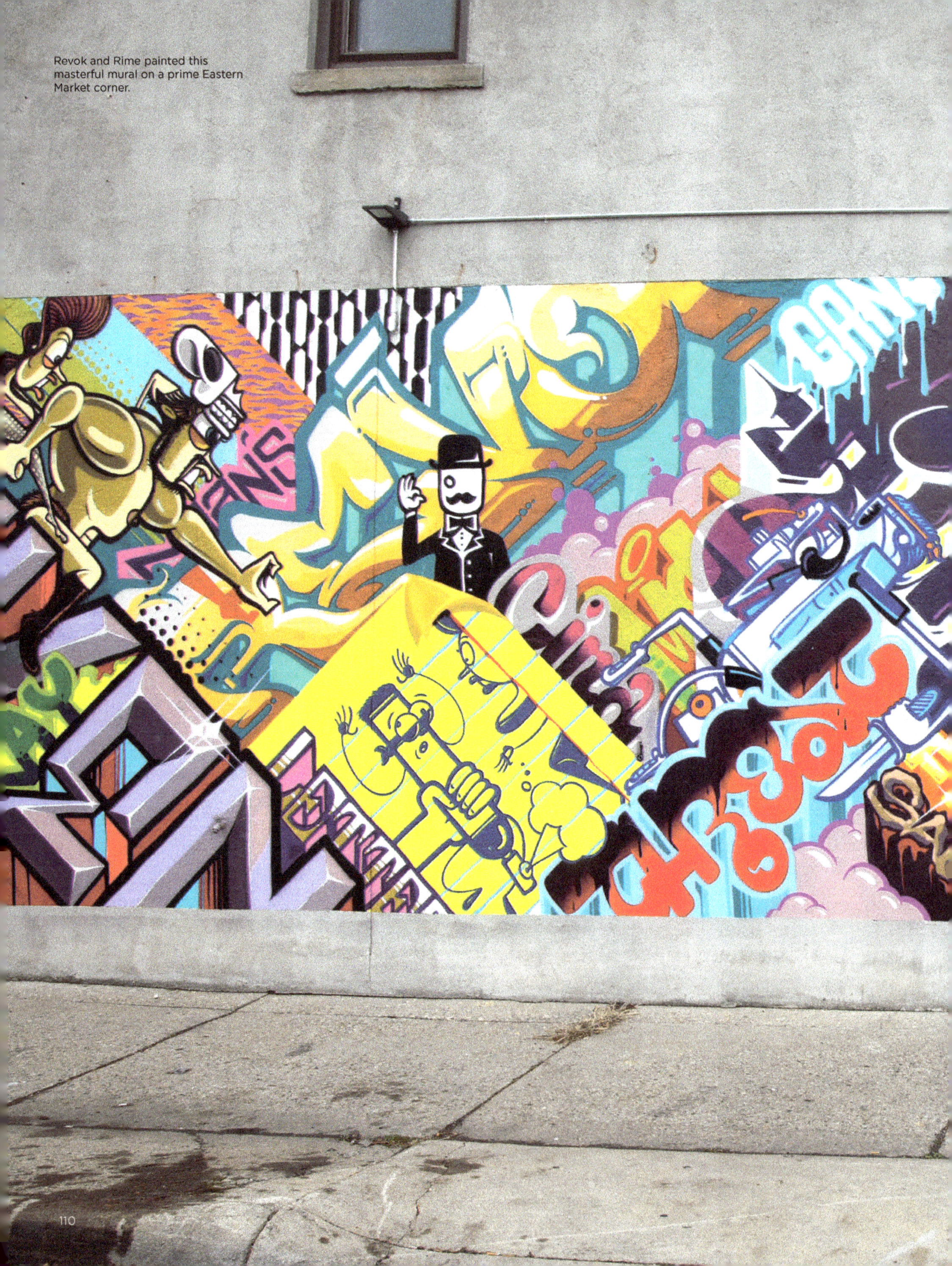

Revok and Rime painted this masterful mural on a prime Eastern Market corner.

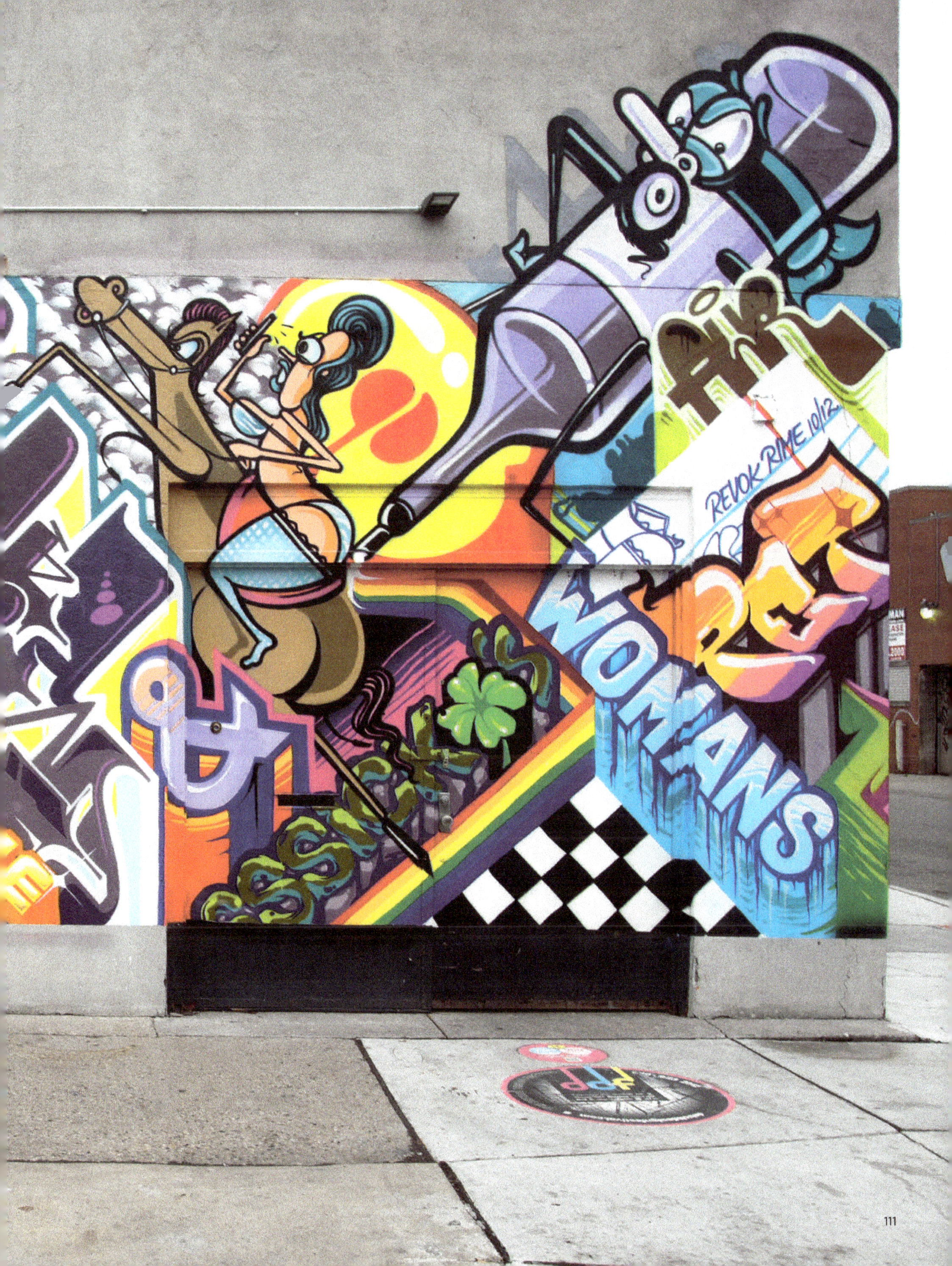
REVOK RIME 10/12
WOMANS

DLECTRICITY

Public Constructions: A Mini Night Park is a series of illuminated flowers fabricated out of construction warning lights that along with seating areas define a mini park. Artists: Reid Bingham and Sean McIntyre. (Photo: Dave Lewinsky)

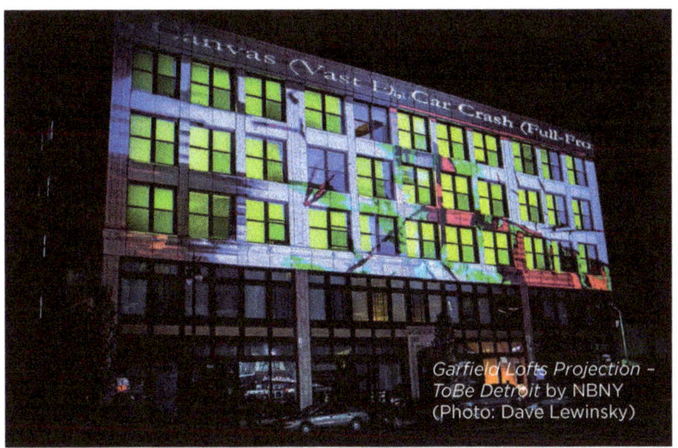

Garfield Lofts Projection - ToBe Detroit by NBNY (Photo: Dave Lewinsky)

In the Detroit art world, few stamps of approval are more valuable than that of Marc Schwartz.

Though he is not an artist, Schwartz is a creative rainmaker who's as dedicated to growing the arts in Detroit as he is to extending the depths of his legendary private collection.

When Schwartz is interested, things happen. Fast.

It was Schwartz who led the way for Detroit's most adventurous arts experiment yet, DLECTRICTY, an after-dark exhibition of contemporary art and light. The 2012 festival spread over two evenings in October and featured installations from thirty-five local, national, and international artists.

DLECTRICITY not only set Detroit aglow, it turned an old, ugly 1980s joke about Motown on its head. The joke went like this: *Will the last person to leave Detroit please turn out the lights?*

With DLECTRICITY, Schwartz and the group Art Detroit Now flipped the switch in a whole new direction, using dazzling displays of light and technology to illuminate art's potential in Detroit.

Under the lights, Detroit looked like a city ready to mesmerize once more. The architectural anchors of the cultural center, the majestic Detroit Institute of Arts and the main branch of the Detroit Public Library, became digital canvases. Light designers bathed the buildings in beams of neon, all part of twenty-five elaborate installations over the festival's two nights.

"The idea of lighting up Detroit resonated instantly. But pulling it together wasn't something that our group was necessarily positioned to do alone," explains Schwartz, acting chairman of Art Detroit Now and a member of the group's DLECTRICITY curatorial committee. Art Detroit Now is an ad-hoc committee of arts leaders and supporters working to create more collaboration among ninety different organizations. "We went forward with a lot of enthusiasm for the concept but we had a few unknowns," Schwartz says.

Perhaps the biggest unknown, says Schwartz, was whether the contemporary nature of the festival, and its abstract focus on light, had enough appeal to lure Detroit out after dark. Taking a cue from well-established light festivals such as Nuit Blanche in New York and Paris, Schwartz says the group and its partner organization, Midtown Detroit Inc., decided Motown was worth the gamble.

Art lovers took a similar gamble. Despite unseasonably low temperatures and rain both nights, Midtown, the heart of Detroit's creative sector, throbbed with excitement. Tens of thousands of spectators lined the streets stunned by 3-D performances, multimedia video projections, even a 3.75-mile Light Bike Parade for festivalgoers who came on two wheels.

"This was a huge experiment that paid off better than any of our expectations. The fact that so many people came out, and in bad weather, showed us a few important things," says Schwartz. "The biggest takeaway for us, if you present art in an accessible manner, there is heightened enough level of interest for real support. It was striking to see the streets so crowded at night. I think it showed, for the first time, that Midtown can really become the pedestrian village that so many people are hoping for."

Schwartz says DLECTRICITY will return. Art Detroit Now intends to make the festival a recurring event.

But to compete against established art cities, he says, Detroit must cement the city's creative appeal. "We have to build a community of patrons and collectors along with concentrated areas where people can go and experience the arts year-round."

Defining such districts in Detroit has become a top priority for Schwartz. He has begun to collect data with the same zeal that he collects art, narrowing his focus to the needs of five to seven pockets of the city and carefully mapping their creative assets.

"There's a lot of money being thrown at the arts right now for various projects, and some artists are understandably coming here as result," he says. "That's a start, but we've got to make sure we're building density and community around art and not just a few good moments. A vibrant city has to have a center."

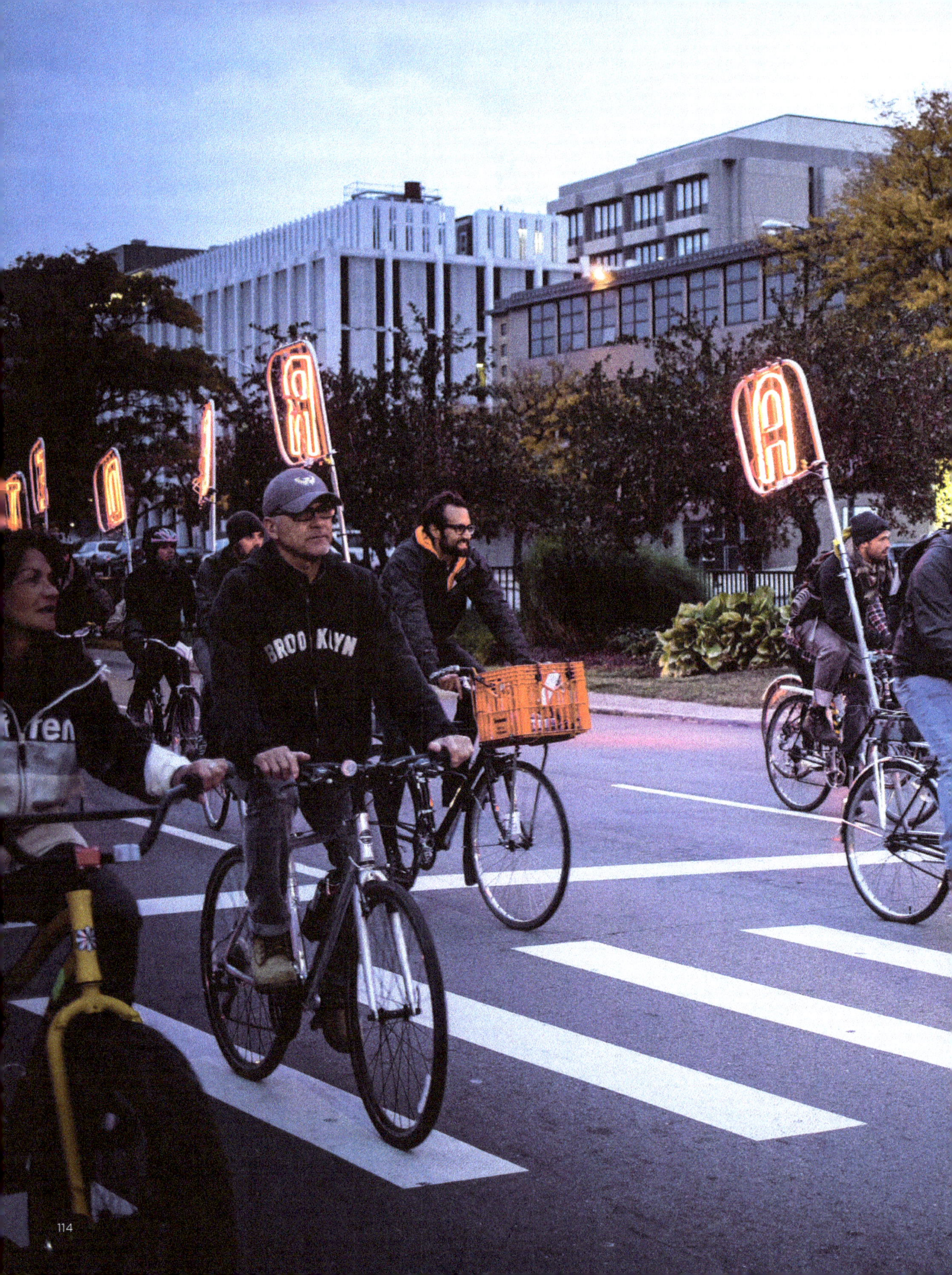
BROOKLYN
A

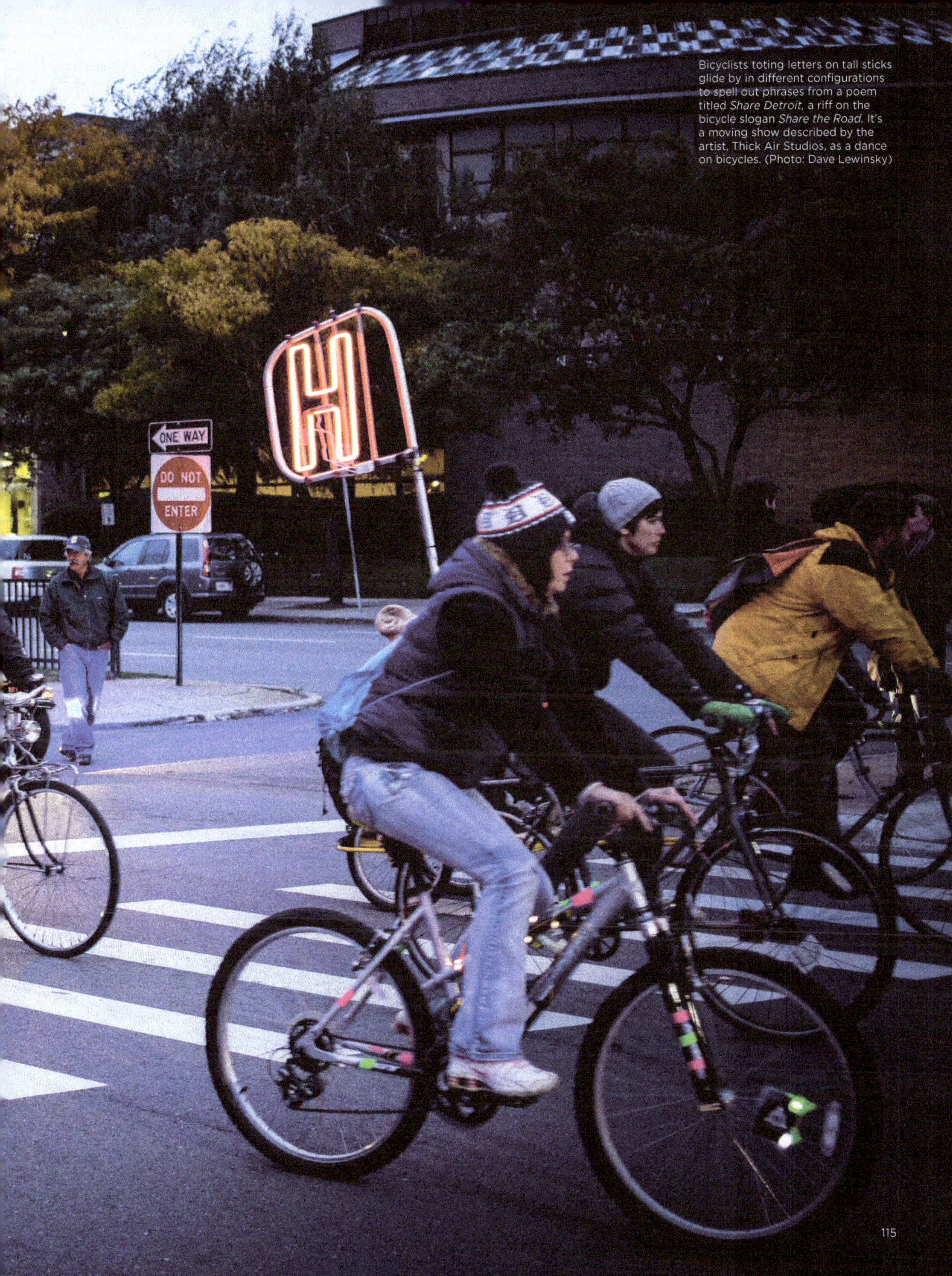

Bicyclists toting letters on tall sticks glide by in different configurations to spell out phrases from a poem titled *Share Detroit*, a riff on the bicycle slogan *Share the Road*. It's a moving show described by the artist, Thick Air Studios, as a dance on bicycles. (Photo: Dave Lewinsky)

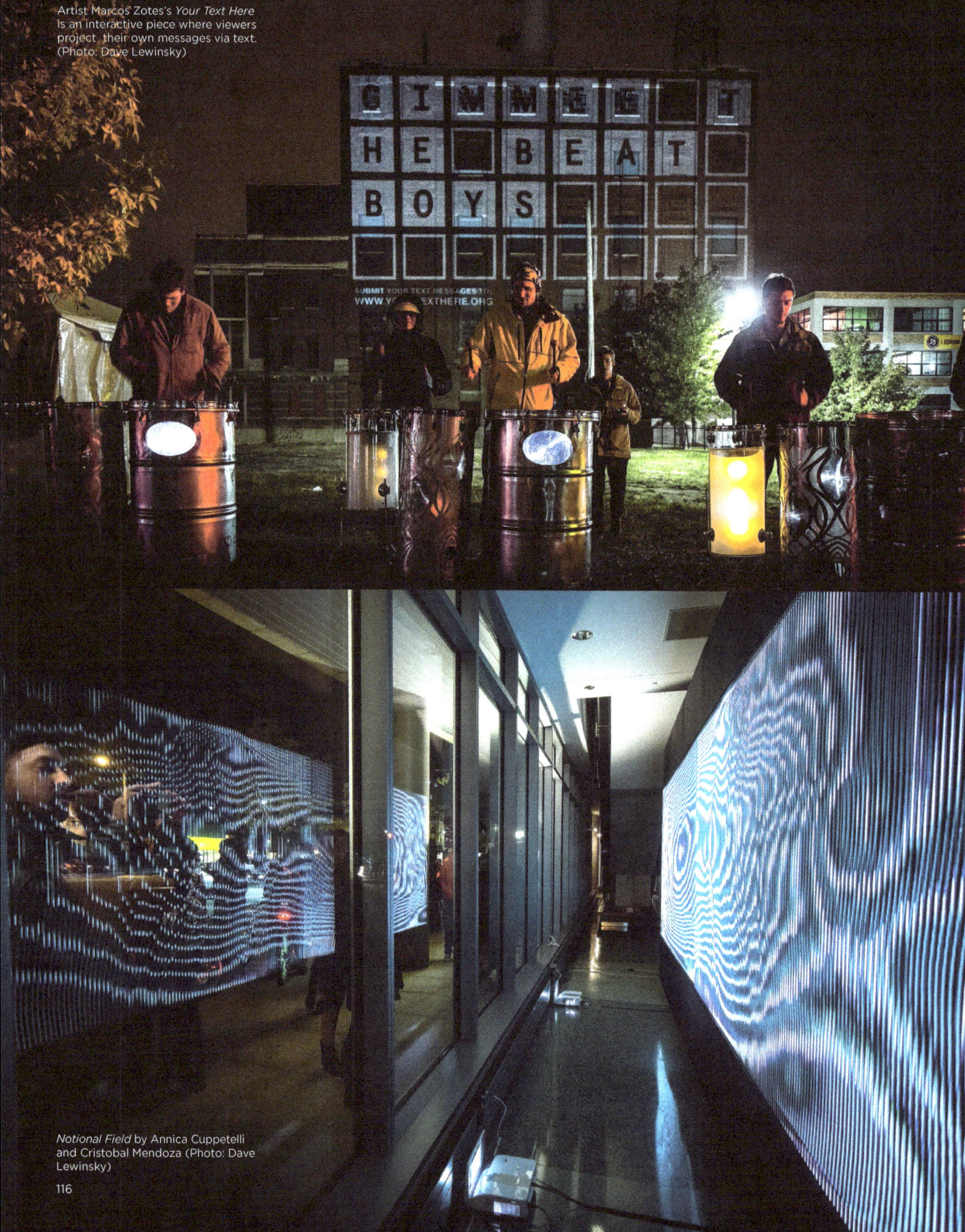

Artist Marcos Zotes's *Your Text Here* is an interactive piece where viewers project their own messages via text. (Photo: Dave Lewinsky)

Notional Field by Annica Cuppetelli and Cristobal Mendoza (Photo: Dave Lewinsky)

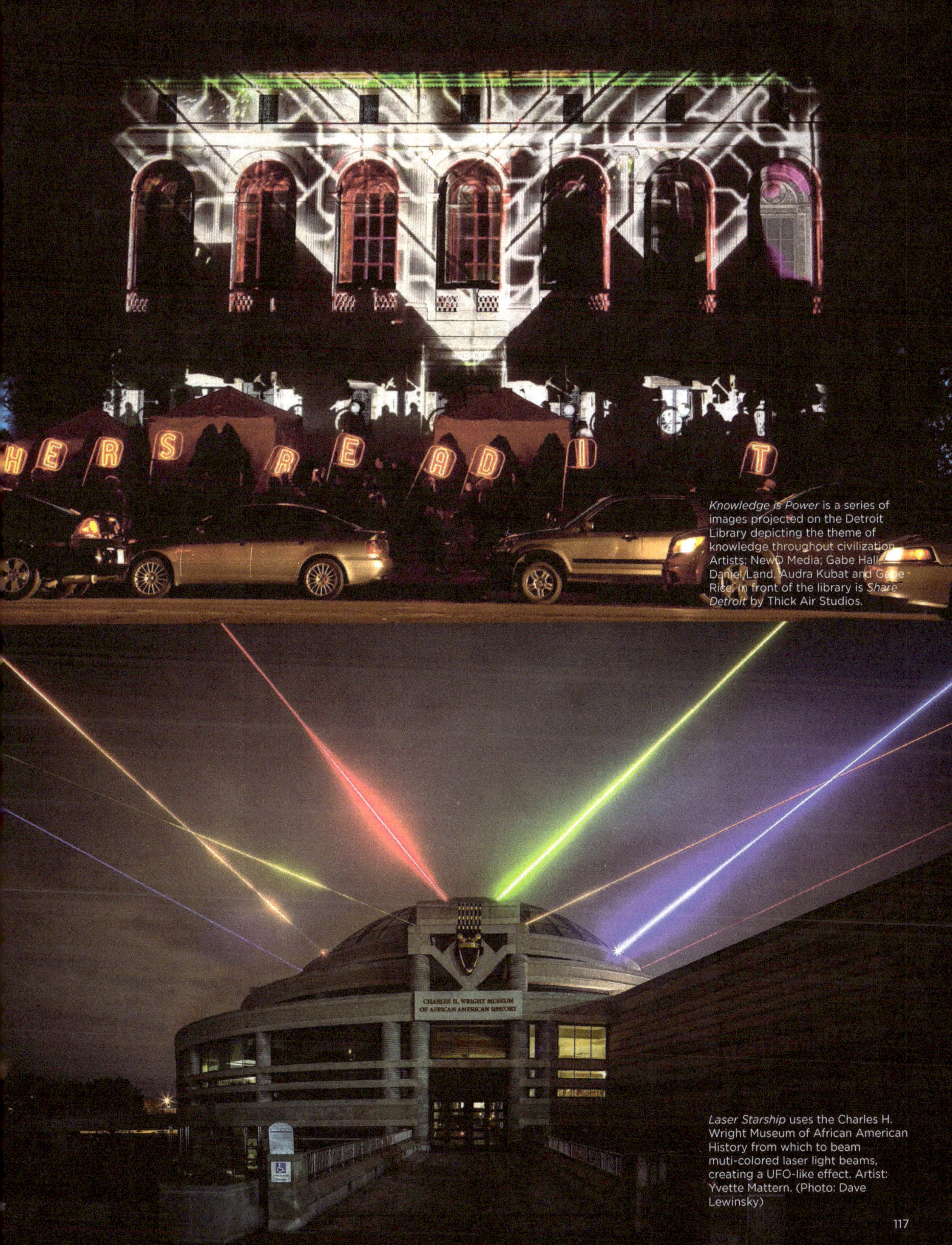

Knowledge is Power is a series of images projected on the Detroit Library depicting the theme of knowledge throughout civilization. Artists: NewD Media; Gabe Hall, Daniel Land, Audra Kubat and Gabe Rice. In front of the library is *Share Detroit* by Thick Air Studios.

Laser Starship uses the Charles H. Wright Museum of African American History from which to beam muti-colored laser light beams, creating a UFO-like effect. Artist: Yvette Mattern. (Photo: Dave Lewinsky)

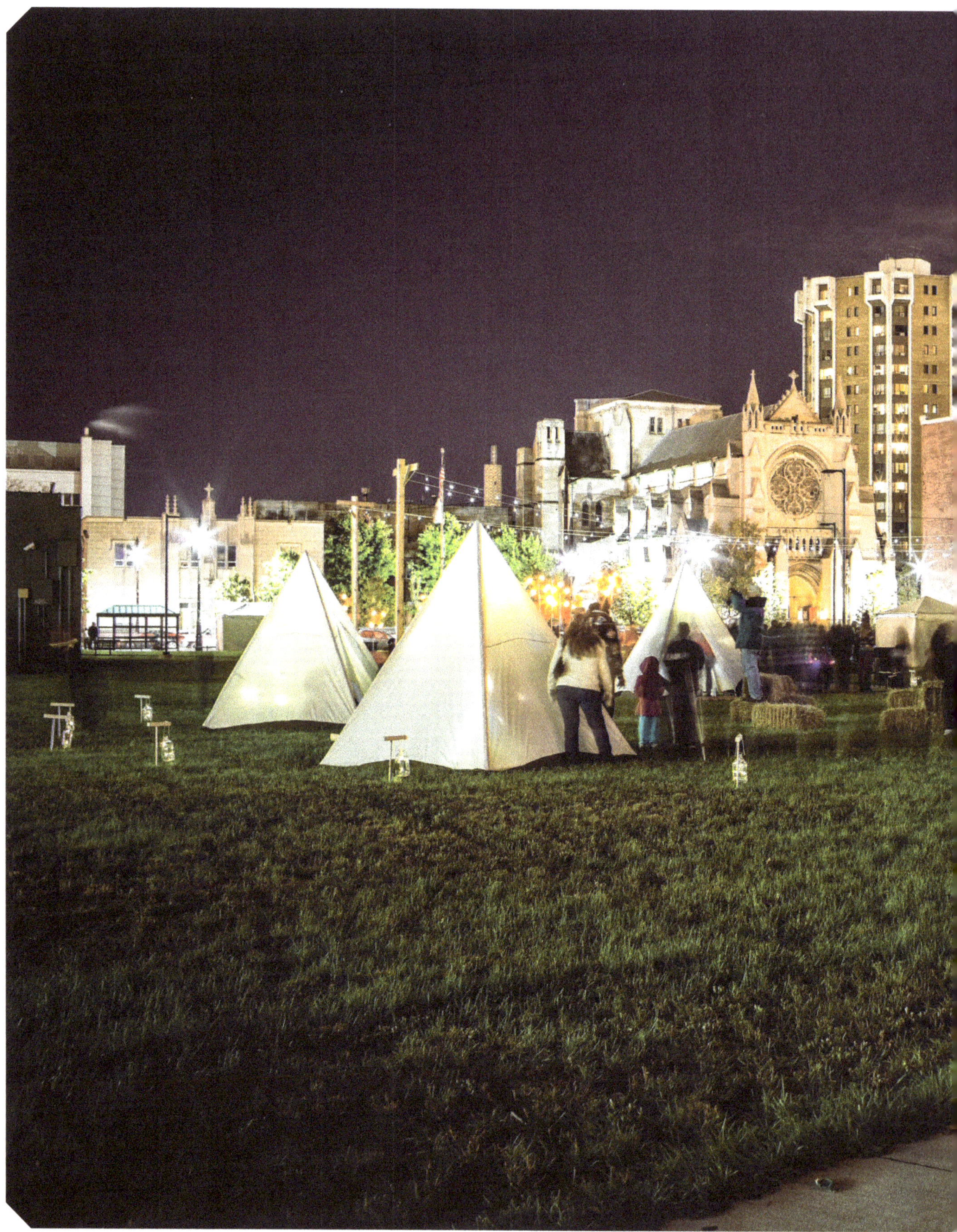

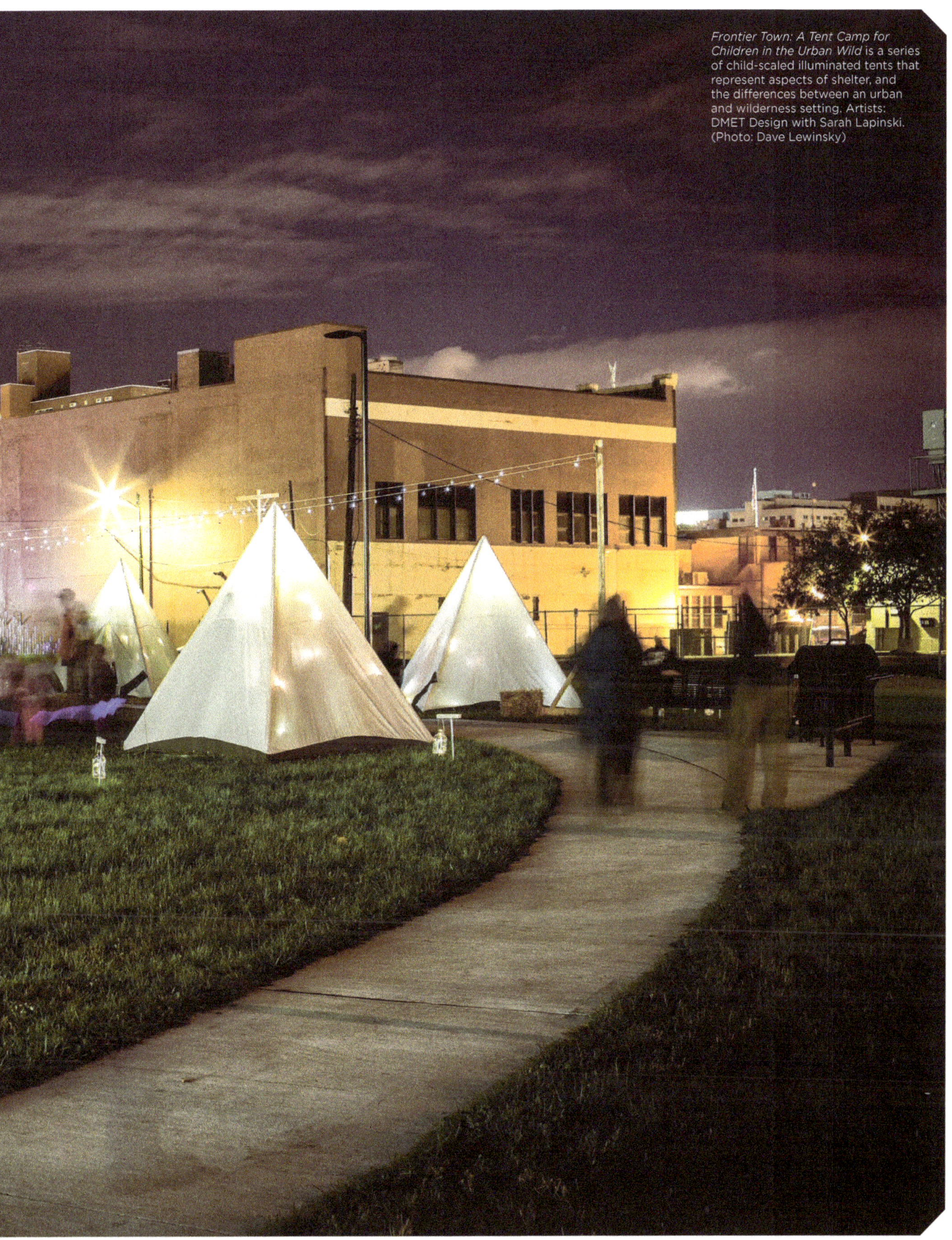

Frontier Town: A Tent Camp for Children in the Urban Wild is a series of child-scaled illuminated tents that represent aspects of shelter, and the differences between an urban and wilderness setting. Artists: DMET Design with Sarah Lapinski. (Photo: Dave Lewinsky)

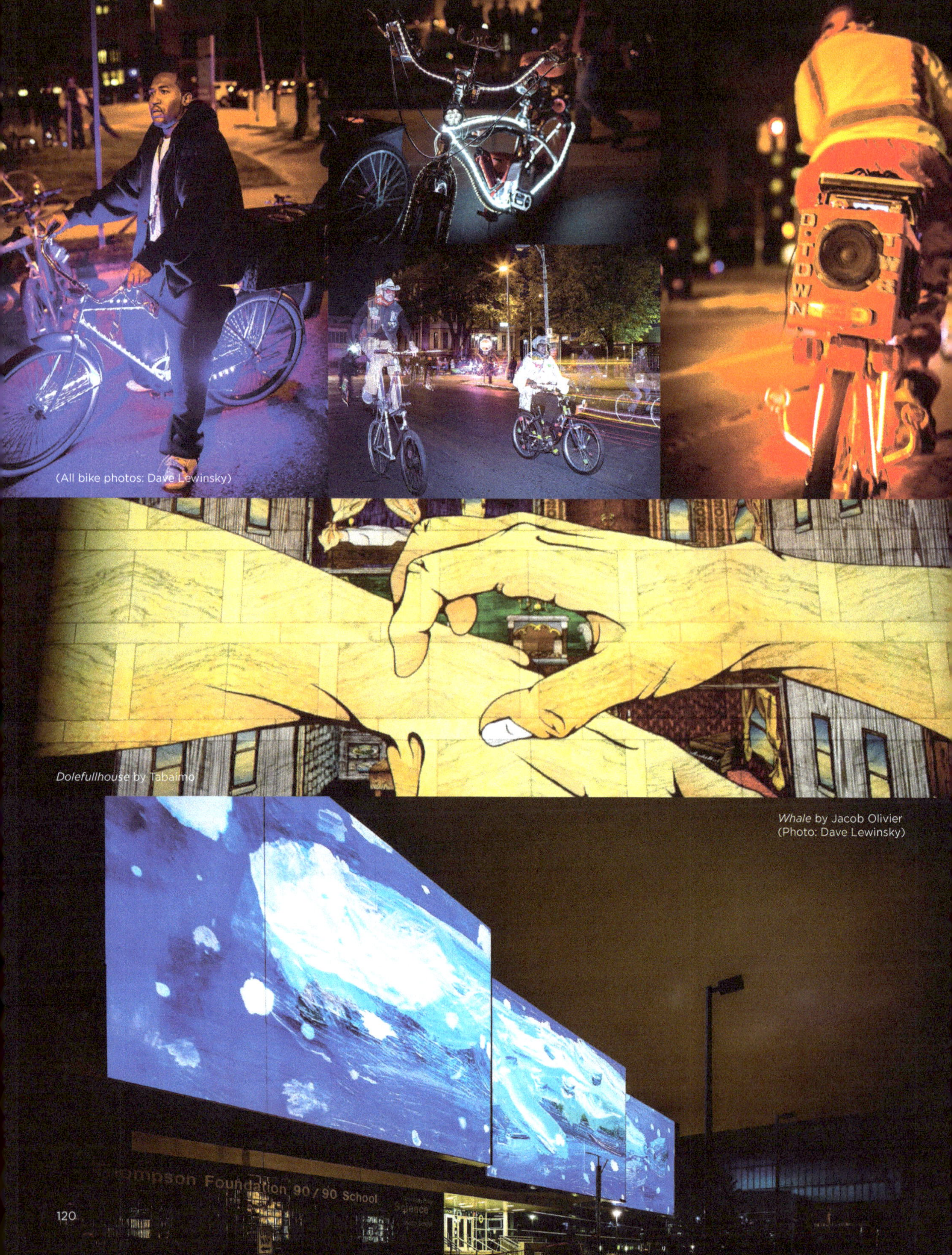

(All bike photos: Dave Lewinsky)

Dolefullhouse by Tabaimo

Whale by Jacob Olivier
(Photo: Dave Lewinsky)

A Ray Array: video by Sarah Rara (Photo: Dave Lewinsky)

The Legacy Lives On by James Dewitt Yancey (Photo: Dave Lewinsky)

64:85:22:11:38

James Dewitt (J. Dilla) Yancey
Feb. 7, 1974 - Feb. 10, 2006

Above, I See You control panel
Below, I See You by Apetechnology

Contour1 by Brienne Willcock & Robert White

Space Monkey Detroit by Dawn of Man

Velociplosion (A Muybridge Influenced Spatial Event) by Jake Chidester and Alisyn Malek

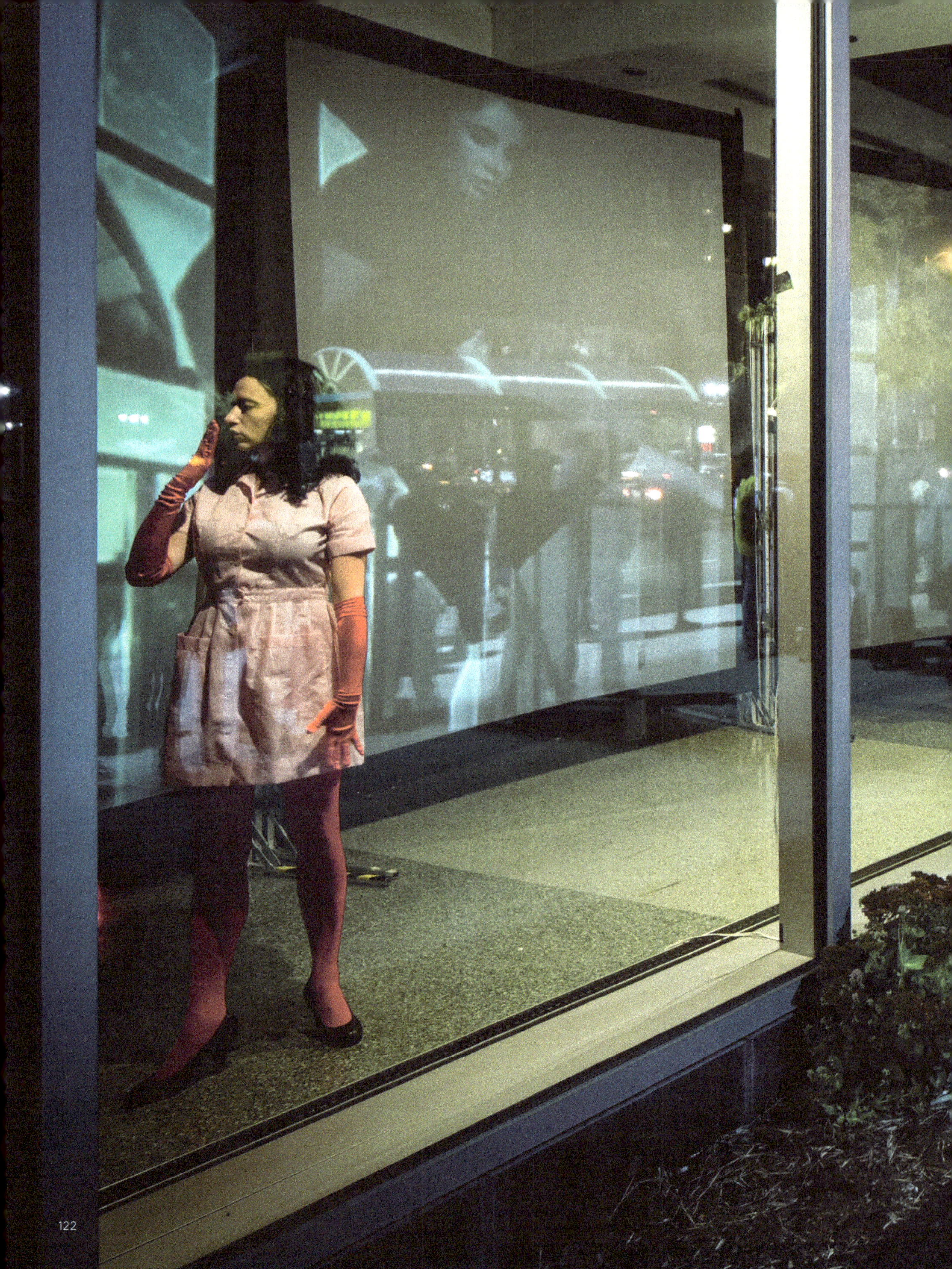

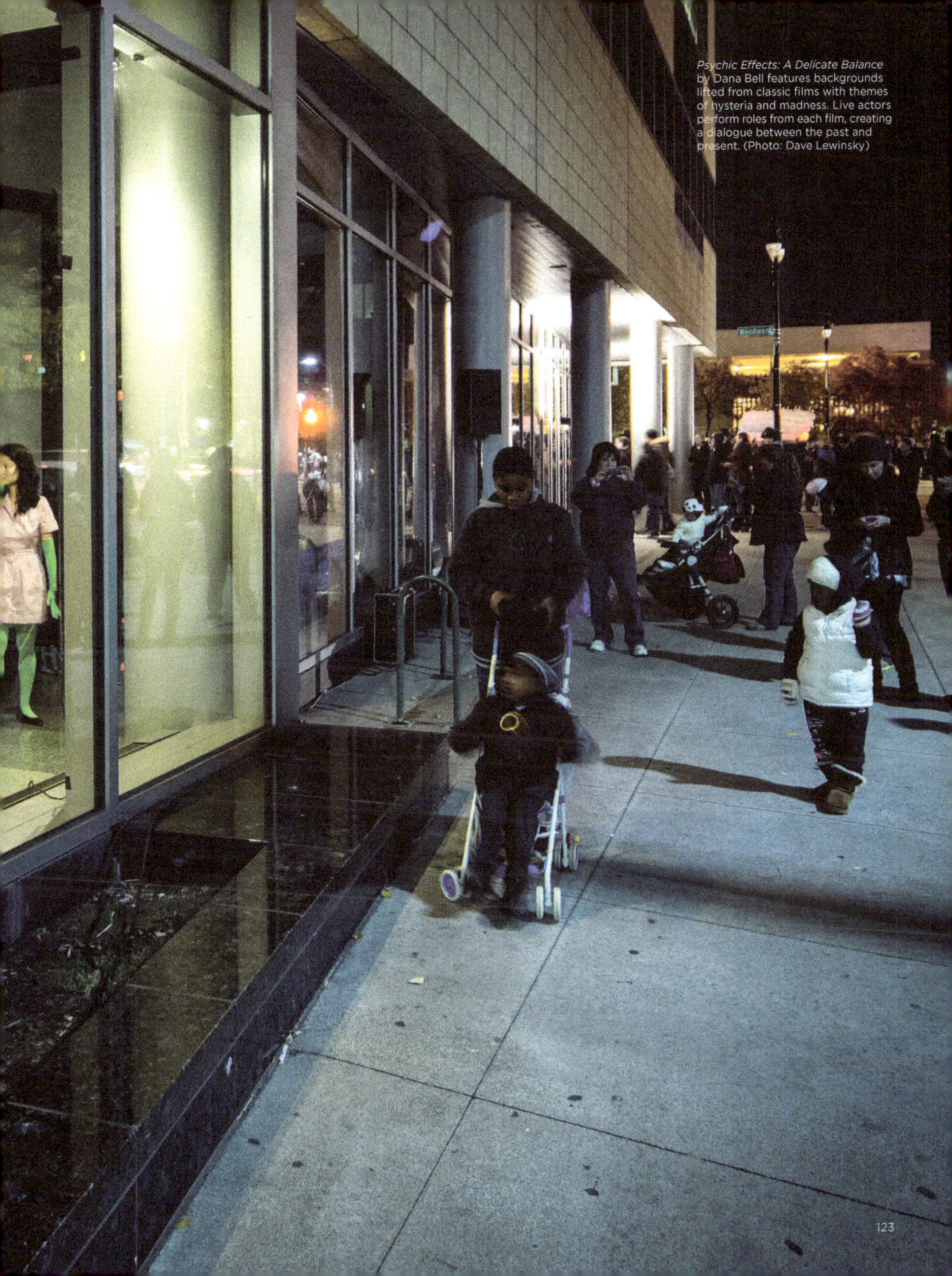

Psychic Effects: A Delicate Balance by Dana Bell features backgrounds lifted from classic films with themes of hysteria and madness. Live actors perform roles from each film, creating a dialogue between the past and present. (Photo: Dave Lewinsky)

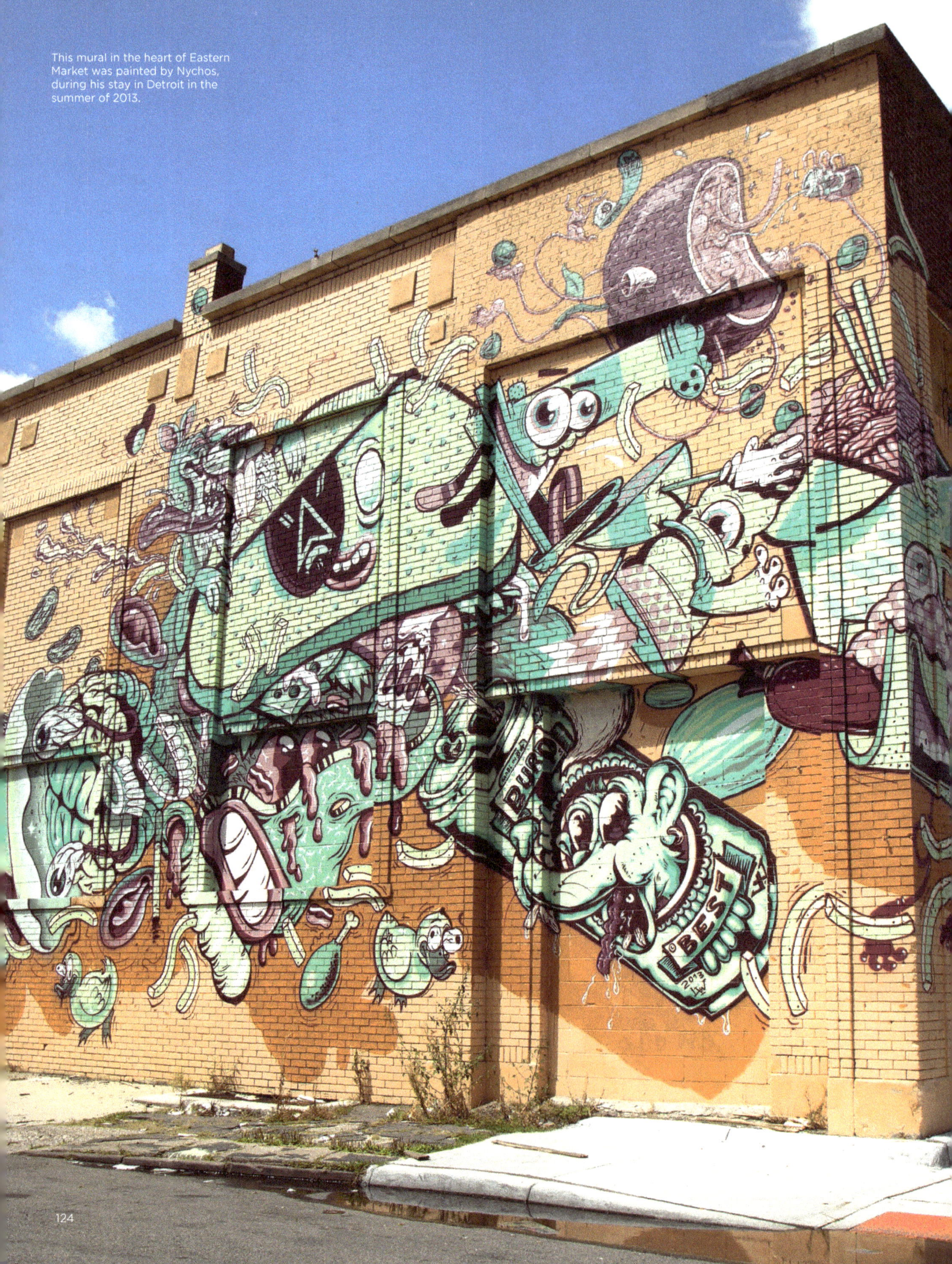

This mural in the heart of Eastern Market was painted by Nychos, during his stay in Detroit in the summer of 2013.

BY John Gallagher

Art and Public Places

Those who think they know Detroit because they've watched movies like *RoboCop* (set in post-apocalyptic Motor City) do not of course know much at all of our city. Take a drive of discovery on the streets of Detroit and you'll see plenty to make you proud and a lot to make you wince. But of all the surprises that await an open-eyed and open-minded visitor, perhaps the most surprising is the abundance of art.

Art peeks out at visitors from graffiti-tagged walls and the banks of Belle Isle, where stone cairns dot the shoreline. Officially blessed artwork includes the glass totems at Campus Martius and Marshall Fredericks's *Spirit of Detroit* at city hall. There's the Joe Louis Fist and the Labor Legacy Monument at Hart Plaza and the ethereal reflecting pool and sculpture garden designed by Minoru Yamasaki at the McGregor Memorial Conference Center at Wayne State University. And lately the Detroit Institute of Arts with its Inside/Out program has begun to playfully post reproductions of classic works in the odd spot here and there around the city.

But unofficial artwork must outnumber the official works by many times. Murals and bits of street art enliven community gardens and vacant lots and sides of abandoned buildings throughout the city. Sometimes the official and unofficial blend together. Tyree Guyton's Heidelberg Project drew so much derision when the artist first began painting his dots more than a quarter-century ago that city crews bulldozed the project twice in the early years. That was before Guyton won acclaim as a genuine American folk artist and his work began showing up in the DIA and other museums. Heidelberg became one of the city's most-viewed attractions for out-of-town tour groups.

This abundance of art in a distressed post-industrial landscape raises so many interesting questions that it's hard to know where to begin. Is the artwork any good? That is, is it any good by traditional art-critic standards? Well, yes, much of it is quite fine, and certainly public sculpture by the likes of Marshall Fredericks or David Barr and Sergio DeGiusti of the Labor Monument would benefit any city anywhere. Harder to define work by folk artists like Guyton and muralist Chazz Miller matches up well with similar street art found in many other cities. And if some of the graffiti that abounds on Detroit walls is unsightly or derivative, and if some of the hammered-together bits of debris erected as totems in community gardens seems more akin to finger painting than art-school work, at least no one can deny the energy behind it.

Beyond the intrinsic quality of the art itself, though, beyond the question of what any particular work means to any one viewer, lie a couple of broader considerations. Art is good for the soul, but it's also good for what architects and planners call "place-making." And however much individual artists may struggle to pay their bills, it appears that art is also good for the broader economy.

Take place-making first. The phrase is now a catchall to mean that lively mix of shops and pedestrian street-life as one finds in the best urban centers from Chicago to San Francisco to Paris. The elements of place-making are better understood today than ever; those elements include sidewalk cafes and moveable benches and chairs in city parks, a wealth of small storefront shops, and enough notable landmarks to fix a spot forever in the public's mind. Art plays its part in this scheme; from the Noguchi fountain on Hart Plaza to Diego Rivera's murals of Henry Ford's factory at the DIA, art not only enlivens a public place but also in many cases defines it.

Urban planners know this, of course, and have long built artwork into their designs. Belle Isle is rich with works of sculpture, mostly in the classical vein, from monuments celebrating Dante and Schiller to Detroit's first great equestrian statue, sculptor Henry Merwin Shrady's tribute to Major General Alpheus Starkey Williams. These works were sited to be focal points, landmarks that help create a sense of orientation on the sprawling island.

Now place-makers are nurturing art and culture in the city's Midtown district to create a lively bohemian atmosphere. There's MOCAD, the Museum of Contemporary Art Detroit on Woodward, plus the cluster of galleries that dot the district and the twin campuses of the College for Creative Studies, all of which populate the Midtown district with artists, art students, collectors, and browsers. And Midtown Detroit Inc., the accomplished civic group active in the district, has sponsored DLECTRICITY, the festival of lights and sounds that includes a bicycle tour for which cyclists festoon their rides with lights. It's all designed to create a lively sense of place that contributes to the overall health of the civic space.

Art contributes to the bottom line as well, something that an increasing number of cities are recognizing. Grand Rapids for the past few years has sponsored ArtPrize, that wide-open competition that brings well over a thousand artists from around the world to place their works in any building or any parking lot, rooftop, or plaza that will have it. ArtPrize runs for three weeks in the fall, and each year brings in tens of thousands of tourists who swamp the hotels and restaurants and contribute millions in revenue to the local economy.

In the same fashion, the former railroad town of Stratford, Ontario, decided some six decades ago that the loss of the railroads was no reason to fold up the sidewalks and wither away. Stratford visionaries attracted top theatrical talent to put on a production of *Richard III* in a rented tent; the Stratford Festival now operates five permanent stages, employs some one thousand staffers, and draws tens of thousands of visitors each year, who fill the hotels and restaurants and who return year after year.

Some critics have argued that mural programs and the like are more a sign of urban distress than urban health; that a work like the Heidelberg Project becomes possible only when a city is abandoned. It's an intriguing thought; but certainly the energy behind even the crudest work of street art belies the notion that Detroit is dead. The murals on the sides of abandoned factories and the rock cairns on Belle Isle and the kinetic sculptures in garden plots around the city proclaim the opposite—

Art is good for the soul, but it's also good for what architects and planners call "place-making." And however much individual artists may struggle to pay their bills, it appears that art is also good for the broader economy.

that there are people in this city who refuse to let Detroit go, who are planting their flag and taking their stand. If art from its very beginnings has, like song, allowed people to sing out what's deep in their souls, that process of art-making and place-making remains vital in Detroit today.

And in a neat irony, RoboCop himself—that half-human, half-robotic fantasy creature that has stood as a cinematic symbol of Detroit's decline—is coming to the Motor City as a work of public art. Where exactly the ten-foot-tall bronze statue will stand when finished and unveiled in 2014 or so remains an open question. But surely its arrival is proof that art, like love, can conquer all, or least can give the populace of an energetic city one more boisterous song to sing in their chorus of their lives.

John Gallagher joined the *Detroit Free Press* in 1987 to cover urban and economic redevelopment efforts in Detroit and Michigan, a post he still holds. He is the author of several books, including, most recently, *Revolution Detroit: Strategies for Urban Reinvention* (Wayne State University Press, 2013) and *Reimagining Detroit: Opportunities for Redefining an American City* (Wayne State University Press, 2010).

RON ENGLISH

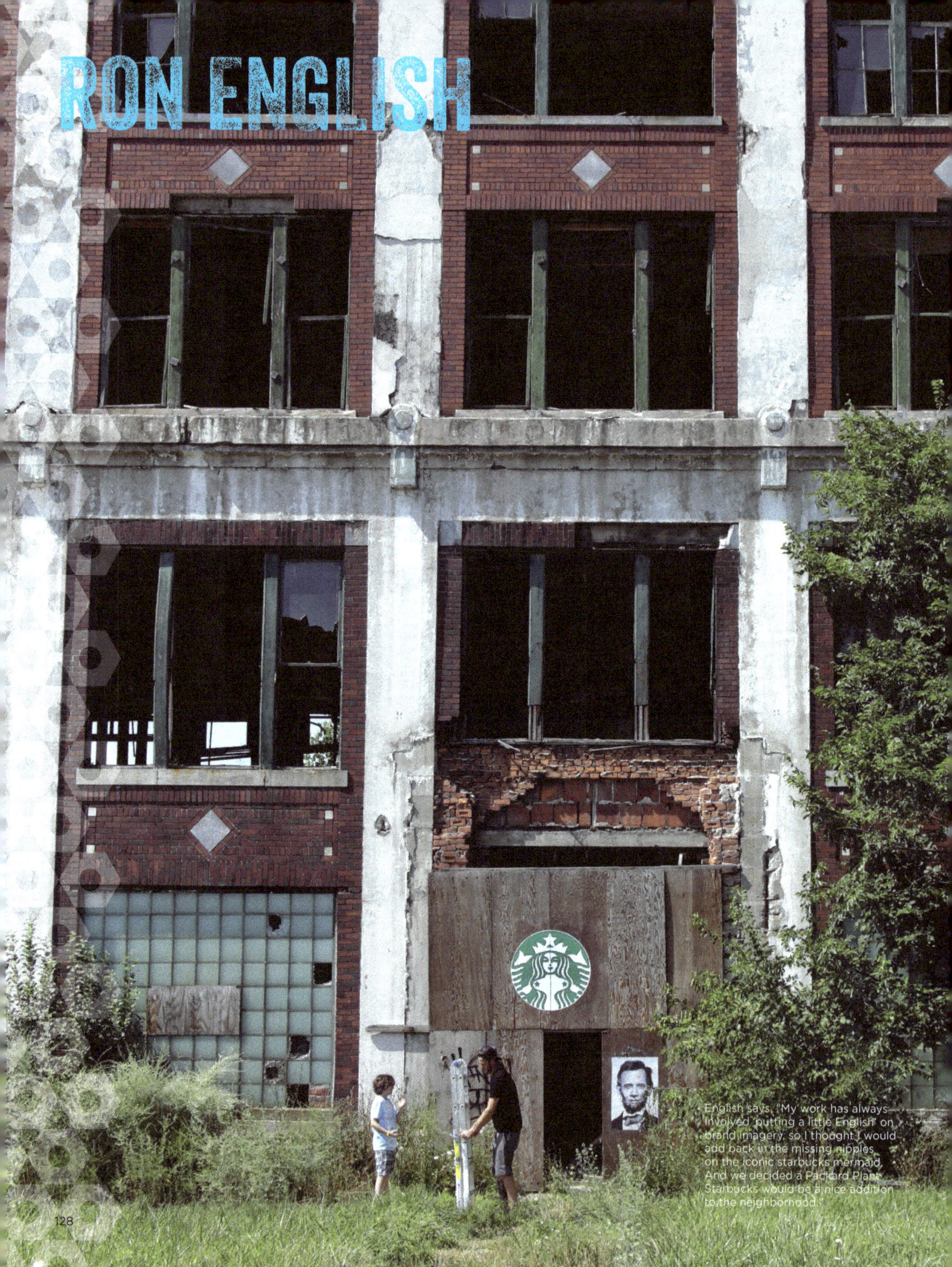

English says, "My work has always involved 'putting a little English' on brand imagery, so I thought I would add back in the missing nipples on the iconic starbucks mermaid. And we decided a Packard Plant Starbucks would be a nice addition to the neighborhood."

On a wild road trip to Detroit, New York-based street artist Ron English got an even wilder creative vision.

In the vision, Detroit stars as the hub of a new kind of creative universe. Think Disneyworld, *small d*, sans goofy.

"It's a great American city with a big void in the middle of it," says Texas-born English. "If I had my way, I would do a huge Disney-esque theme park that would be half outside, half inside. You would invite artists to design crazy rides, and you'd build it inside so that all of the lines were like these art installations. The visual experiences would be the magic of the place. Detroit would be the greatest place to stand in line."

Oddly, English's convictions about the resurrection of Detroit grew out of a visit to one of the city's most iconic ruins, the old Packard auto plant. In 2011, he drove his family to Motown, partly to introduce his children to his wife Tarssa's hometown and partly to leave a few marks of his own on the Packard plant and other places around Detroit.

Like much of the world, English had seen photos, and he'd heard his wife's firsthand stories of the plant's haunting decline. When she was a child, the Packard plant was where she went to play. "I guess I didn't realize how immense it was," English says.

A video camera captured the family's art-making and the antics of their great Detroit vacation. Meanwhile, the city itself captured English.

"Right now there's this global movement called street art that doesn't have an epicenter," says English, known the world over for his photorealist paintings. "If Detroit isn't that, it will be soon. It's really nurturing a new cultural explosion."

For the uninitiated, a word about English: he is POPaganda, widely considered a seminal figure in street art, routinely tagged the king of culture jamming, an art bandit with a penchant for perverting pop culture and making visually provocative statements on pirated billboards. In other words, he's over-the-top. To the extreme is where English goes and where he thrives, painting wherever a muse strikes him, including unauthorized murals on the Berlin Wall and on the Palestinian separation wall.

Yet English insists his vision for Detroit was fueled by the city's realities. "There's a lot of empty space. You have a huge workforce in Detroit," he says. "They already have an infrastructure. They already have hotels. And the city is right there in the middle of the country, so it wouldn't be a hard deal for people to come literally from anywhere."

While it sounds wild, English says, it's wildly possible because of the abundance of artists migrating to Detroit. "If you're not a fifty-year-old blue-chip artist, you're not living in New York anymore," English, fifty-three, says. "What do artists need? They need space and a tolerant environment."

Two years have passed since his road trip to Detroit, and English still talks about the city's "insane possibilities" like a man mesmerized. Credit the Packard plant and its power, after all these years, to energize tourists and thieves.

"When we were there, by mid-afternoon the parking lot was full. People were driving halfway across the country to see an abandoned factory. And to see people still looting it for copper wire; man it's like, that's insane. How do you loot something for fifty years? It just makes you realize how insanely impressive all that was at some point. "

English sees himself returning to Detroit. What he'd paint and the global statements he'd make are sketchy, except that his work would involve prodding people to question the city's emptiness: "I have a lot of love for Detroit, because it's like God, it's so beautiful. I take great pride in the things American people accomplished there. Detroit just needs a huge rethink, that's all."

A POPagandaland, perhaps?

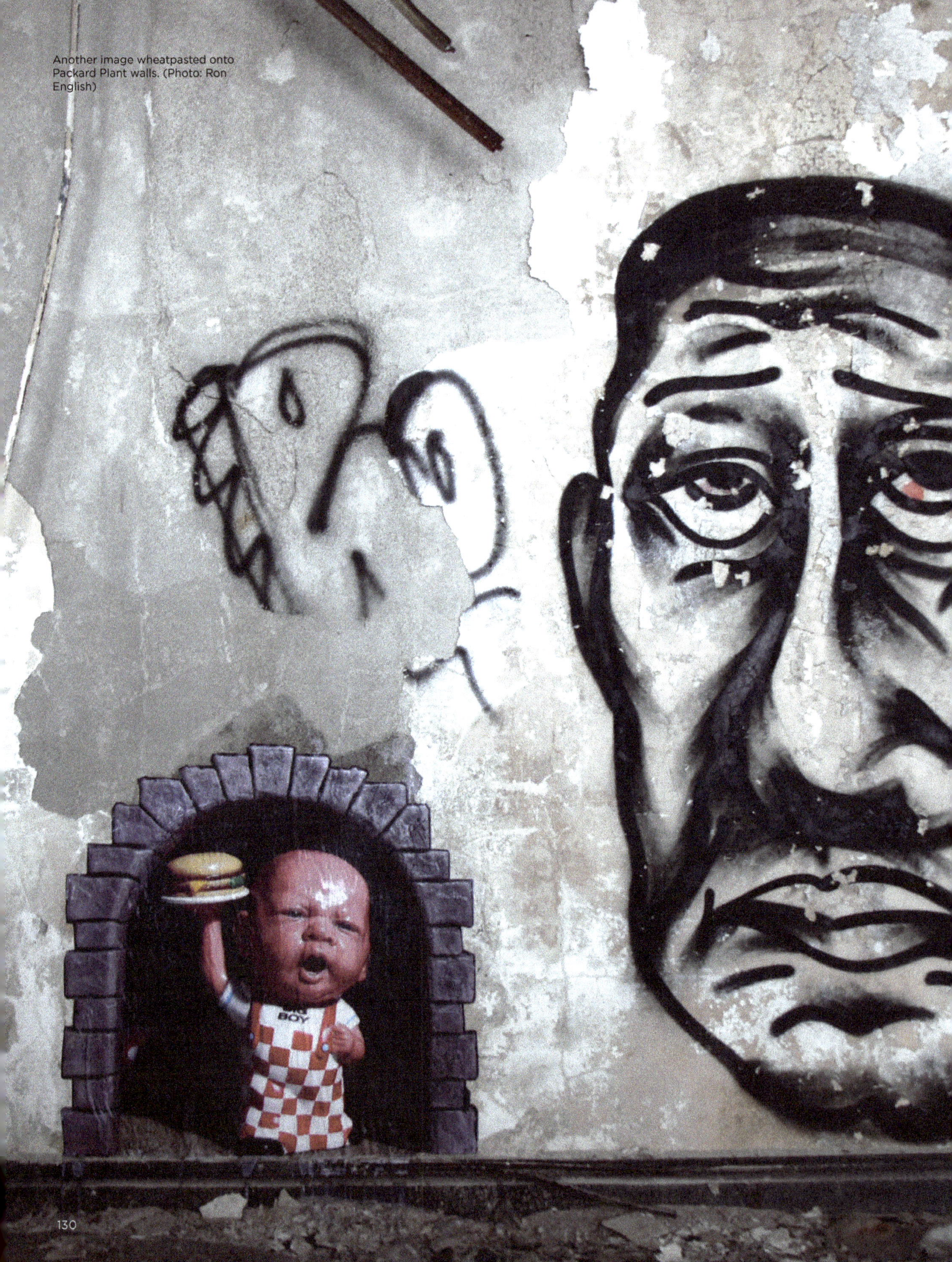

Another image wheatpasted onto Packard Plant walls. (Photo: Ron English)

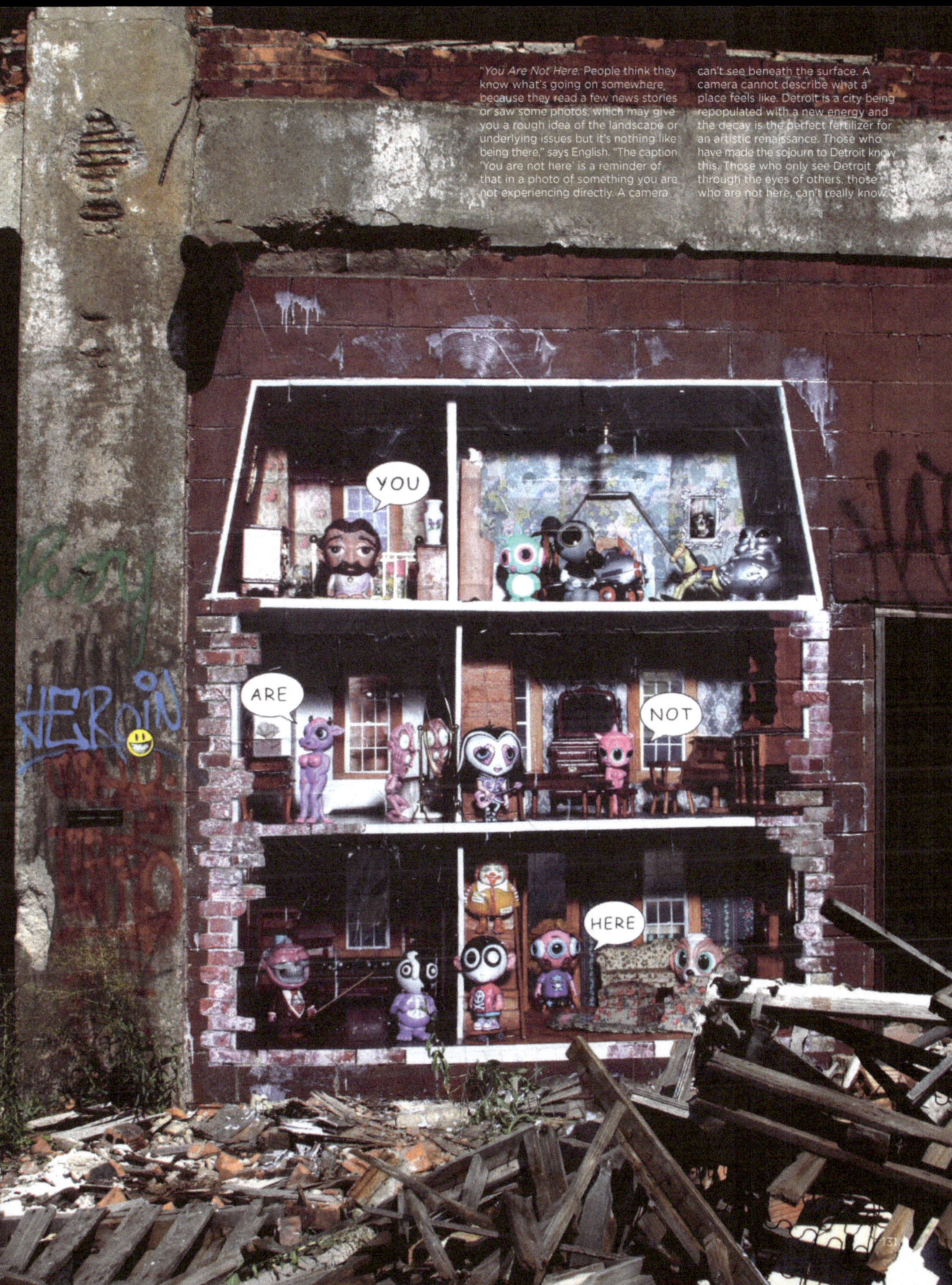

"*You Are Not Here.* People think they know what's going on somewhere because they read a few news stories or saw some photos, which may give you a rough idea of the landscape or underlying issues but it's nothing like being there," says English. "The caption 'You are not here' is a reminder of that in a photo of something you are not experiencing directly. A camera can't see beneath the surface. A camera cannot describe what a place feels like. Detroit is a city being repopulated with a new energy and the decay is the perfect fertilizer for an artistic renaissance. Those who have made the sojourn to Detroit know this. Those who only see Detroit through the eyes of others, those who are not here, can't really know."

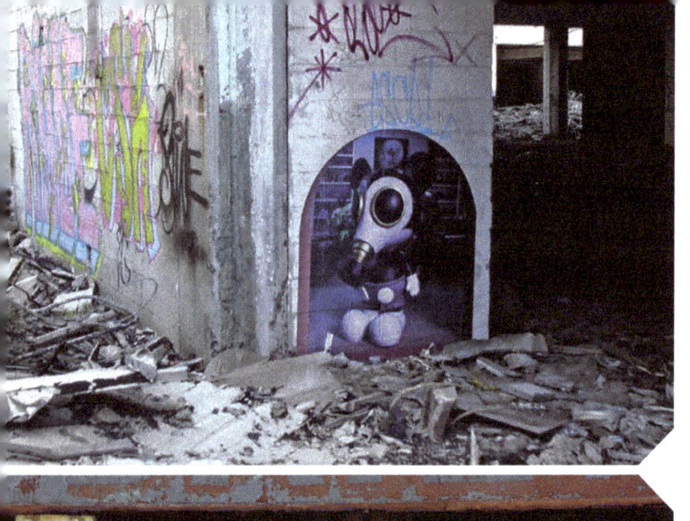

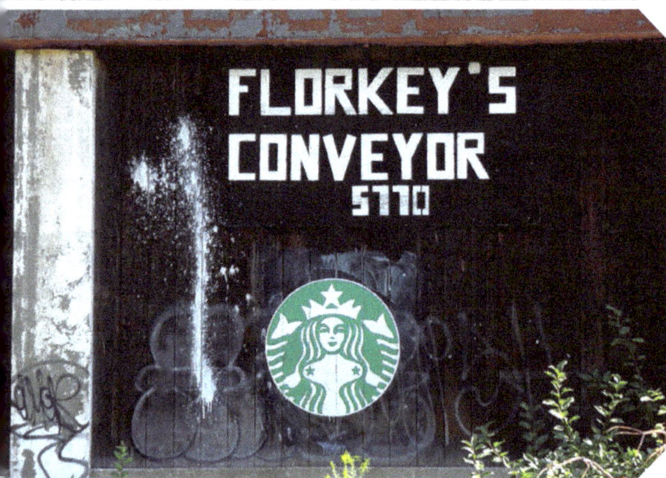
FLORKEY'S
CONVEYOR
5770

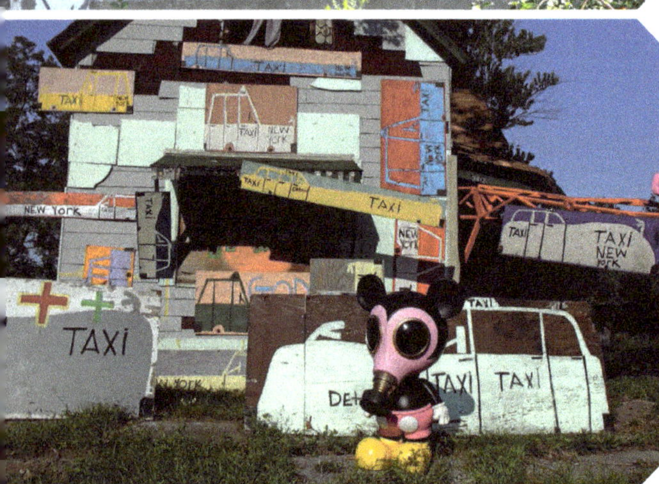
TAXI
TAXI
NEW
YORK
TAXI
TAXI
TAXI

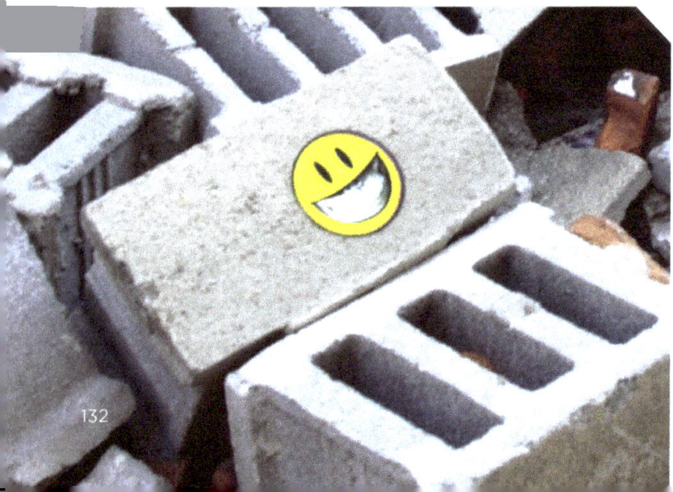

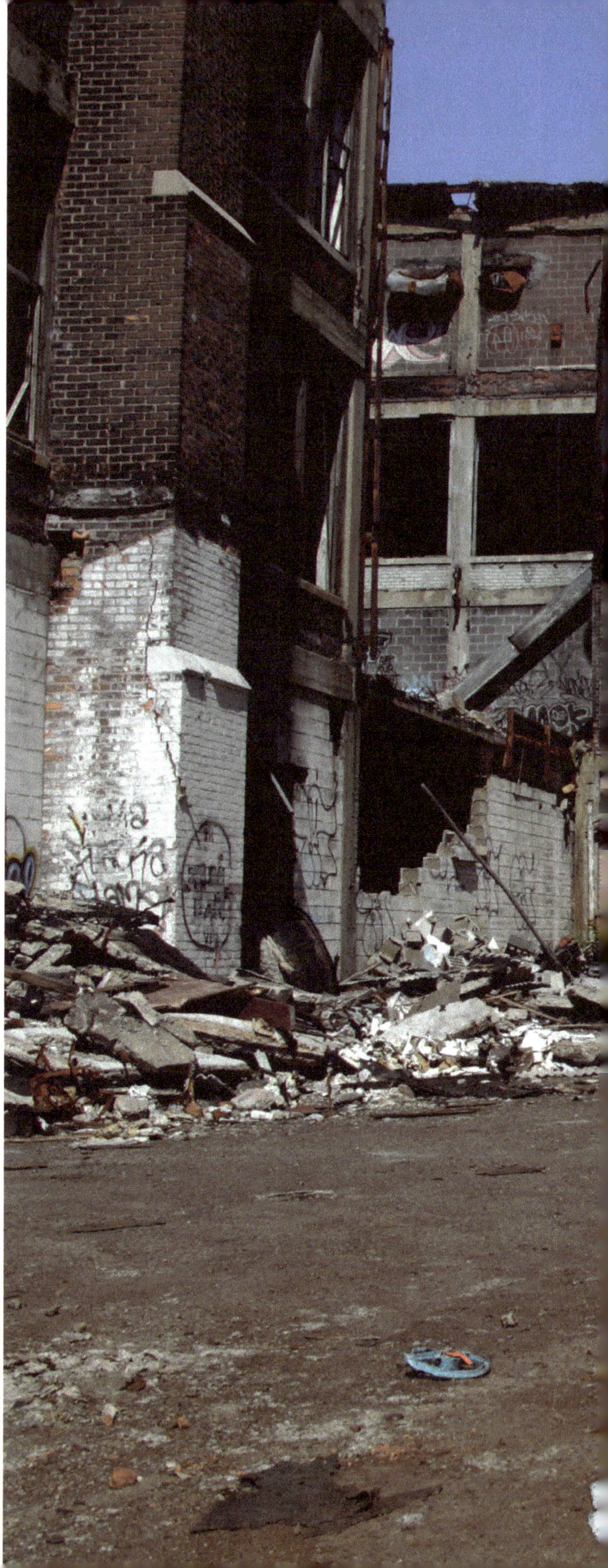

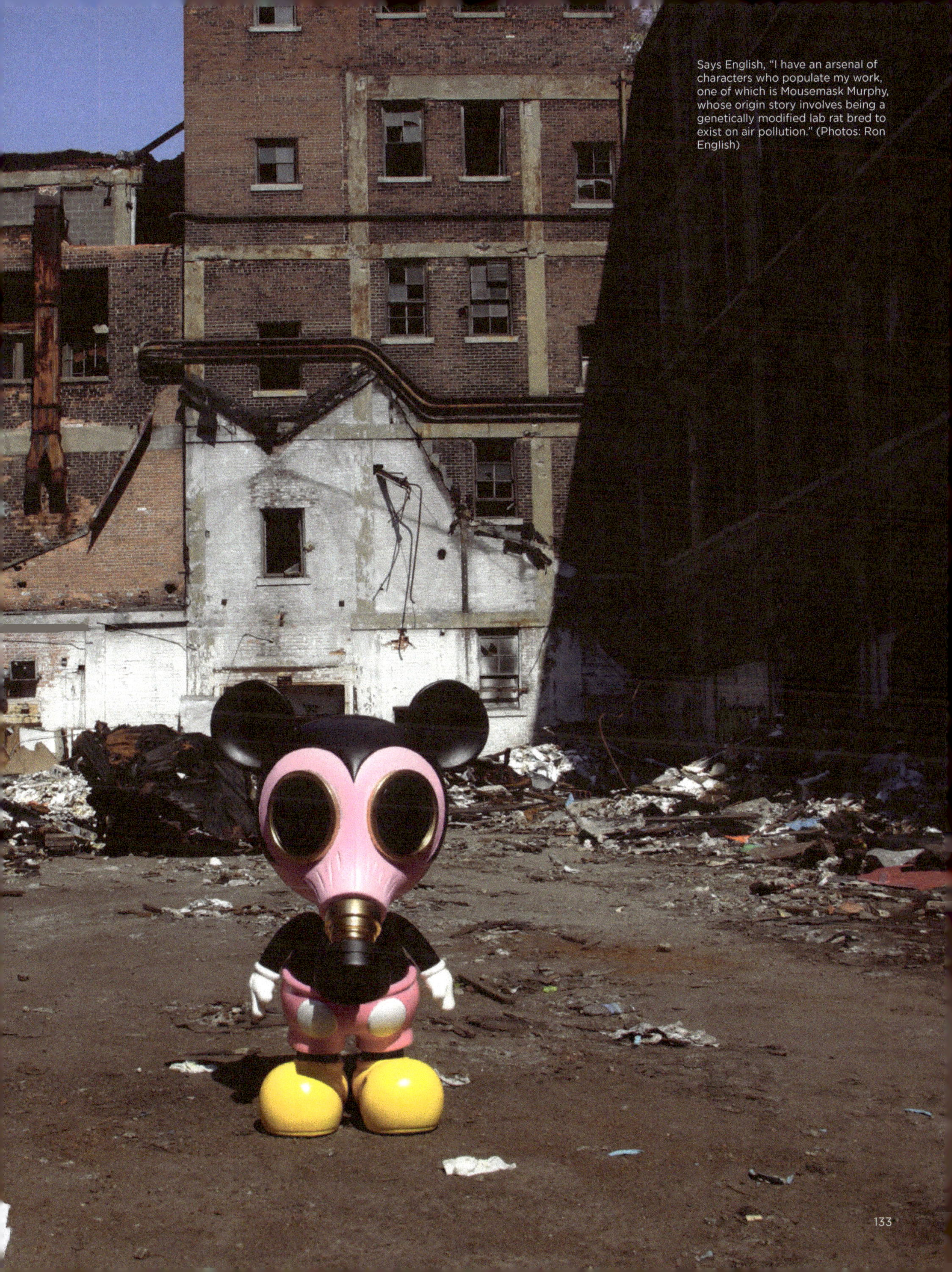

Says English, "I have an arsenal of characters who populate my work, one of which is Mousemask Murphy, whose origin story involves being a genetically modified lab rat bred to exist on air pollution." (Photos: Ron English)

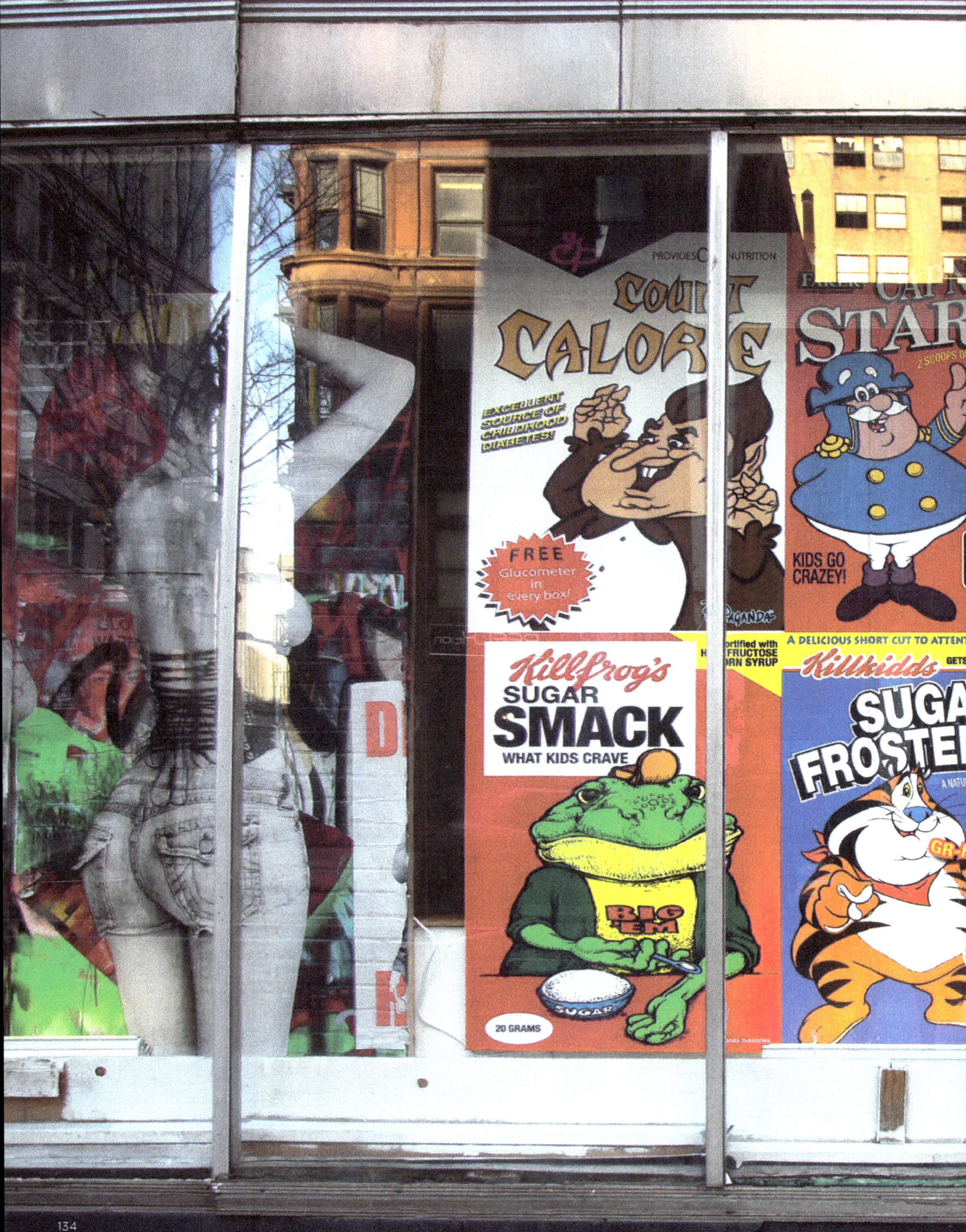
EXCELLENT SOURCE OF CHILDHOOD DIABETES!
FREE
Glucometer in every box!
KIDS GO CRAZEY!
Killfrog's
SUGAR
SMACK
WHAT KIDS CRAVE
BIG 'EM
SUGAR
20 GRAMS
Killkidds

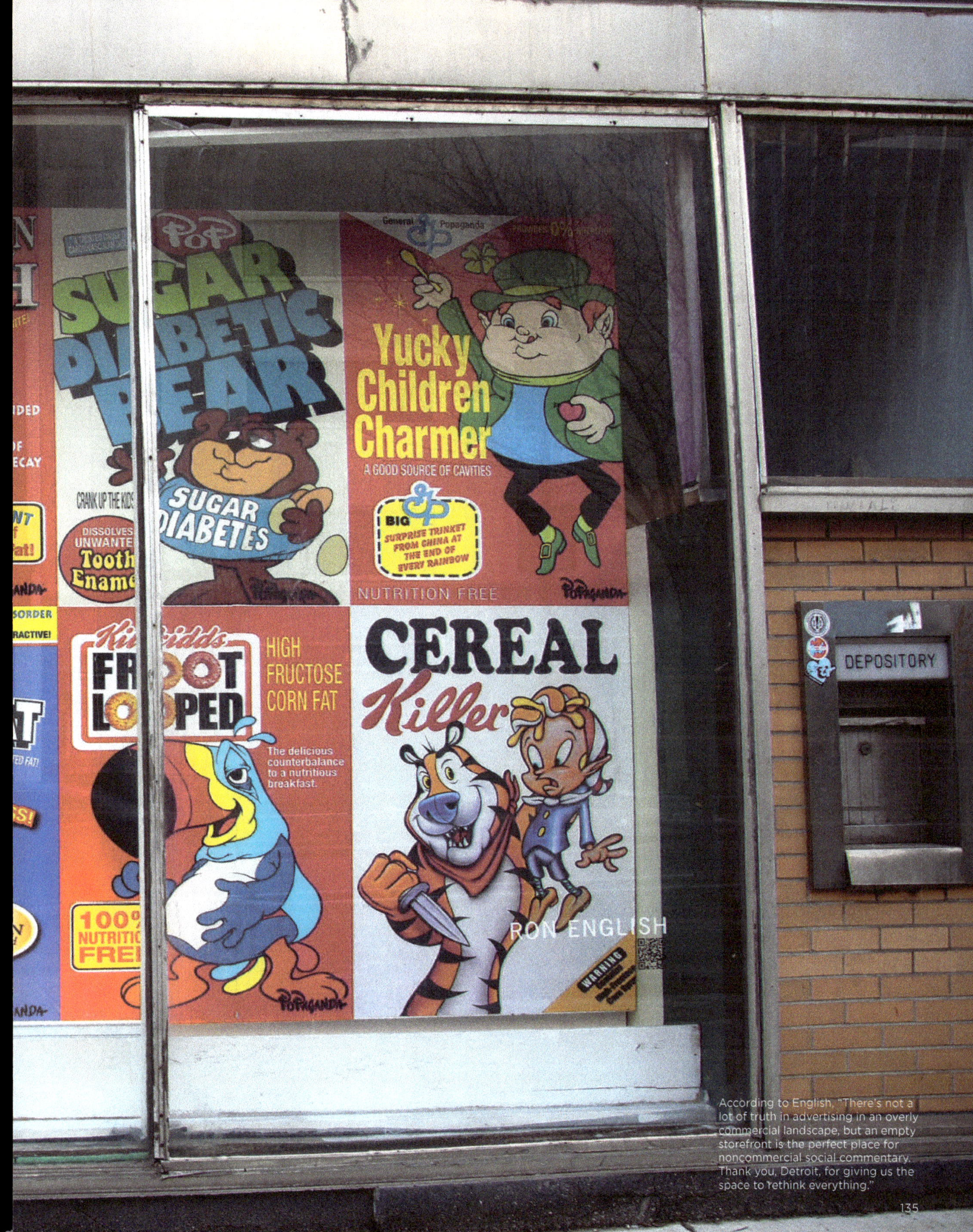

According to English, "There's not a lot of truth in advertising in an overly commercial landscape, but an empty storefront is the perfect place for noncommercial social commentary. Thank you, Detroit, for giving us the space to rethink everything."

GREG FADELL

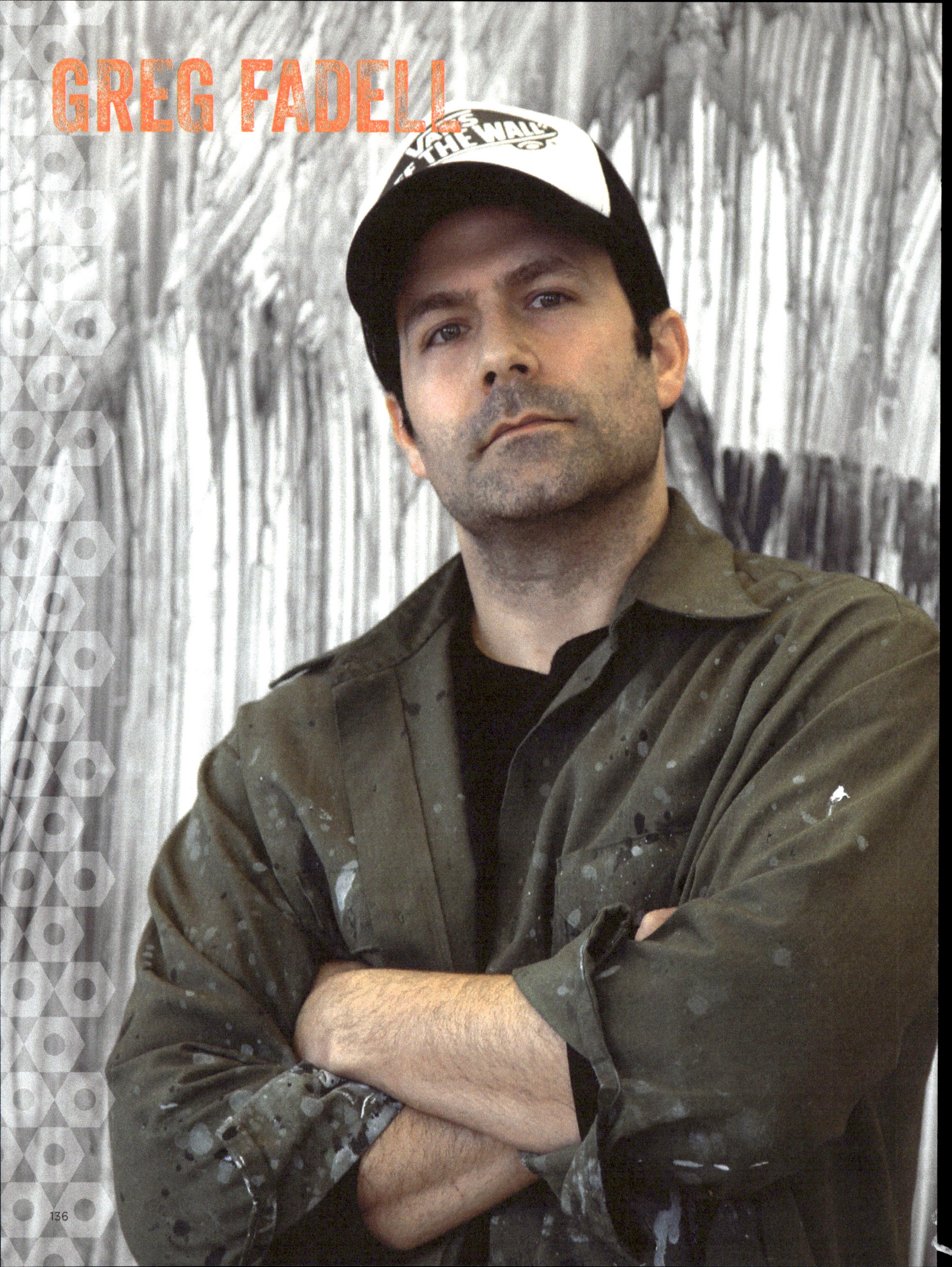

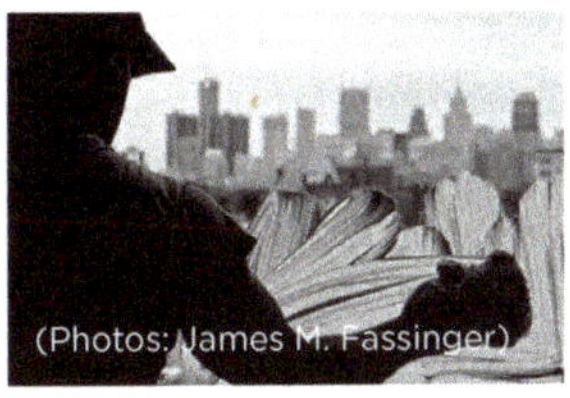

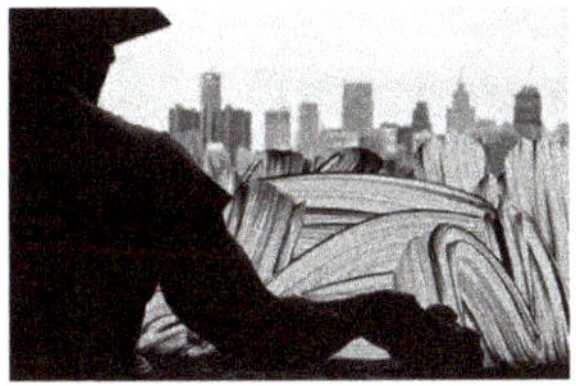

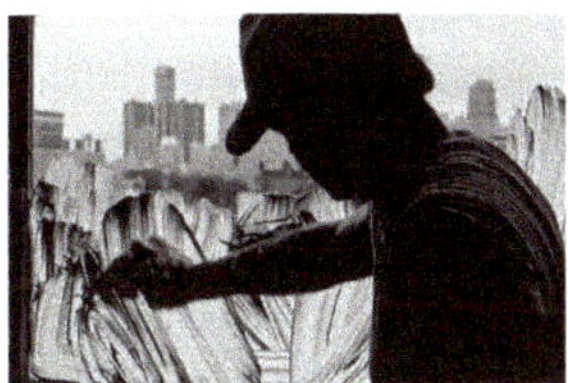

(Photos: James M. Fassinger)

First thing to know about the artist Greg Fadell: he believes in nothing.

Nothing stirs him. He finds form in nothing and nothing pleases him more than illuminating its possibilities to those who believe art must always be about something.

"I don't expect for anyone to think what I'm doing is something," he says. "I'm actually just going, 'You decide.' I'm comfortable with nothing."

In 2012, Fadell took the idea to the extreme, unveiling a brave series called what else but *Nothingness*. Fadell, a University of Michigan-trained filmmaker and photographer and a former professional skateboarder, gave Detroit a major introduction to the concept, covering the walls of the Re:View Gallery with six-to-eight-foot-tall paintings, abstract in every way. No titles other than *Nothing*. No colors other than black and white. No artist's explanations, just the work.

Fadell's fascination with nothing stretched beyond the paintings hanging on the gallery's walls. He made the building part of his exploration, too. In a live installation, Fadell painstakingly "whitewashed" four stories of windows, in unoccupied lofts, with custom semi-transparent paint and dramatic brushstrokes. From prep to finish, he spent seven weeks on the project, which measured eighty feet tall and fifteen feet wide.

During the day, the starkness of the white paint was supposed to prod people to look up as they walked by. The art of Fadell's work emerged at night, as the windows were backlit. They became a glowing column straight through the center of the building. "It was really about looking at transition as art and being comfortable with that," explains Fadell.

The project received modest funding from the Detroit Design Festival, an annual community-curated showcase celebrating design projects and concepts. "The idea fit in perfectly with where Detroit is. You can either look at it as this empty, abandoned place or you can go, 'Wait, I have a vision. I'm gonna make something happen,'" Fadell says.

In many ways, the project, which he titled *Paris of the West*, and the paintings were mirrors of Fadell's transition out of photography and back to a childhood passion for painting.

During a trip to Paris, where he'd gone to sort out his future, Fadell stumbled upon the French custom that would spark his interest in nothing.

"I came back to Detroit and started a new path from nothing," he said. "That's the idea of the paintings; they're about transitions. They're about starting again from nothing and being satisfied. There's a shell there, but you have to fill the shell."

One night while strolling, Fadell found himself awestruck by the way the light hit the whitewashed windows of a building he'd come across. "I was just blown away. I couldn't stop looking at these windows. People thought I was crazy." Fadell was determined to learn everything about the windows. But there was no deep meaning to uncover. The technique, he later discovered, was merely an artful way of signaling a building under renovation.

Still, Fadell kept the idea alive. "I came home and I just started working on painting what I saw. I had hundreds of pictures of windows with whitewash on them."

Fadell didn't just mimic. He developed his own semi-transparent paint to create the illusion on canvas that the paint is dripping and still wet. To achieve the effect, Fadell also designed his own brushes, and he taught himself to build his own canvases and easels.

Fadell's paintings, which list in the low-to-mid four figures, are starting to find homes. His wealth, he says, is in the work and the ability to envision it and create it as he sees fit.

"I tried to get away from art because it is illogical. There's really no reason to do it other than drive. Society isn't set up to support it. What I realized is, I can't worry," he says. "You have to make up your mind to say, Look, I've got a different checklist for success."

Perhaps the best evidence that Fadell's list is different is his determination to succeed from Detroit. He sees no better place.

"People say there's nothing here," he says. "Well then, that means everything's here, because every possibility in the world exists when there's nothing."

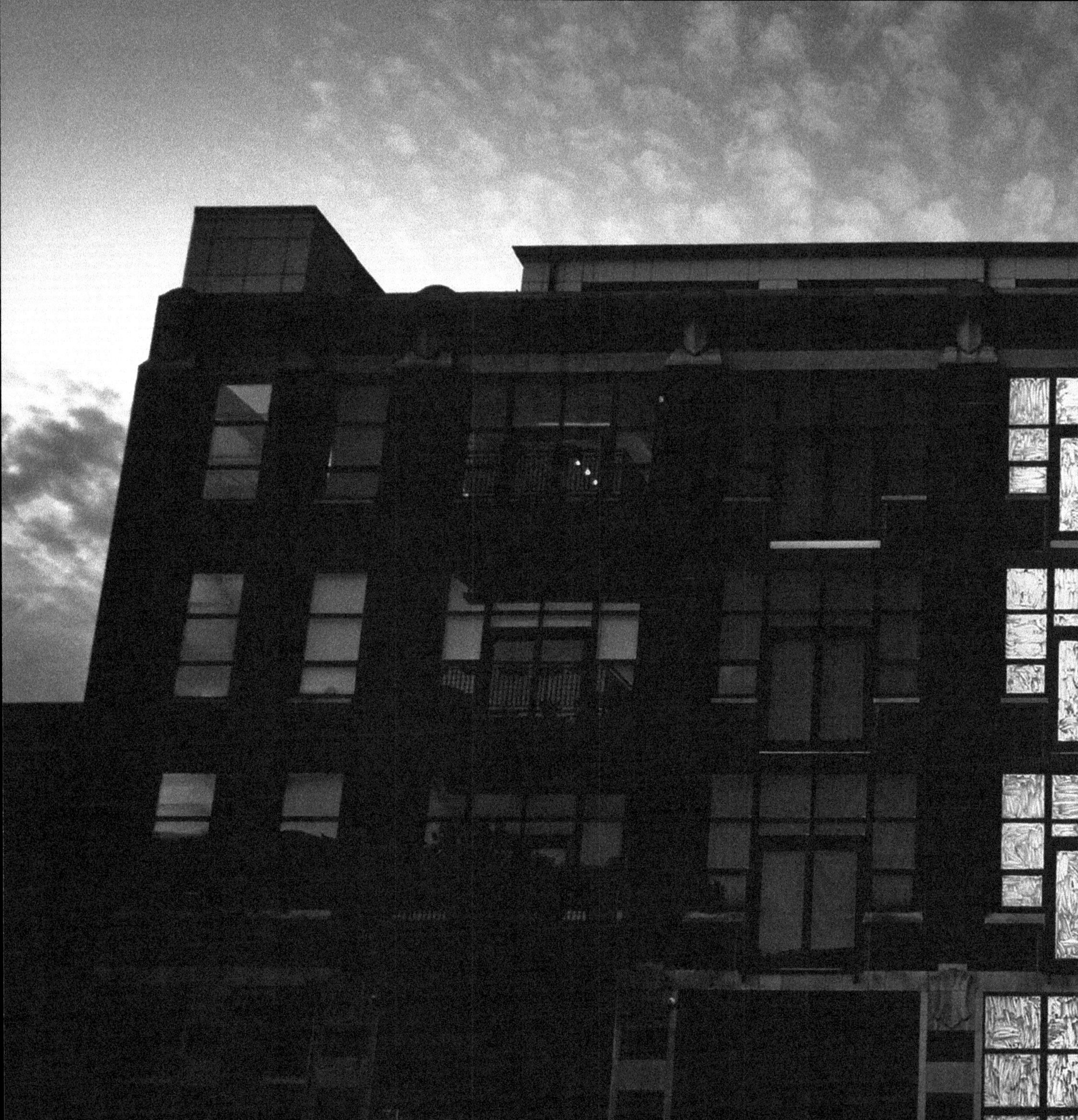

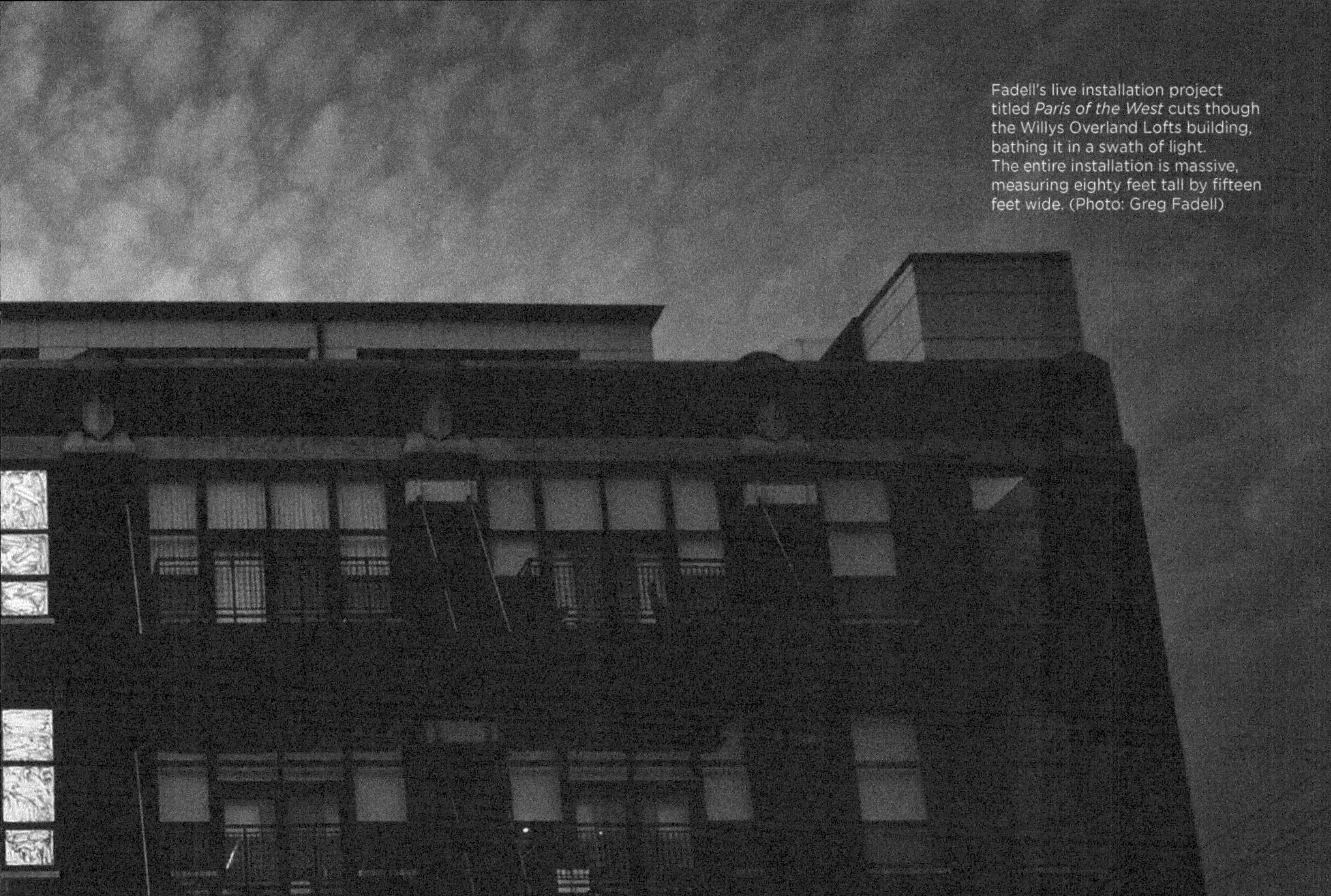

Fadell's live installation project titled *Paris of the West* cuts though the Willys Overland Lofts building, bathing it in a swath of light. The entire installation is massive, measuring eighty feet tall by fifteen feet wide. (Photo: Greg Fadell)

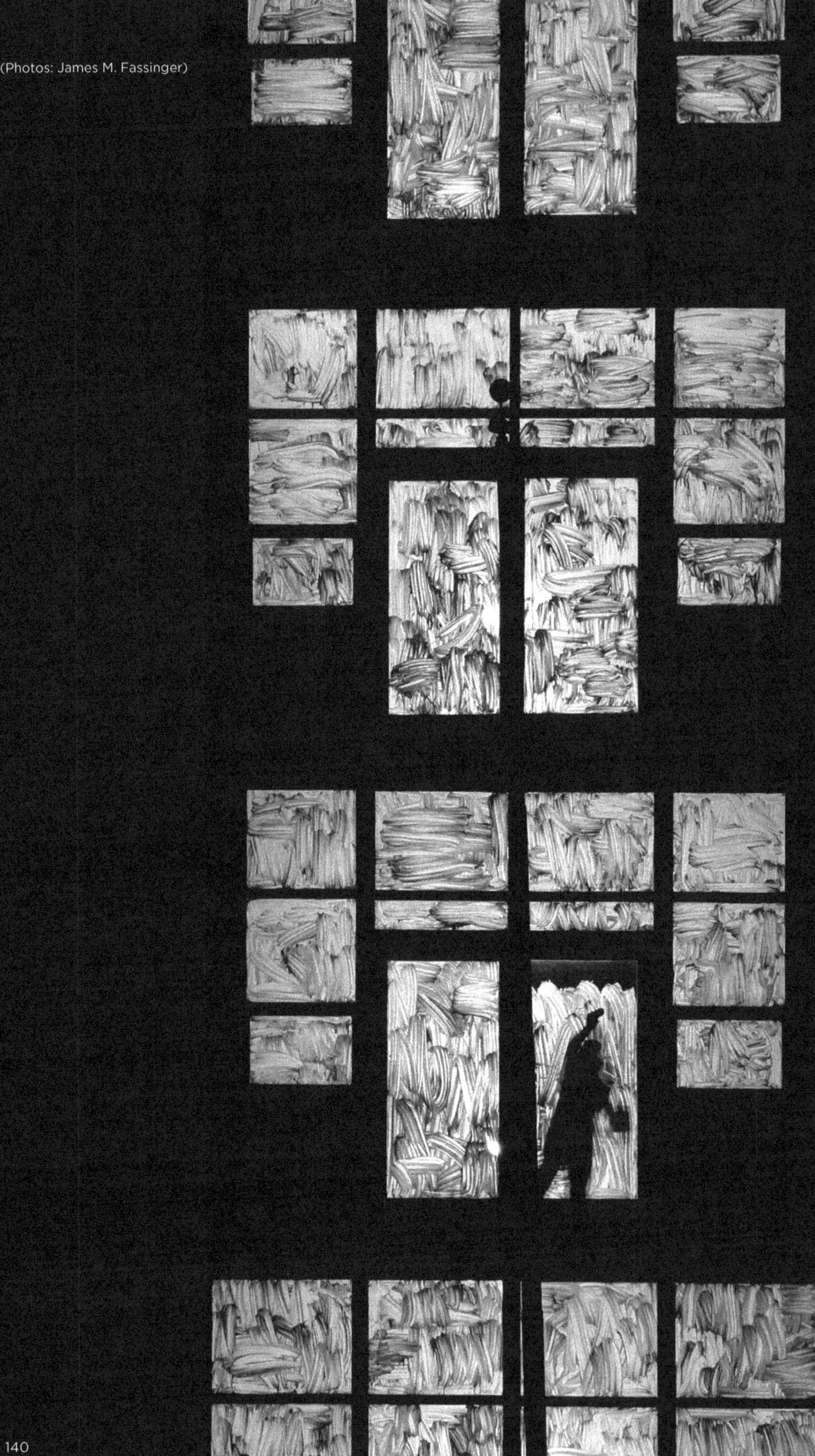
(Photos: James M. Fassinger)

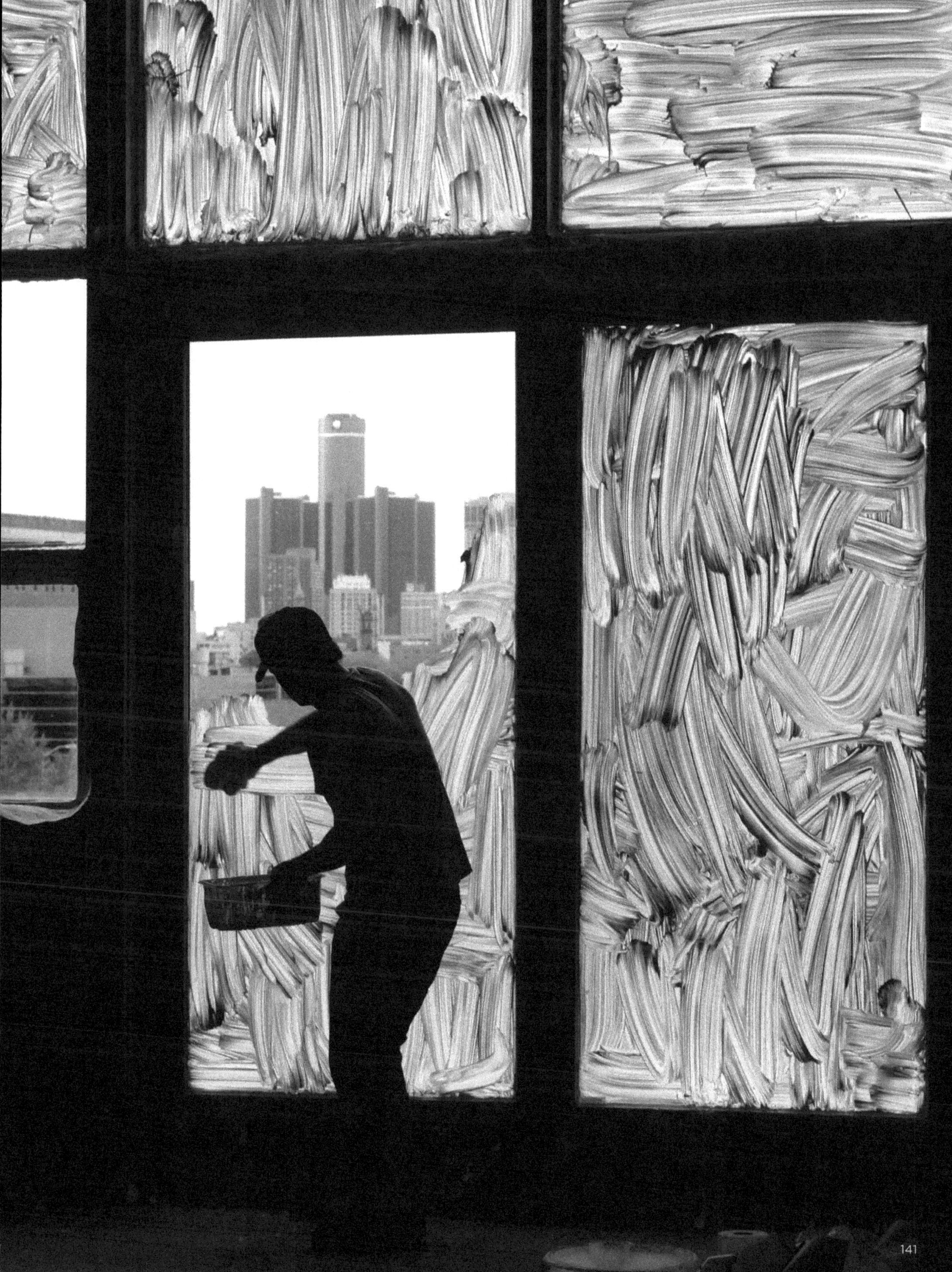

JEROME FERRETTI

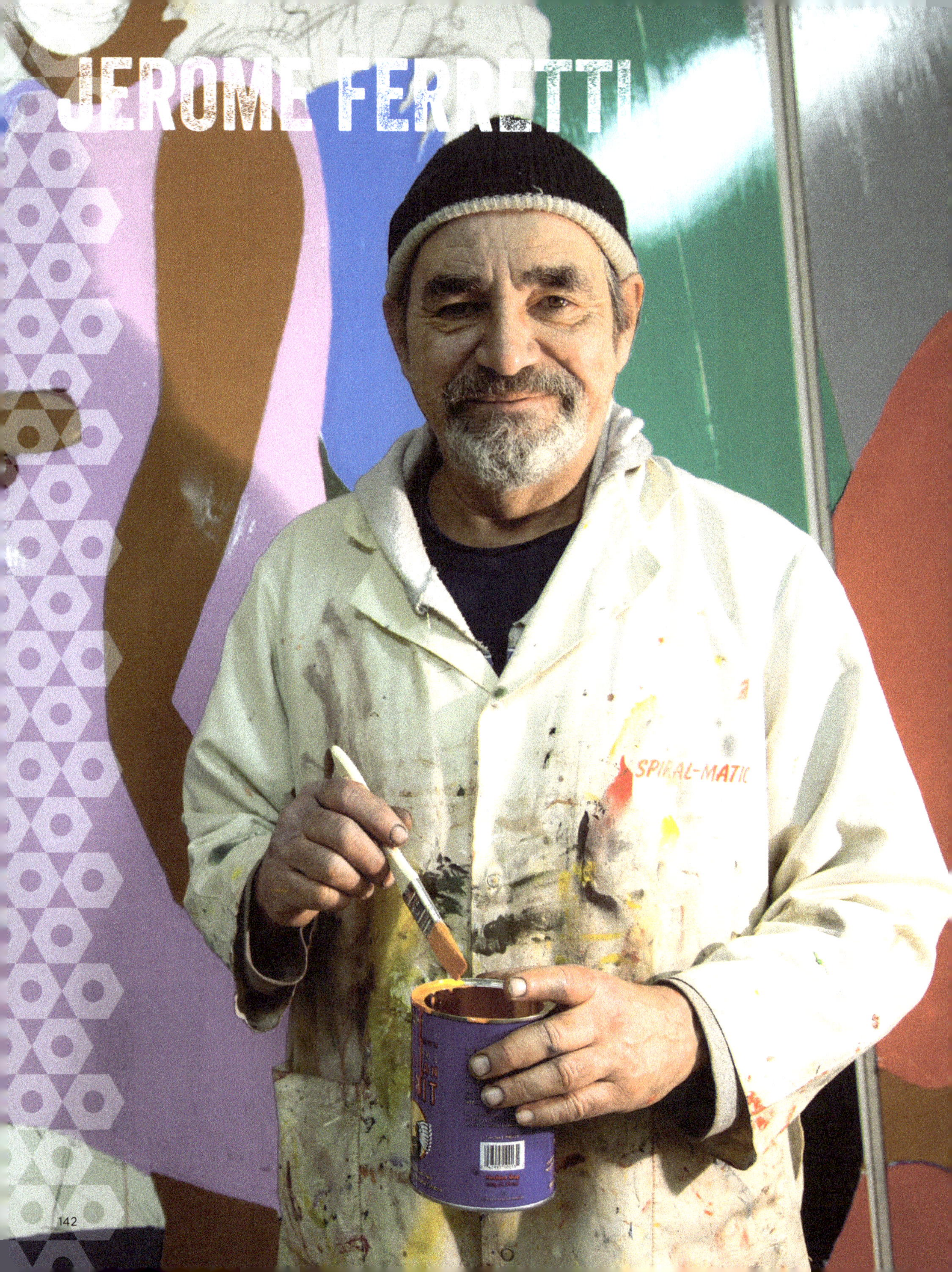

A cat made of bricks, shaped like a dome, and designed as a monument to a famed Detroit neighborhood, put artist Jerome Ferretti on the map.

In Corktown, everyone knows the man who made the cat, the one so big it's called *Monumental Kitty*. When Ferretti, a trained sculptor and painter, set out to design *Monumental Kitty*, he was ironically just trying to help cement the legacies of two neighborhoods, not his own. The cat wasn't even Ferretti's first idea.

In fact, when a Corktown citizens group commissioned him in 2010, Ferretti had no idea at all. "I went insane for two months," said the sixty-year-old Detroit native. "I couldn't come up with anything that stuck, other than wanting to do a geometrical shape, something that would draw the eye in an unusual way."

He also knew his creation had a big job to do. The community group wanted to bring new attention and a new sense of connectedness to Corktown and the old Briggs neighborhood, long divided by a pedestrian footbridge over I-75. Ferretti's vision would serve as an easily identifiable link.

The cat crept to mind by accident, over drinks at the home of a fellow creative whose actual cat wandered into the kitchen and caught Ferretti's eye. In an instant, his imagination unfurled. "It was like a nickel in a bucket. Boom," he said. "I had it figured out just from seeing his nose and his ears."

Though he'd filled thirty pages of drawings with "Irish-themed stuff and a whole lot of stupid ideas," the cat brought Ferretti back to what he views as a fundamental element of art in Detroit.

"You've got all of this history. You can't get around it. You almost have to start with it," he said. "Cats mean something because of the [Detroit] Tigers and the [Detroit] Lions but also there's the sphinx, the symbolism of it being part cat and standing guard on the side of the road, over an important land of riches and gold."

Monumental Kitty certainly lives up to her name. Its dome-shaped head stretches more than seven feet high, dwarfed only by a circular tail whose tip peaks just a few feet higher. Two dome-shaped paws flank kitty's enormous head, nine feet in diameter. "I was fascinated by the question of how do you take something that's flat and square and make it look to the world like it's round. That alone, I thought, would catch people's eyes."

A community-backed Kickstarter campaign helped raise the money to cover Ferretti's expenses. But final approval belonged to the land's owner, the Michigan Department of Transportation. To Ferretti's surprise, the concept of cat as muse didn't immediately wow MDOT. "I think they thought I was crazy," he said. "When I took my drawings in, there was this expectation that I was going to put a 'real' statue over there, you know, a man on a horse or something. A cat was the farthest thing from their minds, too."

Ferretti introduced one other unexpected element to his design, the use of bricks. "It's an unusual art form. Most sculptors use bronze or ceramic or stone," he explained. "But bricks stand for the whole urban experience of building. They're part of the history that's in your face here."

To further illustrate his point, Ferretti used only reclaimed bricks, three thousand of them. He even built special scaffolding from reclaimed and salvaged materials. Each brick, he says, was laid in place as a labor of love, so much so that Ferretti doesn't lament tumbling off of the scaffolding nearly ten times during the six-month project. He says he'd take the creative leap and the falls all over again for a chance to make a lasting creative statement.

That statement, Ferretti says, translates into a giant Detroit-style welcome. "There's a lot we don't have here, but creativity has never been one of those things. In good times and bad times, we're always creating. You name it; somebody is making something," he said. "But now it seems more wide open, like one giant art studio, with lots of wide-open spaces, found materials everywhere, steel and wood and junk, that's all being made into something. You can come up with an idea as wild as a cat made of bricks and you can do it here, if you're willing to step out there with it."

And if you're really lucky, Ferretti says, the idea you dare just might become larger than you ever intended.

"I figure two thousand to three thousand cars a day, maybe a million a year, go by this one statue that's on a service drive that's open twenty-four hours, seven days a week," he said. "I've done a lot of other things in my work, but to have one piece that widely seen—it's pretty monumental."

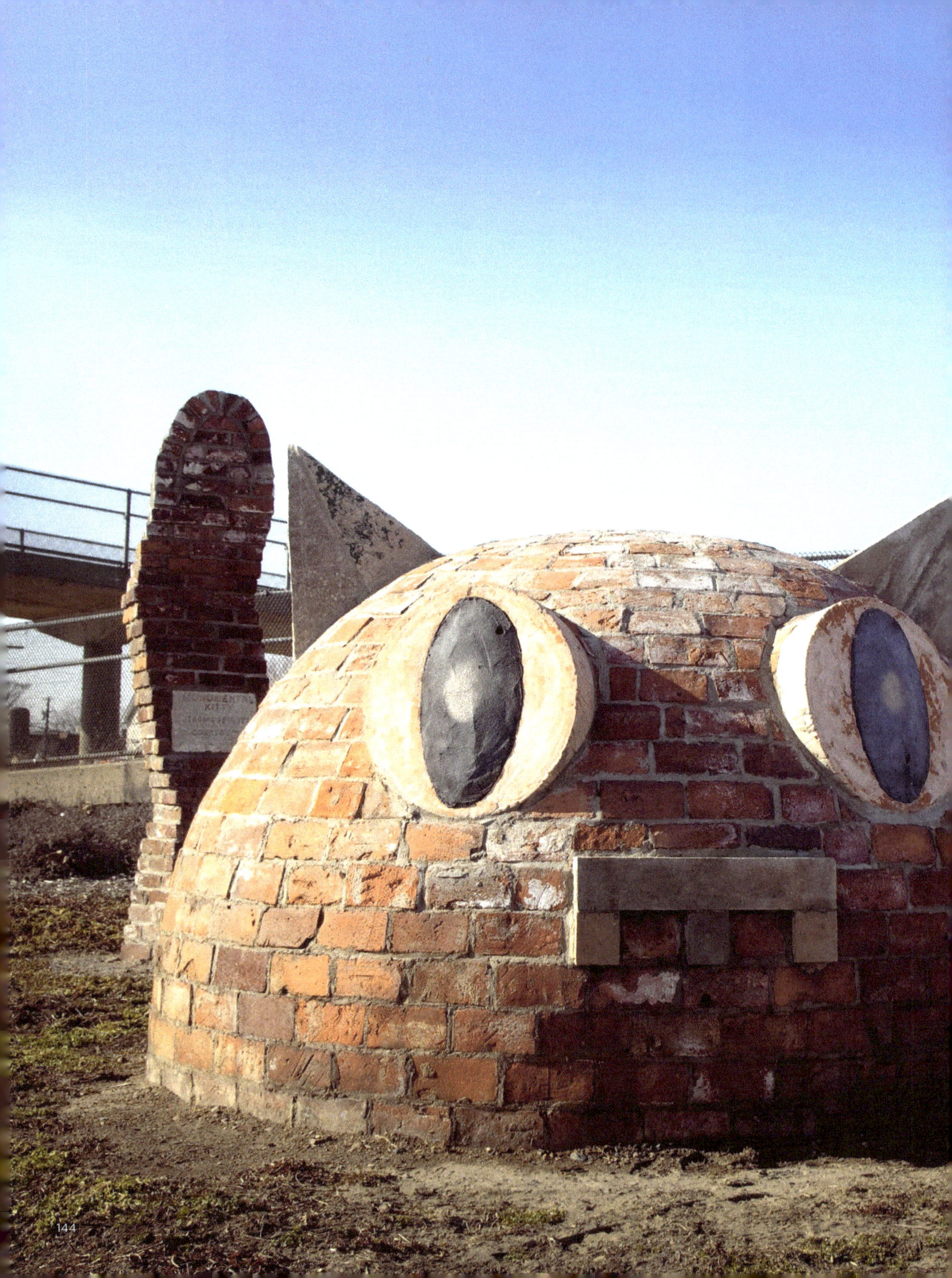

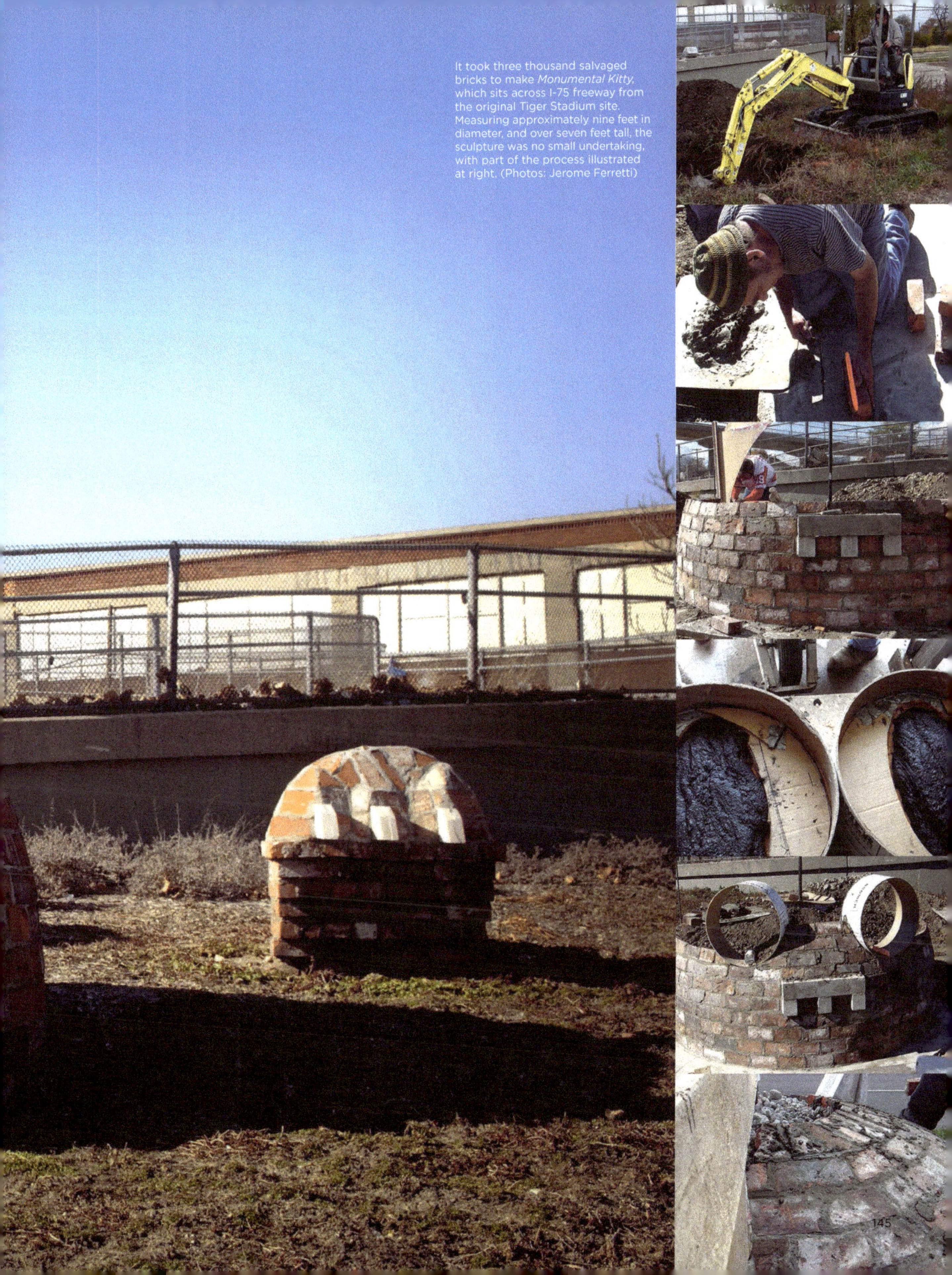

It took three thousand salvaged bricks to make *Monumental Kitty,* which sits across I-75 freeway from the original Tiger Stadium site. Measuring approximately nine feet in diameter, and over seven feet tall, the sculpture was no small undertaking, with part of the process illustrated at right. (Photos: Jerome Ferretti)

FIVE FELLOWS

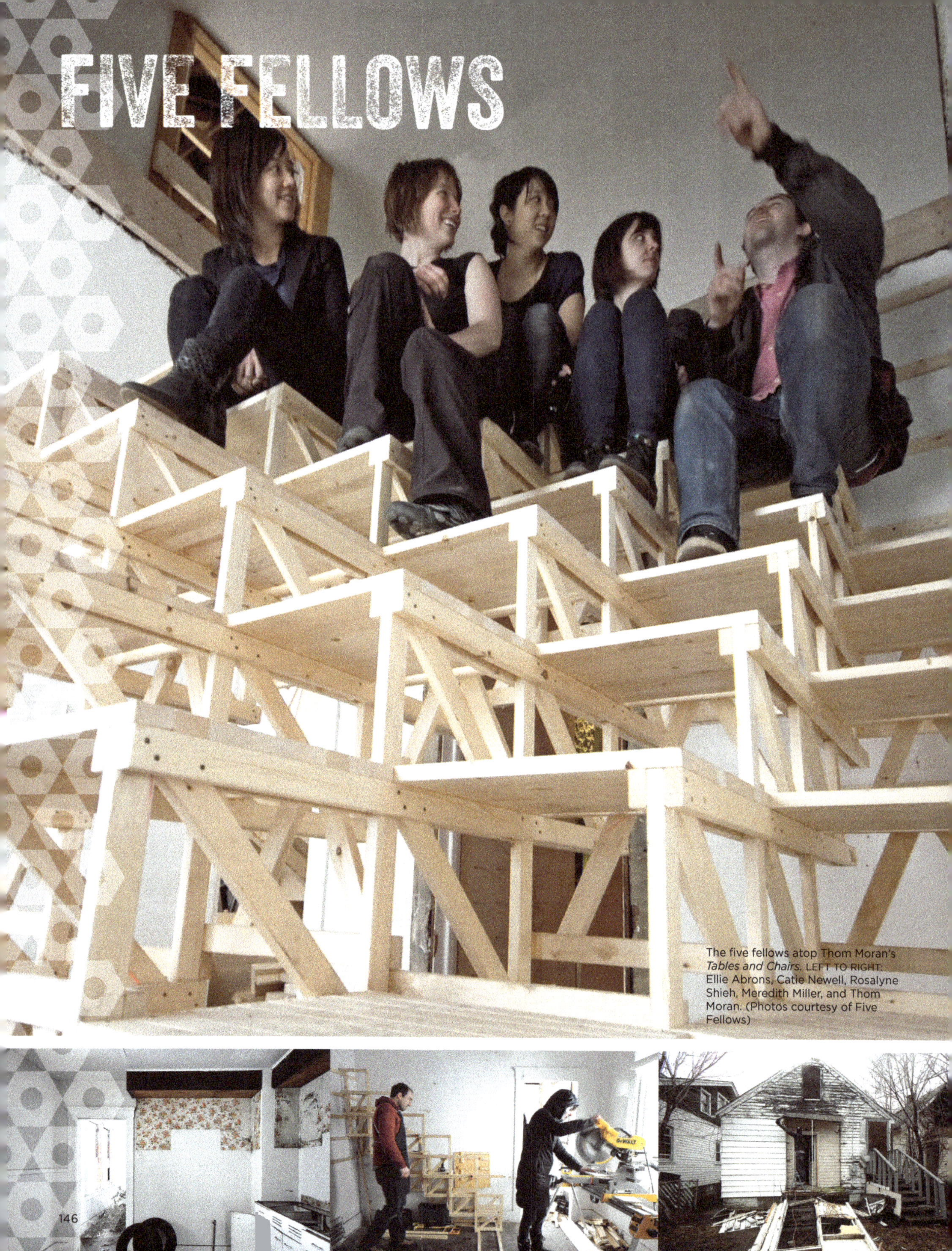

The five fellows atop Thom Moran's *Tables and Chairs.* LEFT TO RIGHT: Ellie Abrons, Catie Newell, Rosalyne Shieh, Meredith Miller, and Thom Moran. (Photos courtesy of Five Fellows)

Ellie Abrons/Meredith Miller/Thom Moran/Catie Newell/Rosalyne Shieh

On a street called Moran, art has taken over.

Virtually every house on the block has a story. Few of the tales are as wildly creative as the one at 13178 Moran.

In that house, the Five Fellows, as they came to be known around Detroit, did inspired things. As artists, they added new dimensions to their creativity, and they stretched the function of architecture, forging five imaginative yet unrelated design concepts under one single-family roof.

People fortunate enough to have seen the work still talk about the *Tingle Room*, the dome-shaped skylight called *About-Face*, the staircase that doubled, by design, as table and chairs, and of course, there was the garage out back. It became an experiment of a different kind, bridging light, sound, and even shifts in weather, as upward of a thousand holes were cut into the structure and filled with a thousand glass tubes to "amplify light conditions both natural and artificial."

Officially, the fellows were: Ellie Abrons, Meredith Miller, Thomas Moran, Catie Newell, and Rosalyne Shieh. Together, they were dispatched to Detroit as collective recipients of a prestigious research and teaching fellowship from the University of Michigan's Taubman College of Architecture and Urban Planning.

Like so many Detroit transplants, the fellows purchased the house at auction for just five hundred dollars. In fact, they got a tip about the house from an art duo that had already begun buying and rehabbing properties on the same block as art.

The fellows' house only vaguely resembled a habitable home. Doors and windows: gone. Plumbing and electricity: gone, too. Even the stairs were history by the time Five Fellows arrived. Their project, officially called Full Scale, was launched in the fall of 2009.

Each of the fellows chipped in a hundred dollars to buy the house that became their design playground. Acquiring the real estate proved easy compared to the challenge of trying to explain the project's value to a block besieged by blight.

In some cases, the answer was simple.

"This project intends to provide the house with its missing staircase," wrote Moran in an artist's statement outlining his contribution to the house. "The bleacher-like quality of the stair makes it a space to move through but also a place to linger. . . . It is something anyone can make with a saw, hammer and nails."

To Abrons, who designed the *Tingle Room*, the collaboration in an unlikely environment marked the project's real innovation.

"The project presents strategies of realization where, out of necessity, architecture is nimble, promiscuous and expedient," she wrote. "Architecture is cast more as a means rather than an ends—a means to finding opportunity rather than solving problems—a technique that resonates with the contemporary conditions of a city like Detroit."

Time seems to have agreed with Abrons's assessment. The house is still standing, surrounded by other houses, each aiming to reflect creativity's untapped practical possibilities.

ELLIE ABRONS

FIVE FELLOWS

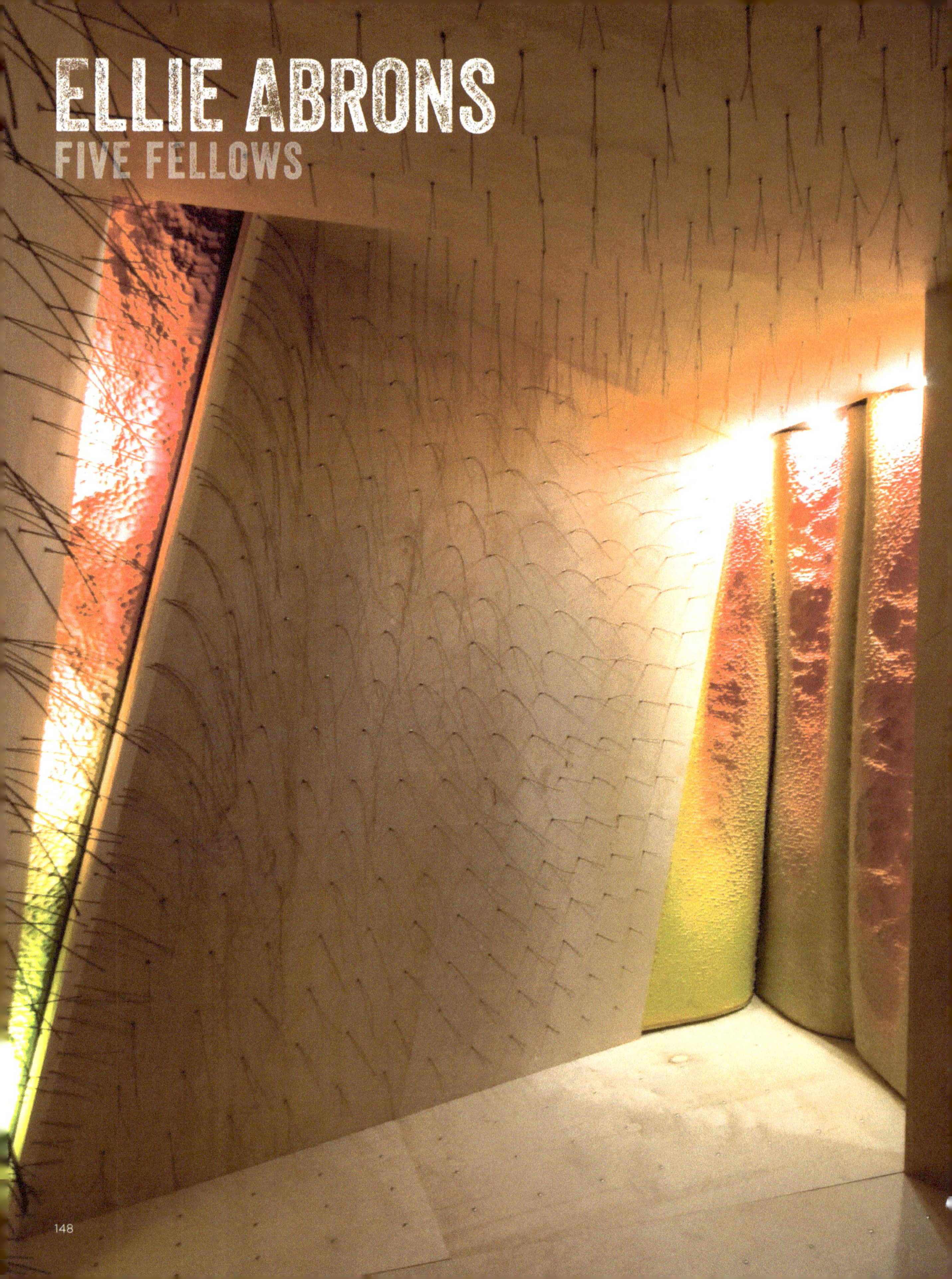

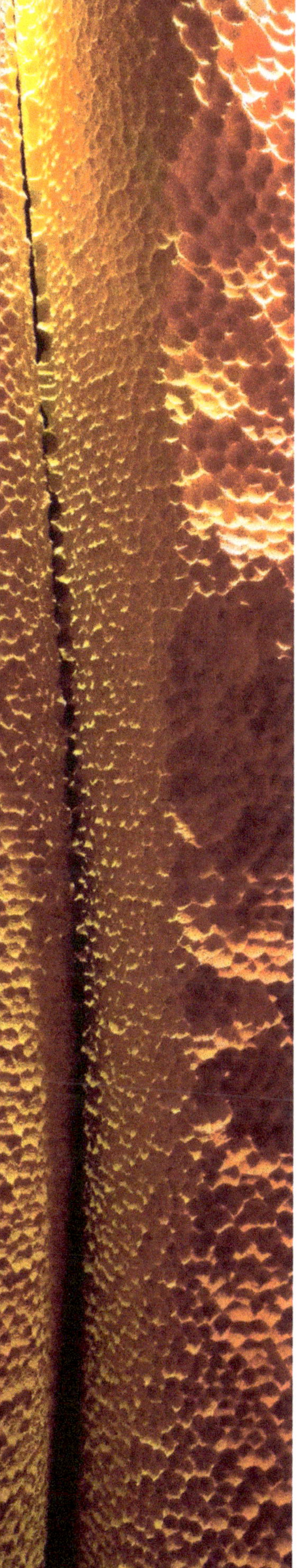

Tingle Room:

1

Abrons and Adam Fure's *Tingle Room* teases the imagination by rethinking the design materials typically called upon in the creation of floors, walls, window dressings, even paint colors. "Materials are carved, painted, smothered, or other-wise manipulated in order to extend their possible qualitative effects," she explains.

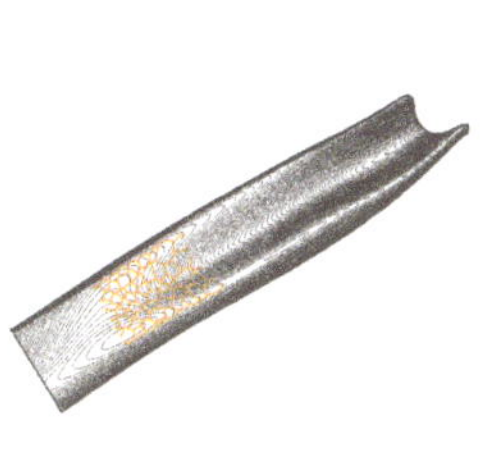

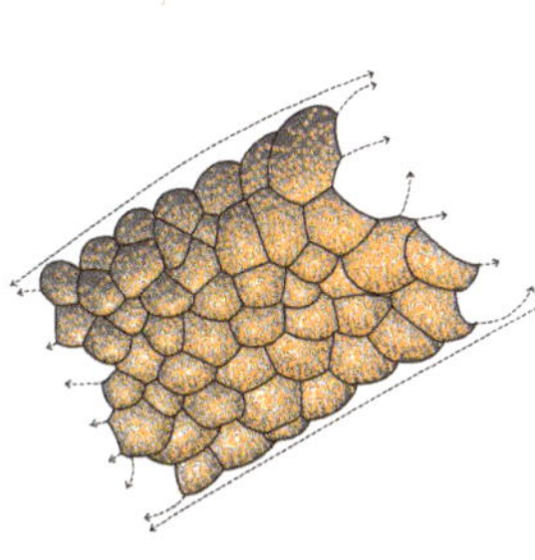

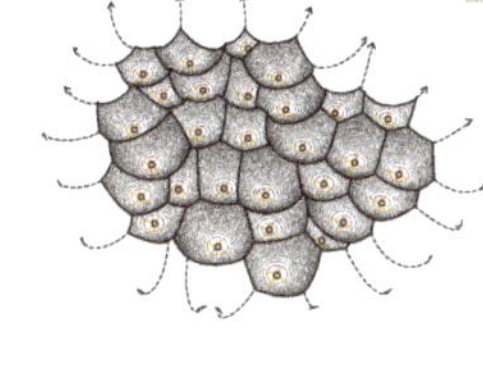

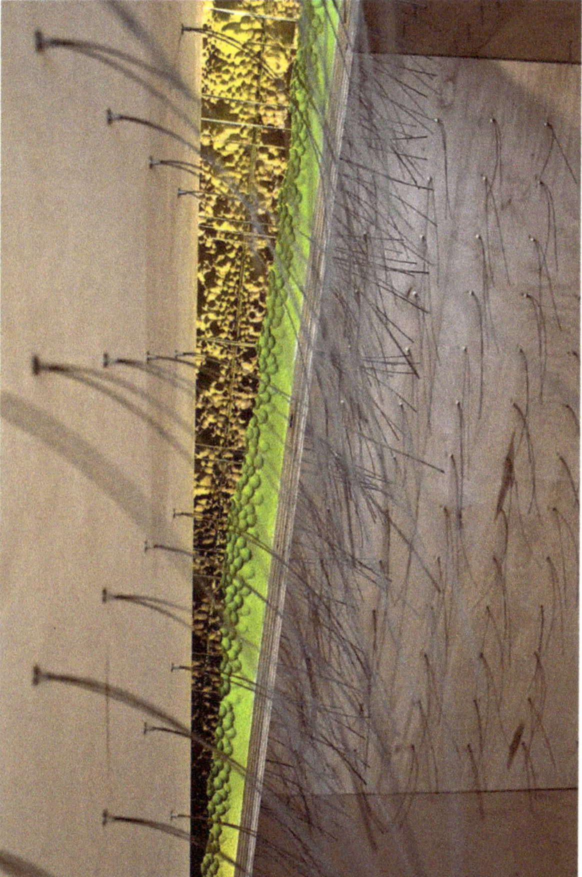

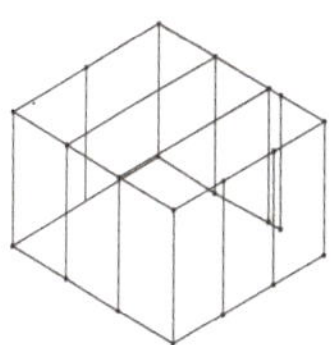

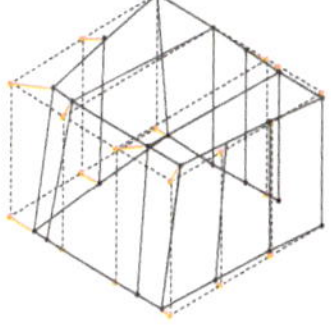

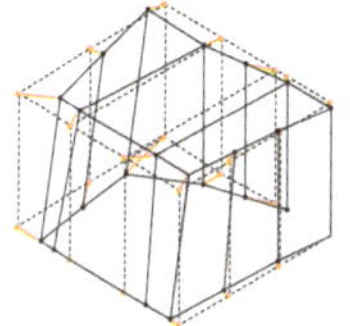

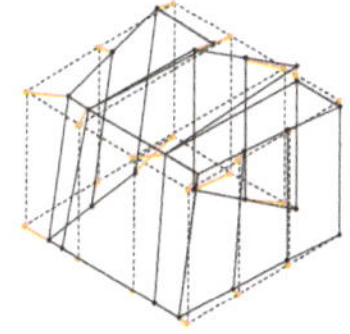

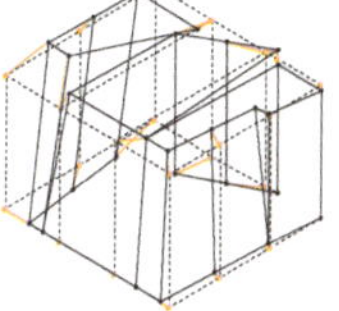

MEREDITH MILLER

FIVE FELLOWS

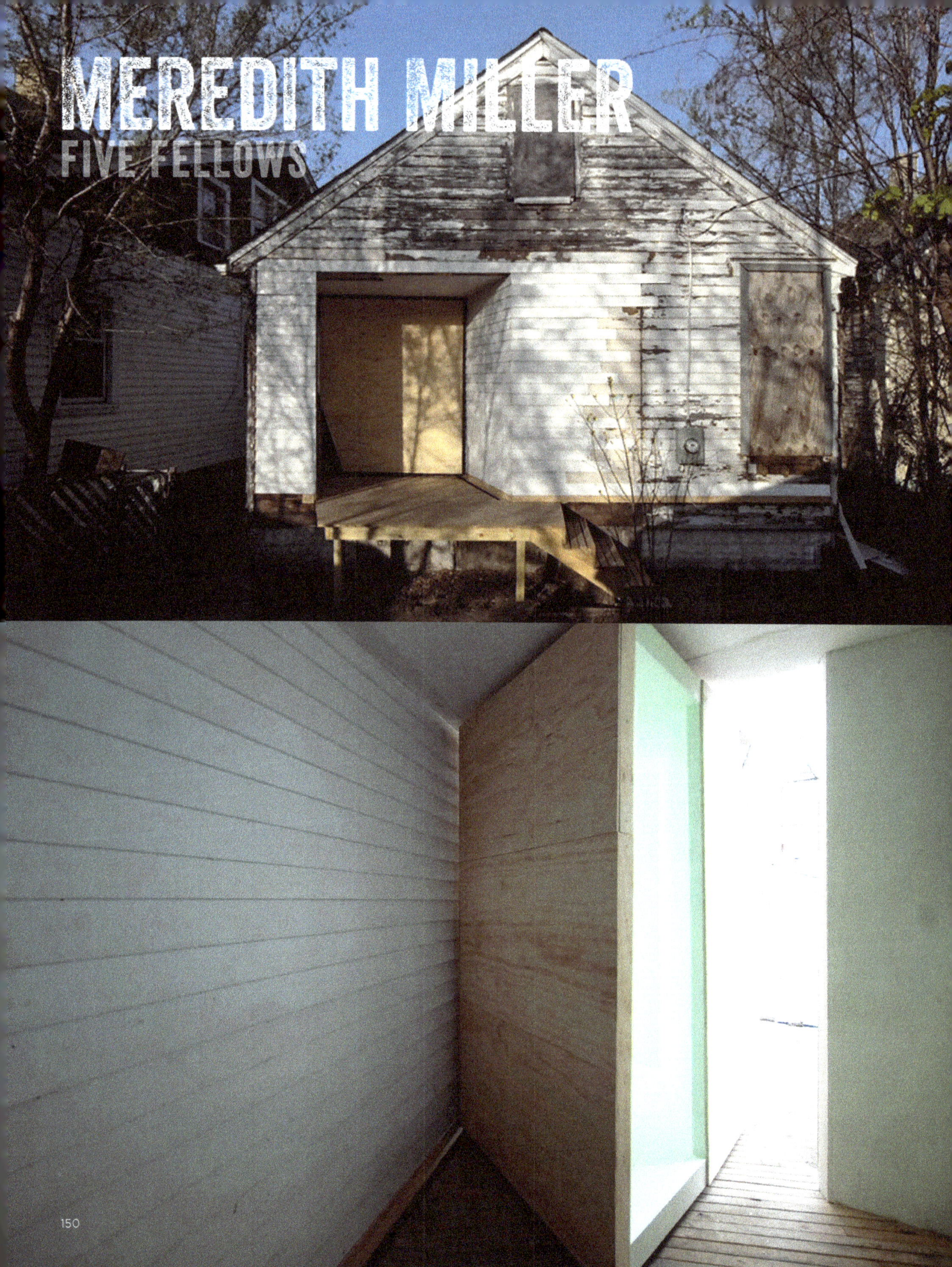

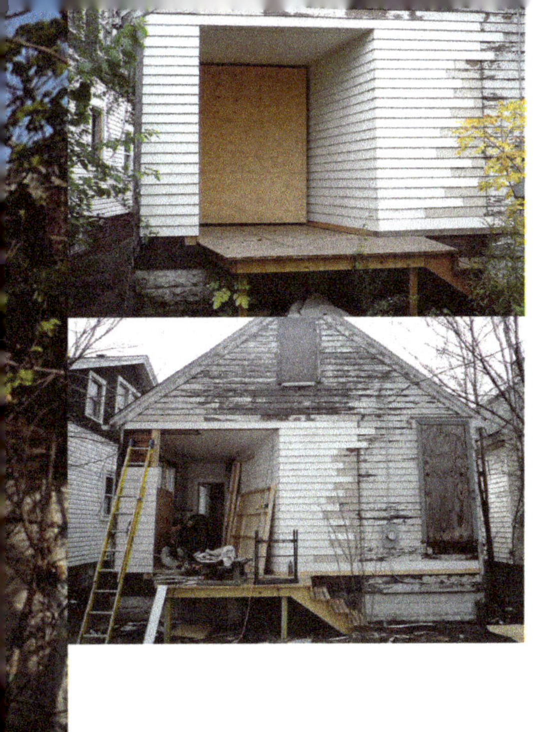

R.O.: 2

Miller created the only design fully visible from the outside of the house, an adjustable door, allowing privacy and security as well as an artful way to showcase the interior to a curious public.

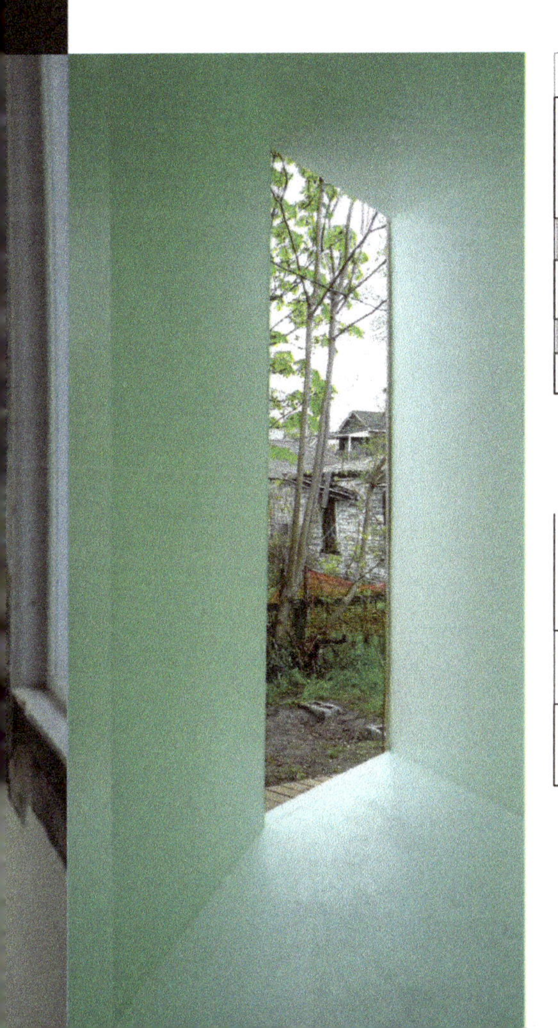

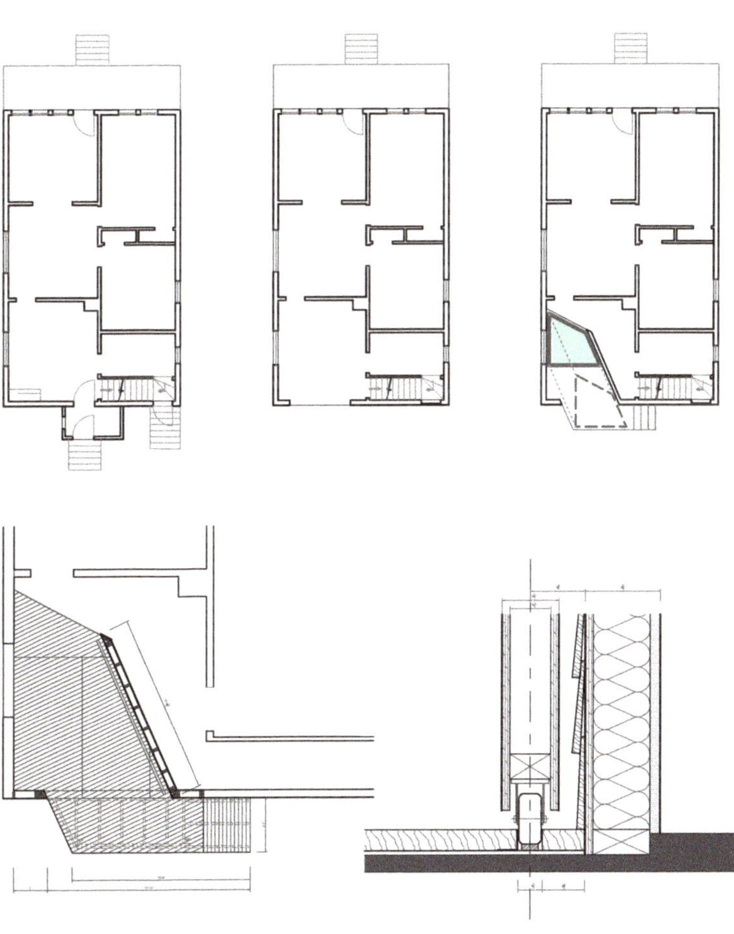

THOM MORAN
FIVE FELLOWS

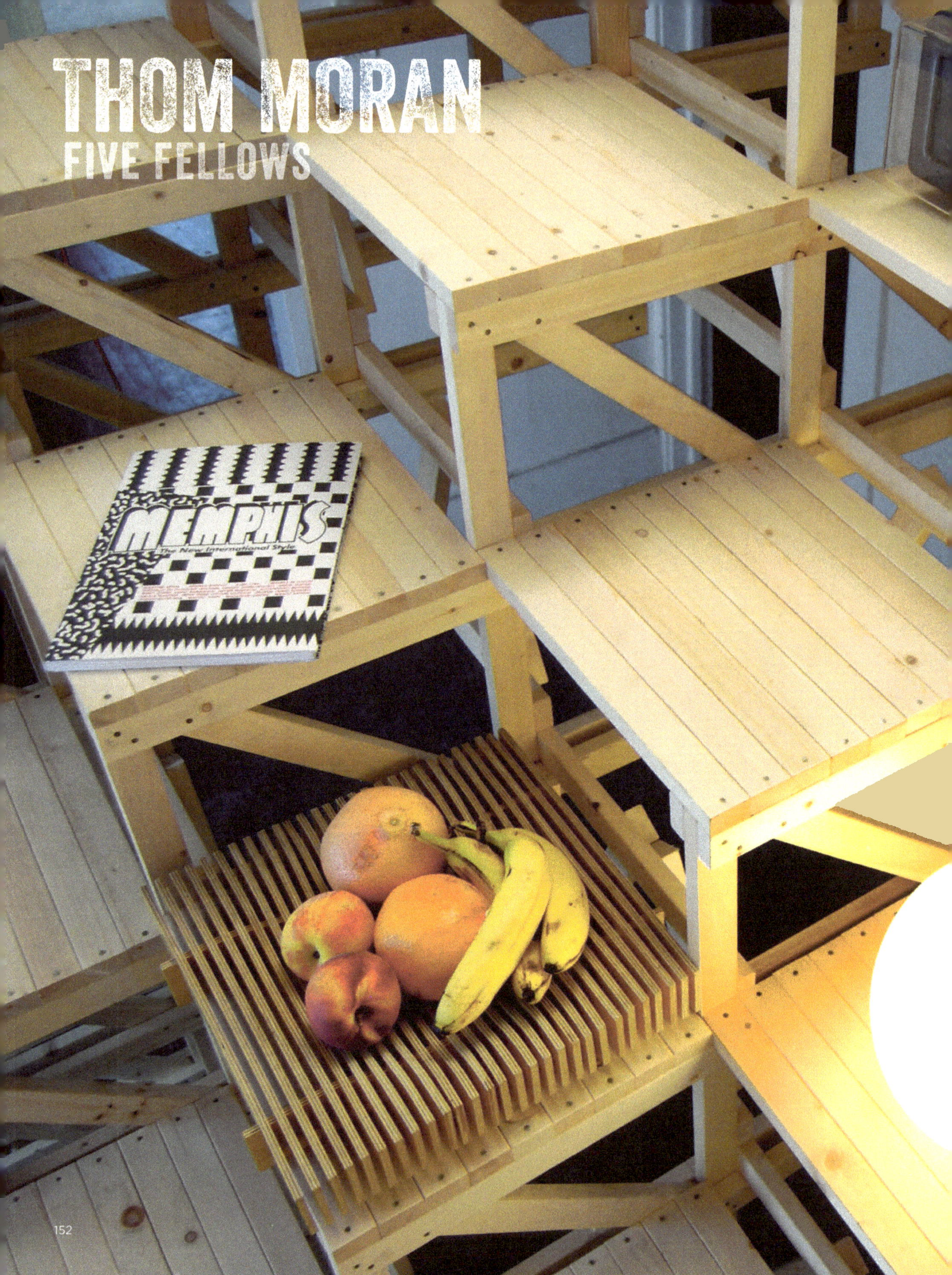

Tables and Chairs: 3

Using minimal supplies and a minimalist's vision, Moran replaced the house's missing staircase, transforming it into a multipurpose, unexpected work of art. With a bleacher-type design, the stairs function as a place to linger, to display items like books, and is a natural place to begin an exploration of the house. "The stair is constructed with only cheap 1x2 boards and nails. It is something anyone can make with saw, hammer, and nails," says Moran.

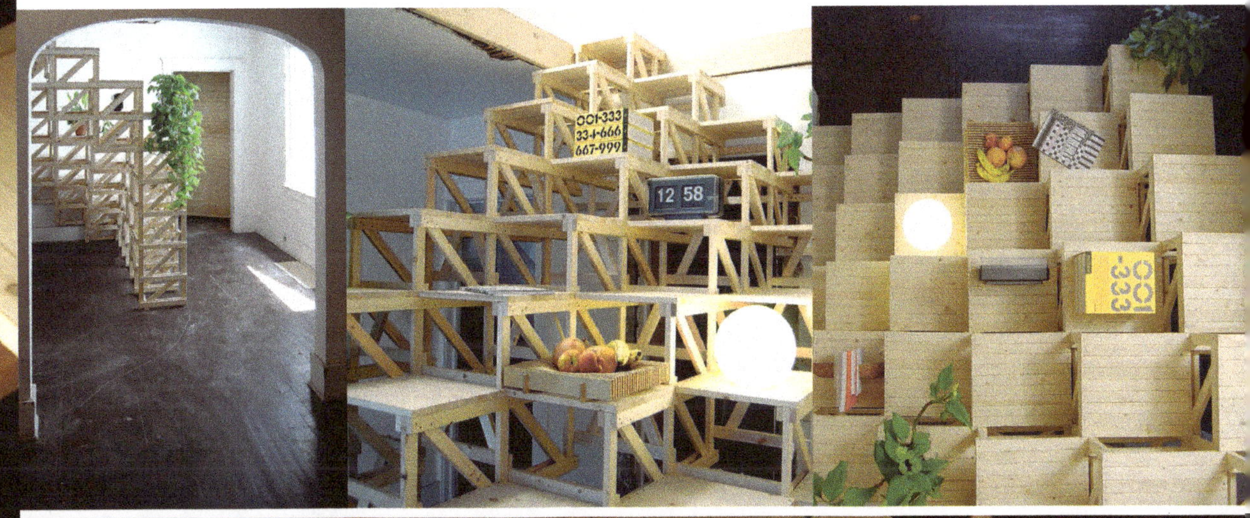

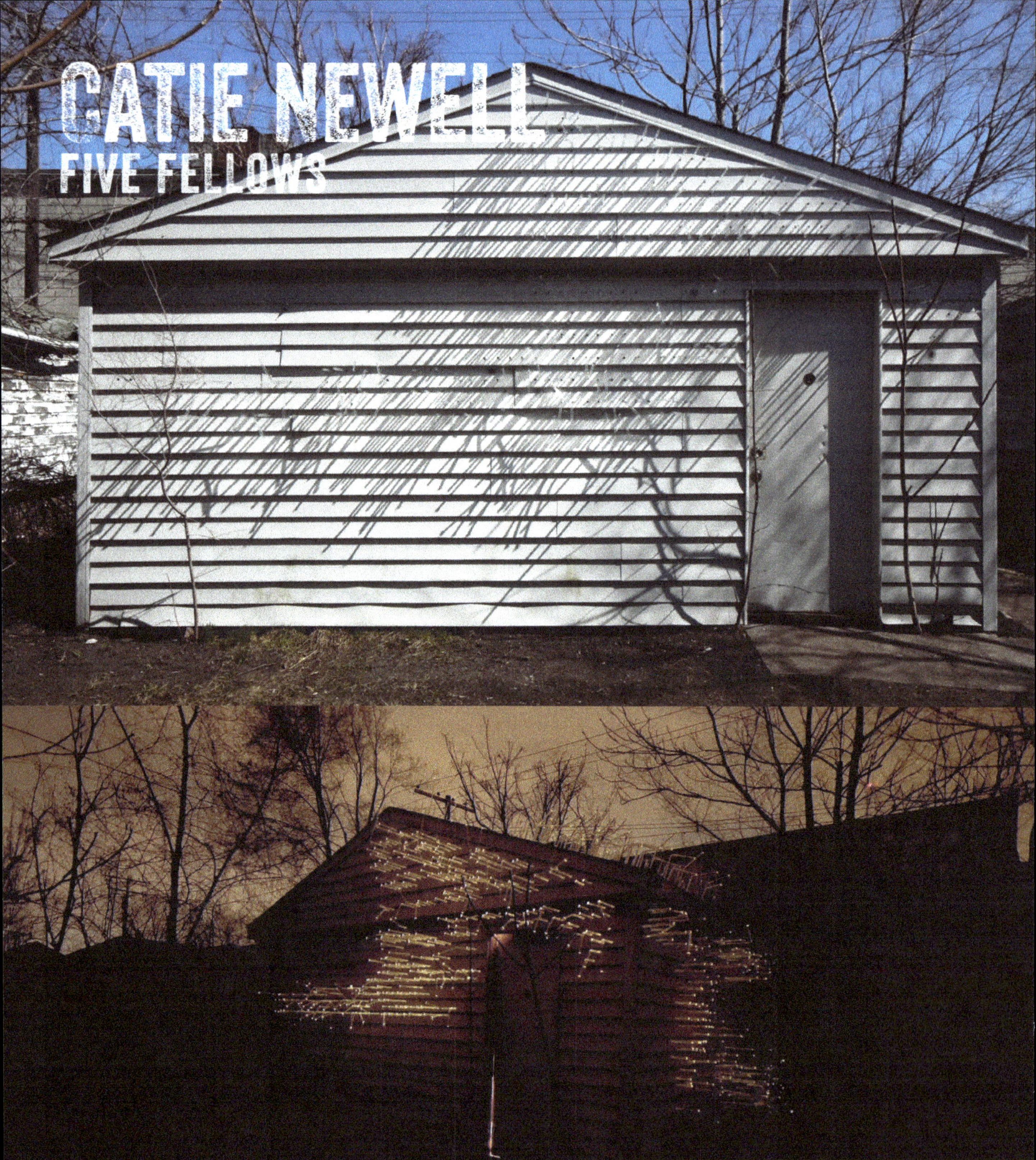
CATIE NEWELL
FIVE FELLOWS

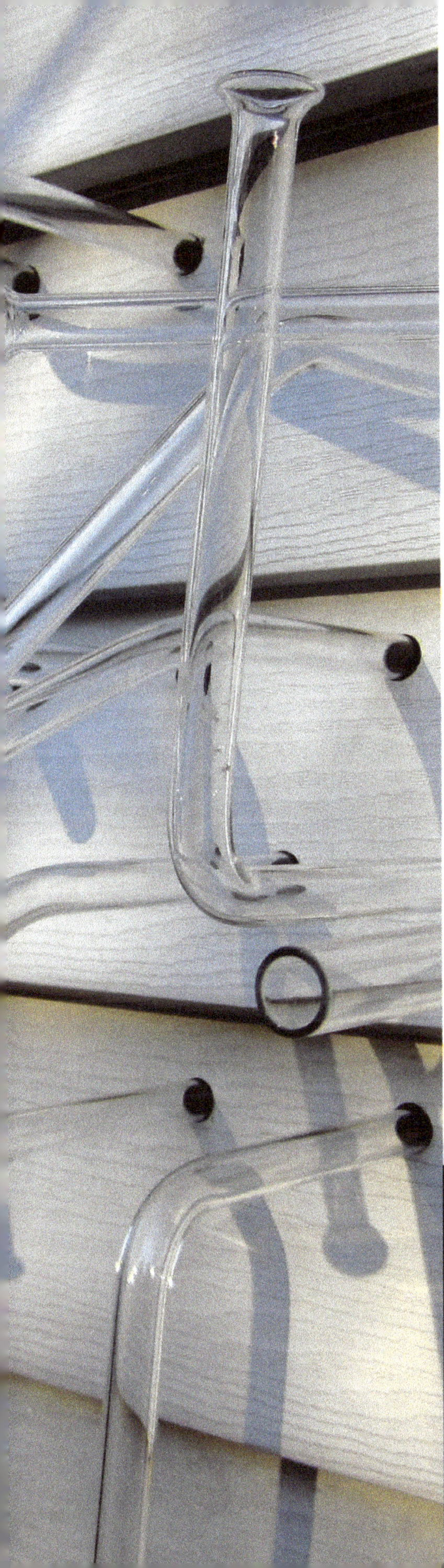

Weatherizing: 4

Newell installed 1,000 glass tubes through the walls and roof of the garage in an exploration of the ways that materials and weather conditions, primarily light, can alter perspective and experience. Newell's use of the tubes, along with solar rooftop panels, created a mysterious glowing effect around the garage at night.

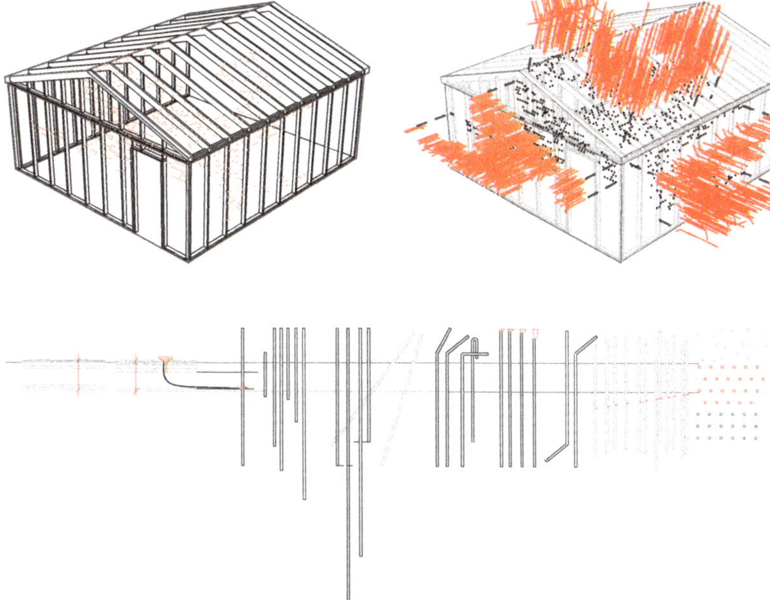

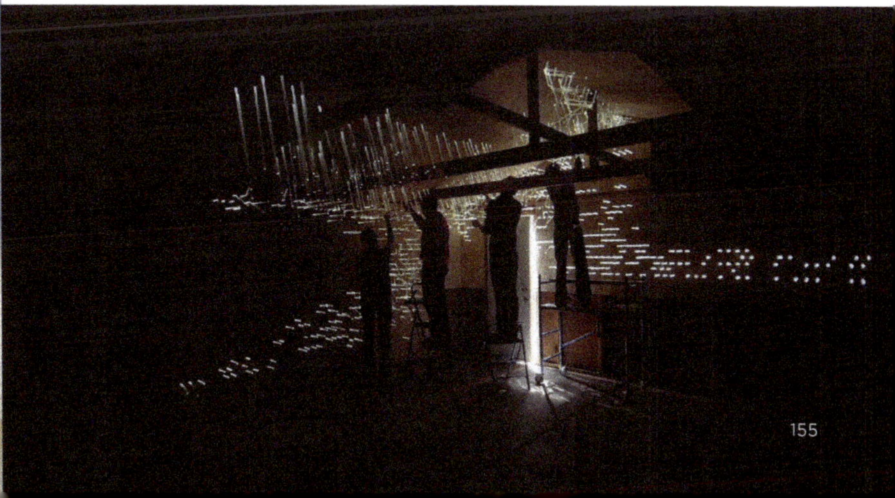

ROSALYNE SHIEH

FIVE FELLOWS

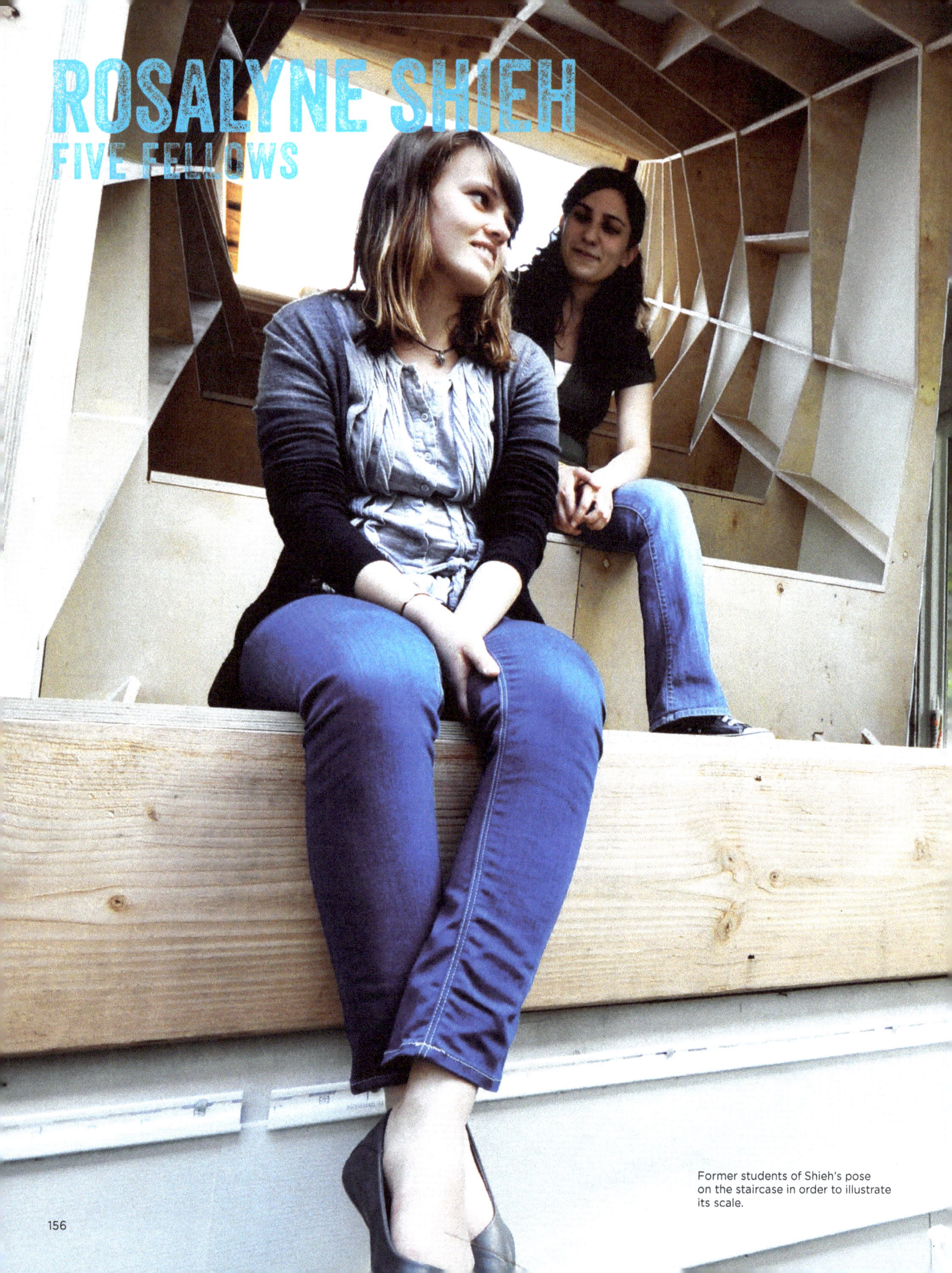

Former students of Shieh's pose on the staircase in order to illustrate its scale.

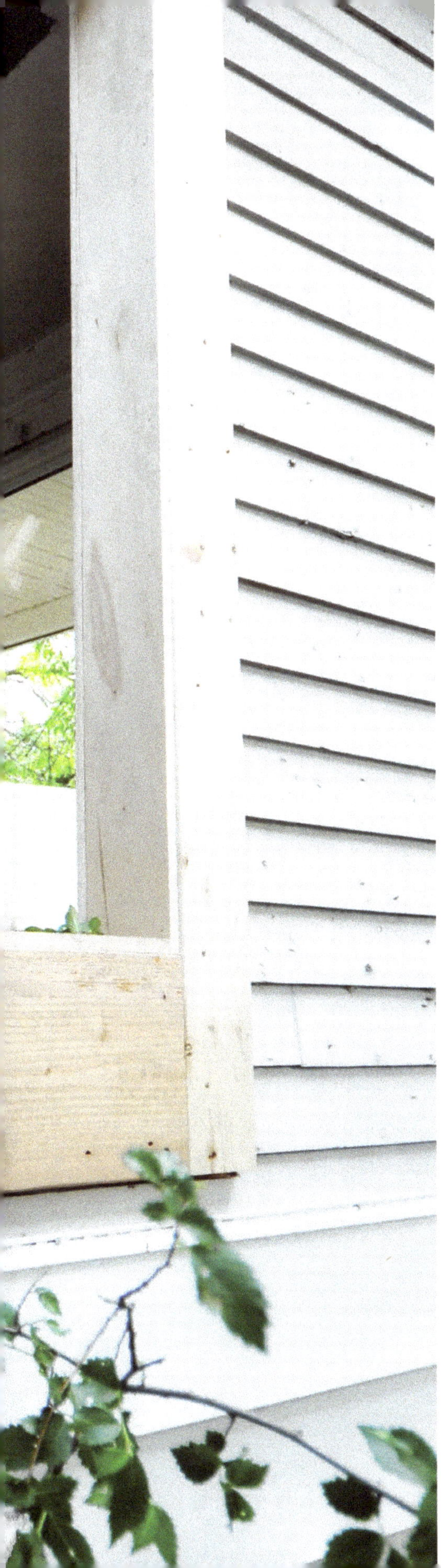

About-Face: 5

Rosalyne Shieh and Troy Schaum redefined the function of a room by slicing a huge diagonal swath through the top of the house to create a skylight space, complete with an octagonal staircase, inviting a new way to see the neighborhood. Shieh's design centered on the hope of "readying the house to turn away from the street and stare down a more distant neighbor."

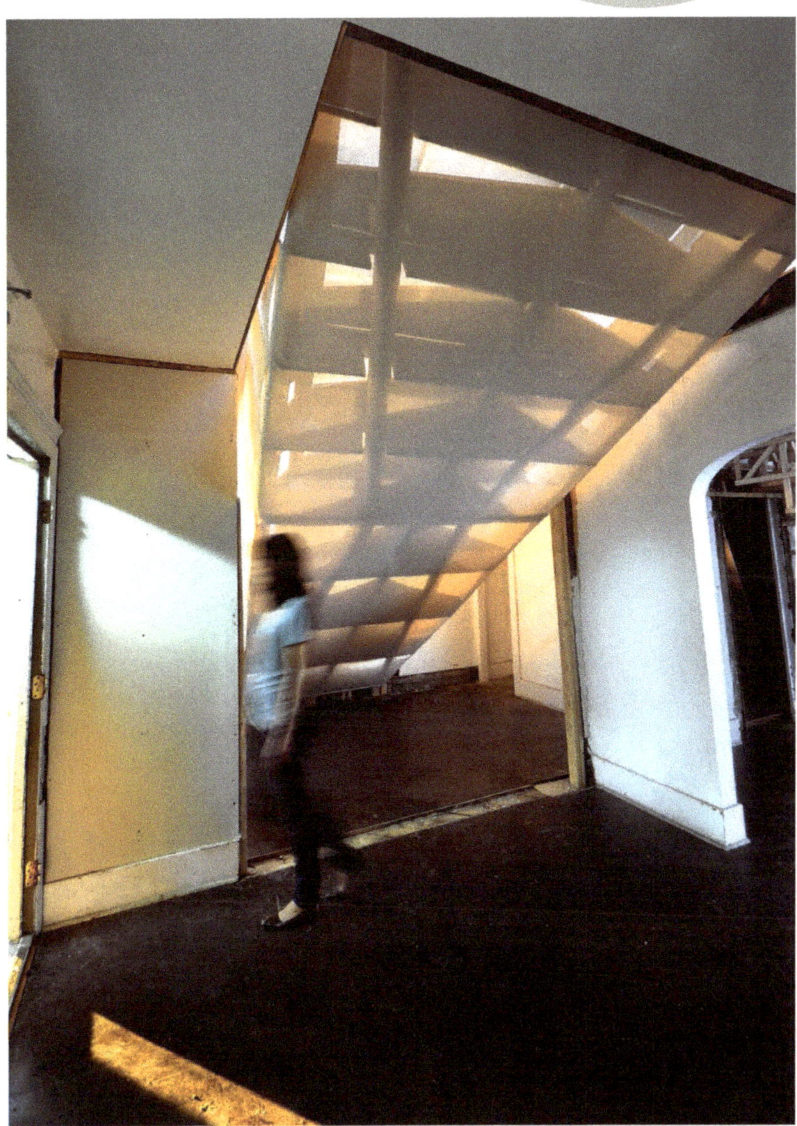

TYREE GUYTON

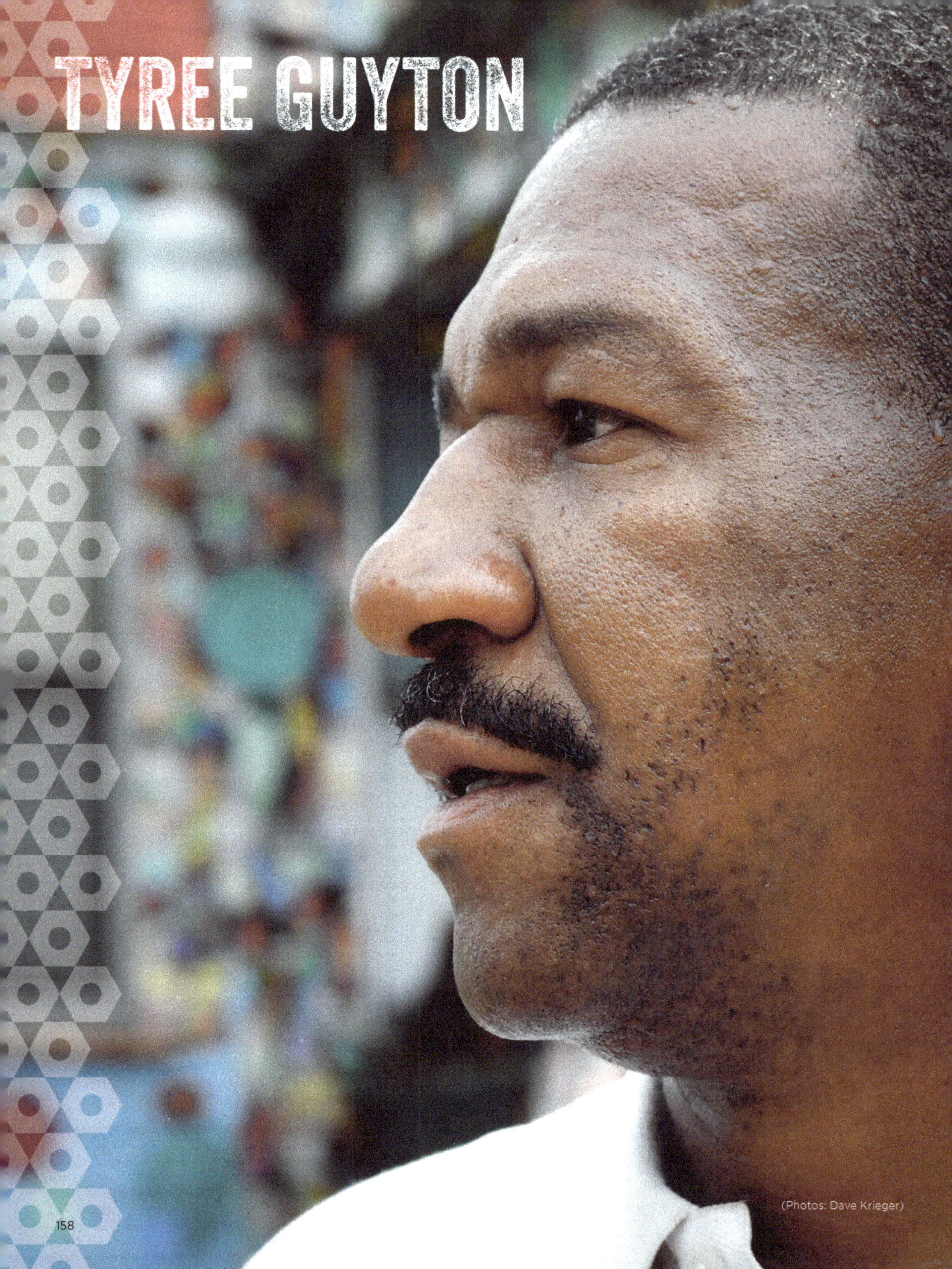

(Photos: Dave Krieger)

My art is a medicine for the community. You can't heal the land until you heal the minds of the people.

–Tyree Guyton

Coming from any other artist, the words above might seem too mighty a declaration to believe. But in Detroit, Guyton is the undisputed godfather of street art. In everything he does, he's proven to be a man determined to build community.

For twenty-seven years, Guyton has made people around the globe look, listen, and linger just long enough to see the beauty in the most ordinary of objects, items that would otherwise be seen only as trash. His most famous creation is a two-block area on Detroit's east side known as the Heidelberg Project. Though it's registered as a nonprofit, the Heidelberg functions as an outdoor arts experience complete with a gift shop and visitor information station.

"My experiences have granted me knowledge of how to create art and how to see beauty in everything that exists," Guyton says.

He covered an entire street with discarded shoes, and adorned abandoned houses with giant polka dots and dolls. Guyton has redefined the look of art in Detroit and beyond.

Joined by his grandfather, a house painter in his eighties, Guyton set out to make people face rather than turn away from the blight consuming his once-vibrant neighborhood and the city. Things left behind found new life in the hands of Guyton, a former autoworker and firefighter.

"I grew up here. I grew up on this block," he says in a video introduction available on the Heidelberg website. "The streets can be very cruel, mean here. People get afraid to come here. What do you do knowing that? I was told that my job as an artist is to come up with solutions. I came up with a solution that makes people put aside the fear and they come here because they got to see it. Once you come here, you can't forget it."

Old cars; junked television sets; empty, decaying houses; torn-apart teddy bears—Guyton used it all. "I saw the need to take found objects from all over the city that people would say was junk," he said in interviews over the years, "and I gave it a new meaning."

Since its launch in 1986, the Heidelberg has become an internationally loved tourist stop, made famous as much for Guyton's unconventional creations as for its symbolism as an artistic battleground. Twice, the City of Detroit sent in demolition crews to level the works that Guyton built. Each time he regrouped, rebuilt, and restored Heidelberg.

At home and abroad, the cheers for his creativity continue. Harvard has touted him. His work has spawned a biographical children's picture book, *Magic Trash*, released in 2011 by Charlesbridge Publishing. In 2012, he completed a coveted residency in Basel, Switzerland, and held the show *Two Countries, Two Cities, One Spirit* in Bern, Switzerland.

Despite the acclaim, Guyton, the painter, the sculptor, the determined Detroiter, remains driven by a belief that art heals. In 2013, arsonists challenged Guyton's faith. Six fires over a six-month period leveled three of the project's most iconic installations: the Obstruction of Justice House, the Penny House, and the House of Soul. Only four of the original seven houses remain—along with a vow from Guyton that beauty will rise from the ashes.

"I'm not going to give in," he told reporters at the scene of the first fire in May. "We're going to use this to make a statement." Hours after the sixth fire he amplified his promise: "We're going to do it bigger and we're going to do it better than before."

If the past is any indication, Guyton will honor his promise.

"I see magic in what I do as an artist," he has said.

Yes, Tyree, the world does, too.

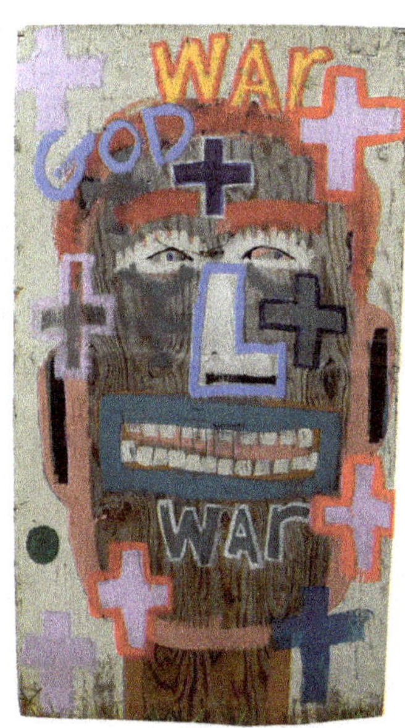

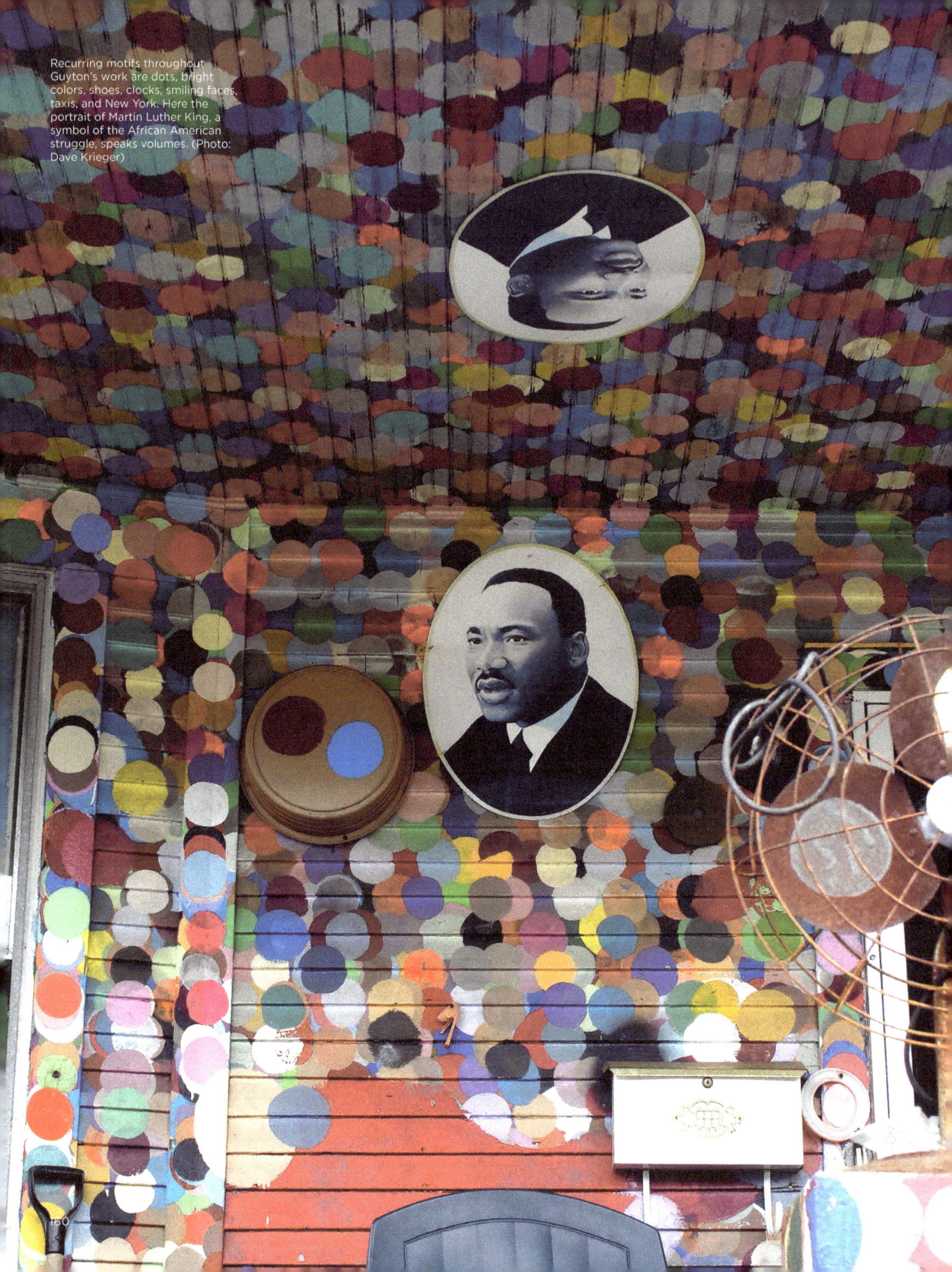
Recurring motifs throughout Guyton's work are dots, bright colors, shoes, clocks, smiling faces, taxis, and New York. Here the portrait of Martin Luther King, a symbol of the African American struggle, speaks volumes. (Photo: Dave Krieger)

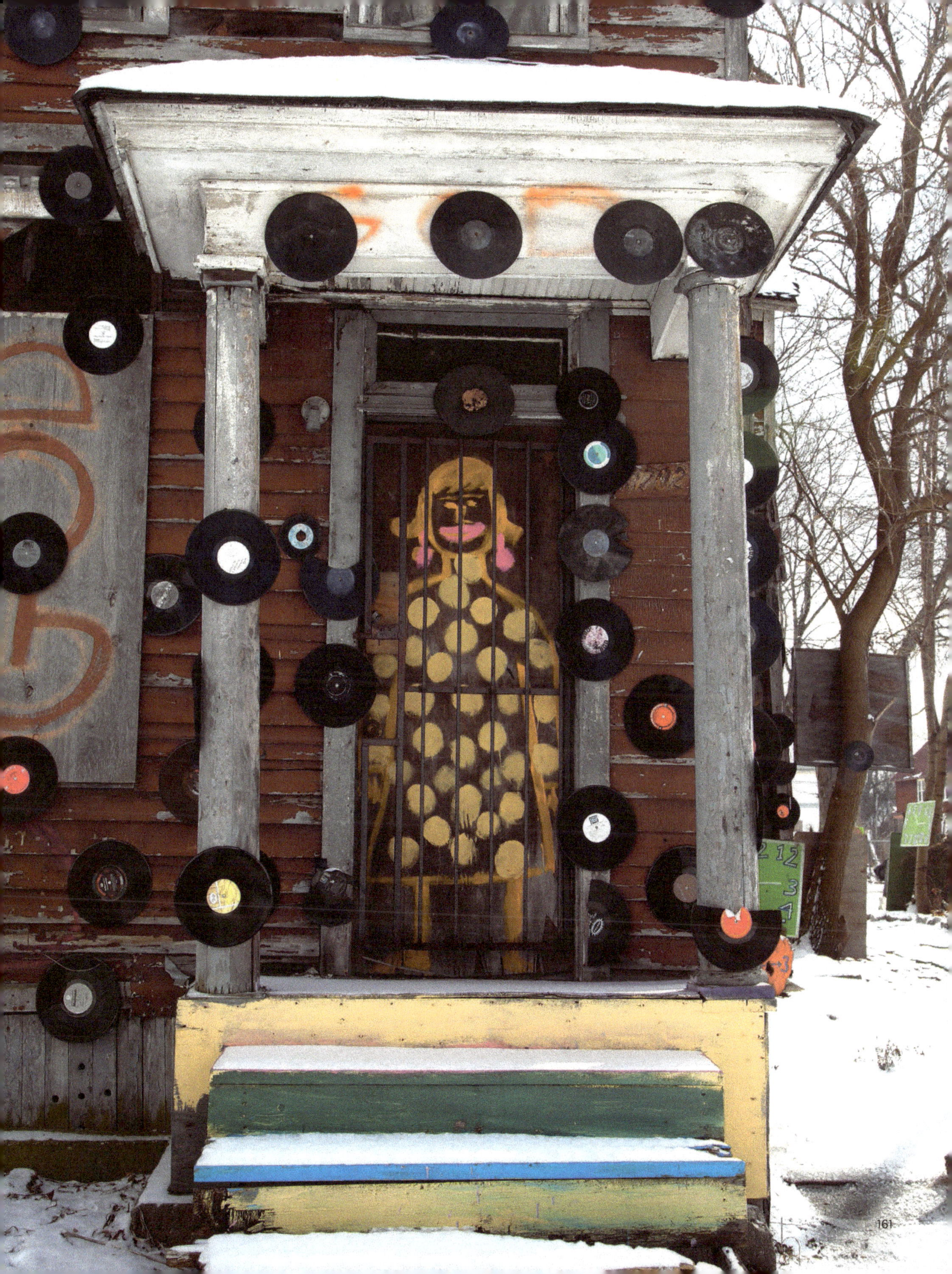

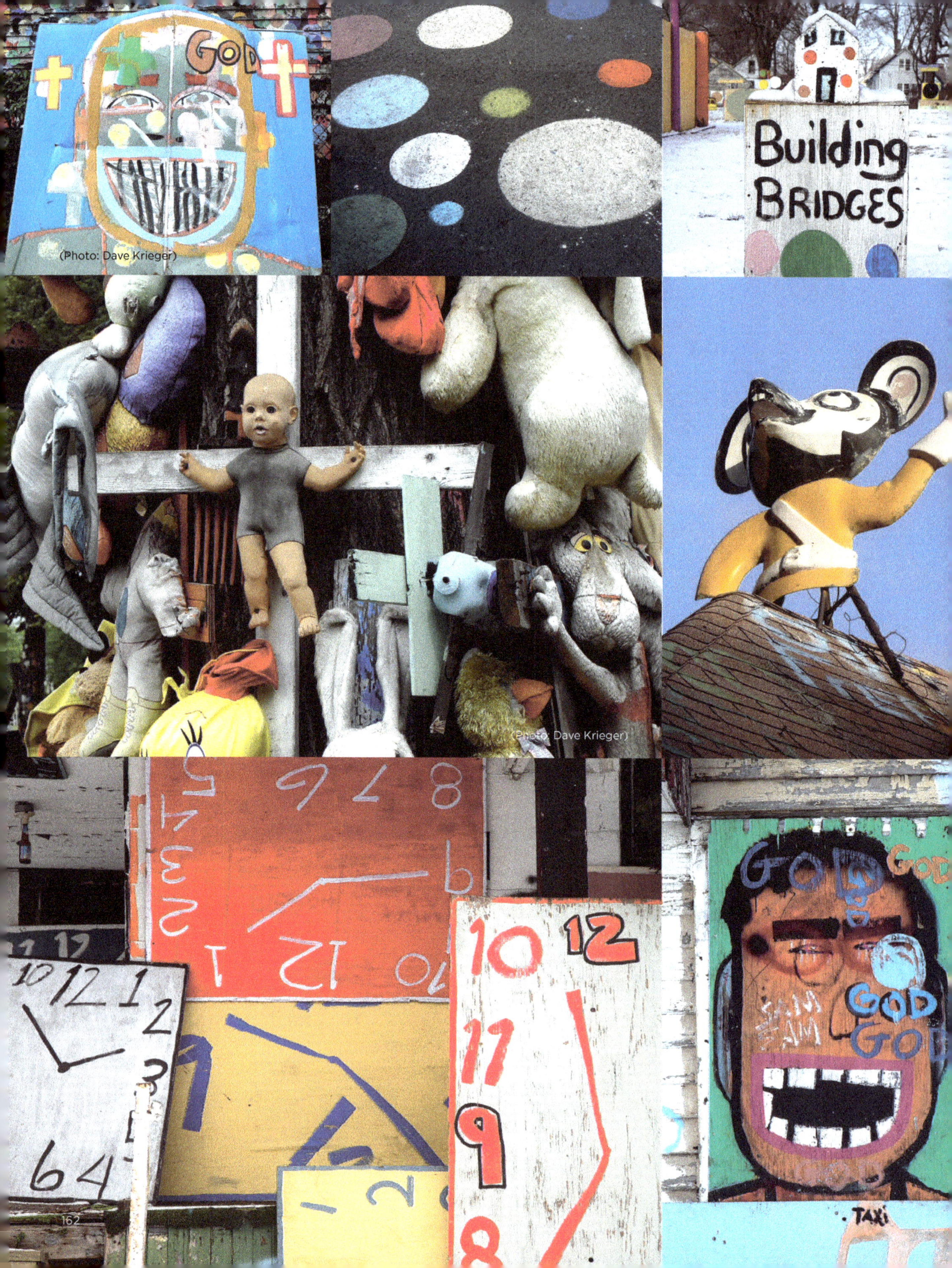

(Photo: Dave Krieger)

(Photo: Dave Krieger)

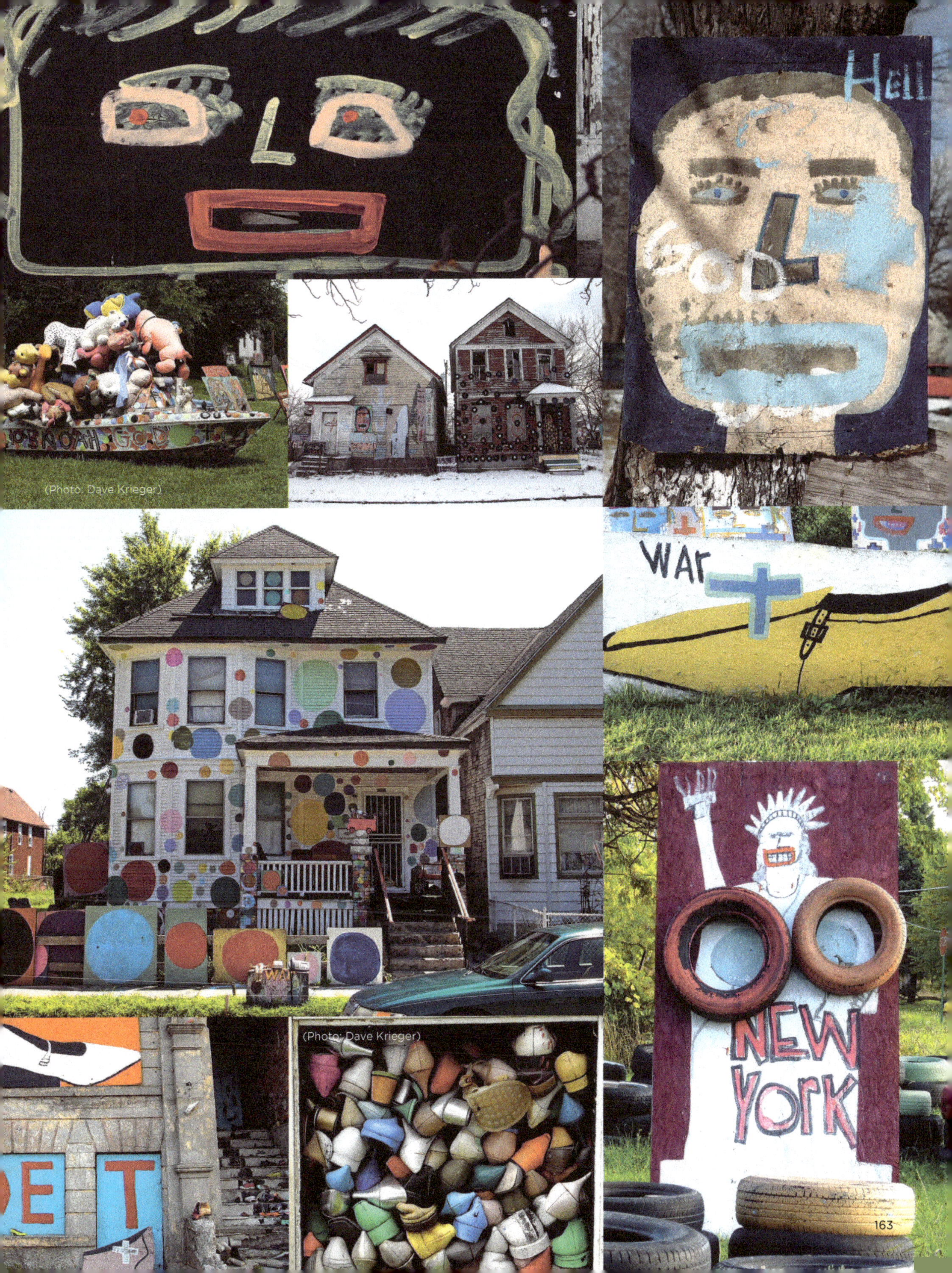

(Photo: Dave Krieger)

(Photo: Dave Krieger)

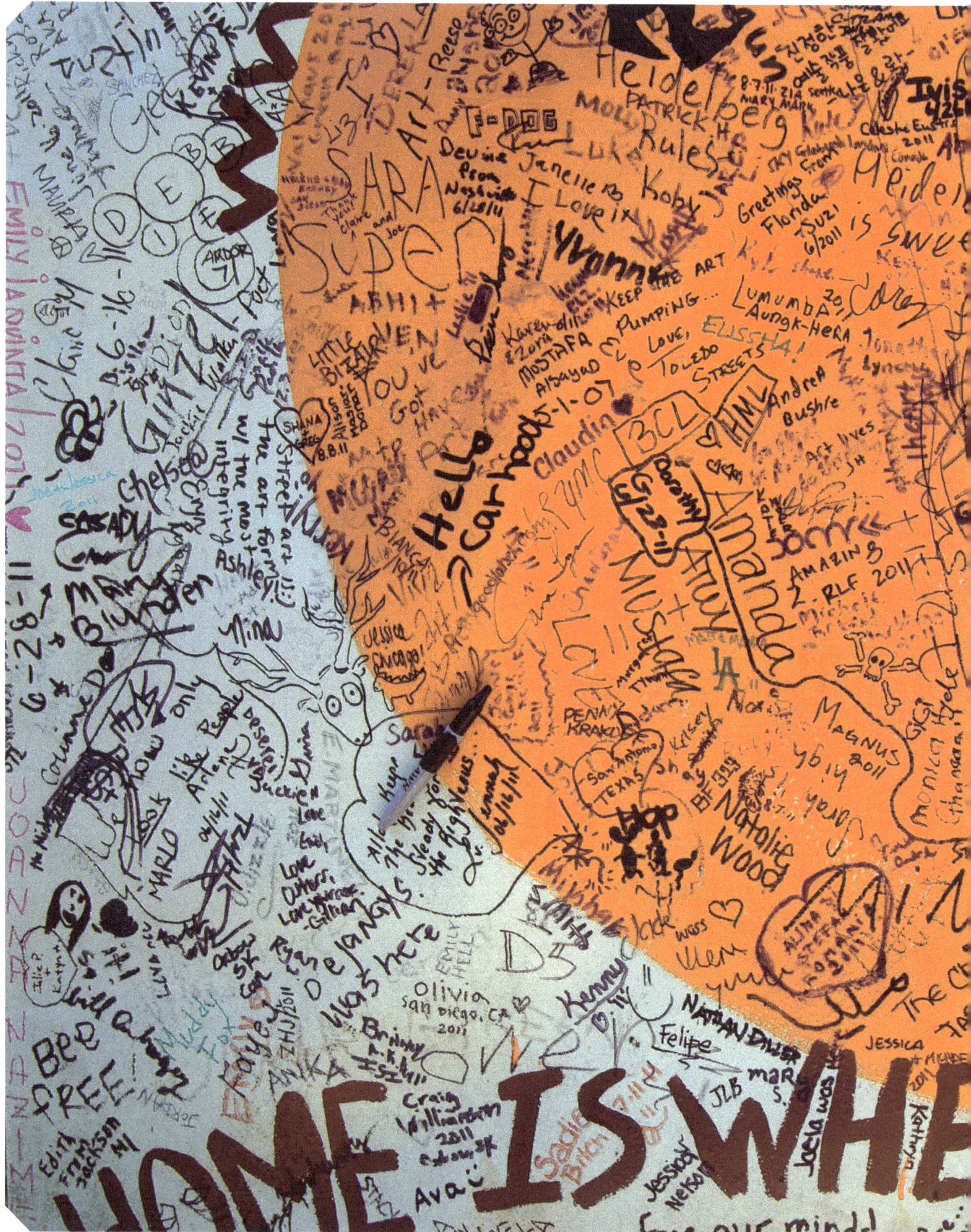

HOME IS WHE
Heidelberg Rules
Art Lives
Hello Car-hoods
Keep the art pumping...
Greetings from Florida Suzi 6/2011
Amanda
Natalie Wood
Magnus 2011
Olivia San Diego, CA 2011
Bee Free!
Free our minds!
Street art is the art form w/ the most integrity
Andrea Bushie
Toledo Streets
Craig Williamson 2011
Jessica
Felipe
EMILY LAQUINTA 2011

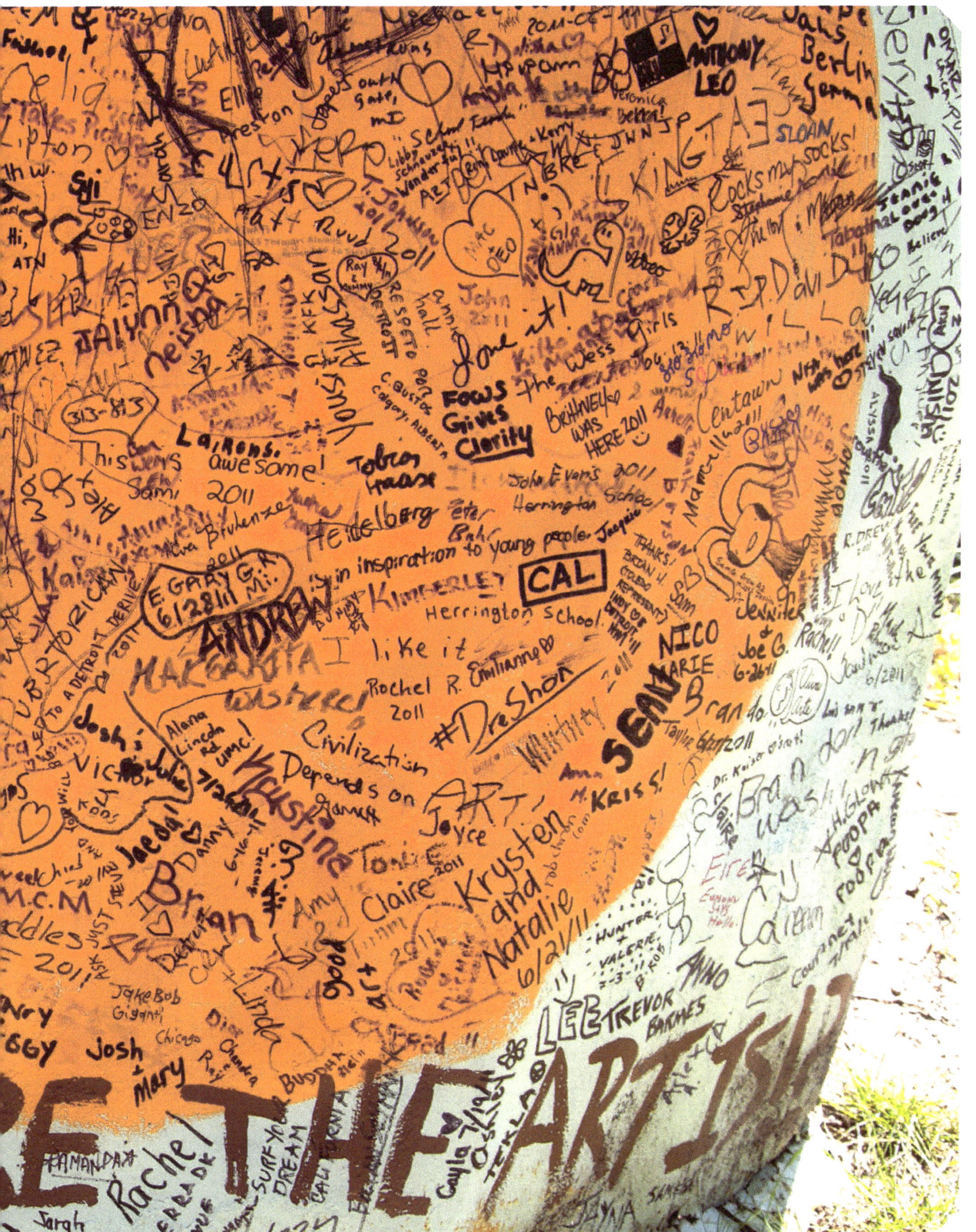

Civilization Depends on ART
Focus Gives Clarity
I like it
Herrington School
CAL
This was awesome
love it!

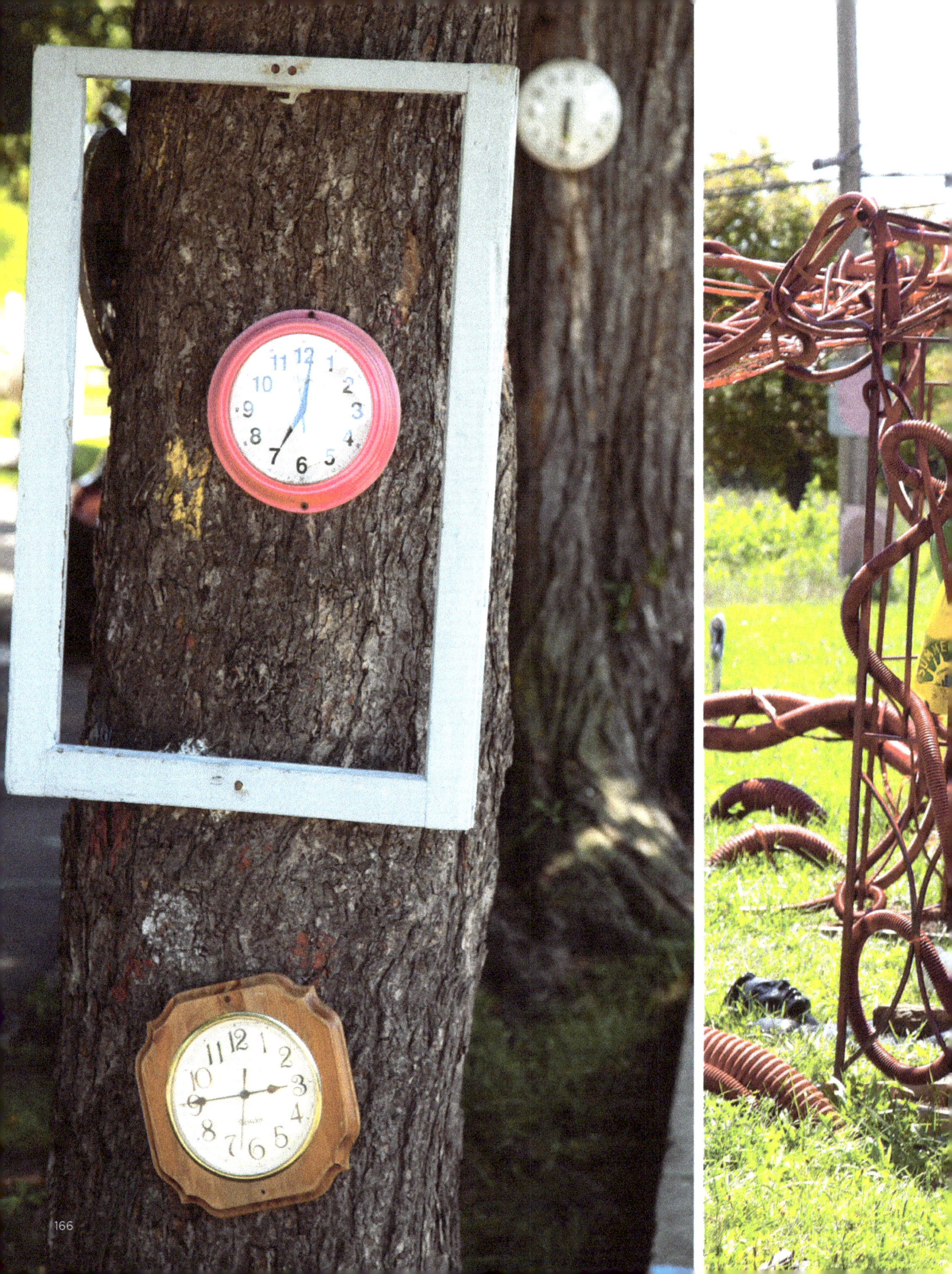

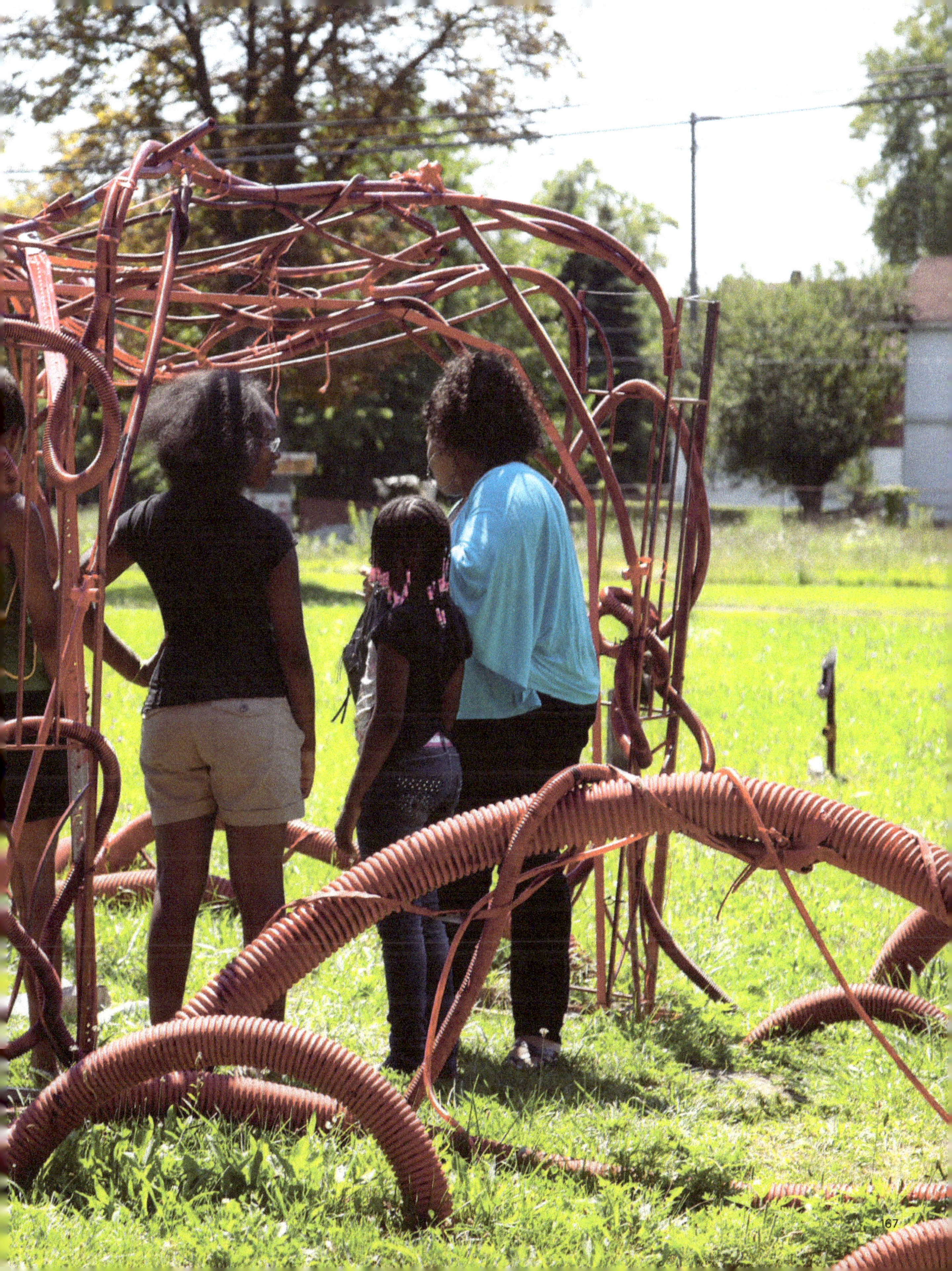

SCOTT HOCKING

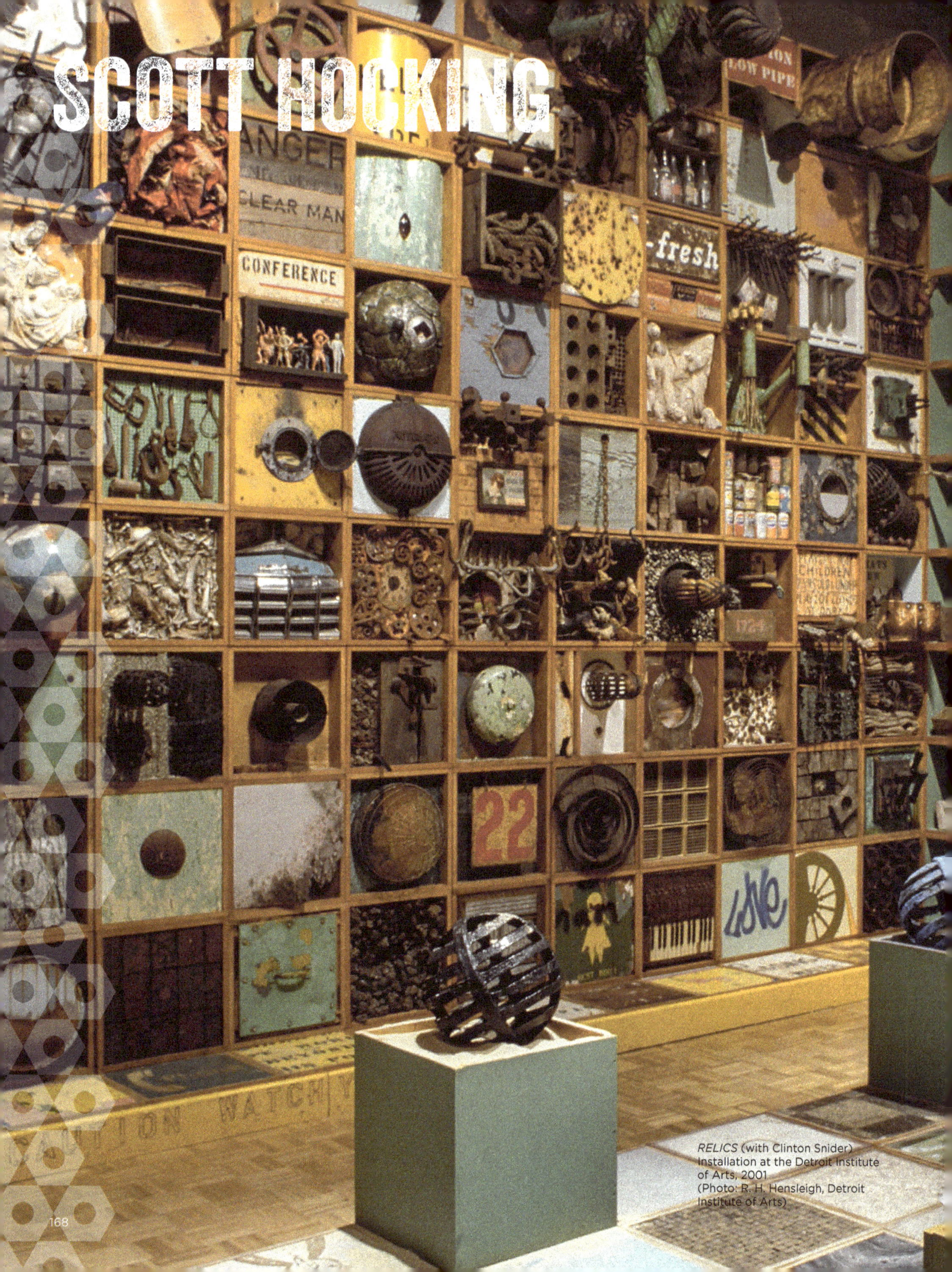

RELICS (with Clinton Snider)
Installation at the Detroit Institute of Arts, 2001
(Photo: R. H. Hensleigh, Detroit Institute of Arts)

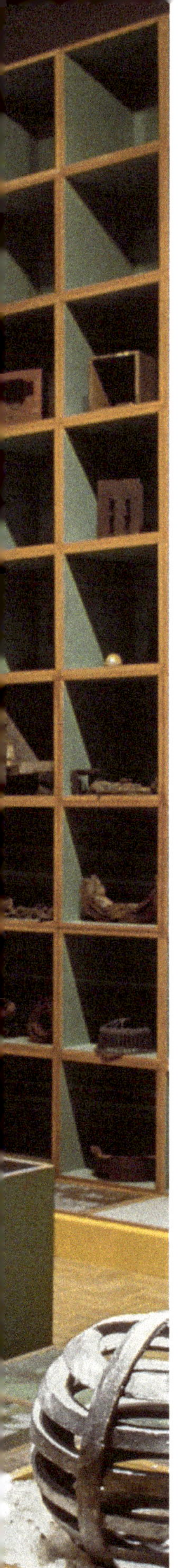

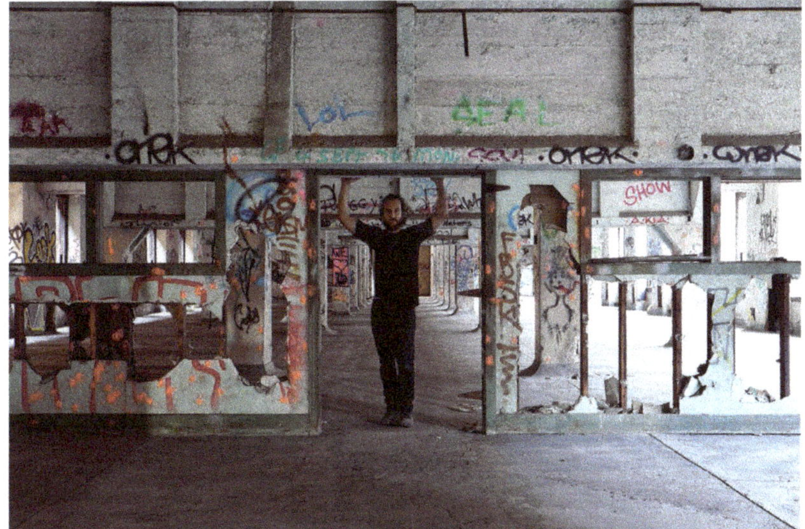

Scott Hocking didn't choose Detroit. Detroit, he says, chose him.

The story is more than a decade old, but it's a foundational tale in the making of one of Motown's most recognized artists. What the world already knows of Hocking is true: he bends the imagination by fusing decaying objects into experimental sculptures and photography displays.

His most famous projects have come to life inside the bellies of industrial burial grounds, abandoned car factories hollowed out by hard times and decades of civic neglect. Predictably, art critics and collectors have come calling. Photos from four of his projects, including Ziggurat, a site-specific sculptural installation made from 6,201 wooden floor-blocks within Detroit's long-abandoned Fisher Body Plant 21, were focal points of the Detroit Institute of Arts' 2012 exhibit, *Detroit Revealed: Photographs, 2000–2010.*

One of the art world's most respected periodicals, *Artforum*, has even lifted Hocking's name.

Still, Hocking says his career might never have happened if a hand had not intervened and saved him from himself. Here's how it happened: He was twenty-one and hell-bent, for the second time, on fleeing the Motor City. At eighteen, he almost got away. But when his engine blew in California, Hocking took the few dollars he had left and hopped a Greyhound bus back to Detroit.

Three years later, he hatched part two of his escape from Detroit. This time, he'd planned to head far west: to Alaska and a life at sea as a fisherman. A silver four-door Toyota that had been his home was fixed up and ready to be sold. But three days before the trip, the Toyota was totaled in a car accident. Hocking landed in the hospital minus insurance and minus a life plan, except for one detail.

"To me, it became very clear I was not supposed to leave Detroit," said thirty-eight-year-old Hocking, who grew up in Redford, a working-class suburb. "It felt like a hand had come down and smashed into my car and said, 'You shouldn't leave.' So instead of trying to get away, I decided to dig in."

Fog Ship, Fisher Body
from Ziggurat and FB21, 2007-2009
(Photo: Scott Hocking)

His life took on new focus. "I realized I needed to figure out what the fuck I was doing with my life." The interests of Scott the boy suddenly transfixed Hocking the man. "The accident put everything into perspective. Things I'd been doing my whole life: being interested in drawing, reusing things, working on gritty stuff, and going to the junkyard with my father; everything just made sense, became pretty organic. I decided I wanted to take a risk and try to be an artist."

At the time, his ideas of being an artist were vague. A trip closer to home helped to fill in the blanks: "I took the Grand River bus to the Warren bus and walked to CCS [College for Creative Studies], found out what the word portfolio meant, and then I made one."

A few months later, Hocking was formally a fine-arts student. The art world has been on his trail ever since.

Today, he's a known artist but still not a wealthy one, at least not by financial measures. In Detroit, there are other success indicators. There's the fortune of being able to live where he creates, on the top floor of a small two-story former industrial building in the city's North End neighborhood. Be sure to also count the steady stream of exhibitions and fellowship invitations he receives from other cities and countries. Once, such invites seemed impossible for Detroit-based artists. Now they come almost as frequently as the evening sun that pours through Hocking's giant studio windows.

"Right now, Detroit is still a pretty good home base for me. I still have ideas, I still want to make work here, and the city's on the art-map more than it's ever been."

Yet Hocking says some of the headlines leading young artists to relocate are misleading. "I think a lot of what people come here thinking they're going to find is false," he says. "I don't think it's a blank canvas. I don't think it's necessarily cheap rent and I don't think it's the kind of place where you can do whatever the hell you want."

Hocking is most disturbed by outside artists whose "gluttony" has birthed its own cliché: ruin porn. "Some of it is just nihilism," he says. "But I do think that there are some people who can't be so easily lumped into a negative category, when what they do might be the same as any generation documenting the time they're in, so future generations can look back."

Hocking insists his work inside Detroit's fallen factories and buildings is done with respect and an eye toward artistic inquiry. "I have a lot of ways I go into buildings that have to do with respecting the area the same way that I would if I was out in the woods. One of the reasons I work in abandoned sites is because I'm interested in changing people's perspectives, maybe shaking up their concepts of what's good, what's bad, what's ugly, what's decaying."

So long as Detroit stokes his curiosity, Hocking intends to continue digging for the art in things left behind. "The same way the accident gave me the sign that I shouldn't leave, I haven't had the sign that I should," he says. "I haven't exhausted Detroit yet."

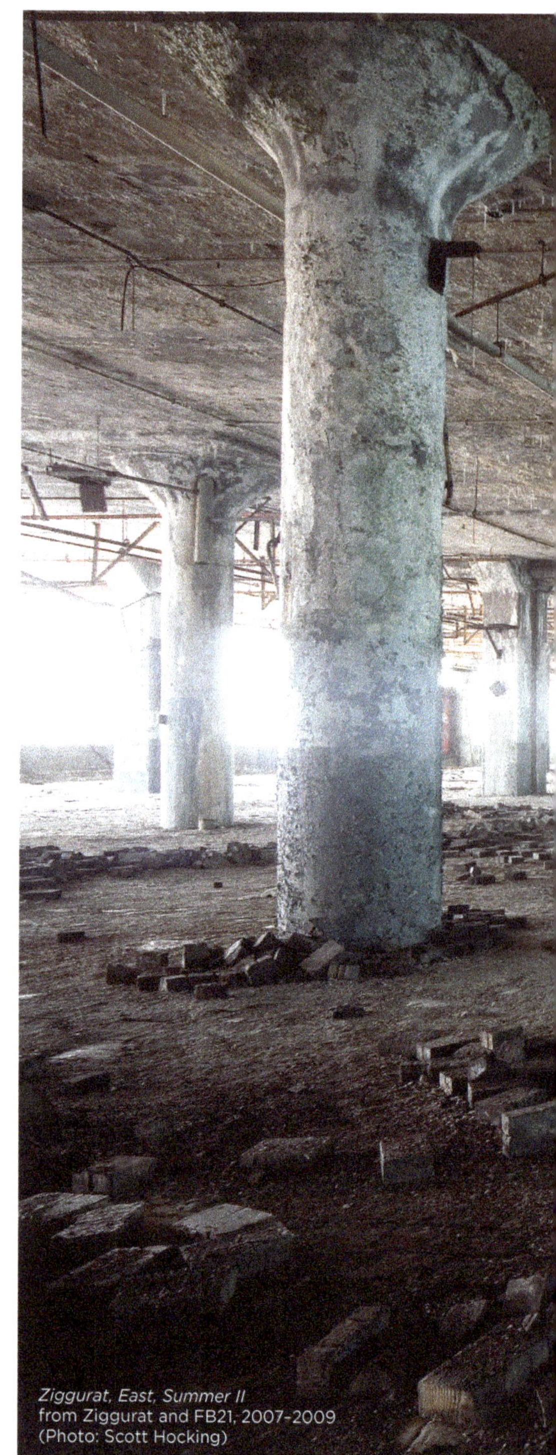

Ziggurat, East, Summer II
from Ziggurat and FB21, 2007-2009
(Photo: Scott Hocking)

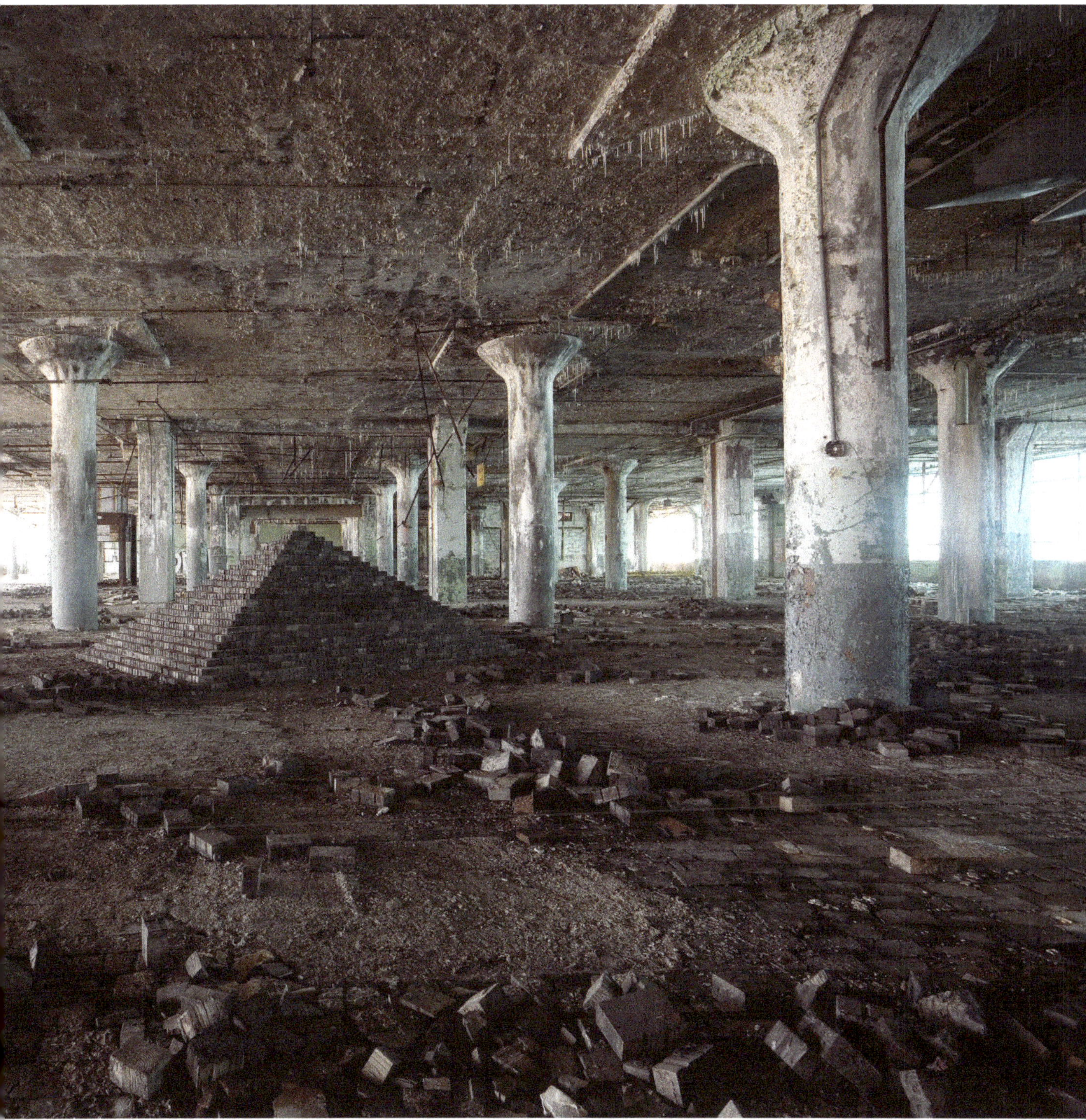

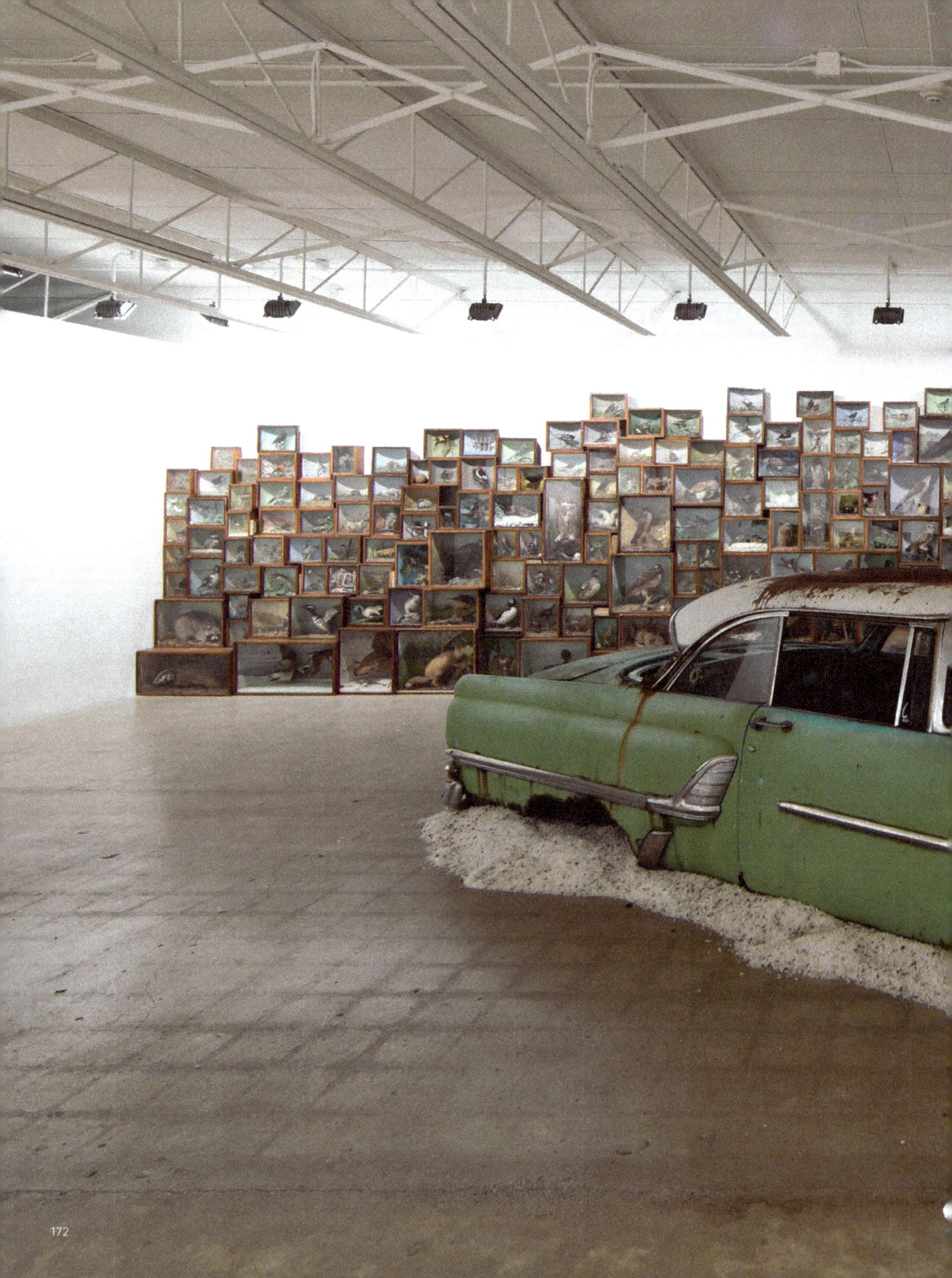

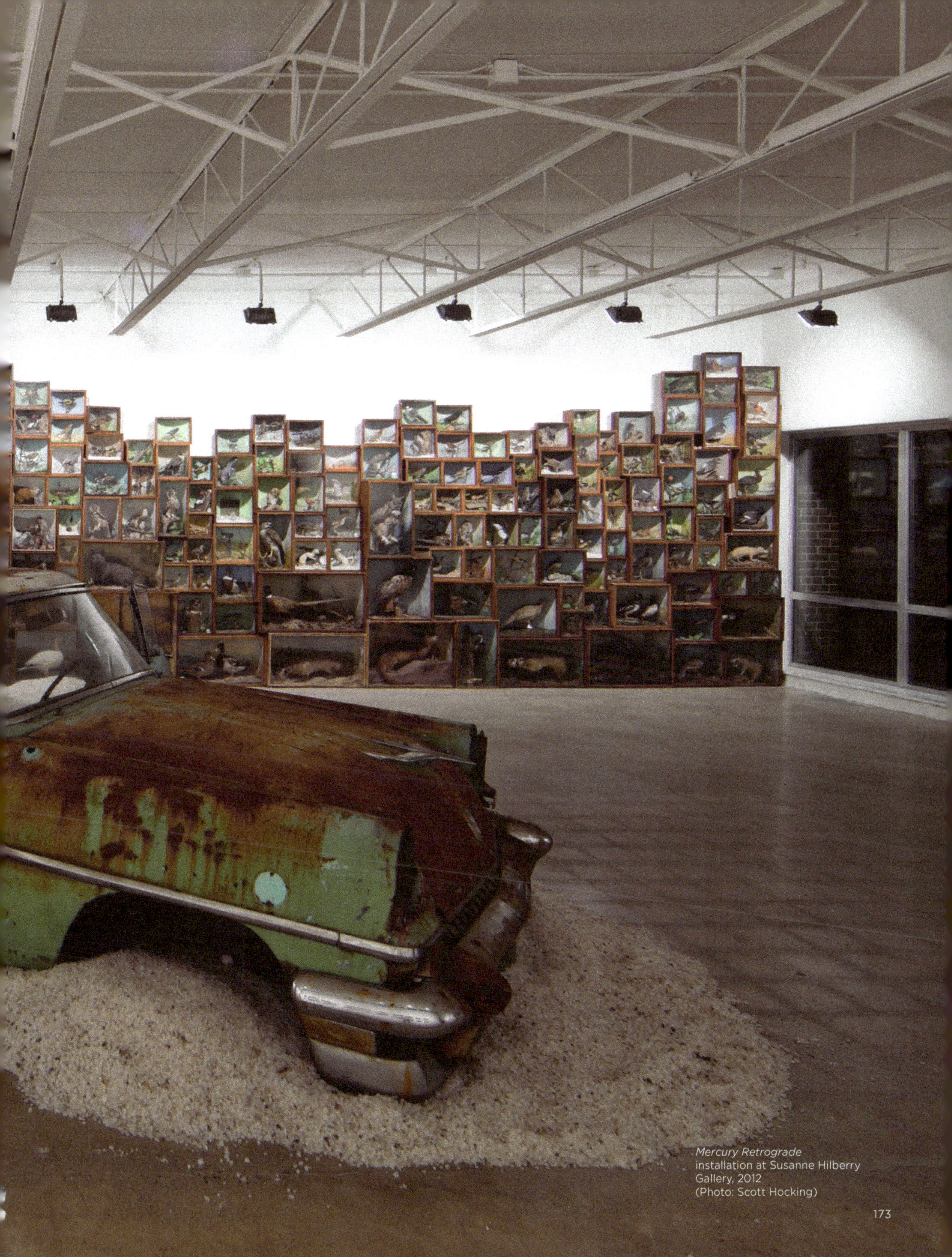

Mercury Retrograde
installation at Susanne Hilberry
Gallery, 2012
(Photo: Scott Hocking)

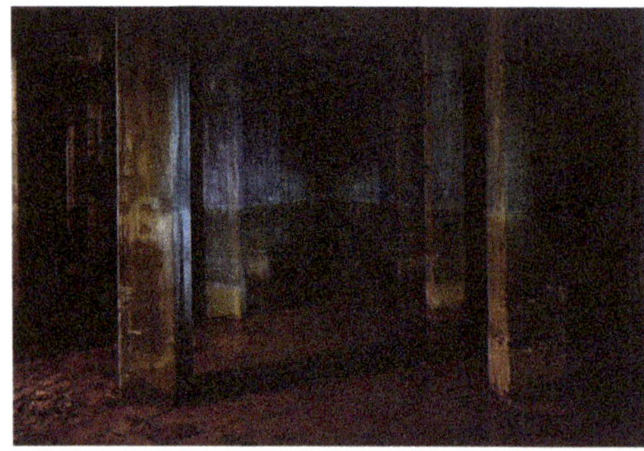

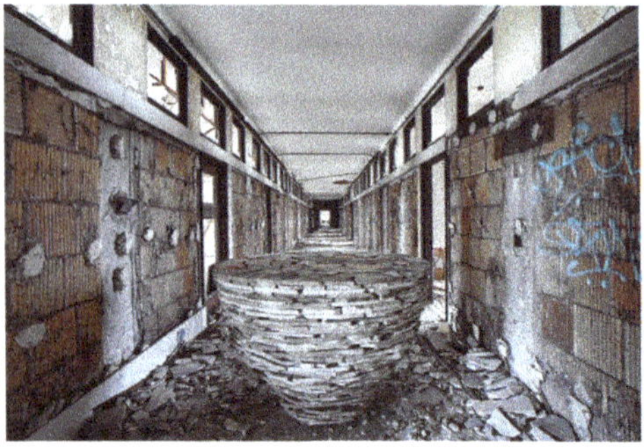

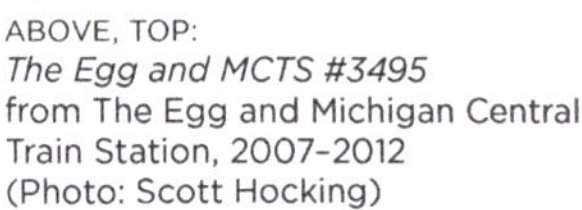

ABOVE, TOP:
The Egg and MCTS #3495
from The Egg and Michigan Central
Train Station, 2007–2012
(Photo: Scott Hocking)

ABOVE, BOTTOM:
The Egg and MCTS #5842
from The Egg and Michigan Central
Train Station, 2007–2012
(Photo: Scott Hocking)

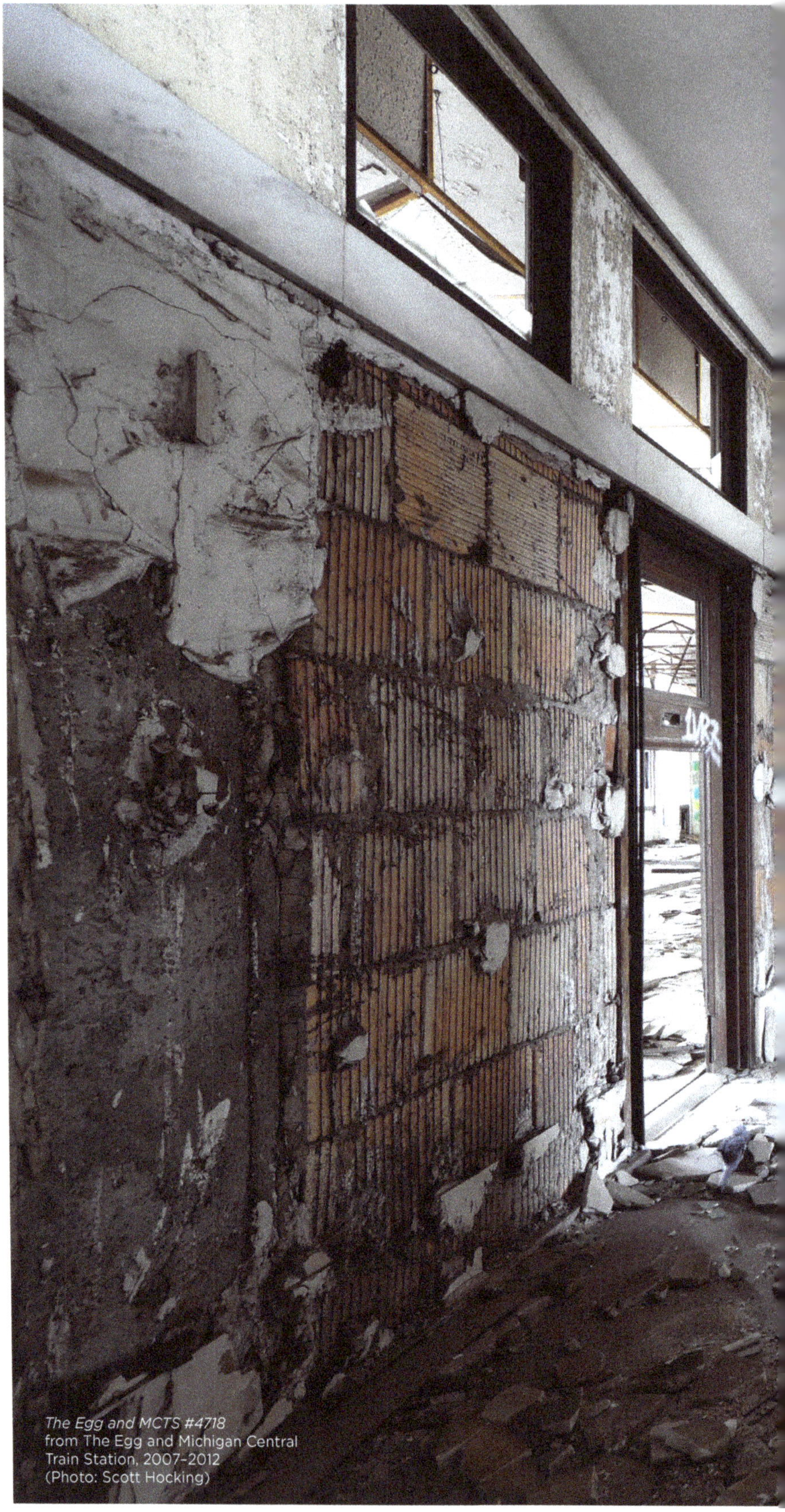

The Egg and MCTS #4718
from The Egg and Michigan Central
Train Station, 2007–2012
(Photo: Scott Hocking)

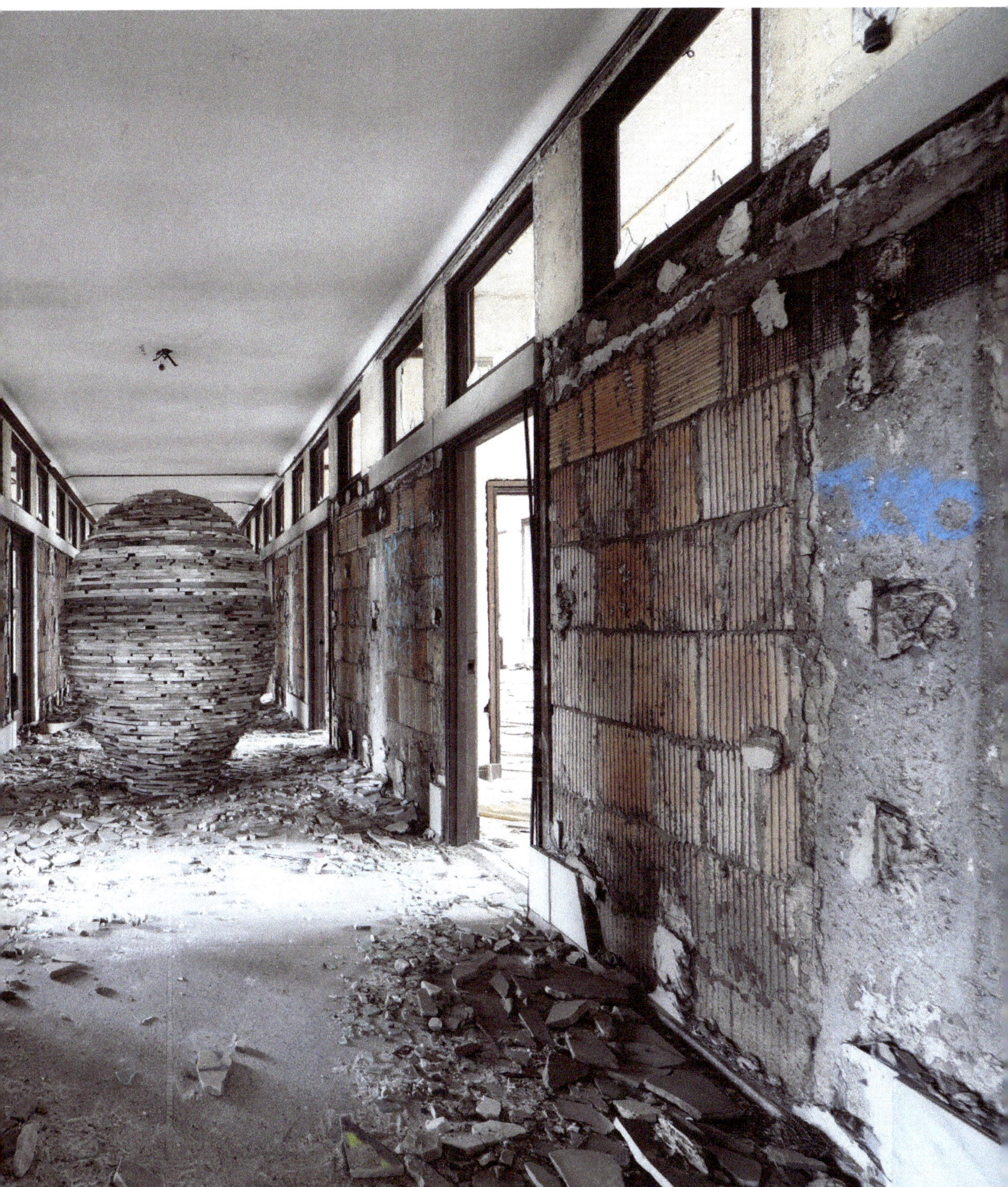

JUDITH HOFFMAN

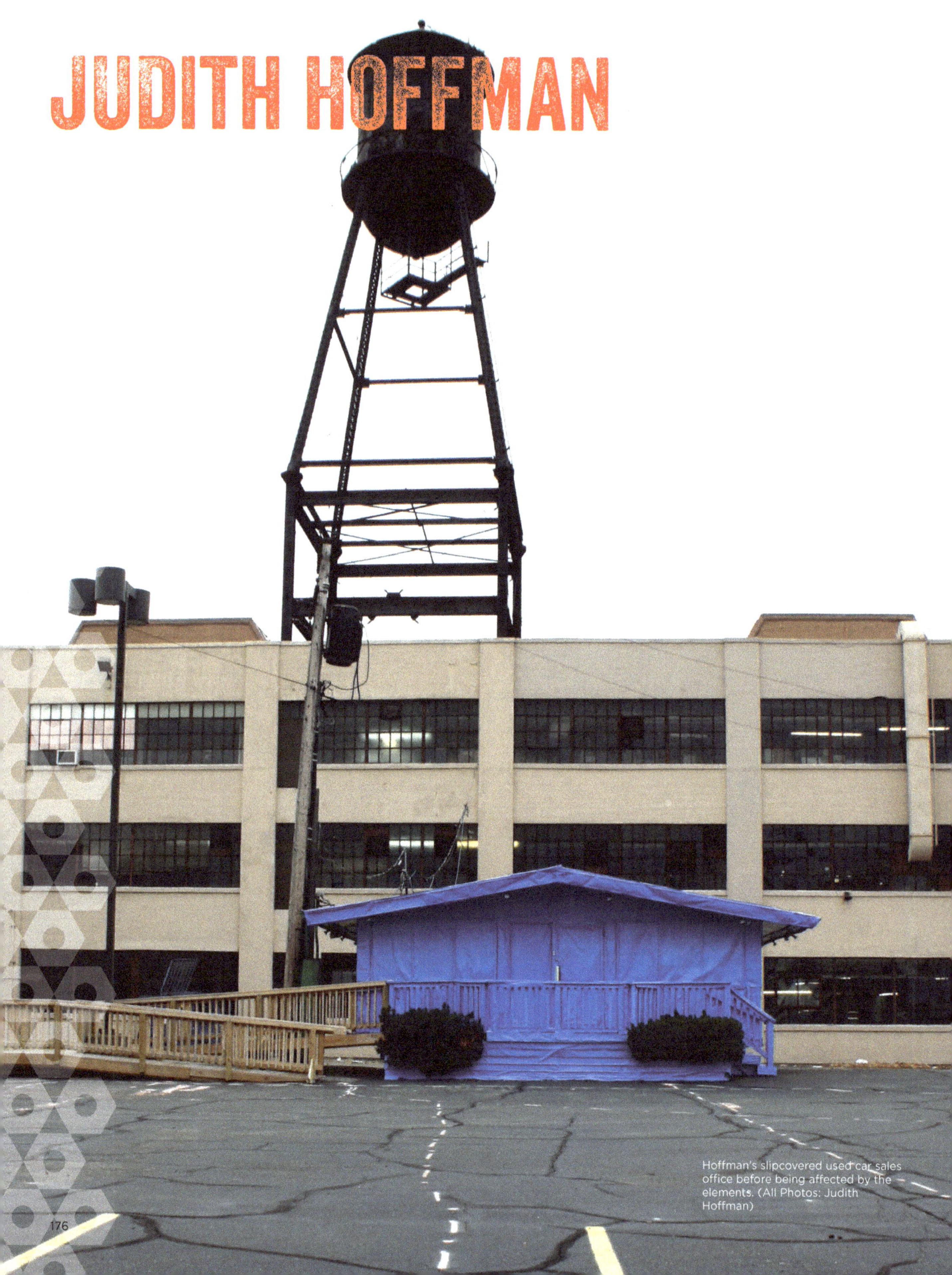

Hoffman's slipcovered used car sales office before being affected by the elements. (All Photos: Judith Hoffman)

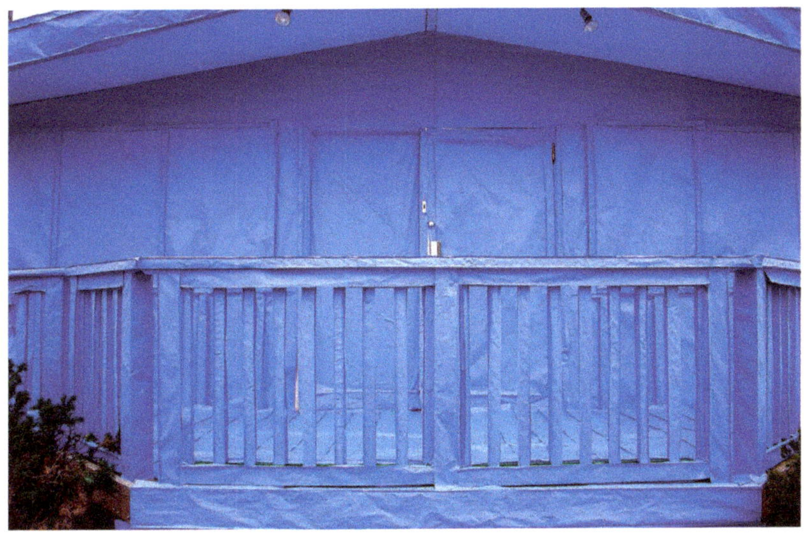

Artist Judith Hoffman's contribution to Detroit exists only in photographs now.

It was always supposed to be this way. Hoffman designed her work in Detroit to be destroyed: by the elements, by time.

A New Yorker, Hoffman was invited to Detroit as a resident artist to pull off a project that on paper seemed too complex to be possible. Her vision: a one-to-one replica of a ten-thousand-square-foot gallery constructed completely out of paper in just one month. To be exact: four thousand pieces of royal-blue paper, carefully sewn together with a sewing machine as a slipcover for the gutsy little gallery that had once been the sales office of a popular Cadillac car lot. The cover was held in place by wooden posts, also painted blue.

With a surgeon's eye for precision, Hoffman attended to every detail. "Being someone who makes large-scale sculpture, I'm extremely concerned with the by-product of the sculpture. For me it's important to consider the environment and to show what's possible using materials that are inexpensive and accessible." The type of paper was paramount. She chose school-grade paper.

Hoffman, who also works frequently with fabrics, worried equally about choosing the right color. "I debated about color for a while." Blue won out as a salute to the city's sports teams and its legacy as a blue-collar city.

The final phase of the piece entitled *In Hoping We Find Ourselves*, involved a time-lapse video, shot every five minutes, chronicling the course of the decay over a month's time. Hoffman also put out a national call to artists for photographs that were projected directly onto the slipcover.

"My work in a lot of ways tries to deal with creating a simultaneous sanctuary and decay," she explained. "I think they're always happening together; it's just a question of whether we're noticing. If I had one aim, that was really it—to inspire some response, a reason for people to notice."

Hoffman surpassed her aim. Three weeks into the project's opening, as the cover was beginning to shred and "look like trash on a building," a janitor from a nearby business took notice in a most extreme way. He wiped the building clean, removing all traces of her work

Hoffman, who is thirty-six, chuckles recalling the irony.

"It was unexpected for sure, but it was just the perfect thing. I was so happy that he did that. It reinforced the idea of Detroit as a place where people may not have a lot of finances but they certainly have dedication and they do care. They really care."

So does Hoffman, it seems. She chooses her words slowly when asked about the city's chances of becoming a nationally respected arts town.

"In all of the United States, Detroit is my favorite place. I love, love it. People absolutely want to support the arts."

Excitement about art, she says, greeted her everywhere and colored her perception about the city that she'd never visited until art opened the door.

"There is this real oasis thing happening because of cheap real estate. But I don't know if, as an artist, you can have a viable living in Detroit long-term. I'd like to believe it's possible because I'd love to come back. There's certainly enough happening to keep you hopeful that opportunities for artists will last."

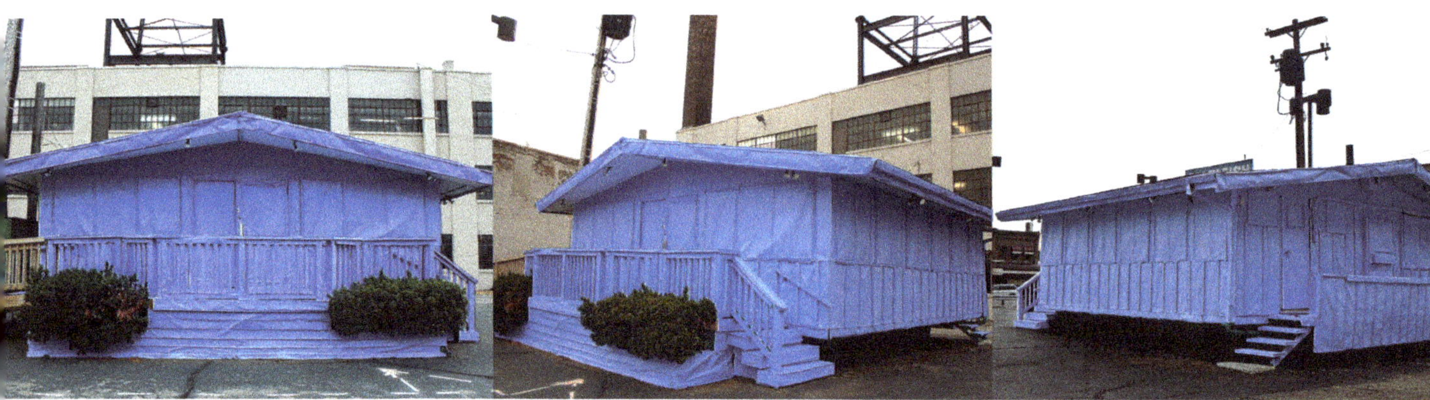

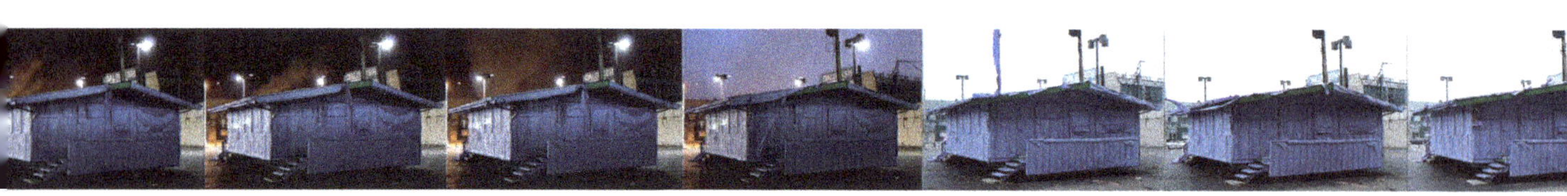

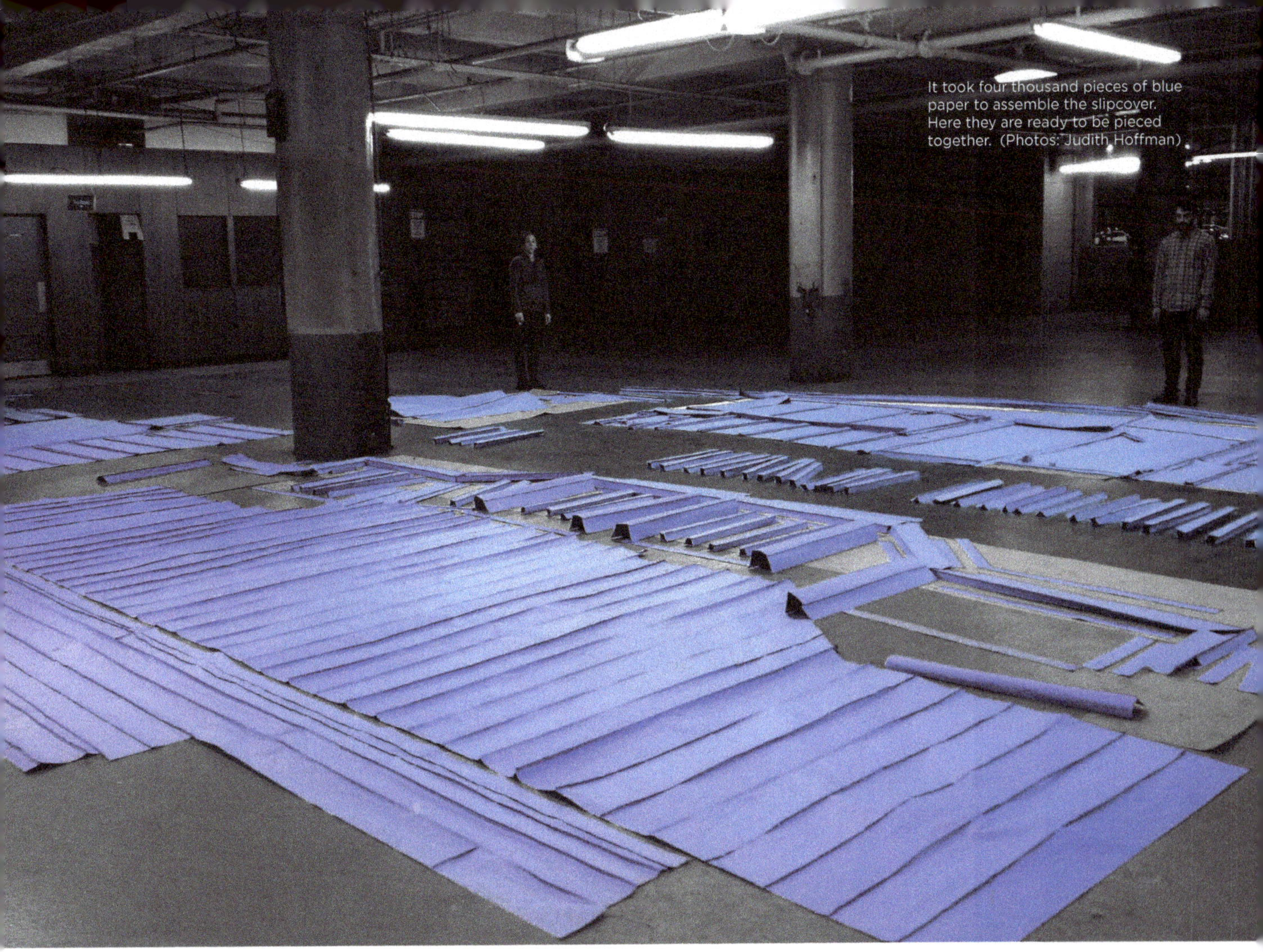

It took four thousand pieces of blue paper to assemble the slipcover. Here they are ready to be pieced together. (Photos: Judith Hoffman)

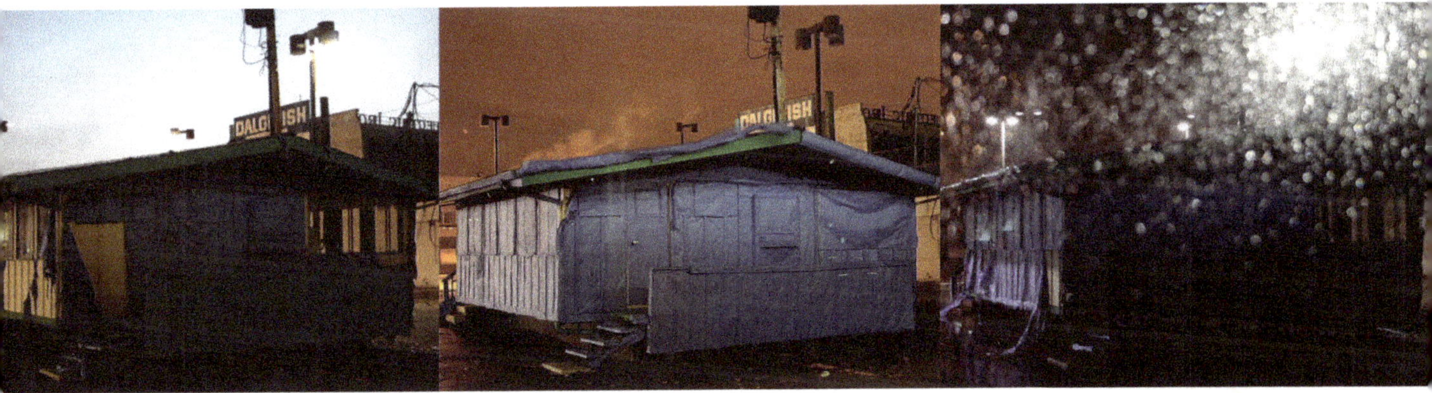

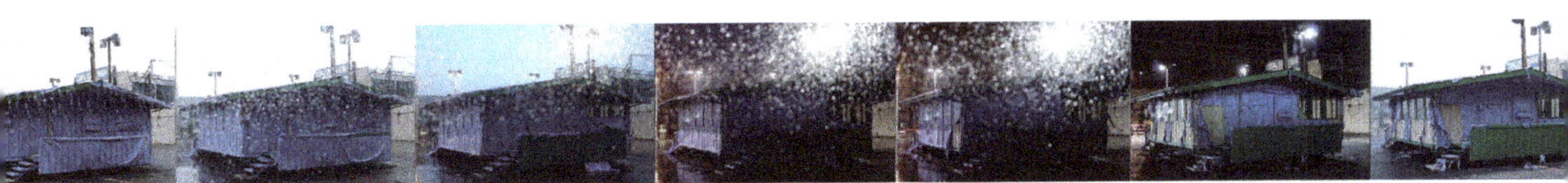

GREG HOLM AND MATTHEW RADUNE

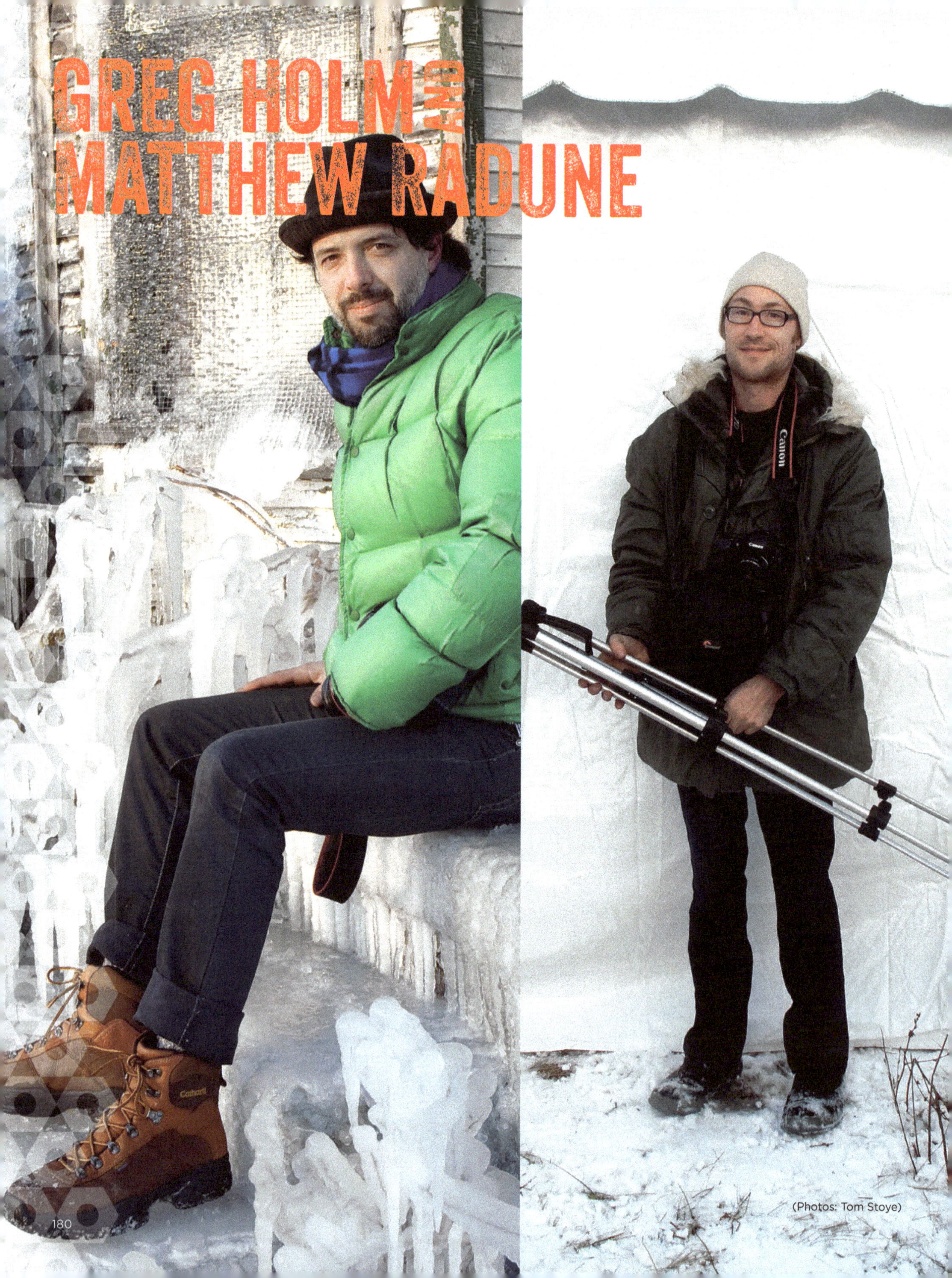

(Photos: Tom Stoye)

Some people paint houses as art. Others find the art in deconstructing and rebuilding.

For the sake of art, Greg Holm and Matthew Radune went a step beyond. On a desolate block on Detroit's east side, in the dead of winter, they completely froze a house. The house they froze back in 2010, a doomed two-story victim of foreclosure, turned heads, drew cameras, inspired awe, and eventually became a series of breathtaking photographs and prints.

In conversations about art in Detroit, the Ice House still stands tall as a go-to example of the way the city is giving life to extreme possibilities. "Obviously, a lot of people thought we were crazy being out in the cold and with water, night after night."

Holm, a photographer and concept artist, says he and Radune, an architect, had been in search of a creative way to illustrate the nation's frozen economy and its disastrous impact on the housing market. No city demonstrated America's economic freeze more than Detroit.

"It just made sense as a really different and beautiful way to represent the times and to look at what was going on with the city and with the housing crisis," says Holm. "Matthew had been thinking of working with ice for a while, and it just all came together in Detroit. With the city struggling the way that it was, it just made even more sense to use ice as a medium."

But as Holm and Radune soon discovered, icing a house is anything but easy.

"Initially, we thought, Oh, this will be really easy, we'll just set up a sprinkler system and it will just do what it does on Belle Isle with the trees and just beautifully freeze," Holm recalled, referring to a long-time Detroit tradition of freezing a Christmas tree on Belle Isle as public art.

Reality hit Holm quickly. "We had prototypes and sprinkler systems that wouldn't freeze. We eventually realized the only way to do this was by hand, dousing the entire thing with a really fine mist, let it sit for five minutes, then every few minutes jut do it all over again."

A new surprise seemed to greet each twenty-four-hour shift during the ten-day project.

"After about a week-and-a-half or two, we realized the top of the house wasn't freezing," Holm says. "We went up into the attic and discovered that it was nearly sixty degrees in the peak of the attic just because of the shingles."

The duo took the first action that came to mind. They busted the windows and turned on fans to create a cross-breeze.

"Within five minutes we had it down to thirty-eight degrees, kind of just learning thermal dynamics on the fly," Holm says. "To look at the end result of what we did, it looked like we just froze a house one day. But it was a mentally taxing project. So much went into making it happen. There was no way for people to see it all."

In fact, Holm says most of the people following the project were so awed by the ice that even they missed its coolest parts: "From the beginning, it was important to us to give something back in the process."

They kept their word in myriad ways. They sponsored a food and clothing drive benefitting homeless men and women near the Ice House. With support from the Michigan Land Bank, Holm and Radune also helped a Detroit mother save her home by paying off nearly five thousand dollars in back taxes. Early on, they'd worked out a deal with the Land Bank to lease a foreclosed home in exchange for their promise to aide a homeowner in need.

"We never wanted to just come to Detroit and create a spectacle," Holm says.

Since Ice House Detroit, he's gone on to stage an opera inside of an old firehouse, starring the Detroit Children's Choir and five prominent New York music composers. Holm has even ventured into architectural preservation. He's personally rehabbing two art deco buildings that he now owns and intends to transform into a restaurant.

In the same way that the city inspired the Ice House, he says Detroit continues to be an improbable yet perfect muse.

"It's still a hard place to live," he says. "Nothing is easy. But I like to be challenged, to feel my worth as a human being and to be creative. Whatever I do here, I know it has a chance to be foundational. The chance to be part of it is what keeps you going in Detroit."

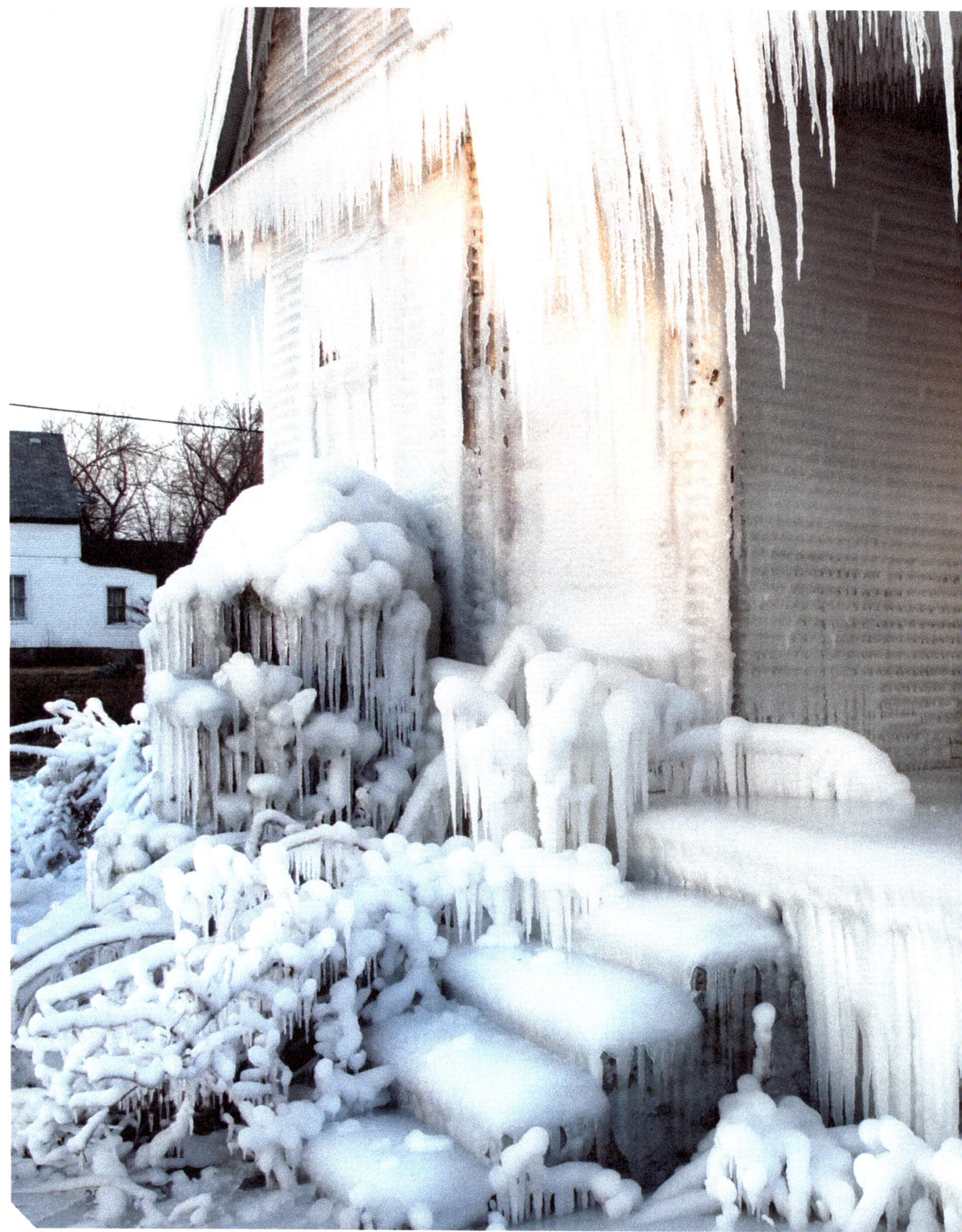

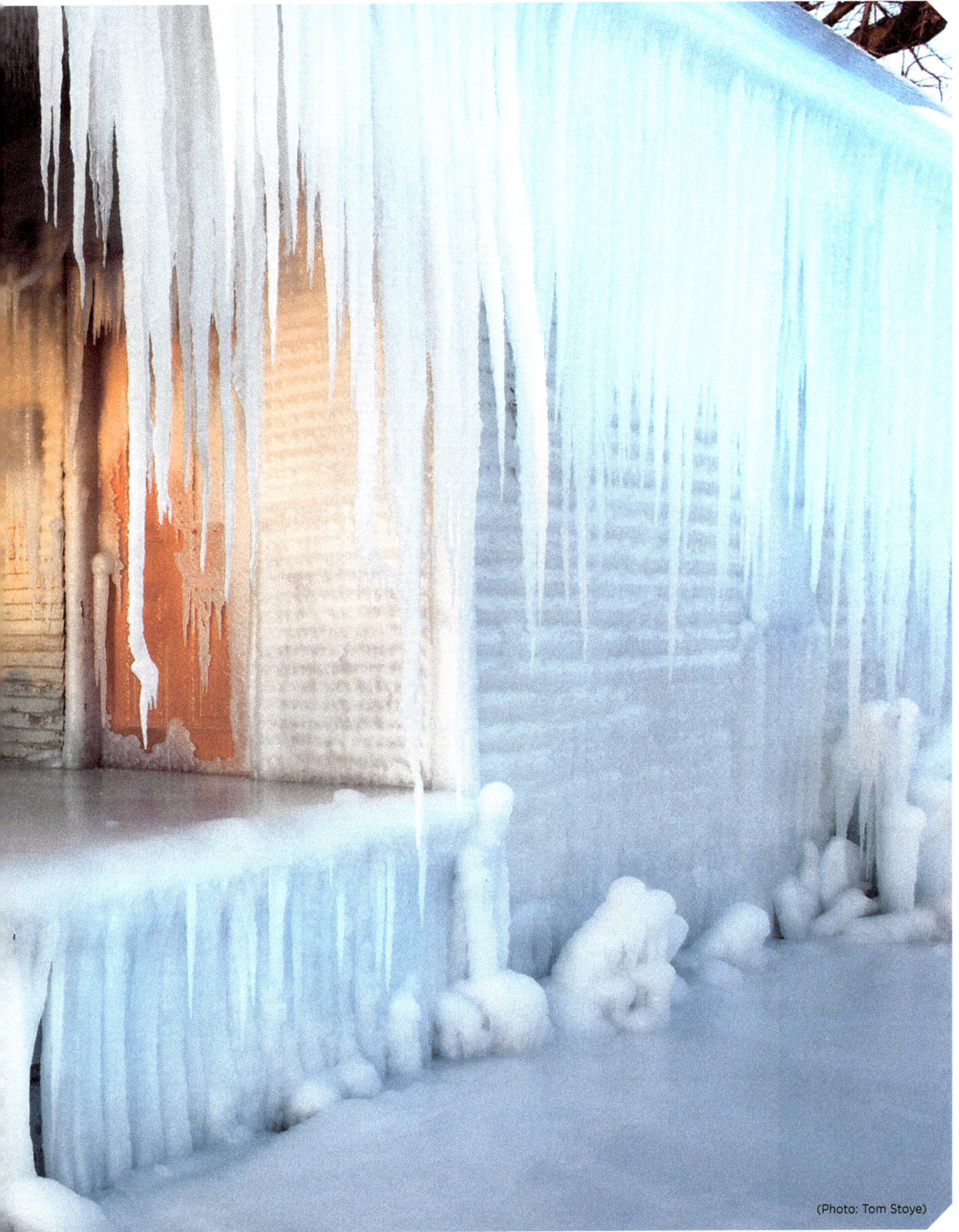

(Photo: Tom Stoye)

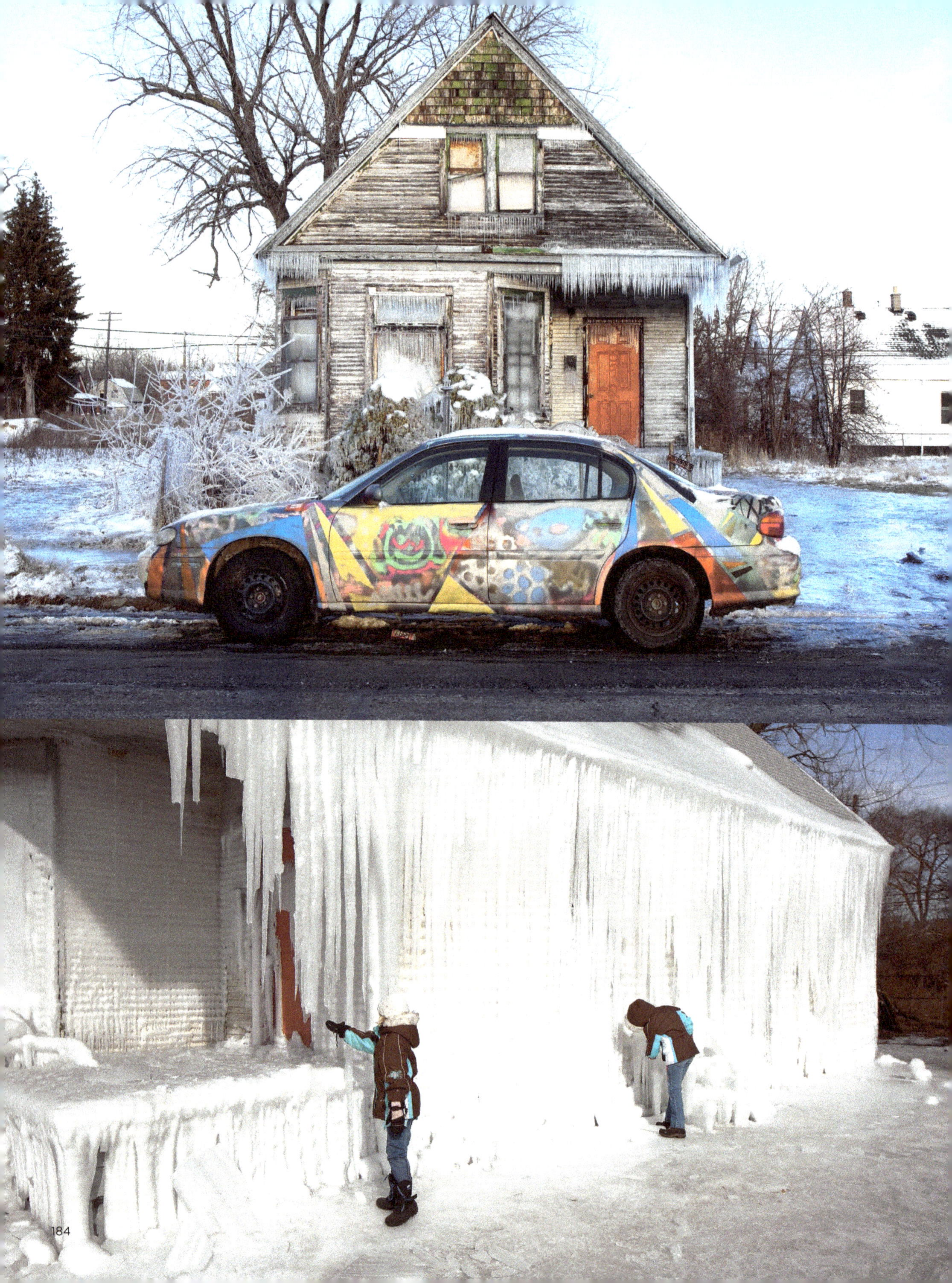

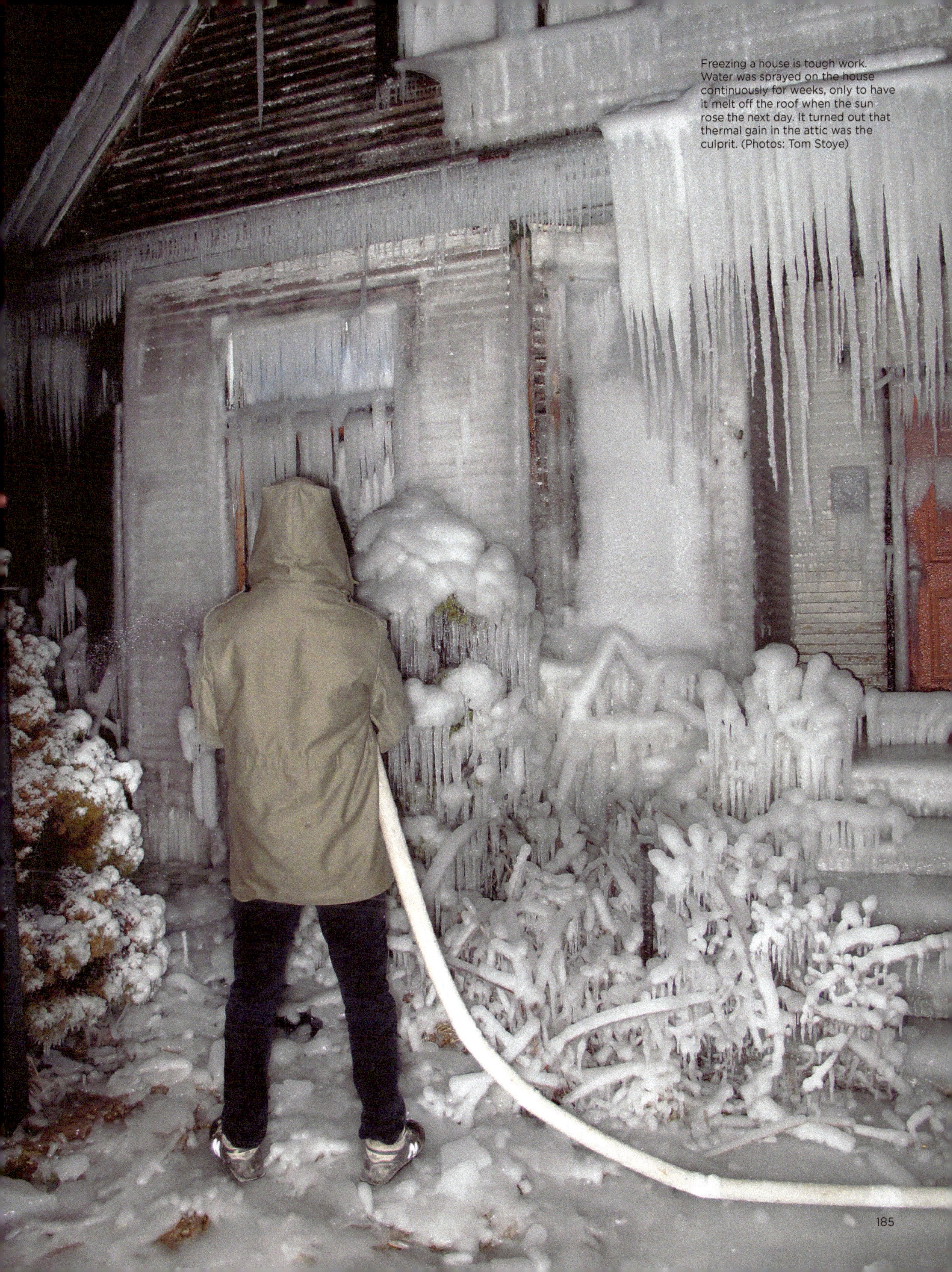

Freezing a house is tough work. Water was sprayed on the house continuously for weeks, only to have it melt off the roof when the sun rose the next day. It turned out that thermal gain in the attic was the culprit. (Photos: Tom Stoye)

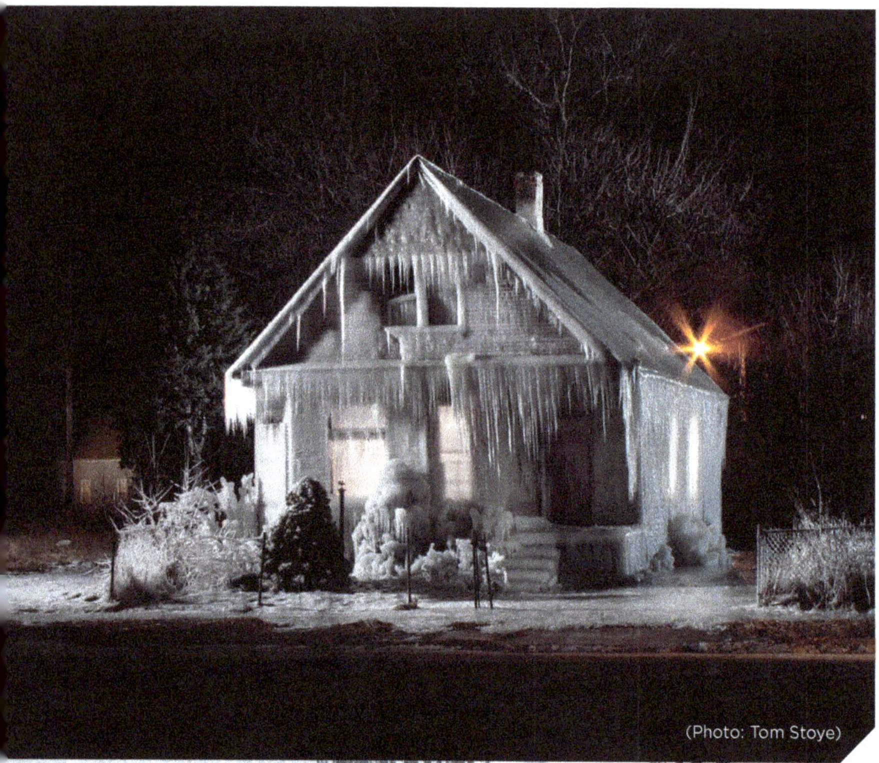

(Photo: Tom Stoye)

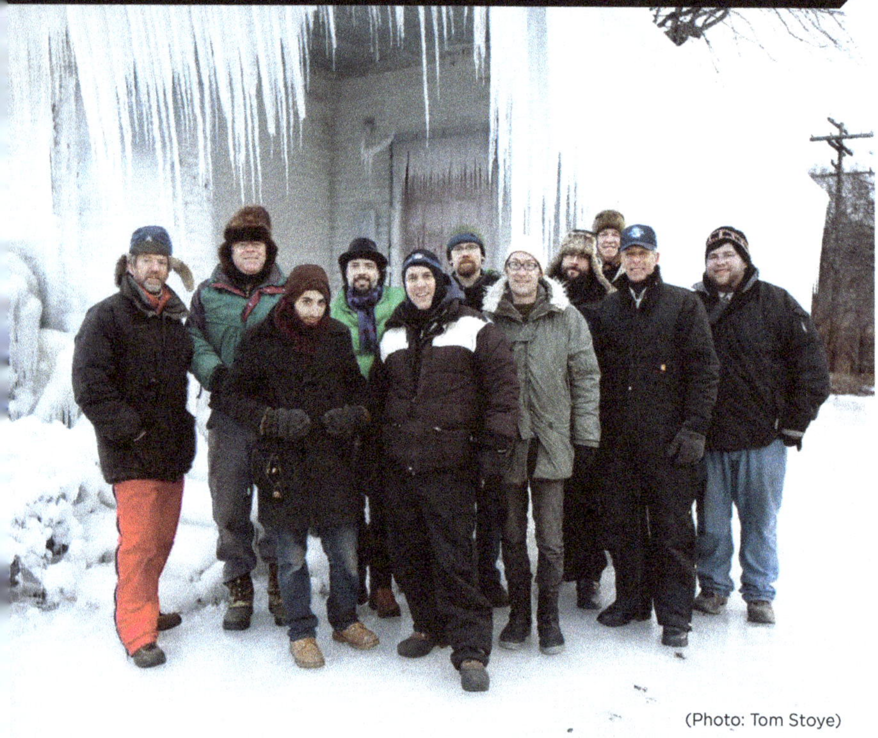

(Photo: Tom Stoye)

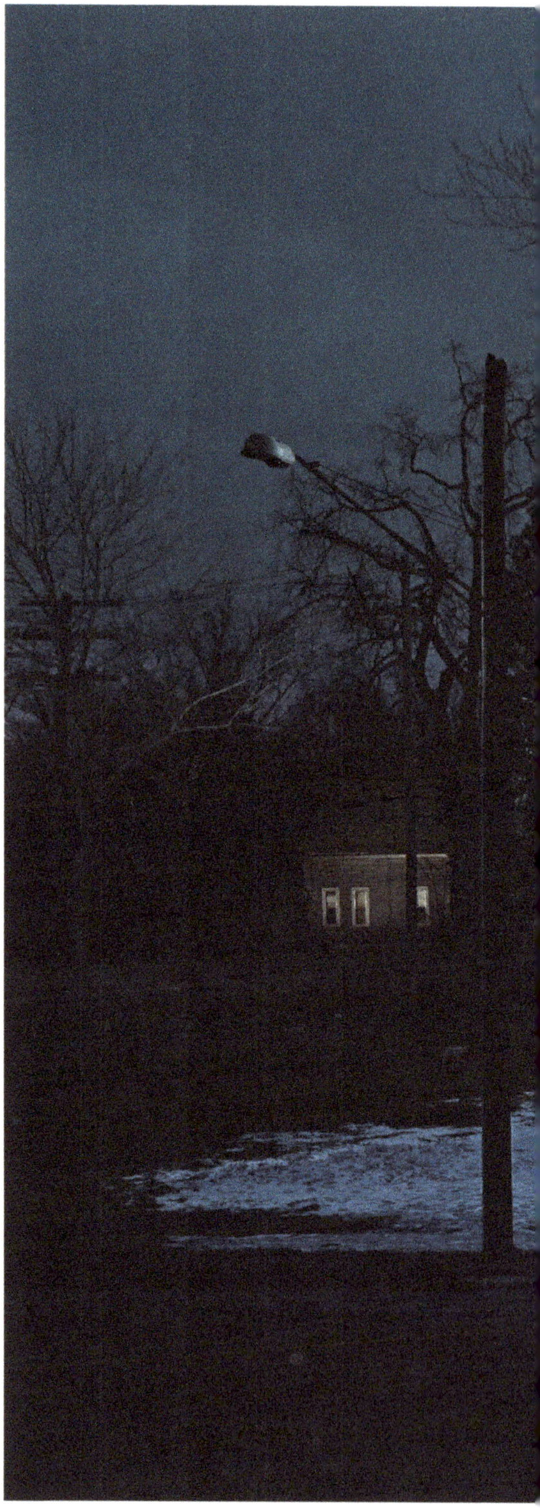

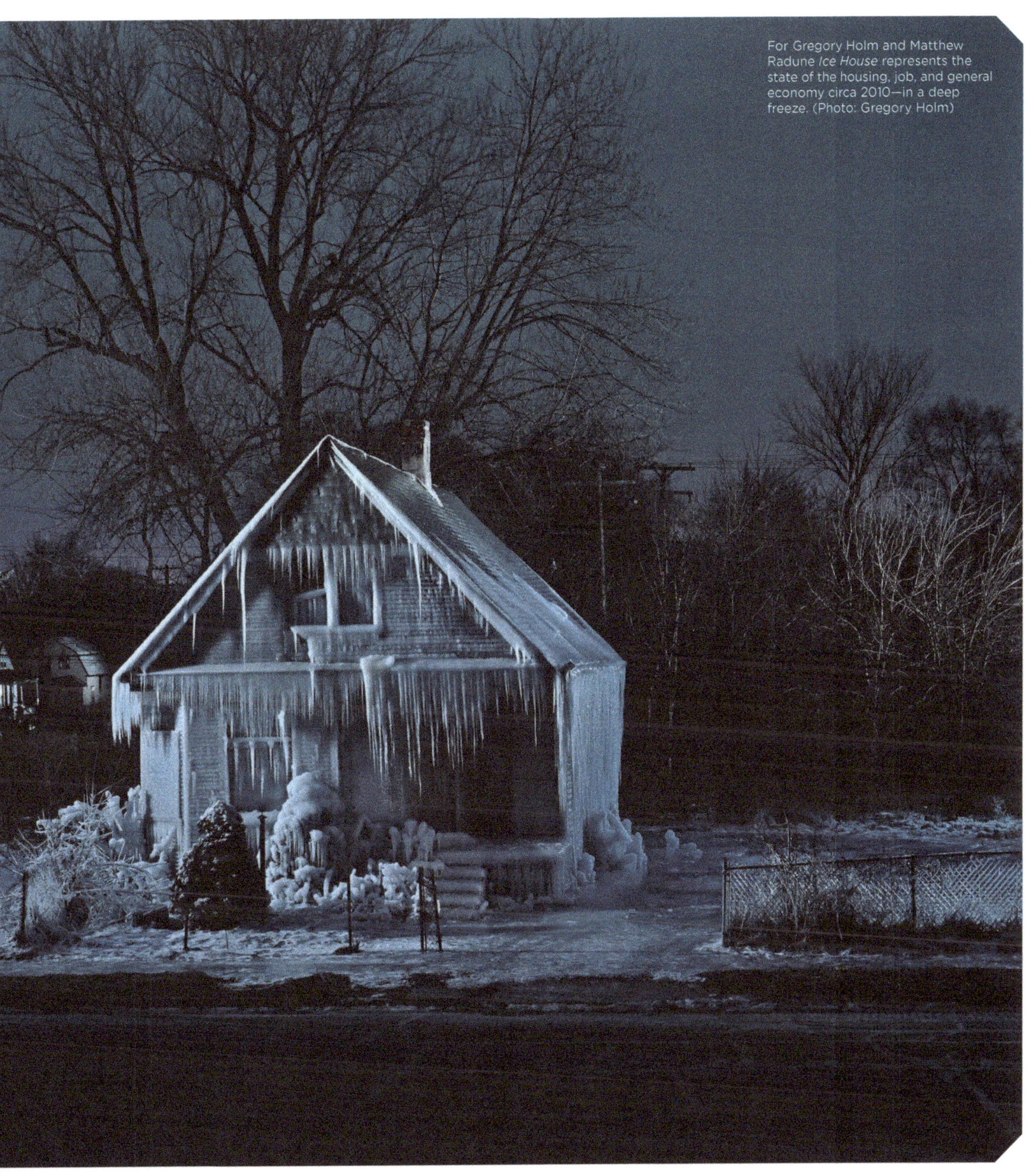

For Gregory Holm and Matthew Radune *Ice House* represents the state of the housing, job, and general economy circa 2010—in a deep freeze. (Photo: Gregory Holm)

HYGIENIC DRESS LEAGUE

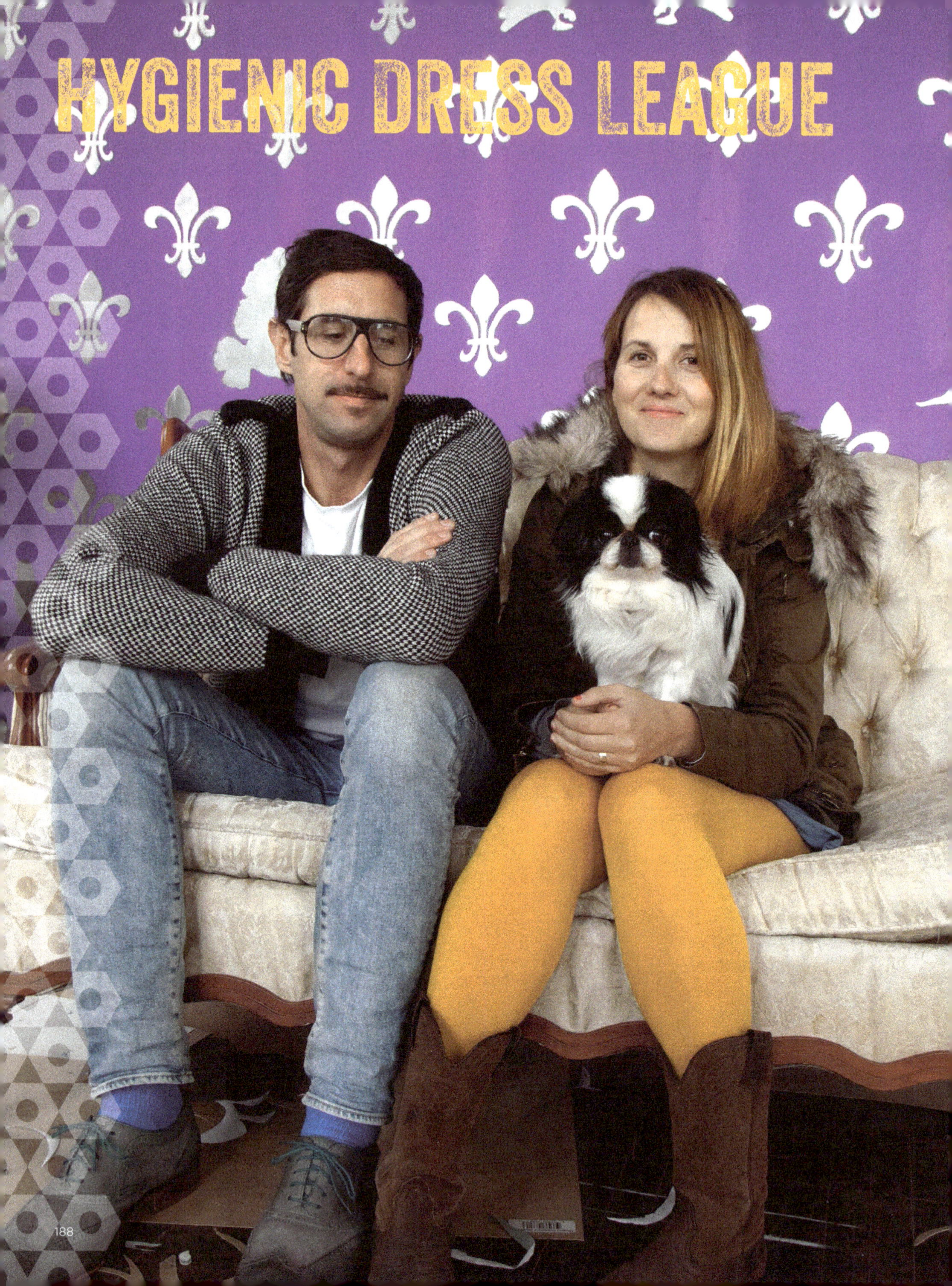

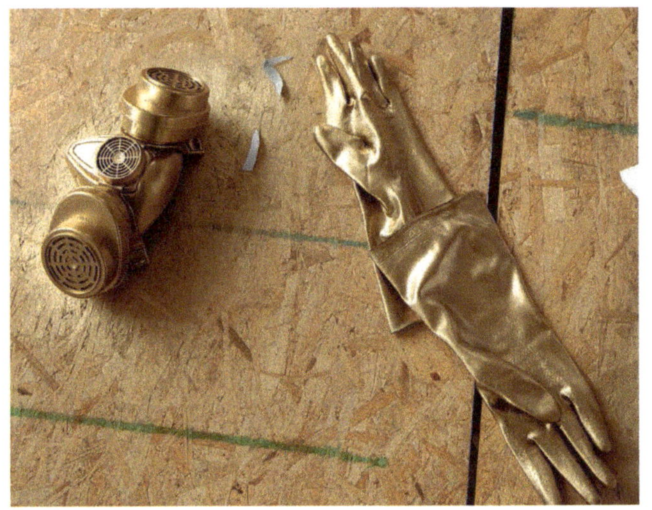

Depending on whom you ask, the Hygienic Dress League is either wickedly creative or totally absurd.

To HDL's founders, multimedia artists Steve and Dorota Coy, all attention is equal and in line with their mission.

Of course, you'd have to be a close observer to know HDL's ultimate mission. Hardly anyone ever guesses that the collective is actually a duly registered corporation. And almost everyone raises an eyebrow when the Coys attempt to explain their post-modern purpose, to promote the absurdity and gluttony of promotion. HDL is all hype, all the time.

"We like to say: 'Our Mission is to Promote our Mission: hygienic dress league,'" says Steve. "It's just absurd enough to provoke curiosity."

Since 2006, they've carefully spread their murals and billboards, painting them on the sides of empty but once-prominent buildings for maximum exposure. "We don't sell anything. We don't manufacture a product. We've created a brand name without a brand."

Still, on each canvas they choose, the Coys create work that looks like advertising, neon promises of "Coming Soon" for products that they vow will never exist. "We lose our conceptual ground the minute we begin manufacturing anything," he says. "Then, we become what any other corporation is, essentially a machine seeking out profit."

Attention is all that HDL craves. Those in the know, know to look for the corporation by its signature promotion, two stylish characters dressed in sleek business attire and wearing golden gas masks. The work is decidedly simple, always colorful and always part-apocalyptic, part-pop culture. They even went so far as to rebrand pigeons as the HDL logo, a play on the fact that pigeons, hardly hygienic birds, thrive in blighted buildings. Another irony made beautiful by the Coys.

While they will never show a profit, the Coys insist that HDL has flown farther than they ever envisioned. HDL has received a trail of media headlines, including star-like status in the 2011 film *Detropia* that can only be explained, they say, by Detroit's rising status and their gutsy decision to choose the city over their easy life in Hawaii.

"It was paradise," Steve Coy said. "And it was beautiful, but we wanted to do artwork in a non-commercial realm, a type of work that wasn't being consumed in Hawaii."

In Detroit, they've found unending inspiration. "From the beginning, we knew Detroit was a place with great history and creative potential," he says. "But I don't think you really understand the symbolism of it until you're here. There's a natural curiosity and creativity and there's also this very real post-apocalyptic feeling. It's had a profound impact on the visual language and aesthetics of our project and the idea of an alternate reality where promotion can become its own machine."

As a native of the Detroit area, Coy says he understands how some people view HDL's work as exploitive, too, taking advantage of the city's glut of empty buildings just because they are empty. He argues that those who take that view misunderstand art's role: "I think of it as just bringing attention, whether it's positive or negative. It gets people rethinking. They start to look at the buildings and maybe even see opportunities. Usually the creative movement acts as a catalyst."

Yet even Coy is unsure of whether HDL can be counted on as a long-term additive to Detroit: "We're not providing services to the homeless. We're not building city infrastructure. We understand there are limitations to what we do," he says. "But I do think the work has its humble place. It's something that wasn't there."

And as long as Detroit remains home, Coy promises there is more: "Coming Soon."

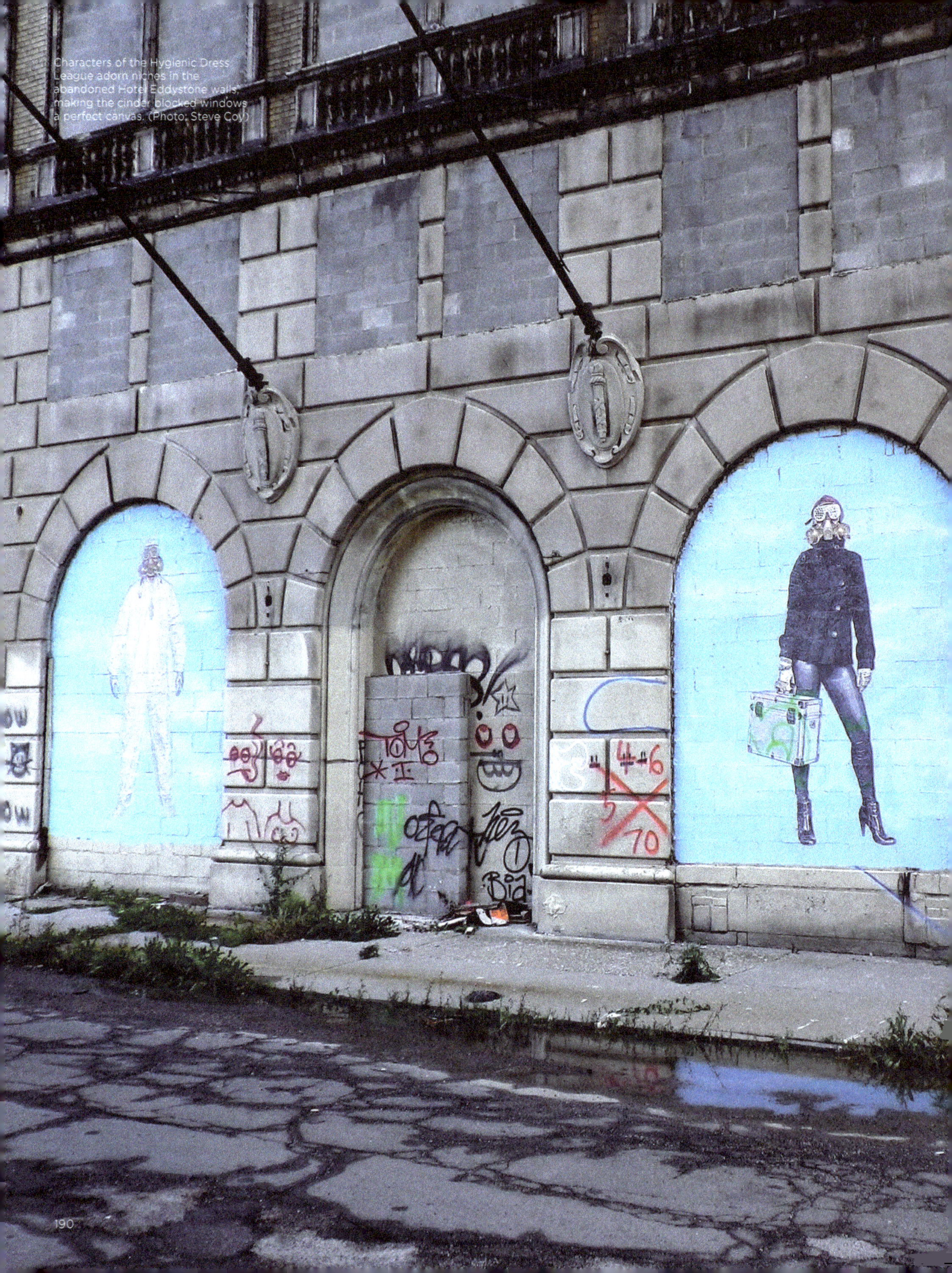

Characters of the Hygienic Dress League adorn niches in the abandoned Hotel Eddystone walls, making the cinder blocked windows a perfect canvas. (Photo: Steve Coy)

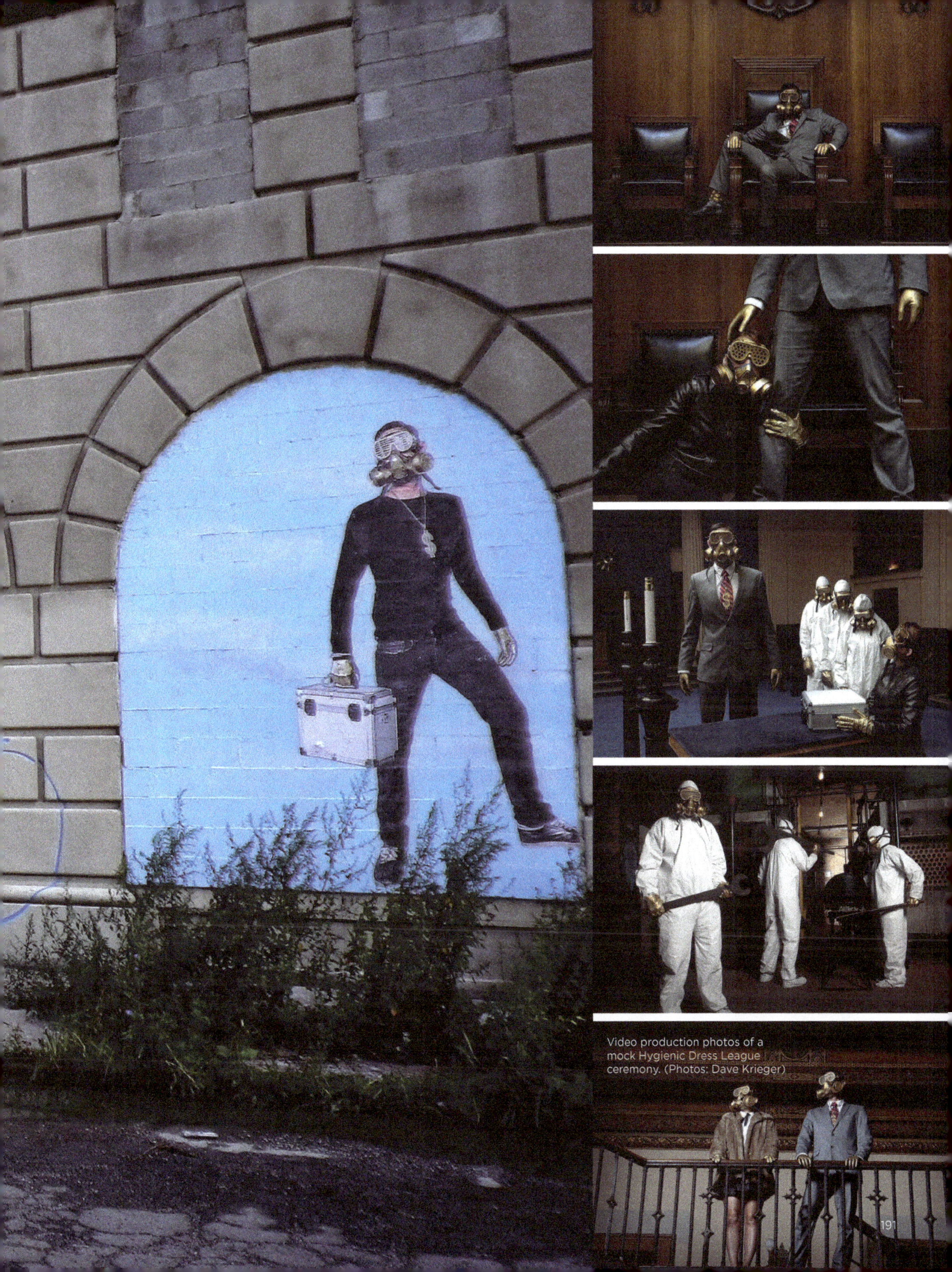

Video production photos of a mock Hygienic Dress League ceremony. (Photos: Dave Krieger)

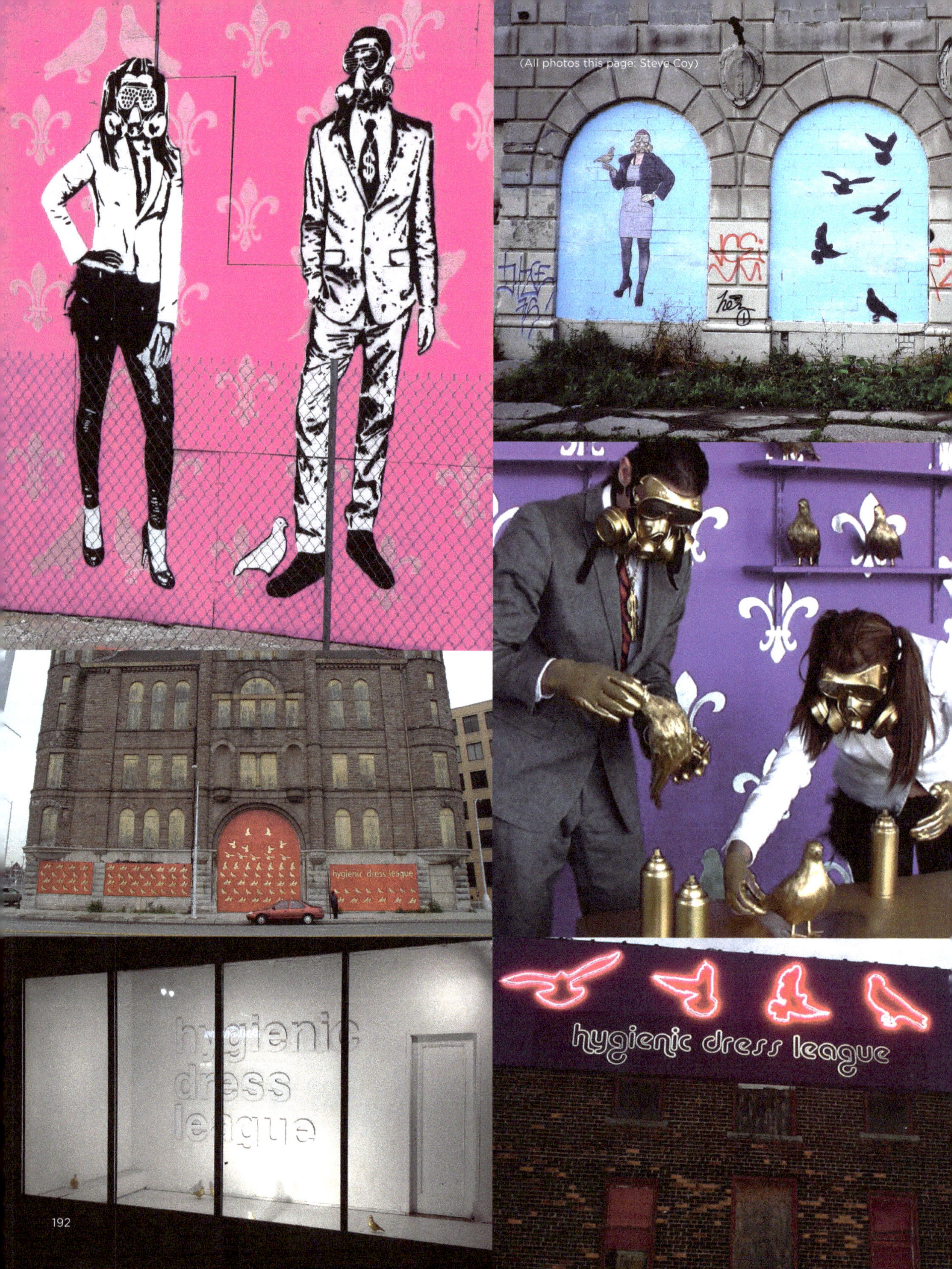

(All photos this page: Steve Coy)

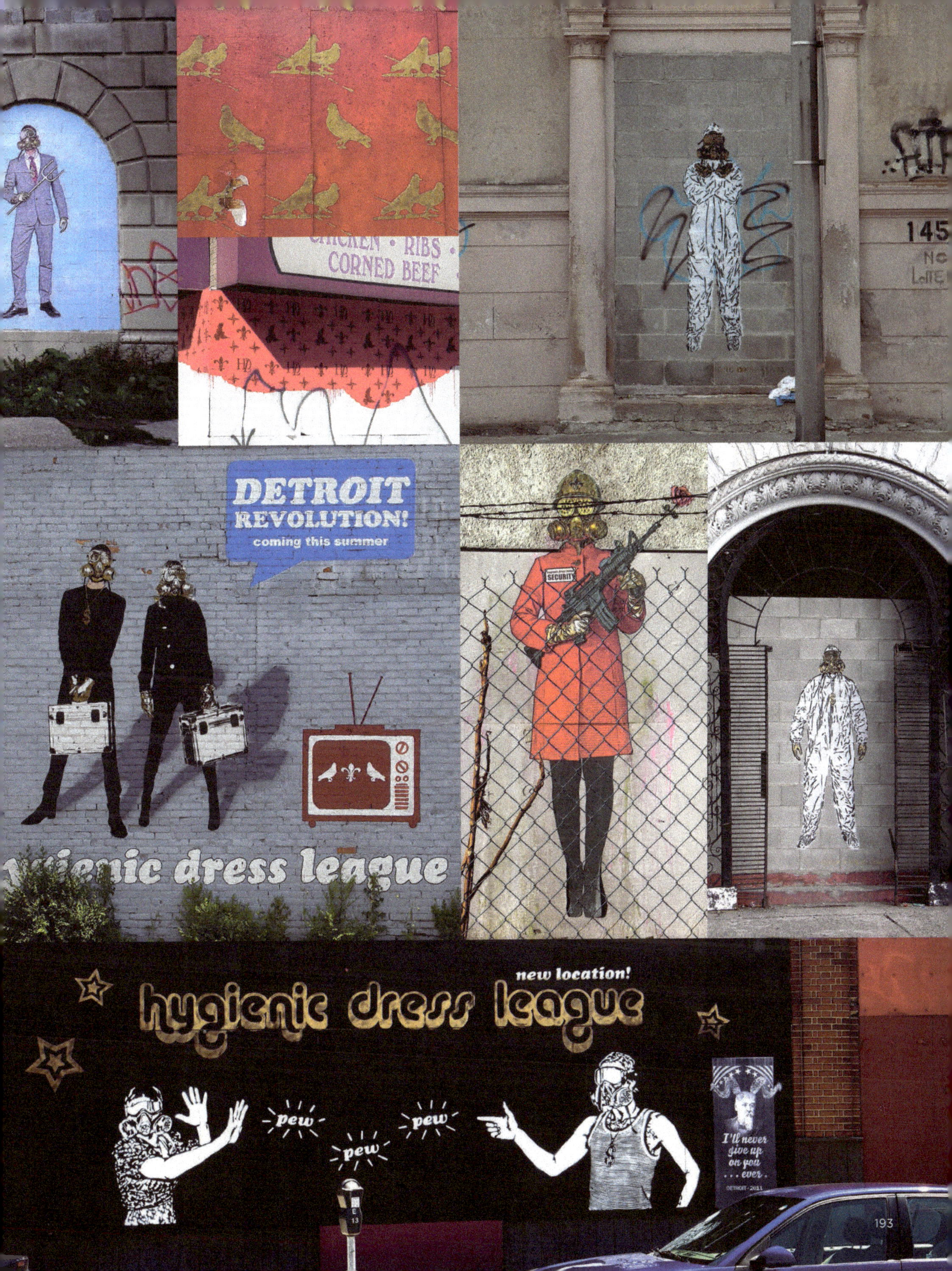
RIBS
CORNED BEEF
145
DETROIT
REVOLUTION!
coming this summer
dress league
SECURITY
new location!
hygienic dress league
pew
pew
pew
I'll never
give up
on you
. . . ever.

KEVIN JOY

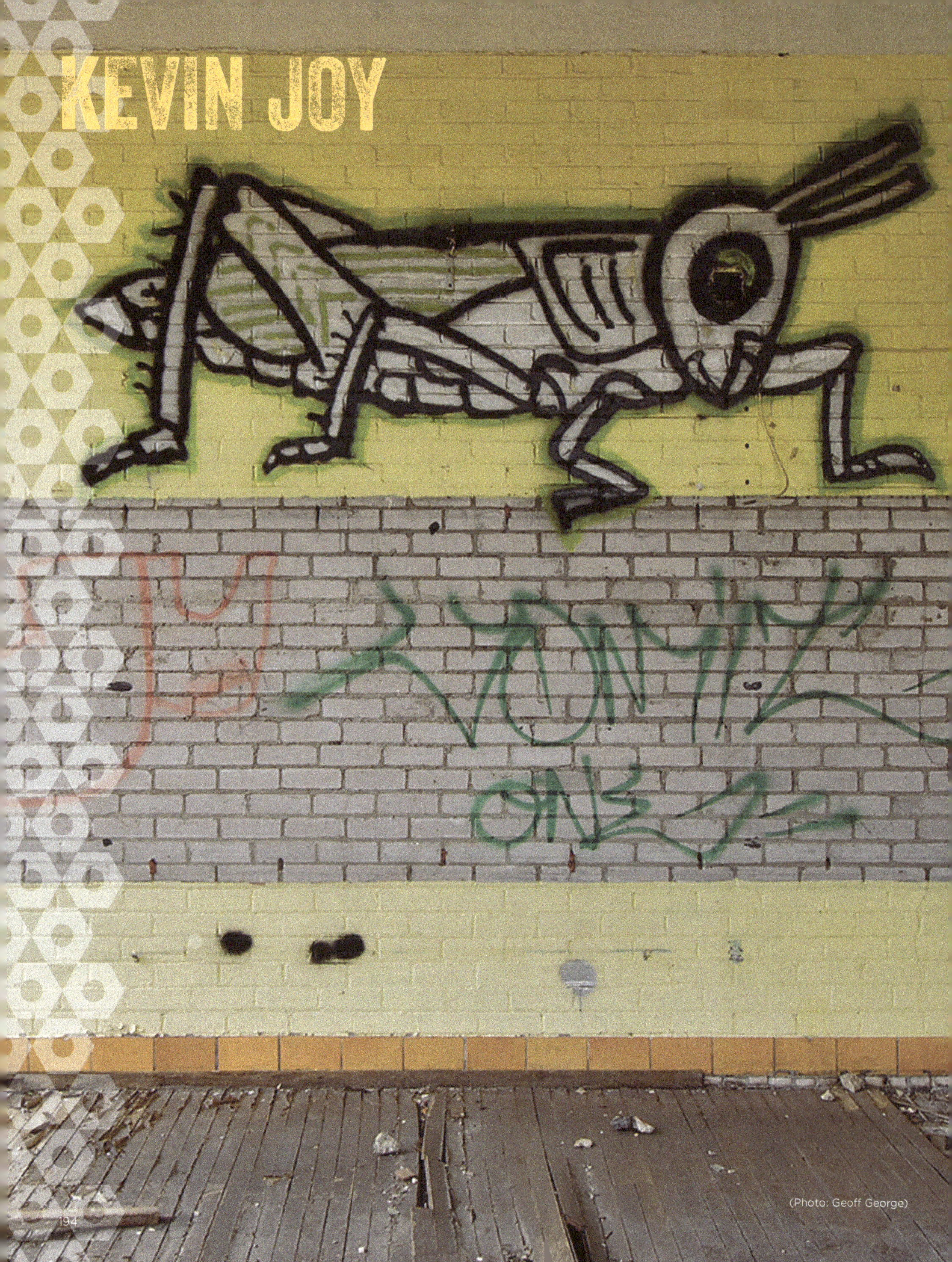

(Photo: Geoff George)

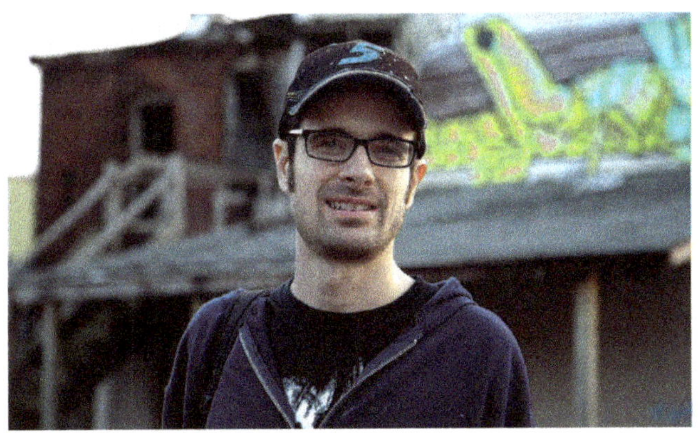

Kevin Joy knows the temptation most people have when they discover his work.

The G-word—graffiti—is often where most minds race to describe his whimsical paintings of grasshoppers, soup cans, and sunrises. Even to Joy, the association is understandable. He has, after all, coveted towering abandoned office buildings as his canvas.

But that's where the similarities end. "A lot of graffiti is solely about the glorification of an ego, the person tagging, saying, `Look at me, look what I did.' They don't even want to be known as artists," Joy, thirty-eight, says. "I'm an artist."

He insists his work is always driven by a singular purpose. "I wanted something pretty to look at on my way to work," says Joy, who grew up in nearby St. Clair Shores. "Seeing abandoned buildings every day takes a lot out of you. You're driving and they're everywhere. It's epic in scope. If you're creative and you care, it's a question of: How can I make it better?"

"It's inspiring to see how the light changes things when it shines through, even in empty buildings," says Joy. "I wanted people like me, driving by, to look and be like, `Hey, someone did something serious. Why is the sun rising?'"

Alas, little of Joy's signature works remain, save for the scrapbook and photos he keeps as a personal archive. As Detroit's efforts at a downtown rebirth have slowly risen, the windows and buildings Joy adorned have all come tumbling down. He witnessed the demolition of both his masterpieces.

"I could be bitter," he says, "But I didn't make the work for me. I did what I set out to do. I gave people something to look at."

These days, Detroit continues to fuel Joy's art. By day, he earns his living making desserts in a Midtown restaurant. By night, he imagines and sketches new creations destined for unknown buildings and windows.

He smiles as he discusses his latest project, a street-level commissioned mural that comes complete with room and board provided by the building's owner. The mural, he promises, will be a whimsical homage to Detroit, "ripping off" some of the reverence and pride he hears in Bruce Springsteen's *Greetings from Asbury Park, N.J.* album. "Some pretty cool things have come out of Detroit," he says.

Joy is also in the early stages of what he calls a "found photo project" focused on Detroit's North End neighborhood. Joy's aim is to link the photos to former residents of now-abandoned homes and paint portraits on the houses they once lived in.

Like much of his other work, Joy expects his latest ideas will raise some eyebrows and maybe make him subject, yet again, to Detroit's great graffiti-versus-art debate.

He's ready. Provoking debate, the soft-spoken Joy says, is both the nature of his work and the fate of anyone who chooses to create in Detroit.

Since 2001, Joy's been offering his response to blight in Detroit with the aid of oil chalks, spray paints, and a fierce determination to lift people's eyes. Rather than confining his drawings and paintings to bare brick walls, Joy has made a name for himself by taking his creations to the top of some of Detroit's tallest eyesores. By painting only on the windows, he says, he restores light to dark places.

Joy's aim to make Detroiters look skyward is no joke, nor is it a small task. He poured more than three years into outlining and painting bright Mayan-styled hieroglyphics onto nearly thirteen hundred windows inside of the eighteen-story United Artists Building. Joy turned heads again by painting a giant red sunrise, covering four stories, on another deserted downtown gem, the fourteen-story Lafayette Building.

"Art in Detroit is all trendy right now, but it's not solving the schools or the crime problem. It's not really changing the big picture yet," says Joy. "If you're comfortable with impermanence, and the kind of resilience where you just keep doing the work, Detroit's still this big opportunity. It's still important to give people something pretty to look at, to wonder about, `Hey, how did that happen?' You can't do that in a lot of other cities on this scale."

"I could leave," Joy adds, "but I don't know if could leave and *stay* away."

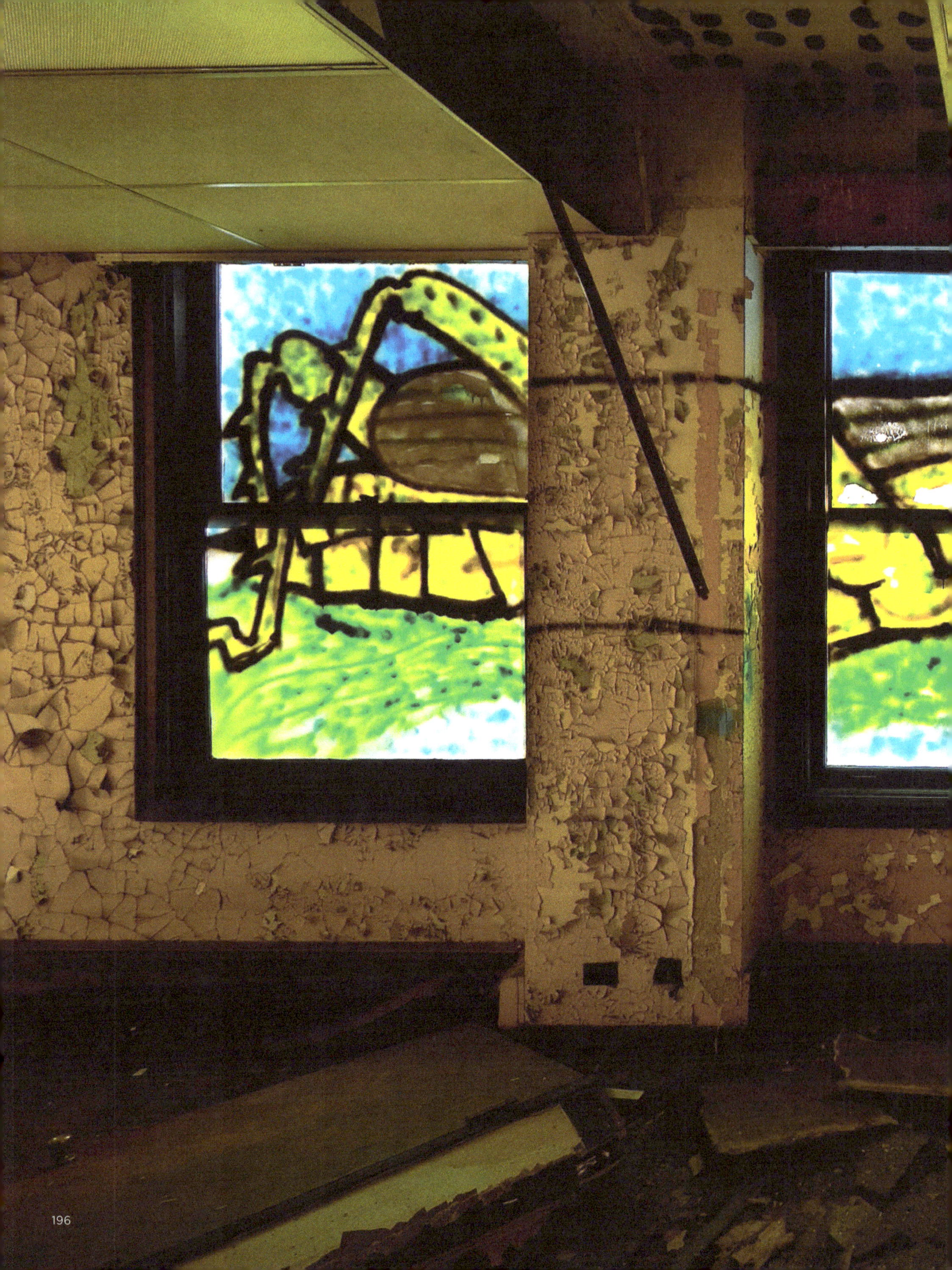

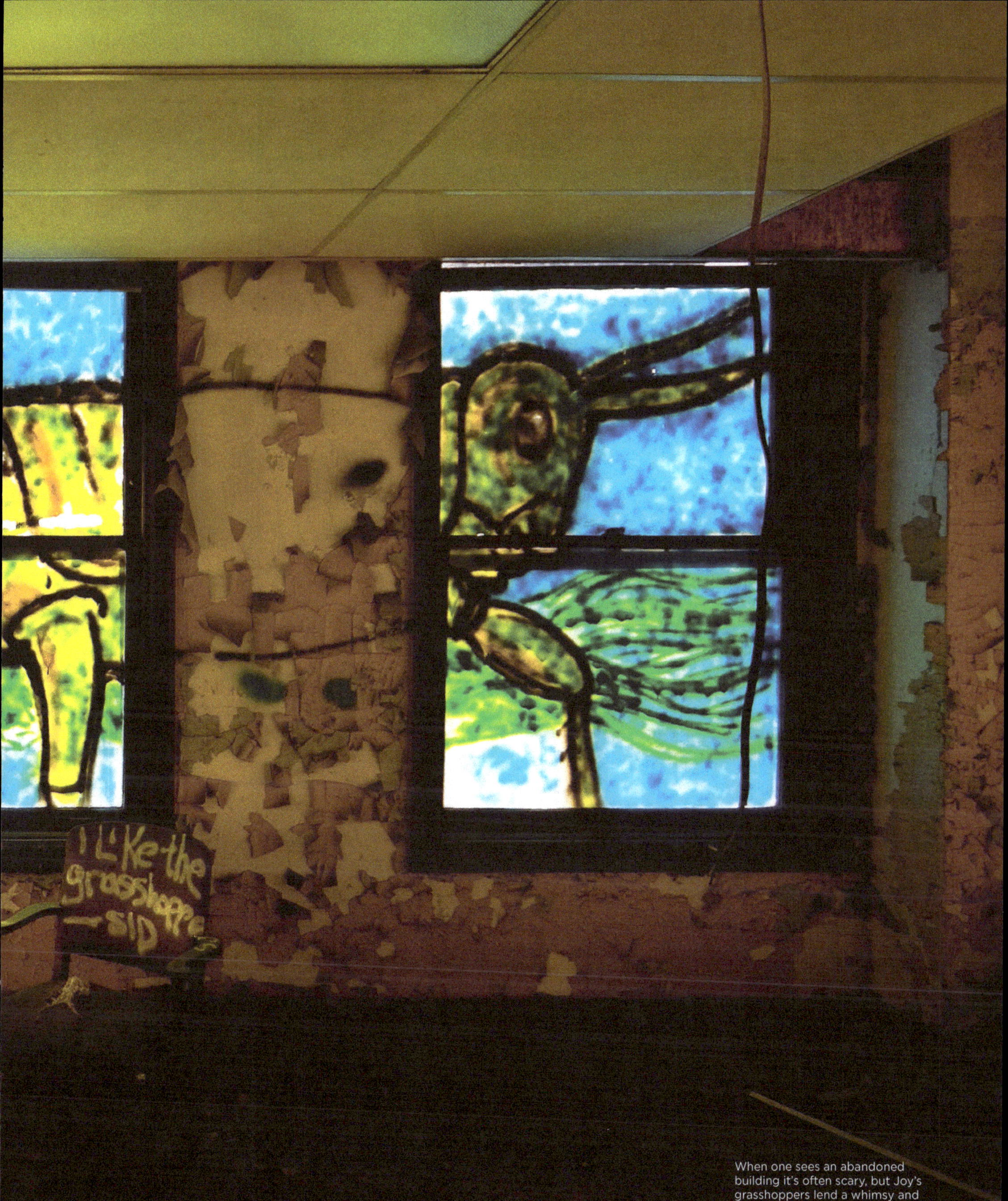

When one sees an abandoned building it's often scary, but Joy's grasshoppers lend a whimsy and

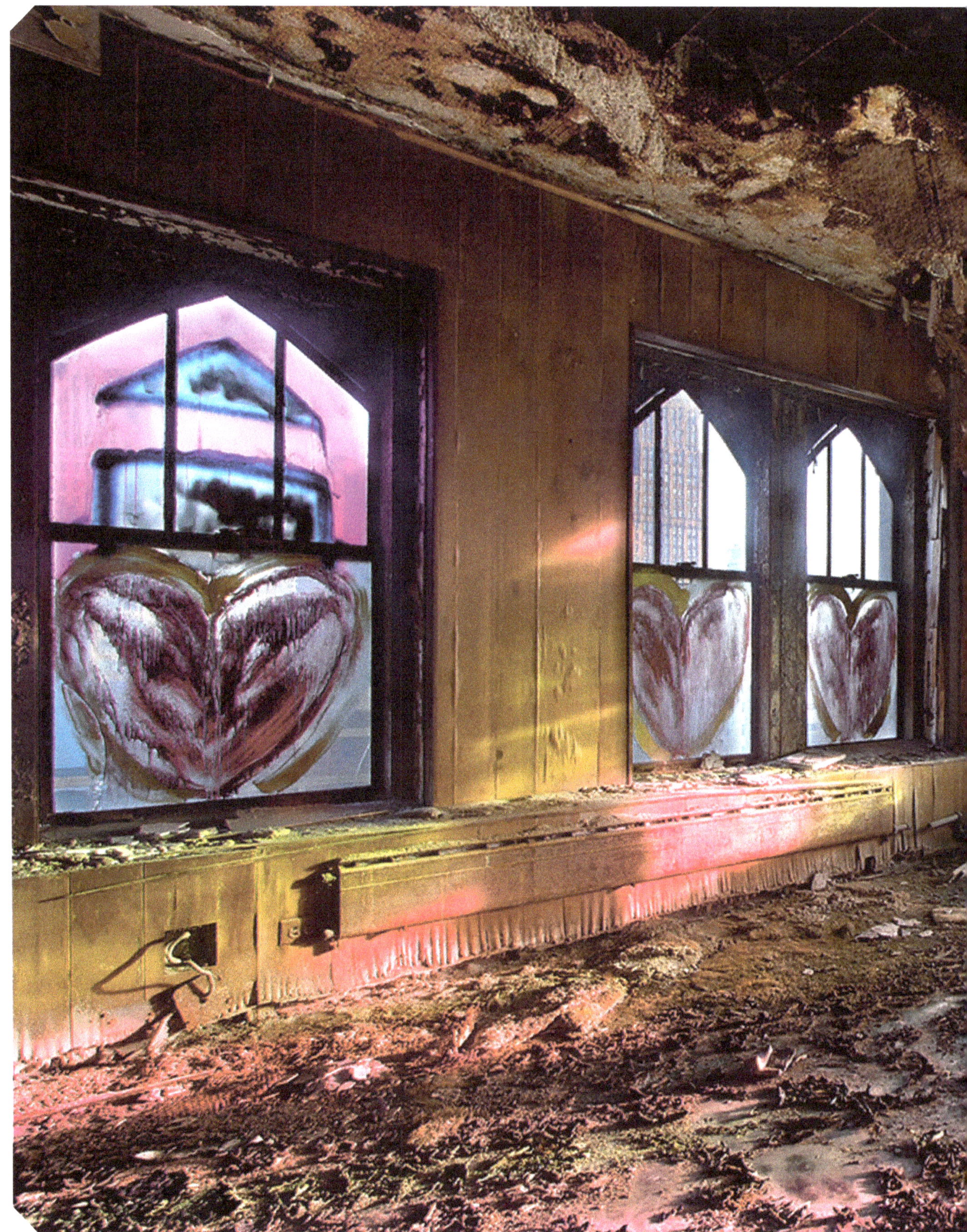

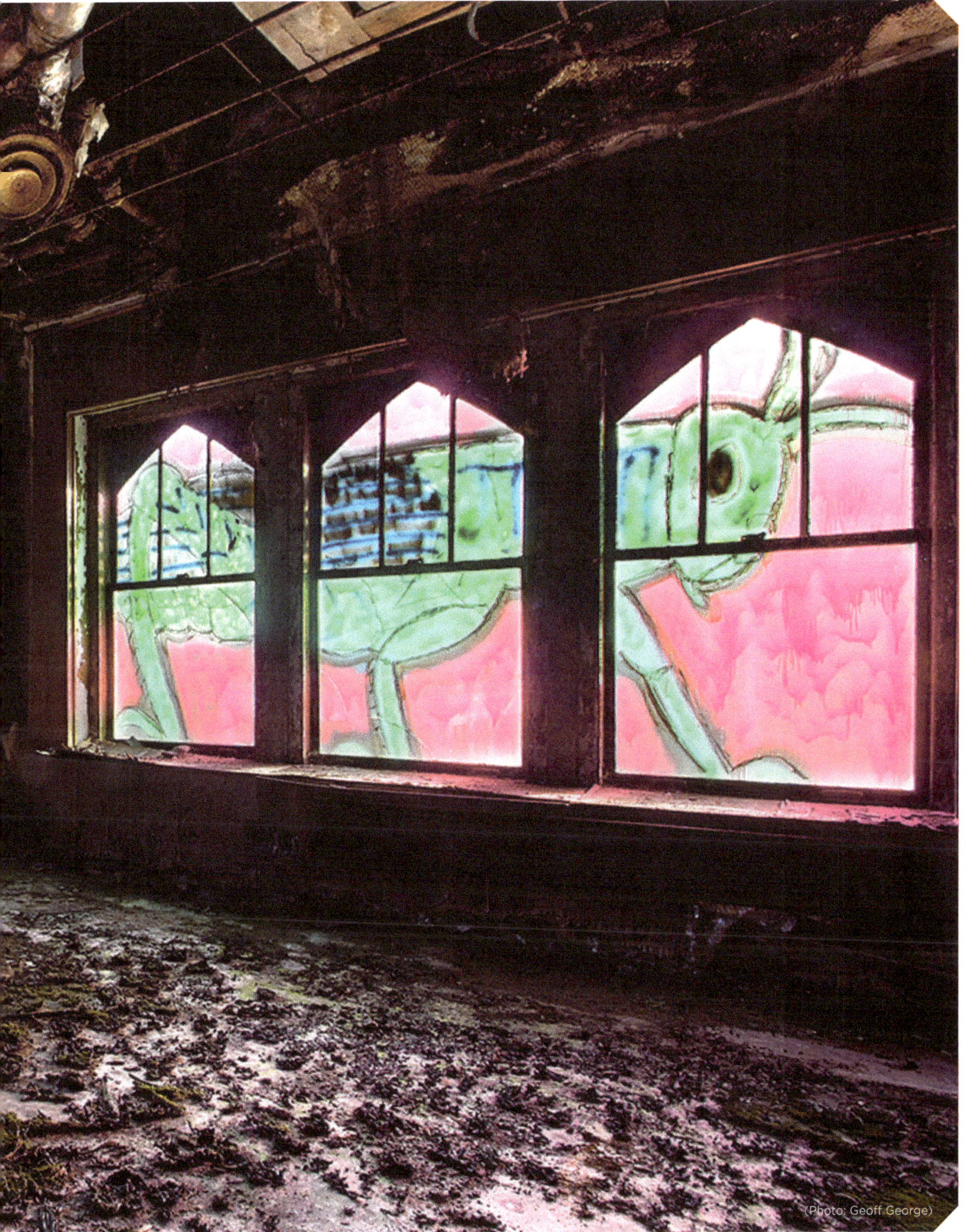

(Photo: Geoff George)

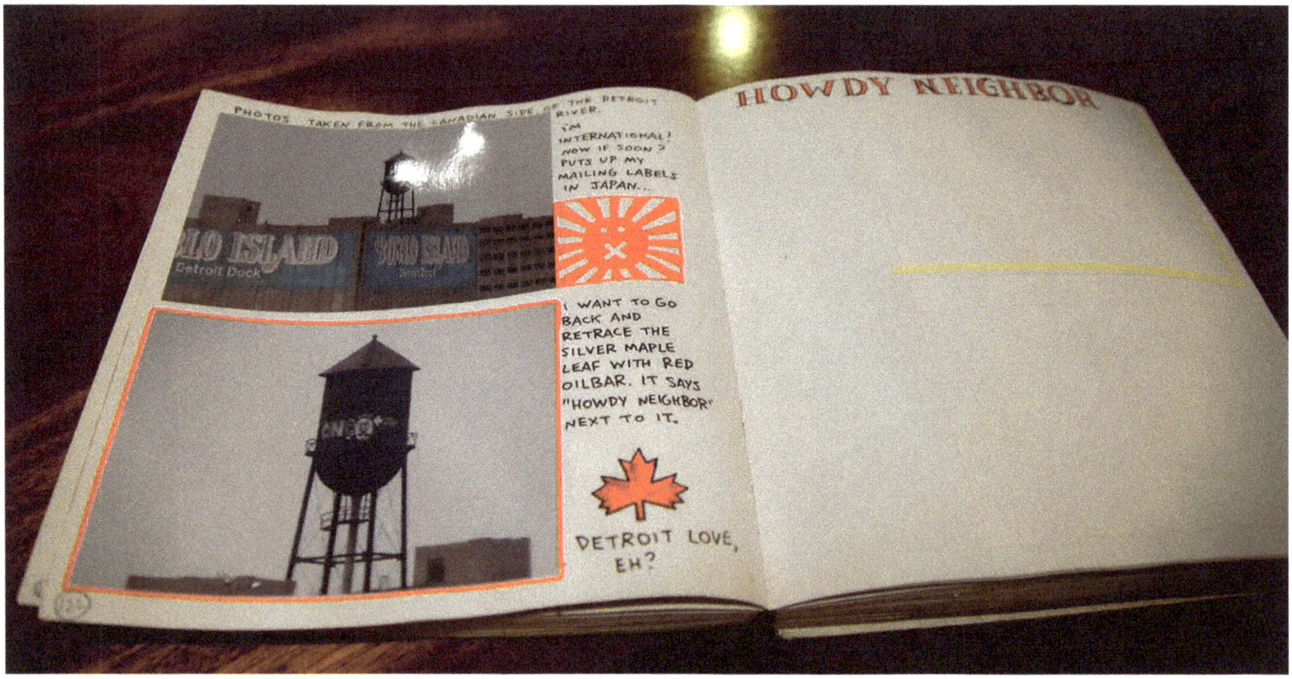

PHOTOS TAKEN FROM THE CANADIAN SIDE OF THE DETROIT RIVER.

I'M INTERNATIONAL! NOW IF SOON? PUTS UP MY MAILING LABELS IN JAPAN...

I WANT TO GO BACK AND RETRACE THE SILVER MAPLE LEAF WITH RED OILBAR. IT SAYS "HOWDY NEIGHBOR" NEXT TO IT.

DETROIT LOVE, EH?

HOWDY NEIGHBOR

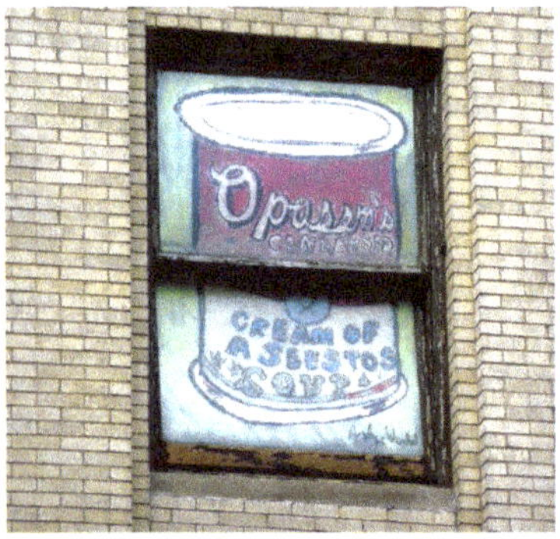

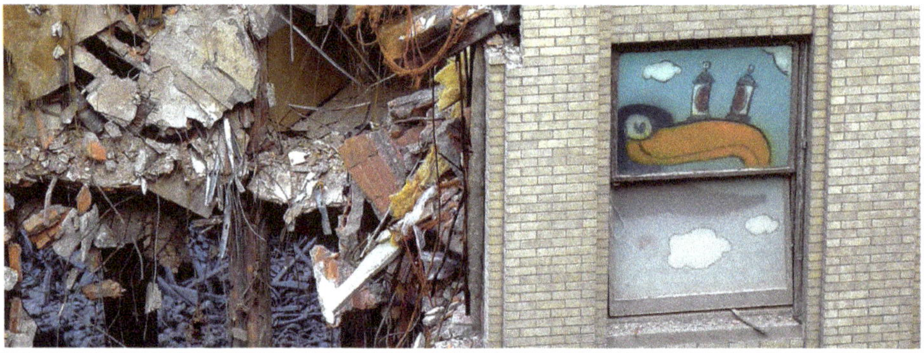

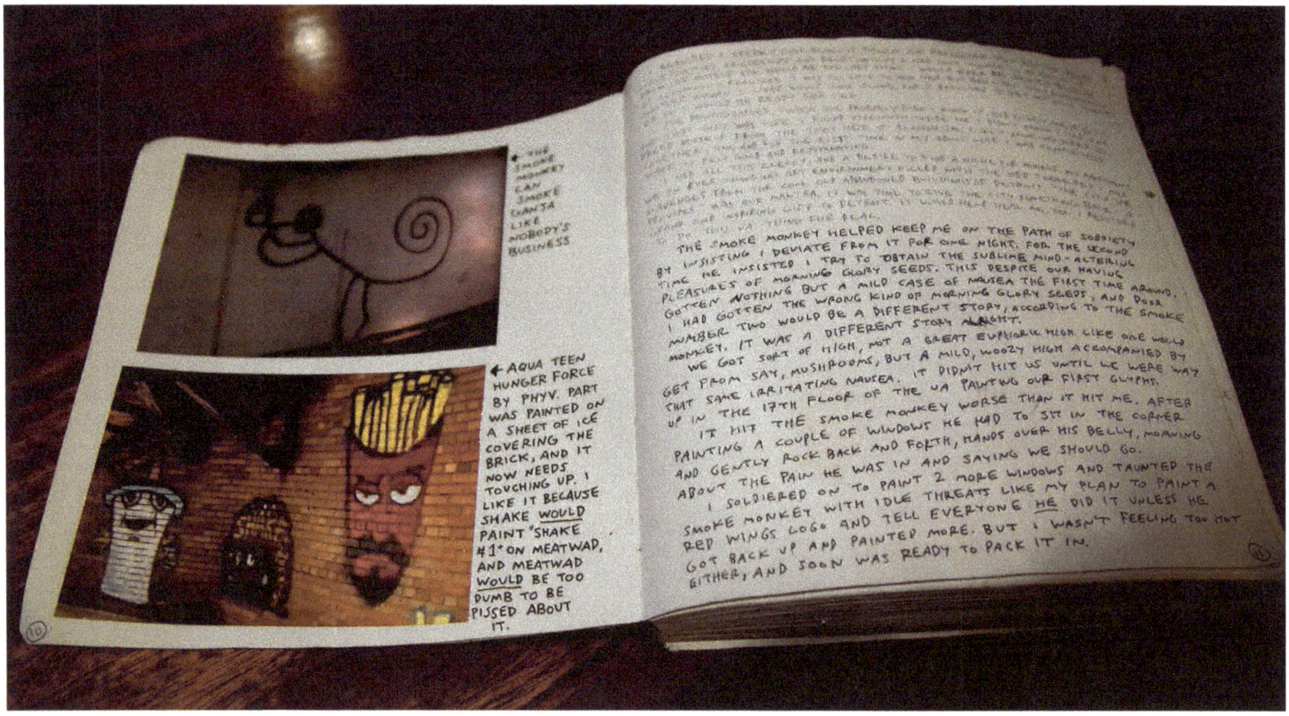

← THE SMOKE MONKEY CAN SMOKE GANJA LIKE NOBODY'S BUSINESS

← AQUA TEEN HUNGER FORCE BY PHYV. PART WAS PAINTED ON A SHEET OF ICE COVERING THE BRICK, AND IT NOW NEEDS TOUCHING UP. I LIKE IT BECAUSE SHAKE WOULD PAINT "SHAKE #1" ON MEATWAD, AND MEATWAD WOULD BE TOO DUMB TO BE PISSED ABOUT IT.

THE SMOKE MONKEY HELPED KEEP ME ON THE PATH OF SOBRIETY BY INSISTING I DEVIATE FROM IT FOR ONE NIGHT. FOR THE SECOND TIME HE INSISTED I TRY TO OBTAIN THE SUBLIME MIND-ALTERING PLEASURES OF MORNING GLORY SEEDS. THIS DESPITE OUR HAVING GOTTEN NOTHING BUT A MILD CASE OF NAUSEA THE FIRST TIME AROUND. I HAD GOTTEN THE WRONG KIND OF MORNING GLORY SEEDS, AND ROUND NUMBER TWO WOULD BE A DIFFERENT STORY, ACCORDING TO THE SMOKE MONKEY. IT WAS A DIFFERENT STORY ALRIGHT.

WE GOT SORT OF HIGH, NOT A GREAT EUPHORIC HIGH LIKE ONE WOULD GET FROM SAY, MUSHROOMS, BUT A MILD, WOOZY HIGH ACCOMPANIED BY THAT SAME IRRITATING NAUSEA. IT DIDN'T HIT US UNTIL WE WERE WAY UP IN THE 17TH FLOOR OF THE UA PAINTING OUR FIRST GLYPHS.

IT HIT THE SMOKE MONKEY WORSE THAN IT HIT ME. AFTER PAINTING A COUPLE OF WINDOWS HE HAD TO SIT IN THE CORNER AND GENTLY ROCK BACK AND FORTH, HANDS OVER HIS BELLY, MOANING ABOUT THE PAIN HE WAS IN AND SAYING WE SHOULD GO.

I SOLDIERED ON TO PAINT 2 MORE WINDOWS AND TAUNTED THE SMOKE MONKEY WITH IDLE THREATS LIKE MY PLAN TO PAINT A RED WINGS LOGO AND TELL EVERYONE HE DID IT UNLESS HE GOT BACK UP AND PAINTED MORE. BUT I WASN'T FEELING TOO HOT EITHER, AND SOON WAS READY TO PACK IT IN.

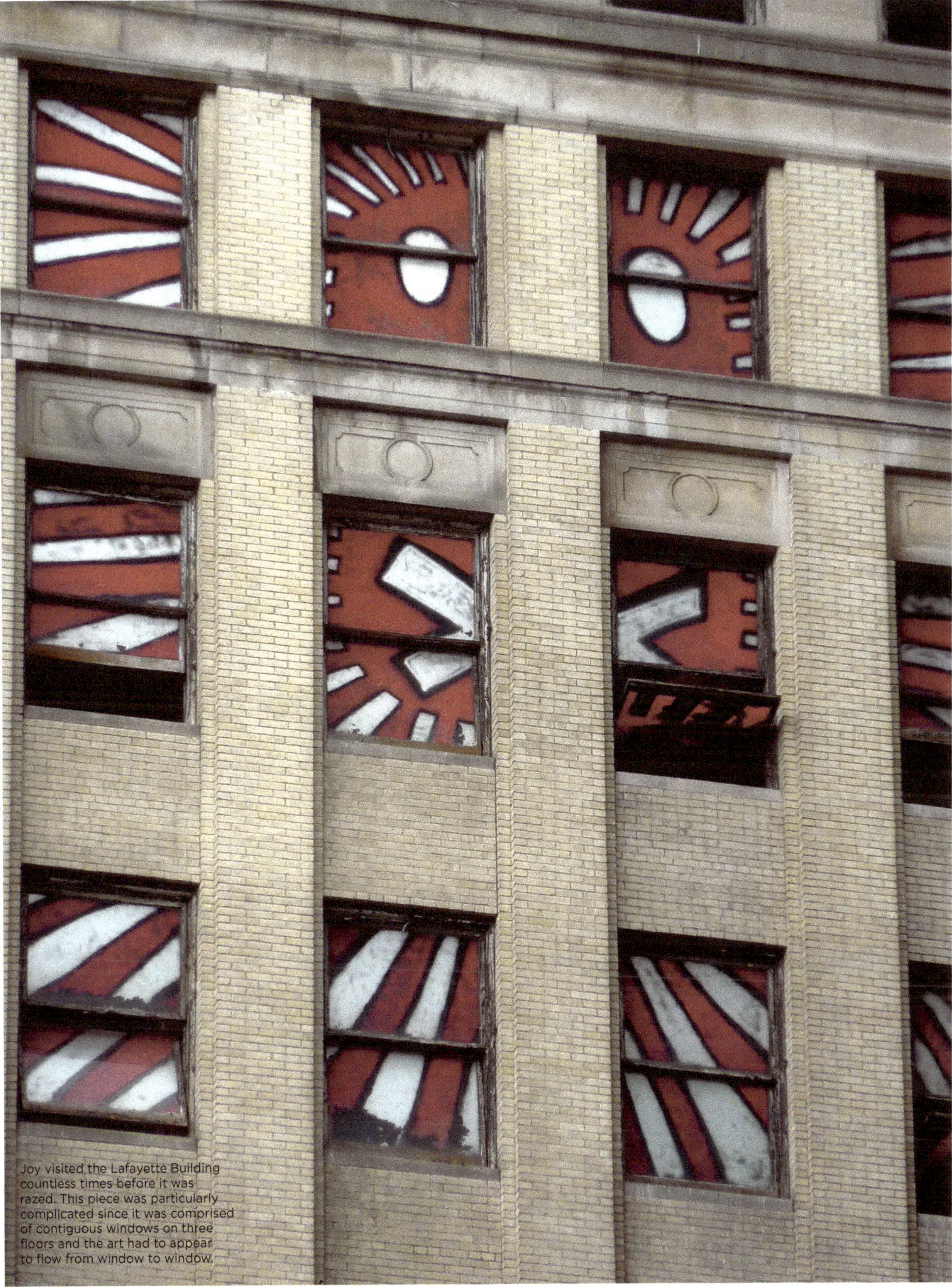

Joy visited the Lafayette Building countless times before it was razed. This piece was particularly complicated since it was comprised of contiguous windows on three floors and the art had to appear to flow from window to window.

ENO LAGET

RIGHT: When Hamtramck teens Ashley Conaway and Abreeya Brown were kidnapped and murdered in 2012, the artist considered what they may have accomplished had their lives not been cut short. What would we have missed if Aretha Franklin had met a similar fate when she was young in Detroit?

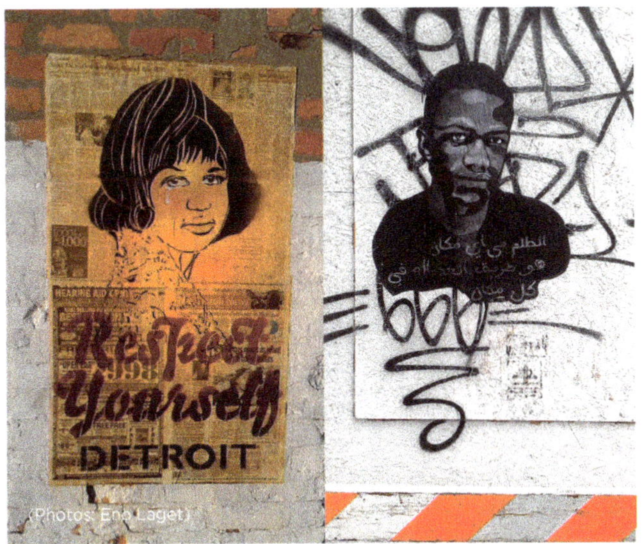

(Photos: Eno Laget)

Artist Eno Laget's work does not last. He likes it like that.

Fans know to watch the streets carefully, for as soon as he pastes one of his massive and edgy street posters, usually 36 by 72 inches, its days are numbered.

"A big part of the process for me is to document the dissolution of what I put up on the streets. It's not made to be permanent," says Laget. "It's not really even about art. It's more like a voice that holds the air for a few moments and just maybe starts some conversation about this place where everything and everybody is throwaway."

While trained in fine arts at Wayne State University, Laget leans artistically toward the streets. His tools are classically street: spray paint, hand-cut stencils, and discarded newsprint. His subject matter is ready made for the streets as well, often ripped straight from the city's hard headlines and its battered history. His posters are as stark in tone as they are in colors, and almost always blur the lines just enough to make viewers wonder.

"Detroit is a tragedy that people are running the hell away from and don't want to acknowledge the responsibility for why things are the way they are," he says.

One of his most famous posters features Hazen Pingree, Detroit's forty-third Mayor, a man often lauded for leading the city into the twentieth century, creating city schools, parks, and even pushing for vacant land to become community gardens. Laget's poster evokes Pingree with Hellboy-style horns atop his head.

"For a while, every time I'd put a Pingree on Woodward, someone would come along and butt out their cigarette on his eyes," Laget says. "I think that's great; any kind of response or interaction that causes people to pause and consider what's going on." He's also painted the Queen of Soul, Aretha Franklin, with a message urging, "Respect Yourself, Detroit."

For twenty years, Laget lived away from Detroit in upstate New York. The distance heightened his respect for Motown as a rare place to be creative.

"We created mobility. We created suburbia. We created the way to the mall, and look what happened to communities. The opportunity to invent whatever it is that comes after what's happened here is just really very real," he says. "If there's gonna be life here, it has everything to do with, as clichéd as it sounds, building sustainable communities. We have a chance to be about more than making a buck."

When he's not creating, Laget is counting the pluses and minuses he sees in the city's changing arts culture. "Let's face it, one of the best things about Detroit, up until now, has been that between the East Coast and the West Coast, we were a no-fly zone," he says. "Now, there are crash pads because certain people have been embedded. They've got a stake."

But Laget is watching for a more telling sign of Detroit's acceptance in the larger art world: "The state of the city makes it real easy for other artists to come here and find materials. But is there going to be perceived value in what's come out of here by those who've been here? Look how long it took Tyree Guyton to go from being outside to moving inside the art world, twenty-five years."

Laget does venture beyond the streets, collaborating with art projects such as The Detroit Print Exchange, an underground exhibition between Detroit and New York print and digital media-makers. As part of the exhibition, twenty of Laget's pieces will travel to New York.

The exposure, Laget says, is nice. But don't expect his motivation to change. "I don't intend to get swallowed by the dominant culture," he says. "For me the conversation that happens on the streets with my work is how I feel my way and stay connected to what reality is."

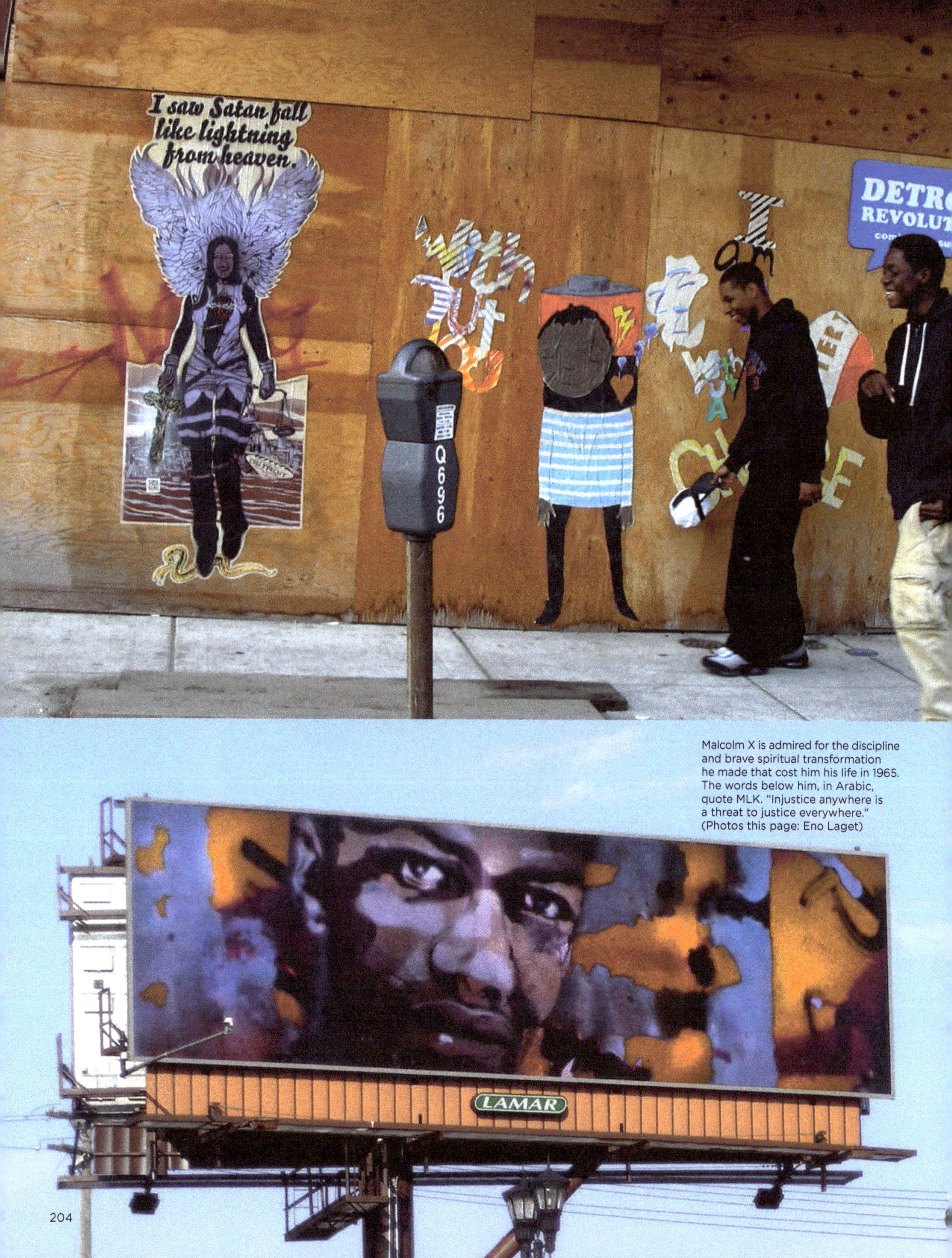

Malcolm X is admired for the discipline and brave spiritual transformation he made that cost him his life in 1965. The words below him, in Arabic, quote MLK. "Injustice anywhere is a threat to justice everywhere." (Photos this page: Eno Laget)

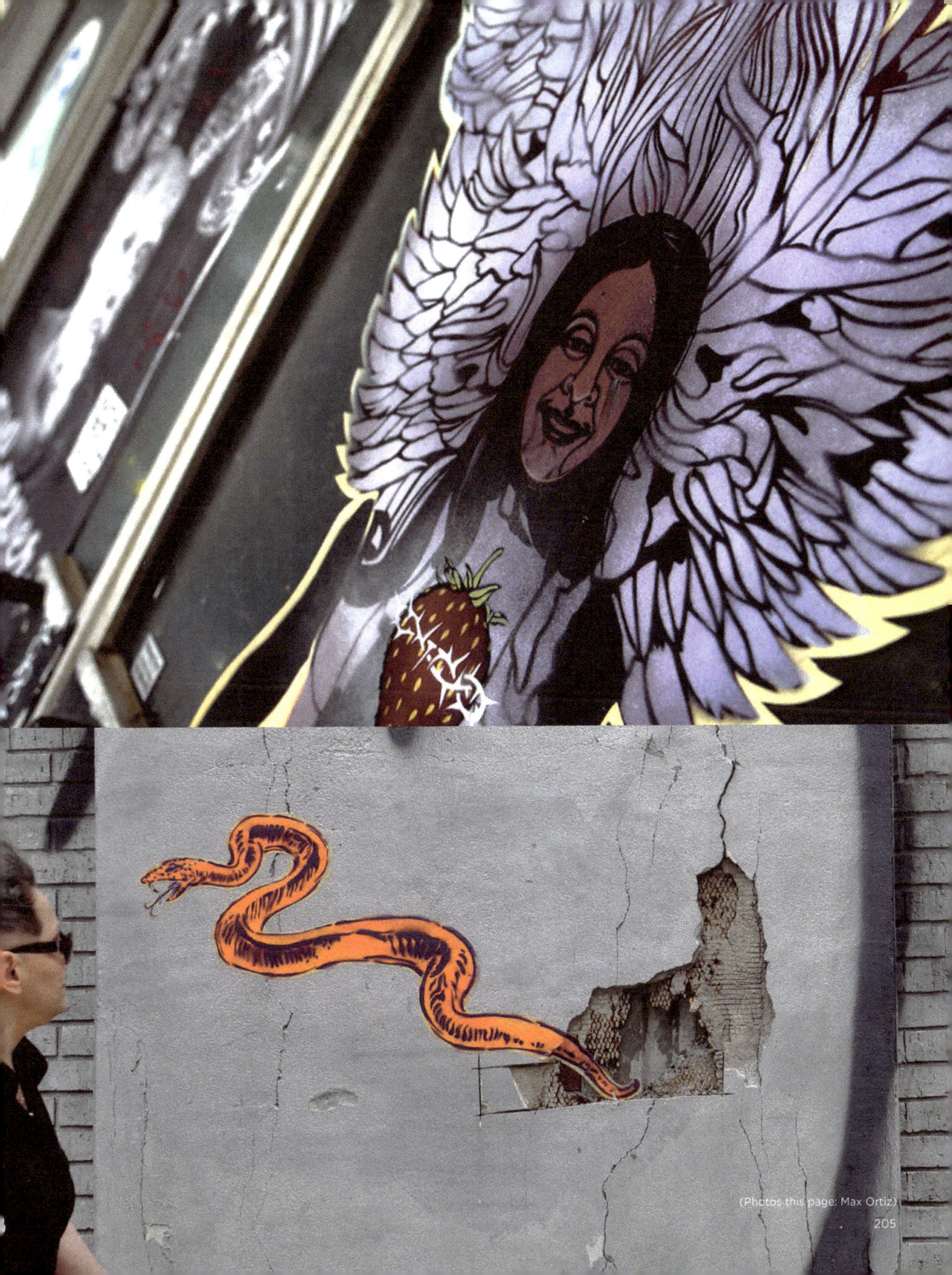

(Photos this page: Max Ortiz)

(Photos this page: Eno Laget)

I'll never give up on you . . . ever .

DETROIT · 2011

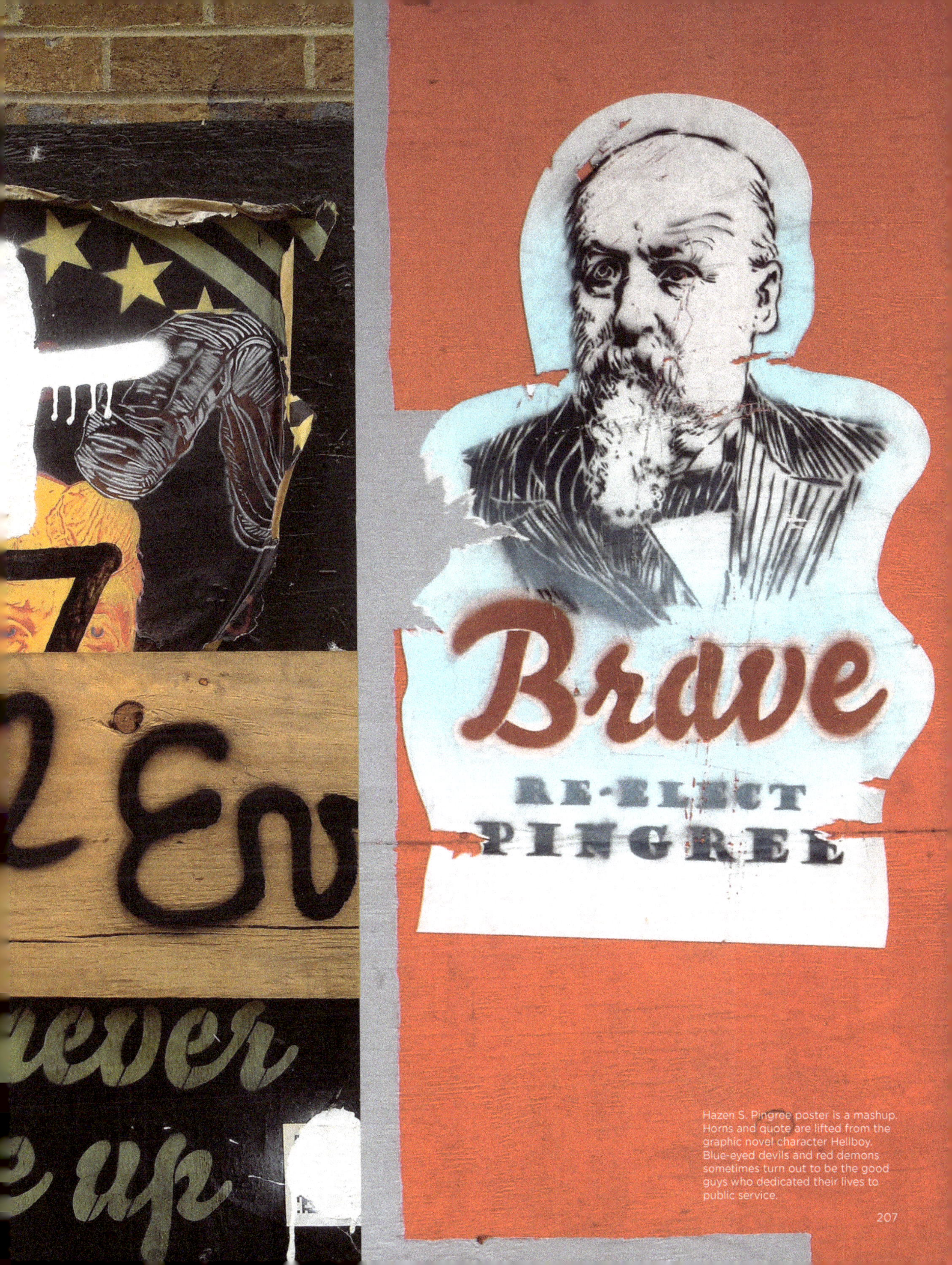

Hazen S. Pingree poster is a mashup. Horns and quote are lifted from the graphic novel character Hellboy. Blue-eyed devils and red demons sometimes turn out to be the good guys who dedicated their lives to public service.

NICOLE MACDONALD

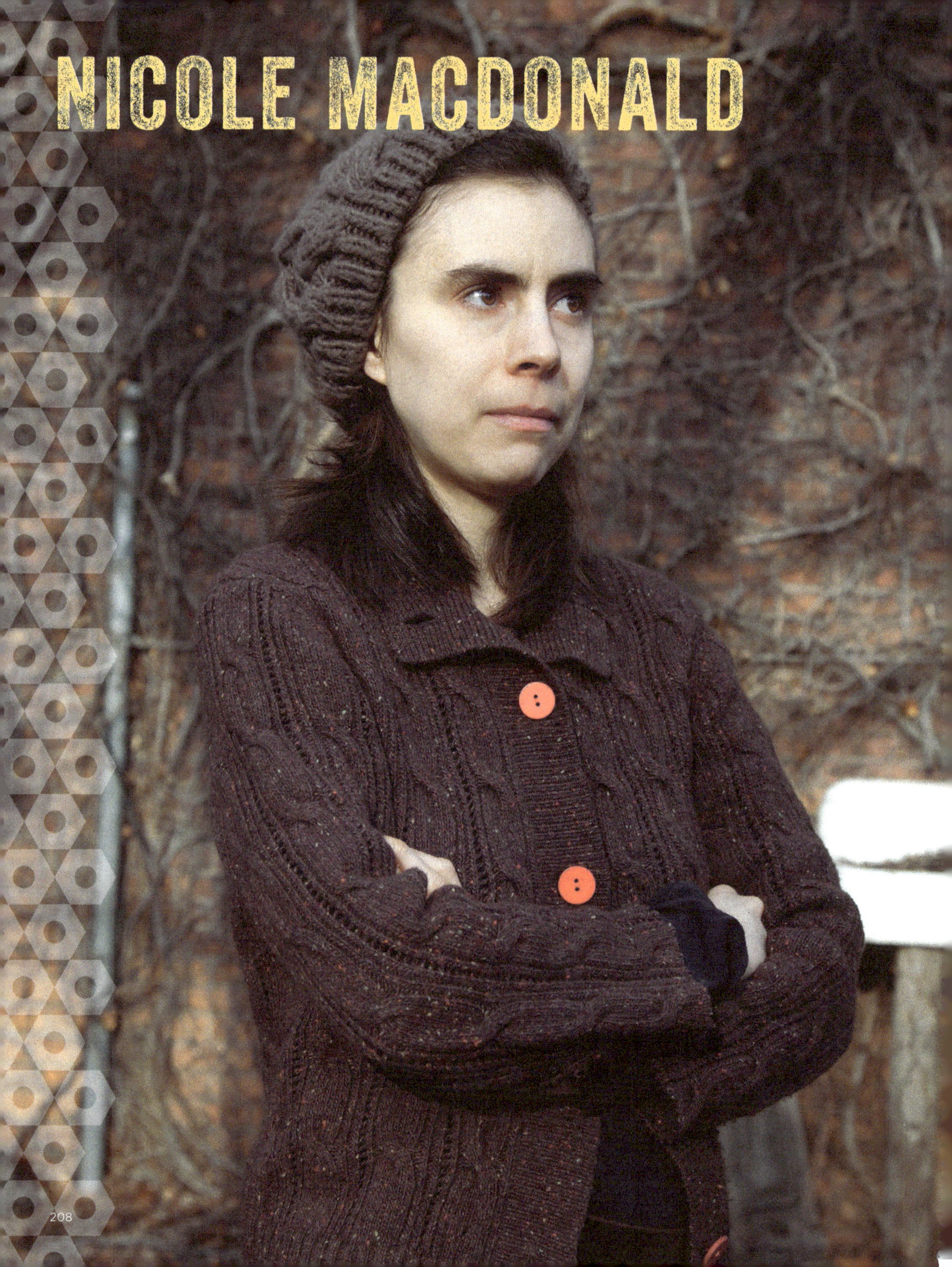

"I'm really driven by an old Italian anarchist idea: Let your voice be heard and do it out on the street."

This is how Nicole MacDonald explains her motivation for moving around Detroit, usually by bike, in search of spaces to leave behind glimpses of the beauty and tragedy she sees.

The images that MacDonald leaves are simple yet symbolically layered 3-D messages on empty corners of decaying walls, outdoor lampposts, even raw concrete—whatever surface she can find that's strong and visible enough to bear the weight of her commentary.

"I'm increasingly interested in the landscape of the city from both an aesthetic point of view and from a social-political point of view. Detroit is really at this great intersection, a city returning to nature, with the challenge of overgrown wild spaces that are peaceful and depopulated and can allow for discoveries," she says. "It's interesting trying to represent that in painting or collages, or photographs. What was here and why was it here?"

To balance the weight of her interests, which range from the city's poor air quality, to its failing transit system and shrinking population, MacDonald chooses to communicate using what she calls the simplest form of street art: hand-cut stencils.

"I like stencils. I understand them because they're straightforward. They force you into a kind of simple delivery, street art 101 really," says MacDonald, thirty-four. "It's an easy and effective way to really see the image. They capture people's attention at a distance, and they really let you focus on the contrasts."

Interestingly enough, MacDonald has found a more focused and immediate voice in stencils than in the art form she was once best known for: filmmaking. She is a former director of the Detroit Film Center, a nonprofit that promotes and supports independent filmmaking in the city.

"There's something about stencils that just translates the urgency of things, and I guess that works for me as inspiration. There are so many relevant burning local issues that I want to make people aware of now."

MacDonald has lost count of how many stencil paintings she's put up around Detroit. Often, she does the work and moves on.

"I'm always surprised by the ones that stay," she says. "It kind of says to me that maybe someone else sees the value of going into these neglected spaces and the time and effort that goes into leaving a little message or a piece of art behind."

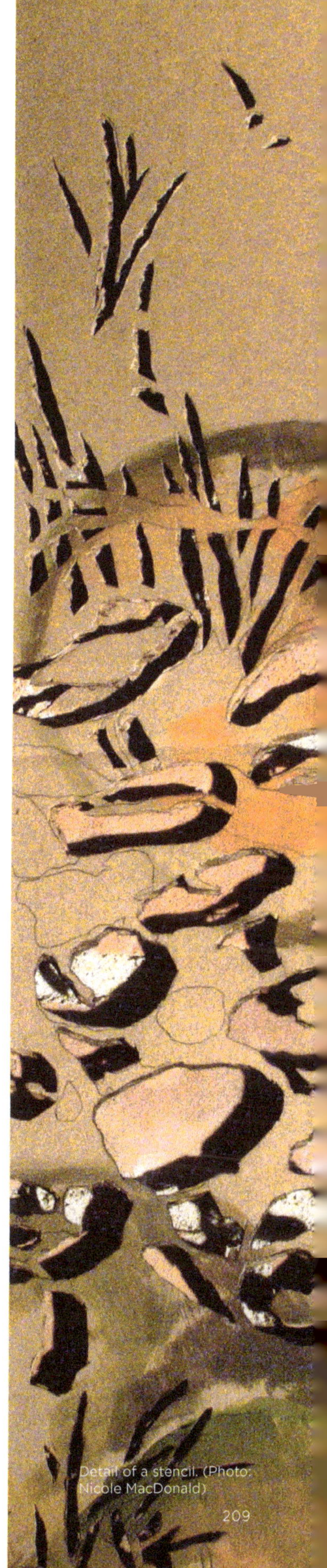

Detail of a stencil. (Photo: Nicole MacDonald)

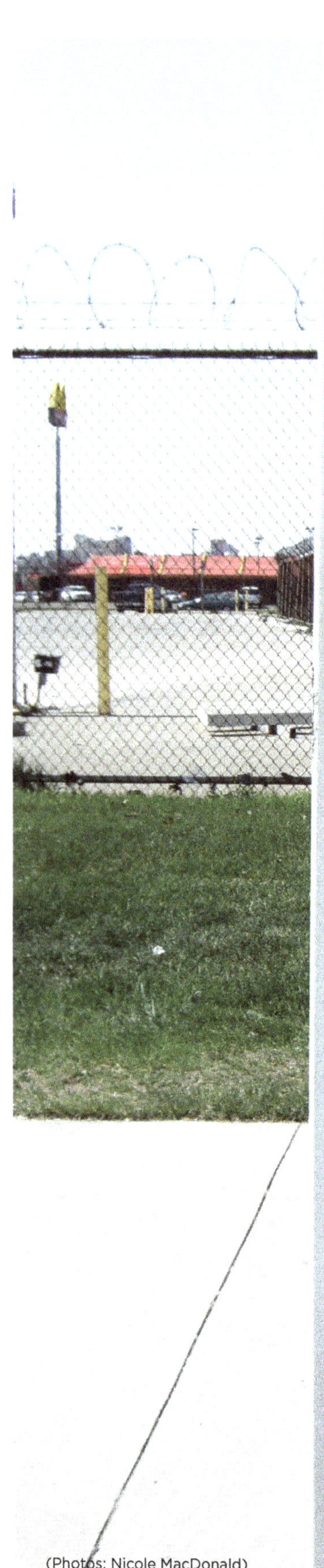

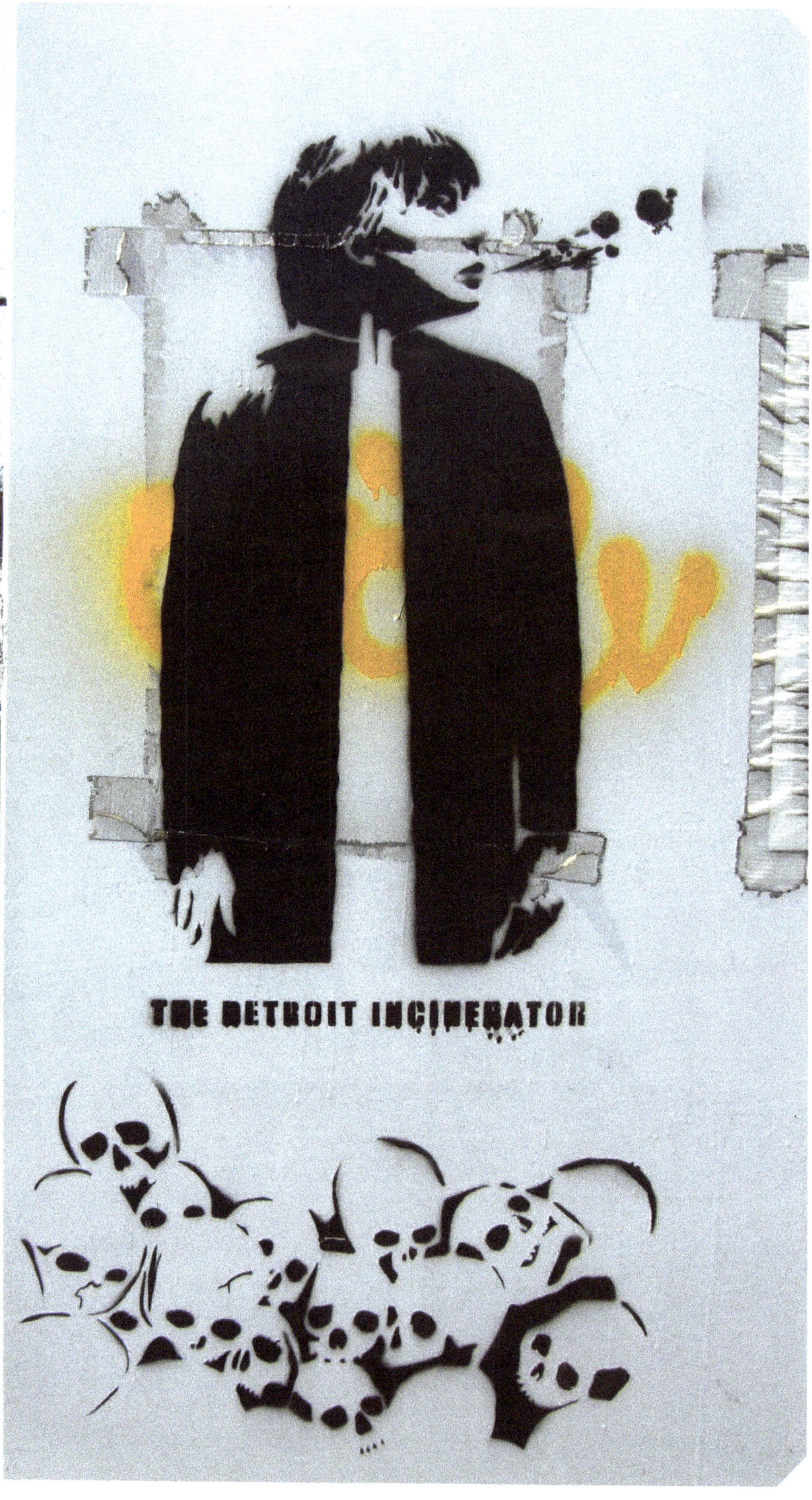

(Photos: Nicole MacDonald)

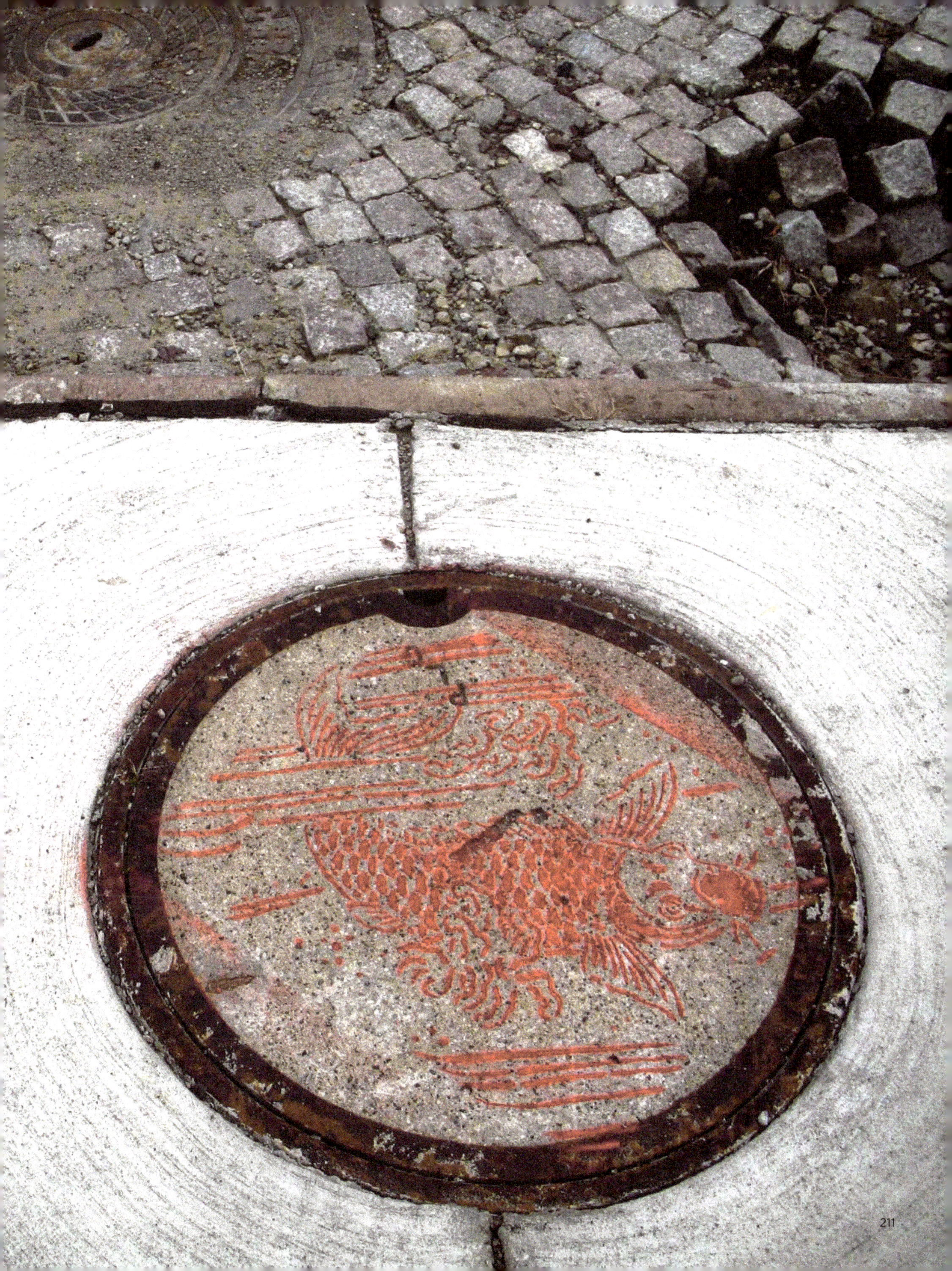

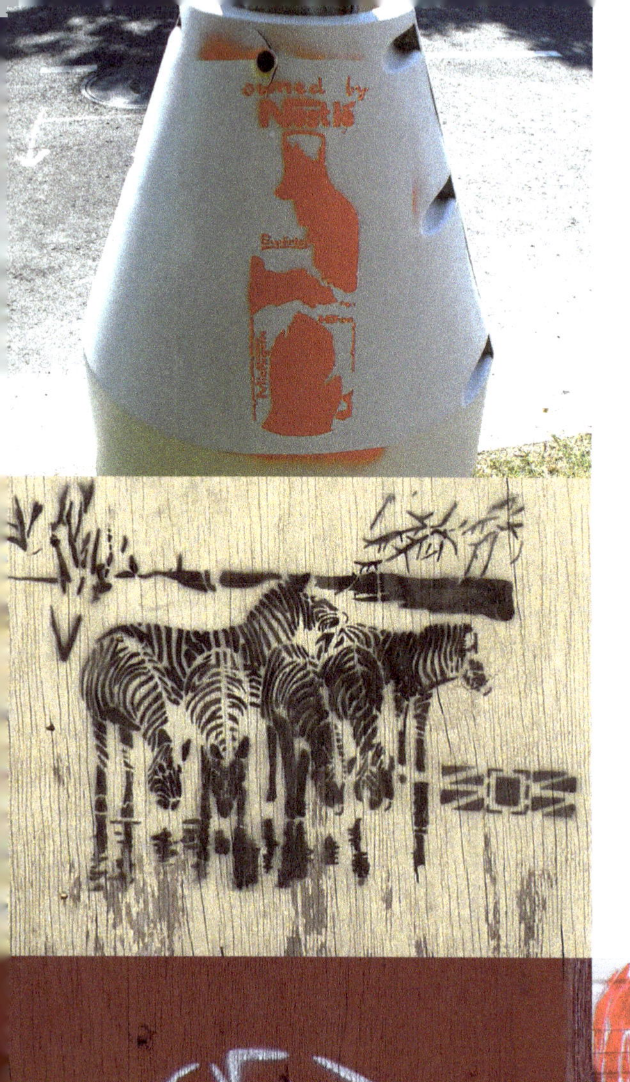

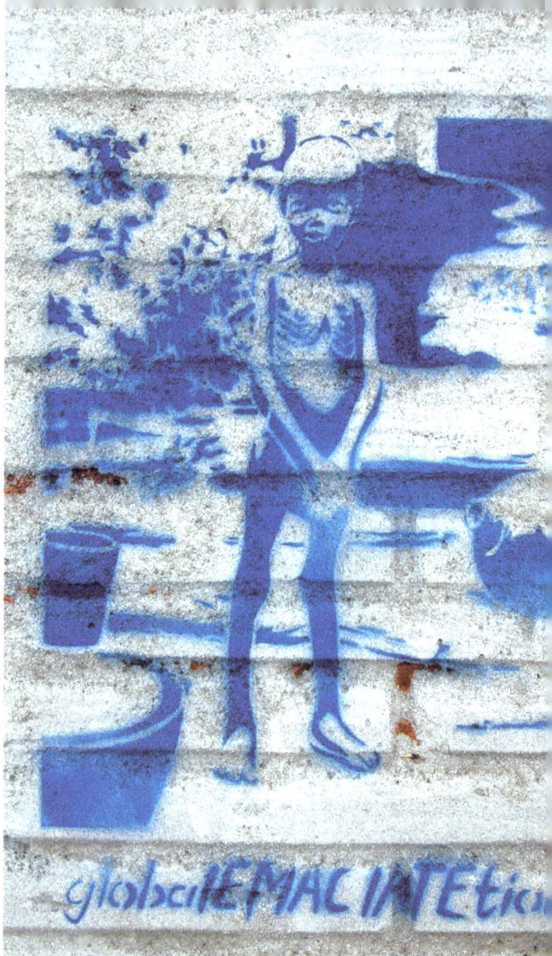

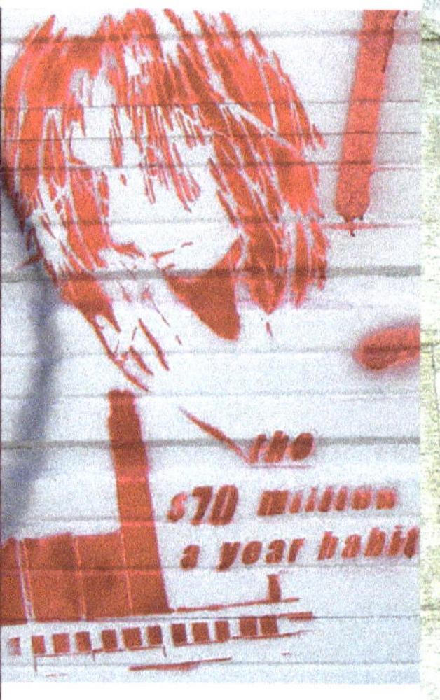
the
$70 million
a year habit

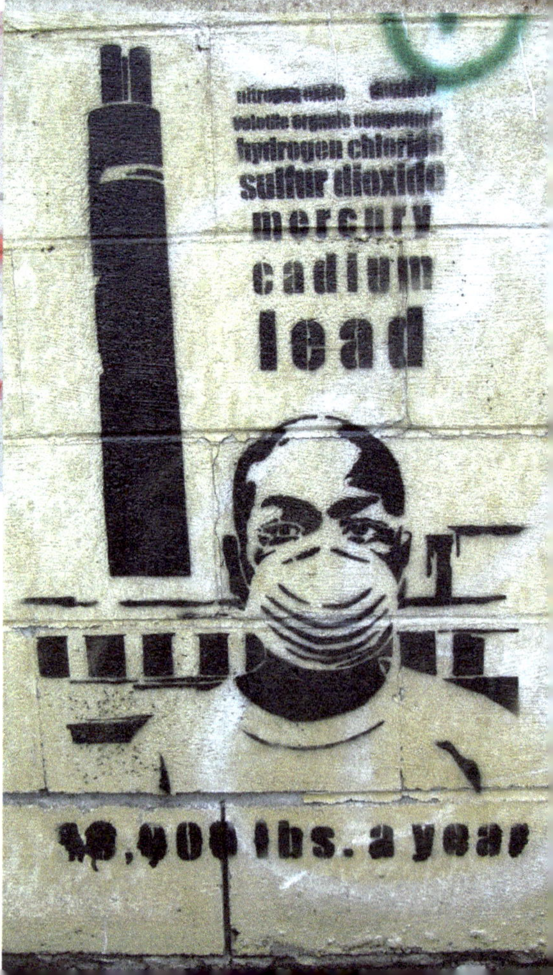

globalEMACIATEtio

hydrogen chloride
sulfur dioxide
mercury
cadium
lead
lbs. a year

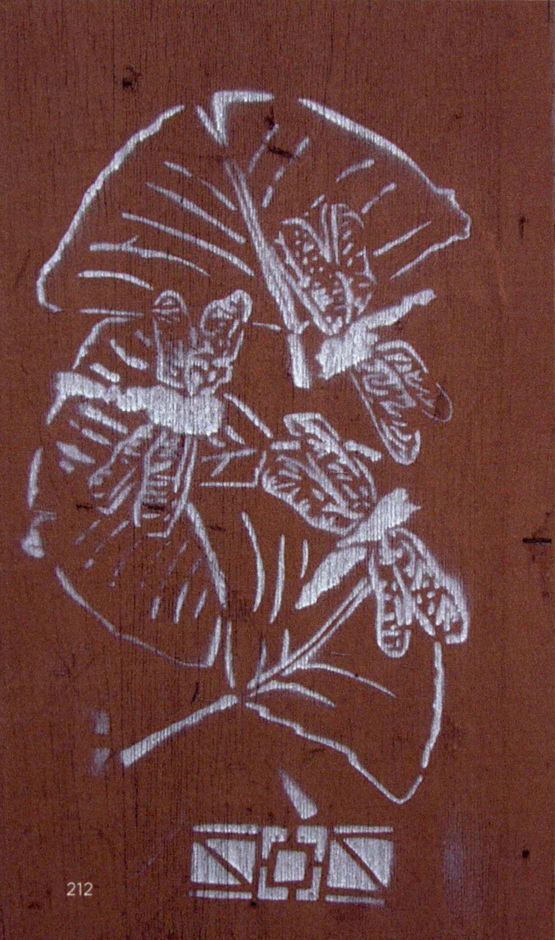

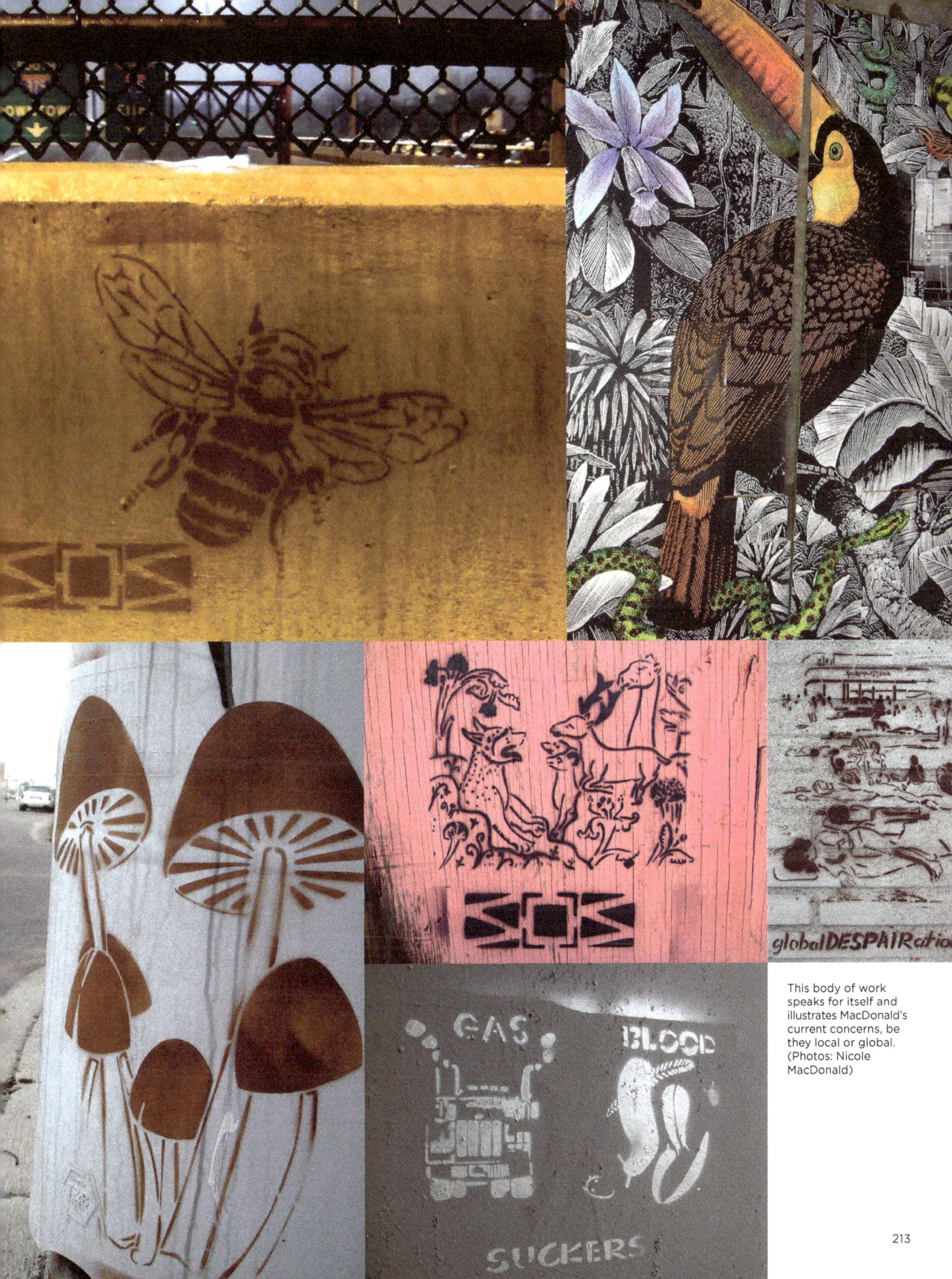

This body of work speaks for itself and illustrates MacDonald's current concerns, be they local or global. (Photos: Nicole MacDonald)

HUBERT MASSEY

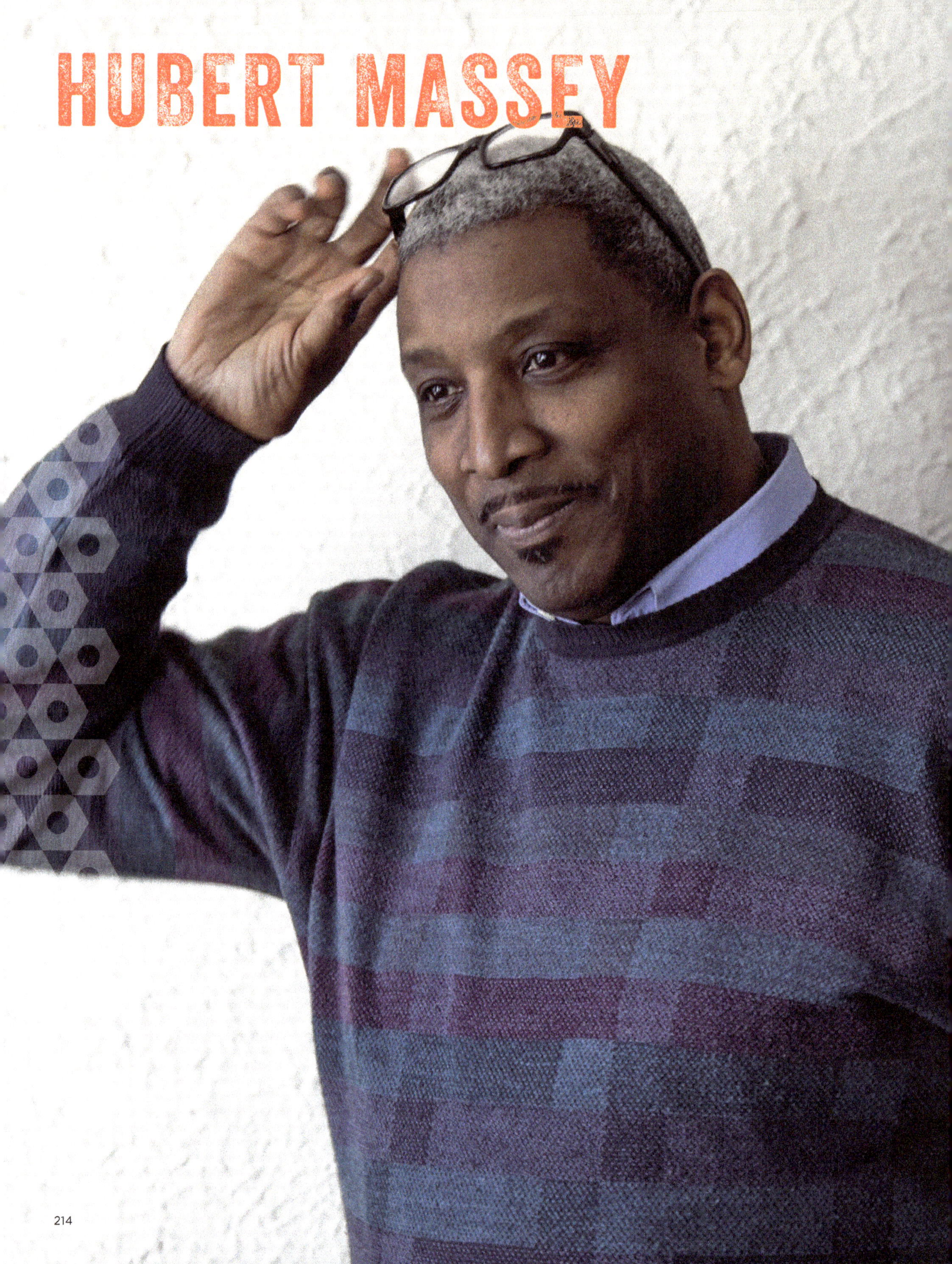

Hubert Massey has covered Detroit, inside and outside, with art.

Before he became a known name around the city, Massey spent his days up in the air, sometimes up as high as two hundred feet, painting photorealistic Gannett billboards, in oil, by hand. For thirteen years, he cranked them out like new cars running down the line.

The money was good, so was the training of facing a blank canvas day after day. "It was one of the best moves I ever made," says the Flint, Michigan, native. "I got to learn by making mistakes and I got paid to do it, forty to fifty signs a week, very detailed, all by hand. It helped me see art on a much larger scale and make bigger connections."

The discipline that Massey developed eventually pushed him into a full-time career as a go-to public artist, with a special affinity for frescos, the complex technique of layered painting perfected by Michelangelo and made famous in Detroit by Diego Rivera. Massey, whose commissioned works command as much six hundred dollars per square foot, studied art at the University of London's Slade Institute of Fine Arts.

He is the only commissioned African-American buon fresco painter in the United States, a testament to the skill he acquired while studying with Rivera apprentices Stephen Dimitroff and Lucienne Bloch. Massey also spent time touring and studying the murals of Mexico City. "I'd still like to see the frescos in Italy," he says.

His artistic footprint in Detroit and around the state is almost as broad as the style he loves, including more than thirty outdoor and indoor murals, sculptures, terrazzo designs, pictographs, even stained-glass window projects. Massey's vision covers the rotunda floor of the Charles H. Wright Museum of African American History. It's a giant, 37-foot tall, circular terrazzo entitled *Ring of Genealogy*, which he designed to showcase the lives of pioneering African Americans.

"I see myself as a storyteller trying to tell the stories of the city through mediums that last and connect people to art," says Massey, who only turned to art after a knee injury sidelined him from his role as a star football player at Grand Valley State University. "I come from the era of community engagement. So, I know how important it is to document the legacies of people and communities."

Massey's installations anchor some of Detroit's most visible cultural sites. He designed and etched images into two granite murals at Campus Martius, a 2.5-acre public park honored by the Urban Land Institute and by the American Planning Association as one of American's Great Public Spaces. More than two million people visit Campus Martius each year.

"I come into communities and I listen," Massey says. "My inspiration comes from having forums and getting people involved in the process."

Commuters between Canada and Detroit eye Massey's work each day as they cross the Ambassador Bridge. Commissioned by the Michigan Department of Transportation, Massey unleashed a torrent of vibrant colors and faces meant to celebrate the history of Latino culture and ethnic diversity in Southwest Detroit. Like virtually all of Massey's murals, the forty-foot mural, "Spiral of Life," features a vivid quilt winding through the work and embedded with recognizable and hidden salutes to Latino culture and Detroit history.

"Public art is powerful when you can translate the story of a community into the work. You give people a voice and the art has a function," he says. "Art has more of a responsibility now than it's ever had to do that, to help create new ideas, give focus and give some direction."

To Massey, the mission of elevating the art in Detroit is personal. "When I was studying in Europe, one of the things that always struck me was the way people make pilgrimages to see art and the places where things started," he says.

"I think Detroit can be a creative capital for America. So many important things started here; it's the ideal place to have the conversation through art: the architecture, the first paved highway. And you have the largest fresco painting done by Diego Rivera, right here. This is the place."

Massey is mindful of Detroit's challenges, its dwindling population, struggling schools, and broken, ineffective government services. Still, his mind is made up.

"Right now, there's a big palette of opportunity, and it's bigger than the self-serving part of art," he says. "I want to be part of the change. I want to be one of the people that help guide us forward. I'm not running from Detroit. I feel privileged to live and create here."

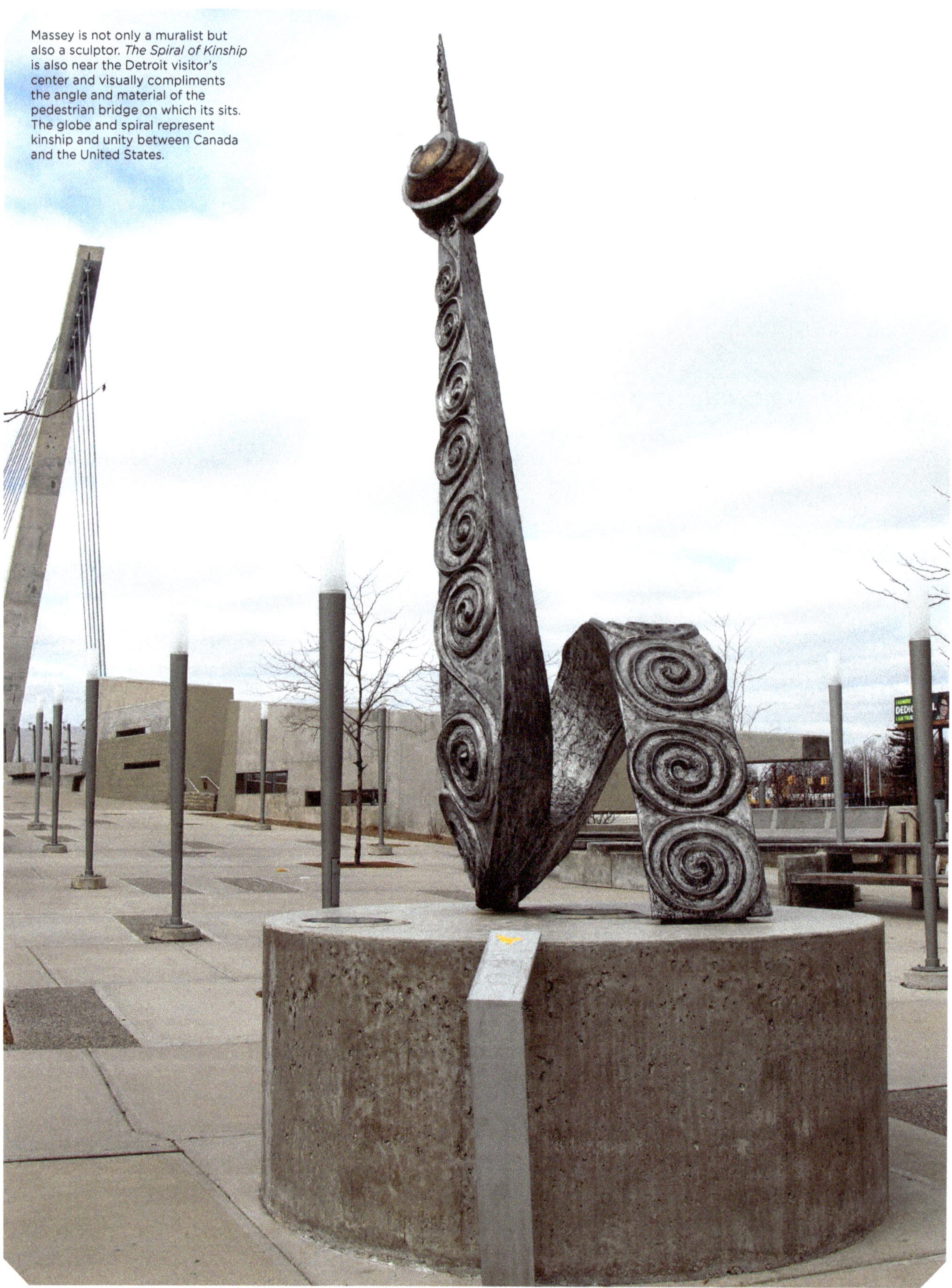

Massey is not only a muralist but also a sculptor. *The Spiral of Kinship* is also near the Detroit visitor's center and visually compliments the angle and material of the pedestrian bridge on which its sits. The globe and spiral represent kinship and unity between Canada and the United States.

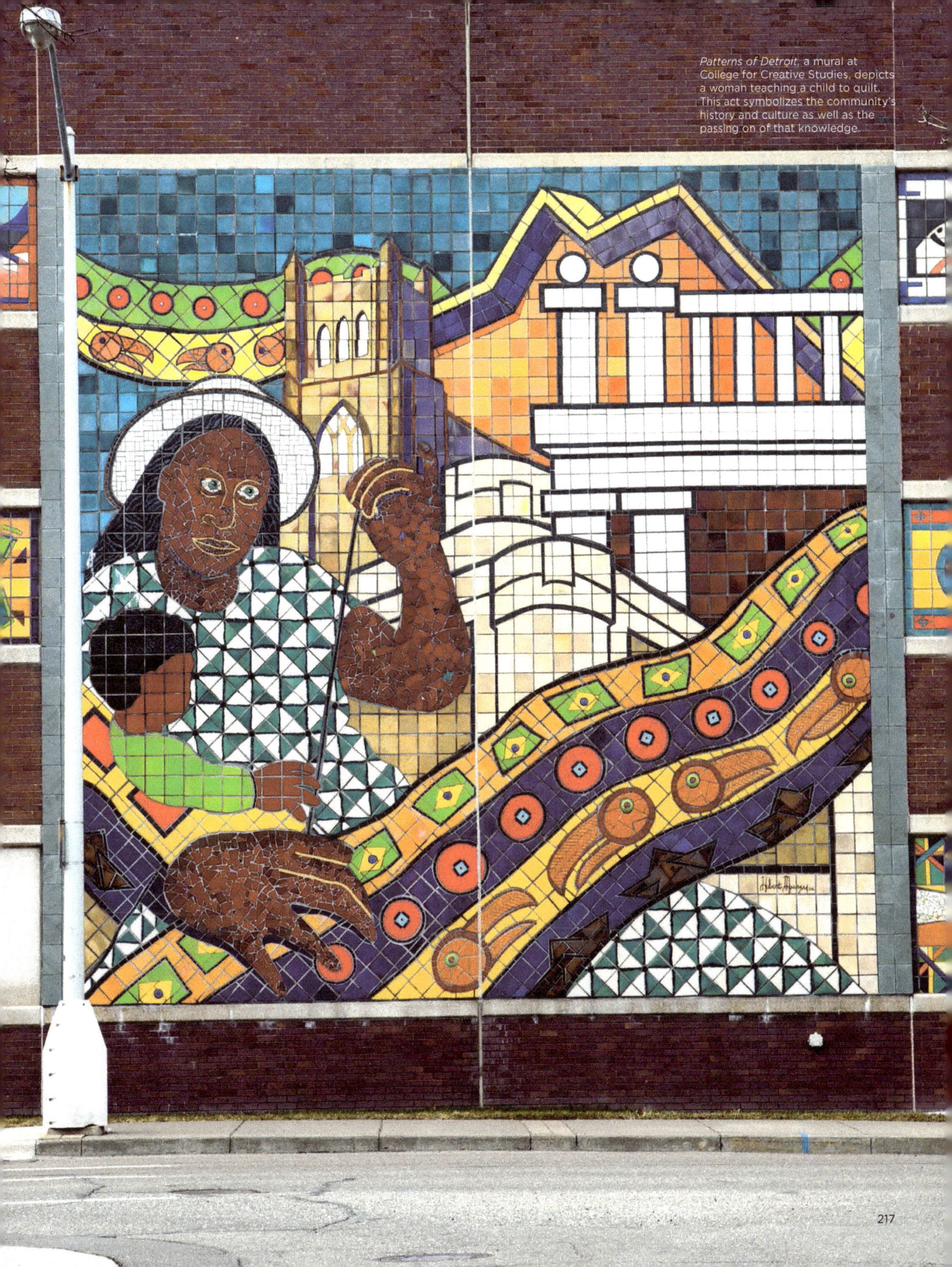

Patterns of Detroit, a mural at College for Creative Studies, depicts a woman teaching a child to quilt. This act symbolizes the community's history and culture as well as the passing on of that knowledge.

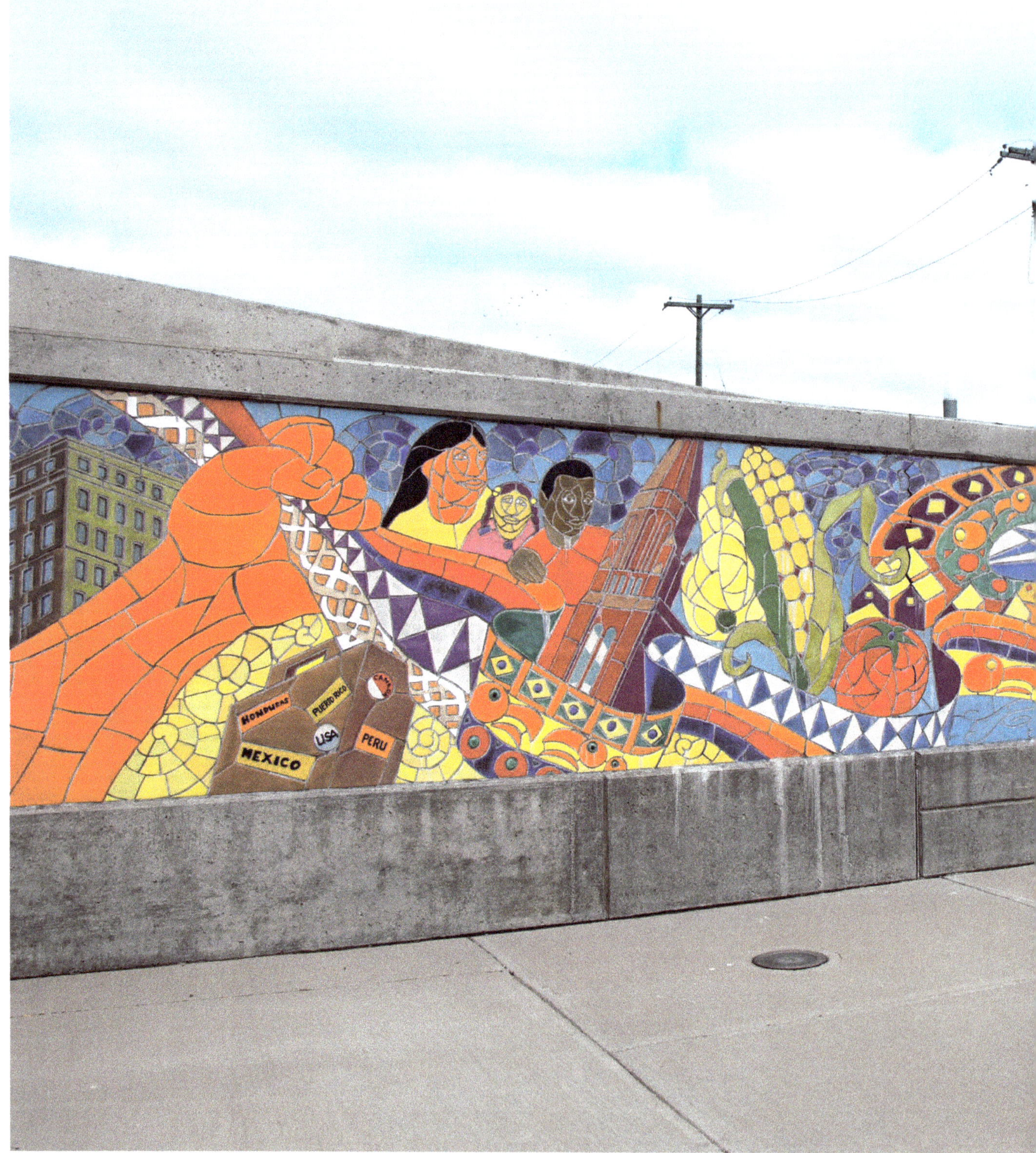

The Spiral of Life was commissioned by the Michigan Department of Transportation. This mosaic leads the eye toward the train station beyond and depicts elements of Detroit, Latino culture, and the ethnic diversity of Southwest Detroit where it is located.

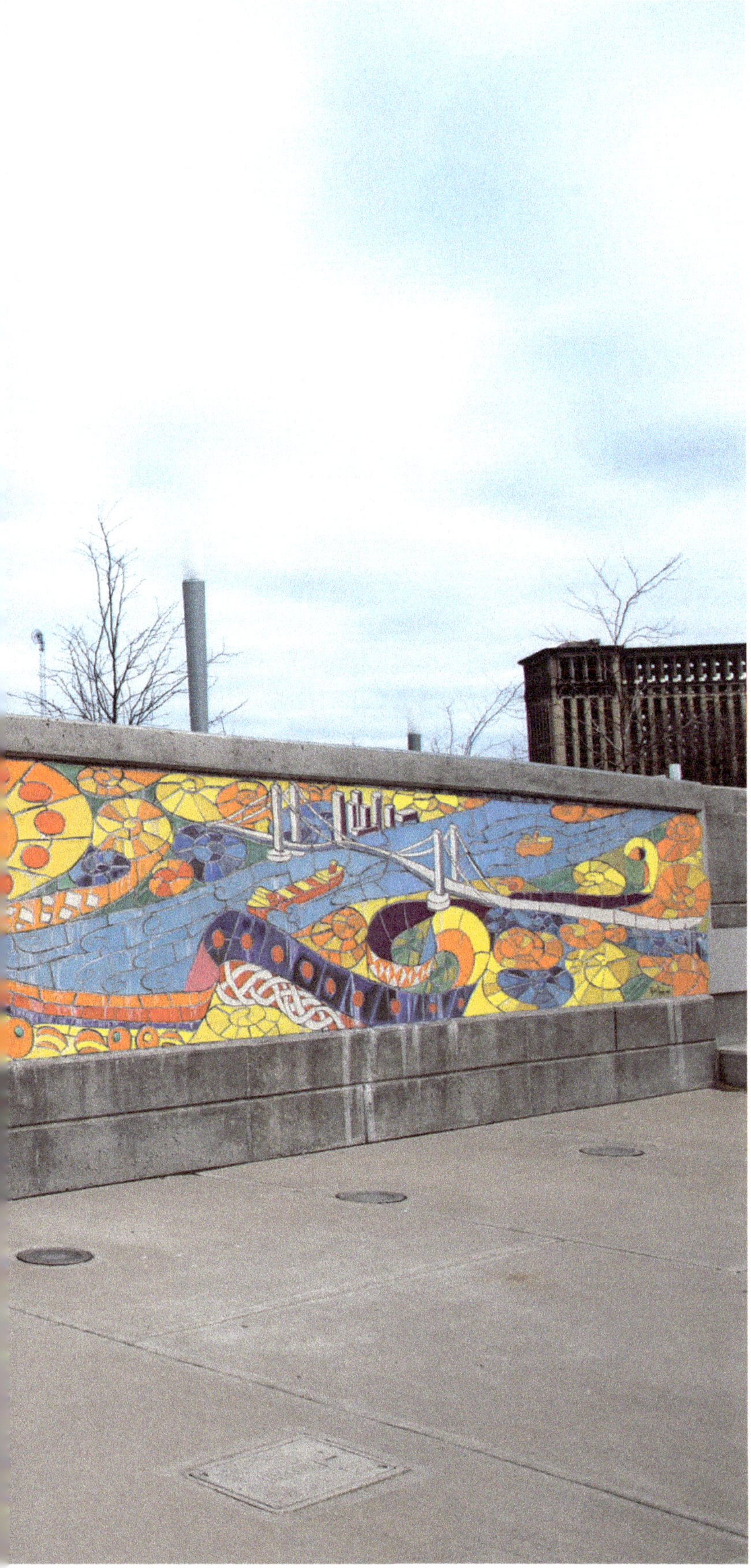

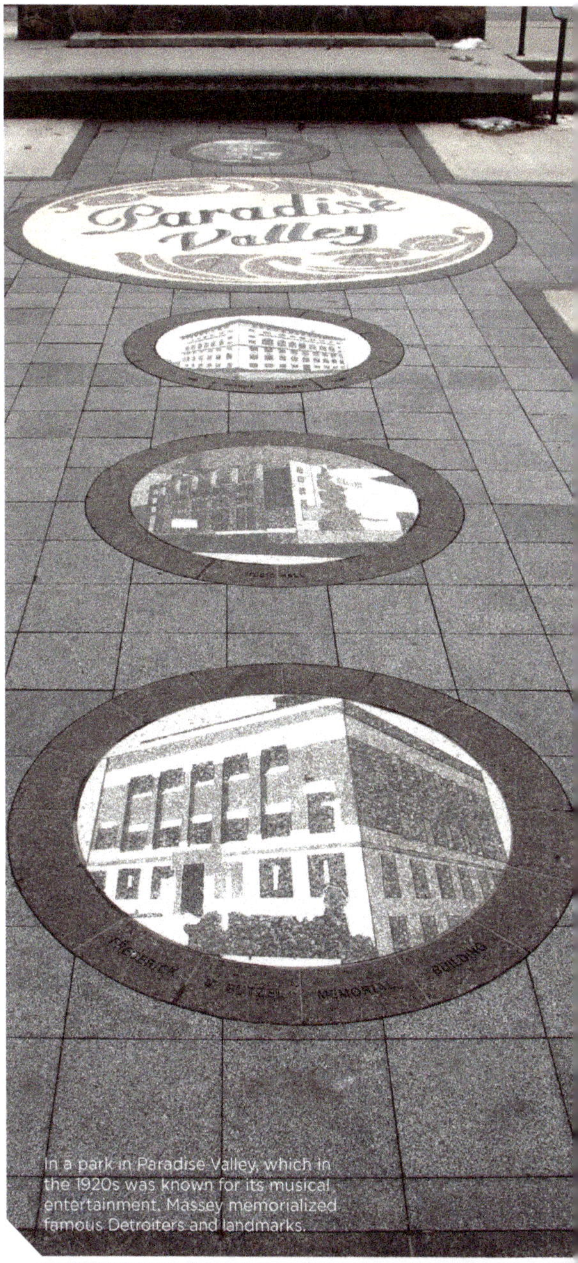

In a park in Paradise Valley, which in the 1920s was known for its musical entertainment, Massey memorialized famous Detroiters and landmarks.

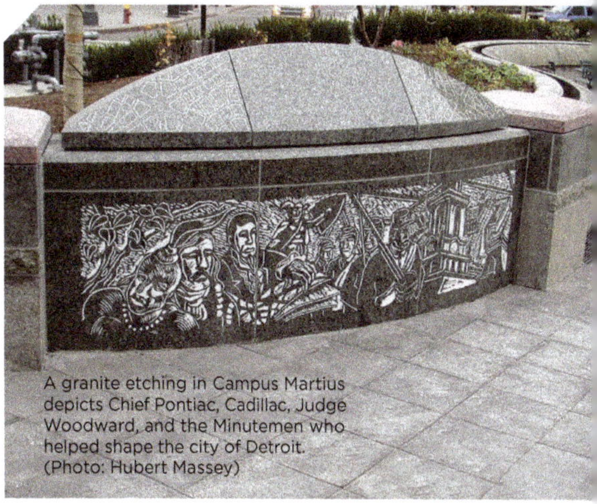

A granite etching in Campus Martius depicts Chief Pontiac, Cadillac, Judge Woodward, and the Minutemen who helped shape the city of Detroit. (Photo: Hubert Massey)

CATIE NEWELL

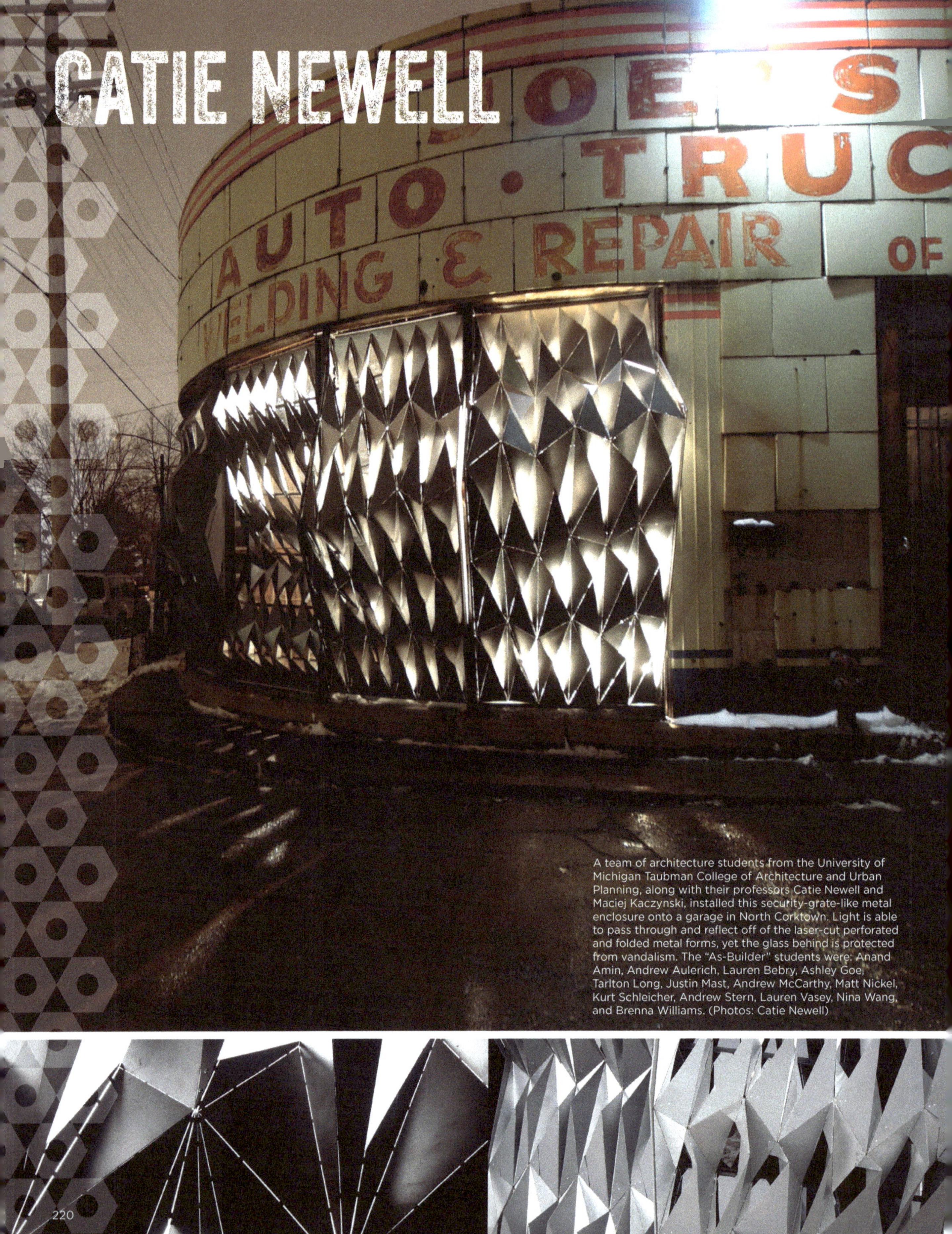

A team of architecture students from the University of Michigan Taubman College of Architecture and Urban Planning, along with their professors Catie Newell and Maciej Kaczynski, installed this security-grate-like metal enclosure onto a garage in North Corktown. Light is able to pass through and reflect off of the laser-cut perforated and folded metal forms, yet the glass behind is protected from vandalism. The "As-Builder" students were: Anand Amin, Andrew Aulerich, Lauren Bebry, Ashley Goe, Tarlton Long, Justin Mast, Andrew McCarthy, Matt Nickel, Kurt Schleicher, Andrew Stern, Lauren Vasey, Nina Wang, and Brenna Williams. (Photos: Catie Newell)

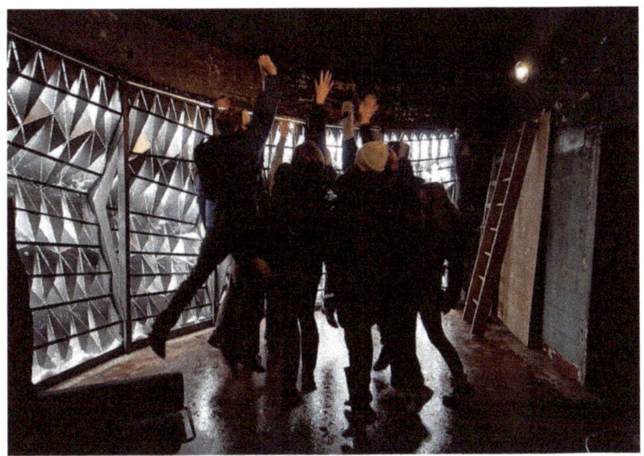

As an architect, Catie Newell likes to listen first.

Each space has a voice, she insists. Sometimes, the space even holds a hint of the form waiting to emerge.

"I like to obscure things, to amplify what's already there but maybe just hidden," she says. "I'm sort of a master environment manipulator."

One of the realms where she is most at home working is with abandoned things and confined spaces. That explains a portion of Newell's passion for creating in Detroit, including the inventive way she and thesis partner Maciej Kaczynski reimagined the exterior of an old North Corktown auto shop that had been boarded up with cinder blocks. Using elaborately fabricated metal, the large curved storefront suddenly became art. "It goes without saying that how this building had been boarded up was doing a disservice to its life as a core feature in the history of its neighborhood."

Newell's fixation with creating alternative uses for space also explains how she came to the idea of designing a room made of charred material from the shell of a house gutted by fire.

When the fire struck, the house was already uninhabitable; though without walls or windows, it continued to stand as a hub for an artists' nonprofit called the Imagination Station. Initially, Newell was brought in to design an installation. But the fate of the space stirred her imagination so, she turned it into an opportunity to curate the demolition.

But in the rubble left by the fire she saw a creative opportunity.

"For me, it would have just been a shame not to look at the materials left behind as a way to ask some questions," says Newell who is also an assistant professor of architecture at the University of Michigan's Taubman College of Architecture and Urban Planning. "It was still recognizable as this house and there was still potential and wonderful texture that could be salvaged only because the house went through a fire."

Newell went about the tedious task of sifting through the debris for usable pieces of lumber. Some pieces she pulled straight from the house's weakened frame. Each piece that she reclaimed was then carefully restacked with an aim of exposing both the burnt nature and reusable quality of the wood. By the time Newell was done, her exploration became a small, visually striking installation, which she called *Salvaged Landscape*.

"As a study of materials and light," Newell wrote in an artist's statement about the project, "the work explores the raw and scorched depths of the wood while simultaneously providing the work and the house with light punctures and the explorations of spaces intentionally left dark."

The next step in Newell's process was nearly as consuming as the selection of salvageable lumber. She lifted the room, which was less than one hundred square feet, right out of its shell into a new life.

Standing alone, it became a tribute to the house that was burned and an award-worthy piece of art at ArtPrize, an international art contest held each year in Grand Rapids, Michigan. At the 2011 show, *Salvage Landscape* was selected a juried winner of the Best Use of Urban Space Award, a designation that netted Newell a seven-thousand-dollar cash prize. Newell's work in Detroit also contributed to her selection as 2011 winner of New York's Architectural League Prize for Young Architects and Designers.

In Newell's eyes, the real prize belongs to Detroit and its growing appetite for creative expression. She says the city's rawness is paving the way for new ideas in art and design.

"There's no other city that's going to let me do what I did," she says. "There is a real richness that comes out of respecting what's already there and being open to the possibilities."

Newell acknowledges that the city's tensions must be observed, too.

"I know my work doesn't fit into fixing the problems or even being functional for typical use," she says. "But I think there can be a lot of value in work that reveals the city's circumstance and starts to ask questions about what can be done with the resources. There's so much that can be reused and reconfigured in Detroit. I think through art, people are just beginning to see how much is possible."

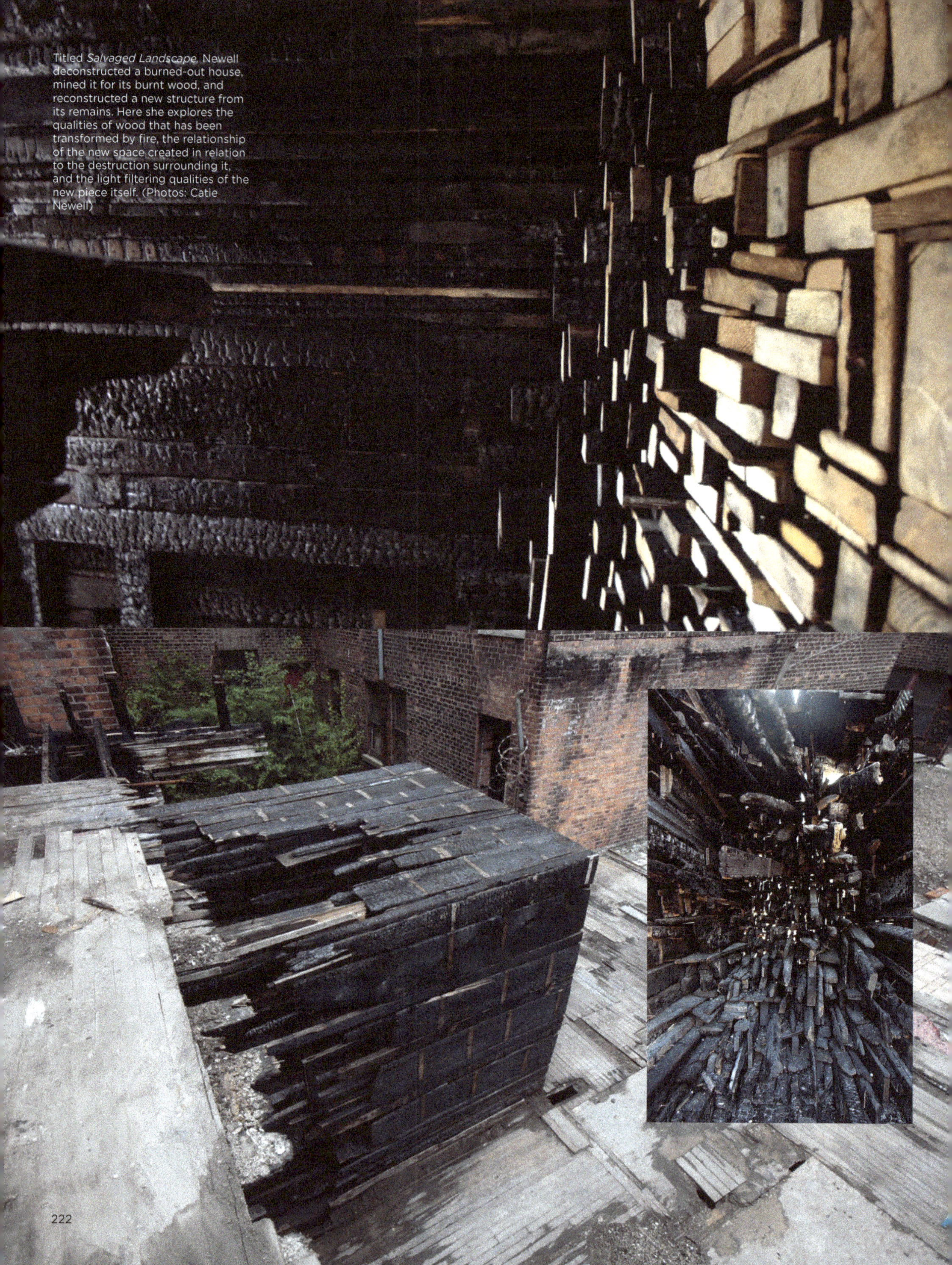

Titled *Salvaged Landscape*, Newell deconstructed a burned-out house, mined it for its burnt wood, and reconstructed a new structure from its remains. Here she explores the qualities of wood that has been transformed by fire, the relationship of the new space created in relation to the destruction surrounding it, and the light filtering qualities of the new piece itself. (Photos: Catie Newell)

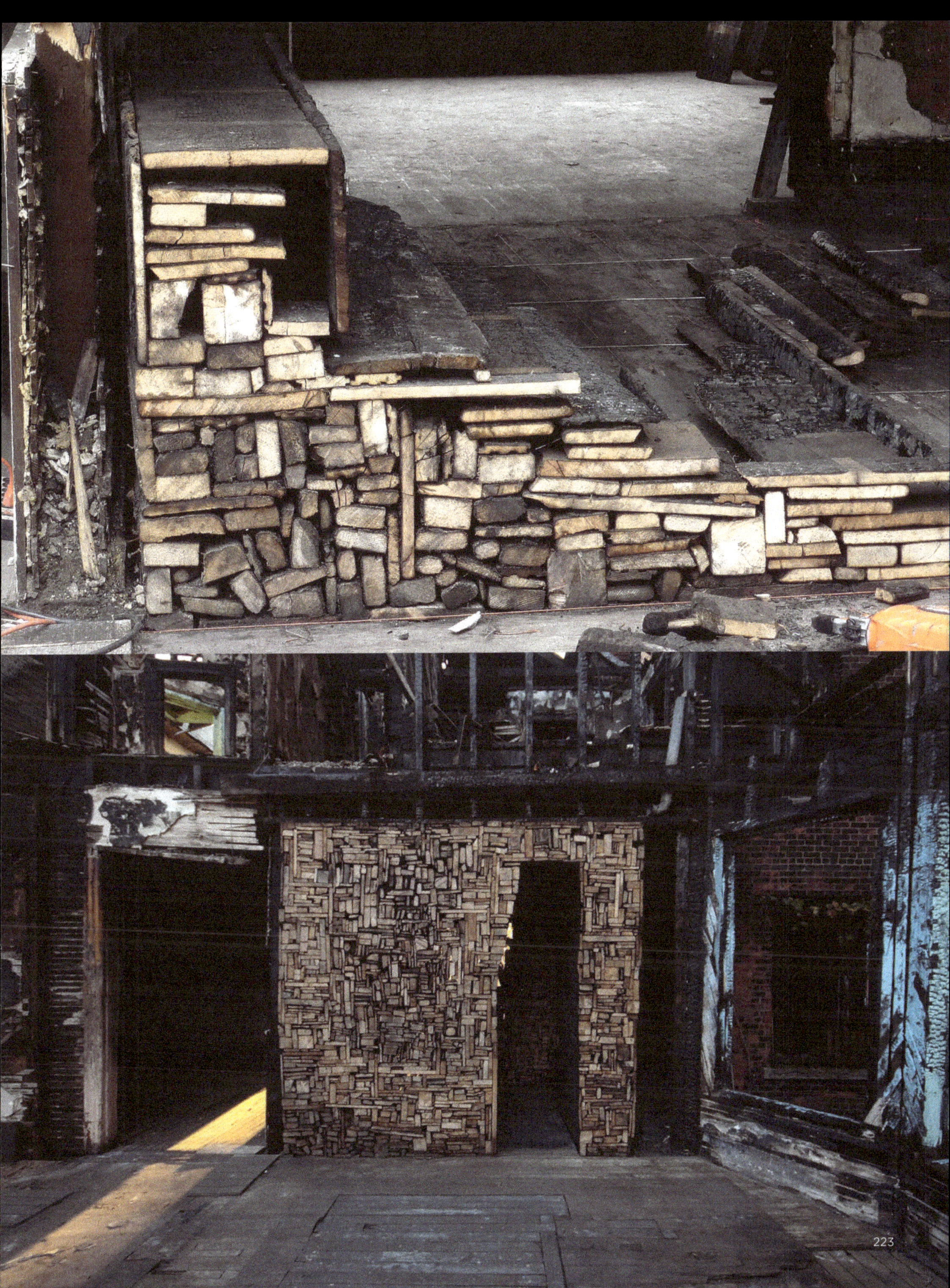

OBJECT ORANGE

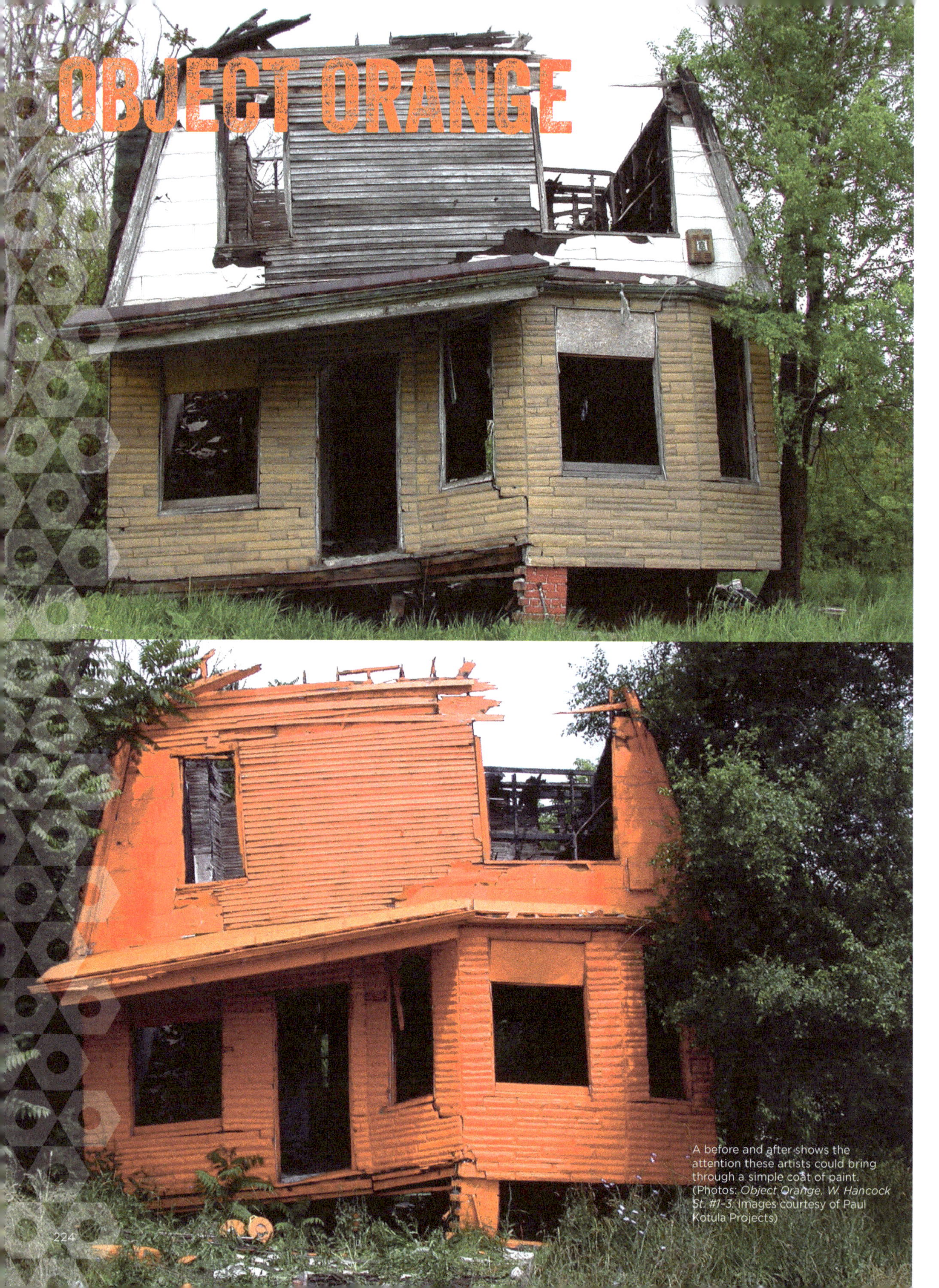

A before and after shows the attention these artists could bring through a simple coat of paint. (Photos: *Object Orange, W. Hancock St. #1-3*. Images courtesy of Paul Kotula Projects)

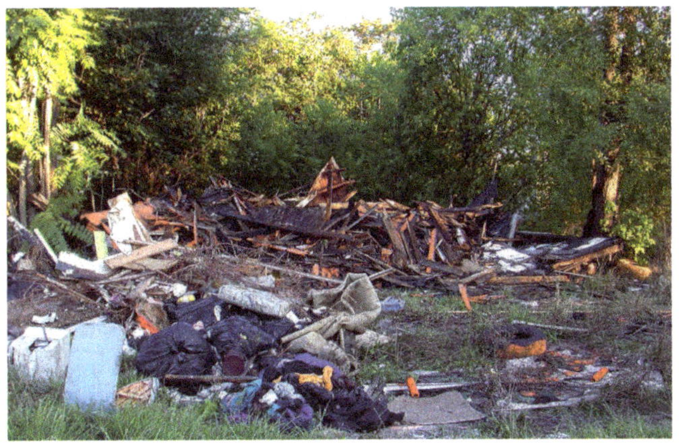

For almost four years, people from the east side to the west side of Detroit asked the same question: "Who's behind the bright orange houses?"

In what seemed like a wave, orange houses began to pop up along the city's major freeways. The color was too halting not to notice, Tiggerific orange to be exact.

To this day, the artists behind the work are still phantoms, identified only by their rather obvious code name: Object Orange. A few other facts are known. They began as a group of four, all artists and all appalled by the number of abandoned homes—thousands of them—left standing, leaning, and crumbling in Detroit.

"For people driving or passing by," explains Greg, an Object Orange artist. "We wanted to create an undeniable feeling that you're in the presence of something odd, and that oddness ought to stick in your head."

From 2006 to 2010, Object Orange painted sixteen different houses, usually as a fast-moving four-man crew but sometimes with as many as fifteen to twenty volunteers. Their work made headlines around the world, always accompanied by striking photos that typically overlooked perhaps the most important detail of Object Orange's mission and style.

"We would only paint the side of the house most visible to the major artery," explained Greg. "The guy living next to the house wasn't the audience we were looking for. He didn't need a high-chroma color to remind him or to shake him awake. He was waking up beside it every day."

Under the cover of darkness, the group selected houses visible enough to bring neon, and eventually national, attention to the problem. "Object Orange didn't start this conversation," says Greg, "But it was a relatively effective way to draw some attention to an outstanding question that Detroit's had to deal with."

At each location, Object Orange managed to cast a high-art effect using very low-tech supplies, little more than brushes, rollers, and a few five-gallon buckets of paint. In the story of how Object Orange chose its color is all the proof needed to show that these were in fact artists in action, says Greg. In fact, the selection of color almost undermined the entire project. "As artists," says Greg, "we felt we had to get the color right."

At a Home Depot, battle lines were drawn over two competing shades of orange Disney paint: Bouncy, Bouncy, versus Tiggerific.

"This was about very carefully getting people to think, and orange is a very useful color in that way. It's a symbol of change, of caution and danger, all things that we saw worthy of calling some attention to."

One outcome not anticipated by Object Orange was the reaction of the City of Detroit. Many of the houses have been demolished, a few almost immediately after being coated in orange paint.

"When we painted that first house, we couldn't have predicted nor were we concerned with the City's reaction. We saw the houses as a form of artistic material and performed an action to draw attention to something. That was the extent of it. As a group do we embrace the City's subsequent tearing down of the houses? I think we do."

But taking note of the unexpected impact of Object Orange's work, says Greg, shouldn't be confused with cheering.

"Just because there are no more abandoned houses deliberately painted orange on the side doesn't mean the conversation has ended or the problem has been solved," he says. "Look around the city today. I think the discussion is still vital and ongoing."

By coating buildings with Tiggeriffic Orange, Object Orange brought attention to the proliferation of abandoned buildings in Detroit. Sites were often visible from highways to allow as many people as possible to see them as they commuted. (Photo: *Object Orange, Auburndale Site #1.* Image courtesy of Paul Kotula Projects)

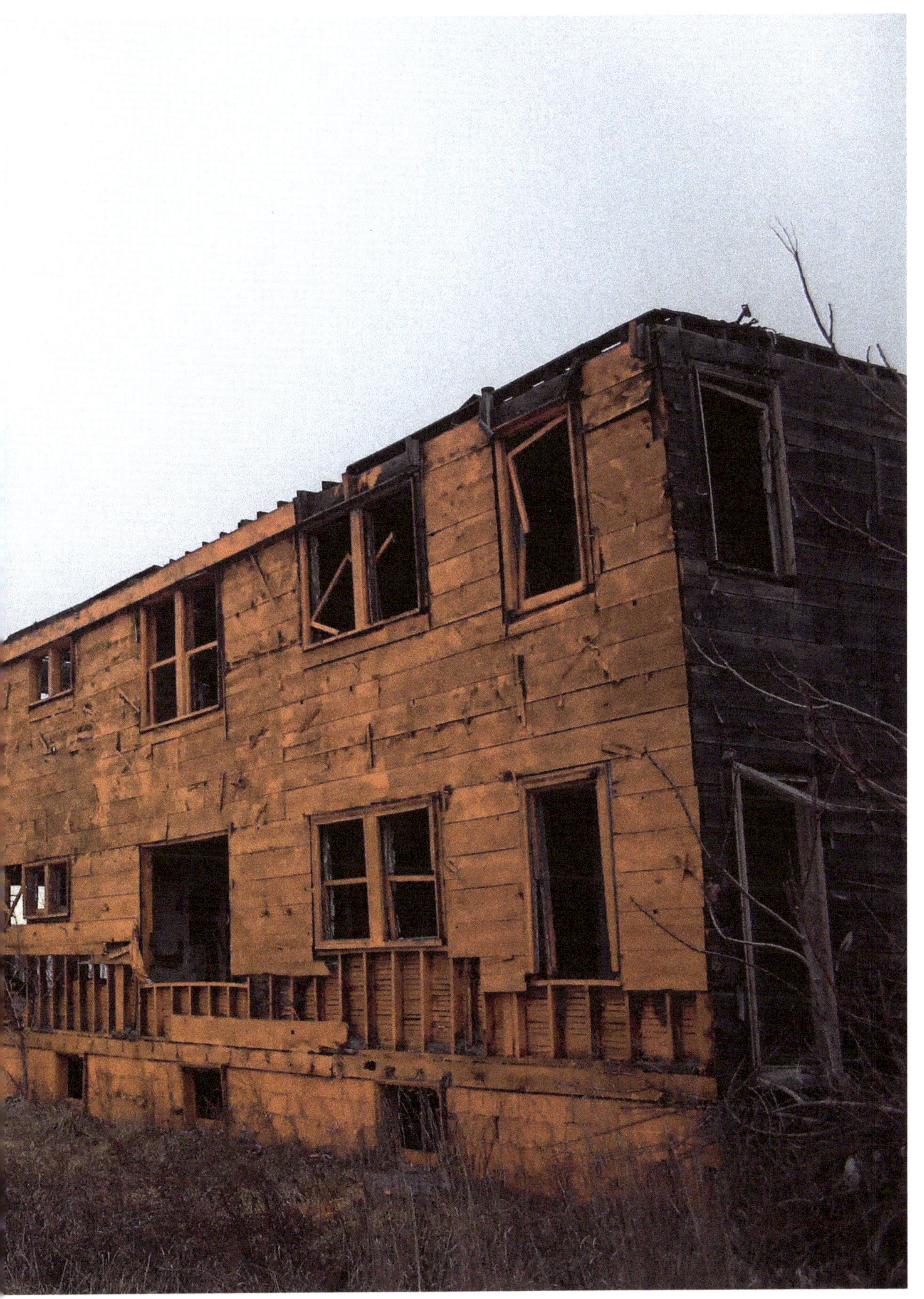

POPPS PACKING: GRAEM WHYTE AND FAINA LERMAN

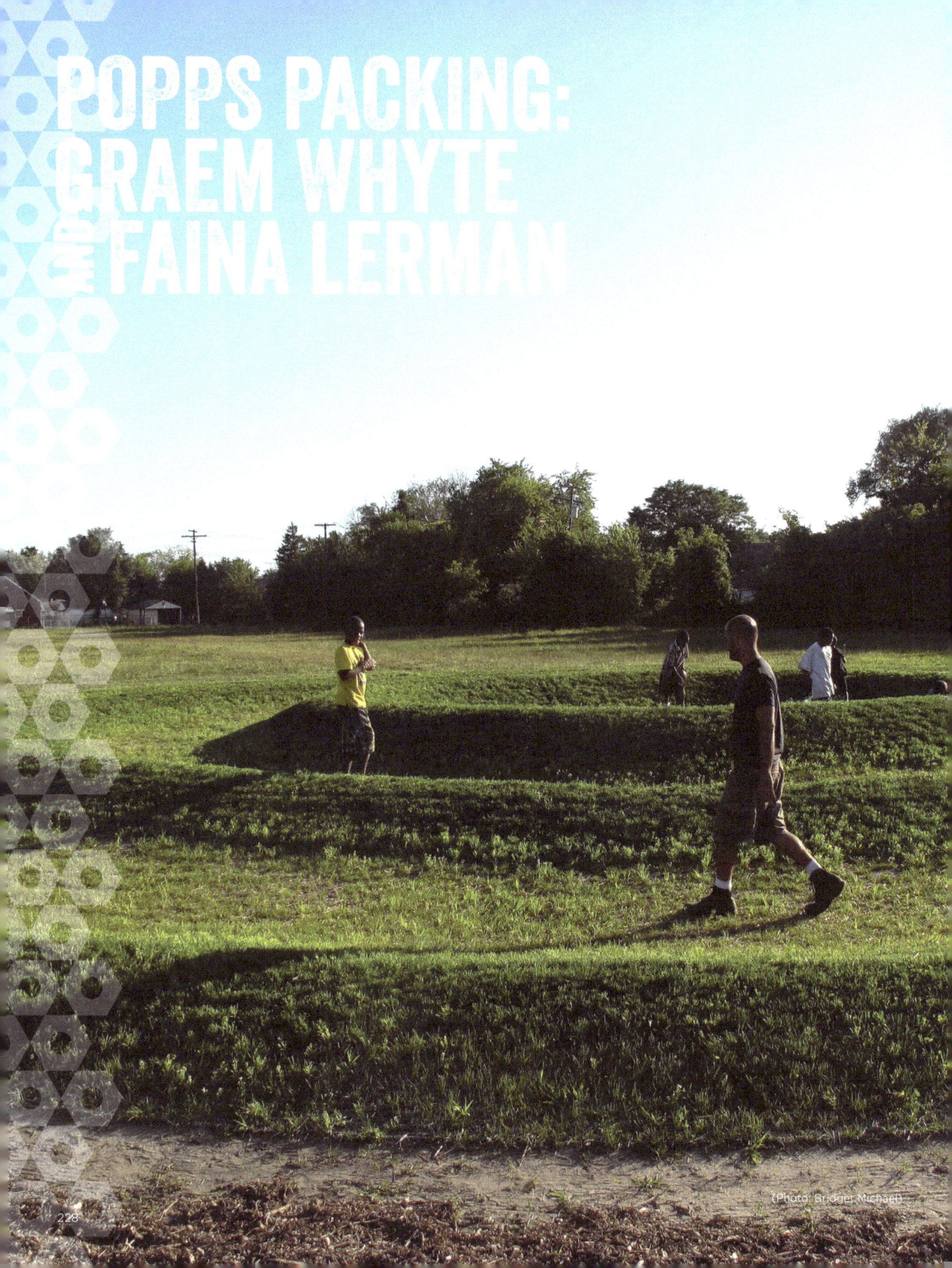

(Photo: Bridget Michael)

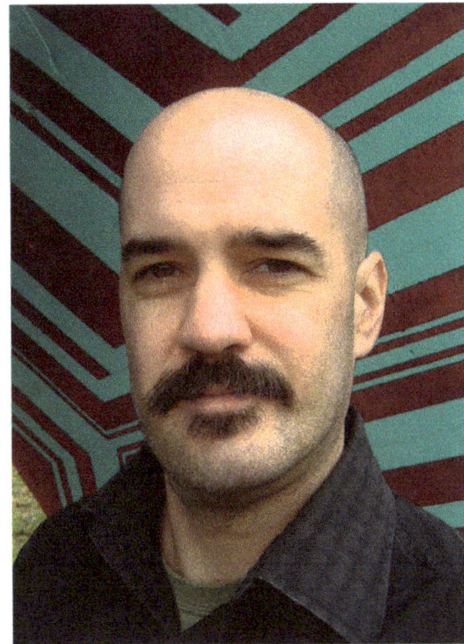

If you must label Graem Whyte, try "creator of space and good vibes."

"Artist," he insists, is too narrow to capture the ways he reimagines and reshapes once-ordinary objects. "I like the freedom of exploring and creating space," says forty-two-year-old Whyte. "I like creating good vibes."

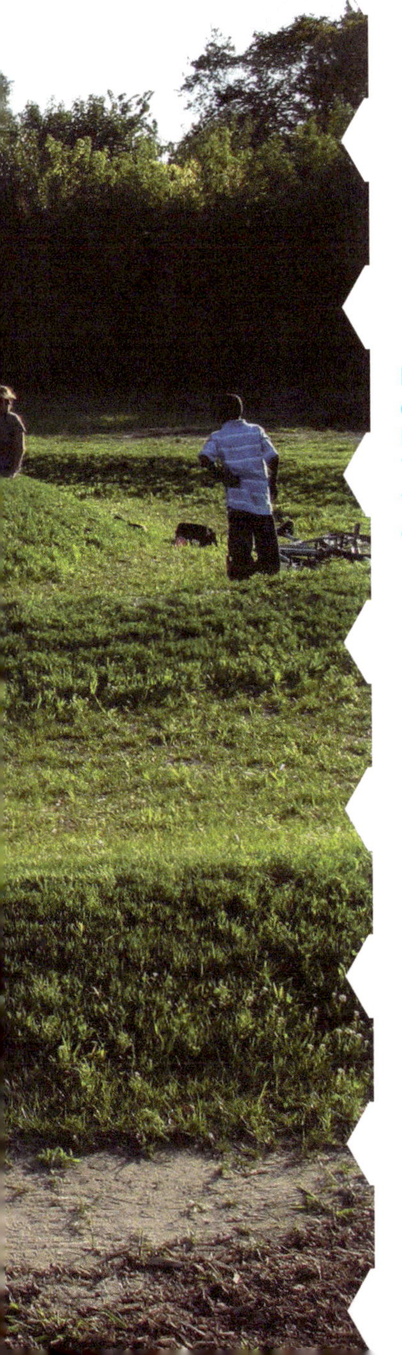

Yet to look at Whyte's body of large-scale architectural installations and miniature landscapes, it's easy to see why so many are quick to pin him with more typical labels such as sculptor. An outdoor sculpture called *Memory Field* is the grandest display of the unique way Whyte works.

With his wife, artist Faina Lerman, Whyte transformed an empty patch of Detroit's Calimera Park into a giant undulating grass sculpture. The art of his big idea lies as much in the shaping of the grass as it does in an underground cistern built as an accompanying feature. The project, funded by the Skillman Foundation, has been called a clever, and giant, example of art meeting need. The scale, 120 feet in diameter, including one three-foot-high ripple, mesmerizes visitors while the cistern collects rainwater to replenish a nearby community garden.

"I see potential in anything. Whatever is at hand has the possibility to become something more," he says. "It's really just about exploring the space. The materials and the steps just have this way of usually presenting themselves."

The same can be said for Whyte's entire journey into art making. "I got a little later start than a lot of people," he says. His plan was to become an architect. After high school, he set out to earn a college degree. He studied at Lawrence Technological University and the College for Creative Studies, but never finished, partly due to a youthful penchant for "hanging out."

By age twenty-eight, Whyte found he had another emerging passion. He was suddenly turning miniature handmade landscapes—using wood, metal, model train parts, and anything else that he could find—into art. "I guess you could say I'm self-educated, always interested in learning news things, exploring new frontiers," he says.

With Detroit as a base, Whyte says the opportunities to reimagine are endless. Take, for example, *Squash House,* Whyte's next project (see pp. 68–69). The vision: redesign a badly burned three-bedroom house into a space for squash playing and squash growing. "The idea just came to me one day," he says. "I've always been interested in games or sports of some sort."

Beyond the fun, the house, owned by the arts nonprofit Power House Productions, is also another invitation to test the limits of space.

"It's not like we're trying to build a regulation-size court. It's more about playing the house for its possibilities, editing out the bad parts, and reimagining a few things." The process includes removing walls and the entire second floor, building a more sculptural roof, and transforming the back of the house into an atrium/greenhouse. "It's a lot of work."

The project is also, he says rather reluctantly, quintessentially Detroit: "Earlier in my career, I think I was trying to not be Detroit. I've never felt the need to get away from the city, but I wanted to make work that could be from anywhere."

Today, Whyte, who also works part time as an adjunct in the foundry at the College for Creative Studies, is no longer torn. "I think being resourceful is who we are and it's who I am. One of the things about making work here is that you're always, always asking: What do I have and what can I do with it?"

Answering that question has led Whyte down some pretty surprising roads, including the creation of Popps Packing. Popps is a 1930s former meatpacking plant turned cookie factory that Whyte and his wife have since converted into their home as well as an experimental art space and artists' residency.

"It's not like Faina and I had this dream of creating a residency program," he says. "We were looking for a house to buy and this opportunity presented itself." For periods of three weeks to a month, artists live and create work at Popps while assisting with ongoing renovations.

Popps's existence, Whyte says, is much like his career—another map-less journey sparked by a willingness to explore and a city hungry for reinvention.

"It's kind of the perfect storm. We've always had quality of work in Detroit, but it's finally getting attention and funding."

But Whyte says pondering the future or sustainability of Detroit's creative resurgence is someone else's job.

"There something really satisfying for me just being in the moment of creation," he says. "I'm just going with the flow and letting things happen of their own accord. We'll see where it leads."

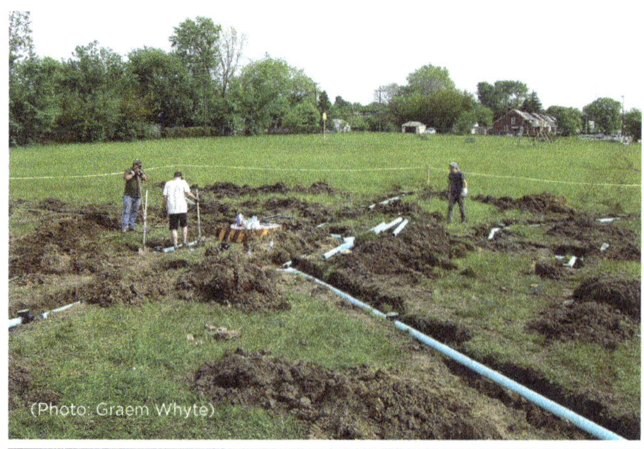
(Photo: Graem Whyte)

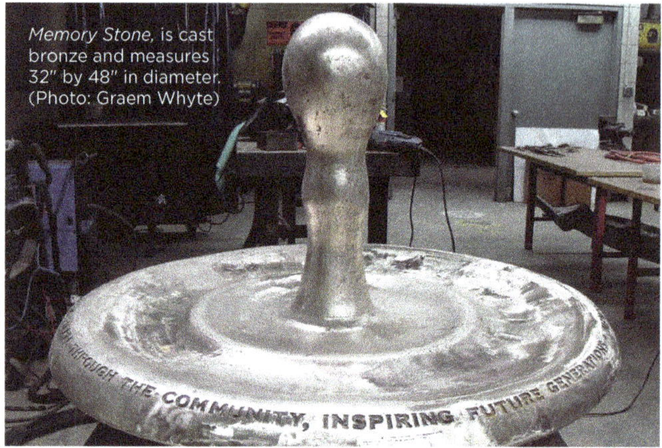

Memory Stone, is cast bronze and measures 32" by 48" in diameter. (Photo: Graem Whyte)

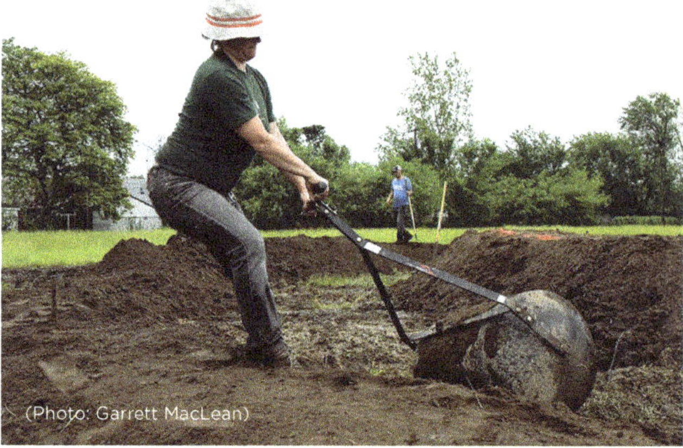
(Photo: Garrett MacLean)

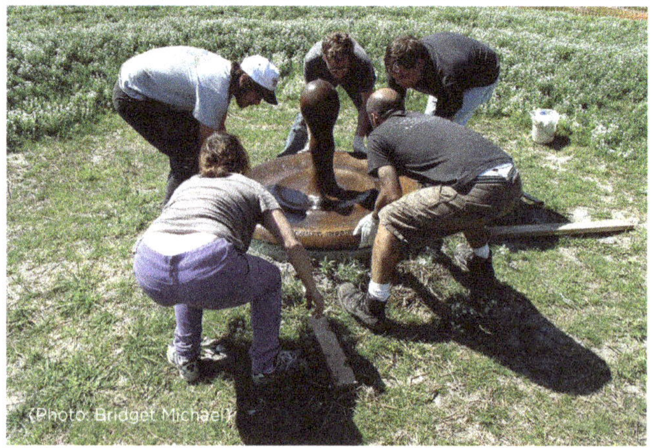
(Photo: Bridget Michael)

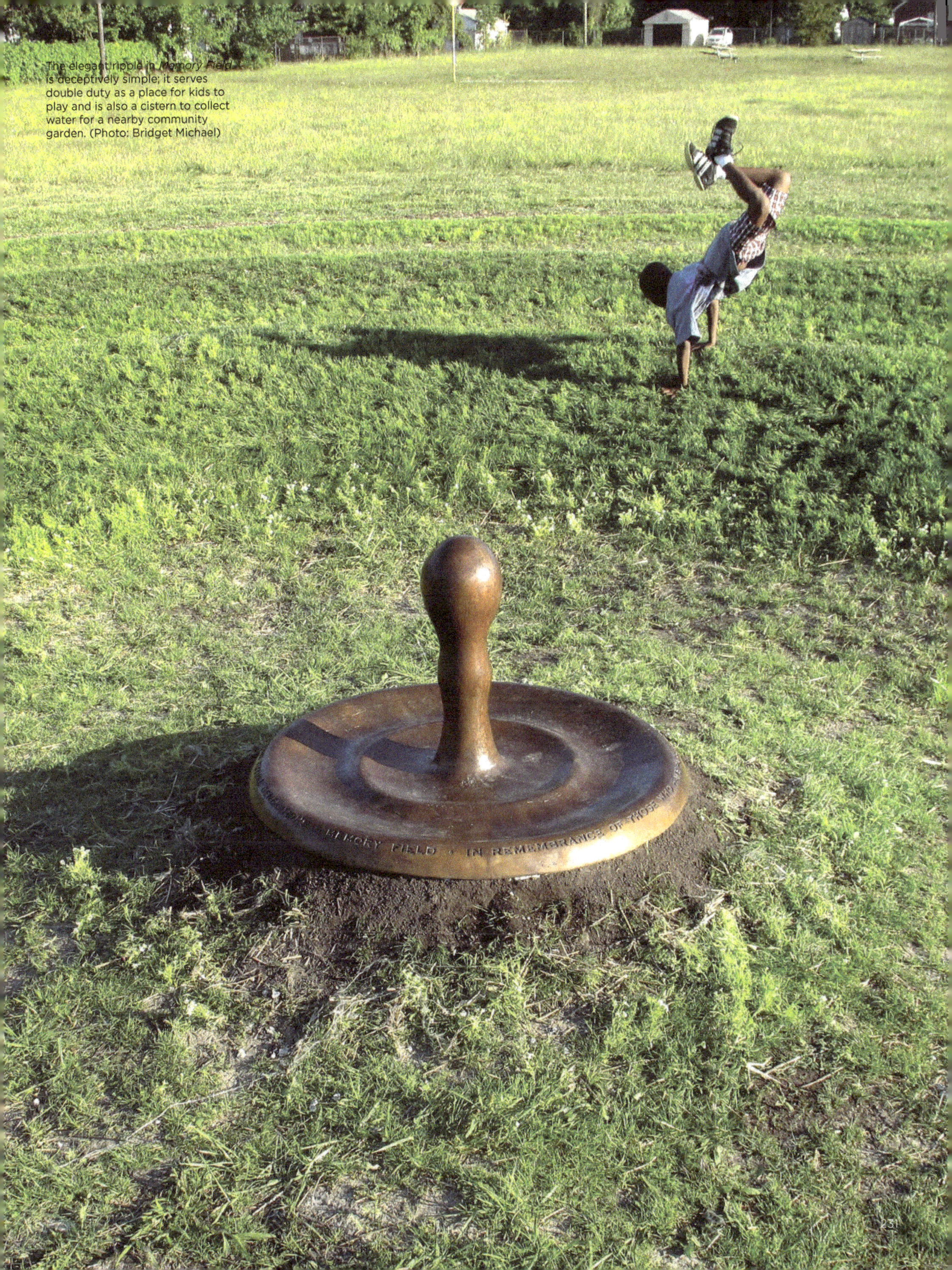

The elegant ripple in *Memory Field* is deceptively simple; it serves double duty as a place for kids to play and is also a cistern to collect water for a nearby community garden. (Photo: Bridget Michael)

YVETTE ROCK

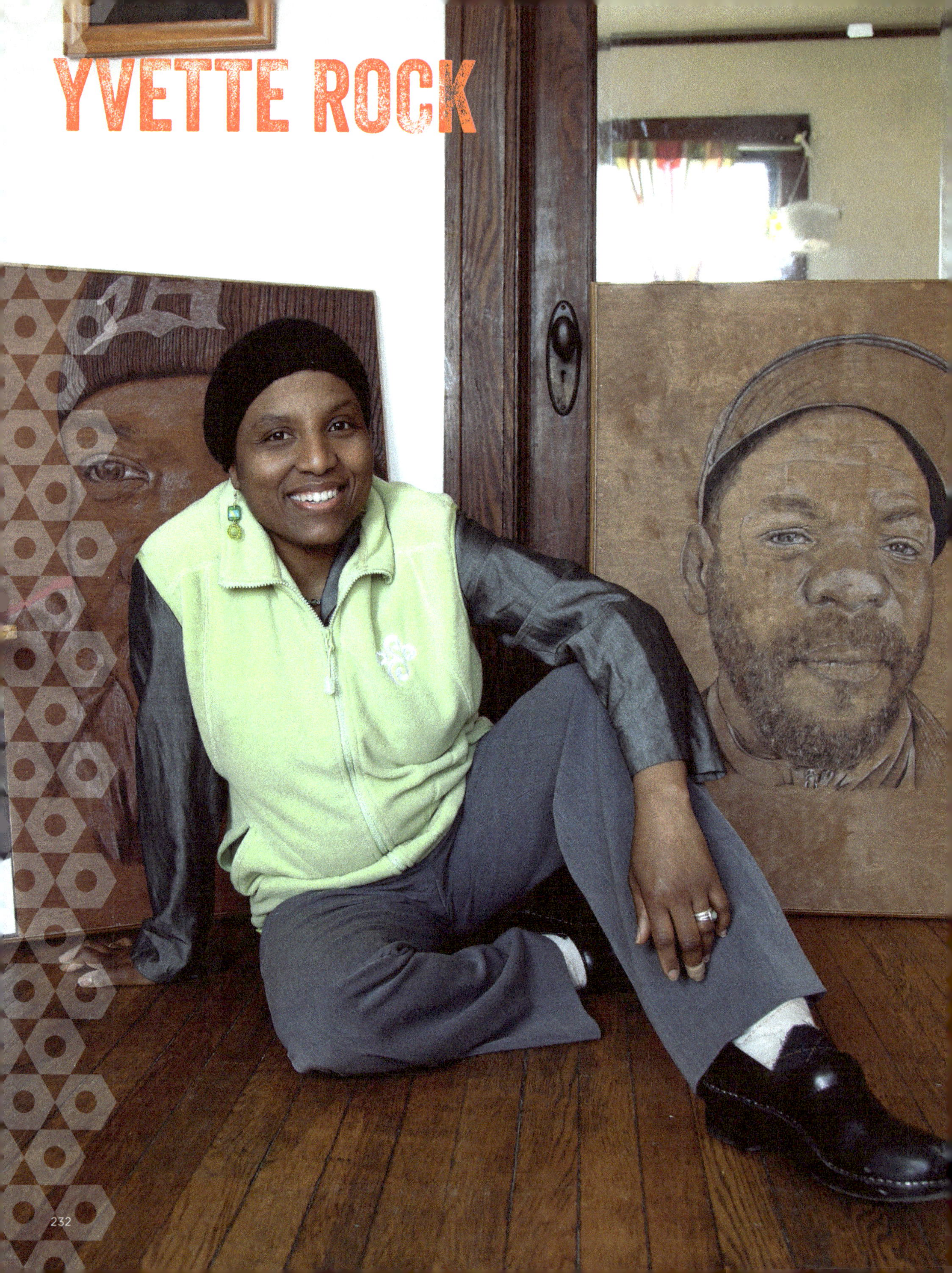

Yvette Rock was born in Suriname.

Yet she is quick to tell everyone she was found, at least as an artist, a world away in Detroit.

"From my first visit, when I was coming to the city as a grad student in Ann Arbor, I was hooked," says Rock, who holds a Master of Fine Arts from the University of Michigan and a bachelor's from Cooper Union in New York.

"I saw something in the city, in the people. It's cliché but this is where I'm called to be."

Since 1999, Rock has rooted herself deeply into the city. She is a self-professed student of all things Detroit: its landscape, its history, even its heartache. "When I'm looking at the city," says Rock, a married mother of four, "I'm actually trying to find out what are some of the root causes for the problems we see."

Everything Rock takes in inevitably returns to her as source material for expansive series of large-scale paintings, photographs, and collages, which she often embeds with objects found during visits to burned-out and abandoned buildings. "My work reflects my passion and concern for the city, hoping that plagues such as addiction are turned to recovery, corruption to justice, abandonment to restoration, and homelessness to sheltered," she says. "I think some people just want to put a Band-Aid on Detroit rather than going deep."

Rock sees herself on a mission. She's spent the last few years carefully completing a mixed-media installation of jarring colors and subject matters called *Ten Plagues of Detroit*.

Her paintings start as sketches, sometimes pencil on wood, and are all infused with religious undertones meant to examine hope's role in restoring broken people and broken places. The paintings explore, for example, the plagues of addiction, illiteracy, arson, abandonment, and social despair.

"There is a truth I'm trying to communicate even if it's hard to take. The truth of the brokenness of the city has to be told from an artistic perspective. I feel very strongly that unless you acknowledge the devastation, you can't move forward in anything," she says.

Rock, who's also lived in Miami and New York, considers herself fortunate to be an artist in a city whose problems are complicated. "Part of art's role is to be a recorder of history, telling the story of Detroit as it is now, but then we can't just leave it at the brokenness. How do we, from the core of it, bring healing, bring redemption to the city, bring wholeness and newness and life again to things that are dead?"

For Rock, the question isn't rhetorical. She recently added community art gallery owner to her list of creative pursuits in Detroit, opening the Live Coal Gallery. The gallery, housed on the first floor of her home, is conceived as a space to educate, curate, and collect the work of emerging and high-school artists. "It's the seed of something new."

Live Coal marks the second time she's built a bridge between art and education in Detroit. In 2000, she designed a University of Michigan course called Detroit Connections. In the course, U-M students partnered with Detroit Public School students to develop and create community art projects.

"I see this as the first step to one day owning a big museum that just features the work of high school artists," she says beaming. "I want people to come here and say, 'Look at what these Detroit kids are doing with art.' I just imagine the feeling of confidence the youth will get from seeing their work and even being able to say, 'I sold a painting.'"

Rock's voice races when she talks about her vision for the gallery. That the space is finally open, she says, proves yet again Detroit is the right place for her.

"Ten years ago, I'd hear people asking, 'Why Detroit? Nothing's happening there.' I think people are starting to see. Even with its brokenness, the city has so much to offer and to teach about life and art. I still feel like I'm just scratching the surface."

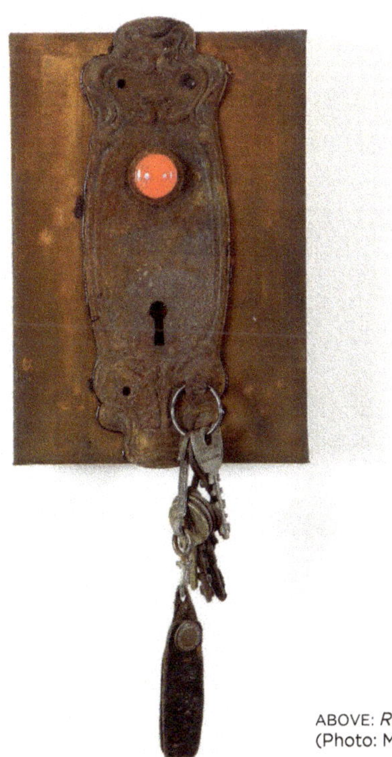

ABOVE: *ReDetroit*
(Photo: Mark Trupiano)

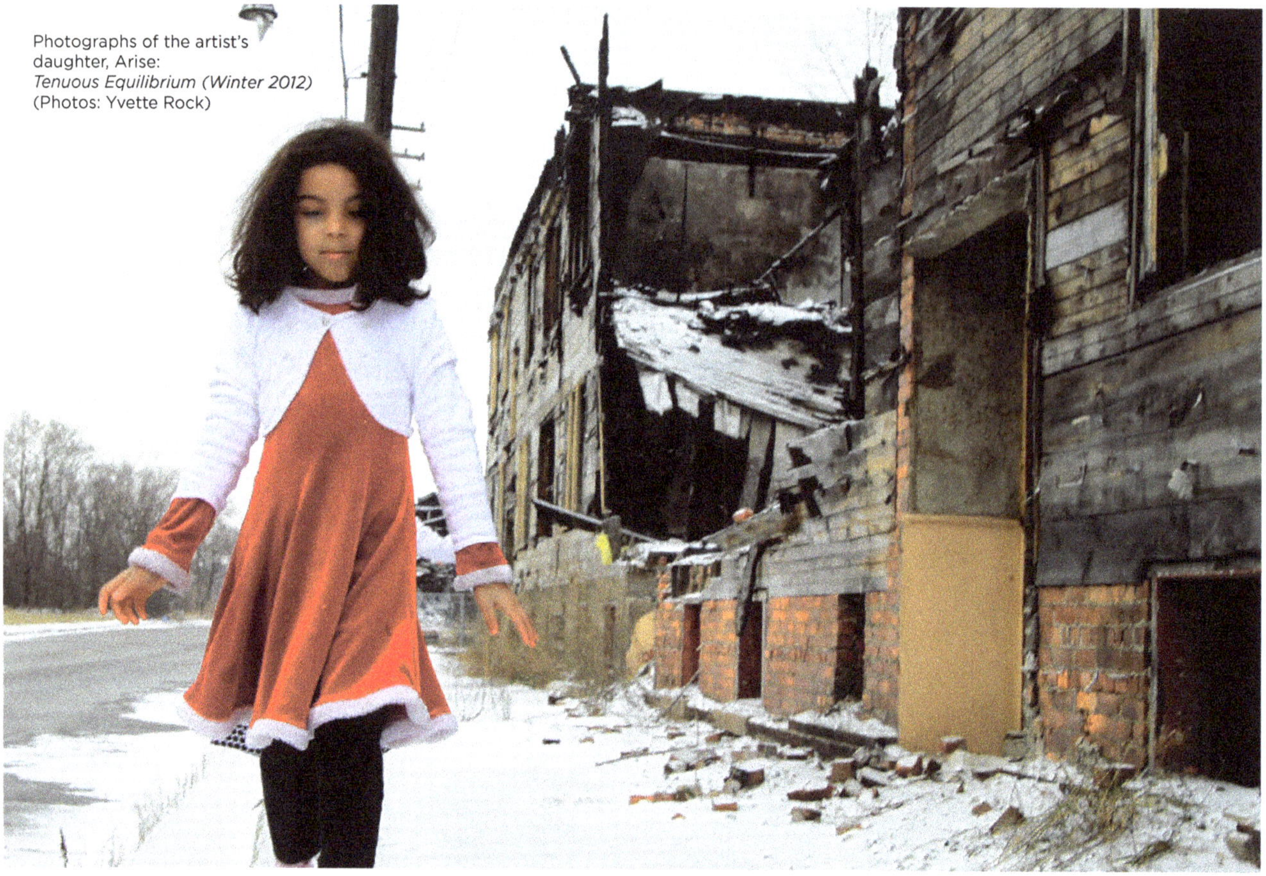

Photographs of the artist's daughter, Arise:
Tenuous Equilibrium (Winter 2012)
(Photos: Yvette Rock)

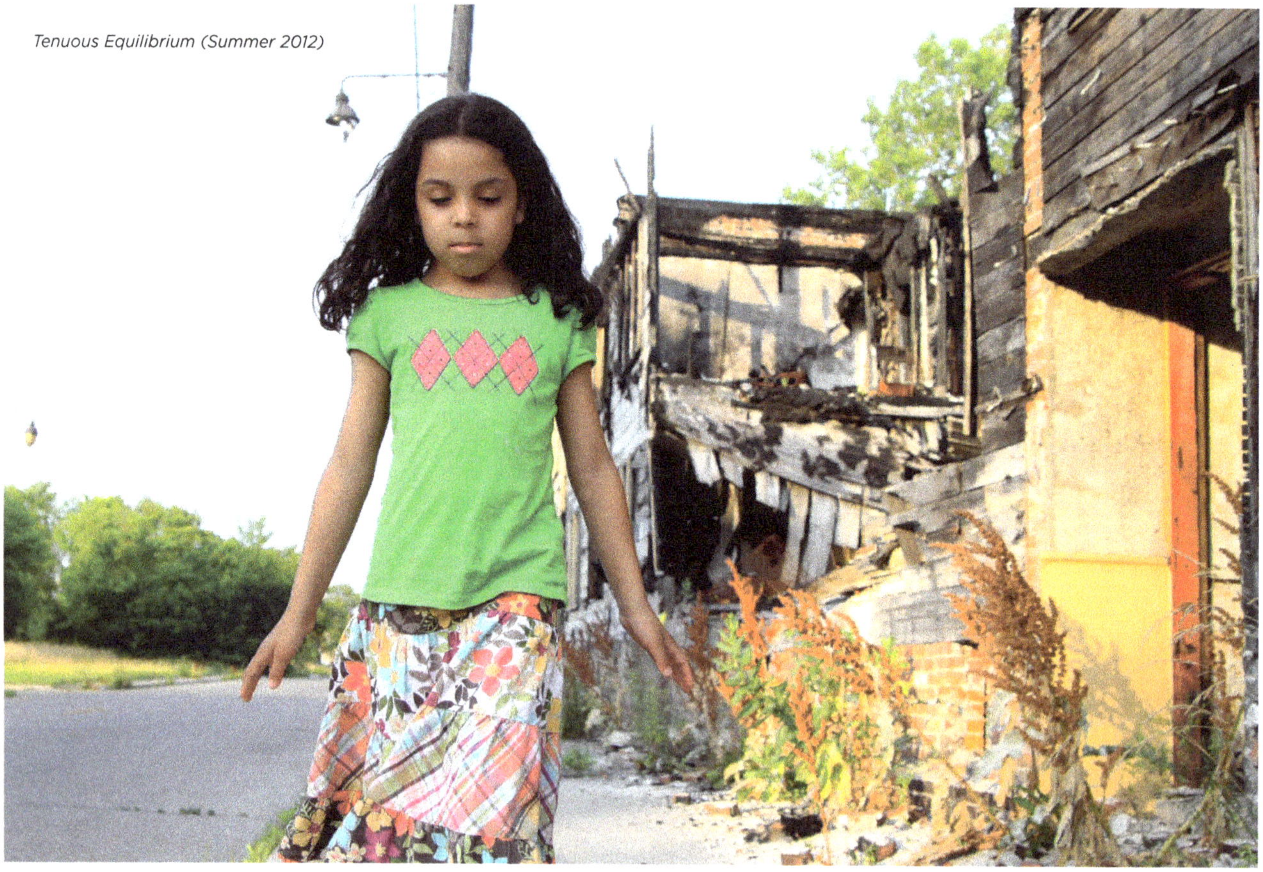

Tenuous Equilibrium (Summer 2012)

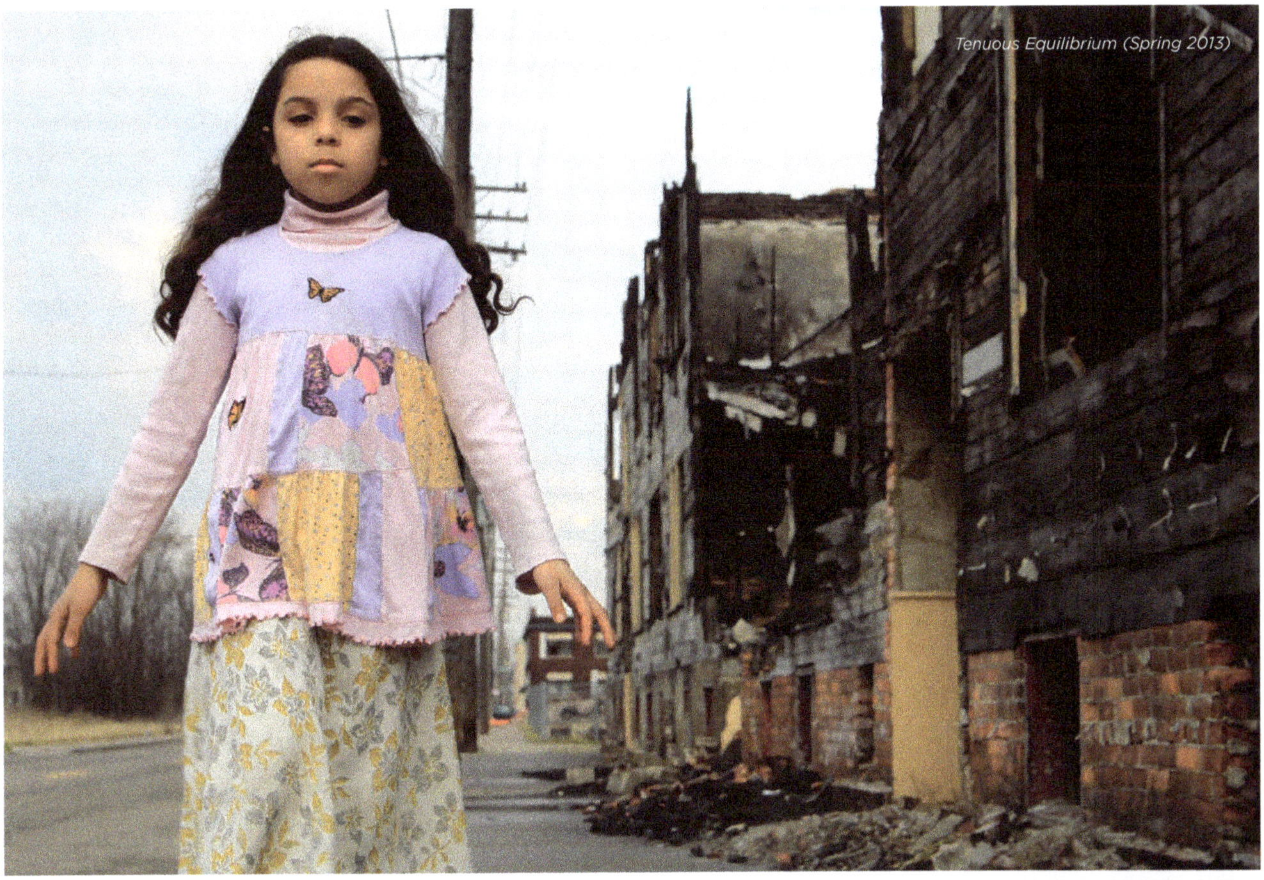

Tenuous Equilibrium (Spring 2013)

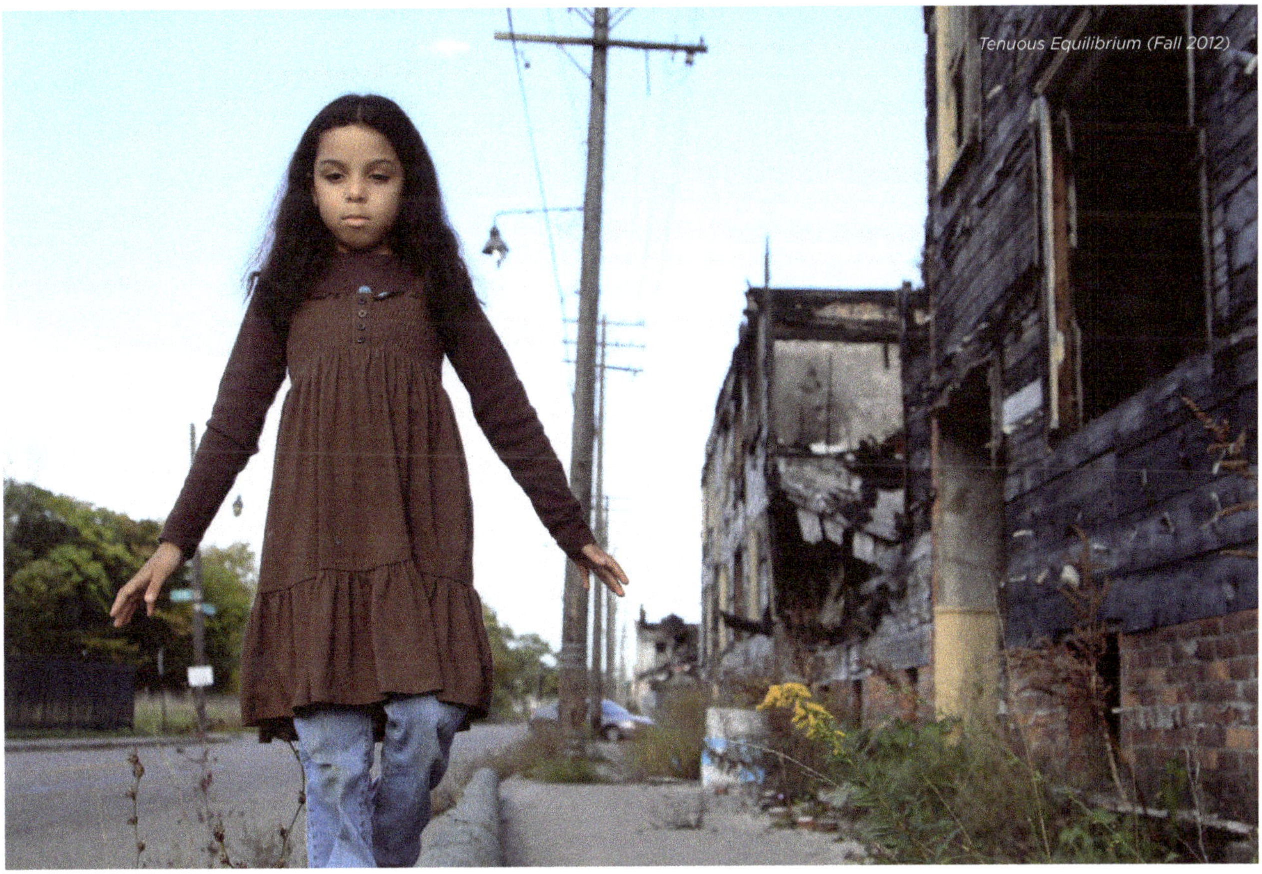

Tenuous Equilibrium (Fall 2012)

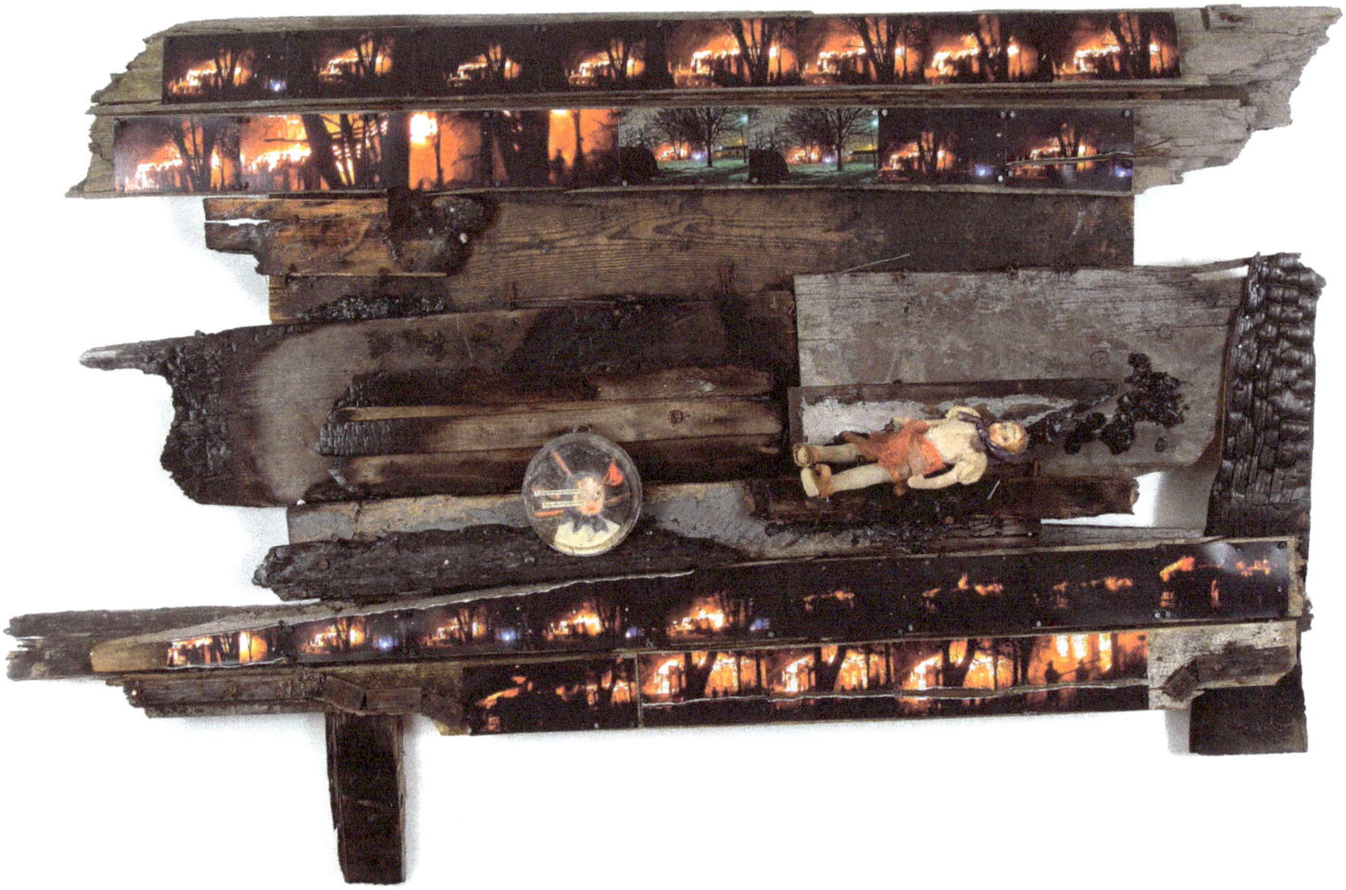

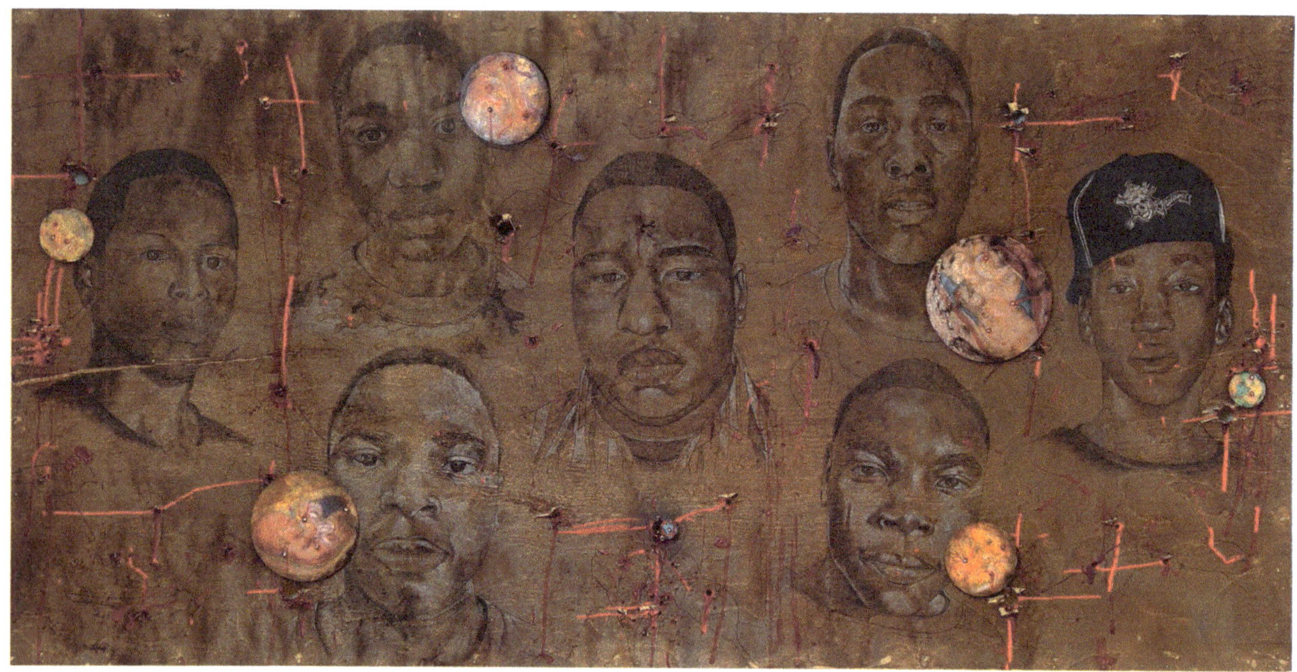

TOP LEFT: *Plague of Arson and Fire: Study 1*
BOTTOM LEFT: *Plague of Violence*
BELOW: *Plague of Arson and Fire*
(Photos: Mark Trupiano)

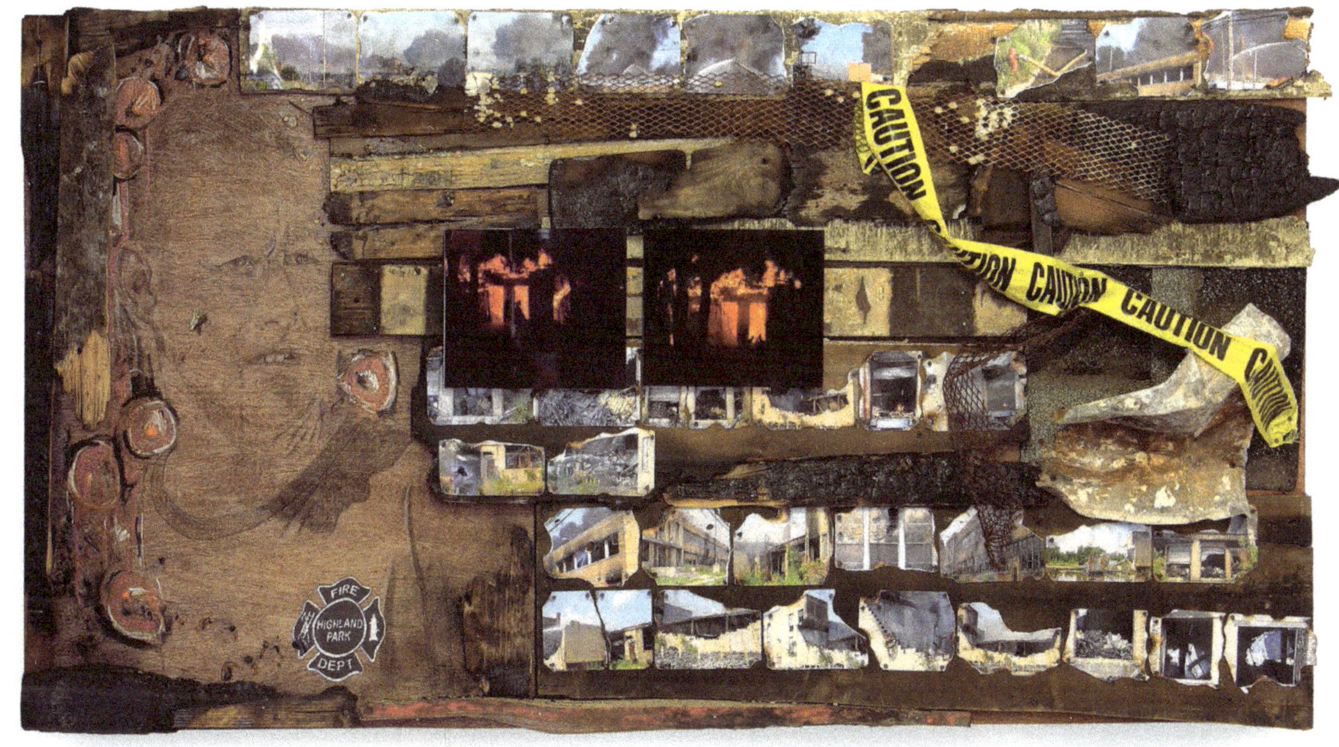

JOHN SAUVÉ

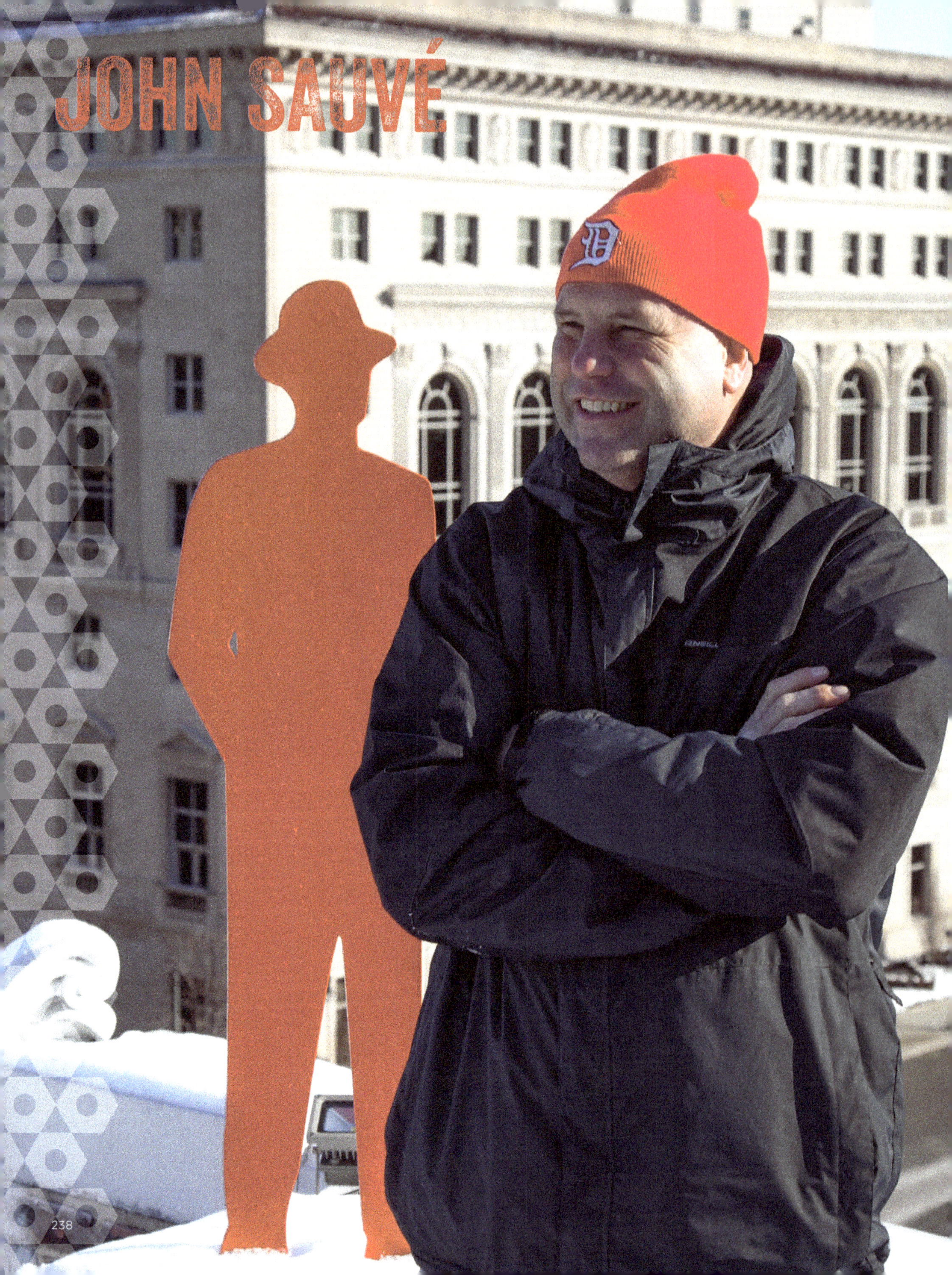

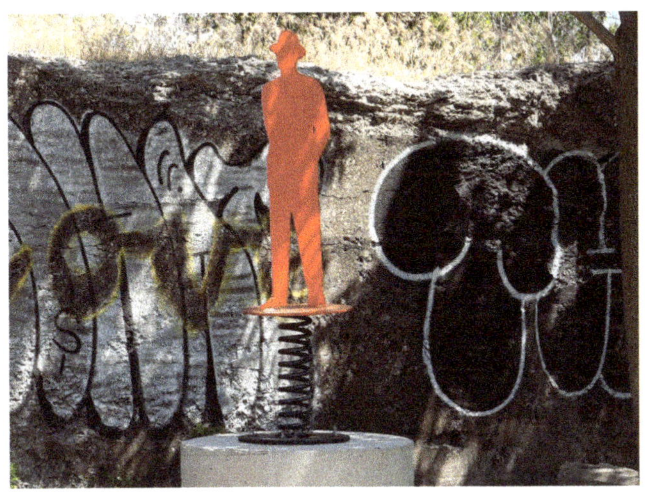

Sculptor John Sauvé does not have a giant name on the Detroit art scene.

He says he doesn't need one. He's enlisted a small army of foot soldiers to make his presence known. They number only thirty but they turn heads everywhere they go, igniting a flurry of curiosity that leads straight back to Sauvé.

Sauvé's soldiers are actually steel statues.

Around the city, the seventy-pound figures have come to be known as "the little orange men." They're perched, like sentries, on the rooftops of some of the city's most prominent and up-and-coming buildings, including the Detroit Opera House and several small shops in the historic commercial district known as Eastern Market.

Despite standing only forty inches tall, some of Sauvé's men can be seen from miles away. He intentionally paints each one burnt orange to ensure that they are hard to miss. Sauvé also personally bolts each statue in place so that they don't stop traffic in more dangerous ways.

People notice the men and they wonder. Some inquire just as he initially hoped when he designed the *Man in the City* installation.

"The dialogue that gets sparked around a project like this—the public awareness that happens—that's what I live for as an artist," says Sauvé, fifty. "I don't need to talk about me. This is about having the men become another reason to look up. Nothing makes you more aware of your surrounding like public art can."

A Michigan State University art history graduate, Sauvé designs and fabricates each of the figures. At first glance, they appear to be randomly scattered throughout the city. But take a tour of the sites he's selected and it's clear that Sauvé applied as much attention to choosing his locations as he did to mastering each angle and cut. Each building is linked somehow to the city's creative history or its new-found appeal among emerging artists.

The statues, silhouettes of a man with one hand in his pocket and wearing a fedora, will be standing tall in Detroit through 2015. Sauvé's orange men first surfaced back in 2008, when he designed a handful of the statues for exhibitions in New York City and later for display in small Michigan communities such as Benton Harbor. In Detroit, he's set the men on a much larger mission.

"Detroit is the hottest creative brand around right now," he says. "We're a little self-deprecating and we may be this underdog in other places around the world, but it hasn't stopped the people here from creating or problem solving. There's something good going on every day that's worth bringing attention to."

While his statues grab attention, Sauvé is more proud of a lesser-known aspect of his work in Detroit. In between scouting for new locations, he also teaches free public art classes for area after-school groups. "It's one thing to go throw your art up and leave, but that just makes it all about you," he says. "It's more interesting to go the extra step so the work becomes part of the community."

He takes students through a simulated project that introduces the importance of goal setting, community networking, and ultimately designing a replica of his *Man in the City* statues. When the class is done, each student receives a miniature wooden replica of the statue, which Sauvé hand-cuts. The students also plan and design a public exhibition.

"I'm not trying to create artists," he explains. "I just want to give kids the opportunity to go through a process that can maybe help them think more creatively about their community. I see it a lot like my approach to the men. They're individual figures. But when you notice them up on the skyline, all of a sudden Detroit looks a little different and you pay a little more attention to things on the horizon."

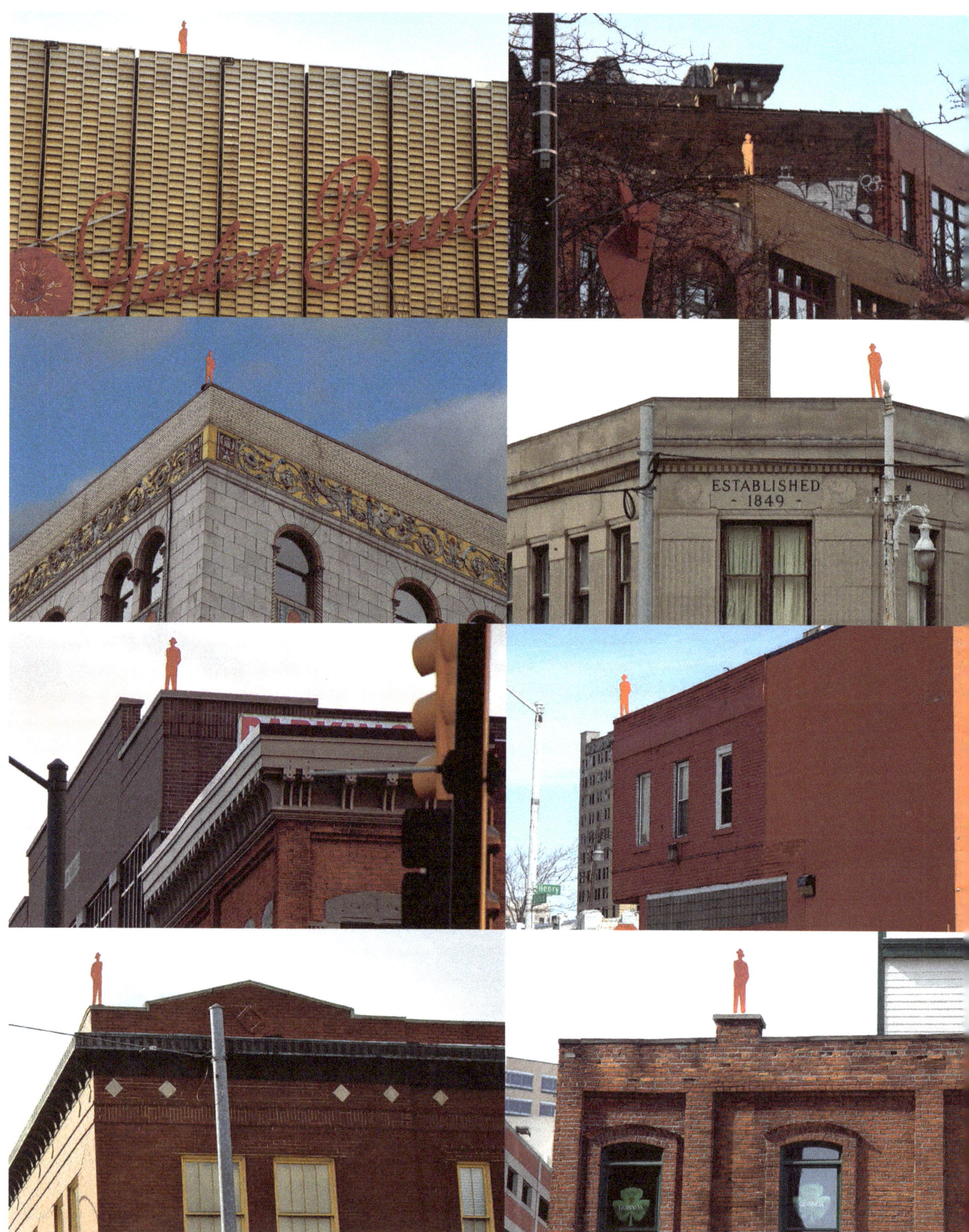
Garden Bowl
ESTABLISHED
- 1849 -
Henry

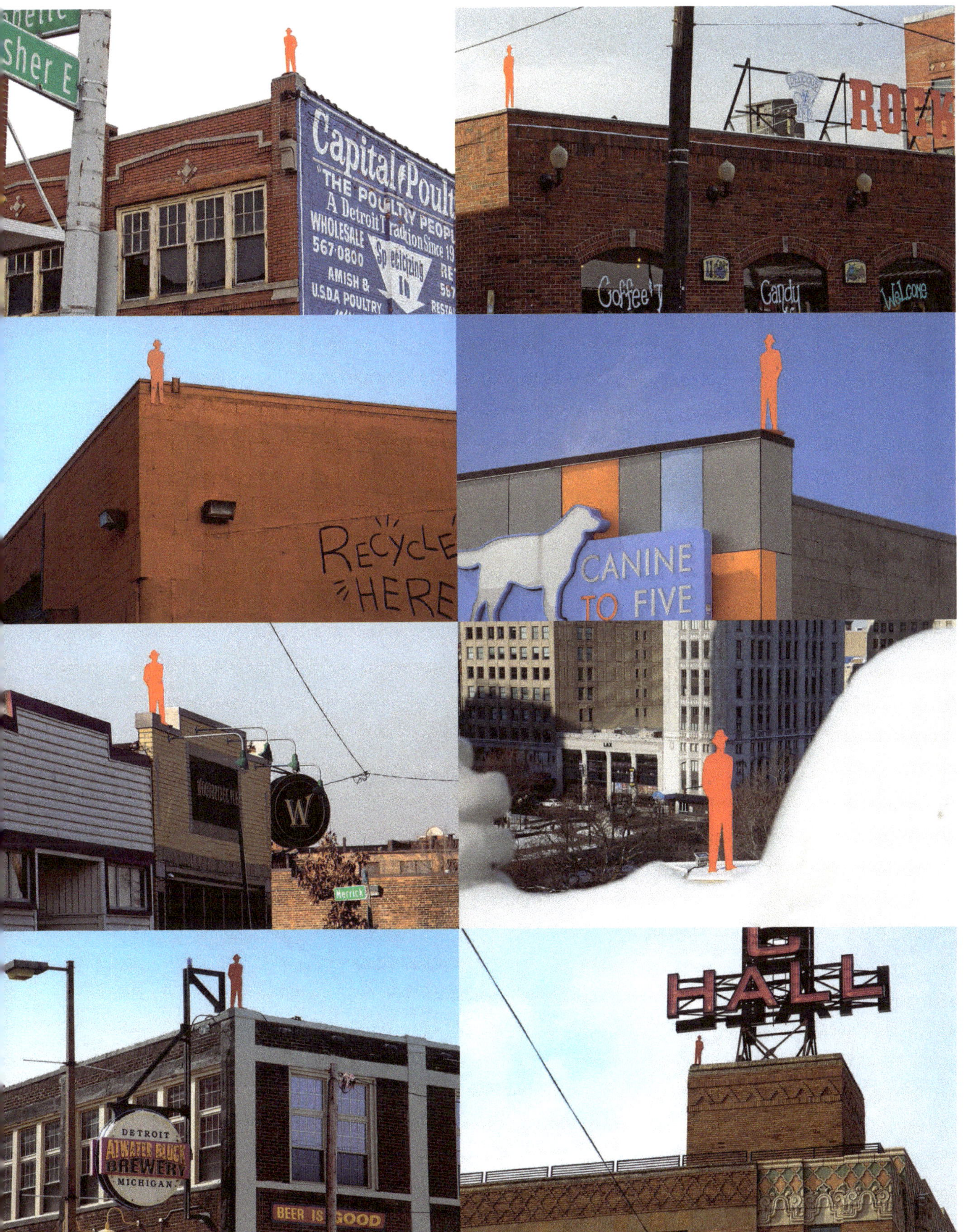

Capital
WHOLESALE
567-0800
AMISH &
U.S.DA POULTRY
Coffee
Candy
Welcome
RECYCLE
HERE
CANINE
TO FIVE
W
Merrick
DETROIT
ATWATER BLOCK
BREWERY
MICHIGAN
BEER IS GOOD
HALL

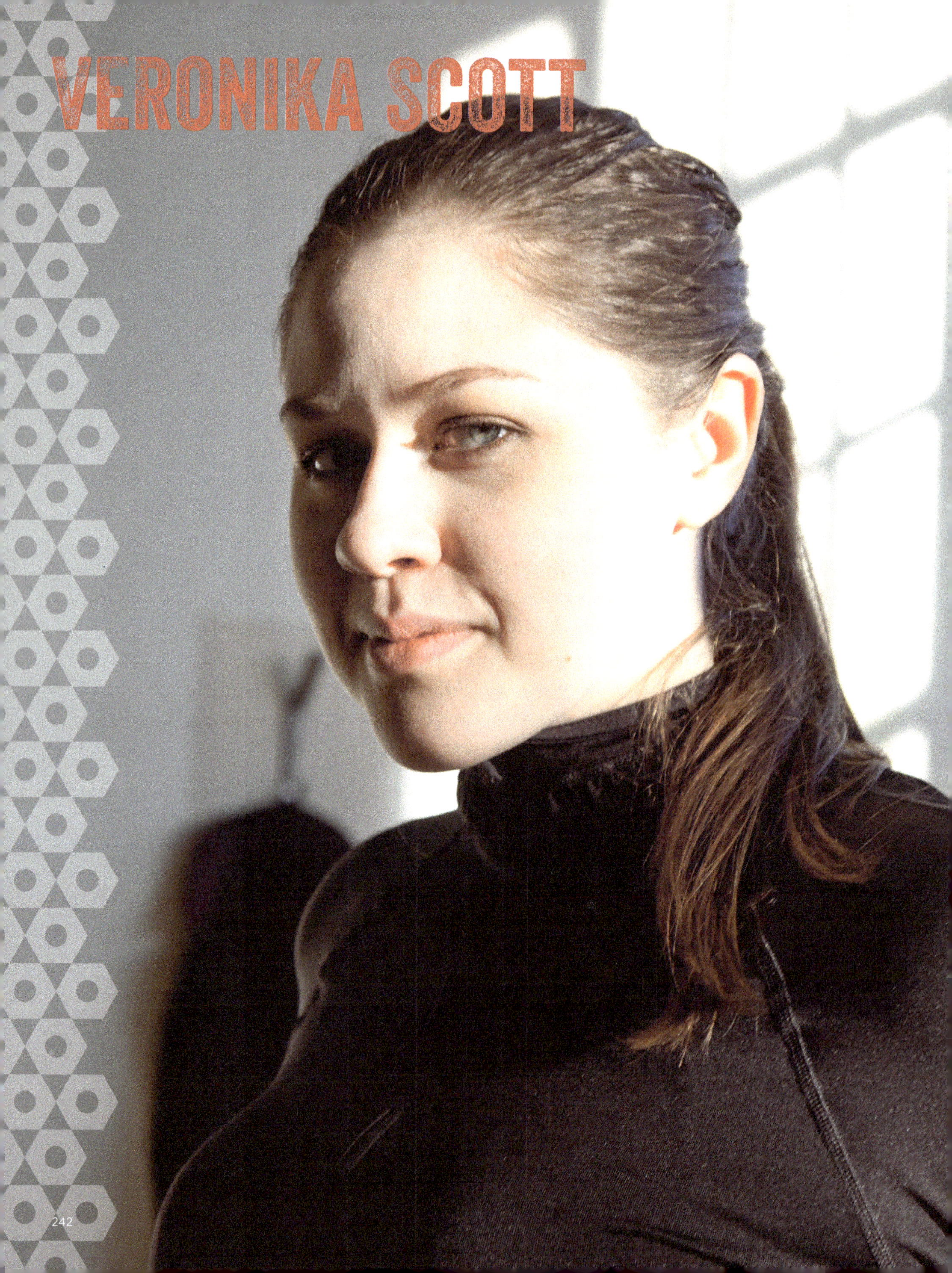
VERONIKA SCOTT

Only in Detroit!

That's how twenty-three-year-old Veronika Scott typically answers the question of how she transformed a class project into a bold example of using design to unravel a great social dilemma: "It couldn't happen anywhere else in the world but Detroit."

Scott's big little idea is almost legend, talked about locally and globally, by those trying to discern whether creativity really can become Motown's next big engine. In Scott, even contrarians find reason to believe. While studying design at Detroit's College for Creative Studies back in 2010, a professor challenged Scott, and others, to devise a design that could respond to a vexing social challenge.

Her attention seized on the streets and research that showed more than thirty-six thousand homeless men and women in need of shelter. Through countless conversations at shelters with homeless Detroiters, Scott heard a recurring theme. "I met a lot of people with a lot of pride," she says, "and they had a very real concern about not having to freeze if they've got to be out on the streets."

So Scott, determined to merge her professor's call to action with the wish list she heard from homeless men and women, decided to create a coat. But the coat in Scott's mind would be fashionable, with a thin black or white quilted exterior and a red interior, yet durable enough to double as a self-heating weather-resistant sleeping bag.

Predictably, the design faced its share of trials and errors. There was the high hurdle of finding cost-effective and lightweight materials for insulation. Production costs had to be kept low also, ideally between seven and ten dollars. Then came the aesthetics of the design itself. Could she make the design sleek enough to disguise its dual-purpose? The coat initially weighed in at a whopping twenty pounds and looked, according to some, more like a "body bag" than an invitation to dignity. The current design weighs in at just one pound, light enough to fold up into an over-the-shoulder bag.

Scott's initial focus was just to complete the project with a viable model. "It really was just a test," she says. "Do we know how to make a coat? Can we teach other people to make them, too? It was so much feeling around in the dark."

Today, Scott is the founder and CEO of The Empowerment Plan, a nonprofit enterprise helping homeless women earn while they learn to become seamstresses. "I'm really surprised that they're trusting in a twenty-three-year-old to make sure that they have food on their table and a chance at real stability," she says of the seven formerly homeless women she's hired. "It's an inspiring reason to work hard." A powerful group of corporate partners, including General Motors and Carhartt Inc., has rallied around Scott and her dreams for the women she employs. She's found factory space "for pennies" in a refurbished warehouse that's become an incubator for creative Detroit businesses. Scott was the building's very first tenant. GM and Carhartt helped resolve some of Scott's more stubborn design challenges: how to insulate the sleeping bag from wind and water. The automaker offered up a solution as novel as Scott's design—the suggested materials used to provide sound absorption for the doors of cars like the Chevrolet Malibu and Buick Verano. "People tend to think that art and business are separate," she says. "But there is a creative energy here right now that's all about redefining art, applying abstract thinking, and asking, 'Why can't we do things differently, in ways that also benefit people's lives?'"

Since 2010, Scott's Empowerment Plan has manufactured and distributed more than a thousand coats in Detroit, Ohio, Chicago, and Buffalo. Some days she finds herself stunned by how much ground her coat has covered. It has also changed her life. "I went to school for art," she says. "I went there only knowing how great painting and drawing skills were and I came out designing products, and I've ended up running a nonprofit business to help the homeless." And she is most proud of the buy-in her idea has received from a "weird mixture" of supporters.

"It's an interesting point and time in the city. There are so many different types of people. There's large entities and small entities, entrepreneurs and creative people like me who look at Detroit like this open landscape," Scott says. "But there are also people who look at the city with a bias of what it used to be or what it may never be for them. We can't just push them aside. There has to be connections between these different worlds. Those of us who see Detroit as a land of opportunity can't be the only ones who feel empowered."

The support she's garnered and the success of the coat invariably bring Scott back around to her guiding thought. "If I was anywhere else but Detroit, a big company like GM wouldn't pay any attention to me. A big company wouldn't think what I was doing was important. But because of what Detroit is slowly becoming, I have big companies like GM and Carhartt supporting me. They also see the possibilities in applying creative problem-solving."

In 2011, Scott further amazed herself by capturing an International Design Excellence Award from the Industrial Designers Society of America. Going forward, she envisions what she calls a one-for-one business model, where one customer's purchase covers the cost of a second coat for a homeless individual. It's a model Scott believes could soar nationally, perhaps even globally. Beyond revenue, Scott has her eyes trained on more personal signs of success. "At the end of the day, I want the women to feel like, 'We can trust Veronika.' This isn't just another program," she says. "It's crazy and it's constantly growing, but it's a model that's also creative enough to become a career, a future if that's what they want. We're building something that's going to last."

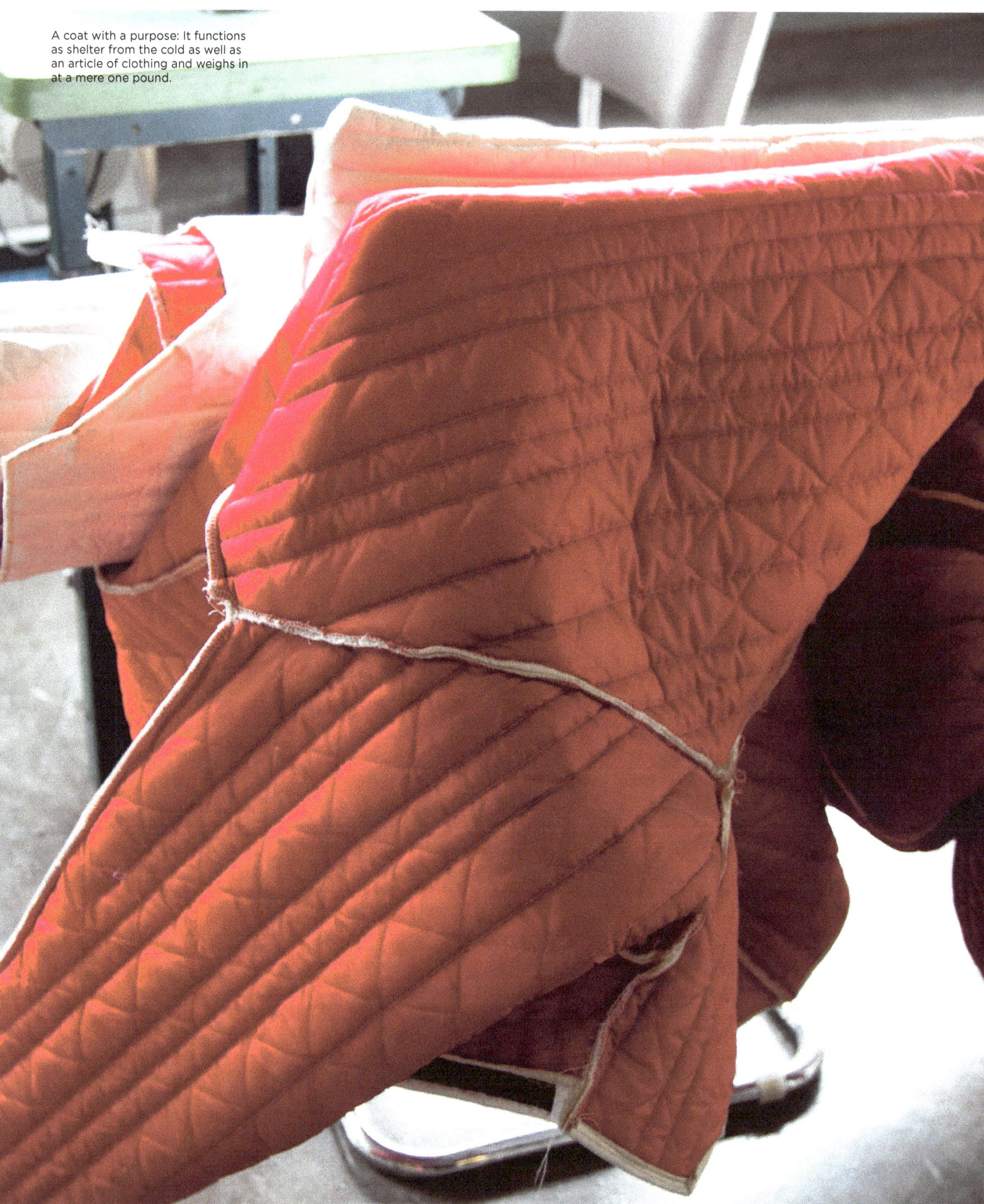

A coat with a purpose: It functions as shelter from the cold as well as an article of clothing and weighs in at a mere one pound.

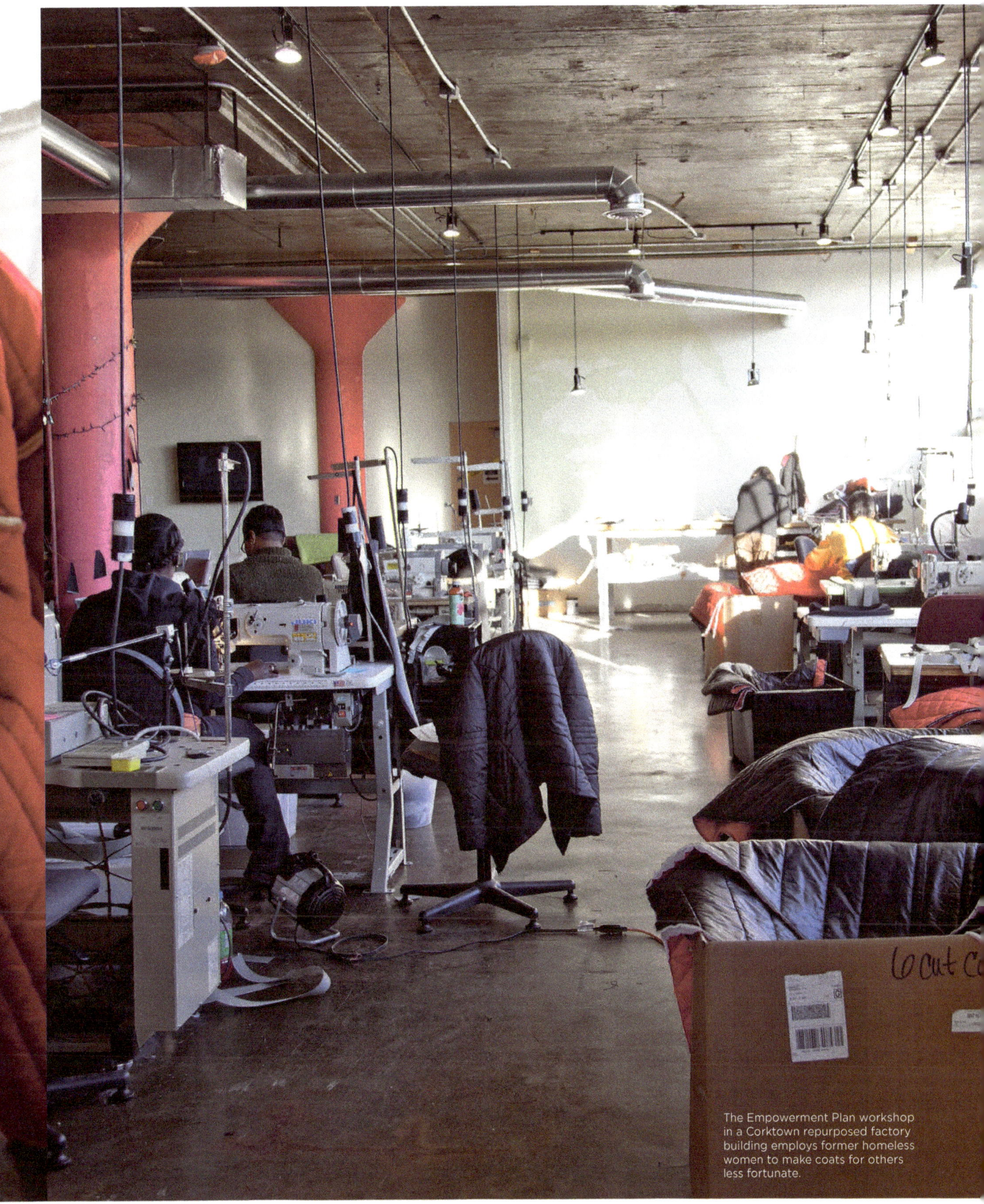

The Empowerment Plan workshop in a Corktown repurposed factory building employs former homeless women to make coats for others less fortunate.

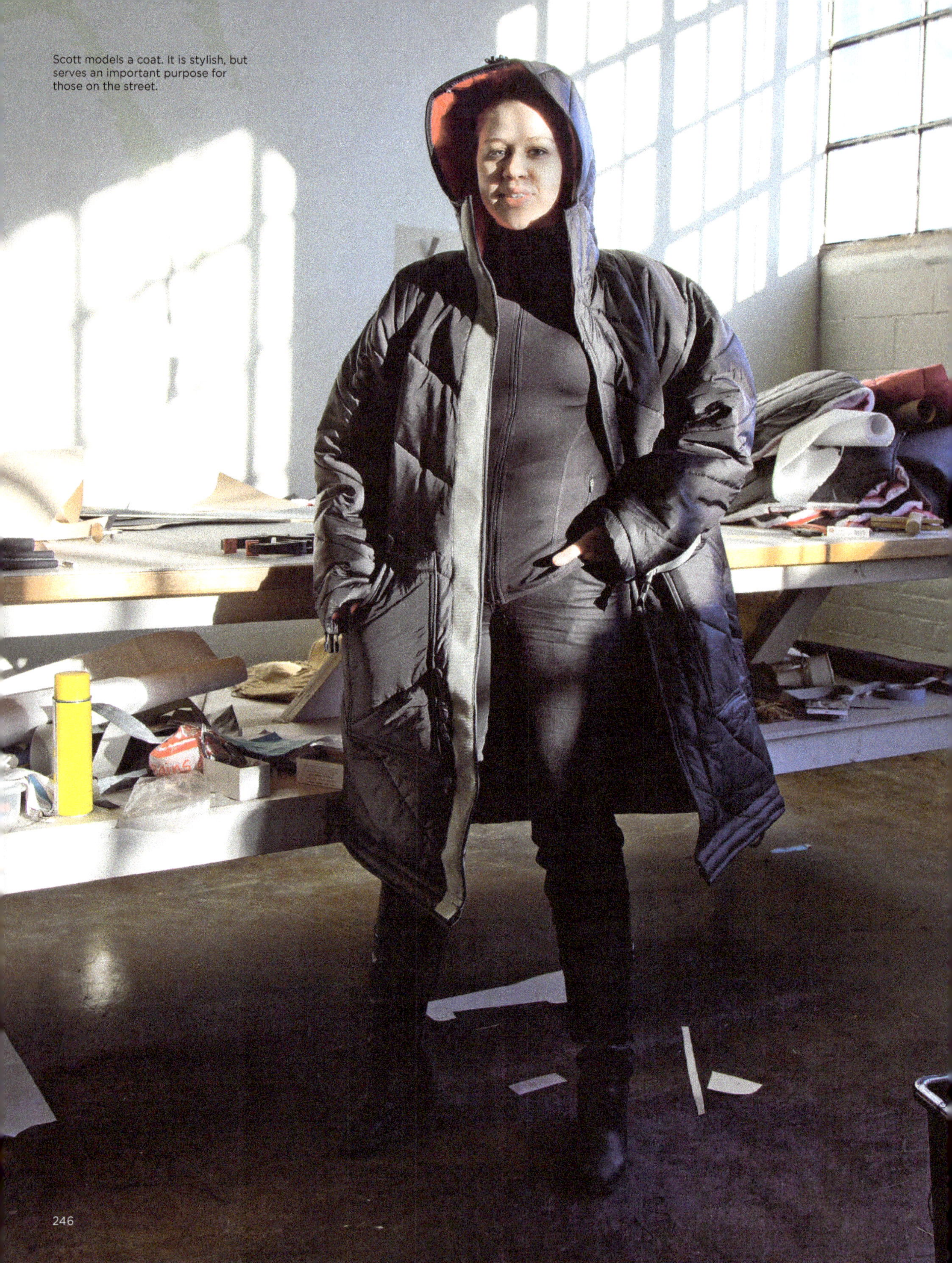

Scott models a coat. It is stylish, but serves an important purpose for those on the street.

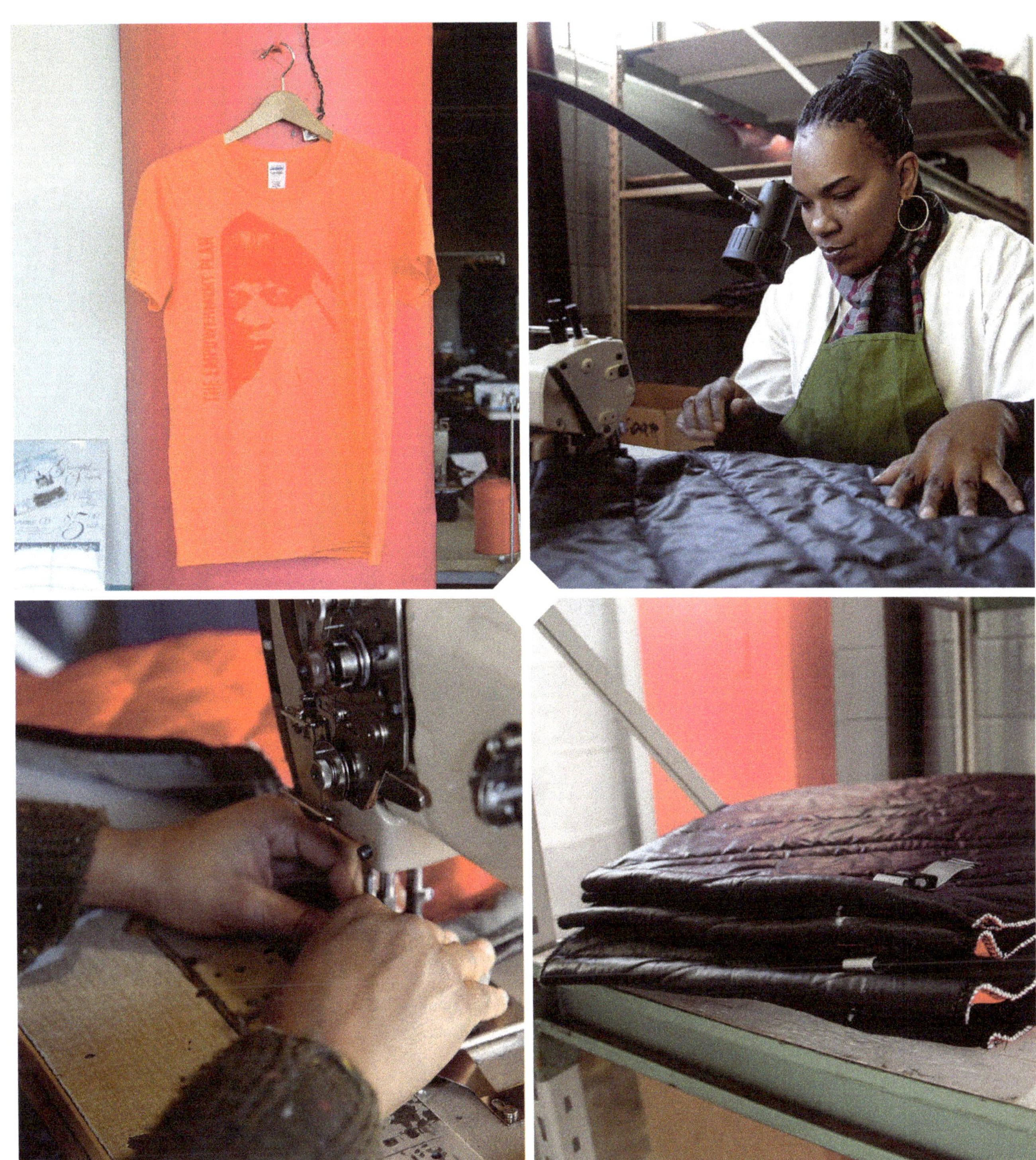
THE EMPOWERMENT PLAN

ROBERT SESTOK

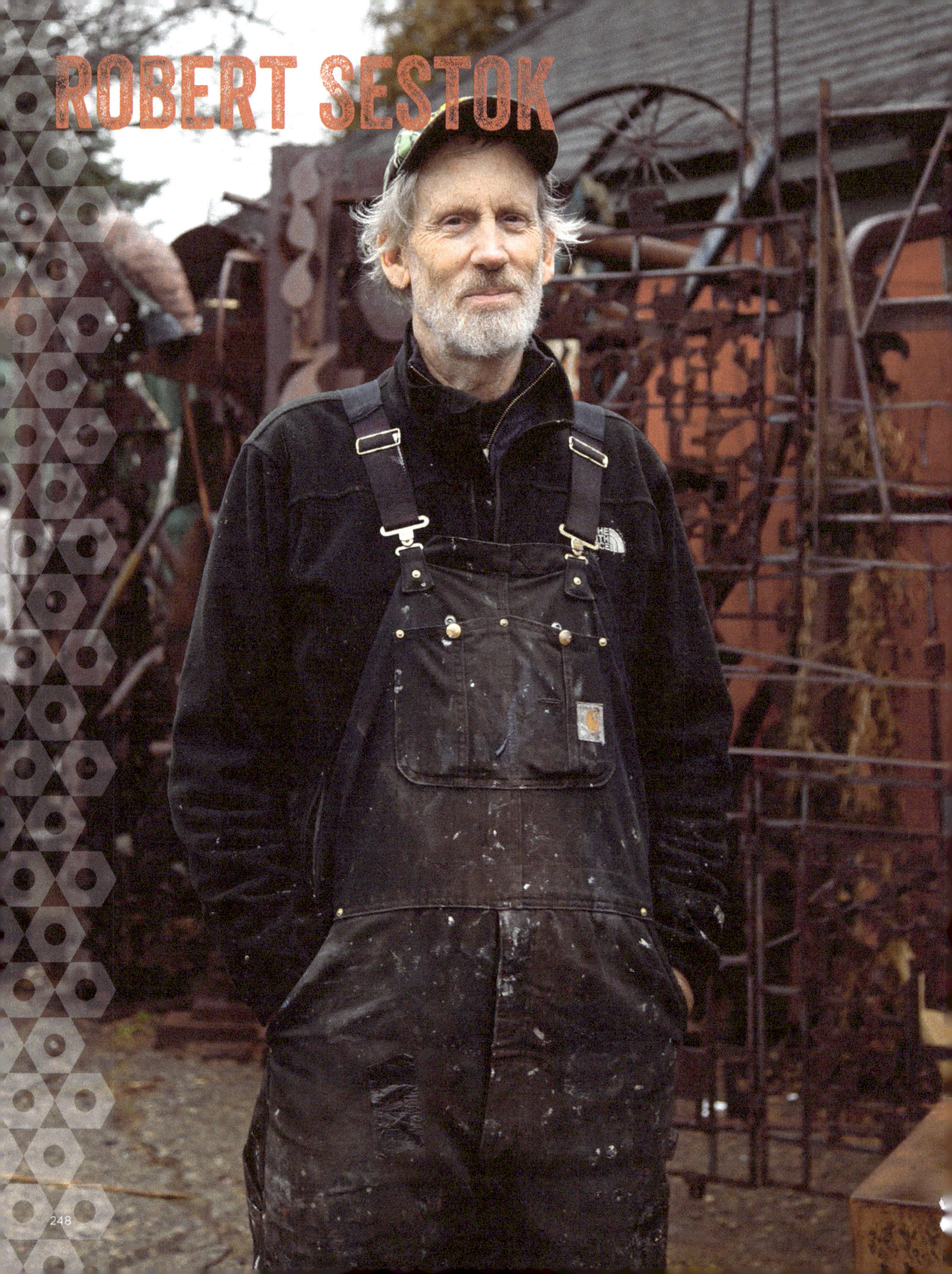

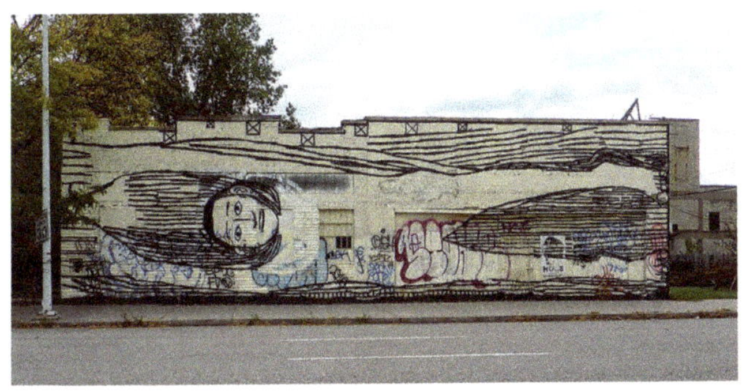

In the late 1960s and 70s, Robert Sestok made a name for himself with his hands.

Renaissance was in the air and Sestok, fresh out of college, jumped right into the action.

"I was thrust into this environment where everybody was making crazy stuff; using found objects, taking things apart and reconstructing them," recalls Sestok, who grew up in suburban Birmingham, Michigan. "The crazier it was, the better."

Sestok immersed himself in the city and putting to work every skill he'd honed as a student at the Detroit Society of Arts and Crafts, the predecessor to the College for Creative Studies. "It was just an inspiring time; Detroit's real renaissance in art right in the Cass Corridor. Artists were establishing the basis for a deconstructivist view of art. The city was falling apart—that just naturally came into play as the theory for a lot of what was being created."

Sestok's works—in ceramics, on canvas, and most notably with metals—helped to earn him a reputation as a seminal figure in Detroit's Cass Corridor movement. He still talks easily about the period, its influence over his current work, and the persistent rumblings that the city is in the midst of another pioneering period in art.

"What's happening right now is very inspiring," he says. "There's a really diverse array of work that's being created, particularly as it relates to street art. But it's not a movement. It's very fragmented; you basically have a lot of people that are really out to get exposure for their work."

Sestok remains very much entrenched in Detroit's art scene, too. He continues to sculpt, dabble in street murals, and is developing new ways of pairing his passions for printmaking and etching. In many ways, he says, the streets have become a muse again. "I'm paying attention. It's hard not to. We're lucky to have so much creativity around the city to experience right now. I don't imitate but I do get inspired by a lot of what I see."

Sometimes he's discouraged, too. "The people who really supported artists in the seventies, they're not here anymore. So, you get to be older and you start to demand more for your work, but it's hard for people to connect. I've accumulated a lot of experiences, a lot of information about techniques from different arts and assembly; there is a value beyond what people want to pay."

Fortunately, Sestok, says, he has already made his name. "I've had lots of opportunities but they were all earned." Everything he creates now is by choice and with a specific focus. "I'm only trying to do things that I think are creative projects that will make the community stronger through art."

When he is not making art, he's mentoring and hard at work finishing renovation plans for a former stamping plant slated to become affordable large-scale studio space for artists. Sestok, who renovated his garage into a barn-style studio, became involved with the project at the invitation of a New Zealand arts investor smitten enough with Detroit to purchase an entire factory.

"Everything I've done has been about working with my hands, from sculpting to painting, to welding, to drawing, to carpentry, to building," he says. "This is just another way for me to use my hands to benefit art."

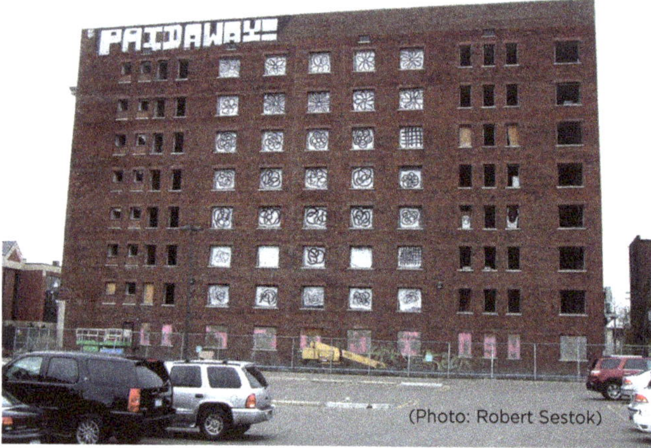

(Photo: Robert Sestok)

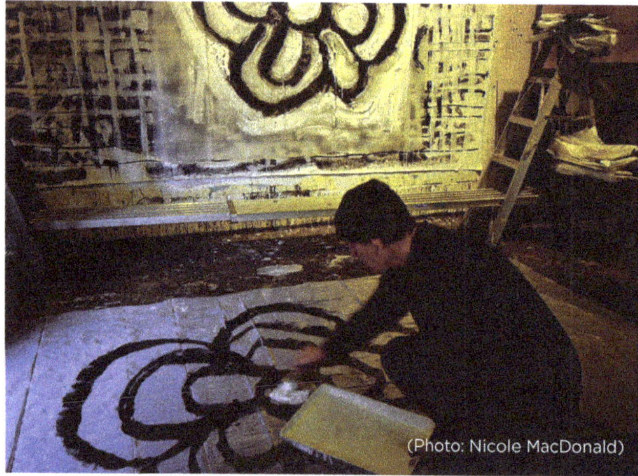
(Photo: Nicole MacDonald)

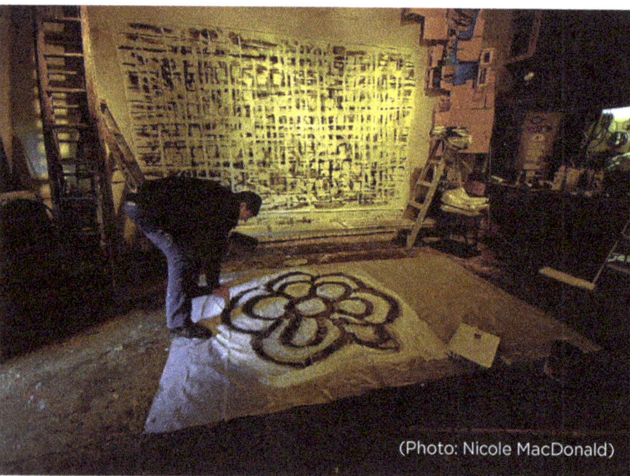
(Photo: Nicole MacDonald)

ABOVE: One day in Midtown Detroit flowers appeared on sheets of plastic covering the windows of an abandoned building. The talented and established artist Robert Sestok was behind the art, which made this skulking behemoth friendly and cheerful.

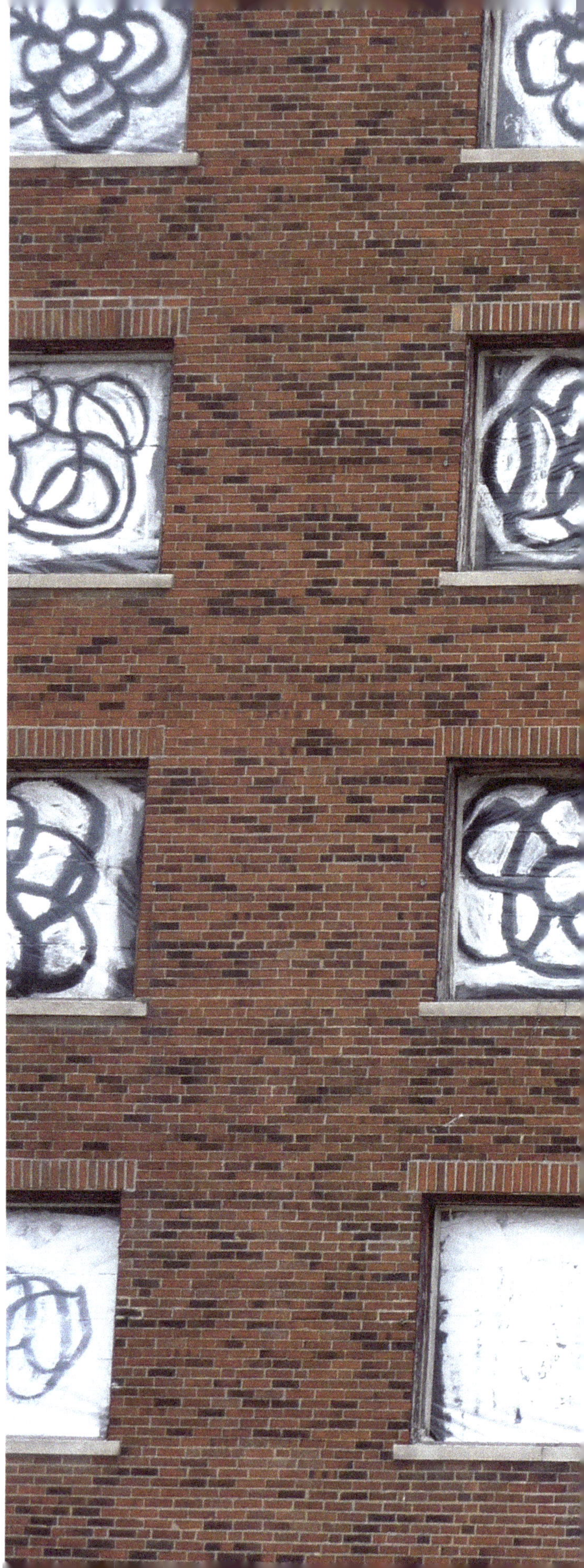

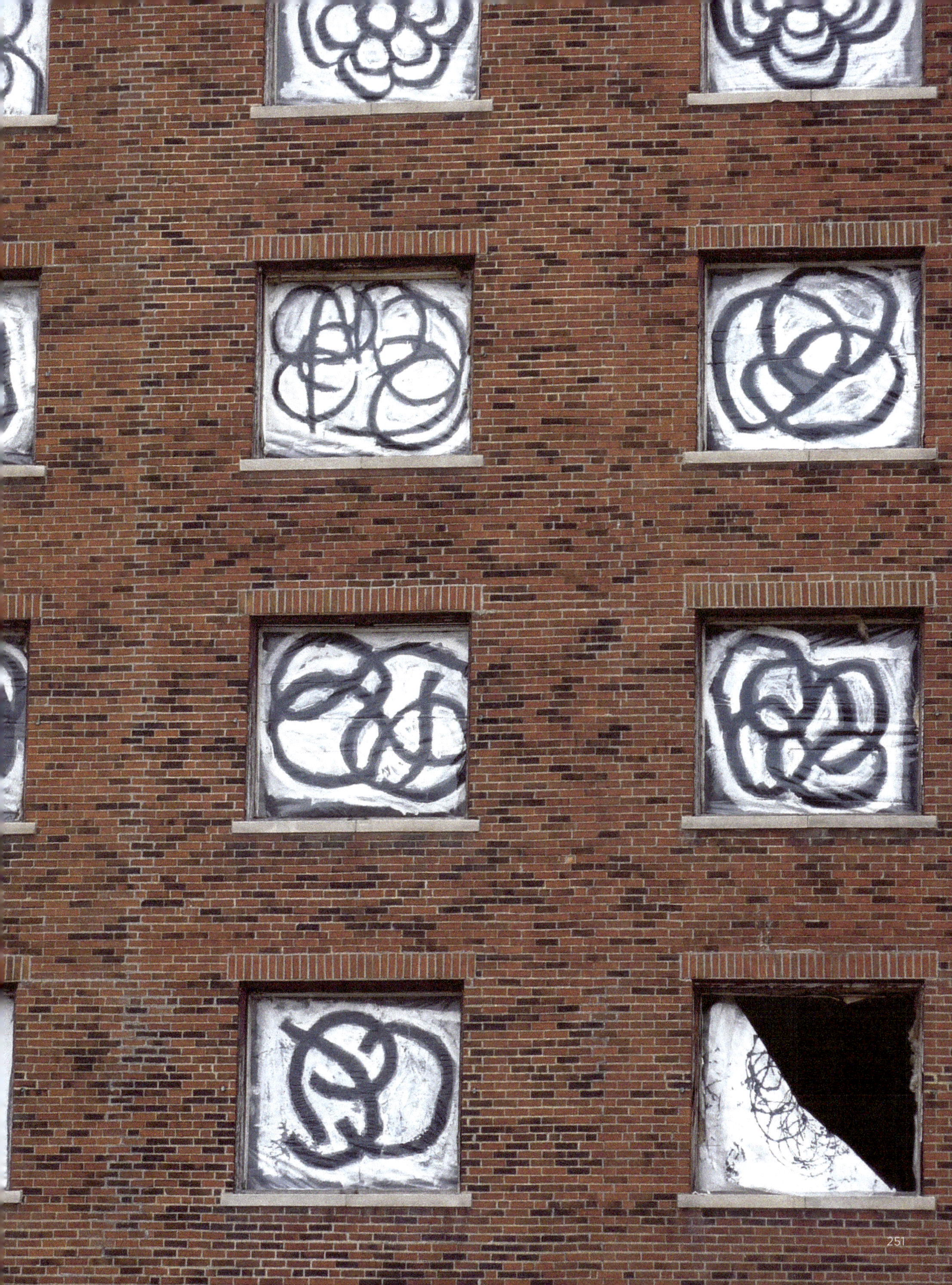

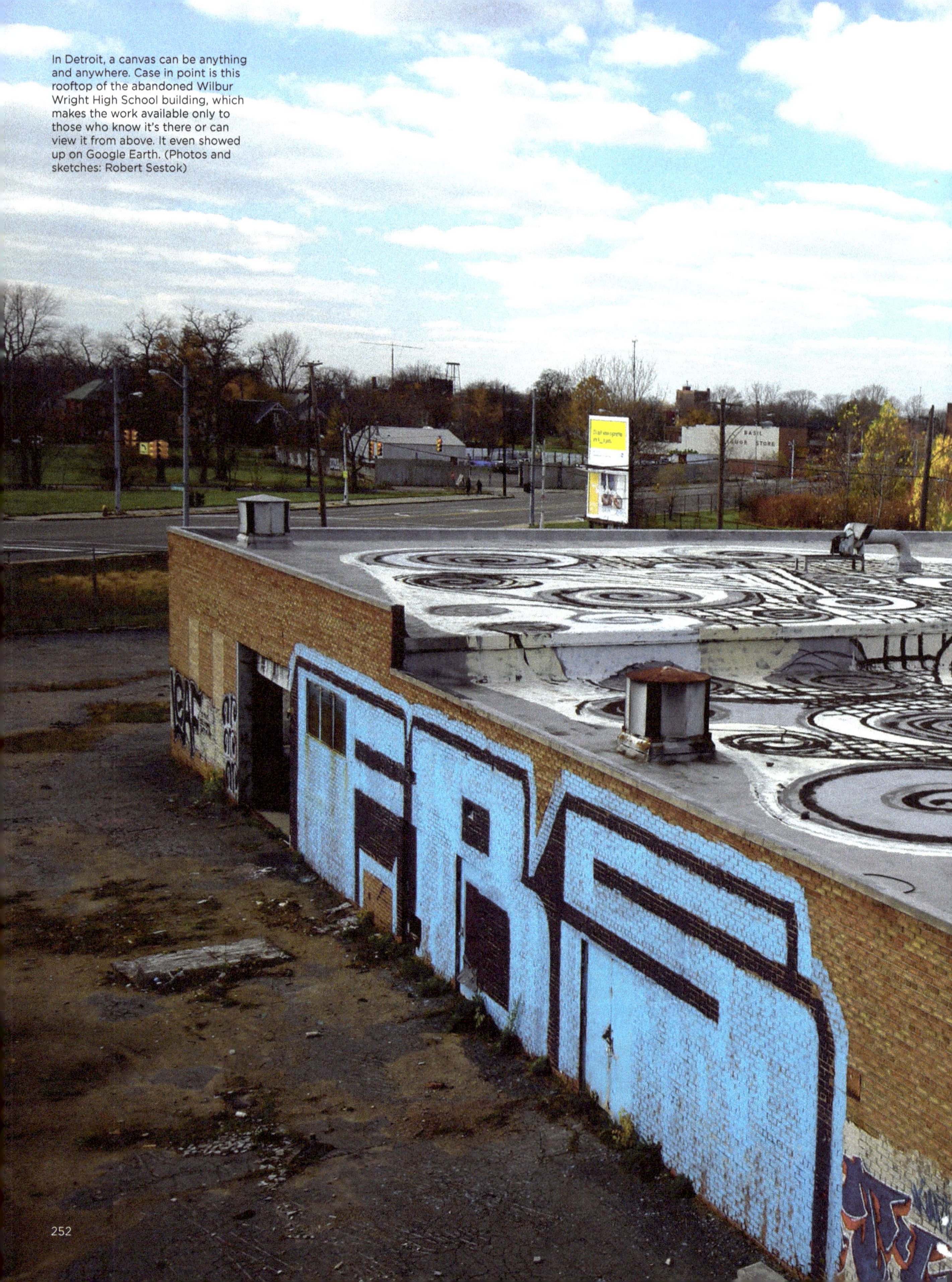

In Detroit, a canvas can be anything and anywhere. Case in point is this rooftop of the abandoned Wilbur Wright High School building, which makes the work available only to those who know it's there or can view it from above. It even showed up on Google Earth. (Photos and sketches: Robert Sestok)

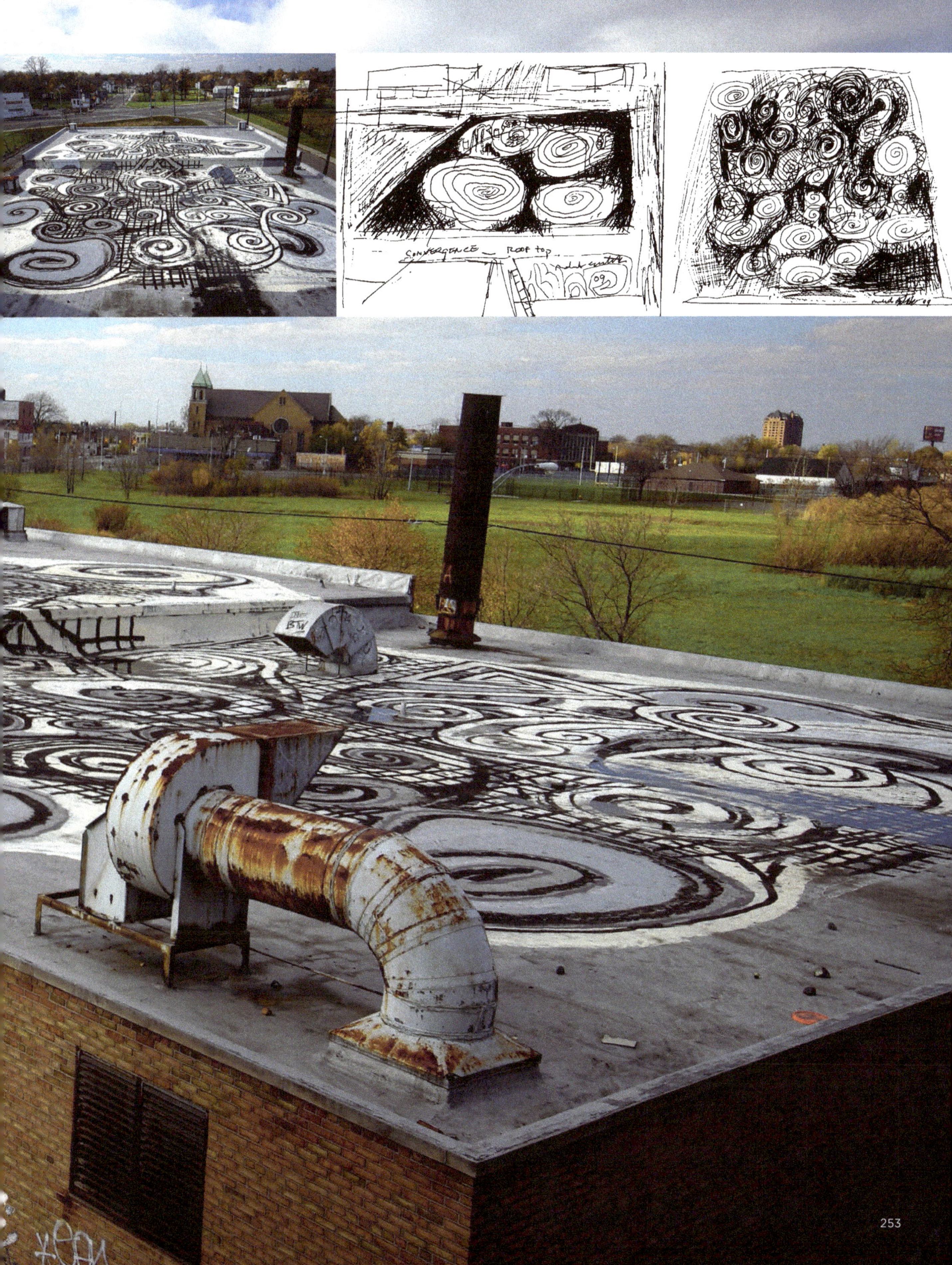
CONVERGENCE — ROOF top

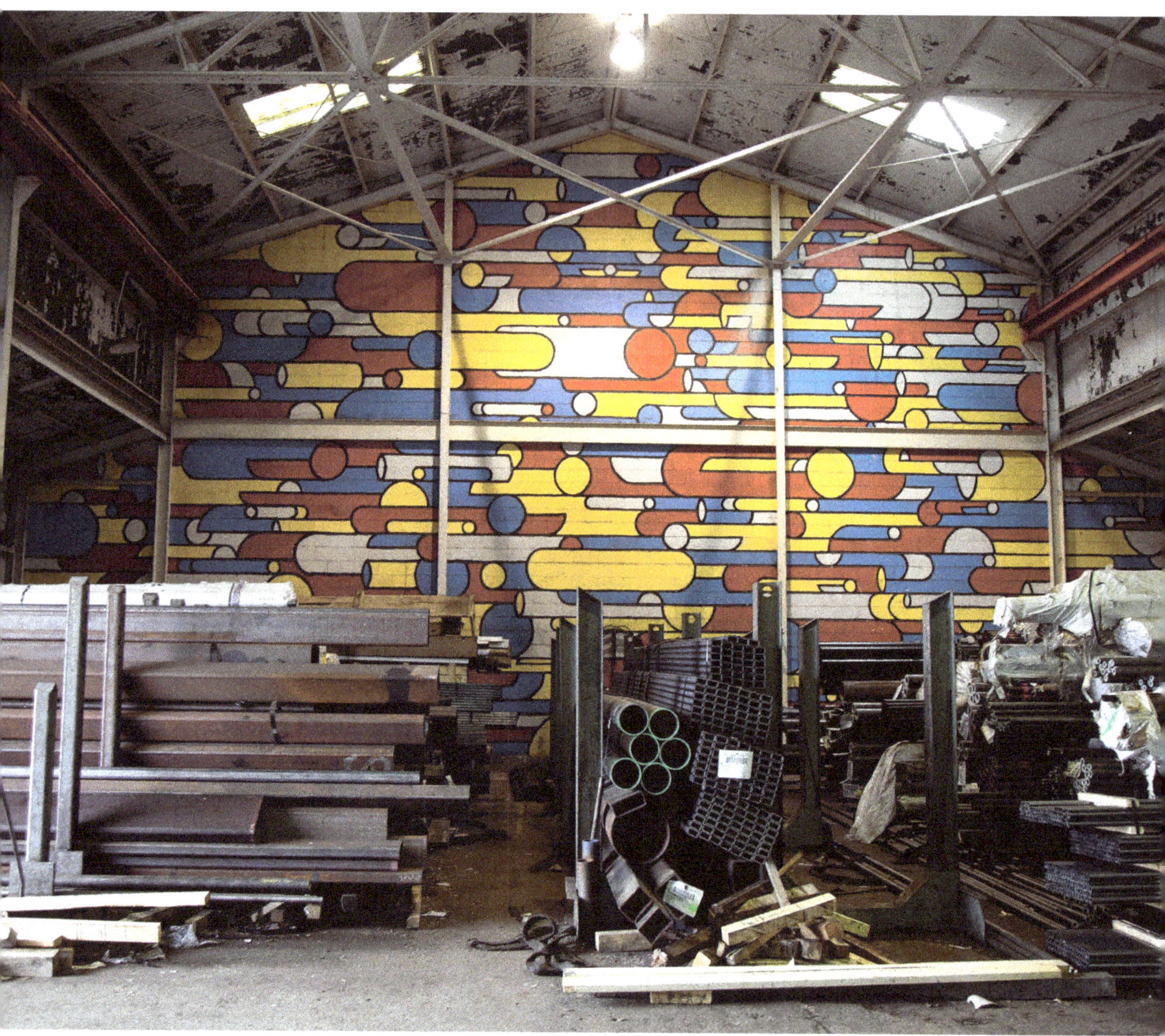

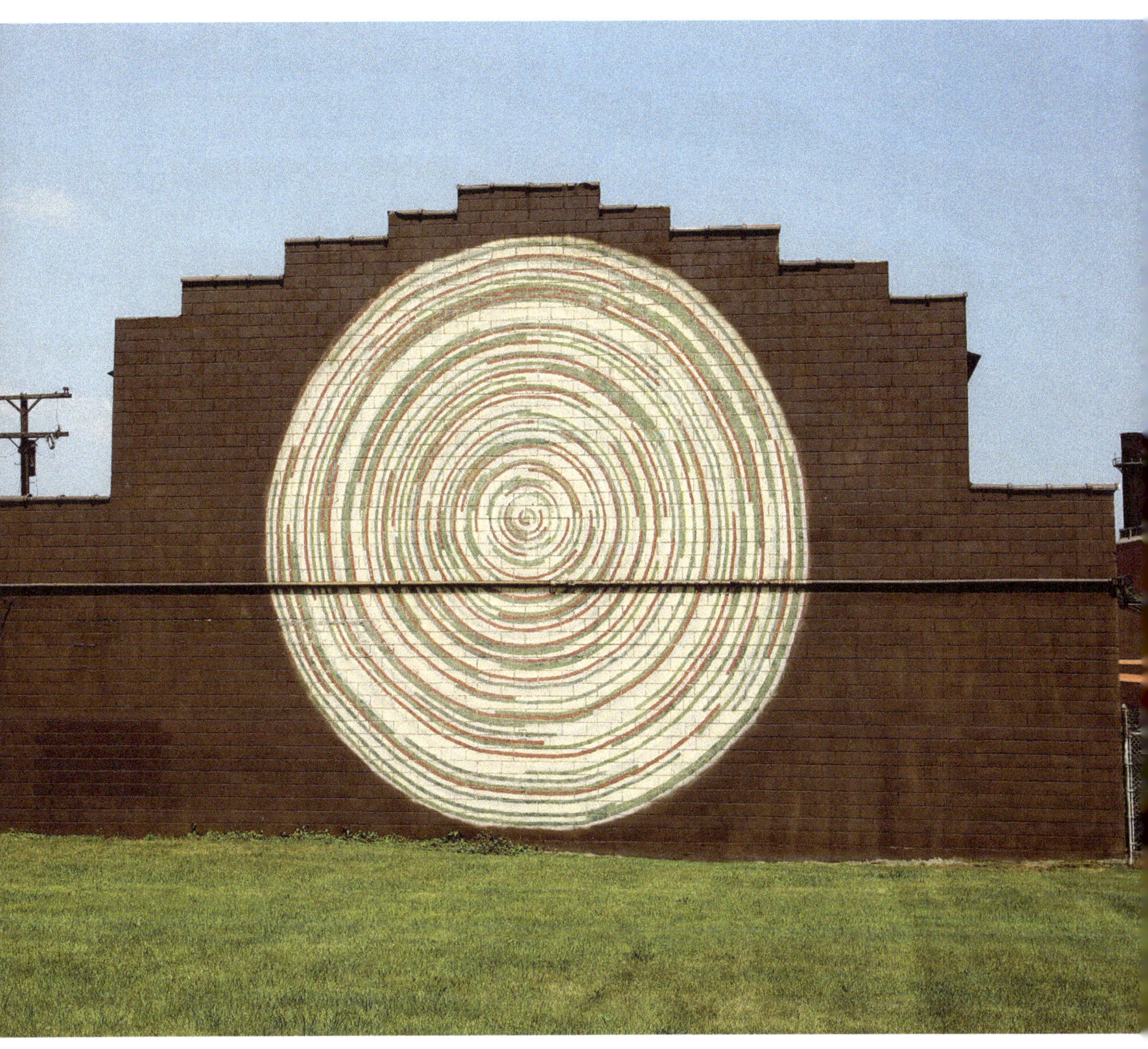

The late James Duffy was a Detroit art patron who owned a successful pipefitting business. He collected local as well as nationally known artists and commissioned Robert Sestok to create these two murals, which still grace his factory although it has changed hands. (Photo, this page: Dave Krieger)

KOBIE SOLOMON

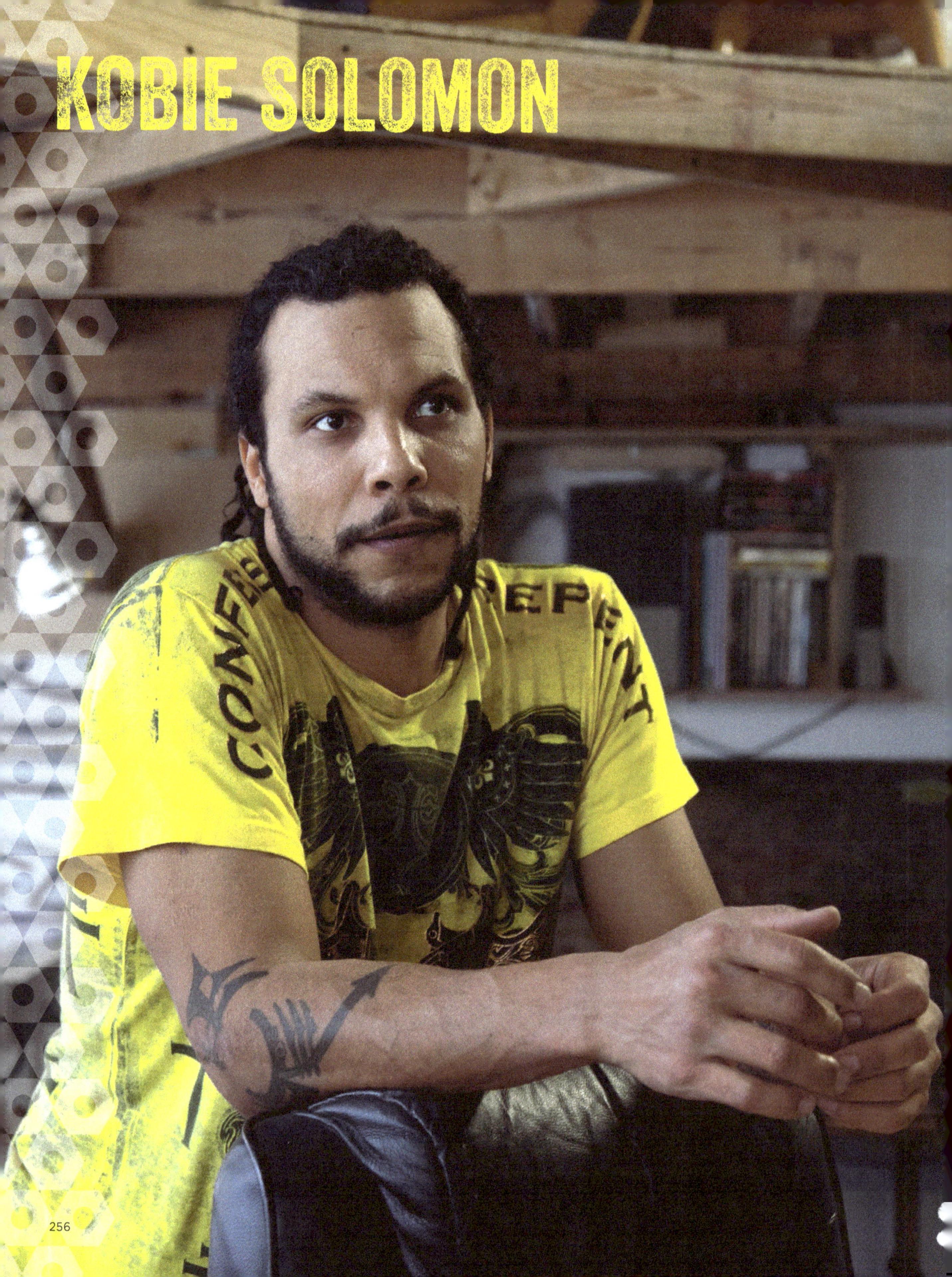

If one image could speak for Detroit, Kobie Solomon says his sprawling Detroit *Chimera* is the one.

Go. Stare. Find the metaphors for yourself.

"Essentially, it's a portrait of the city," he says of the 8,750-square-foot mural, which features, as its central figure, a lion-like creature taken from Greek mythology. "It's obvious if you sit in the parking lot and look at it a bit."

Though tens of thousands of people lay eyes on Solomon's work daily, few venture close enough to take in its intricacies. Most people glimpse the *Chimera* from their cars, drawn in by its jarring colors and the way the creature appears poised to pounce from the wall, ready to guard the Chrysler Freeway and its travelers.

"Some people look and all they see is the sports imagery," he says referring to the fact that while the *Chimera* looks like a lion—a nod to the city's football team—its body is painted in the official colors of the Detroit Tigers baseball team.

"Some people look and they don't know what it is," he says. "They don't even get through to the first layer of the concept, much less the second or third. There's history and culture in there, all kinds of surrealist illusions hidden inside the elements." There are at least seven images waiting to be uncovered. Find the ghost of industry if you dare.

The *Chimera* stands as a monument to another story, too. Solomon keeps that story close, a reminder to him of how far one idea can travel. "I remember the first time I saw that wall," says Solomon, thirty-five. "I was twelve years old, going to visit CCS [College for Creative Studies] with my art teacher. I remember looking out the window and thinking, Wow, what if there was something on there? What if somebody painted it so that it looked like stacks of freight trains?"

While he let the freight train idea and twenty-three years roll by, Solomon says the wall has lived up to all that he'd imagined as an aspiring artist. It's still the ultimate canvas, one hundred feet tall and eighty-five feet at its base. Today, the building, known as the Russell Industrial Center, is a creative hub, housing the studios of more than one hundred Detroit-based artists.

Back in 2010, when the Russell's property manager invited him to create a design, Solomon spent all of forty-five minutes, with a ballpoint pen, unleashing his idea. "I kid you not," he says, "the thing just popped in my head with all of this depth." The only missing detail was how long it would take to transfer what he saw. He spent two and a half years laying detail upon detail onto the wall, often struggling to support himself and the costs of his chosen supplies. "It's been like a battle and a dream at the same time. I put him on the scales sometimes, and I'm still grappling with the costs of doing it.

In 2012, Solomon got a gift, enough support from a Kickstarter to completely repaint the mural, top to bottom, using proper equipment and higher-quality paints that should help the *Chimera* endure.

"Nobody made any cash," Solomon says of the $10,500 supporters donated. By rough estimates, the *Chimera* absorbed sixty gallons of primer and paint, and upward of three hundred cans of spray paint. "It all went back into the work."

Such is the life of an artist in Detroit, he says: "The scene has always been vibrant with a lot of people doing a lot of creative things. There's just not a lot of money for artists."

At times, he's considered leaving. But each time he's stopped by the great irony of creative life in Detroit.

"I think it's like a giant Stockholm syndrome here," he says. "You're in this place that's just so shitty in so many ways and you still, somehow, find beauty. The more you learn, the more you start wanting to change the situation. People here, for whatever reason, change things by being creative. You don't really have a lot of other options," he says.

Bottom line: In Detroit, "You just create."

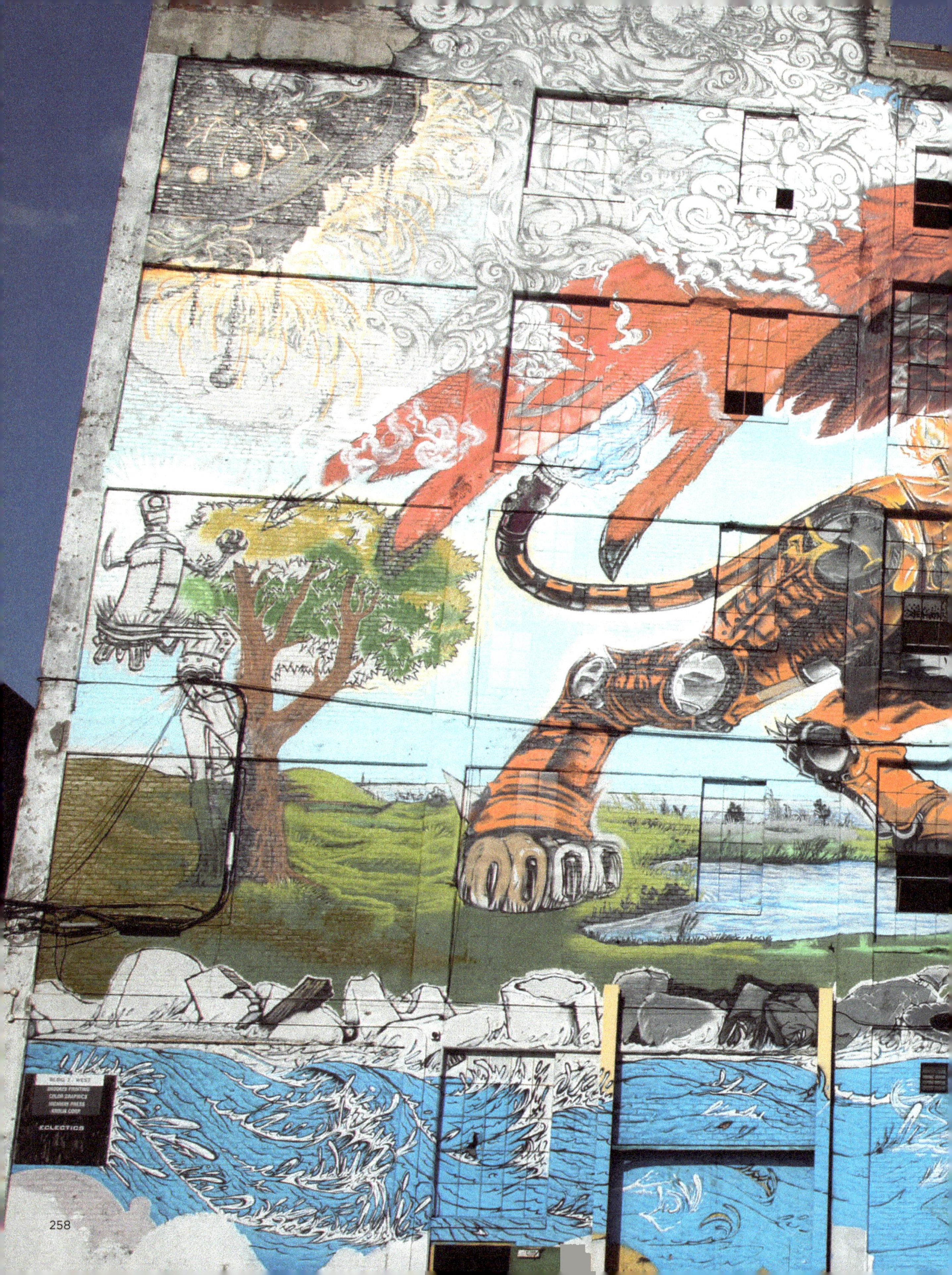
ECLECTICS

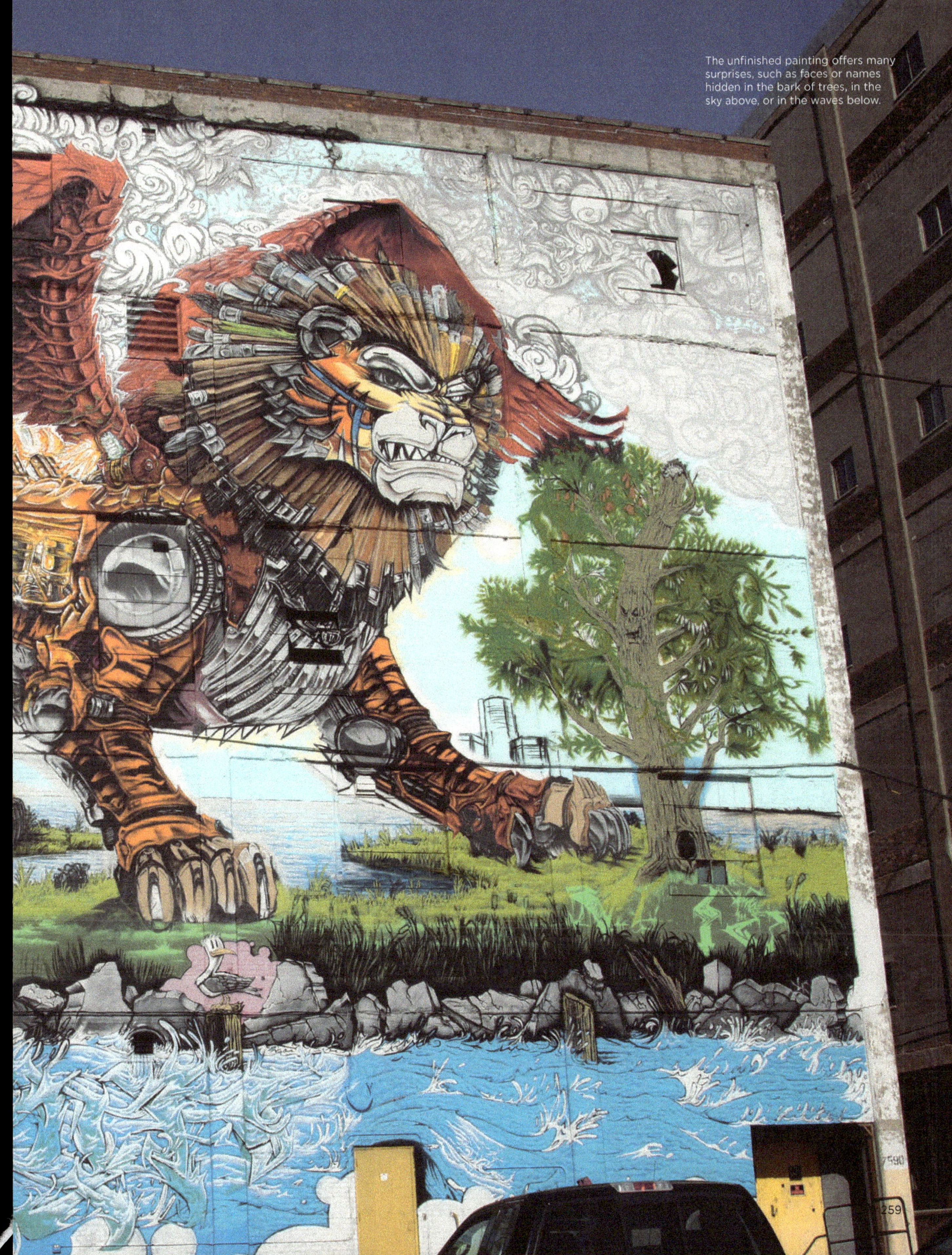

The unfinished painting offers many surprises, such as faces or names hidden in the bark of trees, in the sky above, or in the waves below.

THEATRE BIZARRE

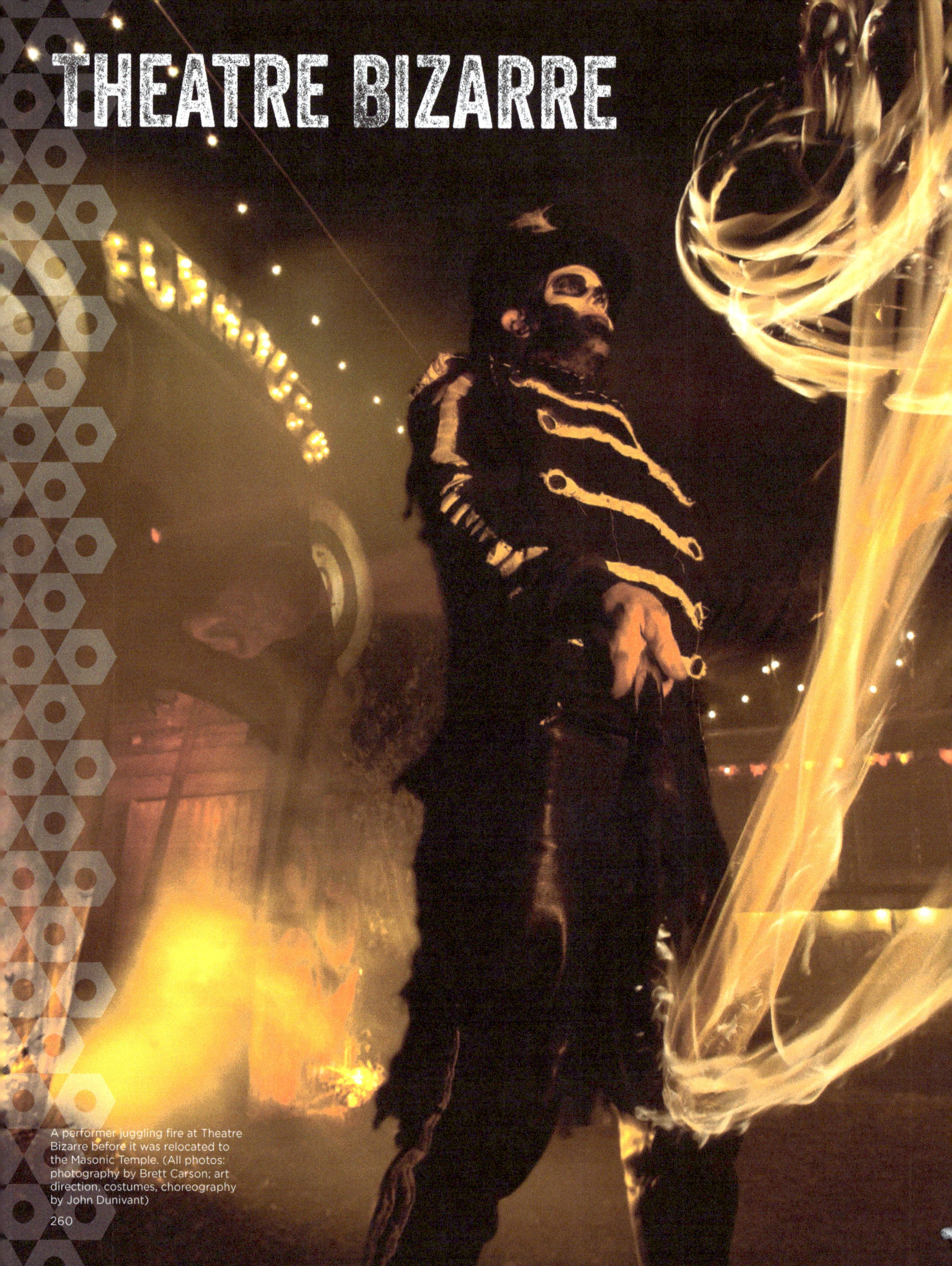

A performer juggling fire at Theatre Bizarre before it was relocated to the Masonic Temple. (All photos: photography by Brett Carson; art direction, costumes, choreography by John Dunivant)

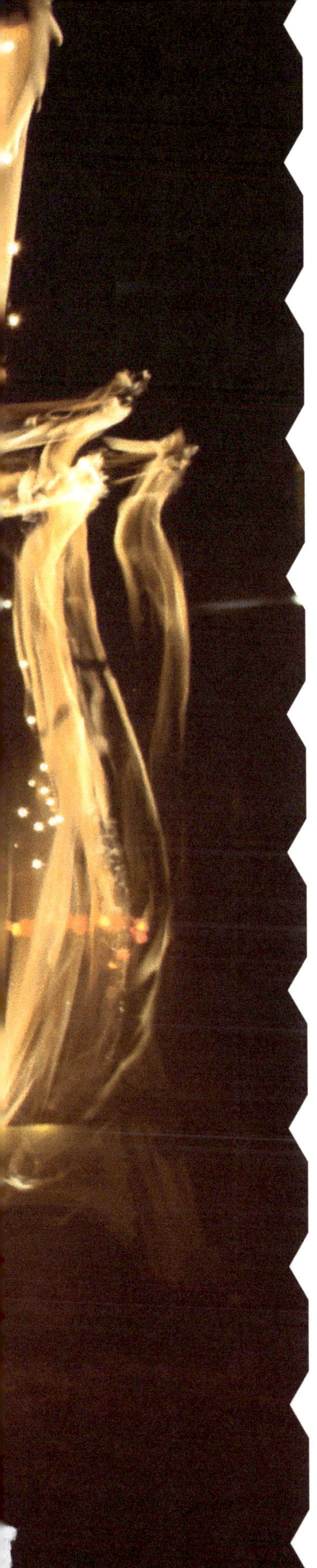

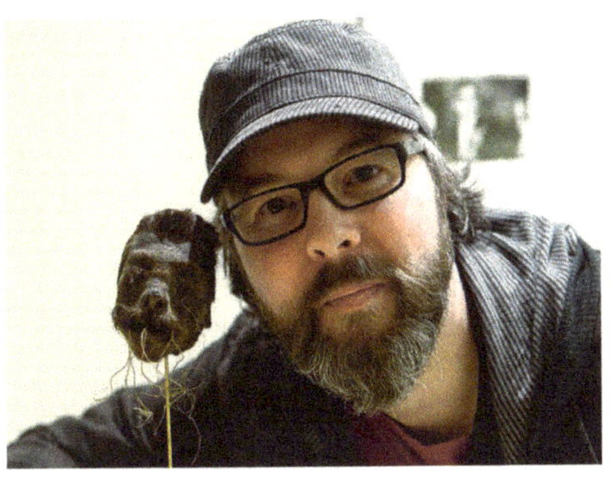

John Dunivant is a master of the bizarre.

His best-known creation is so bizarre even he is loath to give it a label.

Over the years, many have tried, calling the show everything from a macabre backyard costume party to an adult Disneyland on acid, plopped smack in the middle of a hardscrabble section of Detroit near the Michigan State Fairgrounds.

With tickets in hand and fears in check, crowds flock each year eager to take another trip through Dunivant's imagination, also known as Theatre Bizarre. That is, after all, where the magic happens just once a year, each Halloween, with nearly three thousand revelers as willing witnesses. "It's designed to throw you off, to be so immersive that it's disorienting," Dunivant says.

Drawing on skills as a painter, illustrator, set designer, and student of architecture, Dunivant gives life to elaborate handmade sets, stages, costumes, and designs so wild, they seem ripped straight out of a ghoulish burlesque show.

He traces the theatre's start to his childhood. The signs were all around him, but they didn't add up at the time.

"I was an only child with a father who didn't talk much but he loved to drag me to natural history museums, road shows, and terrible civil war museums," says Dunivant. "I was always drawing natural history dioramas. I think it just all blended together into the same aesthetic. I love creating environments."

Dunivant's first foray into creating "immersive art environments" came while staging smaller Halloween house parties.

"The house parties just got too big," he says. "The last one I did, I brought in five hundred trees as well as built a cabin in the center of the space to simulate the feeling of being lost in the woods. I had bags and bags of leaves that I'd collected. I got in some trouble for that one."

Trouble found Dunivant again in 2010, this time with the City of Detroit. The show that had gone on successfully, and quietly, for a decade was suddenly shut down. As if for dramatic effect, the city made its move the day before Halloween.

"I guess we knew it couldn't last," he says. "We were running a giant theme park in the middle of a residential neighborhood. Who does that without running into trouble?"

Looking back, Dunivant, who is forty-two, is shocked that the show went on, uninterrupted, for more than a decade: "Certainly Theatre Bizarre wouldn't have existed without the conditions of Detroit. You could hide in plain sight because there was just so much neglect. The neighborhood was a war zone. The amount of dead dogs we found in just this one three-acre spot just made you sick. No one was paying attention."

Slowly, the show and the crowd grew larger and larger, almost in defiance of its dangerous location.

"In a way, it was like Berlin, just so ravaged that people who chose to stay ended up having more freedom to express themselves creatively than they realized. We took complete advantage of the situation. If you have the opportunity to build a theme park, you build a theme park. How do you not take the chance?"

If you're Dunivant, the dreamer, you go full bore, ignoring every obstacle, even what has become an annual $250,000 price tag. "We figured, let's go for broke until we get caught," he says. Most of the costs Dunivant and his team of ten volunteers pay by credit cards.

The show has now moved indoors to the historic Masonic Temple. While he's glad it endures, Dunivant says he's an artist forever changed by the risks he took outdoors.

"I didn't take any of it seriously at first. It was just lowbrow fun. But after three or four years, all of my influences started to galvanize and I realized this was my voice. I've always cared more about creating spaces and environments. Even as a painter, and doing sculpture and architecture, I was unfocused. Theatre Bizarre combines all of my interests in the best ways."

The only hurdle left for Dunivant and the show is proving that fun can be profitable, too. The show's sixty-five-dollar ticket price barely covers the costs of paint and supplies. By every measure, he concedes, his business model is bizarre.

"Every year, we build a theme park that's only open for one night. We were really just starting to lay the groundwork for something sustainable when the rug got pulled out from under us," he says. "We're still stretching dollars.

In fact, at the Masonic, the staging is even more intense. The show spans seven floors, each offering a different experience. To make the fun happen, Dunivant and his crew build the sets on site, hauling the materials, piece by piece, up the stairs. When they're done, they take it all apart, piece by piece, and haul it back down as many as seven flights of stairs.

"It's brutal and it's insane," he says.

For now, the alternatives are unimaginable. "Starting over anywhere else would be incredibly expensive," says Dunivant.

Plus, he says there is the issue of obeying the muse.

"Creating the world of Theatre Bizarre has also created a language for my art," he says. "I don't really know what else to do. There's still nothing like this in the world. It's pretty crazy."

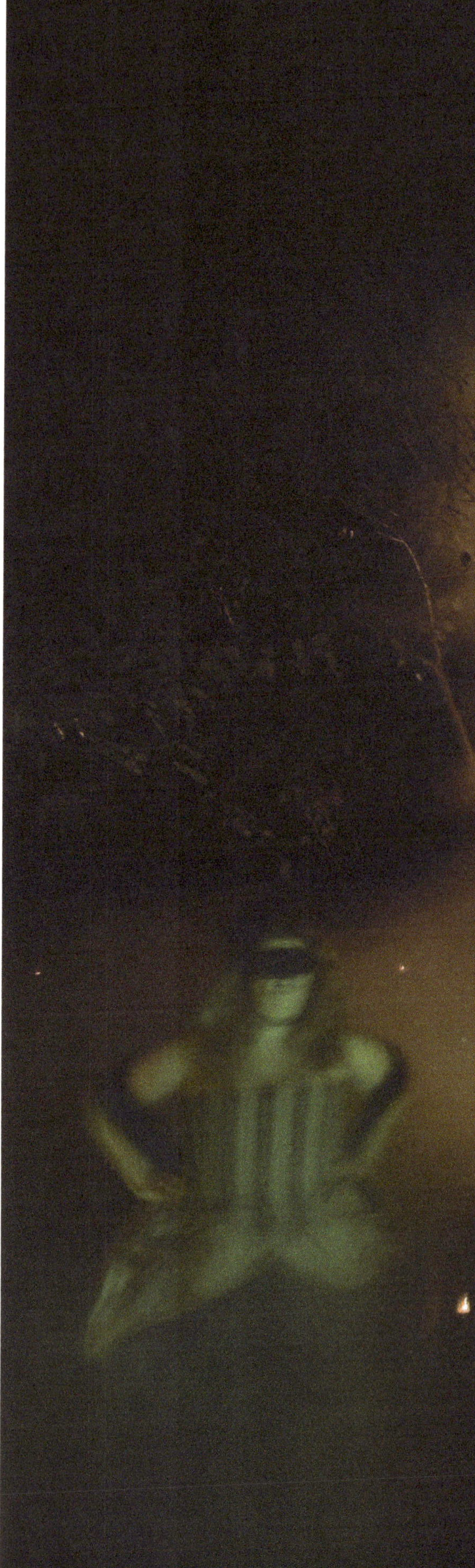

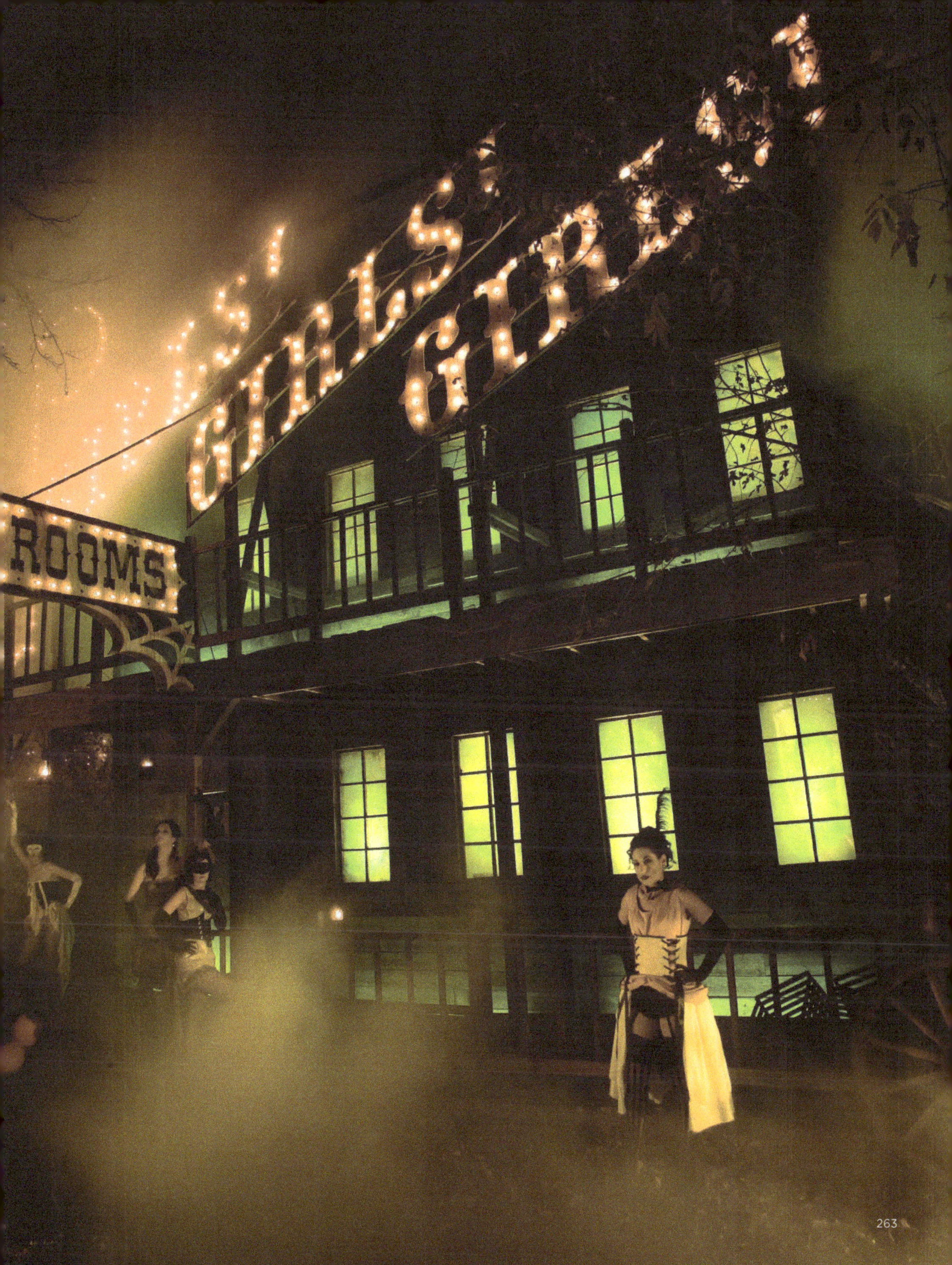
GIRLS
ROOMS

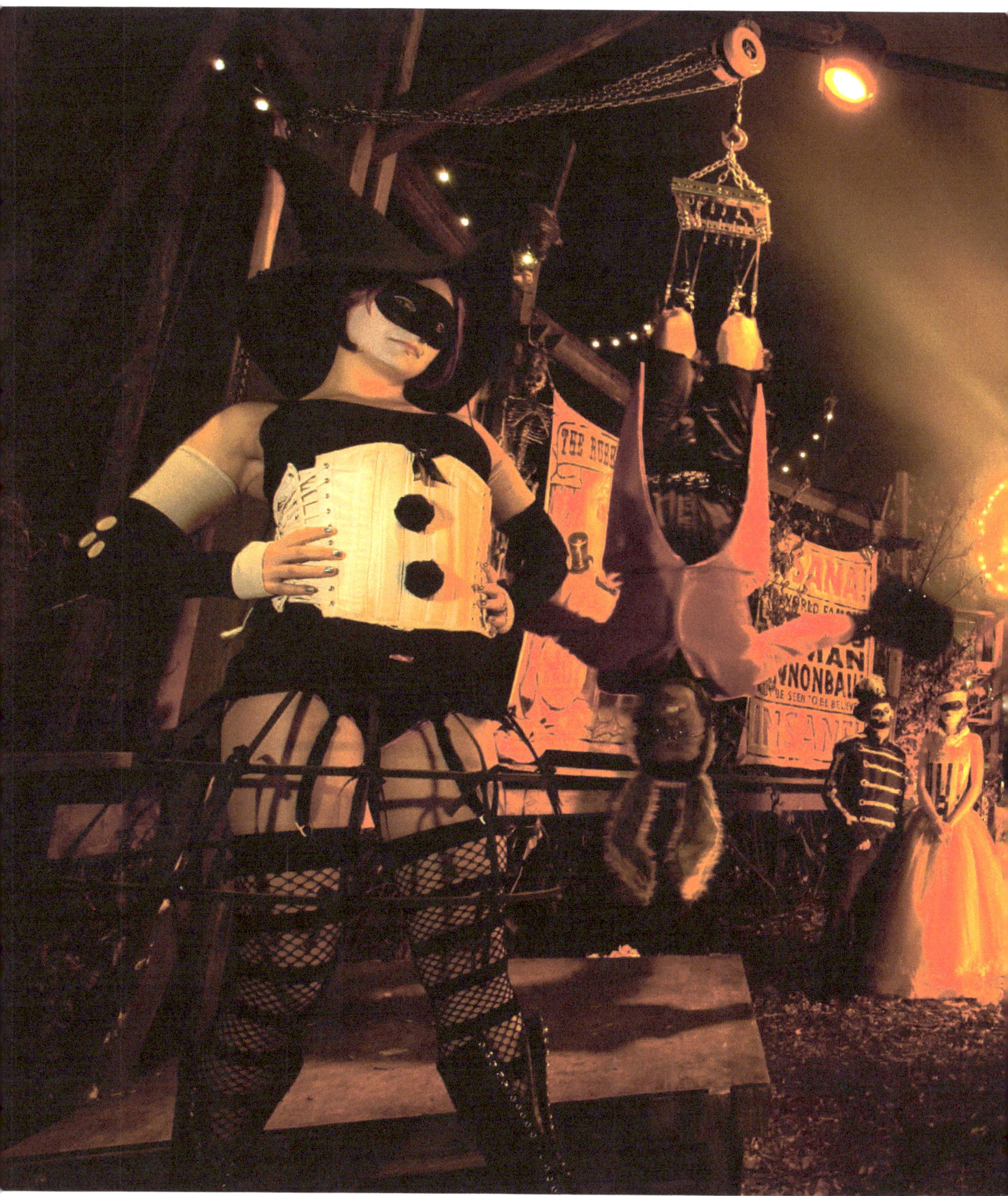

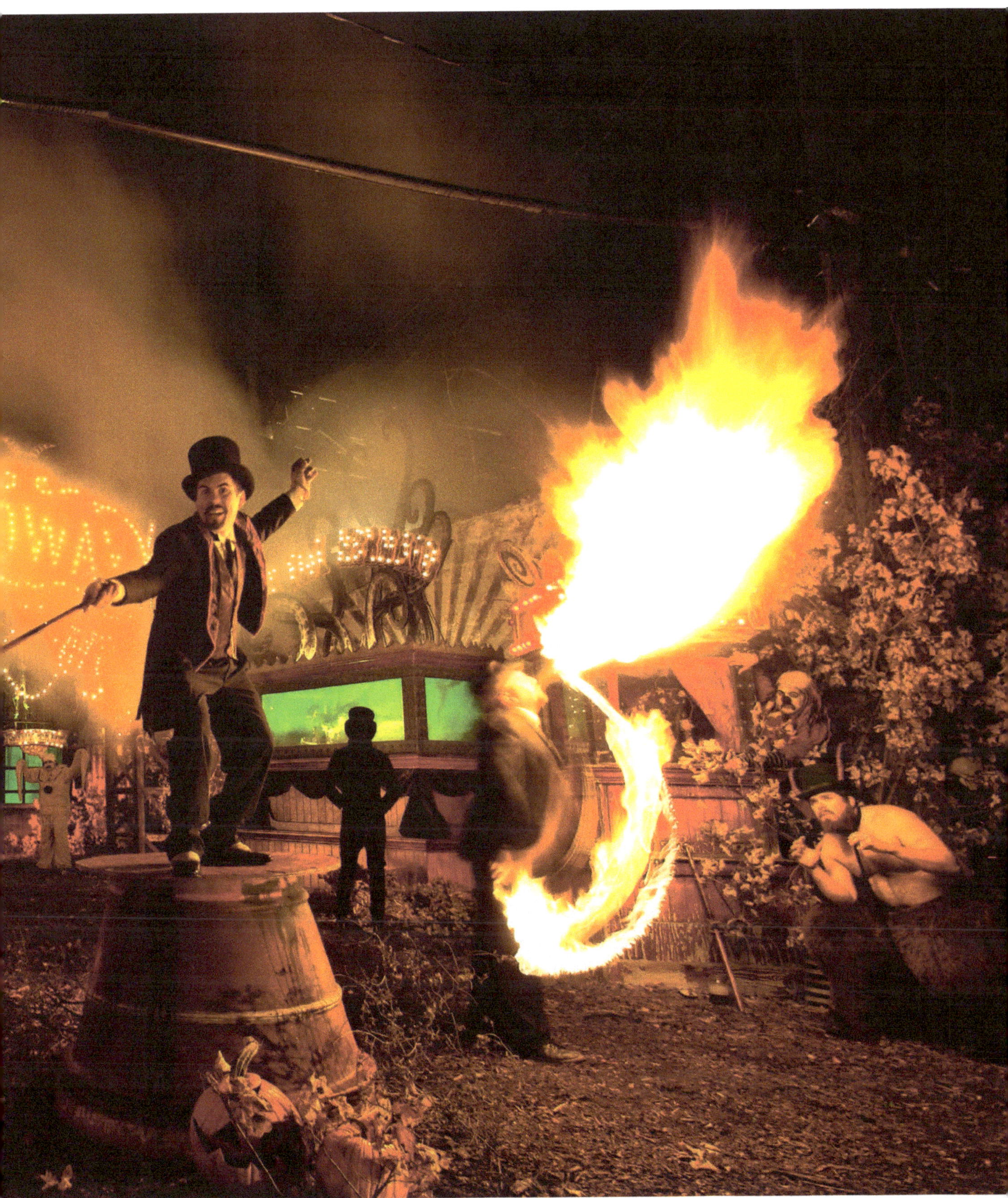

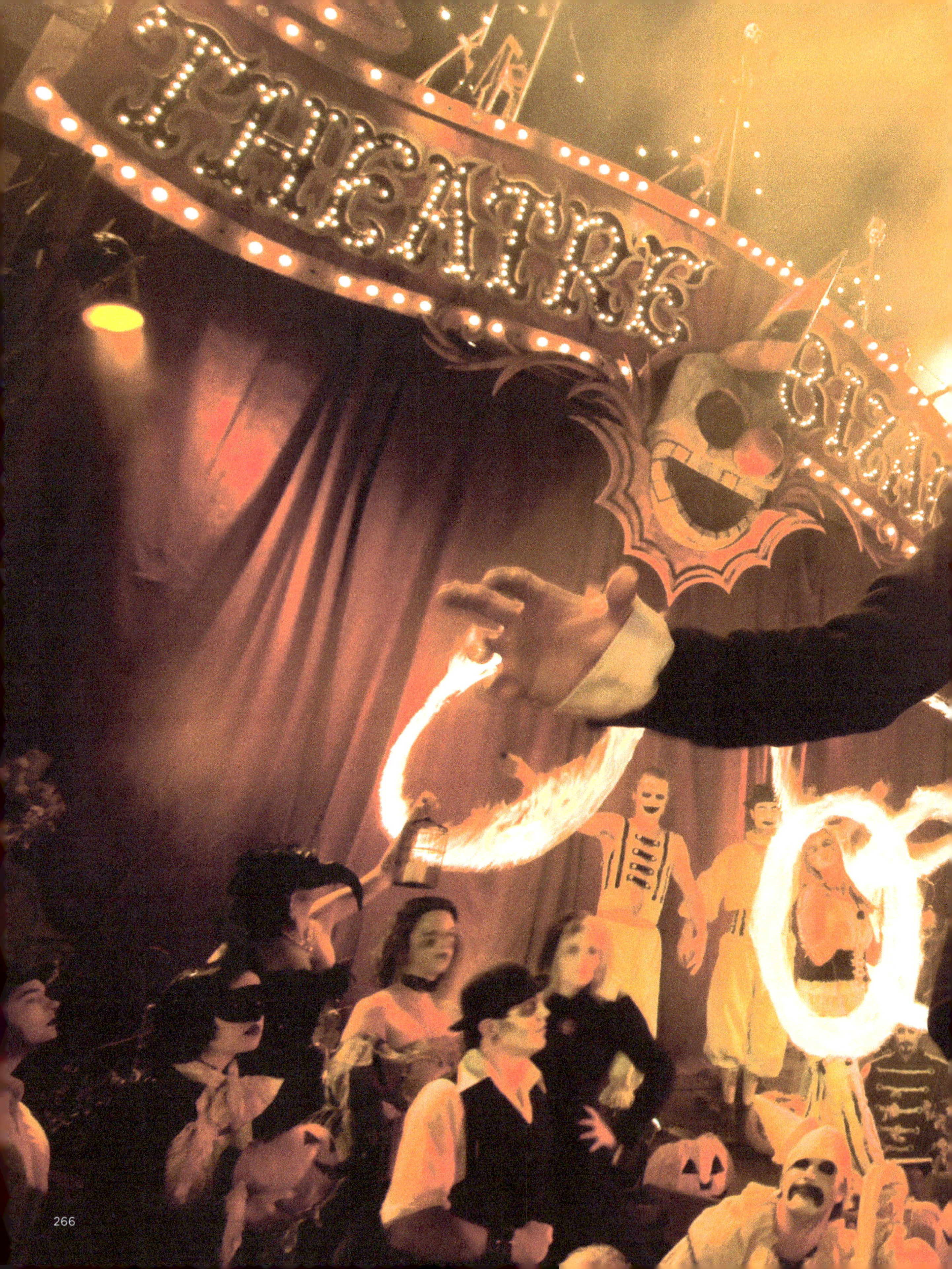
THEATRE

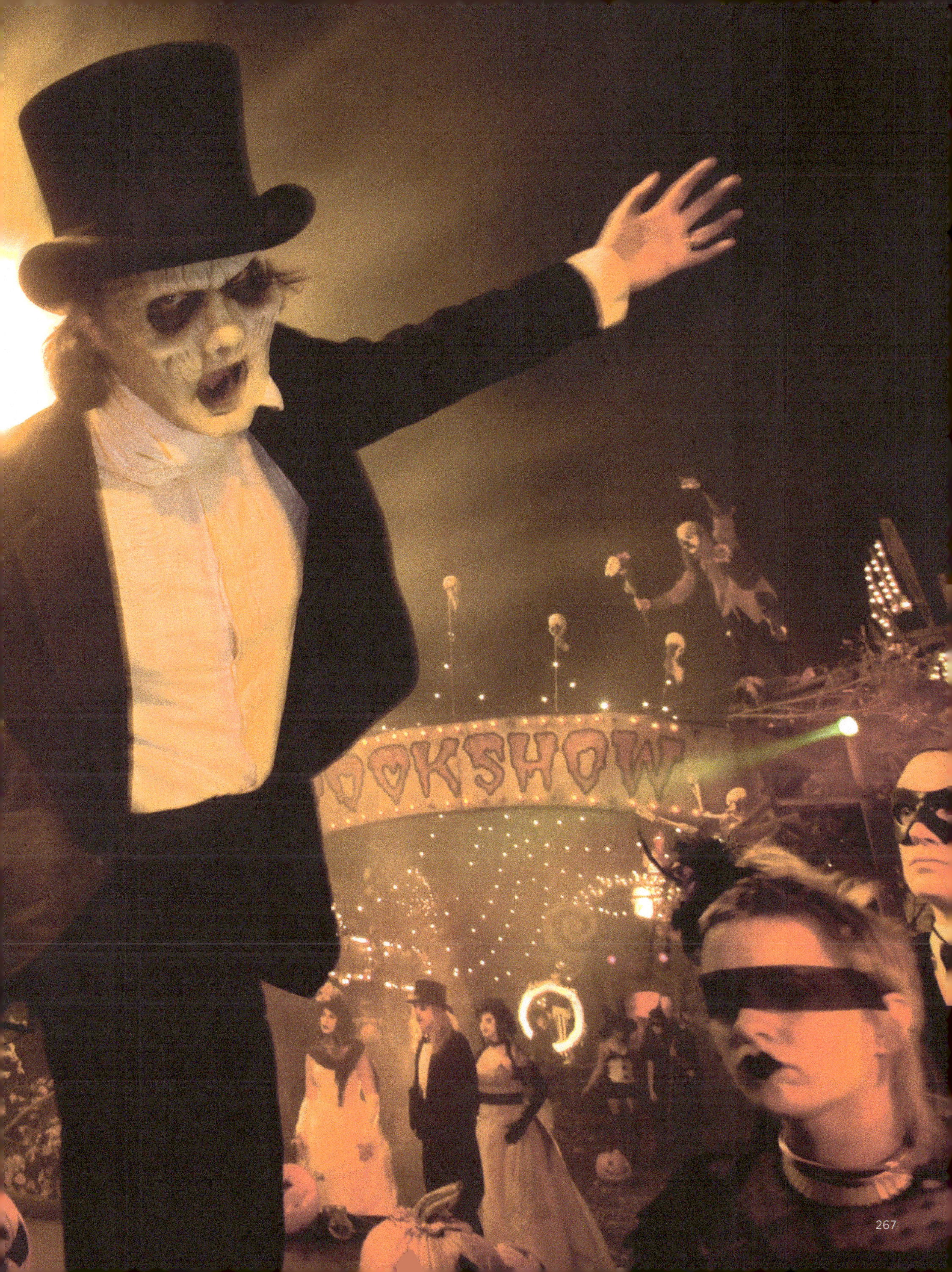
OOKSHOW

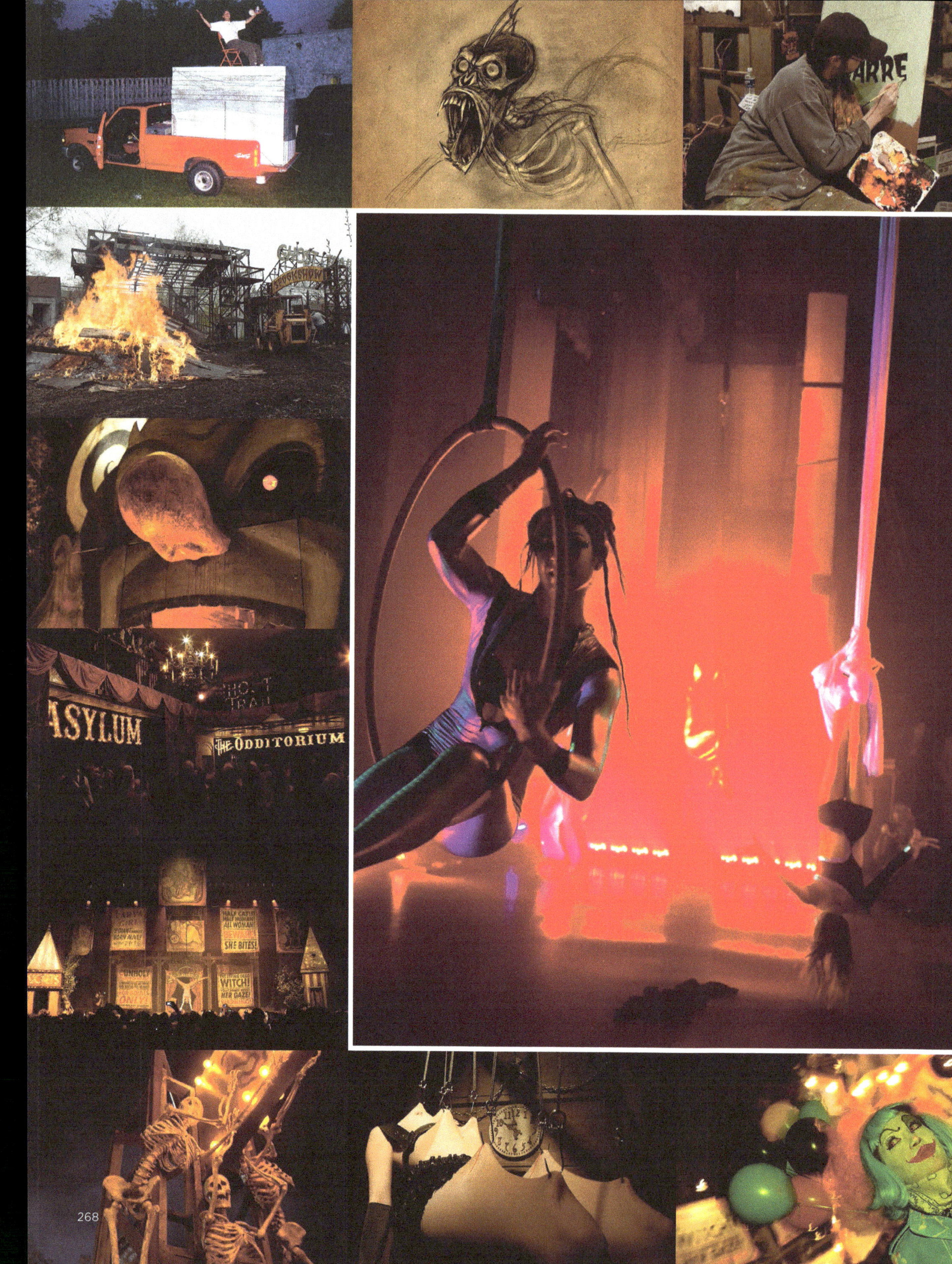
ASYLUM
THE ODDITORIUM
ALL WOMAN!
SHE BITES!
UNHOLY
WITCH!
HER GAZE!

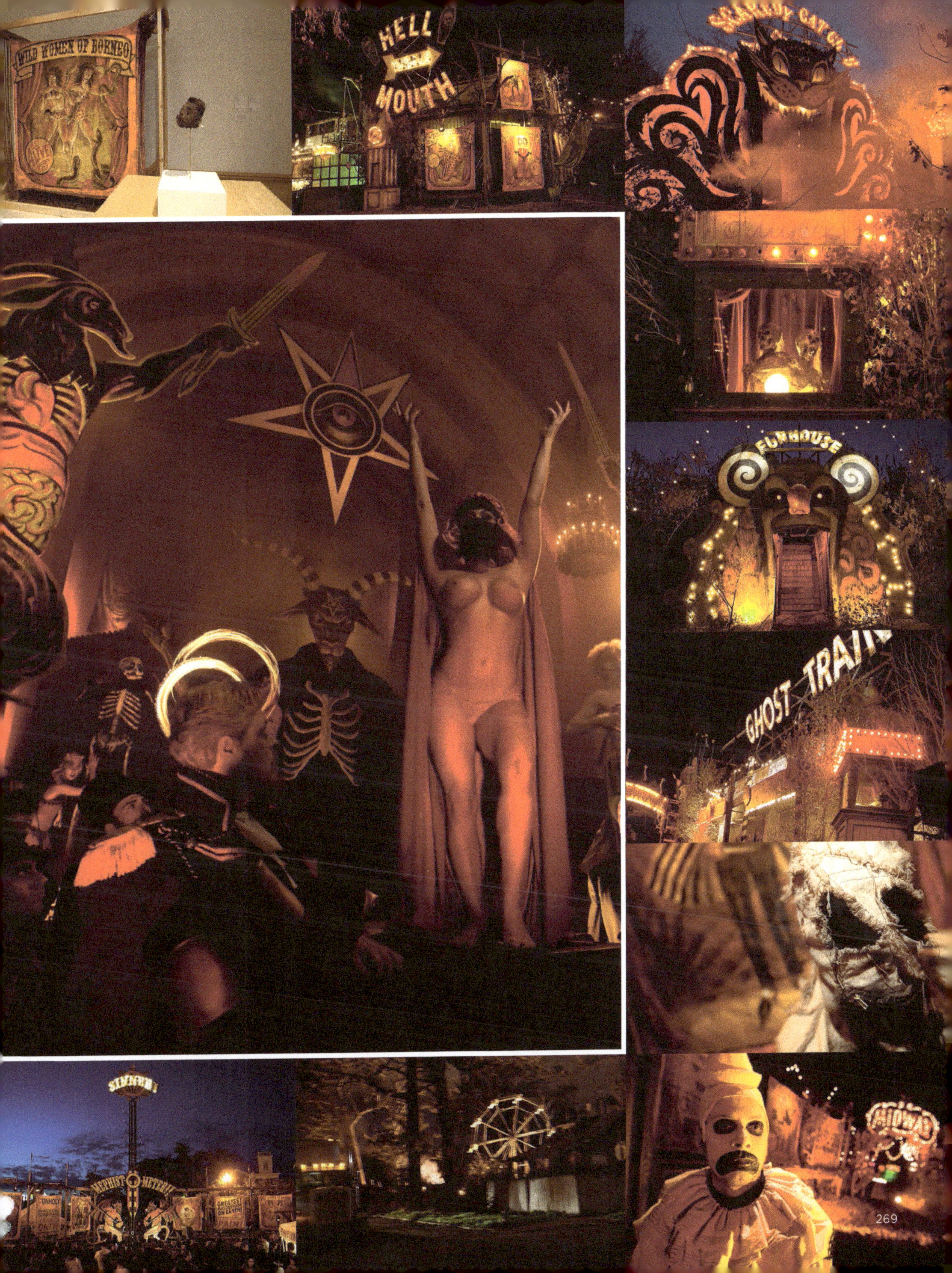
WILD WOMEN OF BORNEO
HELL
MOUTH
FUNHOUSE
GHOST

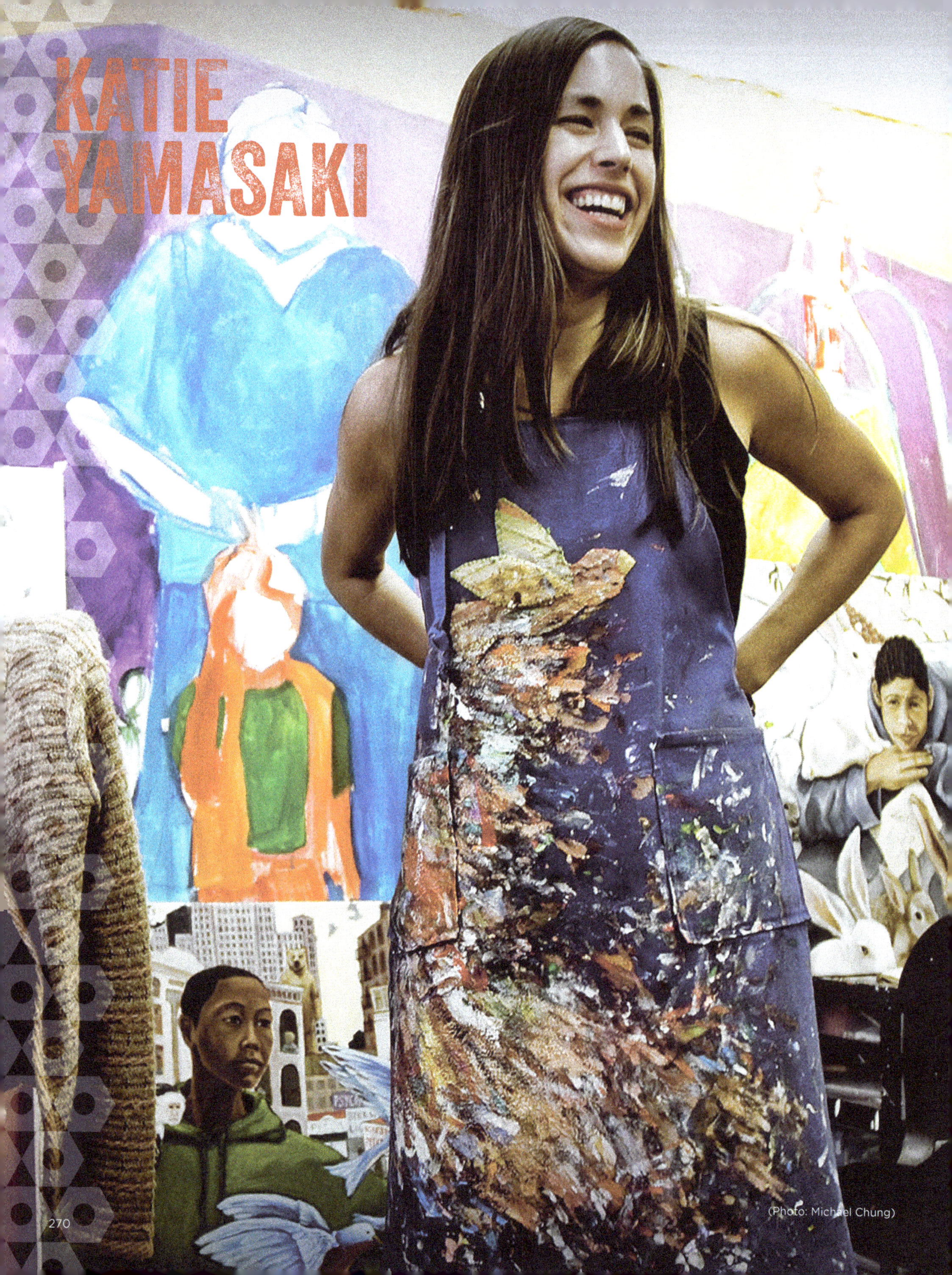

KATIE YAMASAKI

(Photo: Michael Chung)

In Detroit, the name Yamasaki is typically uttered in reference to a lone creative force, the late modern architect Minoru Yamasaki. From his offices in Detroit, he emerged as a global synonym for lean yet elegant structures. It was Yamasaki who laid the vision and captivated the world with his design for the World Trade Center.

But increasingly, art lovers are following the work of another Yamasaki. Like her grandfather, Katie Yamasaki makes art by transforming buildings, from Detroit to Chiapas, into mesmerizing explorations of shapes and expression. She also shares an affinity for Detroit.

The similarities end there, though. Katie keeps her eyes focused closer to the ground, on the barren walls of buildings in communities that view art as a way to build dialogue and bridges. With more than forty murals around the world, the reach of her work is as global as her grandfather's. But few of the cities where she's made art have made as deep an imprint as Detroit.

"It's always felt like a place where people are hungry for engagement and expression," says Yamasaki, who grew up in in the suburbs surrounding Detroit and once worked as a public school teacher in Detroit. "Everybody that I've ever worked with in Detroit has struck me with this total commitment to community, a feeling of how can I make it better despite what's going on around me," she says.

So, whenever organizations in Detroit have asked, Yamasaki has willingly returned with her optimism and one condition. Wherever she chooses to paint, the focus must always be on the community, never the heft of her last name. Detroit is home to three of her large-scale pieces, works she painted essentially as gifts to the Marcus Garvey Academy, the Detroit Catholic Pastoral Alliance, and the Boggs Educational Center. Each mural bears her distinctive style. They're sweeping realistic portraits surrounded by dramatic shapes and colors, choices Yamasaki makes only after listening. (It's a style that Yamasaki also employs in her work as a children's book illustrator, including her latest book, *Fish for Jimmy*.)

"There are a lot of people and populations that get spoken for all the time. Their voices are treated as if they don't matter," says Yamasaki, thirty-six. "Kids get spoken for. Cities like Detroit that are economically poor get spoken for. Murals are a good way for people to speak for themselves and on behalf on their own community."

When she's not travelling, Yamasaki calls Brooklyn home. Yet even on its streets, the air is filled with chatter about the crowning of Motown as the new cheap "it" town for artists.

"I understand the appeal of being in a place where you can afford to make the kind work you want to do, but I also think that a lot of artists, especially young artists just coming up, have this idea that you make it in your art career when you can afford to live off selling your paintings or whatever work you do," Yamasaki says.

Some of the buzz about Detroit—and some of the changes she's witnessed during visits back—worries Yamasaki. Bring on the positive headlines and the influx of open minds, she says, but don't race past the unmet needs of the city's non-creative citizens. "To be an artist, you have to be aware of your context, and not just aware of it in a way that you can benefit from it but aware of it in a way that you're contributing," she says. "The blessing that your environment is giving you in terms of affordability and inspiration, you have to give right back."

One day soon she hopes to give life to a project she's longed to do in Detroit. Imagine, as she does, a "network of faces" spread throughout specific neighborhoods to help agencies and organizations better connect with people in need. "Art can be a really effective tool for bridge building between people who need services, and providers who have the services but can't find an effective way to get the reach they need," she says.

As proof of this concept, Yamasaki points to a mural project she created to help incarcerated women at New York's Rikers Island communicate with their children. For the project, Yamasaki drew on her experience as a former public school teacher in Detroit and as an art teacher in New York. Each group designed a message for the other. The kids painted their mother's design on a wall in East Harlem, while the mothers transformed a wall inside the jail with messages from their children.

The murals set off a chain of dialogue, including reaction from politicians who "had to make a statement about the ways they were going to serve children of incarcerated mothers." Yamasaki imagines art as a catalyst for similar tough conversations in Detroit. "Detroit is so full of walls and so full of need. It's really only a question of whether artists moving there have a vested interest to help preserve culture or an intention to be a part of engaging a new era."

For gutsy artists, Yamasaki sees a chance at creativity's highest reward. "It's a big myth that the successful artist just goes to their studio everyday. That's the lonely artist. You can afford to be *that* in Detroit," she cautions. "But I think a more true measure of success is if your work is good *and* affecting in the world you live in. That's the opportunity I hope artists see in Detroit. It's possible."

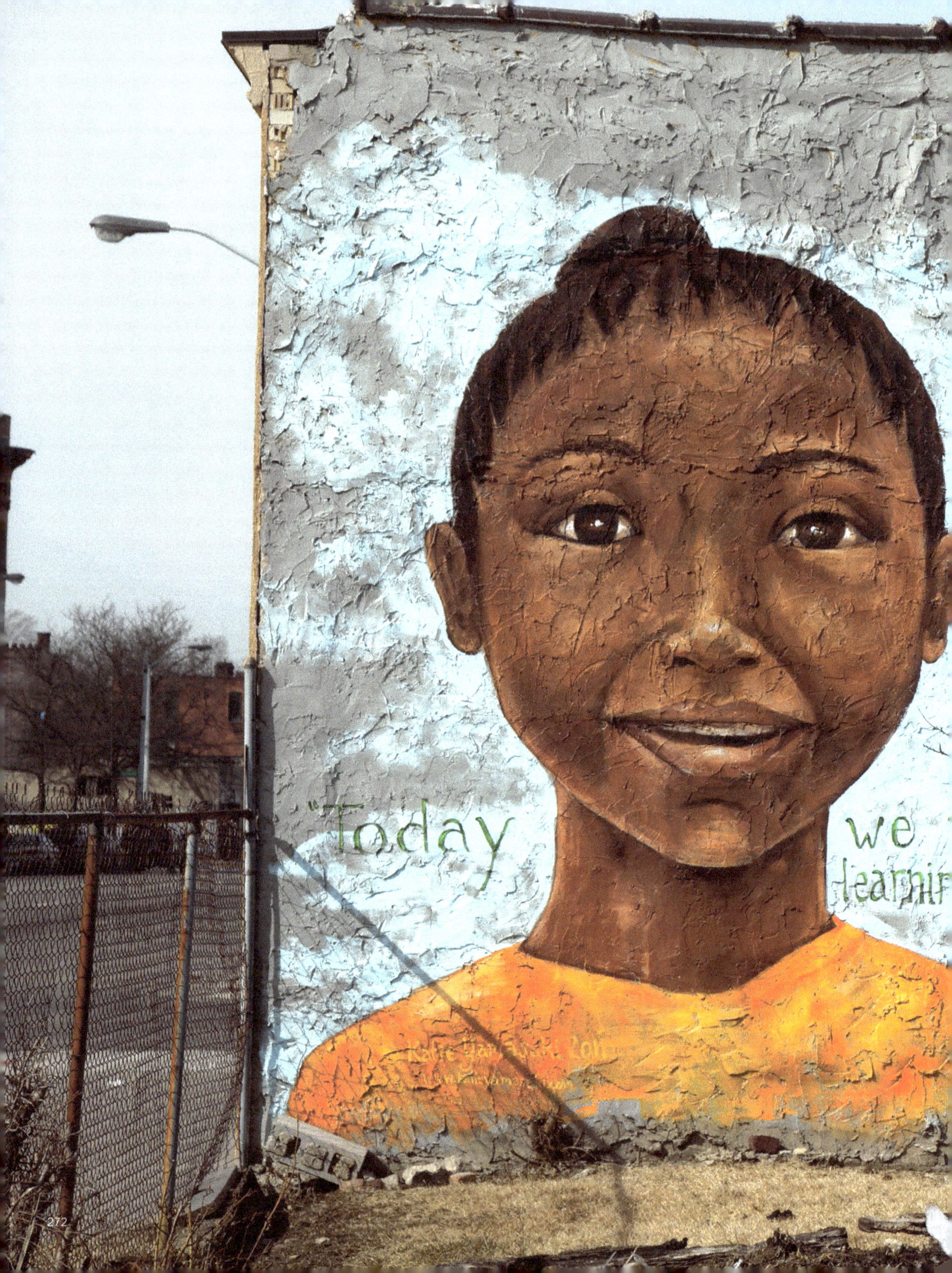
"Today
we

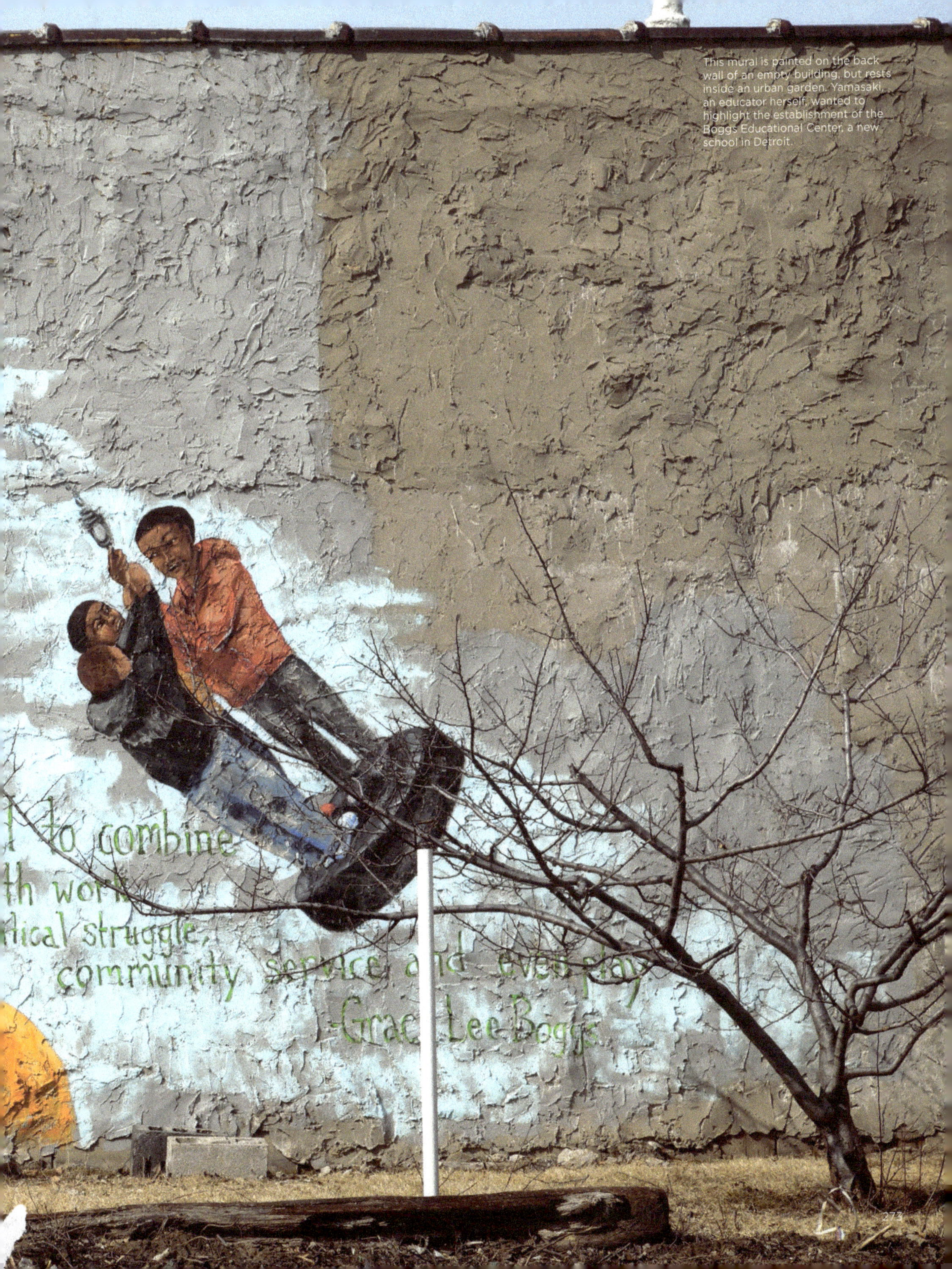

This mural is painted on the back wall of an empty building, but rests inside an urban garden. Yamasaki, an educator herself, wanted to highlight the establishment of the Boggs Educational Center, a new school in Detroit.

Index

www.ingramcontent.com/pod-product-compliance
Lightning Source LLC
LaVergne TN
LVHW070406060826
844660LV00037B/1432

* 9 7 8 0 8 1 4 3 4 4 6 2 0 *